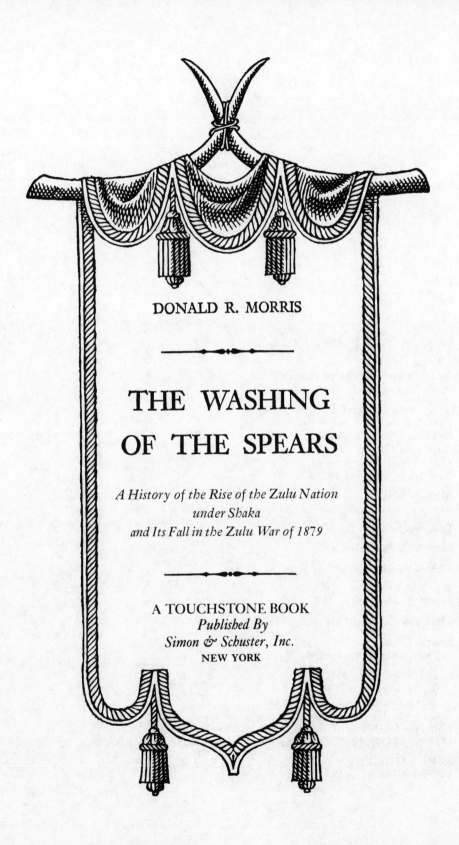

DONALD R. MORRIS

THE WASHING
OF THE SPEARS

*A History of the Rise of the Zulu Nation
under Shaka
and Its Fall in the Zulu War of 1879*

A TOUCHSTONE BOOK
Published By
Simon & Schuster, Inc.
NEW YORK

Simon and Schuster/Touchstone Books,
Published by Simon & Schuster, Inc.
Simon & Schuster Building
Rockefeller Center
1230 Avenue of the Americas
New York, New York 10020

SIMON AND SCHUSTER, TOUCHSTONE and colophons
are registered trademarks of Simon & Schuster, Inc.

Designed by Edith Fowler

Maps by Rafael Palacios

Manufactured in the United States of America

10 9 8 7 6 5 4 3 2 1
10 9 8 7 6 5   Pbk.

Library of Congress Cataloging in Publication Data

Morris, Donald R.
    The washing of the spears.

    (A Touchstone book)
    Bibliography: p.
    Includes index.
    1. Zulus—History. 2. Zululand (South Africa)—
History—To 1879. 3. Zulu War, 1879. I. Title.
DT878.Z9M67   1986   968.4′041   86-13055

ISBN: 0-671-63108-X
ISBN: 0-671-62822-4 Pbk.

For
Colonel Philip J. Noel, MC, U.S. Army
With Deepest Gratitude
20 August, 1958

FOREWORD

I first came across the tale of Rorke's Drift in a long-forgotten collection of stirring deeds written for children. I could not have been more than ten years old at the time; I certainly did not know who the Zulus were, nor even where Natal was. It stuck with me as the story of a fight, however, and it always seemed to me a more satisfactory battle than such better-known events as the Alamo or the Little Big Horn. Many years later Michael Leigh's novel *Cross of Fire*—even more than T. H. White's *Farewell, Victoria*—brought home to me that Rorke's Drift and Isandhlwana were the stuff of high drama, and by 1955 I was planning a magazine article on the two battles. The following year Ernest Hemingway pointed out to me that there had never been a readable account of the Zulu War of 1879, nor, indeed, any account published in the United States, and that it would be a pity to throw the two battles away on a magazine. He was, of course, right, and the present volume is the result.

It soon became apparent, however, that it made little sense to tell in detail the fall of the Zulu nation without explaining who they were or why they had to fall, and this in turn brought me to Shaka and the rise of the Zulu nation fifty years earlier. Then came the realization that the history of the Zulus was also the history of the colony of Natal, and that the framework would also have to include much of the history of southern Africa in the nineteenth century. Although the material was fairly cohesive, the ground thus delineated was extensive, but Robert Gottlieb of Simon and Schuster swallowed hard and bade me proceed. How extensive it was to prove neither he nor I suspected at first; I certainly had no idea, for example, that the story of the Zulu nation would take me as deeply into the history of the schism in the Anglican community as I at one time found myself.

The bulk of the digging was done while I was a naval officer stationed in Berlin between 1958 and 1962. I could hardly have picked a worse vantage point; what materials that were not in England were in Natal, and I was forced to purchase virtually all of my secondary sources. (And I here wish to acknowledge the services of two book firms—C. Struik of Capetown and

3

Charles Sawyer of London—who were frequently able to locate Africana when other sources failed.) A score of libraries and their staffs played their usual indispensable roles. I am particularly grateful to Mr. D. H. Simpson and Mr. D. E. Dean of the Royal Commonwealth Society, to Mr. O. H. Spohr of the University of Capetown, to Professor Vernon Tate of the United States Naval Academy, to Mr. Eben Gay of the Boston Athenaeum, and to Mr. J. A. Tuckson of the Art Gallery of New South Wales, as well as to personnel of the University of Natal, the Durban Municipal Library, the London Library, the British Museum, the Navy Department Library and the Library of Congress.

I was both astonished and deeply touched by the number of people who came to the aid of a total stranger to provide documents and information about their immediate ancestors. Their response was invariably generous and unstinting. The Right Honourable the Viscount Chelmsford not only gave me access to his grandfather's papers but also rallied his family to my support, and His Honour Arthur Thesiger, Mr. Justice Gerald Thesiger and Mr. Richard Thesiger were all most kind and provided valuable help, as did Admiral Sir Bertram Thesiger. The family was not able to locate one particular collection of papers concerning General Lord Chelmsford despite an intensive search. (It fortunately was quoted extensively elsewhere.) The institution they thought might house it denied possession, but was most helpful in directing my inquiries elsewhere. Only after the manuscript had been submitted for publication was the collection finally located—in the original institution.

Lieutenant Colonel Sir Benjamin Bromhead provided much valuable information concerning his great-uncle, including Gonville Bromhead's personal copy of *The Zulu Army* and the hitherto unsuspected fact of his deafness, which resolved a number of mysterious references. Margaret Stewart Roberts, great-niece of Colonel Arthur Harness, sent me the whole of his correspondence from the Perie Bush and Zululand in 1878 and 1879, which helped to flesh out the bones of the campaign. Mr. Charles M. Wynne and his two brothers provided information and excerpts from the journal their father, Brevet Major W. R. C. Wynne, R.E., had kept during the siege of Eshowe. Mrs. W. Oxford provided information about her father, Private Hitch, V.C.; and Lieutenant Colonel P. R. Butler about his father, Major William Butler. Mrs. Muriel Durnford, the widow of Anthony William Durnford's nephew, was most helpful in providing information about his family, and Mr. Dennis Pratley and Mr. William Fielding provided information and documents about their grandfather, John Williams Fielding, who enlisted under the name John Williams and won a V.C. at Rorke's Drift. Colonel H. C. Lugg, a distinguished Zulu linguist and historian, provided letters his father, Harry Lugg, had written from Rorke's Drift and showed me the carbine and the hunting knife he had carried during the battle.

The editors of the *Illustrated London News* kindly gave me permission to use several woodcuts from 1879, provided information about Melton Prior— and showed me the helmet he had worn during the Zulu campaign. Mr.

Ralph Varns, Secretary of the Capetown Branch of the World Ship Society, traced early ship movements for me; and Dr. R. E. Stevenson of the National Monuments Commission provided information about the battlefields of Zululand. Mr. T. V. Bulpin, historian, helped to sort out several generations of Henry Francis Fynns; and Barbara Tyrrell, whose magnificent work records a rapidly vanishing native garb, provided information about Zulu dress.

Many people freely made available the fruits of their own labors. Miss E. G. F. Eastwood, biographer of Cetshwayo, placed the results of her own researches at my disposal and was invaluable in tracing the antecedents of John Dunn. Mr. C. T. Binns, also a Cetshwayo biographer, helped to interpret the geographical complexities of early Natal and Zululand. Thomas E. Jones, Bishop of Willochra, devoted most of an interminable flight from Melbourne to Johannesburg to introducing his seat-mate to the intricacies of Church law and administration; if he was unable to rescue me from theological error, he did save me from a host of mistakes in terminology. To all of these good people I owe a deep debt of gratitude. The responsibility for what I have made of their material is mine, and I sincerely pray that they are content with the use I have made of that material and with my treatment of their distinguished forebears.

Several debts are even greater. Mr. Sighart Bourquin, Director of Bantu Administration in Durban, is an outstanding authority on Zulu history. Time and again he was able to track down information for me, or to correct a point. His collection of photographic material on Zulu history is unparalleled, and he has made available for this book those illustrations marked "Coll Collection."

Mr. Ian Player, Senior Ranger of Zululand, offered me his services by mail (little realizing what he was letting himself in for) and then proved indefatigable in providing information that ranged from Zulu ethnology through flora to cattle diseases. He was then my host during two subsequent visits to Zululand, and with him I visited Rorke's Drift, Isandhlwana, Kambula, Hlobane and Ulundi. Further local guidance was provided by the Reverend Peter Harker of St. Vincent's Mission at Isandhlwana and by Colonel Jack Vincent, then Director of the Natal Parks, Game and Fish Preservation Board.

Major G. J. B. Egerton (as well as his predecessor, Lieutenant Colonel E. N. G. Earle), Regimental Secretary of the South Wales Borderers, provided material from the 24th Regiment Museum at Brecon, and gave considerable help in clarifying early regimental records.

I owe a special debt to Mr. W. Godfrey Winckler of Durban, an expert student of John William Colenso's life and times. He gave me freely the results of his own exhaustive researches, and his comment and help were invaluable. He was never too busy to aid a distant friend.

I owe the greatest debt of all to a most remarkable person, Dr. Killie Campbell of Durban. She has worked industriously and largely alone for more than half a century to preserve the vanishing traces of the early days of southern Africa, and she has assembled what is undoubtedly the most important collection of Africana in private hands today. This book—as is true of a score of others—could not have been written without the riches of the Campbell Library, nor without the many kindnesses and the friendship of its director. I am indebted to Dr. Killie not only for the materials and the facilities she made available but for a host of introductions as well. She and her staff, notably Mary McQueen and the late Kay Collins, found books, manuscripts and photographs for me and did all they could to ease my research. I humbly salute a very gallant woman.

And—of course—my thanks are also due to my own family; to my wife, whose warfare against bad writing I resisted only to my own disadvantage, and to Sally, Michael, Julia and Margaret, who endless times honoured the depressing excuse: "Father is working."

DONALD R. MORRIS

Forest Home, North Carolina
July 20, 1964

FOREWORD
TO THE NEW EDITION

In 1956, when I began work on what was to become *The Washing of the Spears*, the literature not only on the Zulu War of 1879, but on the entire rise and fall of the amaZulu, was thin indeed.

There was no lack of material; there had been a spate of workmanlike accounts by participants and the odd journalist in the years following the war, and then a sprinkling of books at sporadic intervals through the decades. Most were by enthusiastic amateurs, or at best by professional writers untrained in historiography, fascinated by some aspect of the story and eager to tell a good tale. Some primary sources on the early history of the Nguni Bantu existed— Nathaniel Isaacs and Henry Francis Fynn—but neither was a facile, let alone a trained, writer. Some—A. T. Bryant—were serious researchers collecting and collating as best they could priceless oral material; others produced sketchy and anecdotal accounts. Many—Frances Colenso and Gerald French—provided valuable material but were primarily grinding axes. One or two—T. V. Bulpin—were both knowledgeable *and* readable (a rare combination), but essentially "popular" historians who neither listed nor analyzed their sources.

Almost all the amateurs had fed at dubious springs, and a host of minor errors had been passed from one to another over the years. Only one trained, professional historian had ever glanced at the Zulu War—Reginald Coupland, in *Zulu Battlepiece*, and even he had been only briefly interested in one or two aspects of Isandhlwana, and had passed on several minor errors himself (referring to Chard and Bromhead as "barely out of their teens").

I was not a professional historian either; I, too, was an enthusiastic amateur. I claim credit only for doing my homework before writing, starting with the primary sources and then combing through the secondary sources to trace the accounts, and some of the errors, back to their origins. The myth that Durnford had been engaged to Frances Colenso, and that they would have been married had he survived, evaporated when I discovered that he had a wife who survived him, and there were other twice-told tales that finally vanished.

In one or two fields I did break fresh ground. There had been, before, no account of the transport, and as I researched that story I realized how completely the struggle to collect oxen and wagons, and to cope with them, had controlled Chelmsford's strategy and even the British tactics. There had been, moreover, no account of how the war had been seen from Ulundi, of what was passing through Cetshwayo's mind. The evidence was scant and had never been collected, but it was possible to trace out the messages he had sent, when and where he had sent them, and why, and to reestablish at least the dim outlines of what he had been trying to do.

Even as *The Washing of the Spears* appeared in 1965, the floodgates were at long last opening. F.W.D. Jackson the same year published an account of Isandhlwana, the first reconstruction of the battle to be based on a long overdue re-examination of the official records.

There were one or two further accounts after 1965, but then, finally, professional historians began to work on the material. They came largely from South Africa, where until the 1970s the history departments of the English universities tended to point their graduate students at Charles II or the French Revolution, while the Afrikaner universities were busy with their own history. It was—a derogatory term which suddenly popped up—all very "albocentric"; native history was largely ignored. But a new generation of South African historians was emerging—Andrew Duminy (who at long last "Africanized" the History Department of the University of Natal), Charles Ballard (an American), Colin Webb, Jeff Guy, Adrian Preston, Sonia Clarke, Philip Gon and a score of others—who for the first time began to examine and reconstruct native economies and political structures, with something more than an anthropologist's eye. Collected papers—Wolseley, Harness, Jervis, Bulwer—for the first time were competently edited and published; and competent biographies were now replacing the inadequate efforts of earlier times.

Were I working now, some thirty years later, there would be minor changes. Some of the phrasing used in discussing the early history of the indigenous peoples of southern Africa reflects a vocabulary in common usage then, which has long since changed. And there are minor factual errors.

A number of writers were under the impression that the last time Colours were carried into action uncased was at Ulundi; they were carried uncased at Majuba Hill, on February 27th, 1881.

I reviewed the inconclusive evidence that James Adendorff actually stayed to fight in the defense of Rorke's Drift, after bringing word to the garrison of the destruction of the camp at Isandhlwana. I am still of the opinion that he in all probability deserted Dartnell's force the night before the battle, and certainly left Isandhlwana just as the battle was commencing. A more detailed account by Lieutenant Chard of the defense of Rorke's Drift has subsequently been found in the Royal Archives at Windsor, in which Chard gives Adendorff a specific place in the defense, and mentions a Zulu shot "I believe, by Lt. Adendorff." This would appear to settle the question of his presence at Rorke's Drift during the fight.

A curious controversy has arisen concerning the ammunition supply at

Isandhlwana. I made much of the difficulty of opening the stout wooden boxes, closed with two copper straps, held in place by nine screws—to open the box, the three front screws of each strap had to be removed.

It was well over a half hour's walk (for the drummer boys, who brought fresh ammunition packets in their helmets to the troops in the line) from the most distant companies to the site of the ammunition wagons and back, and the Zulus, who had been pinned down by the fire as long as the ammunition held out, charged forward and overwhelmed the line when the fire dwindled.

Even before 1879, a "Mk IV" ammunition box had been designed, converted from the old ones. A quick-opening top had been devised by cutting out the wooden top between the copper straps; it was fitted with tongue-and-groove sides and held in place by a split pin, and the top could now be slid out without unscrewing the straps. Such boxes were present in Natal in 1879, and F.W.D. Jackson places them at Isandhlwana, and questions whether an ammunition failure played any role in the defeat of the British forces. Two schools of thought seem to have formed on this topic; my account, apparently, is known as the "traditional" version. I still maintain that the Mk IV boxes were *not* at Isandhlwana.

I have since come across a clipping from the October 29th, 1937 *Dean Forest Guardian*, covering an interview with Regimental Sergeant Major Henry Buckingham Andrews, late 2nd Battalion, 2nd Warwickshires, who marched out of Isandhlwana under Colonel Glyn to reinforce Major Dartnell the night before the battle. He lists as a contributing cause of the disaster the great difficulty in opening the ammunition boxes, which was only possible with a screwdriver, of which there was usually only one in each battalion; as a result of the battle, the ammunition was *subsequently* packed in boxes with a split pin attached.

I have before me on my desk even as I write mute but eloquent evidence that there were *no* Mk IV ammunition boxes at Isandhlwana. It is a stout, twisted, corroded copper strap, found, half buried in the soil and hidden by grass, in 1962, on the site of Durnford's last stand around the ammunition wagons. It had lain there 83 years, unnoticed by the countless visitors who had combed the site for souvenirs.

There are six screw holes in the strap, and the end of the strap (with the three front screw holes), has been bodily snapped away. The last screw hole has been forcibly prised up over a screw head, and beside it is a high undulation in the copper, formed when a bayonet was thrust under the strap in the desperate effort to pry it up.

Such winds sweep even the distant hills of kwaZulu. Endless trickles of pilgrims still wend their way to South Africa, their goal the grim mount of Isandhlwana, and the mission station now standing on the site of Rorke's Drift. But Mntwana Mangosuthu Gatsha Buthelezi, the Chief Executive of kwaZulu, sees that as "redcoat history," and the history of kwaZulu is far more than "redcoats." A professional archaeologist has restored the royal kraal at Ulundi and the four-room hut which served Cetshwayo as a palace, and a fine museum there bears witness to the fact that Ulundi was a royal seat and the capital of an empire; the fact that a battle happened to occur nearby, over a century ago, is almost incidental. Throughout kwaZulu, historical markers and restoration work invite modern attention to the rich course of Zulu history, not just to the fleeting events of a few months in 1879.

The story of kwaZulu and its people is just beginning to be told.

DONALD R. MORRIS

The Houston Post
Houston, Texas
March 25, 1986

PREFACE

Man's eternal quest for political self-determination has long since reached black Africa—that last stronghold of the mixed blessings of European colonialism. Progress varies from the first quickenings to full independence, but progress of some sort can be found in every corner of the continent but one—southern Africa.

This seems strange, because the factors that give impetus to such a quest are all to be found there. The native population is large, and it outnumbers the European civilization three to one. Although it is composed of scores of divergent tribal components, it is ethnically and linguistically considerably more homogeneous than other groupings which have already achieved independence elsewhere. Because much of it is in close contact with an advanced and prosperous European civilization, it can observe firsthand the material benefits of political independence, and for the same reason it is acquainted with such political tools as the ballot, the major communications media, and the organization. It has suffered the loss of all these tools, and all weapons as well, so that the only weapon left is its own numerical superiority, and it is not yet aware that this in itself is a weapon.

There are, of course, many reasons why this particular native population has not yet tried to better its lot. For one thing, it is not really a colonial population, because the European civilization that dominates it is itself indigenous. Indeed, in the most developed part of the country, the European civilization was present for almost a century and a half before it even encountered the dominant element of the native population. The predominant native element, moreover, has no strong tradition of cohesive political activity. They are a people, one historian commented dryly, whose annals are empty because they have nothing to put in them. And, finally and decisively, the European civilization watches and controls the native population with a stern eye and a heavy hand, so that the first spark of political progress has always been snuffed out before the tinder caught.

The situation is strange for another reason, for within the memory of living man much of the predominant native element was not only independent, but a part of it was possessed of great power as well. As the Na-

11

poleonic Wars were coming to a close, a petty native chieftain, whose clan numbered less than 1,500 souls inhabiting an area perhaps ten miles on a side, started to forge a nation. When he was murdered twelve years later, he controlled 2,000,000 people inhabiting hundreds of thousands of square miles, and even larger areas had been totally depopulated by the ravages he had unwittingly initiated. So powerful was the monolithic political entity he created that it survived the mismanagements of two incompetent successors, and in 1878, fifty years after his death, its irresponsible power posed a considerable threat to the continued existence of the European civilization in its vicinity.

The European civilization, therefore, waged a preventive war against this native state and destroyed it. Even though the European civilization invoked only a fraction of the might at its disposal, it had to exert considerably more strength than it had at first thought necessary, and before the native state was broken, it had inflicted on the European civilization a defeat more grievous than modern troops have ever suffered at the hands of aborigines.

This war largely determined the place of the native population within the European civilization in southern Africa, and it freed that civilization (which was facing grave internal problems of its own) from any need to listen to the voice of black Africa while it worked out its own destiny. The war was a minor, encapsulated incident, and because it had relatively little effect on the course of the European civilization—it only removed a threatening obstacle from its path—it has had scant attention from history. It was, however, the last truly major challenge that the native population offered the European one, and for this reason alone it is worth the telling.

This, then, is the story of the Zulu nation—of its rise under Shaka and of its fall in the Zulu War of 1879.

CONTENTS

MAPS

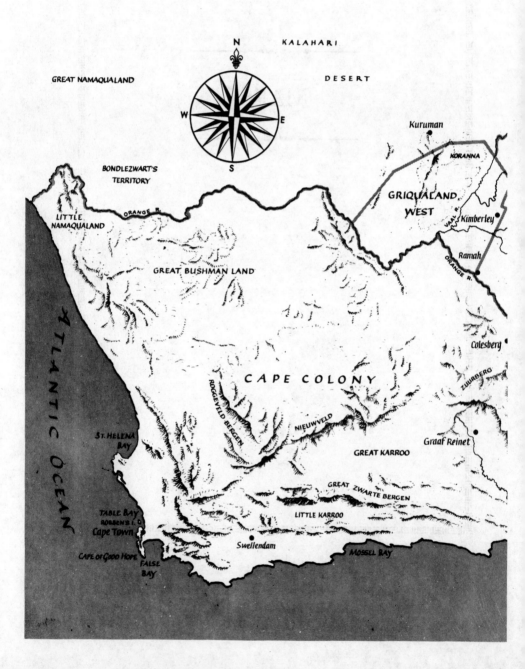

SOUTH AFRICA
Before 1879

TRANSVAAL

LIMPOPO R.

MARICO R.

OLIFANTS R.

LIMPOPO R.

BAPEDI

Sekukuni's
Kraals

Lydenburg

Rustenburg

Pretoria

Middelburg

Lourenço
Marques

DELAGOA
BAY

BARALONG

LEBOMBO RANGE

HART R.

VAAL R.

VET R.

KLIP R.

Wakkerstroom

MAPUTA R.

BATLAPIN

Platberg

ORANGE FREE STATE

Vecht Kop

SAND R.

DRAKENSBERG

Utrecht Luneberg

SWAZI

INTOMBE

PONGOLA R.

TONGA

ZULULAND

ST.
LUCIA
BAY

Winburg

MODDER R.

Bloemfontein

RIET R.

Thaba Nchu

BASUTOLAND

Boom Plats

TUGELA R.

CALEDON R.

Philippolis

ORANGE R.

DRAKENSBERG

Aliwal North

STORMBERG

TAMBOOK

MPONDO

UMZIMVUBU R.

GREAT WINTERBERG

FINGO

TEMBU

BRITISH KAFFRARIA

Somerset

GAIKA

PERIE BUSH

Kingwilliamstown

GCALEKA

GREAT KEI R.

TRANSKEI

Umtata

Port St.John

EMANG WA NENI

Dundee

RORKE'S
DRIFT

Ulundi

ZULU

UMVOLOZI R.

WHITE

MTETWA

Helpmakaar

TUGELA R.

Weenen

Eshowe

QWABE

Greytown

BUSHMAN'S
PASS

Pietermaritzburg

Stanger

NATAL

Verulam

Durban

PORT NATAL

GRIQUALAND
EAST

Kokstad

UMKOMAZI R.

BLACK

GREAT FISH R.

BASHEE R.

East London

Grahamstown

uitenhage

ALGOA BAY

Port Elizabeth

INDIAN OCEAN

0   Miles   200

palacios

Potter's Store

ITYENTIKA MT.

HLOBANE

BEVANE R.

PENVANE R.

to Pretoria

Utrecht

X KAMBULA

ZUNGUIN MT.

NOABA KA HAWANE

Boundary beaconed off
in 1864

BLACK UMFOLOZI R.

BLOOD R.

LY-N SPRUIT

BEMBA'S KOP

WOLF HILL

Tinta's Kraal

SALTE SPRUIT

Ft. Napoleon

CONFERENCE HILL

DISPUTED
LAND

MUNHLA HILL

INHLAZATYE MT.

INCENCI HILL

BUFFALO R.

BLOOD R.

KOPPIE
ALLEIN

TOMBOKALA R.

ITELEZI HILL

Ft. Cambridge

DEATH OF THE PRINCE IMPERIAL

DOORN RAND

ITYOTYOSI R.

Ft. Newdigate

WHITE UMFOLOZI R.

SUNDAY R.

VEG KOP

NAPOLEON
KOPPIE

SAND SPRUIT

LANDMAN'S
DRIFT

BASHEE R.

NDITU RANGE

SECOND
INVASION

Dundee

Dingane's Kraal

Harrison's Kop

IBABANANGO

RORKE'S DRIFT

ISANDHLWANA

Ft. Marshall

Ft. Evelyn

FUGITIVE'S
DRIFT

FIRST
INVASION

ISIPEZI HILL

BUFFALO R.

Helpmakaar

N

Umsinga

MIDDLE
DRIFT

TUGELA R.

KRANZ KOP

Ft. Buckingham

MOOI R.

THE BORDER ROAD

Ft. Cherry

Weenen

Miles

0   10   20

palacios

Greytown

to Pietermaritzburg

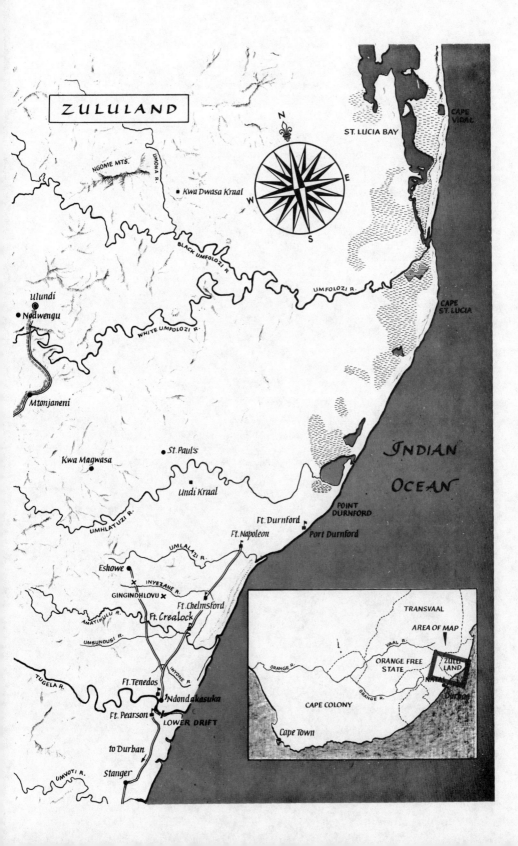

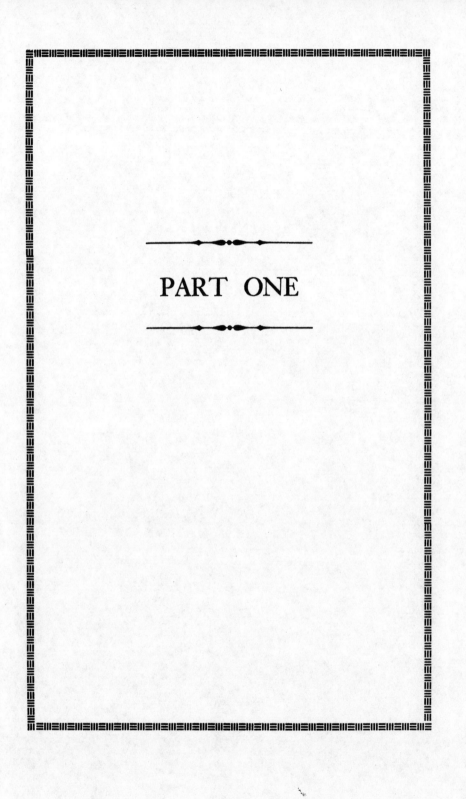

PART ONE

PART ONE

PROLOGUE

IT WAS an endless land of scattered riches and infinite variety. The continental divide crowded the eastern coast, fencing off a well-watered belt that rounded the southern end of the divide and broadened out into a fertile country. To the west of the divide, and north of the fertile country, was a high plateau, drained by sluggish, rocky rivers that ran westward to the Atlantic. Here were found desert and swampland, mountain and grassy plain, tropical forest and arid veld. There was a profusion of game on the open plains, the rivers that drained the eastern coastal strip were choked with crocodiles and hippopotamus, monkeys chattered in the forest and baboons scrambled about in the mountains. There was everything but man.

There had been prehumans in the river valleys, but they had disappeared thousands of years ago, and some time after their going a scattered race of hunting people had spread out over the land. These were the Bushmen, full-fledged humans, but so primitive that even today their survivors are a cause for wonder. They lived in small family groups, with no concept of a higher political structure, and they built no permanent habitations. When they camped in the shade of a clump of trees, they might pull the grass growing about their werfs into a protective screen, but of roofs they knew nothing. Their only weapon was a flimsy bow with poisoned arrows, and they lived on an erratic diet of game, eked out by wild fruits, roots and grubs. They were hunters, and so close to the level of existence on which their prey itself lived that their skill in tracking has never been equaled. They had a language of delicate complexity, with an array of weird phonemes— clickings, cluckings, croakings and raspings. They knew music, and they covered the rock outcroppings of the land with colored drawings of high artistic merit.

Their physiology was peculiar. Not true pygmies, they were nevertheless stunted, and their skin was loose and wrinkled even in child-

17

hood. They had peppercorn hair and small lobeless ears, and their wary eyes were set in flat faces with high cheekbones, broad bridgeless noses, and wide lips. The males' penes were set at a perpetual semierect angle, and the females' labiae formed an external flap that looked like an apron. They were steatopygic: in times of plenty they stored fat in their buttocks and thighs until a solid shelf stood out a foot and more behind them, and the fat accumulated in such a fashion that it did not hinder their movements. In lean times they lived on this fat, going for weeks on end with little or no food. Because they were only hunters, they went where the game went; and because they left no mark on the land except for their rock paintings, higher orders of people could pass through their territory without seeing a trace of them. It was only when the game began to disappear that latecomers learned of their presence.

At least a thousand years ago, a new race entered the southern part of the continent, traveling slowly down the western coast until they finally rounded the southern tip and started east and north again. These were the Hottentots, and no one knows where they came from or what mixtures of blood their veins held. Somewhat larger than the Bushmen, they were also small yellowish Negroes with peppercorn hair and a modified form of steatopygia. They knew the bow but depended on the spear, and they traveled in clans that were still based on kin but went far beyond the immediate family groupings of the Bushmen. They were ruled by hereditary chieftains, and they kept cattle and tended crops. Seminomadic, they followed their cattle, and since good game land was also good cattle land, their advance, in far greater numbers than the Bushmen, drove the game out of the lands they entered. The main stream of the migration was south along the west coast, but great eddies were deflected by rivers and mountain ranges, and offshoots gradually filtered into pasture land wherever it was found. The Bushmen fell back with the game, but not without resistance, and since domesticated cattle are easy marks for poisoned arrows, the Hottentots suffered. They were too strong to drive off, however, and in the end it was the Bushmen who gave way. They went no farther than they had to; to the lower foothills and the less favorable grasslands, and from there they struck out at the fringes of the Hottentot tide.

The first Europeans came by sea, pushing farther and farther south, until the Portuguese, under Bartholomew Diaz, rounded the Cape of Good Hope in February of 1488 and anchored in Mossel Bay. Diaz was then some 1,400 miles farther along the African coast than anyone had been before, in command of two storm-wracked ships of fifty tons burden manned by a half-mutinous handful of homesick mariners. He landed to replenish his water casks, and the Hottentot herders fled inland with their cattle. Returning with reinforcements later, they mustered enough courage to attack the interlopers with a shower of stones, and Diaz, snatching up a crossbow, drove a quarrel through the nearest native. The rest fled again. The watering party returned to its ships, and after a suitable interval the Hottentots came back to the beach to inspect the first example of the white man's handiwork in southern Africa.

Diaz sailed only a few days farther along the coast before his men demanded that he return them to Portugal. A decade later Vasco da Gama reached India. In December of 1497 he had passed the farthest point Diaz reached, and on Christmas Day he was sailing north along a harborless coast whose wooded hills and alternating sand and rock beaches sparkled in the midsummer sunshine. He named the area Natal.

In the century and a half that followed, the thread-line of trade Diaz had pioneered was woven into a thick cable that stretched from Europe to India. As the Portuguese established their routes, the cable was anchored by bases. The winds determined these routes. On the voyage out, anxious to beat the monsoon, the ships rounded the Cape of Good Hope and touched at the Portuguese bases in East Africa; coming home they clawed around the Cape to the fresh water, fruits and wild cattle with which St. Helena Bay had been stocked. They had no need of a base at the Cape itself, and every landing was marred by a fresh clash with the Hottentots. Events along the Natal seaboard were hardly happier; the coast was uncharted and rocky, and in the course of the sixteenth century a number of vessels homeward bound from India came to grief. Small bands of survivors struggled off to the north in hopes of reaching one of the Portuguese trading stations north of the Limpopo. Few made it; starvation or exhaustion finished most of those who survived the contacts with hostile native clans. The remnants of these groups were in no condition to note that the natives they had encountered were not Hottentots but a vastly superior agrarian people. The Portuguese posts were often based on earlier Arab trading settlements, and these natives were simply known by the Arab word for infidel—Kaffirs.

By the middle of the seventeenth century, the Dutch had driven the Portuguese ships from the India trade, and because the Dutch were better mariners and lacked bases in East Africa, they struck out for India and beyond by sailing south of Madagascar. This made Table Bay the only landfall out and back for the Dutch, and on April 6, 1652, one Jan van Riebeeck arrived there with orders from the United Chartered East India Company to build an earthen fort, plant a vegetable garden, and acquire cattle by barter from the Hottentots.

The handful of settlers who landed with Van Riebeeck established a colony at Table Bay much like a score of other colonies on other bays—Massachusetts and Havana, Botany and Manhattan. The earthen fort was duly built, as well as a few rude huts of logs and mud, and ragged fields were planted to wheat, millet and other grains. The Hottentots were willing to barter cattle; indifferently at first for beads and gimcracks, and then with more enthusiasm for tobacco and brandy. The early history of Table Bay differed from other colonies only in the greater indifference with which it was regarded by its parent company. Most colonies were seedlings, backed by companies that hoped they would develop roots to suck the riches out of the hinterland. The United Chartered East India Company looked on the hinterland at Table Bay with animosity; the colony existed solely to service the score or so of ships that touched there sailing for India or returning, and the unexplored surroundings simply diverted the attention of employees from company business to private enterprise.

For five years everybody at Table Bay was a company employee. In 1657 a few men took their discharges and started to farm in the vicinity. They were mostly Dutch; a few, mercenary soldiers, were German. The company did not object, providing produce was sold to the company stores and not directly to visiting ships. A few settlers came out to what was known as Hottentot Hollandia, and in 1688 a stream of French Huguenots, refugees from the Revocation of the Edict of Nantes, began to arrive. The French added almost 200 settlers, and they brought a heritage of rebellion against oppression. They made common cause with their Dutch predecessors against certain unpopular company policies, and they were quickly absorbed.

Within fifty years of Van Riebeeck's landing there was a town at Table Bay and a suburban farming population. Within a century a new race had been born and was seeded 200 miles to the east along the coast. It was a peculiar race, and geographic, political and economic factors gave it a homogeneity from which it drew enormous strength. It was an agricultural race—the word "Boer" means farmer—and because the land was free and seemingly endless, it developed notions about farms that would have staggered contemporary Europeans. The average Boer holding was a block of land comprising about 6,000 acres, on which cattle and a few sheep were grazed, and as much land put to cereals, vegetables and orchards as the supply of native labor permitted. Most Boers wanted two such farms, one for winter and another for summer, and instead of subdividing they sent their numerous progeny to the limits of the settled area to stake out new claims. It was only necessary to register the new farms with the Chartered Company, which theoretically owned all land and charged a nominal rental—

which it had no means of collecting. Hottentots already in place were easily driven away. Until 1780 expansion was untrammeled by law behind or enemy in front, and if the land was never settled thickly, the frontier raced eastward with great rapidity.

As the frontier advanced, the ties with Capetown faded and those with Europe disappeared. Capetown was still in touch with the contemporary world, but its influence petered out beyond the tilled plots. There were no ports to the east, and the frontier Boers, who visited Capetown perhaps once in a lifetime, soon grew intolerant of even the lightest controls. Each Boer farm was a self-sufficient community, with no need for outside authority. The simplest trade mechanisms sufficed, and among themselves the Boers generated few problems they could not solve by what amounted to the decisions of tribal elders. No government, consequently, could offer the Boers anything they wanted except armed help against the natives, and this the Chartered Company was not prepared to provide. Since they wanted nothing from a government, the Boers saw no reason to support one by paying taxes or rendering service, and the demands of the Chartered Company were easily evaded on the frontier. The situation led to a brand of individualism and a sense of personal independence rarely matched by other pioneering folk.

The Boer attitude toward the natives exemplified this intransigence. In the very first years of the colony the natives were despised not because they were black and savage but only because they were pagan. When the company barred further white immigration after the advent of the Huguenots, however, the settlers turned to black labor. All manual service, and some artisan work, was performed by natives, so that the natural Boer independence was reinforced by the social stigmas that attached themselves to working for another. A justification for slavery was found in the Old Testament, and as a fundamentalist religion grew and its ranks closed against outside pressure, what had started as rationalization ended as a basic creed.

Even as the Bushmen fled before the Hottentots, so the Hottentots crumbled before the Boers. In the settled areas there was no room for organized clan life, and the Hottentot was suffered only as a slave or a worker. The border area itself, constantly shifting eastward, was in a turmoil. Brandy and tobacco sucked in the cattle, and with the cattle gone, Hottentot choices were few. They could pass into indentured service, which was equivalent to slavery, or they could raid to regain their cattle. But raiding led to savage retaliations, and the survivors could only flee to fresh clans in the east.

The remaining Bushmen were hunted down for sport by Boer and Hottentot alike, and this activity continued well into the nineteenth century. By then such minuscule bands as were left had taken to semi-deserts or mountain fastnesses where neither herder nor planter was likely to follow. Only their infant children were spared; they were in great demand in Boer households as domestic servants. In 1713 small-pox wiped out the bulk of the Bushmen and snapped the weak clan organization of the Hottentots.

For the next fifty years the frontier Boers were undisputed masters of the southern rim of the African continent. They dotted the rolling watered landscape with thatched mud farmsteads, tended their cattle and raised their crops. A few Jewish pack peddlers brought them powder and lead and the small artifacts they could not make them-selves, and the Hottentots provided them with labor. Where farms were close together, an occasional itinerant schoolteacher might hold a season of classes, and at least once a year each Boer family would try to attend communion. They developed in utter isolation, and the outside world moved past them.

As the Boers waxed, the fortunes of the Dutch waned. The British had entered the trade to the Indies, and a series of wars sapped Dutch maritime strength. By the end of the eighteenth century the majority of the ships that touched at the Cape were British, and in 1793 the English took Capetown away from the Dutch. The following year the United Chartered East India Company, long moribund, went bank-rupt, and although the Dutch regained Capetown in 1802, they lost it again in 1806. This time the English stayed.

THE BANTU

For five full generations the infant Boer race oozed eastward along the southern rim of the continent. Some 12,000 families were thinly sprinkled over the 500 miles stretching out from Capetown; they developed customs and usages of their own, and the High Dutch with which they had started picked up new words and was stripped of much of its grammatical complexity. The thin edge of the tide moved on apace. There were always Boers who could not abide even the weak trammels of their own political structures—men who felt hemmed in if they had neighbors within twenty miles. There were always younger sons in search of land—always one farm flung out beyond the rest that for a few months would be the edge of settlement until it in turn was leapfrogged. By the 1750's there were farms at Algoa Bay, by the 1770's the frontier had turned and started to follow the long smooth coastal curve to the north. Then, in the valley of the Great Fish River, the process was abruptly halted.

The frontier had passed through the ephemeral Bushmen, it had detribalized and absorbed the Hottentots. The Boers were vaguely aware of the existence of a third division of the Negro race—tall, well-formed specimens who dribbled south in small hunting parties from some reservoir in the limitless north. They were known generically as Kaffirs and they were obviously superior to the Hottentots. Their attitude toward Bushmen approximated that of the Boers themselves, but little else was known about them or the lands from which they came. Now, on the Great Fish River, the foremost Boers collided with the Kaffir reservoir itself. Beyond lay native settlements and grazing lands that came down almost to the river.

There was a year or two of cautious contact, and there were a few daring Boers who crossed the river and settled beyond, but the frontier itself had stopped. The borderlands filled, and the pressure from behind mounted, and the unending clashes over cattle increased. Then

23

there was a concerted heave or two, and the truth finally dawned. The Kaffirs were themselves the fringes of a tide. Even if they had been willing to recede—and they exhibited infinitely greater resistance to pressure than the Hottentots—they could not move. The free land had run out, and Africa was no longer endless.

The meeting was one of great mutual surprise, since neither side had ever before encountered anything quite like the other. The Kaffirs had seen few white men, and most of those had been shipwrecked mariners hardly likely to give an impression of strength. Boer opinions of natives were based on Bushmen and Hottentots, both of whom had existed only in disorganized fragments for over fifty years. The contact now was between two well-organized societies both of which were based on cattle and both of which required ever-broadening lands in order to survive.

The collision stopped both groups in their tracks and led to immediate friction. There was to be a "Kaffir problem" for the next century and more, and the solution to the land problem was only reached in the creation of a social problem which cankers southern Africa to this day.

It is worth looking closely at these Kaffirs, and what lay behind them, for directly and indirectly they have determined the history of the entire African continent south of the Sahara. It will, however, be hard to bring them into an exact focus, because they defy precise classifications. They can be broken down by blood, by language, by social and political organizations and by custom; but such breakdowns lead only to imprecise and overlapping boundaries which are, moreover, in a state of flux. Even modern terminology changes, and the term "Kaffir" itself has become one of opprobrium—on a par with "nigger"—but because all 50,000,000 people originally embraced by the term speak one of a family of over 200 related languages, they are generally known as the Bantu, a philological word coined in the course of the nineteenth century. It comes from *abaNtu*, meaning "people," and is the plural of the word "man"—*umuNtu*. These languages vary enormously, and mutually unintelligible dialects run into the hundreds, but over wide areas they shade almost imperceptibly one into the next, so that most groups can communicate with their immediate neighbors. All of them retain certain grammatical features which point to a common origin at the dawn of human speech, and it has even been possible to reconstruct an Ur-Bantu.

The Bantu are magnificent physical specimens. Their natural diet embraces meat and dairy products, fruits, cereals and vegetables. They live in the open and are a cleanly people, although not all of their ideas of sanitation would meet with favor in a Western civilization. Warfare has played a sufficient part in their heritage for a process of natural selection to weed out the physically unfit, and blood admixtures here and there have varied the blue-black basic stock to a bewildering array of shades and features.

No one knows from whence the Bantu came, and by the time modern man turned a scientific scrutiny on the problem a century ago, the layers of evidence were irrevocably tangled. Halfway between settled farmers and nomadic herders, they probably entered Africa with their cattle from the Fertile Crescent something over 10,000 years ago, and because their civilization was based on cattle, they could go wherever their herds could graze. Their roots were never very deep, and if their few possessions could be packed and ready to move on an hour's notice, their crops might hold them back for a season or so.

They seem to have passed up the Nile Valley and disappeared into the Sudan before the quickening of civilization in the Eastern Mediterranean. Then they were lost for some thousands of years. Once past the Saharan latitudes and pointed south and west, they had the continent to themselves, and only the ubiquitous Bushmen and the Hottentots, who may have passed along the same road themselves, lay ahead. They were not very closely related to the peoples of the African Horn, but they passed through their fringes, and their languages and social structures retain faint Semitic influences from the Arab world. They filtered into East Africa; they populated Central Africa and the reaches of the western coast, and always they worked to the south, driven by vague pressures probably of their own making and connected with cattle.

They traveled in family groups, at the pace of the cattle, which is the pace of all folk movements in Africa, and they moved whenever the pressure exceeded their low level of toleration. The moves were never farther than necessity dictated, and were controlled by rivers and mountains and pastures, so that their progress was slow and confused. Offshoots eddied and swirled and doubled back, and all over Africa the tiny seedlings they sloughed off in the course of the centuries rooted and grew apart in language, culture and even physical characteristics from the purer strain that continued the advance.

By the fourteenth century they were south of the Zambesi in numbers, and somewhere in the Rhodesias they seem to have paused long enough to experiment with political structures. Stopped by the Kalahari wastelands, they expanded to the west, pinching the Hottentots against the Atlantic and propelling a wave of them down the coast, where Diaz found them. Then they abandoned whatever they had been about and slanted off to the southeast. By the sixteenth century a large subdivision was inhabiting what is today the Transvaal. This was the Nguni family, consisting of several hundred small clans, all speaking a common language. Groups of these clans mixed with Venda-Karanga strains from the north and new subdivisions developed, whose language and customs began to grow apart. The new groups mixed again with the pure Nguni strain, and elements of all these brachiations presently filtered down into the pleasant coastal strip that lay between the Drakensberg Mountains and the Indian Ocean a hundred miles beyond. This movement was general and rapid, for the coastal strip was occupied only by the Bushmen, and the lure of uncrowded, well-watered grazing brought the Bantu tumbling down through the mountain passes. Once on the rolling plains below, they settled in the river valleys, jostling for position, blurring ethnic lines and spawning still fresh groups.

Three of these Nguni groups, the Mtetwa, the Lala and the Debe, settled in what is today Natal, while the Tonga clans moved off to the north and the Xhosa and Ntungwa groups spread out to the south. The Xhosa, pushed on by fresh clans still entering the coastal strip from the north, moved farthest south of all, until they too found the grazing and the water they sought in the valley of the Great Fish River.

It was, in fact, the last free movement, and therein lies the Bantu tragedy. History had offered them a continent, and had given them 10,000 years to fill it, and they had dallied a little too long. When Van Riebeeck landed at the Cape in 1652, the nearest Bantu were 500 miles to the north and 1,000 miles to the west, and in this generous toehold the newcomers flourished, so that when the two civilizations finally met in the 1770's, the Bantu encountered not an artificial colonial outpost but a full-fledged vigorous folk, rooted and growing, with a vested interest in its hinterlands. Because they did not know they were in a race, with a continent for a prize, the Bantu lost it. The hare, in the twinkling of a century, had outstripped the tortoise.

It is these eastern Nguni groups, from the Xhosa on the Great Fish River to the Tonga groups on the Pongola River at the northern end of the coastal strip, who have played the largest role in the history of southern Africa, and their culture is sufficiently homogeneous to permit a final focus. Each of these ethnic groupings was composed of aggregates of clans, and each clan in turn was composed of from five to fifty or more families, all of whom claimed descent from a common, and usually prominent, ancestor. The clans were ruled by hereditary chieftains, and were both small and numerous; the 800 or so in Natal alone ranged from a few hundred souls through an average of one or two thousand up to a few giants that verged on 10,000 people. Each clan was a distinct political entity, and while he was aware of other gradations, it was primarily as a clansman that the Nguni Bantu lived and fought and died.

Since the clans varied in size, and individual chieftains of course varied enormously in their capabilities and personalities, the political scene was constantly shifting. Strong chieftains tended to kill off possible successors, and weak chieftains invited usurpers, and most reigns were short. If a chieftain was strong, his neighbors were usually weak, and he might indeed be regarded as a paramount chieftain and tend to absorb his neighbors, and so come to rule a tribe; and if the process was continued, something very like a nation might be seen. Such amalgamations, however, were rarely cemented with anything stronger than a paramount chieftain's personality, and with his death the structure would collapse and assume a new form.

The incessant regroupings led to a cultural homogeneity, reinforced by a common geographical setting, and insured continuity by the practice of exogamy, which forced the men to seek wives from neighboring clans and thus prevented inbreeding. The wives, in moving from clan to clan, served as cultural carriers, passing on to their children the customs and mores of their childhood homes. The tendency toward cultural homogeneity among the coastal groups, however, was limited by the natural barrier of the Drakensberg Range, and a linguistic barrier existed between all of the coastal groups and the Sutu-Nguni Bantu who had remained on the inland plateaus.

Exogamy, however, produced an occasional quirk. The Bushmen, as usual, had been displaced, and those that were not exterminated took refuge in the Drakensberg Range. From their rocky fastnesses they struck back at the coastal clans, and when the clans went after them, they killed the men and kidnaped the women. These Sabines passed on to three or four Nguni groups the weird phenomenon of the Bushmen tongue clicks and such customs as amputating the last joint of the little finger, mute evidence of forgotten genocide.

By the middle of the eighteenth century the coastal strip had filled, and almost all the clans belonging to the original groups had come down through the mountain passes; only the Sutu-Ngunis were left inland. The coastal groups were isolated geographically, and because the area was limited by the Boers to the south, a subtle shift in the political patterns began. The clans had always been able to ease the tensions of proximity by movement; they were now nestled cheek by jowl in an area where movement was cramped and possible only at the expense of a neighboring clan, and the tensions began to rise. The entire political structure of Bantu civilization had been predicated on free movement, and the structure now proved inadequate.

The tensions rose slowly at first, and the old order was able to prevail for a while because the clans were not only political entities but were also economically self-sufficient. Although the clan was the basic political unit, it was not the lowest economic unit; this was the kraal, each of which was inhabited by a single family. The kraal was thus economically self-sufficient but not capable of political independence, and it is in the kraal that we can finally focus on the microcosm of Bantu civilization.

It is difficult to consider any one facet of Bantu civilization, how-ever—even such an ultimate facet as the family—without at once being forced to consider other facets, for in very few civilizations do the same basic values so permeate the entire structure. The shape and arrangement of the Bantu kraal, for example, make little sense without foreknowledge of the Bantu family structure, and neither kraal nor family makes any sense unless one is aware of the overriding impor-tance of cattle. It might, in fact, be best to start with the cattle, for all the Bantu world was nothing but a gigantic mechanism for the care of the herds.

They were small scrubby beasts, long-horned, and of every conceiv-able color. Something was known of selective breeding, but it was not extensively applied, and a beast in itself was so valuable that compara-tive conformation or milk yield hardly mattered. When a kraal had amassed cattle beyond any dreams of avarice, it might breed herds true to color, and this was almost the only form of ostentation known to the wealthy. With a quinary system of numeration that made counting high numbers hopelessly complicated (ninety-nine, for example, was "tens five and four, and five and four"), a herdsman could describe with great accuracy each animal in a herd running into the thousands, and would notice at once when one was missing. Ears were notched for identification, horns trained into fanciful shapes, and patches of hide were tied up with cords in a form of scarification. There were hundreds of words to deal with color variations alone. Some beasts were trained to be ridden, some to be raced for sport, and one or two clans developed special herds trained to charge as an adjunct to war-fare. The greatest of the Bantu monarchs found no finer pleasure in life than in having his herds driven past him by the hour for his inspection.

Milk curds—amaSi—were the diet staple, and so much a foundation of the family unit that this food alone could not be offered to stran-gers—although hospitality was widely practiced. A man who had eaten the amaSi of a kraal stood forever afterward in a special relationship to that family. Although women performed all of the endless round of household chores and carried the entire burden of agricultural pursuits, they were not permitted to care for cattle. This was the province of the male, from herding to milking. Women, in fact, were not permitted to enter the cattle pens of strange kraals and were only allowed in their own under special circumstances; when menstruating, their shadow alone sufficed to endanger the cattle.

Goats and sheep were also kept, but served mainly as lower denominations of the only form of currency. Each kraal also practiced a form of diversification: portions of the main herd could be let to other kraals, paying for their care from the natural increase. This was especially common with royal herds, which were usually much too large to be supported in the vicinity of a single kraal. Each kraal in a clan, therefore, might tend a portion of the chieftain's herd, as well as that from other kraals, so that a complex network of cattle bound the kraals of a clan together, and served to adjust such matters as taxes, fines and loans.

The Bantu families that tended these herds were tightly knit polygamous units. The wives were purchased with cattle, but the exchange was not an outright sale. If the wife for any reason returned to her parents, the purchase price—*lobola*—had to be refunded. (Wives proving barren, however, were simply replaced with a sister.) Missionaries were to wage a hot fight against what they regarded as sinful polygamy and the sale of human beings, but the practice was not a form of slavery. The Bantu wife had a surprising degree of status; her price gave her a definite economic value, and daughters were always welcome to parents who depended on the lobola to support their old age.

Lobola made marriage a serious business and contributed to the stability of the family unit. A man could not take a wife until he had demonstrated his responsibility and general efficiency by the acquisition of cattle, and even a single beast represented a sizable investment. Survival as a bachelor was unthinkable—no man would deign to produce or prepare any form of food except meat and milk—and it might take years of labor tending herds before the lobola was in hand. The practice, in modified form, exists to this day, and it could never have been uprooted without destroying the entire Bantu social fabric.

Most men had three or four wives, chieftains might have twenty or more, and one or two paramount chieftains maintained harems that ran into the hundreds. Since the first wives were usually purchased before a man had achieved any particular economic status, the Great Wife, chosen for dynastic reasons, was never the first one. It was also necessary to cleanse oneself of impurities on common wives before mating with a Great Wife. Great Wives were expensive, and wars had resulted when a clan thought the lobola offered for their chieftain's daughter was insultingly low.

The kraals which housed these families were of identical configuration, usually facing east on sloping ground near water, fuel and grazing. A circular cattle pen lay at the center, surrounded by a low barrier of woven branches and grass, with a single gate, barred at night by heavy poles. This area, in which the herd was enclosed at night and to which it was returned for the noonday milking, had a great ceremonial significance. The ancestral spirits were thought to cluster around it, and here all ritual was performed. The kraal's winter grain reserve was stored beneath it in deep clay-lined pits, and the area served as a meeting place, a parade ground and a court of justice. Calves were penned in a special enclosure at the upper end, and in royal kraals a tree or two might be left standing, beneath which the chieftain held his court.

The huts, one for each adult woman and her minor children, were set in order around the pen, and a stout circular outer barrier, which might have thorns woven into it, surrounded the huts. The Great Wife—the *inKozikasi*—dwelt in the central hut at the far end from the gate, behind the calves' enclosure. The hut of the first wife was placed to her left, and that of a substitute Great Wife to her right, thus dividing the kraal into an *inKhohlwa* side ruled by the first wife and an *inGqadi* side ruled by the substitute Great Wife, both under the supervision of the Great Wife herself. Chieftains maintaining harems placed such women in a special section known as the *isiGodlo* near the hut of the Great Wife. The paterfamilias took his meals in the Great Wife's hut but slept where his fancy led him. Additional wives, grown sons and daughters, and various retainers had huts descending toward the gate. Chieftains' kraals were usually military establishments; they were considerably larger than normal kraals (although of similar configuration) and contained numbers of additional huts housing batches of unmarried warriors.

The huts were hive-shaped structures, light frameworks of woven saplings to which grass thatching was applied. The center of the roof was supported by a pole, and the only access was a single low door through which one scrambled on hands and knees. The floor was a polished surface of clay and cowdung, ground to a lustrous green, and cooking was done in earthen pots over an open fire on a low hearth. Everybody slept on grass mats, rolled during the day and hung from the walls on wooden hooks which also held the family's other possessions. Goats and sheep might also be given shelter.

The huts were rainproof, warm in winter and cool in summer. They were cheap and durable, and could be erected in a few hours. (An entire kraal, in fact, could be erected in two or three days.) The huts, however, had a number of disadvantages. The walls were usually alive with cockroaches, and because the door, which was barred at night, was the only opening, the interiors were always dark and choked with smoke. The structure was also highly inflammable, and on the open plains frequently struck by lightning.

The kraals varied only in diameter. A poor man with two wives and a handful of goats might live in a kraal barely twenty yards across, and a paramount chieftain with scores of wives and thousands of soldiers might rule an establishment well over a mile in diameter; and if the paramount chieftain's hut was larger, so that a whole cluster of poles had to be used to support the roof, he still had to scramble in and out on his hands and knees, and the royal eyes watered just as badly from the smoke. He also, undoubtedly, had many more cockroaches.

The children born into this society had to adjust to a bewildering series of relationships. In addition to learning the relationship of their own kraal to neighboring kraals and to the chief kraal of the clan, they had to learn where their clan stood in relationship to other clans. They then had to cope with complex family ties. Each child possessed a mother and father, but his father's other wives counted as mothers too, and his father's brothers also counted as fathers. He might easily have a "father" younger than he was, and in any event his father's eldest brother would loom considerably larger on his horizon than his real father. He saw little enough of his real father at first, because he would be nursed for three or four years, and his father would not sleep with his mother again until he was weaned. He would at least have an exclusive claim on his mother until he was five years old or so, and thus was in no danger of being pushed out of the nest by his siblings.

Female relatives of his father carried more weight than male relatives of his mother, and he had a separate terminology for elder and younger brothers and a simpler one for sisters, and all of these siblings might be full or half. The relationships verged on chaos when they dealt with cousins—there were scores of Zulu words to deal with a phenomenon that English dismisses with a single noun. And cutting across all considerations of age and sex and blood were the social gradations inherent in the three sections of the kraal—the Great Wife's, the Right and the Left.

His religious life began during his mother's pregnancy, a time of especial concern, since almost every act she performed and every object she touched might affect her child. She had to avoid crossing the tracks of certain animals and had to abstain from all manner of special foods, lest her child take on such unpleasant characteristics as long ears or blue eyes. Her husband, on the other hand, went out of his way to partake of these foods, and also had to avoid water, as he was particularly vulnerable to drowning.

The birth, attended by the old women of the kraal, might take place in various huts, depending on the mother's social status, but boy or girl, it was a joyous event unless it resulted in a deformed child or twins. Defective children and all but one of multiple births were suffocated at once by an earthen clod stuffed into the mouth, and the survivor of a multiple birth enjoyed a peculiar status. He was neither lucky nor unlucky, but he was certainly different. He had to have ashes put on his head after each haircut, he was never counted when a family was enumerated, and when he married there would be no dancing at his wedding. On the other hand, he could foretell weather and would be especially brave in battle.

The first year or so of infancy was marked by a series of strengthening ceremonies which carried off more infants than disease did. Babies were smoked in fires, buried up to the neck in holes and abandoned for short periods, and had reeds thrust up their rectums and twirled till the blood flowed, all in the name of hygiene.

The early years of childhood were passed in the kraal with an extraordinary degree of freedom. Discipline was firm but never severe, and play consisted of simple games and tentative excursions into the adult world. Toddlers tried to help with the milking, and little girls balancing miniature pots on their heads helped their mothers draw water from the streams. (The pot-balancing led to a graceful walk but almost universal lordosis among the women.) At five or six, children would be set to tending younger siblings.

At six or seven, the boys took up herding duties, starting with sheep and goats in the immediate vicinity of the kraal. With other boys their own age they formed an *iNtanga* which would move through life together. Every few years the iNtanga that was about ten years old would have its ears pierced in a mass ceremony that marked the advent of responsibility. Thereafter each boy was regarded as fit to help herd the kraal's cattle on the open pasture land.

The herdboys took the cattle out at dawn and stayed till dusk, returning only for the noonday milking. They played games with clay pebbles representing their fathers' cattle, they wrestled, fenced with sticks, and hunted small game with toy assegais. They fought herders from other kraals for the choice grazing, and they grew to a strong, confident manhood in the open among their peers.

INtanga ears were pierced together, but the puberty ceremony was individual, for each boy after his first nocturnal emission. On the morning after this event the boy would arise long before dawn, drive the kraal cattle far out into the veld by himself, and attempt to hide them. The entire kraal would search for him, and the harder he was to find, the greater the success predicted for his future life. When finally located, he was brought back with the cattle and isolated while a feast and a ceremony were prepared in his honor. His father gave him his first adult assegai, and all his old clothing (which wasn't much) was burned or given to his younger brothers. His father gave him a new *umuTsha*, a slit skin loin covering, which he added to his *umNcedo*. This was a light box made from leaves of the wild banana, which covered only the end of his prepuce, and had up to now constituted his customary garb. He also got a new name, which had to be used by all younger than he.

Circumcision was once universally practiced, and, over wide areas, for females as well, but the custom inexplicably died out in a single generation among the Nguni of the northern coastal strip. There were, however, various ceremonies practiced by all the clans, so that the Bantu all moved through life by stages, each set off from the other by appropriate ritual. At some point, all the clans imparted mass instruction in sexual matters. Moral standards were severe, but based not so much on the prevention of illicit intercourse as on avoiding the birth of children out of wedlock. Sexual play among preadolescents, therefore, was open and permitted, and was only hedged with proper behavior standards in the dangerous period between puberty and marriage. Even then, however, a form of external intercourse known as *ukuHlobonga* was permitted under certain circumstances, and the technique was passed on to adolescents.

After most of the boys in an iNtanga had passed through the puberty ceremony, a leader would be appointed from the next highest age group. The kraals in a particular area of a clan's territory were under the supervision of an *inDuna*, who thus served as a district administrator and was responsible to the clan chieftain. The inDuna appointed the iNtanga leaders, collected taxes, settled disputes, and in time of war served as a military leader for the forces in his district.

Periodically the older iNtangas would be summoned to the chieftain's kraal for a ceremony known as *ukuButhwa*. This marked the men's transition from herders to full-fledged adults and warriors. In a large clan the young men would spend much of the year at the chieftain's kraal, ready for various services, and tending the royal cattle by which they were supported.

These military groups were akin to regiments, but the analogy was not precise in the early days. INtangas varied enormously in size, and in small clans might be composed of less than a dozen boys. In time of war most clans were content to field all the adult males, the iNtangas mixed together, with no group breakdown of what was frequently a pathetically small force.

Justice was dispensed by the kraal elders, sitting in something close to a formal court. Witnesses were heard and evidence weighed, and majority rule prevailed. Only the most serious cases were taken to the inDuna, and very rarely to the chieftain himself. The only punishments levied were cattle fines, and death for serious offenses. In the case of flagrant transgressions the death sentence might be extended to the malefactor's entire kraal.

The artifacts this civilization produced were simple. Plates, spoons, combs and pillows were carved from wood; calabashes and clay pots served as containers, as did woven bags and baskets, some so finely plaited that they were used to hold beer. Household utensils were made from bone and ivory, and horn was used for such items as snuff containers and the small spoons from which snuff was inhaled; used as nose reamers, these spoons also doubled as handkerchiefs, and when not in use were carried with the snuff horns in the pierced ears.

Torches were made from reed bundles impregnated with tallow and cowdung; they were smoky and feeble, and people went to bed with the sun. A paste of bruised herbs and berries was used as soap, applied after the body was anointed with fat.

Shells, beads and copper were used for ornamental dress, as were special furs and feathers. The beads were woven into delicate patterns, which constituted the closest approach to a written language the Nguni possessed. Various emotions were represented by colors, and much could be said by sending a present of a beaded belt. Aside from the copper ornaments, the only metal artifacts in demand were hoe and assegai blades. Certain families specialized in ironworking, and the tradecraft was passed from father to son.

The forges were primitive. Iron ore, collected on the surface, was smelted in clay receptacles. Goatskin bellows blew air through wooden pipes with clay nozzles held in place on the ground by large stones. Heavy stones embedded in earth served as anvils; other stones as hammers. Iron hammers were used for the final finishing work; they were produced only at the cost of enormous effort, as the artisans could neither cast nor drill and had no way to punch a hole through a mass of metal to insert a handle. Both hoe and assegai blades were attached to their hafts by pointed tangs which were first heated and then driven into the wood; the joint was then bound with wet rawhide. Nothing was known of steelmaking, but enough charcoal from the fires usually worked its way into the iron to make an acceptable product.

The spiritual life of these people was wrapped in an all-pervading magic. Religious doctrine had been replaced by a species of codified superstitions. There was, for example, a Creator—who had made mankind in a bed of reeds—but he occupied no particular place in a divine hierarchy. He was neither worshiped nor placated; he was simply a convenient answer to the question posed by existence. Ancestral spirits were far more immediate and frequently appeared, usually in the form of small snakes, to remind their descendants of their presence. There were spirits everywhere, in animals and plants and geographical features and meteorological phenomena, and their propitiation necessitated endless attention.

Superstition is frequently based on practical considerations; a poisonous plant may be avoided because it makes people ill, and in time the avoidance may be graced with a religious taboo. Bantu superstitions, however, were more of a hindrance than a help, and a high percentage of available food stuffs went to waste because of inane taboos. Almost half the slaughtered meat, for example, was simply abandoned because various groups, depending on age, sex and social status, could not touch certain parts. Scores of game species, available in abundance, were never eaten because fancied characteristics might be passed on to the consumer.

Medicines, designed either to cleanse or to strengthen, formed a part of every ceremony, but the significance lay in the ceremony and not in the ingredients, which depended more on the imagination of the concocter than on any pharmaceutical properties. All sorts of animal organs and discharges found their way into repulsive mixtures which might be boiled, charred or turned into an unguent. Comparatively few medicines were destined for internal consumption; some were simply burned, scattered or buried, and those that were not smeared on the body were taken into the mouth and then spat, squirted or sprayed on the ground, on fires, at the sun, or on other people. Human ingredients were also used on occasion, but while this added enormously to the potency of a medicine, it never became as great a fetish among the eastern Nguni as it did among some of the Sutu clans.

Religious rituals were frequent and time-consuming. There were ceremonies for planting and at harvest time, at the investiture and death of a chieftain, and there was a protracted strengthening and purification for the chieftain and the entire army before any active service. The ritual slaughter of cattle occurred in all these ceremonies; at the harvest ceremony a bull was strangled by unarmed men.

One superstition had a decided effect on military activity. A warrior who killed an opponent stood to develop a serious ailment, culminating in madness, unless he took immediate preventive action. The first step in the cleansing process was to rip open the fallen foe's abdomen with a single slash of the assegai, in order to allow his spirit to escape. The victorious warrior then had to eat and sleep apart from the other men until his cleansing was completed. This involved travel to his home kraal, but before resuming relations with his wives he had to have intercourse with a woman not of his own kraal; this transferred the disease to her in latent form, and she in turn would pass it on to the next man to have intercourse with her. If no woman was available, the warrior could resort to sodomy. The superstition led to short campaigns, since after every battle most of the victorious army at once decamped for home.

Witchcraft was universal. All illness, and indeed all evil, was caused by *abaThakathi*—wizards who made use of primal forces. An umThakathi was disembodied, and might inhabit an animal or a plant or even a rock while blighting a neighborhood. It frequently inhabited a human being—anyone but a witch doctor or a chieftain, who was actually an umThakathi (but a benign one) himself. The unfortunate host would be quite unaware of the parasite until a witch doctor pointed it out; witch doctors could *smell* abaThakathi.

An accusation of witchcraft was fatal; once the wizard had been smelled, no defense was possible, and because the host was quite unwitting, no plea of ignorance, purity of action, or innocence of intention could stand. Whenever the presence of an umThakathi was suspected, the chieftain would summon the entire male membership of the clan, which assembled in a large circle with the witch doctors in the center. These worthies, bedaubed with clay and bedecked with outlandish ornaments, had long since worked themselves into a frothing frenzy of concentration. They slowly strutted around the circle, chanting a single word to a low counterpoint from the clan. They paused in front of each man, sniffing and howling, passing on and suddenly darting back to terrorize anew someone just starting to breathe again, and as a really likely prospect was approached, the chant would rise in volume. The volume peaked as the witch doctors passed, and died away beyond the suspect. The clan might think the rising volume was the witch doctors' making, but they in their turn were merely sounding out public opinion, cleverly reinforcing nuances of sound until they were certain their choice met with popular approval—a rich but miserly kraal head, or the transgressor of some social taboo. The witch doctors would pass him and return, until finally they were leaping and screaming before some poor wretch on his knees. Bounding clean over him, they flicked him with a gnu's tail, whereupon he was at once dragged off to have sharpened stakes pounded up his rectum, while an impi was dispatched to exterminate his family root and branch, destroy his crops, and burn his kraal. His cattle were simply added to the royal herd with, of course, a cut for the witch doctors.

The process was naturally abused by many of the paramount chieftains, who would complain of being bewitched, summon a "smelling-out," and indicate quite clearly to the smellers-out just whose cattle they coveted. Sometimes even this sham ceremony was dispensed with, and the first indication a man might have of an accusation of witch-craft would be an impi arriving at his kraal in the dead of night.

Witch doctors also waxed fat on private practice. They were called in as consultants for every form of minor crisis, and rarely failed to secure the payment of at least a goat. The vicious grip in which they held the people was made possible by an implicit and universal belief in magic; not even the victim of a smelling-out was indignant. He might register horror or fear or remorse, but not even in his final painful moments did he doubt the existence of the wizard that had possessed him.

The military institutions these people had developed were simple but served their needs. A mild and almost continual warfare was the norm. It was, in the beginning, a casual warfare with limited objectives. Gratuitously aggressive clans were rare, and the rights to grazing lands the major source of tension. A clan defended itself against encroach-ments on its territory, and it forced weaker neighbors to vacate adja-cent territory, but the defeated clan moved and the tension vanished. With the *casus belli* settled, there were no hard feelings or bitter blood feuds to pass on to subsequent generations.

Every adult male was a warrior, and those that had survived child-hood were hardy and strong, inured to the elements by long years of herding, and well versed in the use of their weapons. Modern civiliza-tions in times of crisis can deliver perhaps one man in twenty to the armed forces; the Bantu habitually sent one in ten and on occasion one in four. They fought in a mob, called an impi, and there was little or no internal organization, although the men of a particular iNtanga tended to support one another. Because the men of all clans were the products of identical environments and all were armed alike, most conflicts were settled by weight of numbers, and only a very rare chieftain was able to infuse into his clan a spirit that allowed it to cope with a numerically superior foe.

Warfare was primarily an extension of the hunt—in which the Bantu was peculiarly inept. The exquisite tracking skill of the Bushmen was unknown; entire clans participated in an occasional roundup and slaughter of game, and the same weapons and techniques were used that served for human foes.

Bows and arrows were rarely used, since no really suitable bow woods were available. The Bushman archer depended on poison, mak-ing use of a feeble bow that simply served to convey the poison to the game. The eastern Nguni fought and hunted with the assegai—a light six-foot throwing spear with a six-inch steel tip. It could be hurled perhaps sixty or seventy yards with some degree of accuracy, and each warrior carried a handful of them, retaining the last one to be hefted overhand for a stabbing weapon at close quarters. The only other weapon was the knobkerrie, a spindly stick with a heavy burled end which was used for braining.

The single means of defense was an oval cowhide shield, measuring almost three feet across and giving cover to the entire body. It was held on the arm by leather strips woven into parallel slots running the length of the shield and a central stick that also served to brace the hide. Only two such shields could be cut from a single hide, the hair was left on, and the color served as identification. The shields were light, handy and tough, and they could turn or blunt the force of a thrown assegai. They were also effective in a melee; a strong man could use one to batter an opponent, and an agile one could catch and turn the point of a thrusting assegai.

Most clan conflicts were settled in a frequently prearranged battle. The two clans met at a convenient location, often facing each other over the banks of a small stream, and the women and children assembled on a nearby hillock to shout encouragement and watch the fun. A long preliminary period was devoted to shouted boasts and taunts, and individual warriors ran forward to *giya*—howling self-praises and dealing death to imaginary foes. The two mobs then edged toward each other, hurling assegais as the range closed. Eventually one side or the other would sense a moral ascendancy and hazard a charge, which usually sufficed to send the enemy bolting. The defeated clan lost cattle and land, and captives had to be ransomed, but crippling damage was rare and extermination unheard of.

Tactics were nonexistent. There might be an attempt to surround an enemy, but if a sufficient numerical advantage was at hand for such a maneuver, a battle was hardly necessary. There were, however, occasions on which such sport assumed more serious proportions. In crowded areas a clan could be forced off its territory and fail to find new land. It then had little choice but to go marauding, in a desperate attempt to secure a new home by displacing another clan. Traveling fast, it would engage in predawn raids, burning kraals, driving off cattle, and slaughtering its victims as they scrambled, one by one, out of their burning huts. The grim displacements continued until some final, minuscule clan had been displaced and disintegrated, or the trail of burning kraals had led to a new and still unsettled area where expansion eased the pressure.

When a marauding clan appeared on the horizon, defense was simple. The kraal was never meant to be defended—it was primarily a defense against predatory animals and cattle thieves—and a threatened kraal drove its cattle into the bush while the people hid out in the surrounding countryside. This eliminated any substantial target, and rather than attempt to winkle such scattered bands out of the bush a marauding clan would usually move on. If they were in force, they might simply settle on the abandoned lands, forcing the scattered clan to hide out until starvation finally drove them in. Some such scattered clans existed for decades under the noses of more powerful neighbors. If the marauders moved, the scattered clan rebanded, and the kraals were rebuilt in a day or two.

These, then, were the Kaffirs the Boers had met on the Great Fish River. They were an aimless people, happy and careless, with little sense of time and less of purpose. They lacked written records, they lacked wheels, horses, trade mechanisms and all forms of machinery, and they had little to pit against the strange race now barring their path but a boundless vitality and their own ubiquitous numbers. The storm was about to break.

THE RISE OF THE
ZULU NATION

B Y THE closing decades of the eighteenth century, the ethnic
stage had finally been set. The Bantu actors were on the
boards; the European cast was in the wings. The clans were still performing their ageless shuffle, but their languorous drift had been
stopped, the ancient pattern of movement was no longer possible, and
the setting needed but a spark to touch off a conflagration.

The tinder was unwittingly provided by Du Prè Alexander, Earl of
Caledon, who as Acting Governor of the Cape Colony in 1807 decided
to send an expedition overland to the Portuguese settlement at Delagoa
Bay. He picked a military surgeon, Robert Cowan, who set out in two
wagons with a Griqua guide and twenty Hottentots of the Cape Regiment under a Lieutenant Donovan. The party picked its way north
through a chain of mission stations in Bechuana territory, hiring a few
bearers, and then plunged into the unknown lands to the northwest. It
was never heard from again.

The spark flashed in Natal, far from the sight of the white actors. In
the coastal region south of the White Umfolozi River dwelt a large
clan called the Mtetwa. These were Tonga-Nguni people, surrounded
by Ntungwa-Nguni clans, and they had drawn their wives from the
clans around them, so that even the vestiges of Tonga pronunciation
were fading from their speech. They numbered perhaps 4,000 people,
and they were firmly emplaced on good land.

In the early years of the nineteenth century they were ruled by an
aged chieftain named Jobe, who wielded an autocratic but essentially
stagnant scepter. He would neither die nor, apparently, reign, and
eventually his impatient heir, Tana, decided to hasten the process. He
was abetted in his plotting by a full younger brother named Godongwana, but before he could take a decisive step, his father got wind of
his intentions. Aged Jobe might be, but he was far from senile, and an
armed band shortly raided Tana's kraal. Tana died in his sleep, but

40

Godongwana, with a barbed assegai in his back, scrambled out of his hut and clawed his way through the kraal fence into the darkness.

Hiding in the bush, he was secretly tended by a sister, but he could not tarry in Mtetwa territory, nor even linger among such neighboring clans as the Mtetwa dominated. He struck out upcountry, passing from clan to clan until he found refuge among the Hlubi people in the foothills of the Drakensberg Range. Here he seems to have been employed as a herdsman. To hide his trail he dropped his name and called himself Dingiswayo—"the Troubled One."

After two years of exile, Dingiswayo met a single white man, who with a few Bechuana and Sutu bearers had come through the Drakensberg and was trying to reach Delagoa Bay. He was mounted and armed, and since it was later remembered that he made use of surgical skills on the injured knee of a Hlubi chieftain, he was almost undoubtedly Robert Cowan. By the time he was ready to set out for the coast, rumors of Jobe's death had drifted inland. Dingiswayo was anxious to return to his homeland, and he offered to serve as a guide.

Somewhere in Qwabe territory the white man died. He may have caught fever, or he may have been murdered—perhaps even by Dingiswayo, although this is unlikely. At any rate the remnants of the party broke up, and Dingiswayo possessed himself of a horse and the gun. (Forty years later Dr. Livingstone met a native who as a child had lived in the kraal where this white man had died. His family had eaten one of the horses, and he remembered that it tasted like zebra.)

Dingiswayo was now near his home, and he rode into Mtetwa country. A younger brother, Mawewe, was on the throne, but Dingiswayo was not to be denied. The scar on his back established his identity; the horse and the gun—both unknown to the Nguni clans in Natal—established his might. Mawewe fled, to be lured back later and killed, and Dingiswayo took over as chieftain of the Mtetwa.

His reign was unique in native annals. With Mshweshwe's founding of the Basuto nation, it ranks as one of the only two exhibits of true statesmanship in Bantu history, and where Mshweshwe founded a nation, Dingiswayo forged an empire.

He started with an army. At the outset the Mtetwa could field perhaps 500 warriors, and while Dingiswayo made no radical military innovations, he did provide a brand of driving leadership which had been absent before. The Mtetwa were surrounded by weaker clans; Dingiswayo incorporated drafts from these clans into his own forces and set out on a course of political amalgamation that went far beyond a simple attempt to enhance the Mtetwa. His objective was political submission, and once he had attained this goal, he left each clan in peace. At most, he would replace a recalcitrant chieftain with a pliant one, or designate a particular heir, and he sought to strengthen the bonds of this novel confederation by a series of dynastic marriages. Since every chieftain could marry as often as he liked, and everyone worth his salt had swarms of eligible daughters, the process was considerably easier than it would have been in Europe.

As the Mtetwa empire grew, so did Dingiswayo's army. Each submissive clan tendered a quota of men, and as the amalgamated clans grew, so did the size of the iNtangas in which they were tendered. The iNtangas consequently came to be regarded as military drafts, and the regimental concept received a strong impetus.

Dingiswayo's political innovations may have been motivated by the contemporary scene. The coastal strip was full of people, and although the Natal clans had never encountered the white race at the southern end of the strip, the crowding had disturbed the previous pattern of movement and a measure of desperation was already visible in the incessant warfare. It seems clear that Dingiswayo hoped to regulate this conflict by pinning each clan into place, replacing a thousand discordant foreign policies by a single cohesive domestic one.

The motivation for his experimentation in another field is not so clear. Dingiswayo made strenuous efforts to establish a regular trade with the Portuguese at Delagoa Bay. He sent them a large shipment of hides and ivory, and then tried to foster a factory system in his kraals. Over a hundred men were gathered at a site devoted to the preparation of hides, and he continually sought new artifacts which might create a demand. He even set a group of woodcarvers to reproducing European furniture, but since his workmen carved each chair from a single block of wood, the effort was not practical. The Portuguese, interested only in gold and ivory, made little effort to respond; and the system called for a division of labor for which Bantu society was not designed, so the trade never flourished.

In the eight years that he reigned, Dingiswayo established a Mtetwa hegemony over fifty major clans and scores of minor ones. His rule was liberal, enlightened and altruistic. The clans within his territories lived in peace with one another, and the continual petty bloodletting that had characterized Bantu civilization came to a temporary halt. It is clear that he was a highly intelligent man with a distinct nobility of character, but the concepts he forwarded were utterly alien to his own culture. Such ideas as political amalgamation rather than extermination, international commerce, and even the degree of military skill he exhibited could only have come from an outside source, and this in turn could only have been Robert Cowan. The difficulties of such an exchange must have been considerable, especially since the contact could hardly have lasted more than a few months and the two men had no common language. Cowan, however, was trying to reach Delagoa Bay to open an overland trade route to the Portuguese, and the promptness and zeal with which Dingiswayo made that goal his own show that something of the sort took place. The spark, weak and flickering, had truly caught.

Each of the Nguni clans in the Mtetwa paramountcy had its own history, but very few of them could trace their story back more than a generation or two. In the absence of any written records, or of any oral epic tradition, there was little enough to go on. Clans could recite the direct genealogy of their chieftains for perhaps a dozen generations, but the names that came so readily to the lips were of people whose lives and deeds had already dropped into limbo. Every Nguni chieftain had *iziBongo*, formalized laudatory phrases, which were awarded for specific incidents and recited on ceremonial occasions, and in the case of paramount chieftains these iziBongo might run to scores of praise names. They were, however, cryptic and were meant to serve only as *aides memoire*, on which story tellers could elaborate. Such phrases as "the Green Water Snake," "the Black Elephant," or "He Who Cut the Reeds" yielded no historical information once the reference had been forgotten, even though the iziBongo remained.

It is known, for example, that late in the seventeenth century a Nguni chieftain named Mandalela had wandered down from upper Natal into the coastal regions along the Mfkune River. He had, in all probability, less than a hundred people with him, and he lost a few of them one night when darkness fell before all of them had crossed a small stream. Mandalela wanted to continue in the morning, but those still on the far side had discovered a patch of melons and refused to cross, so he went on without them. The *emaGladeni* clan—"Those Among the Melons"—eventually grew out of the tiny group he left behind, and Mandalela finally drifted back inland to a small patch of land on the White Umfolozi River, where he settled.

His family grew, and Mandalela died, and his son Zulu mounted the throne. The few souls that had migrated with Mandalela were in all probability only a fragment of a clan, and if they had a name, it has been forgotten. Little is known of Mandalela, and even less of Zulu, but by the time Zulu died, the group was indeed a clan, and it adopted his name. It meant "the Heavens," and the clan was proud of its title of *amaZulu*—"the People of the Heavens."

Punga followed Zulu, and Mageba (who may have been his brother) followed Punga. Ndaba followed Mageba, and Jama followed Ndaba, and about the time that Jobe, Dingiswayo's father, succeeded to the Mtetwa, Jama's son Senzangakona was born.

Senzangakona came to the Zulu throne in the years the Xhosa clans collided with the Boers to the south, and no rumors of that event, or any inkling of its significance, troubled the kraals in the Umfolozi valleys. The Zulus by then may have numbered 1,500 people—certainly no more—and their kraals were scattered over the rolling grassy hillocks of an area that measured perhaps ten miles on a side. They were a small clan, and they bickered with small neighbors, and all of them were very much in the shadow of the weightier Mtetwa, off to the southeast.

One of these small neighbors was the eLangeni clan, immediately adjacent to the Zulus and closely related to them. Their chieftain had recently died, and among his orphaned children was a wild, strong-willed maiden named Nandi. This girl one day caught a glimpse of Senzangakona and fell in love with him. Marriage was out of the question, since Senzangakona's mother came from the eLangeni, but Nandi determined to have at least a flirtation and soon contrived a trailside meeting. Senzangakona already had two wives—he was to leave ten—and of course he knew perfectly well who Nandi was. As a chieftain, however, he felt no qualms in flouting the strict rule of exogamy, and since Nandi was attractive, he saw no objection to such love-play as the Nguni called "the pleasure of the road." UkuHlobonga occurred.

A few months later the Zulu elders were startled by a messenger from the eLangeni who announced that Nandi was pregnant and requested Senzangakona to fetch her. The tidings reflected no credit on Senzangakona. Dalliance was permissible, but ukuHlobonga did not extend to full intercourse, and a Zulu chieftain was expected to show better judgment than to dally so close to home, and with a chieftain's daughter to boot. The entire clan had been publicly humiliated by the act, and the elders sent back word that it was obviously no case of pregnancy but merely the work of *iShaka*, a convenient intestinal beetle on whom menstrual irregularities were usually blamed.

The eLangeni swallowed the slight and bided their time. In due season a second messenger arrived at the royal Zulu kraal and dryly bade Senzangakona collect Nandi and her "iShaka." In some annoyance he sent for them and quietly installed Nandi as his third wife. This must have been about 1787.

Senzangakona could face down the fact that his third marriage verged on an incestuous relationship—in a pinch he could always declare a seduced maiden the head of a *new* clan—and once installed, Nandi was in a sense legitimized. The marriage nevertheless had scandalous overtones and could not be properly celebrated. Nandi was in disgrace, and the stigma extended to her infant son.

For about six years the royal couple tried to make a go of their marriage. There were quarrels and separations and reconciliations. A daughter named Nomcoba was born to them, and Senzangakona tried to reduce the friction by shifting Nandi from one kraal to another—which did nothing to enhance her status with the Zulus. Finally, just as Shaka was starting out as a herdboy, he lost a pet goat of Senzanga-kona's he had been set to watch, and the resulting spat was too much for the easygoing monarch. Nandi was sent packing, lugging Shaka and his infant sister, back to the eLangeni.

Nandi was considerably less welcome among the eLangeni than she had been among the Zulus. She had disgraced her clan, and had now forced a return of her lobola; she had no male to fend for her, and her strident personality did nothing to smooth her arrival. Until he was fifteen, therefore, Shaka grew up fatherless among a people who despised his mother and him as well, and he spent ten years herding cattle with an eLangeni iNtanga which made him the butt of every cruel and painful joke it could devise. To add to his other burdens, he seems to have had undersized genitals until he reached puberty, and since herd-boys wore no clothing at all, he was not allowed to forget it for an instant.

As might be expected, he grew up lonely and embittered. The sole human being to whom he could turn was his mother, whose own life was daily made miserable, and shoulder to shoulder they faced a hostile world. His high intelligence and his natural sensitivity were forged in the fires of his frustration; he was acutely conscious of his royal blood and the plebeian origins of his tormentors. To the end of his days he retained a mortal hatred for the eLangeni.

In 1802 a heavy famine struck the area, and Nandi was evicted from the eLangeni kraals. With no cattle and no adult male to provide for her, she and hers were extra mouths in a season in which the clan could barely sustain its own. She took up her children and went to a man called Gendeyana, who belonged to a subclan of the Qwabes. She had already borne this man a son named Ngwadi, and the record here is a little shadowy. Nandi was still married to Senzangakona, and however little interest he may have displayed in his marital rights, he would still have regarded a second liaison on Nandi's part as open adultery. The episode is indicative of her character; in all probability only her royal blood and her fiery disposition kept a charge of harlotry in the background.

Her stay with Gendeyana was happy but short. Shaka, with the advent of puberty, was beginning to show signs of physical prowess, and both the Zulus and the eLangeni were pressing for his return. However little use both clans had for the mother, they were interested in the son, for a good warrior was always a welcome addition to a small clan. There was no question of his succeeding to the chieftainship of either clan—Senzangakona by now had a number of other sons, one of whom, Bakuza, was his recognized heir—but Nandi's disgrace extended to him only by association, and the eLangeni at least were willing to let bygones be bygones. Senzangakona, however, may have had some idea of getting Shaka back simply to put him out of the way. He seems to have made overtures along these lines to a neighboring chieftain, and on the last occasion on which he had seen Shaka, when the boy reported to him for the puberty ceremony at which he received his first umuTsha, the son's arrogance and hostility had caused a final terrific quarrel.

Shaka, therefore, from hatred of the eLangeni and fear of his father, would have none of either clan. Nandi thereupon fled to her aunt's kraal, among the emDletsheni clan, which dwelt directly under the powerful Mtetwa and their aging chieftain Jobe.

For the next six years Shaka lived among the Mtetwa. His mother was at last accepted, and they were quiet and happy years, although exciting ones for the clan. Tana was killed and Godongwana escaped; Jobe died, and Godongwana returned on his horse as Dingiswayo, established his rule, and embarked on his course of Nguni consolidation. All this time Shaka served as a herdboy, growing to a magnificent manhood that made him the natural leader of his emDletsheni iNtanga. At full growth he measured six feet three inches, with a heavily muscled build in due proportion. He grew expert in the use of the light throwing assegai, and tackled such game as the deadly black mamba and, on one occasion, a treed leopard. For the latter success he was awarded his first head of cattle, which he proudly drove home to his new foster father Mbiya.

For all his normal life the scars of his childhood were still upon him. He could lead his contemporaries, but he could never join them, and he spent much of his time apart, brooding in lonely silence. Despite the affectionate relationship he had established with Mbiya, his mother was still the only person he trusted. He was unquestionably a latent homosexual, and despite the fact that his genitals had more than made up for their previous dilatoriness, so that he always took great pride in bathing in full public view, he was probably impotent.

Shaka was twenty-three years old when Dingiswayo called up the emDletsheni iNtanga of which he was a part and incorporated it into the *iziCwe* regiment. He served as a Mtetwa warrior for the next six years, and his own star rose with the Mtetwa empire.

Dingiswayo's policy of planned aggression provided ample opportunity for combat. Clan after clan fell into line as the ferocious retribution which befell the first startled victims taught more distant clans the futility of resistance. Shaka at first played no part in Mtetwa policy.

He went where the iziCwe was sent, and he fought whom he was told to fight. He found in battle an outlet for the pent-up frustrations of a lifetime, and his political philosophy began to crystallize. Where Dingiswayo saw combat as an unfortunate but inevitable necessity when palaver had failed, Shaka saw it as the one safe and sure method of political growth. Dingiswayo would at once accept submission and chain the dogs of war, but Shaka saw that an undefeated clan, temporarily left in peace, was always free to turn on a paramount chieftain in a more propitious season. The iziCwe had more than once been sent to deal with a clan they had already vanquished, and Shaka preferred to smash such a clan the first time, incorporating the fragments into an organization of his own making. He took this attitude into his battles, and he fought for total annihilation. He despised a show of force designed merely to convince an enemy that resistance was useless; he attacked with brutal weight and welcomed hand-to-hand combat. His pursuits were tenacious and bloody.

He regarded the light throwing assegai as a ridiculous toy, and fretted at its flimsiness. He soon devised a new assegai, with a heavy broad blade and a stout shortened haft. He hefted it underhand, making of it a thrusting weapon similar to the short sword of the Romans, and the haft served to balance the point. It was called *iKlwa*, an onomatopoeic term imitating the sucking sound it made as it was withdrawn.

He even converted his shield into an offensive weapon. Hooking its left edge over the left edge of his opponent's shield, he could spin a foe to the right with a powerful backhand sweep. Shaka's left was covered, and his opponent, off balance and askew, could find no opening for his assegai, hampered by his own shield which had been dragged across his front. The shield dragged the left arm over with it and turned his left armpit to Shaka, who could sink his iKlwa in it in a movement that was a natural continuation of the shield-hooking. Then, as the victim slid off the assegai blade, Shaka would shout, "*Ngadla!* (I have eaten!)"

He also threw his oxhide sandals away. On the frequently stony soil, his bare feet added to his speed and increased the surety of his footing. In a country filled with thorns, the innovation was not generally adopted.

The new weapons proved themselves in their first battle. When the Mtetwa moved against Pungashe, chieftain of the Butelezi, Shaka's iziCwe were in the forefront. Shaka's half brother Bakuza, the son of Senzangakona and his last wife Sondaba, was fighting with the Butelezi. When a Butelezi warrior sprang forward to giya, Shaka dashed out of the iziCwe, killed him with a single blow and then charged the stunned Butelezi alone. The iziCwe gathered their wits and followed him, and when Dingiswayo called a halt to the subsequent slaughter, Bakuza lay amongst the slain. Pungashe and his clan accepted Dingiswayo's suzerainty.

As a by-product of this victory the neighboring Zulus also passed under the light Mtetwa yoke. Senzangakona, mourning Bakuza and unaware that Shaka had fought with the Mtetwa, had in the past matched strength with the Butelezi on a number of occasions. The feckless Zulu chieftain had invariably lost, and the Butelezi kraals were richer by many cattle that the Zulus had paid to ransom him after his periodic defeats. He saw no point now in fighting a clan which had so easily beaten his own conquerors.

As a further result Shaka came to the direct attention of Dingiswayo, who at once recognized his qualities of leadership. He saw more in Shaka than a mere soldier: he saw a potential chieftain for the Zulus, who were far upcountry on the fringes of the Mtetwa hegemony, where they might someday serve as a buffer to more powerful clans to the north. Under his tutelage Shaka rose to command of the iziCwe and participated in the councils where the Mtetwa policy was hammered out.

There were continual expeditions, and Shaka experimented with his new command. He divided the regiment into three parts and drilled them, seeking to pin an opposing clan down with the central group while the two flanking parties raced out to surround it. He made use of the iKlwa mandatory, and taught his own methods of infighting. He refined his charge, teaching his men how to advance with their shields at the proper angle, covering their bodies and poised to send thrown assegais glancing off while from a crouch they still had free vision beneath the raised brim. He also developed the *uDibi*, senior herdboys of fifteen or sixteen. He assigned one to every three warriors to carry sleeping mats, cooking pots, extra assegais and small amounts of grain and water.

Once during these years Dingiswayo summoned Senzangakona, aging and fat, to his kraal and confronted him with the son he had not seen in a decade, pointedly suggesting that Shaka would make an excellent substitute for Bakuza. Senzangakona professed himself delighted and returned to his kraal. He then allowed his Great Wife, Mkabi, to talk him out of the idea, since she naturally favored her eldest son Sigujana.

In the Mtetwa councils, nothing was known of what lay beneath Shaka's prepossessing exterior. His ferocity in battle was a known quantity, but in council he was modest and sage. His advice was quiet, and met with Dingiswayo's approval, and among his more disarming traits was a decidedly unusual concern for morale in the ranks; most of the gifts of cattle he received from Dingiswayo he passed on to his warriors.

When Senzangakona died in 1816 Dingiswayo immediately released Shaka from his service and sent him on to the Zulu kraals. Since he was under no illusions about the validity of a distant chieftain's promise, he lent Shaka a strong escort from the iziCwe.

Long before he arrived he heard that Sigujana had mounted the throne. Shaka was then twenty-nine, and had not lived among the Zulus since he was six; if Senzangakona had even reported his promise to anyone but Mkabi, it had long since been forgotten. Shaka sent his half brother Ngwadi ahead—Nandi's son by Gendeyana—and when he himself stalked into the Zulu kraals, in a deadly silence, Sigujana's body was floating in a nearby stream. Something of Shaka's adult reputation may have preceded him, but he was still the son of the disgraced Nandi, a stranger and more of a Mtetwa than a Zulu. The leaderless and hostile clan took wary stock of the man they had not seen in almost a quarter of a century, but there was no hesitation on Shaka's part. Almost ignoring the iziCwe escort, he took up his scepter and commenced his rule as if there had never been any question of his right to do so. From the day of his arrival the Zulus left forever the ranks of sleepy upcountry clans and commenced their march to greatness.

There was much to be done. The clan was in a state of confusion, a natural outcome of the two rapid changes in leadership. Courtiers who had filled various posts under Senzangakona and Sigujana hardly knew where they stood with Shaka, the army was pitifully small and totally lacking in organization, and most of the royal cattle seemed to have disappeared. To add to the turmoil, a younger half brother named Dingane returned from a visit to the Qwabes with some idea of disputing the chieftainship. He was shocked to find Sigujana dead and forgotten, but after his first glimpse of Shaka he hastily dropped whatever he may have had in mind and made obeisance. The new chieftain greeted him courteously and left him in peace; it was the worst mistake he ever made.

Shaka went to work vigorously, treating the Zulus as so much clay to be molded in accordance with his personal wishes. He dealt instant death at the slightest sign of hesitation. It was his right as chieftain, but not in the memory of the clan had this right been exercised so freely, so suddenly, or with such appalling callousness. All half-formulated opposition disappeared.

First was the matter of his kraal. He had no desire to take over Senzangakona's, of unhappy memory to him. He built a new one, and ominously named it *kwaBulawayo*—"At the Place of He Who Kills— With Afflictions." Then there was the matter of his personal attendants. He found Zulu cookery inadequate—uncouth, in fact—and he sent to specified clans for his chefs, who taught the Zulus how Shaka wanted his amaSi prepared. Any anti-Zulu medicine a future enemy clan might want to prepare would have to be based on Shaka's *inSila*, or "dirt"—which ranged from excreta to fingernail parings—so a whole series of attendants was appointed to deal with it. The Royal Barber, who paid with his life for the slightest nick in the royal chin, had daily to collect the shaven stubble, burn it, and scatter the ashes in a river. There was also a Receiver of the Royal Spittle (his back served as a receptacle), and even a Wiper of the Royal Anus.

Shaka then began to rectify the absence of the cattle. At first he borrowed from neighboring clans, who made haste to comply, since his personal reputation outstripped that of his clan. Among the borrowings was the nucleus of what eventually became his fabulous herd of snow-white cattle.

His most immediate concern was the army. If the Zulus were to rise—and Shaka had no intention of lording it over such a minor clan as had satisfied his father—it could only be through the army. He knew by now precisely what kind of a military machine he wanted, and he built it from scratch.

He had refined his early experimentations with the iziCwe into a standard formation that required at least four separate groups, although each of these four tactical units could be composed of numerous subdivisions. The strongest of these was the "chest," the main body that in battle closed at once with an enemy and held it fast. The two "horns" raced out and surrounded the enemy impi until the tips met, whereupon both horns turned in and worked back to the center. The fourth unit consisted of a large reserve known as the "loins," which was placed behind the chest and remained seated with backs to the fight so as not to become excited. The commander took station on any convenient elevation, from whence he could communicate with all parts of the field by runner, sending the reserve in wherever the enemy threatened a breakout. The formation sounded simple, but its execution depended on several mass movements which had to be carried out, frequently over broken ground and at top speed, silently, while maintaining perfect alignment.

Shaka had also sensed that his own fighting spirit could best be infused in his warriors through the mechanism of the regiment; his men had fought better for the honor of the iziCwe than they had for the honor of the Mtetwa. An *élan* could be milked from such tightly knit and highly polarized groups that would never come from mere membership in a clan. The escort from the iziCwe, owing allegiance to Dingiswayo, had returned to the Mtetwa as soon as they had seen

Shaka safely installed, so he now called up the entire adult male strength of the Zulu clan.

It is doubtful if even 400 men answered this summons, and it was a mixed lot that Shaka surveyed. Perhaps half were *iKhehla*, who wore the *isiCoco*, a headring donned by fully mature males just prior to their initial marriage. This ring, unique to the Zulus, was made by sewing a fiber circlet into the hair and plastering it into place with beeswax. The ring was then greased and polished, and the hair around it shorn. Only those with headrings had had any previous military experience; most of them had survived one or more of the humiliating defeats administered by the Butelezi. Those without headrings—men about to marry or senior herdboys proudly answering their first call—had seen little or no service.

Shaka immediately formed four regiments—the minimum he needed for his tactics. He placed all the older men, headringed and married, into the *amaWombe*. He allowed them to keep their wives, but he built them a new kraal, to which they all had to move, and he placed it under a maiden aunt, Mkabayi, who had once been kind to Nandi. (He had immediately executed those who had shown her hostility, including Mudli, his own uncle and the man who had sent the eLangeni the original insulting message about "iShaka.") Another group, perhaps thirty years of age, had already taken the headring but had as yet not married. Shaka banded them together as the *uJubingqwana*—"They of the Headring Ukase"—for he made them all shave off this sign of maturity and reduced them all to boys again. The balance of the mature men, still without headrings, were organized as the *umGamule*, and since both regiments were scanty in numbers he brigaded them together as the *izimPohlo*, or "Bachelors' Brigade."

This left the herdboys, fresh from their years in the open, and the youngest of the bachelors, scarcely more than herdboys themselves. From this group Shaka fashioned the *uFasimba*—"the Haze"—and the one group which could be trained in his methods from the start of its career. It became his favorite regiment, "Shaka's Own"; here he placed his greatest reliance and it became the prototype for the regiments that followed.

Shaka at once collected all the throwing assegais, threw away the hafts, and sent the blades to every smithy he could reach to be turned into stabbing assegais. While he was waiting for their return, he started drilling his men. They practiced the new movements until they dropped with weariness, until each group knew its function and could carry it out instantly and silently in response to signals. Zulus, already hardy from a life in the open, were pushed and prodded until the regiments could travel fifty miles in a single day, trotting tirelessly over the rolling trackless hills, living off cattle and stored grain from the kraals they passed, and accompanied only by the uDibi boys with their sleeping mats and cooking pots. (European troops, on paved roads, prided themselves on their ability to cover fifteen miles from sunup to sundown.)

Shaka drew further on his earlier experience and ordered the army to discard its rawhide sandals. This innovation led to grumbling, which only ceased when he arranged a dance on a bare area he had sprinkled with thorns, and then executed every warrior whose mind did not appear to be fully occupied with the rhythm. The Zulu feet toughened immediately, and the army never went back to the sandals.

He also cut new shields, larger than the old ones and wetted and dried to toughen them. He matched the shields to his regiments by a color code; he himself carried a pure white one with a single black spot in the center. Each regiment also adopted its own song and war cry and, making use of various ornaments fashioned from feather and fur, its own uniform. Shaka wore a golden kilt made from twisted strips of civet fur, a collar of the same material, and, fastened under the knees and over the elbows, circlets of leather with long white cowtail fringes. In his headband he bore a long blue feather from the tail of the lory bird, which only he might wear. He never married, and never wore the isiCoco. So fiercely individualistic did his regiments become that— much to his delight—their kraals had to be widely separated, since a fight resulted whenever two of them met.

When the new assegais arrived, he drilled his men in their use and in the hooking manuever he had developed with his shield. The drills were incessant, and before his first year was out, he had forged a weapon the likes of which black Africa had never seen before. The Zulu army was then perhaps 350 strong, still untried, and neither his own name nor that of his clan meant much in particular to anyone but his immediate neighbors.

There was, at first, a heavy check on his activity. As long as Dingiswayo lived, Shaka was a vassal of the Mtetwa, and even had he borne his paramount chieftain animosity, the Mtetwa were far too powerful for Shaka to attack or even annoy. He was far enough from the center of the Mtetwa influence to permit independent action, and he knew perfectly well that Dingiswayo, rather than being annoyed, would look with favor on any dependent buffer state he might be able to construct. Dingiswayo, indeed, expected something of the sort; but he would not be permitted to build indiscriminately, or to dominate a coalition that would threaten the Mtetwa themselves. He would have to proceed with caution.

He started with the small clans in his immediate vicinity. The first of these were the eLangeni, who awoke one morning to find the Zulu impi surrounding their main kraal. There was no resistance. Shaka paraded the entire male population of the clan and searched out the members of the iNtangas who had made his life a torment as a child. One or two, those who had done Nandi such small services as helping her find a new grindstone and the like, were dismissed with the gift of an ox, but asked to stay long enough to see how much they owed these long-forgotten acts. The remainder were impaled on the sharpened stakes of their own kraal fences; Shaka put an end to the agony of those surviving at sundown by firing the kraals.

The bulk of the eLangeni were incorporated into the Zulu clan, lock, stock and cattle. The men were drafted into the existing regiments, rigged out with the new assegais and shields, and taught the new tactics.

Shaka sopped up other small clans in the vicinity in similar fashion, several submitting without a fight. He next turned to the Butelezi, but Pungashe proved to be pugnacious. Already defeated by Dingiswayo, he saw no reason to suffer additional humiliation at the hands of the Zulus, whom he still equated with the weaklings of Senzangakona's days. He drew no particular conclusions from the fact that their upstart chieftain had participated in his losing battle with the Mtetwa.

The subsequent battle, the first real test for the new Zulu army, was a triumphant vindication for the recent innovations. Slightly outnumbering the Butelezi, Shaka bunched his regiments at the outset, and made the men carry their shields on edge, so that his force seemed small. Then, when the horns raced out, each warrior turned his shield toward the enemy, and the army seemed to double in an instant. The horns encompassed not only the Butelezi impi, but also the clan's women and children, watching from a nearby elevation. The disciplined regiments smashed into the Butelezi and reduced them to a bloody welter, and when some of the fleeing warriors sought shelter amidst the women, the slaughter started there as well. When Shaka finally called a halt, there were only a few scattered survivors.

Pungashe himself had fled. Escaping to the north, he crossed the Black Umfolozi and sought refuge with Zwide, chieftain of the powerful Ndwandwe. Zwide had been defeated twice already by Dingiswayo, to whom he was related by marriage, but that magnanimous chieftain had on each occasion released him. The Ndwandwe were too far upcountry for the Mtetwa to control; they blocked expansion to the northwest and their size and Zwide's capricious treachery made them a threat to all the clans that dwelt in their shadow. Dingiswayo's hopes for a buffer state in the vicinity of the Zulus, in fact, were based on the Ndwandwe threat. Zwide now heard Pungashe's story and then killed him.

In token of fealty Shaka sent the Butelezi cattle on to Dingiswayo, who approved of his recent activity and returned the bulk of the cattle. There were, this time, no surviving drafts to incorporate into the Zulu regiments, but Shaka took such Butelezi maidens as survived and established at kwaBulawayo a seraglio that was eventually to number 1,200 women. This was his *umDlunkulu*, and he carefully referred to its inmates as his "sisters"; they were never his "wives." During the twelve years of his reign the umDlunkulu did not produce a single heir of record. Shaka maintained that he had no desire for offspring who might some day oppose him, and by tradition he would only engage in ukuHlobonga, but in view of the utter lack of control that characterized every other facet of his personality, it is far more probable that he never managed to consummate a full relationship.

By the beginning of 1817 the Zulu territories had quadrupled in size. The army numbered some 2,000 trained warriors, and there were 800 men in the uFasimba alone. None of the three junior regiments had been allowed to marry. Between campaigns they lived in enforced celibacy in their military kraals.

That autumn Shaka received word that Mbiya, his foster father in the emDletsheni, was dying. He journeyed the seventy miles to the coastal regions to bid him adieu, and then went on the twenty miles to Dingiswayo's kraal to confer with his overlord. The two men decided on a major expedition against a chieftain named Matiwane, whose powerful emaNgwaneni clan was nestled in the foothills of the Drakensberg Range. Matiwane, a short brawny man of great intelligence but with a ferocious temper, lived even beyond Zwide, well outside the Mtetwa influence, from where he was able to keep the Mtetwa borders in a turmoil.

The expedition was scheduled for the winter month of June, and because a general mobilization had been decreed, Matiwane learned well in advance that he was to be the target. He made what preparations he could, and he asked a neighbor, Mtimkulu of the amaHlubi, to guard his clan's cattle in the mountains until the fighting was over. Mtimkulu, the son of Bungane, the chieftain who had sheltered Dingiswayo during his exile, agreed.

To Shaka's disgust, the fighting was inconclusive. Dingiswayo accepted a quick surrender, topped it off with a lecture on good relations, and departed, leaving Matiwane's forces largely intact. With the Mtetwa army gone, Matiwane sent to Mtimkulu for the return of his cattle. To his astonishment, Mtimkulu refused.

While Matiwane was pondering his next move—the amaHlubi dwelt among some rugged mountains and a campaign against them was not to be undertaken lightly—Zwide with his Ndwandwes fell on him and evicted him from his lands. Zwide had rightly assumed that Matiwane would be an easy mark after his brush with the Mtetwa, and he himself was far enough removed from Dingiswayo to be careless of possible retaliation. In forcing the emaNgwaneni out of their territory, however, he unleashed a disastrous chain of events.

The eastern Nguni were far more crowded than they realized. The check in the distant south had corked the coastal strip a generation before, and by now almost all the interstices between the clans had filled. Despite the continual bickering the past century had constituted a Golden Age; the climate was benign, the country fruitful, and the clans and their cattle had been breeding at a terrific rate. The area was approaching an overpopulation problem for which there was no peaceful solution. The Boers blocked the south, and the west was blocked not only by the natural wall of the Drakensberg Range but also by innumerable Sutu clans who had settled the inland plateau almost as thickly as the Nguni had settled the coastal strip. The way to the north was barred by Tonga clans and a broad, swampy and fever-infested belt along the lower reaches of the Pongola River.

Zwide's attack on Matiwane raised a brand-new problem. In the past Dingiswayo in victory might take a percentage of a clan's cattle, and Shaka might actually exterminate a small clan, but Zwide had now for the first time deprived a sizable mass of people of all means of livelihood. Matiwane's choice was simple; he could let his people starve, or he could fall on the nearest source of cattle and land with a ferocity born of desperation. He naturally chose to fall on the amaHlubi, which he did with a grim purpose that even Shaka would have approved. He massacred all the major Hlubi kraals, recovered his cattle, and then as a preventive measure went on a rampage among the Hlubi subclans before they could organize an effective resistance. The remnants of these clans cleared out in a body, and because there was no room for them on the coastal plain below, they crossed through the passes of the Drakensberg Range and descended on the startled Sutu clans beyond. A deadly game of musical chairs had started.

It is necessary to trace out Matiwane's subsequent history before we return to Shaka, because the chain reaction that had now been initiated had a profound effect on the history of southern Africa. While the amaHlubi were looking for land and cattle among the Sutus, Matiwane abandoned most of their territory and settled his clan in a crowded patch lower in the foothills. The amaHlubi had been mountain folk, and their kraals were dotted on hillsides far too steep for the liking of the emaNgwaneni. Tightly compressed in a vulnerable position, they enjoyed a few years of comparative peace until 1822, by which time Dingiswayo and Zwide were both dead and Shaka reigned supreme between the mountains and the coast. The Zulu impis were ranging farther and farther afield, and when they approached Matiwane that year, they were infinitely more powerful than the Mtetwa army that had moved against him in 1817. Matiwane also knew that Shaka would never be satisfied with the negotiated peace that Dingiswayo had once accepted, so he abandoned his land and cattle and fled over the Drakensberg with his entire clan.

He was unable to settle his people in the vast central plateau beyond the mountains. The kraal economy could not be built overnight, since not only land but a season of peace was required to grow the crops. The only alternative was pillage, so that Matiwane and his emaNgwaneni, as well as the amaHlubi, who had been at it for the last five years, moved through the Sutu clans in great destructive arcs, scattering freshly displaced groups ahead of them who in turn were also forced to go marauding.

In 1823 Matiwane unexpectedly blundered against the main body of the amaHlubi, who were finally showing signs of settling down. The clans attacked each other in deadly enmity—this was no mere question of displacement—and after a savage battle that flickered and flared over five days, the amaHlubi were broken, with only a few tiny bands fleeing to escape the massacre that followed.

From here on the record is confused. Something is known of the early history of the coastal Nguni, because Europeans arrived in the area while Shaka was still alive and the events of the preceding generation were still fresh in living memory; but except for a few missionary outposts far to the south, there had been no penetration of the main reservoir of the Sutu clans, and nothing of their early history had been recorded. What occurred now, therefore, passed virtually unnoticed by either the coastal Nguni or the white civilization south of the Orange River. Only on occasion did the seething cauldron of humanity fling a spatter of wreckage up over the rim that gave a hint of what was going on in the interior.

The movements of Matiwane can be traced, and the names of some of the clans he jarred loose are known, but the rest is chaos. As each clan was shaken loose, it attacked a fresh area, and the groups of refugees grew smaller and smaller, and their courses shorter, until something over two and a half million people were stumbling back and forth over the land, sometimes running away from something, and sometimes striving to reach something, but always in search of food and a security that no longer existed. Over scores of thousands of square miles, not a single permanent kraal existed, nor a single clan staunch enough to avoid being sucked into the maelstrom. Cannibalism, which was fully as repugnant to Bantu civilization as it is to our own, became common, and reached the point where entire clans depended on it and nothing else to feed themselves. Nameless, formless mobs coalesced and began to move, acquiring strength from individuals who saw the only hope of safety in numbers, and these mobs rolled across the blighted country and stripped it of everything edible. For decades their aimless tracks were marked by countless human bones.

One of the larger Sutu clans, for example, was the baTlokwa, led by a formidable woman named Mantatisi. They were among the first clans the amaHlubi had displaced, and they set off in a vast circle of destruction of their own. Woman chieftains were a rarity, and they generally had to demonstrate a considerable force of personality before a clan would accept them; this Mantatisi did in ample fashion, rampaging across the land with a ferocity that matched Matiwane's. She scotched one threat that appeared while her men were off foraging by lining up all the women and children in a military formation and trotting the unarmed mob straight at her erstwhile attackers, who promptly fled. As the baTlokwa curved one way, the amaHlubi curved the other, and they met and caromed off each other just before the amaHlubi met their final destruction at the hands of Matiwane.

Mantatisi's specialty was rapid travel, and she sopped up the clans she passed over like an enormous sponge. By 1823 she had worked her way far to the south, traveling with an immense horde of some 50,000 people, totally uprooted and forced to move every day in order to feed the large herd of cattle penned up in the center of the unmanageable mass. Hundreds of people attached to this horde died daily, unable to find food, to find water, bewildered, lost and utterly spent.

This vast concourse, known to history as the Mantatee Horde, rolled down from the north and eventually approached a small baTlapin settlement to which some white missionaries from the Cape Colony had attached themselves. The baTlapin were all for flight, but the missionaries stiffened them and sent for help to the Griquas living to the west under their chieftains Waterboer and Kok. These Griquas (who also answered proudly to the sobriquet "Baastards") had evolved from miscegenation between the early Cape settlers and the Hottentots. They were by now a distinct race precariously perched between civilization and savagery. They farmed, owned horses and guns, and many of them dressed in European fashion, but they lived in isolation. They now rallied to this appeal for help, and perhaps a hundred mounted men started for the baTlapin settlement. It was a close race, and the baTlapin, with the Mantatee Horde already upon them, were

packed and poised for flight when the first Griquas streamed into their
kraals.

The Griquas had only a few dozen rounds of ammunition apiece,
and their baTlapin allies, reinforced by a few scrapings from other
clans, were terrorized and useless. The Griquas nevertheless sallied
forth to reconnoiter the amorphous fringes of the Mantatee Horde.

Their first sight of the enemy, recorded by one of the missionaries,
was an eerie one. In the gray dawn an outflung group of some 15,000
armed men huddled on a hillside around their dying campfires, looking
for all the world like a still-smoking patch of burned-over grass. Only
when the men discovered the Griquas and stirred, so that the rising sun
caught their assegai blades, did the illusion disappear.

There was no question of engaging such a force bodily, or even of
making a dent in the mass of humanity. All that the Griquas could do
for the next five days was to herd the ponderous body, trotting back
and forth along its fringes, slashing and snapping, and dexterously
avoiding its thrusts. The baTlapin ran from each attack, returning later
to hack and stab at the women and children who had been separated
from the mass. The mob was finally stopped, turned, and then slowly
started back on the long path to the north.

On their retreat they attacked a small Sutu clan led by a young
chieftain named Mshweshwe. They forced him out of his area in a
conflict known as the War of the Pots because the baTlokwa lost all
their crockery in the fighting. Mshweshwe was appalled at the destruction by which he was surrounded, and alone refused to join in the
general pillaging. He gathered his clan, perhaps 2,000 people, and led
them south, into the western foothills of the Drakensberg (his grandfather Peete was eaten by cannibals on the way), and here he found a
most unusual mountain. Thaba Bosiu—"the Mountain of the Night"
—was a flat-topped hill in a deep, hidden valley, with 150 acres of good
pasture and a spring on the summit. The plateau was surrounded by a
steep scarp with only three access trails. Mshweshwe established his
clan on top and supplied each trail with enormous mounds of boulders,
which could be rolled down to break up attackers. Perched on this
stronghold, he formed the only island of sanity in a sea of madness, and
over the years was able to build his clan into the Basuto nation. He
pieced it together from debris cast up in the general havoc, offering
succor to the fragmented groups that eddied and swirled through the
foothills. His security was greatly enhanced by a carefully planted
rumor that the mountain grew to an immense height at night and
subsided to its normal 300 feet during the day.

The Mantatee Horde rolled on to the north, where it eventually fell
apart from the strain of its own weight. Mantatisi died, and was re-

placed by her son Sikonyela, but the baTlokwa remained a major nuisance until Mshweshwe, by then a power in the land, finally finished them off in 1852.

Matiwane, meanwhile, had angled off to the southeast, passing through the fringes of Mshweshwe's new domain, where the latter was already too strong to be budged. He fought back against Matiwane with all his strength, even calling on Shaka for help at one point, so that either a Zulu impi or some other force from the coastal strip came to his aid. Matiwane finally left him in peace, and by 1828 had come to a temporary halt in Tembu country, having crossed the southern end of the Drakensberg Range.

Unbeknownst to him, a Zulu expedition had that year ranged all the way south in the coastal strip to the Great Kei River. This was perilously close to British Kaffraria, and a mixed force of British regulars, Boer commandos and native allies sallied forth to drive them back. The presence of the emaNgwaneni was known, but the British had confused them with the Zulus and thought they were all part of the same force.

On July 26, 1828, a Major Dundas with thirty Europeans and a small force of native allies bumped into Matiwane, introducing him to the wonders of gunpowder. Dundas reported his location to a Colonel Somerset, who had with him the 55th Foot (today the 2nd Battalion of the Border Regiment), a large party of Boers, and close to 18,000 Tembus. By the time Somerset reached the scene, the Zulus were long gone, but Matiwane was still there. Kaffirs were Kaffirs, so on the twenty-eighth of August Somerset cheerfully attacked him on the Umtata River and smashed him. He then retired, still under the impression that he had beaten the Zulus.

The battle scattered the emaNgwaneni and broke Matiwane's spirit. For over a decade he had led his people—the Nomads of Wrath—on a broad highway of ruin and death, and now his people were gone and he was almost alone. With a few wives and their children and a handful of retainers he started a lonely retreat to the north, with some idea of throwing himself on Shaka's mercy.

He passed up the western side of the Drakensberg and neared the vicinity of Thaba Bosiu. Given Matiwane's history, any other Bantu chieftain would have murdered him out of hand, but the incredible Mshweshwe offered him sanctuary. Matiwane sorrowfully refused—he was simply homesick—and, leaving an ill wife and her children with Mshweshwe, he pressed on to his distant homeland. This was Zulu territory by the time he reached it, and Shaka's successor sent for him, pondered his future for a while, and then gouged his eyes out and killed him by driving wooden pegs up his nostrils.

This period of history on the inland plateau is known as the *Mfecane* —"the crushing." At least a million people, and more likely two, died in a decade that virtually depopulated what is today the Orange Free State. On the coastal strip it took the frontier almost a century to move the few score miles north of British Kaffraria, which had been spared the total annihilation of the interior. When the Boers trekked north-west of the Drakensberg in 1836, however, they passed freely for hundreds of miles through a fertile countryside peopled by more skeletons than living natives.

The toll in the interior has usually been added to Shaka's reckoning, but while he was certainly responsible for the havoc on the coastal strip, he had little enough to do with the destruction in the interior. The onus here falls on Zwide and Matiwane and Mtimkulu, but ultimate responsibility, perhaps, should be assigned to Bantu civilization itself. Bound through the centuries to a rigid pattern, it depended on free land to supply the flexibility it lacked, and in the end it proved too brittle to adjust to a single footloose clan.

Following his subjugation of Matiwane in 1817, Dingiswayo turned his attention to Zwide. Although the Ndwandwe had never set out on a course of aggrandizement of their own, they were potential trouble-makers. Always, at the most inopportune moment, it was Zwide who lashed out like a snake, touching events that might have had a more fortuitous ending had he left them alone. Zwide had been a friend of Dingiswayo's father, and despite Jobe's attempt to murder his son, Dingiswayo had always respected the friendship and left Zwide in peace. He had, however, increasing difficulty in mastering his ire, and in 1818 an involved family dispute arose between the two, during the course of which Zwide murdered Dingiswayo's son-in-law. This was too much for Dingiswayo, who sent a message to Shaka to join him in an invasion, and then set out with his army for the Ndwandwe borders. Just before matters reached an open break, however, Zwide made a final effort to smooth over the rupture, and he sent Dingiswayo a peace offering in the form of a highly attractive addition to his isiGodlo.

Dingiswayo went right ahead with his preparations, but he accepted and made use of the gift. This charmer then slipped out of his kraal one night and returned to Zwide, bearing a smear of Dingiswayo's semen, which was turned over to the war doctor. The Ndwandwe were overjoyed. No more potent form of inSila could be imagined.

For some reason the Zulus were delayed, and the Mtetwa army waited on the Ndwandwe borders for them to catch up. Zwide was busy with his defenses, relying heavily on medicine made with the semen, which was used to doctor the river fords on the border. The

witch doctors were only too successful—it was just such blind luck
that has kept witchcraft alive to the present day. Dingiswayo, for no
good reason whatsoever, left his army and wandered into Ndwandwe
country unarmed and accompanied only by a bevy of girls. He blundered straight into the arms of a small patrol. Zwide could hardly
believe his good fortune. He had Dingiswayo brought to his kraal,
treated him courteously for a day or two while making certain no
trick was involved, and then cut his head off and gave it to his mother,
who collected such things.

The leaderless Mtetwa army lost all heart. Shaka arrived with his
forces just as Zwide attacked, and all the Zulu discipline sufficed only
to win a retreat in good order.

An incompetent half brother followed Dingiswayo on the Mtetwa
throne, and the clan's power declined. For a year or so, while Shaka
and Zwide warily watched each other over a single buffer clan, the
empire seemingly remained intact, but when a few minor disturbances,
which Dingiswayo would have quelled immediately, went unpunished,
it was suddenly apparent that while the bright beads of the Mtetwa
hegemony still lay in their old positions, the thread that held them
together had vanished.

There were now three potential contenders for the rich prize of
paramountcy. The Qwabes, a large and potentially dangerous clan
between the Mtetwa and the Zulus, showed signs of entering the contest, and Shaka was hemmed between them and the Ndwandwe. Both
clans were over twice the size of the Zulus.

Zwide moved first. Regarding himself as invincible, he sent a large
force against Shaka, who at once snapped up the buffer clan and
moved to meet the threat. Abandoning his usual tactics (the Ndwandwe army was far too large for the Zulus to think of encirclement), he
took a strong circular defensive position around the summit of a conical hill topped by a deep depression within which he was able to hide
his reserve. He also sent the Zulu cattle off with a small escort, deliberately leaving the herd visible to draw off a portion of the enemy in
pursuit.

The Battle of Gqokli Hill opened in the early morning, when the
Ndwandwe surrounded the rise and made the first of a series of frontal
assaults. All were uniformly unsuccessful. As the attackers clambered
up, their front narrowed, and by the time they reached the Zulus, the
terrific press hampered their movements. They were in any event
armed only with the throwing assegais, and unprepared for the Zulu
skill at close quarters. By midafternoon the Ndwandwe were exhausted, and in addition to heavy casualties had suffered the loss of
scores of men who had wandered off in search of water. (Shaka, well

supplied on the summit, had carefully chosen a location some miles from the nearest spring.) The Ndwandwe now staked everything on a last endeavor. Leaving half their force in a semicircle at the foot of the hill, they formed a heavy column with the remainder and launched it at the Zulu ring from the other side, hoping to drive the defenders over the top and into the arms of the men waiting beyond. Shaka grabbed his chance, and when the column was almost at the top sent his fresh reserves streaming down on either side, to surround and annihilate it. He then circled the hill to attack the remainder of the Ndwandwe, whose view of events had been blocked by the summit. This group broke, and just managed to rejoin the body of men returning from the cattle chase.

The surviving Ndwandwe were now together, and in some force. They had, moreover, captured almost all the Zulu cattle, and had easily beaten off the attacks of the small uFasimba escort that had originally driven the cattle away as a lure. Shaka was now outnumbered and, under continuous attack, was forced to retreat to his kwaBulawayo kraal, where he was reinforced by the last scrapings of his reserve and small parties streaming in from their pursuit of the Ndwandwe defeat at the hill. The Ndwandwe finally withdrew, taking all the Zulu cattle with them. They had been savagely mauled, but were still largely intact. Zwide, who never accompanied his forces, had lost five sons in the course of the day.

Shaka was well pleased with the results of the first real test of the Zulu army. Despite grievous losses, he had beaten off a clan more than twice the size of his own, and now his army was being swelled by a growing stream of individual volunteers, as well as by whole clans which joined him while they still had a chance to do so on terms of good will. Shaka made all welcome, and promoted newcomers on the basis of merit, often over the heads of his own original inDunas. One of these was a Kumalo named Mzilikazi, a petty chieftain from the north and a grandson of Zwide, who had fled when Zwide killed his father. Another was Ndlela, who, somewhat to the disgust of the men serving under him, was an ex-cannibal.

He also formed new regiments, although for a while he simply incorporated the incoming parties into his four original regiments. These were by now swollen in size, and composed of subdivisions, many of which still retained their own names, so that the regiments in fact became brigades. Whatever their source, all recruits were armed with the iKlwa and subjected to the Zulu drill and discipline.

Zwide was also regrouping. His own forces were augmented with sizable levies from the Swazi clans he controlled in the north, and he made a belated effort to copy the iKlwa. In May of 1819 he invaded Shaka's territory for a second try.

Shaka was well prepared. He had invited the Qwabes to join him, but their chieftain had preferred to await the outcome of the Zulu-Ndwandwe dispute and had returned a surly answer. Shaka struck him at once, won an easy victory, and added the Qwabes to his own force. Now, with no opposition left behind him, he faced the Ndwandwe army, under the redoubtable Soshangane.

The Ndwandwe were 18,000 strong, a huge force for the warfare of the day, and Shaka left no tempting targets in their path. He had driven the cattle of all the clans he controlled off into the forests, to be followed by the women and children, and he had even emptied the grain pits in the kraals. Then, for a few days, he kept his compact force in the path of, but just beyond reach of, the exasperated Ndwandwe. As usual, he was well supplied by his uDibi, who for this campaign were reinforced by herdboys from iNtangas well below the usual age. The Ndwandwe, however, had no supplies, and could find none in the deserted area they traversed. For the better part of a week Shaka led them a wild chase, until, ravenous and frustrated, they decided to retreat.

They camped for the last night in a thick forest, and Shaka sent small parties among them to stir the sleeping host. The few casualties the Ndwandwe suffered were mostly self-inflicted, but the rumpus cost them a night's rest, and it was a starving and exhausted army that started to retreat in the morning. Then, finally, Shaka attacked. The battle raged for two days over a series of contested river fords, and when it died down, the Ndwandwe were smashed. Shaka then led a fresh reserve the seventy miles to Zwide's kraal and ordered his men to sing a Ndwandwe victory chant as they approached in the dark. The royal kraal turned out in a body to greet the returning heroes, discovered their mistake when it was too late, and died in the ashes of their own kraal.

Zwide himself escaped, gathering a handful of the scattered refugees and striking out for the north. He settled for a while among the baBelu, a Sutu people, and seemed in a fair way to reconstitute his clan, when he fell foul of a chieftainess named Mjanji. This awesome woman reigned over a small baPedi clan, which lived in a hidden valley in peace and comfort with never a thought of war—no clan in its right mind would dare attack her. She was the Queen of the Locusts, and could send deluge, drought or insects against anyone who opposed her. She also had four breasts, so pendulous that she could sling them over her shoulder and suckle an infant borne on her back. She was by repute immortal, and it was death for a stranger to look on her. The baPedi took care to keep both beliefs alive, and were consequently never bothered by outsiders seeking to find if she were still alive. She was reported living as late as 1896. Mjanji let it be known that her magic was herewith directed against Zwide, and Zwide obligingly died.

Soshangane also got away, taking the nucleus of an army with him. He also worked his way north, nursing his forces, and he eventually drove the Portuguese out of the country beyond St. Lucia Bay to found a Shangane nation outside the Zulu sphere.

Shaka had now been on his throne three years, and had so consolidated his rule that not a tribe in all black Africa could have opposed him. Less than a year after Dingiswayo's death his rule went far beyond the Mtetwa hegemony, and his grip on his subjects far exceeded that enjoyed by his milder predecessor. For all his power, however, only a few minor clans in his immediate vicinity had felt his weight, and only the Ndwandwe had been broken up. Hardly a ripple had as yet disturbed the placid surface to give a hint of the monstrous force hidden in the depths.

The Zulu domain now stretched from the Pongola River in the north to the Tugela River in the south, and from the coast inland to the Blood River. The original hundred square miles had increased to 11,500; the army now numbered 20,000, a long way from the 350 who had answered Shaka's first call. This area was Shaka's heartland, and a new phenomenon now began to manifest itself. There were scores of clans within Zululand, but such chieftains as survived had been relegated to a status hardly higher than inDuna, and their royal blood, no longer of political significance, was only a matter of social standing. The clans began to identify themselves with the Zulus, even to refer to themselves as Zulus, and the clan basis of activity began to fade. The political voices of the future would speak not for two or three thousand clansmen, but for a nation of a quarter of a million.

Shaka's military activity to date had been forced by events. As he had one by one removed the threats to his existence, each step had been dictated by the last one, and the sequence had been logical. Now, for the first time, he was free to act as he pleased, and all logic disappeared. Dingiswayo had been motivated by a Grand Design, a closely reasoned dream of political union to which he had devoted all his skill and power. Shaka displayed no such motivation; having consolidated his base, he could conceive of no further objectives for which to use his power, and he employed it blindly, striking out wherever his whims led him. He waged war for the sake of war, and the Zulus grew rich on the hundreds of thousands of cattle the impis brought back from their raids. What became of the clans they had been lifted from, or what ravages occurred beyond his ken, interested him not a whit. If he felt any goad, it was one all tyrants have discovered to their sorrow—the fact that a large standing army cannot be maintained in idleness.

In 1820 he attacked two of the largest clans across the Buffalo River. Ngosa, chieftain of the Tembu, and Macingwane, leader of the Cunu, called up their minor dependent clans and defended the river crossings. The Zulu army, divided, fought two simultaneous actions. It defeated the Tembu, slaughtered most of the women and children, and brought off tens of thousands of cattle, but the division thrown against the Cunu was forced back over the Buffalo. The Cunu stayed where they were for the nonce, but the Tembu streamed south into Natal proper and made good their losses from the intricate network of clans still jostling each other in the coastal strip.

For a season or two Shaka busied himself with his own domains, resettling clans in the deserted Ndwandwe area and gathering in the last few holdouts in Zululand. Then, in the winter of 1822, he invaded Natal. (It was from this invasion that Matiwane finally fled over the Drakensberg.) The Tembu and Cunu attempted a final stand, but the Zulu weight was too great for resistance. They broke and started for the south, touching off a replica of what was even then beginning in the interior.

There were differences, but the net effect was the same. The chaos in the interior was total, with no focal point of disturbance. The movement on the coast was not as aimless, and the stampede, general as it was, proceeded only to the south. Clan after clan crumbled and ran; there were feeble attempts to stem the tide, by vague coalitions that dissolved half-formed. The refugee stream poured south, spreading fresh disaster, and finally petered out on the border itself, where the Xhosa clans were embroiled with the European frontier.

By 1824 it was over. Not a single clan remained in a belt a hundred miles wide south of the Tugela River; in an area that had teemed with bustling clans only thousands of deserted kraals remained, most of them in ashes. A few thousand terrified inhabitants remained, hiding out in the bush or forest in pitiful bands, and cannibalism flourished. No one dared to till crops or build kraals.

The clan structure in the far south held, although strained to the limit. Two major tribes were formed from the debris: the Fingoes of British Kaffraria—reduced almost to helots—whose very name had been taken from their cries of want as they entered the area, and the Bacas, who led a precarious existence in the hunted corners of Natal until the coming of the white man provided them a shelter from the Zulu wrath.

Other Zulu expeditions harried the north, where some scattered Sutu clans had spilled over from the Transvaal. Shaka placed Mzilikazi in charge of one of these raids, and, in Ndwandwe country, he stopped off at the kraal where his father had once ruled before Zwide killed him. His reception was heartfelt, and, his raiding mission successfully accomplished, he settled at his father's kraal with the cattle he had brought off—and the two regiments entrusted to his care.

Shaka, noting the discrepancy between the reports of the cattle taken and the token numbers Mzilikazi had sent him, requested the balance, but Mzilikazi made no reply. Such defiance was more than sufficient to call for heavy retaliation, but Shaka sent only a light impi to collect the cattle, and Mzilikazi defeated it. Even then Shaka was inclined to let the matter drop—Mzilikazi had been a favorite—but the Zulu elders would not condone such resistance from a young foreigner. Shaka regretfully sent a second impi in force, and Mzilikazi decamped for the interior.

He had with him only some three hundred warriors, but they were Zulus and they added their measure of ruin to that caused by the baTlokwa, the emaNgwaneni and the amaHlubi. Mzilikazi hammered a tribe—the Matabele—out of his original band and such Sutu clans as he could swallow. Where Mshweshwe had been based on an impregnable fortress, working with people speaking a single tongue, Mzilikazi was adrift on an open plain and forced to cope with a language barrier. The nation he forged, however, was even more powerful than the Basuto, and after cutting a wide swath of destruction, he finally came to rest in the northern Transvaal. He stayed there until the Boers drove him out in 1836—he offered the only effective resistance encountered by the Great Trek—and he then took his tribe so far to the north that he did not become a problem to European civilization for the next sixty years.

As the Zulu impis destroyed the clan structure in Natal, there were concurrent changes within the homeland. The Bantu economy produced few surpluses except in manpower, and the military system Shaka had by now perfected had sopped up this surplus, holding upwards of 20,000 marriageable males in enforced celibacy. The female iNtangas had also been organized into groups which corresponded to the regiments, although they performed no military function. Shaka now gave his senior regiments permission to don the headring, and ordered them to seek their wives among the girls of the eldest guild. These men, between thirty-five and forty years of age, were permitted to scatter to their home kraals and settle down, although they were still subject to call in the event of an emergency. On rare occasions he also vented the pressure that built up in the younger regiments by giving them mass permission to engage in ukuHlobonga with particular female guilds, although any resultant deflorations or pregnancies resulted in cattle fines.

There were also changes in his personality. Until he was thirty he had been subject to the orders of others, and even in his first few years as a chieftain he had been vassal to Dingiswayo and forced by circumstance to tread warily in the presence of larger clans. All these checks had now disappeared, and even as his foreign policy displayed a wanton capriciousness, so was his domestic policy careless of consequence. His rule was based on a fear so profound he could afford to ignore it; his subjects would no more think of resisting him than a mouse would gainsay an elephant. He moved through his daily routine surrounded by a retinue that included a group of executioners, who, a dozen times daily, bashed in skulls or twisted necks at a flick of Shaka's hand. The lives he snuffed out in this fashion were guilty of no great crimes; they might have sneezed while he was eating, or made him laugh when he was serious. It was no set policy that made him act like this, nor was it cruelty, which implies a desire to inflict pain. It went beyond cruelty, it ignored pain, and the people he killed meant no more to him than so many ants.

The greatest change of all, however, was just in the offing. History was about to introduce a new factor.

PORT NATAL

THE COASTAL strip filled with Bantu, the Mtetwa empire rose and fell, and the Zulus came to the fore, but no hint of these events reached the European civilization to the south. Shaka was at the height of his power in the early months of 1824, but from the Kieskamma River in the south to the Portuguese settlements at Delagoa Bay not a single white man lived or traveled amongst the Nguni Bantu of the coastal strip. The Dutch had been in Africa for 172 years, the British had been at the Cape for eighteen, but only Robert Cowan had slipped down through the Drakensberg passes to reach Natal from the west.

The littoral, however, was far from unknown. Vasco da Gama in the *San Gabriel* had named the northern reaches of the coastal strip Natal on Christmas Day in 1497, and in the years that followed, other Portuguese vessels homeward bound from India had nosed along the coast. These ships were poorly constructed, badly navigated, and invariably overladen, and on June 24, 1552, the first of a number of disastrous shipwrecks occurred. The *San João*, with a complement of 610, went ashore near what is today Port St. John. Of the 500 people who got ashore, only 25 survived the long walk to the nearest Portuguese settlement at Sofala.

The *San João* was followed by a half a dozen major shipwrecks in the following century before the Portuguese misfortunes came to an end. Close to 3,000 souls had landed on the coast, of whom a bare 500 were eventually rescued. Each wreck produced a miserable caravan of survivors, who faced an uncharted country filled with hostile fauna and a succession of strange clans with a rapacious appetite for trinkets and little food to spare. The caravans dropped women, children, the aged and the infirm at every kraal, and Portuguese sailors and slaves simply deserted to merge into tribal life. Almost every shipwrecked company encountered survivors from previous wrecks—ten, twenty and even forty years before.

The Portuguese eventually faded from the India trade, and the English ships that replaced them were stouter and manned by more skilled crews. The first English wreck occurred in 1683, and in the next few years two English wrecks and a Dutch wreck decanted a handful of hardy sailors on the shores of Natal. Some died, one was trampled to death by an elephant, but several tarried for a while to explore the surroundings and to collect ivory before trying to walk to civilization or accepting rescue from passing ships. Some of the rescued men reported meeting a Portuguese survivor wrecked 42 years before, who had been circumcised and dwelt amongst the amaMpondo with his wife and children and had "forgotten everything, his God included."

The stories that filtered back to the Cape from rescuers and rescued excited a mild interest, and in October of 1689 Governor Simon van der Stel sent a Captain Timmerman back in the galiot *Noord* to purchase Port Natal. Timmerman found a chieftain named Inyangesa, handed him a thousand guilders' worth of trade goods, and secured his mark on a document deeding the area to the United Chartered East India Company. Timmerman ringed the harbor with stone beacons and sailed away—to be wrecked near Algoa Bay. Only four of his complement of eighteen reached Capetown, where Van der Stel was far more upset by the loss of the bill of sale than by the loss of the ship and fourteen men.

In November of 1705 the galiot *Postlooper* under Captain Johannes Gerbrantzer was sent back to Port Natal to initiate exploitation of the sixteen-year-old purchase. Gerbrantzer had been a survivor of the *Noord*, and he found Inyangesa dead and his son reigning in his stead. He also made several interesting discoveries about Bantu business transactions: the concept of land transfer by written contract was only dimly understood, and contractual obligations were not regarded as binding on subsequent generations. Gerbrantzer wisely sailed away, "having no instructions from the Company concerning the matter." To southern Africa's sorrow, the lesson he learned at one sitting had to be taught over and over again.

Ships continued to touch at Port Natal, and in 1718 one of them logged a social note: "Here lived in Anno 1718, a penitent Pirate, who sequestered himself from his abominable Community and retired out of Harm's Way." The next year a British slaver anchored off Port Natal and purchased 74 boys and girls for the Rappahannock plantations in far-off Virginia, noting that "these are better slaves for working than those of Madagascar, being stronger and blacker." The visit provided one of the few instances in which maritime records served to pin down an event later salvaged from oral tradition. Timmerman in 1689 had not bothered to record the name of Inyangesa's clan, but according to native lore it had been replaced at some point in the early eighteenth century by a small clan of amaTuli under a chieftain named Shadwa, who had led his people down from the north, where the amaQwabe had been making difficulties. It is quite possible that Shadwa arrived at the bay he called *iTeku*—"One Testicle"—it being an oval landlocked harbor—in March or April of 1719, because the Bantu rarely sold their children, and the ease with which the British acquired 74 boys and girls for a few brass rings hints at a recent change of ownership in the vicinity.

The Natal coast was clear of major wrecks for the next sixty years, until the East Indiaman *Grosvenor* blundered ashore on the night of August 4, 1782. (The captain was convinced he was still 300 miles offshore, and he ignored the frantic warnings of a lookout.) The survivors set out blithely enough for Capetown, which the captain assured them they would reach in a fortnight. His estimate of latitude was even worse than his estimate of longitude; four months later six emaciated survivors staggered up to the farm of a frontier Boer—still 400 miles from Capetown. A relief expedition eventually rounded up another dozen, and for years there were rumors that some of the *Grosvenor* women had been taken to wife by Bantu chieftains. In 1790 a party investigating these tales stumbled onto a kraal on the Umgazana River whose 400 inhabitants were descended from three aged European women who as children had survived some unrecorded wreck. There were half-caste children, culturally full-fledged Bantu, with names like Bessie, Betty and Tommy, and corruptions that might once have been Geoffrey, Thomas and Michael, but the wreck they stemmed from was never identified.

On March 17, 1796, the East Indiaman *Hercules* went ashore a few miles from the wreck of the *Grosvenor*. The captain, an Englishman named Stout, lived up to his name; he got his entire complement ashore and shepherded all 64 to Capetown, which he reached in three months. He was back in London for Christmas.

The *Hercules* was the last of the major recorded shipwrecks on the Natal coast before the first permanent settlers arrived. The assorted comings and goings since 1497 left curiously little trace behind. Whatever European blood mixed into the Bantu clans dropped from sight—even the kraal of half-castes disappeared—and by the nineteenth century only one or two of the coastal Bantu could trace descent from a shipwrecked European. One of these was a Mpondo chieftain named Faku, who co-operated with Major Dundas in 1828 when Matiwane's emaNgwaneni visited his parts; another was an early convert to Methodism. Among the Bantu all knowledge of European civilization had gone; there was only the vague and curious story that a white race dwelt on the sea bottom and collected beads, occasionally riding to the shore on animals with great white wings in search of the ivory on which it fed.

Almost every wreck had its chronicler, and some of these had been observant and even articulate men, but their material was far from scientific and it was never collated. Modern researchers, puzzling over these accounts, have deciphered some of the garbled names, pinning down a river here and identifying a clan there, and they have found some evidence for the presence of Hottentots on the coastal strip before they were inundated by the oncoming Bantu. All further knowledge of the political history of the eastern Nguni Bantu came from later contact with permanent settlers.

The long period of haphazard maritime activity along the Natal coast, which had failed to provide a cohesive picture of the Bantu life in the interior, was now drawing to a close, and the first permanent European settlement lay in the immediate future. It was a direct out-growth of the Pax Britannica which had started with Waterloo; the commercial ferment of the English nation was finally released from the grip of the Napoleonic Wars, and hundreds of young officers set out to carve their careers in the far corners of the earth. They were followed by settlers, who gave impetus to a colonial movement that had been stagnating for a generation, and the English system of primo-geniture sent out younger sons from the best families of the realm. The magnificent instrument of the Royal Navy was freed for survey work, and helped to weave the colonial threads into the fabric of empire.

In September of 1822 Captain William FitzWilliam Owen, R.N., left Capetown for Delagoa Bay in H.M.S. Leven, charged with the survey of the southeast coast of Africa. Neither Captain Owen nor any of the officers in the three ships in his squadron knew much about survey work, but they were competent mariners and willing to learn. Owen raised the question of interpreters before he left Capetown, and the administration supplied him with three "excellent, trustworthy" con-victs from the penal colony on Robben's Island. Owens was pleased to note the fluency these men demonstrated in their native dialects, but he was unable to capitalize on it, as the convicts unfortunately spoke nothing else. He made an effort to rectify this failing by berthing them with his sailors, in the hope that they would pick up sufficient English to be of some use, but the arrangement caused more damage to the "domestic economy" of his crew than the linguistic progress was worth, owing primarily to the table manners the convicts displayed.

They refused to touch the standard fare of the mess deck, and showed a distressing predilection for raw entrails.

One of these interpreters showed mild signs of initiative, and he had a fragmentary smattering of English words and the simplified Dutch which was the speech of the frontier Boers. He could hardly be called fluent, but he was at least more advanced than the other two, and his progress was rapid. This was Jakot Msimbiti (he has come down in history as Jacob), an epileptic Xhosa cattle thief whom the British had captured on the Cape Colony frontier. He had been shipped to the penal colony in a small trading brig, the *Salisbury*, James Saunder King commanding, and had then been turned over to Owen with the understanding that he would eventually be granted his freedom if he performed satisfactory service.

Owen put into Delagoa Bay, the northern end of his assigned stretch, and commenced his survey. There was considerable activity in the harbor; merchant adventurers were beginning to investigate the area's potential in gold and ivory, and among others Owen encountered a John Robert Thompson, a thirty-four-year-old Bristol man who had settled at Capetown in 1809 and had there founded a trading company. The vicinity of Delagoa Bay was blighted by malaria, Thompson was down with the fever, and it shortly struck viciously at the *Leven*, but the survey work continued. Parties from the English ships investigated the interior, inhabited by a motley array of small clans, and in the course of one of these expeditions encountered a small invading army of a few hundred Bantu warriors, infinitely superior to the local variety, under the command of a chieftain named Soshangane.

The Portuguese, abysmally ignorant of ethnology, thought these were Bushmen, and the local natives, taking their terminology from long-gone Dutch ships, referred to all strangers from the south as "Hollontontes," but the invaders were in fact Ndwandwe, whom Soshangane had led north in flight from Shaka's Zulus. After making Portuguese lives miserable, he was to go on to found the Shangane nation.

One of the *Leven*'s survey parties had an inconclusive brush with this band, in the course of which Soshangane was wounded. The log described the Ndwandwe's approach: "Their appearance was warlike, and had a striking effect as the extensive line moved through the various windings of the path. The grass being wet, they were observed taking particular care to keep their shields above it, as the damp would render them unserviceable; the spears attached to them, being thus elevated, were often seen glittering in the sun above the brow of the hill." It was a fair description of a scene the British were to encounter time and again in the next half-century.

Captain Owen, growing progressively more unhappy with Jakot's English and general behavior, picked up a local native called Shamagwava to replace him. Known as "English Bill," he had seven wives (and a local chieftain for a son-in-law), and in addition to his native tongue, a Tonga dialect, spoke passable English, Portuguese, Dutch and Hindustani.

When the work at Delagoa Bay was finished, Owen collected his little squadron and started south, charting the coast as he went. It was grim work. Sand bars and bad weather kept him away from the coast, so that he was forced to leave Port Natal unsurveyed, and the malaria laid low half his crews and a goodly number died. Point Durnford, Cape Vidal and Boteler Point honored the officers who charted them, but Morley Shoal, Watkins Creek and a number of other features recorded the memory of shipmates dead and buried at sea. Back at Capetown, there was a grand ball on the *Leven*, and English Bill was even received by the Governor.

The *Leven* was due to sail on a second expedition in June, 1823, and even before she left, her reports stirred a certain amount of activity in Capetown. A joint stock company had in fact been formed by the John Thompson whom Owen had encountered at Delagoa Bay, one Francis George Farewell, a boardinghouse keeper named Peterson, and a number of other citizens. The Farewell Trading Company hoped to found a settlement at a suitable location in Natal, and it chartered the brig *Salisbury*, still under James Saunder King, and sent her out a few weeks ahead of the *Leven*.

Both King and Farewell were former officers of the Royal Navy. King, born in Halifax in 1795, joined the service as a ship's boy in 1806 and resigned as a midshipman in 1815; by 1822 he commanded the *Salisbury* in the merchant service, ferrying troops between Capetown and Algoa Bay. Farewell, born in Tiverton in 1791, had moved somewhat faster. Joining in 1807, he served in nine ships, was wounded several times, and commanded the defenses of a small island in the Adriatic before he went on half pay as a lieutenant in 1815. He had since commanded merchant ships trading between India and South America and had been wrecked off Rio de Janeiro. Shortly after his arrival in Capetown in 1822 he married Elizabeth Catherina Schmidt. Her father was a member of the Farewell Trading Company, and she was to see very little of her husband in the next few years.

The *Salisbury* was in Algoa Bay on June 27, 1823, when H.M.S *Leven* sailed in and anchored. Farewell and King visited Captain Owen, talked over old days in the Navy, and spoke of hoping to open up the coast of Natal. Owen, delighted to meet such zeal in a private group, turned over what information he had in return for a promise of the results of whatever surveying the party accomplished. When the lack of an interpreter was mentioned, Owen, secure in the possession of English Bill, happily turned over Jakot, who now found himself back in the *Salisbury* with his freedom as far away as ever.

The *Salisbury* sailed north along the coast, missing Port Natal in a storm. The bay at St. Lucia looked promising, however, and two boats were put over to try for a landing. Both capsized in the surf, six men were drowned, and Farewell only struggled ashore with the help of Jakot, who was a remarkably good swimmer. One of the other survivors, a man named Alex Thompson, decided Jakot was responsible for upsetting the boat and promptly attacked him. Jakot, already unhappy with one thing and another, was deeply offended by such ingratitude and promptly disappeared into the bush. This left a dozen men shivering on the beach with no means of communicating either with the *Salisbury* or with the local natives who were now approaching. It was five weeks before the *Salisbury* managed to bring them all off safely, but Jakot had vanished, apparently for good.

The *Salisbury* put in to Algoa Bay to replenish supplies, and then returned to the Natal coast. Another storm broke and drove her over the bar and in to Port Natal, where she anchored. King surveyed the area—Salisbury Island was named at this time—and the party decided that this was the place for their settlement. Despite the sand bar that made entry and exit perilous, the bay was spacious with good holding ground, and the vicinity was green and well watered. Hardly any natives were observed. The *Salisbury* returned to Capetown in December and the Farewell Trading Company set out to drum up interest.

King at once booked passage for London, where he passed himself off as the surveyor of a new and important harbor, much to Captain Owen's subsequent disgust. A frosty Admiralty turned down his request for a lieutenant's commission, but Earl Bathurst, the Secretary of State for War and Colonies, gave him a letter of recommendation to Lord Charles Somerset, Governor of the Cape Colony. The letter called for little in the way of active assistance, but it was equivalent to permission for King to settle at Port Natal on his own responsibility if he chose to do so. He at once sailed for Capetown to share in the development.

Farewell did better. He scraped up sufficient cash to purchase a small sloop, the *Julia*, and to charter the brig *Antelope*. He then induced some thirty people to join him in starting the settlement. Twenty of these were Boer farmers looking for free land, and the balance Englishmen frankly out for adventure and trade. Farewell took three Hottentot servants—Michael, John and Rachel. The first half of this expedition left Capetown in the *Julia* in April of 1824, and by the end of the month was safely ashore at Port Natal.

This group was led by a young partner of the Farewell Trading Company named Henry Francis Fynn. Born in England in 1803, he had been educated at Christ's Hospital and had worked in London for a while as a surgeon's assistant. Finding the work too dull, in 1819 he joined his hotel-keeping father and two brothers in Capetown, and in the next few years he visited Delagoa Bay and then worked for a while at Somerset East. Fascinated by the natives, he made something of an effort to learn their languages, starting with one of the Xhosa dialects, and he was even vaguely aware of the existence of a chieftain named Shaka somewhere in the north. Such qualifications were well-nigh unique at the time.

Farewell stayed behind in Capetown for six weeks after the *Julia* left before proceeding with the balance of his party in the *Antelope*. His major problem was a legal one. Port Natal was located in an area known simply as Independent Kaffraria, which meant that it was presumably under tribal rule, and it was, of course, without diplomatic representation. The would-be settlers, British citizens all, would naturally take their citizenship with them, and thus the Union Jack, and they were therefore objects of some interest to the Governor of the Cape Colony. Lord Somerset was not averse to the expansion of trade, but he had decided objections to the expansion of British territory in southern Africa. New acquisitions invariably meant fresh expenses, and Somerset was having quite enough difficulty with the territories for which he was already responsible. When Farewell, therefore, petitioned on the first of May for permission to found a new settlement, Somerset granted it five days later, but added a *caveat* about acquiring new land.

Fynn's party trooped ashore from the *Julia* late in April, and the men set out to erect shelters and to explore the environs. There was, at first, no sign of native life, but within a few days one or two natives had been coaxed out of the bush, and Fynn learned something of recent Nguni political history. The story was not one to cheer potential farmers. The natives belonged to the small amaTuli clan, which had enjoyed undisputed possession of the bay until a series of petty neighborhood squabbles had driven them to a kraal site on the thickly wooded bluff bordering the harbor. The natural cover and general inaccessibility of this location provided security, but the site was unsuitable for both cattle and crops. The clan survived but did not thrive. Sometime before 1820 a regent named Fica took over for the rightful heir, Mnini, who was still a minor. The clan was very weak at this point, and had already turned to fish for a diet staple, a most unusual choice for a Bantu.

Fica was to have an adventurous regency. By the early 1820's Zulu impis were in almost continuous passage through amaTuli territory. The clan was far too insignificant to become a Zulu target, but it suffered repeatedly from foraging parties. Goaded to desperation, it finally attacked a small Zulu patrol that was making off with its scant cattle, and much to the clan's surprise it exterminated the patrol. Then, horrified by the likely consequences of such rashness, the clan scattered, breaking into small bands which hid out in the bush. It became impossible to plant any crops or tend any cattle, and the groups with access to the tidal pools subsisted on shellfish, while the families farther inland turned to cannibalism.

When Fynn arrived, Fica was still hiding on the bluff with perhaps thirty amaTuli. The clan gradually realized that, far from being a threat, the settlers provided a fine defensive shield, and after a few months the amaTuli crept out of their hiding places and re-established a semblance of normal kraal life in the open.

Fynn thus learned that all of Natal was more or less Shaka's personal property, and he determined to visit kwaBulawayo, which he thought lay a few miles to the north. (It was actually over 120 miles away.) Gathering Michael and John, he started out along the beach to the north of Port Natal.

Twelve miles on his way, and over the Umgeni River, he sat down on the dunes to rest and was suddenly given an opportunity to confirm what the amaTuli had told him. Hearing a dull roar that gradually impressed itself over the rhythmical pounding of the surf, he glanced down the beach and saw a dense column of Zulu warriors trotting along the packed sand above the water. Michael and John promptly disappeared inland, and Fynn, all alone, smiled weakly at the astonished inDunas who led the column. They finally made signs indicating that they recognized him as one of the bead-gathering race, and without pause the black avalanche trudged past him. Fynn could scarcely credit his computations, but there were at least 20,000 Zulus in the party; it was part of the main Zulu army which was returning from a campaign in the south of Natal. It had apparently skirted Port Natal, as none of the other settlers saw it, and had reached the beach between Fynn and the bay.

Fynn called Michael and John out of their hiding places, fell in behind the impi, and continued his march. At each kraal he passed he sent on word of his impending arrival; he had covered almost the entire distance when Shaka at last returned his answer. He was not yet ready to meet Fynn; he sent him a gift of ivory and forty head of cattle, and bade him return to Port Natal. Fynn turned around and tramped back, arriving just after Farewell entered the bay in the *Antelope*.

The *Antelope* landed her party, some stores and a few horses, and left at once, her charter having expired, but the *Julia* stayed on till September. She then made a trip to Capetown to return nine of the Boer farmers, and by December was back at Port Natal to bring off the remaining eleven Boers. The farmers had decided to a man that the vicinity was most unsuited to peaceful agriculture, and their eventual departure left eight Englishmen and three Hottentots to found the colony of Natal. The *Julia* caught fire on her return trip to Capetown in December and was lost with all hands, leaving the settlers marooned and the Farewell Trading Company virtually bankrupt.

Contact with kwaBulawayo, however, had been established before the Boers started to go and, indeed, had hurried them on their way. Shaka had sent an inDuna on Fynn's return trail to spy out the settlement and, receiving reports of a mere handful of men, invited them to visit him. Farewell and Fynn, therefore, together with Captain Davis of the *Julia*, Peterson, Henry Ogle and Joseph Powell from the Englishmen, the two male Hottentots and a Boer named Zinke, all mounted their horses, packed an assortment of gifts and set out in mid-July. Shaka provided an escort, and Farewell wore his lieutenant's uniform.

With this visit in July of 1824 the eastern Nguni Bantu finally passed from the realm of sporadic reporting into the pages of continual recorded history. Fynn, still a youth and essentially a freebooter, kept a few rough notes which he amplified into odd papers in his later years. His active, inquiring mind was backed by a sound education, and he had the sense to ask, listen and evaluate and the ability to record; and if his later memory for dates was chancy, the scenes of his early manhood remained vivid. Much of what is known of the story of Dingiswayo and of Shaka's origins and rise stems from him.

The party hardly knew what to expect as it approached kwaBulawayo. The miserable native hovels in the Cape Colony and the small kraals on the frontier or at Delagoa Bay were no preparation for the sight that greeted them as they topped the last rise. The vast royal kraal was spread over a gentle hillside a mile away across a shallow valley, as if it had been tilted for their inspection. The central cattle pen, black with people, was over a mile in diameter, the pen was surrounded by upwards of 1,500 huts and the outer fence was more than three miles in circumference.

The chief of the escort bade the group wait by a tree while he reported to Shaka. He returned shortly and asked the group to gallop around the kraal several times, which it did, and he then finally led them into the cattle pen, where Shaka was waiting for them. There were 12,000 warriors in the upper half of the pen alone, and Shaka was so surrounded by his inDunas that he could not be distinguished. The head of the escort then made a long speech, to which the whites had been instructed to lend support by *yebo*'s at every pause; they knew this meant "yes," but not even Fynn had an inkling of what they were assenting to.

In the middle of the interminable tirade, Fynn suddenly spotted Shaka, whose great height and royal bearing stood out even in the midst of his huddled warriors. Fynn nudged Farewell to point him out; Shaka caught the movement, grinned in delight, and waggled a finger at him.

The speech finally over, one of the inDunas presented an elephant's tusk as a gift, and then Shaka suddenly sprang to his feet and flung his arms out against the shields of the men beside him. The entire body of 12,000 men then ran to the lower end of the pen, leaving Shaka in magnificent isolation before the awed Europeans. Only one man remained by his side. Glancing at him, Farewell to his acute horror recognized the grinning features of the ex-convict Jakot.

Farewell had last seen him trotting off into the bush the previous year at St. Lucia. Jakot at that time had good reason to hate Europeans, and especially the members of the Farewell Trading Company. Although his presence here, in an obvious position of trust and influence, boded ill for the party, Farewell's immediate fears were groundless. Jakot had made his way to the Zulus, where his tales of European ways shortly brought him to Shaka's attention. He had been renamed Hlaba-manzi—"the Strong Swimmer"—and was now installed as Shaka's interpreter and intermediary with the Europeans. Since his elevated position depended on the presence of the whites, he had no desire to work them harm, and his still abominable English helped to eke out Fynn's sketchy command of Zulu.

The meeting was a momentous one, and Shaka knew it. Dingiswayo had evidently passed on something of his own heritage from Robert Cowan, and Jakot had filled this tenuous framework with details culled from his own knowledge of the frontier and Capetown itself. Shaka, supreme in his own world, knew that the men he faced came from a civilization vastly superior to his own, but eager as he was to learn more about it, his royal dignity would never permit him to acknowledge the superiority in public. He now went to some pains to put on a show, so that his visitors might be suitably impressed by the power he commanded.

He ran his warriors past them, dancing and shouting, in the disciplined formations he had taught them. He had the hordes of girls from the isiGodlo dance for them, making sure the white men understood that all of them (and there were close to 1,200 in all) belonged to his personal seraglio. And, wealth beyond imagining, he had the vast royal herds, each bred to a single color, driven past for their inspection.

Fynn once counted one of these herds, stung by the implication that the number was beyond computation. He made it 5,654 head of cattle, but his announcement was greeted with derision, as he had not once made use of his fingers.

As the afternoon wore on, a repeated occurrence caused concern. Time and again, for no discernible reason, Shaka, with a flick of his hand and no further attention, ordered the execution of some member of his entourage. It was a phenomenon that was noted on every occasion on which a European paid a visit to the royal kraal, and despite the initial impression that Shaka merely wished to impress his visitors with his absolute powers, it gradually sank in that the executions were a normal part of Zulu court life, and that Shaka gave as little heed to the impression left on his visitors as he did to that made on the victims or their families. The power was indeed absolute, and it had reached the ultimate corruption.

The party was housed for the night in a special kraal erected close to the main gate. It had been furnished with an ox, a sheep, a supply of corn, and eight gallons of native beer. Before retiring for the night the group salvaged something of the white man's honour by firing a salute of eight musket shots and sending up four skyrockets. The ensuing consternation in the main kraal was balm to their tired souls.

The group was summoned again the following morning—to find Shaka taking his bath. This public ceremony was a daily event; the king covered himself with a paste compounded of fat and ground meal, rinsed it off with water, and then rubbed red ocher and a final layer of sheep-tail fat into his glossy skin. He then dressed himself in his finery, holding court the while and shaded by a page-boy who held his shield aloft.

Farewell's party stayed for a fortnight, while Zulu and Briton took each other's measure. Shaka's curiosity was insatiable; he insisted on endless comparisons of the Zulu world with European civilization, and to Fynn's frustration he was able to hold his own with ease. His arguments were untutored but logical, Jakot was too obsequious to translate the full force of Fynn's comments, and many arguments foundered on philological rocks. Shaka developed an immediate brotherly interest in King George, and assumed he was the ruler of all the whites, even as he himself was ruler of all the blacks. Of what use, however, to attempt to describe the glories of Buckingham Palace to a monarch who could conceive of no architectural structure that differed from his own thatched hut, and who could not even grasp the concept of a window?

Shaka easily fielded the few arguments Fynn did manage to translate. A mild remonstrance over the continual executions led to an explanation of the English penal system—savage enough at the time—but Shaka, utterly indifferent to bludgeonings, twisted necks and impalements, was horrified by the idea of imprisonment. He regarded execution as much the milder choice. Openly impressed by firearms, he continued to regard his impis as the best of all possible military machines. He noted at once the weakness of the muzzle-loader—the length of time it took to reload—and pointed out that while Europeans were reloading, the impis would be upon them, and that clothed in their ridiculous fashion they could neither fight nor run away.

Shaka was more amenable in private, and displayed all the traditional attributes of the untutored savage in the presence of gewgaws. He was delighted with small mirrors; he was fascinated by burning glasses and at once tried them out on the arm of his nearest subject. Fynn's medicine chest was the greatest treasure of all, and each instrument and pill must needs be explained. Shown the laxative pills, he gulped two of them, and then, suddenly suspicious, ordered the disgusted sixty-three-year-old Peterson to swallow six.

The party finally left to return to Port Natal at the end of July. Fynn remained behind at Shaka's request, keeping Michael with him. The Farewell Trading Company had permission to remain at the bay, and Fynn, whose Zulu was improving daily, wished to explore the possibility of acquiring some sort of formal diplomatic recognition. His chance came sooner than he expected.

A few days after the others had gone, Fynn spent an afternoon reading by his hut while an interminable dance dragged on in the cattle pen. The ceremony continued into the night, and Fynn finally wandered over to the main kraal to inspect the scene by the light of the flaring reed torches. He had no sooner arrived than a terrible shriek arose, the lights were dashed out, and the wildest confusion broke out. Fynn was only able to gather that Shaka had been stabbed while dancing; he at once gathered his medicine kit and sought out Jakot to get particulars. Jakot chose this moment to have a fit, so Fynn fought his way through the mob to Shaka's hut. There was a dense press around it, his torch was extinguished, and he could not force his way through. Some of the isiGodlo women kept plucking at his arm, and since the crowd was growing hysterical and his own position dangerous, he allowed them to lead him away. The women took him to a hut in their own section of the kraal, and there, much to his amazement, he found

Shaka. The monarch had indeed been stabbed; an assegai had penetrated his left arm and struck so deeply into his side that he was cough-
ing blood. A witch doctor inspected the wounds for evidence of poison and then purged and vomited him; Fynn washed the cuts with
camomile tea and bandaged them. Shaka cried pitifully the whole night,
not from pain but because he was convinced he was going to die.

Fynn stayed with him until dawn, dimly aware of the continuing
clamor outside the crowded, stuffy hut. When he finally stepped out
into the morning light, he could hardly believe his eyes. There were
close to 30,000 people in the cattle pen, more thousands outside the
kraal, and immense hordes were arriving every minute from more
distant kraals as the news spread. Leaderless, each individual had taken
his behavior cue from an equally bewildered neighbor, and the chaos
was general as men, women and children wept, shouted, wailed and
threw themselves on the ground to roll in paroxysms of grief. No one
had eaten or drunk since the day before, hundreds had collapsed from
exhaustion, and scores had died. They had also started to kill one
another, slaying all who flagged in their expressions of grief. Those
beyond tears were rubbing spittle into their eyes. The isiGodlo women
were in a particularly piteous condition; already tired from the long
dances, they had led the wailing throughout the night, pressed together
in a compact mass. They were now totally unable to care for themselves, strewn in huddles of inert heaps about their huts. Fynn procured a few pots of water and dashed them over the nearest piles, and
even this feeble directed act served to restore some order to the immediate area.

Shaka lay at death's door for four days, and then began a rapid
recovery. Six other Zulus had been stabbed, and it was thought that the
assassinations might be connected with the ceremonial *iHlambo* hunt
required for Zwide, chieftain of the Ndwandwes, who had recently
died. Two regiments were accordingly dispatched to Ndwandwe territory, where that scattered clan was beginning to filter back into its
original lands. The impi overtook three men on the road, slew them,
and returned the bodies to kwaBulawayo. They were assumed to be
the killers; their ears were cut off and burned and the ashes scattered,
and then each of the 30,000 Zulus in the royal kraal and its neighbors
passed by the bodies and beat them with sticks. The impi went on and
rescattered the Ndwandwe, burned several kraals, and returned with
800 head of cattle.

Fynn's position was now assured. Needing additional medicaments,
he had sent after Farewell's party on the morning following the assassi-
nation attempt, and the group was back by the first week in August.

Farewell at once drafted an imposing document and presented it to

Shaka for his signature. It was nothing less than a deed granting Farewell outright title to Port Natal and about 3,500 square miles of the surrounding territory. Since Farewell knew absolutely nothing about the geography of the interior, his description of the area involved was somewhat imprecise, and since his knowledge of legal terminology was equally sketchy, the jumble of phrases he tossed in did not even make grammatical sense.

The document was signed on the seventh of August, Shaka and a few of his inDunas making their mark, and the Europeans signing their names. (One of the seamen, however, proved to be no better equipped for the task than Shaka himself was.) Shaka enjoyed the ceremony hugely. He had, of course, not the slightest intention of parting with any of the land involved—at most he simply intended to give permission to live on it—and it is thus quite clear that he did not properly understand either the document or the significance of placing his mark on it. He was, in fact, later to sign similar documents deeding much the same area to two further visitors. Francis George Farewell, sometime officer in His Britannic Majesty's Royal Navy, had let his greed run away with him, and by a mean confidence trick besmirched the credit that was rightfully his for founding the colony of Natal.

The party now returned to Port Natal, and on the twenty-seventh of August Farewell ran the Union Jack up at the fort he had started but never completed. He proclaimed the area British territory, fired a salute, and sent his land grant to Capetown when the *Julia* sailed in September. Lord Somerset naturally paid no attention to it.

The *Julia* returned, picked up the rest of the Boers, and sailed away again in December, never to be heard from again. The small party of stranded Englishmen was not alarmed as the pleasant summer months went by. Each man had constructed a rude hut, and one or two of them were beginning to assemble groups of retainers; Michael and John in particular lost no time in starting kraals. Their clothing gradually deteriorated, their language proficiency improved, and they built up a small stock of ivory. Rachel seems to have been kept busy.

In January of 1825 the *York* visited Port Natal. She had been sent by the Cape Government, since there had been no word from the settlers since the *Julia* departed Capetown after discharging the first group of returning Boers. Fynn had just left to explore amaMpondo territory in the south, taking Ogle with him. Farewell and John Cane, the gigantic carpenter, were away on a short exploration of the interior. Those still at the bay refused to leave without them, so the *York* returned to Capetown, reporting that the settlers might shortly be in need of help.

There now appeared upon the scene the most engaging of the pioneers. Nathaniel Isaacs was born in Canterbury in 1808, into a family active in the Anglo-Jewish community of the nineteenth century. One cousin, Sir David Salomons, was to lead the struggle for the removal of Jewish civil and political disabilities; another, Saul Isaac, gained fame as the projector of the Mersey Tunnel and was eventually to become a member of Parliament for Nottingham. Nathaniel's father died when the boy was still young, and when he was fourteen, he was sent to his uncle, Saul Solomon, a merchant who had settled on St. Helena in 1796.

The trip south was harrowing. It had been planned to send him even earlier, but until Napoleon Bonaparte died in 1821, the controls were so stringent that permission could not be obtained for even a twelve-year-old boy to move there. When permission finally did come, Isaacs was entrusted to an inebriated captain, who devoted most of the interminable, calm-plagued trip to an attempt to seduce him. On his arrival Isaacs was put to work in his uncle's counting house. He found both the work and the locale dull.

Determined to get off the island, he secured a position as supercargo on a small vessel setting out to trade with other South Atlantic islands. The ship was no sooner out of sight of land than it sprang a leak, shipped four feet of water and ruined the cargo of trade goods, and barely made it back to St. Helena. The venture was abandoned, and Isaacs returned to the counting house.

Rescue came in June of 1825 in the form of the brig *Mary*, James Saunder King commanding. After his unsuccessful suit at the Admiralty, King was working his way back to Capetown, hoping to help reap the benefits of whatever progress the Farewell Trading Company had made in his absence. Discharging a cargo consigned to Solomon, he formed an intimate friendship with his nephew and offered to take the lad along. The uncle assented, and Isaacs jumped at the chance.

The *Mary* reached Capetown on the first of August. Here King was greeted by the *York*'s report indicating that the settlers were in some distress and hoping to be rescued when they were all together. The reported distress may have been somewhat exaggerated, since none of the marooned adventurers then or later made any really strenuous efforts to extricate himself, but King capitalized on the report to have the *Mary*'s expenses underwritten, and gallantly sailed to the rescue on the twenty-sixth of August.

Dropping a missionary passenger and his wife at Port Elizabeth in Algoa Bay, King arrived at Port Natal on the first of October. There was a strong onshore wind, and King anchored outside the bluff, with some idea of sending the longboat in through the heavy surf breaking on the bar. The attempt failed, and the *Mary* began to drag. King slipped his cable and then, unable to beat to sea in his sluggish command, decided to chance the bar. The *Mary* struck, broached, and lost her rudder, and then swept into the bay at the mercy of the tide, crosscurrents and the wind. She floundered about for a few hours, and the combined efforts of King and Hatton, the mate, only sufficed to ground what by then was a waterlogged total wreck in a position which could be easily reached from the shore. All hands got off safely, although one sailor had to be rescued by a Newfoundland dog.

The party was welcomed by six naked amaTuli, Rachel, and the only Englishman then at the Port—Thomas Holstead, who proved to be mentally deficient. Farewell and Cane were visiting Shaka again, and Fynn and Ogle had not yet returned from amaMpondo territory. The situation was anything but pleasant; the crew had jettisoned the entire cargo to lighten ship for the attempt on the bar, and the carpenter's tools and most of the crew's personal possessions had been lost in the wreck. It would be months before another rescue attempt might be mounted from the Cape (where Lord Somerset was beginning to find the antics of the Farewell Trading Company a bit tiresome), and in the meantime the party would have to make the best of it with only the clothes on their back to help them—and in some cases less than that.

Isaacs was nothing loath. He was seventeen years old, without a care in the world, and motivated by nothing more complicated than a healthy curiosity. He had the sense to start a scratch journal, and he seems to have had an inkling that he was witnessing a part of the earth and a way of life that was virtually unknown to Europe and that might someday fade away. He was utterly untrained in observation—he misnamed almost every plant and animal he saw—and despite an eventual fluency in the language, his attempts to transliterate Zulu surpass anything else in the field—but he reported on everything he saw with zest and ingenuity and a surprising insight into the characters of the men he met. He strove mightily to achieve the florid, polysyllabic style he thought was expected of a gentleman, but his forced elegance was always more noticeable at the beginning of his entries than later, when he had warmed to his work.

King, Hatton and the seven sailors spent a few days salvaging what they could from the wreck, recovered a few tools, and decided to build a new ship. They set up their dockyard on the southern shore of the bay, where timber was handy, and commenced their labors. The task ahead of them was not a light one, and it was most likely adopted in sheer desperation. King and Hatton may have been financially involved in the loss of the *Mary*, but the sailors most likely were not. Their only chance, however, of getting their pay, and even of getting to a place where they might be able to collect it, lay in constructing a vessel to take them out. If completed, such a ship might represent a sizable amount of capital, and King must have promised them shares to get them started. Even by stripping the *Mary* of her cordage, sails and fittings they got little to get them started. Practically none of the lumber was usable, and the timbers and planking had to be hewn and sawn by hand.

Isaacs explored. The earlier arrivals had constructed mud-daubed wattle huts, for the most part windowless, and Isaacs took over Farewell's, which was the most substantial. Some of the natives had placed typical kraal huts among the wattle structures, but aside from the half-finished Fort Farewell, no other work had been taken in hand. Holstead did not have a horse, and was using an ox for transportation. He was living with Rachel, who warned Isaacs not to venture out at night since the area was infested with leopards and packs of wild dogs.

Determined to better his lot, Isaacs commenced trading operations on a small scale. His first exchange was a small quantity of tobacco for seven assegais and two carved calabashes. Rachel told him he had been cheated.

On the fifteenth of October Fynn returned from his trip to the amaMpondo. Ogle was still with him, and he had a retinue of close to a hundred natives. He had been gone for nine months or so, and had a quantity of ivory to show for his tramp 200 miles to the south. His appearance was bizarre; young and tall, with a striking face, he was sunburned to the bone and had neither shaved nor trimmed his hair for some months. He had been going barefoot for over a year, and the only article of European clothing he still owned was a frazzled, crownless straw hat. To this he had added a single garment—a tattered blanket tied around his neck like a kaross.

Farewell showed up five days later, having broken short his visit to Shaka when word of King's arrival reached him. Somewhat disconcerted to find his old friend as marooned as the rest of them, he cautioned them all not to let Shaka know the full extent of their plight, as Jakot's glowing accounts had given him a somewhat overinflated picture of the white man's power. Since Shaka had installed a minor chieftain and his kraal in the vicinity for the express purpose of providing him with information about events at Port Natal, the warning was probably superfluous.

A week later Farewell and Fynn departed to present King to Shaka, taking two seamen and forty natives with them, and leaving Isaacs in charge at the Port. This established his status as a great man, and he was at once called in to treat a native with a terminal throat cancer. Isaacs did his best with chicken soup, Epsom salts, soap liniment and a red woolen bandage, and so impressed the bystanders that his patient's prompt death was not held against him. He also tried to plant a vegetable garden, but failed to interest any of the natives in working on it—not unnaturally, as they regarded this as women's work.

Farewell's group returned on the eleventh of November, driving 107 head of cattle which Shaka had given them. The gift capped the mission with success, and one of the sailors had once and for all impressed Shaka with the true power of European civilization. Shaka, always fascinated by firearms, had insisted that the visitors join him in an elephant hunt. The men would have been equipped with surplus military muskets—smoothbore .69 caliber muzzle-loading flintlocks without any form of rear sight, and unreliable and inaccurate at anything beyond point-blank range. Loaded with shot, they made passable if clumsy fowling pieces, but a more inadequate weapon for elephant could hardly be imagined. Farewell had a lively idea of what would happen to white prestige if his firearms were put to such a test, but one of the sailors, blissfully ignorant, made a lucky ear shot and dropped a tusker with a thud that shook Shaka's faith in the superiority of his assegais.

Later that month Norton, second mate of the *Mary*, and three of the sailors stole the longboat and set off for Algoa Bay. This reduced Hatton's work force to four men, and slowed his progress even further. The dockyard was near the timber, isolated from the other settlers, and the leopards were particularly active in the vicinity; one of them even carried off the lifesaving Newfoundland.

Farewell now lent Isaacs his horse and sent him after a store of ivory he had cached near the Tugela River. Isaacs took Holstead with him, and made use of the opportunity to see Shaka for himself. To his surprise, he found a Portuguese trader from Delagoa Bay at kwaBulawayo; Shaka at once determined that the two men represented different nations, and urged them to fight one another. His visitors were only able to scotch the suggestion by insisting that the death of either of them would have incalculable diplomatic repercussions, as a treaty was in effect between their respective countries. Isaacs left with the gift of twelve cattle, plus an additional two given for Farewell's dog, to which Shaka had taken a fancy.

The year 1826 was ushered in with a dance at Fort Farewell, to which all the Port Natal natives were invited. There must have been quite a number of them, for the attendant festivities made serious inroads in the cattle, and by February it became necessary to plan another trip to Shaka's kraal to purchase more. The settlers were short of gifts by now, and finally decided on the figurehead of the wrecked *Mary* as the most suitable item. It was accordingly hacked loose, and Isaacs set out with Fynn and two of the natives to deliver it. The Tugela was in flood, however, and forced them to return. On the way back, Isaacs almost achieved scientific immortality. Chatting with a kraal head, he heard a description of a wondrous beast at a distant kraal which, if he could trust his elementary Zulu, could only be a unicorn. He set off in great excitement and after an arduous journey found the animal exactly where his source had stated. One-horned goats, however, were nothing new to science, and Isaacs ruefully abandoned his dreams of glory.

The rivers stayed high for another month, and in mid-March a messenger arrived from Shaka. He was on the banks of the Tugela, and requested the whites to send him one of their small boats, of which he had heard. Only the skiff remained, so Isaacs set off with a small party of natives to manhandle it to the Tugela. He hoped to recruit fresh bearers at each kraal, but in mid-journey he found himself alone with no source of labor in sight. He thereupon complained to the next kraal head he encountered that the last set of porters had "abandoned the King's property," and was horrified when that worthy promptly attacked the deserters' kraal and killed forty people, including two of his own brothers and five sisters-in-law. When Isaacs protested at such a drastic reaction to his complaint, the kraal head pointed out that anything less would have drawn Shaka's wrath on his own head, and that royal property was not to be treated lightly. The boat reached the Tugela with no further difficulty.

The river was still in spate, but Isaacs launched his craft and set out to find Shaka, who was somewhere downstream. Shaka, however, received reports of the skiff's lively performance in the turbulent current and, rather than chance a public refusal to entrust himself to the boat, returned to kwaBulawayo, sending word to Isaacs to join him there. Three of the four messengers who delivered this summons were drowned in the crossing.

Isaacs now learned that Shaka was at war, and that one of the temporary coalitions in the south had been brash enough to send an impi north of the Tugela. It was obvious that Shaka merely wished the settlers to lend their military aid, but despite the necessity of staying in his good graces, the Europeans were not anxious to get involved in the local warfare. Isaacs in his various travels had passed numerous abandoned kraals littered with bones and splintered skulls, and thought it best to steer clear of the quarrels that had led to such drastic underpopulation. He finally decided to go, however, as he feared the results of a direct refusal.

On his arrival at kwaBulawayo he found that the invading impi had retired, and that the court was busy with a series of executions stemming from the recent death of a local chieftain. Since chieftains were technically immortal, their deaths from any cause led to smellings-out to locate the abaThakathi responsible. Isaacs was amused by the care Shaka displayed in maintaining his dignity; the monarch never took any public notice of the gifts he received, merely watching impassively his inDunas' excited reactions, until in bored tones he ordered the gifts to be taken to his hut. The instant he was alone, however, he dropped all pretense of indifference and frankly admitted the superiority of the European artifacts. He expressed a desire to have missionaries visit him, and wanted to learn how to read and write.

Only in the matter of firearms did he prove immovable. Isaacs explained the principle of mass firing from a square, showing how the kneeling front rank and the standing rear rank implemented each other's fire. The Zulus grasped the concept at once, but were still convinced that an energetic charge could overpower such a formation, provided one were prepared to accept the initial losses. The question would be put to the test in precisely those terms fifty-odd years later.

Isaacs stayed a fortnight and then started back with six head of cattle. He was hurried on his way by a message that had arrived from Delagoa Bay, where a Captain Colledge of the familiar *Salisbury* had heard of the wreck of the *Mary* and now promised to call at Port Natal on his return voyage. Halfway back Isaacs met a second messenger, sent out by King from Port Natal. H.M.S. *Helicon*, alerted by Norton's arrival at Algoa Bay in the stolen longboat, had been at Port Natal for a week. She could wait no longer, and King, unwilling to miss this opportunity to return to the Cape, had taken passage in her. He apologized to Isaacs for abandoning him, and promised to send help in the near future. Isaacs had now been at Port Natal for over six months, and for the first time lost faith in his eventual rescue.

Fynn paid Shaka a visit in June, taking Michael and John with him. The two Hottentots were in a peculiar position. Technically in Farewell's employ, they came from a race the Zulus despised, but, half-civilized, they had been permitted to associate themselves with the Europeans, and they made the most of their status in dealing with the Port Natal natives. Both men were armed, and had constructed their own kraals and collected large groups of retainers. Farewell, interested in giving his settlement as much weight as possible, had encouraged the process, and Fynn, Ogle and Cane (with whom Rachel was now living) were well on their way to founding their own clans. Fynn, at least, does not seem to have taken any of the native women to wife, although Ogle definitely did. Many years later, when the English-woman he subsequently married died, a native walked in from the bush, claimed to be his natural son, and contested the inheritance. To the acute horror of a number of the older colonists, he won his case.

The two Hottentots now courted serious trouble. Getting drunk on native beer, they picked a fight with a Zulu and then knocked Fynn down, in Shaka's presence, when he attempted to separate them. Shaka was all for executing them out of hand, but Fynn interceded, pointing out they were Farewell's "property" and that he would handle the matter himself. Back at the Port, Farewell convened a kangaroo court. The Hottentots' kraals were destroyed, their people taken away, and the two men were lashed.

Shaka sent for all the settlers a few days later, asking them to bring a tent. Sikhunyana, one of Zwide's surviving sons, was approaching with a newly constituted Ndwandwe impi. Isaacs set out again, accompanied by John and Frederic, a native who had picked up some English and was serving as an interpreter. He also took ten Port Natal natives to whom he had taught the use of muskets.

The trip was a hard one. Isaacs' clothing was in rags, and he had finally been forced to abandon the remnants of his shoes. Much of the country was covered with thorns, his feet had not hardened, and it was all he could do to force himself on. Overnighting at convenient kraals, his sleep was frequently interrupted by rats and mice that gnawed at the soles of his feet, attracted by the salve with which he had smeared them. On occasion they ate out his toenails without awakening him. He finally converted a pack ox to a mount, but the beast kicked him in the groin one day, and Isaacs in disgust reverted to shanks' mare until his feet eventually hardened.

Shaka welcomed Isaacs and the tent—which he wanted simply to scare his enemies—but expressed surprise that the others had not come, and sent Isaacs back after them. He was unable to leave for ten days or so, since a boil on the sole of one foot made all progress impossible. He finally allowed a native doctor to treat it—successfully, much to his surprise.

Zulu court life ran true to form during his convalescence. Shaka reviewed a few of his regiments and then asked Isaacs how many soldiers King George had. When he was told as many as he had men, women, children and cattle, he developed a suspicion that King George might attack him someday, and, voicing this fear, he got into an argument with his inDunas, which ended with his ordering eight of them to be executed. The exchange was somewhat beyond Isaacs' Zulu. "The cause for this I could not comprehend, neither could I elicit it from any of the natives," he commented sadly.

Just before he left, Isaacs got word from Shaka that John and Frederic were to remain behind. He sneaked them out of kwaBulawayo at once, but he had no sooner left the kraal than he was intercepted and brusquely ordered to return. An irate Shaka threatened him with death and accused him of cowardice; Isaacs manfully replied that the English feared nothing but King George, who only wanted them to collect ivory and make friends. Shaka subsided, grumbling that the best way to make friends with *him* was to support his military projects, and he let Isaacs go with three head of cattle against his promise to return promptly with all the others—except Farewell, whom he regarded as too much of an old woman.

On the road back John and Frederic deserted. Isaacs overtook them and, when Frederic became insolent, disarmed him. He was contemplating the next move when Farewell and Fynn, on their way to Shaka, joined him. Isaacs, mindful of his promise, decided to return to Port Natal, leaving Farewell and Fynn to deal with Shaka—and the two servants. Isaacs got back on the second of August, and on the eleventh got a message from Farewell that the others need not report after all, but that he himself and Fynn would have to accompany Shaka's expedition.

For the rest of August and all of September Isaacs puttered about Port Natal. Hatton's new craft was slowly taking shape, but since all the timber had to be hacked out with a few worn hand tools, the four sailors were growing restive. The settlers, doing no manual labor, were leading lives of indolence and lording it over their growing kraals, and the shipbuilders would much have preferred to join them.

On the sixth of October the schooner *Ann*, Captain Dunn commanding, arrived at Port Natal. She bore Lieutenant King and—to the great consternation of the nearly naked settlers—Mrs. Farewell, come to join her husband. Isaacs was overjoyed to see King again, and hurriedly borrowed canvas trousers and a jacket from the schooner's crew. There had been no word from Farewell since August, and the settlers showed Mrs. Farewell the local sights while they waited. Isaacs, ever the gentleman, was in a nervous agony over her possible reaction to the hordes of curious and unclad savages that followed her about, but the first white woman to settle in Natal was made of stern stuff and was not to be discomposed. The *Ann*, which brought Isaacs the first mail he had gotten since leaving St. Helena, left shortly, bearing away his gift of a bullock for his uncle.

Farewell and Fynn finally returned at the end of the month while Isaacs, a bit prematurely, was off purchasing food for Hatton's vessel. The two men had been off with Shaka and 40,000 Zulus on a successful expedition against the Ndwandwe.

Shaka, in fact, had taken them clear to the north of the Pongola River, to a rocky mountain near the Intombi River, where the Ndwandwe were encamped near the summit. The Zulus advanced in formation to within twenty yards of the enemy, and late in the afternoon Jakot opened the battle with an unsuccessful musket shot. The

Zulus then charged, and an hour and a half later the Ndwandwe clan had ceased to exist. The Zulus collected 60,000 head of cattle and then began to slaughter the women and children, who were stunned by the men's defeat. Fynn begged for and was able to save only a single infant. Sikhunyana himself got away, hiding until dark in an elephant pit, and then striking out to establish contact with Soshangane. The latter, however, suspected treachery, and drove him north of the Mumiti River, where he disappeared forever.

When Isaacs got back from his food-gathering jaunt, he found that Farewell had quarreled with King. The nature of the quarrel is shrouded in mystery, since Isaacs always refused to describe it, although he referred to it often enough. As King's partisan, he had little use for Farewell, but it is apparent that neither man was blameless. The settlers had made an informal arrangement whereby Farewell was to appear as their principal in all transactions with Shaka. The reasoning was sound; they were few and the Zulus many, and the appearance of a united front was obligatory. In consequence, all gifts to Shaka were to stem from Farewell, and he was to take custody of all that was given in return. The difficulty was that Shaka did not particularly care for Farewell, who had an unfortunate personality. He much preferred Fynn and King and, for all his youth, Isaacs. King now wished to present certain gifts in his own name, and Farewell objected, apparently more worried about the cattle or ivory Shaka might give in return than about the united front. As a result, King and Isaacs now commenced to operate independently—as Fynn had been quietly doing for some time.

Isaacs now made another trip to kwaBulawayo to present King's gifts. (They were peacock feathers, and Shaka was something less than enthusiastic.) During his stay Shaka massacred 170 young men and isiGodlo girls as the result of a suspicion of adultery. Isaacs, for the first time, was really afraid of him, and made haste to get away. For all his horror at the continual executions, he was able to accept them as a part of Zulu court life, but this was something new. Shaka had announced his departure on a long trip and then made a sudden return, and Isaacs had seen what was coming from the start. So abnormal were Shaka's actions on this occasion that Isaacs even observed him beating Nandi.

Given Shaka's impotence, the effect on his pride of even a single pregnancy in the isiGodlo can be imagined, and pregnancies were frequent. There was a considerable volume of nocturnal traffic over the isiGodlo walls, and even Isaacs seems to have engaged in the sport. Barred from a public admission that he knew all pregnancies were the result of adultery, Shaka adopted the pose that he simply wished no heirs to trouble his later years, and he killed a number of isiGodlo infants with his own hands. Nandi once smuggled a newborn male out and started to raise it in great secrecy, under the impression that it was her long-awaited grandchild. Shaka came across the situation quite by accident, and although Nandi whisked mother and babe to a distant kraal, there is no record of the child ever having attained maturity.

Late in November Shaka moved his kraal to kwaDukuza, on the present-day site of the village of Stanger. This placed him on the coast fifteen miles south of the Tugela River and within an easy two days' march of Port Natal. He gave no reason for the shift, but with the Ndwandwe threat removed, his attention was now drawn to the south, and he undoubtedly wished to be closer to the Europeans, who were beginning to figure largely in his plans.

Isaacs drifted through the land during the pleasant summer months of December and January of 1827. His feet had hardened, his Zulu was perfectly fluent, and he thoroughly enjoyed the primitive life he led. The phrase "Shaka's friend" gave him security and deference wherever he went. With King, he picked up 700 pounds of hippopotamus ivory Fynn had cached on an earlier trip, and the two men then planted the Union Jack at the mouth of the Umlalazi River. At the beginning of February, 1827, Isaacs was staying at a kraal a few miles from kwaDukuza, when the Great Wife of his host burst into his hut one morning to inform him that Michael and John, at gunpoint, had just raped the young wife of a local chieftain.

Isaacs and King caught up with the two Hottentots, confirmed the main outline of the story, and ordered them back to Port Natal. They then hurried to kwaDukuza, where the news had preceded them. Shaka was in a cold fury and threatened death to the entire settlement, but despite King's apprehensions Isaacs detected signs that Shaka's rage was in large part assumed and for the benefit of the inDunas. His own major fear was that one of the inDunas might misinterpret Shaka's rantings and take it upon himself to order a massacre.

John Cane now arrived with a message of apology from Farewell and an offer of restitution for the outrage. Shaka gradually allowed himself to be mollified, and then announced he would again require help for one of his military projects. It was thus arranged that Isaacs, Cane, two seamen and seven armed natives would make themselves available for the proposed expedition. The negotiations were still in progress when Michael and John unconcernedly put in an appearance at kwaDukuza; Isaacs hurried them out before Shaka learned of their presence. Their cattle were again taken up and added to the royal herds.

Shaka, in fact, was quite pleased by the turn of events, and the rape had given him a lever for which he had long been searching. He was faced with an annoying military problem to which the muskets promised a solution. Between kwaBulawayo and the ravaged Ndwandwe country lay the Ngome forest, an almost impenetrable tangle of undergrowth-choked woodland situated on steep and rocky hills. This forest was the stronghold of a chieftain named umBeje, whose Kumalo clan had been driven into it by Zwide some years before. Mzilikazi, who had taken the Matabele out of the Zulu fold, had also been a Kumalo, and Shaka had reason to view the clan with suspicion. When umBeje had refused Shaka's demand for aid in the previous Ndwandwe campaigns, Shaka had immediately turned on him, but for once the Zulu might was helpless. The first Zulu impi had failed to locate any signs of the errant clan in the dense jungle; the second, a regiment detailed to the task on its return from the Sikhunyana campaign, had penetrated a short distance into the forest and had then been wiped out. Shaka then sent still a third impi, which for the past three months had been circling the forest, unable to work out a solution and afraid to return to Shaka. So unusual was this resistance that "umBeje is in the Ngome" remains a Zulu proverb to this day.

Isaacs was happily unaware of this background as he set out to join the Zulu forces. In addition to Jakot and the guides Shaka had provided, he had ten men armed with muskets and a contingent of twenty Port Natal natives armed with assegais. Shaka had ordered the Kumalo exterminated root and branch; Isaacs privately decided to keep the fighting to a minimum and to see if umBeje could be induced to surrender. The Zulu inDunas on the scene were in hearty accord with this plan, as they were at a total loss as to how to proceed.

The ensuing hostilities were ludicrous. Isaacs, eighteen years old and with no military experience, found himself in command of a Zulu army of over 5,000 men, faced with a fairly intricate military problem. His ignorance was so abysmal that he failed to recognize the perplexities, and he consequently proceeded as if no problem existed.

Brown, one of his sailors, observed the bulk of the Kumalo cattle grazing on the fringes of the forest, walked over with his companions, and took the cattle away from the herdboys. The herdboys called up the Kumalo army, Isaacs called up the Zulus, and the two forces were suddenly face to face on the outskirts of the wooded area. Isaacs saw no reason why they should not have a battle, so as soon as the Zulus were doctored, he ordered an advance.

He had marched his party of ten musketeers to within fifty yards of the nearest Kumalos when he perceived that he was unsupported. The Zulus had retreated instead of advancing, and the nearest were now on a small hillock over the creek at his back. In the absence of Shaka or an inDuna imbued with his spirit, the Zulus were no better than any other Bantu clan of identical stock and rearing.

Isaacs, with ten men, was now facing over a thousand Kumalos, but he was still determined to have his battle. He consequently approached the nearest Kumalo band, an outpost of about fifty men, and fired on it. The results were catastrophic. Neither side had encountered fire-arms before, and Isaacs had not reckoned on the shock effect. The entire Zulu army dropped to the ground and crawled under its shields, and the Kumalos broke and ran away in confusion. They had assumed that the muskets were merely knobkerries and failed to connect them with the reverberating flashes and the greasy clouds of white smoke. They thought the white men were spitting.

All hope of a proper battle was now gone, but Isaacs reloaded and continued his advance up the rocky slopes, heading for such individuals as were rash enough to put in an appearance. He shot one man who hurled an assegai at him, marveling at the force and the fact that he could duck in time. Small groups defended themselves with assegais and stones, but despite the efforts of one brave inDuna to rally them, the Kumalos refused to coalesce. Isaacs pressed on. In the act of firing, he felt something strike him from behind; he ignored the blow and reloaded, and then, glancing over his shoulder, was amazed to observe an assegai handle protruding from his back.

He now called off the attack, and first Cane and then Jakot tried unsuccessfully to remove the barbed weapon. His servant finally managed to extract it by inserting a finger in the wound, which while not deep was severely lacerated. Feeling weak from loss of blood, Isaacs returned to the Zulus and requested help; this was refused, and when he threatened the men with his musket, an entire regiment scattered. He got back to the kraal from which he had started by sunset, and after a night of excruciating pain ordered another advance.

The Zulus had by now pulled themselves together and set off to make the attack. Isaacs was left at the kraal, where a witch doctor soon appeared to tend to him. Isaacs merely wanted some food and to be left in peace, but, since he had killed an enemy, the witch doctor was determined to cleanse him before he could again drink milk or visit Shaka—otherwise all the Zulu cattle might sicken. Isaacs watched in fascination as the witch doctor killed a heifer, removed the excrement from the entrails, parboiled it with the gall, and ordered him to drink three sips and sprinkle the rest over his body. He refused point-blank, but the furious witch doctor told him he would be given no food until he did as he was told. The witch doctor carefully explained that the medicine was to be followed at once by a second concoction—equally unappetizing—which would make him vomit up the first drink. Isaacs finally took his three sips and then gulped down the second mixture. To his horror—and the witch doctor's annoyance—it failed to have the desired emetic effect, but the witch doctor finally declared the ceremony over and allowed his shaken patient to have some milk.

The Zulu army returned in the evening. It had been on the point of attacking when three Kumalo envoys appeared and offered a full surrender, rather than face the white men again. They brought the balance of their half-starved goats and cattle, which the Zulus joyfully accepted. One of the sailors thereupon suggested that they throw in ten young maidens, "by way of cementing their friendship by nuptial ties." The Kumalo gave them up as willingly as they had the cattle.

After three days of pain so intense he was unable to write, Isaacs determined to return to kwaDukuza. Litters were unknown to the Zulus, whose wounded either walked away from a battle or were dispatched by their comrades on the spot, so Isaacs set out in a stretcher formed from a green bullock hide slung from poles. The hide dried, unevenly, and the bearers made no effort to keep their burden on an even keel in hilly country. They also left Isaacs broiling in the sun every few miles or so while they impressed fresh bearers, so that before the journey was over, Isaacs gave up and finished it on foot. The Zulus gave him the praise name of *uDambuza* (which Isaacs rather freely translated as "the Brave Warrior Who Was Wounded at Ngome"), and Shaka gave him four milch cows and pardoned the Hottentots, but only after informing him that he would have killed any warrior of *his* who returned to him with a back wound.

Isaacs stayed at kwaDukuza until he was fully recovered and then made a trip inland to open trade with a new clan. He returned to Port Natal in mid-April to find Hatton and his four sailors exhausted and on the verge of downing tools, although the schooner was almost completed. (The ten Kumalo maidens may have had something to do with this decision.) King threatened to burn the ship on the stocks and to take his party overland to Delagoa Bay, there to take his chances on finding a passage back to Capetown, and he actually sent Isaacs to get an escort from Shaka. Hatton thereupon gave in and returned to work with his men.

The settlers were by now running short of medicines and they needed numerous small fittings for the schooner, so King decided to try for Delagoa Bay after all. He chose John Ross, his fifteen-year-old apprentice, for the round-trip tramp of over 600 miles through unexplored territory, and the red-headed Scots lad set out with a sum of money and a small Zulu escort under an inDuna named Langalibalele. No European had ever made the trip before; Powell, one of Farewell's original party, had tried it in 1824 and had never been heard from again. Ross was back in three weeks, having averaged better than thirty miles a day. The Portuguese were friendly enough, but they thought him a spy sent by Shaka, as they were convinced no Christian would have sent a boy on such a journey. A French slaver was so impressed he supplied all his wants, so that Ross only spent two dollars, but when the slaver started to eye his Zulu escort the boy started back at once. Isaacs and King, fearing that Shaka might try to relieve him of his purchases, set out to intercept him before he reached kwaDukuza, but Ross had anticipated the danger and avoided the royal kraal. With only a small escort and no knowledge of Zulu he had completed a trip on which a number of well-equipped shipwrecked parties had foundered. Forty-five years later a native chieftain in Natal named Langalibalele was in grave difficulties with the law of the colony, and on the off chance that this might be his friend, John Ross wrote a letter in his defense to a Natal newspaper. He described his trip and the good service Langalibalele had rendered. His own true name, he added, was Charles Rawden Maclean; he had taken the name of Ross when he ran away to sea at the age of twelve.

Work on the new ship continued slowly while the settlers marked time. The small party at Port Natal was riven by tensions which only the overriding fear of Shaka could bridge. Farewell was unable to exert his leadership over the group he nominally led, and he ran a poor second to King in Shaka's esteem. King for his part was collecting ivory on his own and, with the schooner nearing completion, was financially in a much stronger position than Farewell was. Shaka was aware of these dissensions, and planned to make use of them. He could easily have wiped the settlement out, and the presence of refugees from his tyranny among the Port Natal natives gave him cause, but the forceful personalities of such men as King and Cane, and of such striplings as Dunn, Isaacs and Ross impressed him deeply. Port Natal was a never-ending source of wonderful gifts and arguments, and he was also fascinated by the concept of his distant brother-monarch King George.

Shaka had, in fact, determined to send a mission to King George, making use of King's schooner when it was finally launched. His motives were mixed. There was a natural tendency to advertise his own importance by exchanging courtesies with a fellow sovereign, and for a while he even considered (although not very seriously) going himself. There was a much more practical reason, however. Shaka had by now thoroughly depopulated his environs, and he was planning a major expedition to the southern reaches of the coastal strip, inhabited by Xhosa-Nguni peoples as yet unscathed by the Zulu impis and by masses of refugees from the clans which had fled Natal. The largest of the still-settled clans, the Tembus and the amaMpondo, lived hard by the Cape frontier, and Shaka wanted to sound out the possible reaction to his contemplated campaign. He had no wish to draw on himself massive retaliation from a European civilization, and while he would not have put it in such blunt terms, he wanted permission from King George to wage war in King George's front yard.

He had still a third reason, and it is hard to escape the conclusion that in the dark recesses of his mind this one was by far the most important. On an early visit Farewell had somehow mentioned England's leading hair dressing—Rowland's Macassar Oil. One wonders how the subject could possibly have arisen, but arise it did, and Shaka thereafter lusted for it beyond all earthly treasures. The nostrum—which had never seen a Macassar nut, but was compounded of one dram of oil of origanum to a pound of olive oil—not only soaked scores of thousands of contemporary scalps but also had the happy effect of turning gray hair black. Shaka decided it must be a rejuvenator, and he wanted it for the aging Nandi and for the gray hairs that were beginning to pepper his own thatch. Isaacs idly promised him a bottle, and never heard the end of it.

On July 24, 1827, therefore, Shaka suddenly proposed to Lieutenant King that he send a diplomatic mission to King George. The idea took the Europeans by surprise, and raised some new complications.

To begin with, it was perfectly obvious to all of them that Shaka had no very clear idea who King George was or where he resided or, in fact, what the British structure of government was. He obviously had King George confused with the Governor of the Cape Colony, and he thought of the white world as a large, somewhat superior, but essentially Bantu clan. Intimately acquainted with every hillock and stream in his own domains, his knowledge of geography faded outside the coastal strip, and he would never understand or accept the delays that distance and civilized administrative procedures might impose on his ambassadors. He was, however, an independent monarch with a perfect right to send diplomatic missions wherever he chose, so the idea had to be accepted.

Before the mission materialized, however, an event occurred that marked a permanent change for the worse in Shaka's twisted personality. In early October he was off on an elephant hunt (Isaacs having impressed on him the importance of ivory in the European world), and he was some eighty miles from kwaDukuza when a messenger arrived with word that Nandi was seriously ill.

Fynn was with him; Shaka at once abandoned the hunt and between late afternoon on the ninth of October and noon the next day had covered the entire distance afoot. He sat down by his hut, surrounded by several elder chieftains, and sent Fynn to inspect and report on his mother's condition. The *inDlovukazi*—"the Great Female Elephant"— had dysentery and was obviously dying. Fynn drove a crowd of mourning women out of her smoke-filled hut and gently told Shaka the case was hopeless. Shaka sat quietly for an hour, brooding, until word came that she was dead. He then entered his own hut, emerged in full war regalia, and went to Nandi's hut. Here he stood for perhaps twenty minutes, with his head bowed on his shield, and Fynn saw that he was crying. He then sighed deeply, his feelings became ungovernable, and he broke into frantic yells. What followed made Fynn's earlier experience of Zulu mass hysteria pale in comparison:

The signal was enough. The chiefs and people, to the number of about fifteen thousand, commenced the most dismal and horrid lamentations. The people from the neighboring kraals, male and female, came pouring in, each body as they came in sight, at a distance of half a mile, joining to swell the terrible cry. Through the whole night it continued, none daring to rest or refresh themselves with water; while at short intervals, fresh outbursts were heard as more distant regiments approached. The morning dawned without any relaxation, and before noon the number had increased to about sixty thousand. The cries now became indescribably horrid. Hundreds were lying faint from excessive fatigue and want of nourishment; while the carcasses of forty oxen lay in a heap, which had been slaughtered as an offering to the guardian spirits of the tribe. At noon the whole force formed a circle with Shaka in the centre, and sang a war-song, which afforded them some relaxation during its continuance. At the close of it, Shaka ordered several men to be executed on the spot; and the cries became, if possible, more violent than ever. No further orders were needed; but, as if bent on convincing their chief of their extreme grief, the multitude commenced a general massacre. Many of them received the blow of death while inflicting it on others, each taking the opportunity of revenging his injuries, real or imaginary. Those who could no more force tears from their eyes—those who were found near the river panting for water—were beaten to death by others who were mad with excitement. Towards the afternoon I calculated that not fewer than seven thousand people had fallen in this frightful indiscriminate massacre. The adjacent stream, to which many had fled exhausted to wet their parched tongues, became impassable from the number of dead corpses which lay on each side of it; while the kraal in which the scene took place, was flowing with blood.

Nandi was buried on the third day, with ten handmaidens, their arms and legs broken, buried alive to keep her company. A regiment of 12,000 men was set to guard the grave for a year, supplied with 15,000 head of cattle taken up from every kraal in the country.

Shaka then set the conditions of mourning. No crops were to be planted for the following year, nor was milk to be used; it was to be poured on the ground as it came from the cow. (Since milk curds formed the diet staple, the order was equivalent to national starvation, once the limited stores of grain and the cattle themselves had been eaten.) All women found pregnant during the next year would be killed, together with their husbands. The regiments fanned out to enforce the edicts and to punish those who had not attended Shaka when Nandi died.

Isaacs, off on a hippopotamus hunt, heard of Nandi's passing but missed its significance until he reached a kraal on the heels of one of the enforcing impis. The charred bodies of women and children in the smoldering ashes of their huts convinced him a major event had occurred.

The insane commands and the killings continued for three months, and on three occasions Shaka called the nation together to help him mourn. On the last occasion he ordered everyone to bring all their cattle with them, so that the bellowing of a single gigantic herd could be added to that of his people. Still not satisfied with the din, he ordered every kraal head to rip the gall bladder out of a calf and pour the contents over him; the mutilated animals were then released. Cows were then killed, so that even the calves might know what it was to lose a mother.

Finally one brave man, goaded beyond endurance, publicly bearded Shaka and took him to task for the damage he was doing to the Zulu nation. His name was Gala, and it deserves to be recorded. He bade Shaka stuff a stone into his stomach, and had the temerity to point out that Nandi was not the first person to die in Zululand. Shaka, on whom mourning was beginning to pall, rewarded him with cattle and called off the edicts.

In February of 1828 the schooner *Buckbay Packet* put into Port Natal en route to Delagoa Bay. The settlers traded some of their stored ivory, but their own vessel was so close to completion that no one took advantage of this opportunity to leave. Then, in March, the *Elizabeth and Susan* (named for Farewell's wife and King's mother) was finally launched. She had been two and a half years in the building, and Hatton had reason to be proud of her. The four *Mary* sailors, Biddlecome, Nicolls, Brown and M'Koy, were on hand to man her.

The *Elizabeth and Susan* sailed for Algoa Bay on April 30, 1828. In addition to King, Hatton and his sailors, she carried Isaacs and Farewell and his wife. Also aboard was Shaka's mission to King George, consisting of the ubiquitous Jakot, Shaka's body servant Pikwane, and two leading chieftains named Sotobe and Mbozamboza. (He was usually referred to as Unbosom Boozer.) King carried a lengthy document of his own phrasing, lately signed by Shaka with an imposing scrawl and witnessed by Jakot's mark and Isaacs' signature. The document empowered Sotobe and King to act for Shaka in concluding a treaty of friendly alliance with King George, and specifically enjoined King to return to Shaka to report the results. Then, since no European could apparently resist the opportunity to take advantage of Shaka in one of his signing moods, it went on to grant to King more or less the same broad rights and the same extensive area Shaka had previously granted Farewell.

King was in a delicate position on a number of accounts. The loss of the *Mary* might still cause him complications, and he was now appearing as the owner of a new craft of uncertain registry. His current status as a Zulu envoy was somewhat irregular, and was certain to pose a problem for the British authorities—he had undoubtedly inserted the phrase directing him to return to Shaka to extricate himself from any possible detention. Farewell was also an unknown quantity. He had patched his quarrel with King sufficiently to accept passage for himself and his wife on King's schooner—and the inclusion of "Elizabeth" in the name was a nice touch on King's part—but Farewell undoubtedly had prior rights at Port Natal, and in addition to his pique at the selection of King over himself as an envoy, he could hardly have taken kindly to King's brazen coupling of the land grant to his letter of diplomatic accreditation. To cap it all, Shaka was on the verge of striking south to the very Cape border (under the excuse that Nandi's death required a ceremonial iHlambo hunt), thus making hypocritical nonsense of his request for a treaty of friendly alliance. He had, moreover, only allowed King and Farewell to depart on Fynn's promise to remain behind as a hostage until they returned, and he had made a promise, which he obviously did not intend to keep, not to move south for at least two months after the mission departed.

The situation in what was known as the Zuurveld was indeed touchy. The border, far from stable, still lay along the general line of the Great Fish River, and the Cape Colony was now aware that a powerful Bantu nation in Natal was responsible for the pressure on the frontier clans and the debris that continually flooded the area. General Bourke, commanding troops at Grahamstown, was already involved in a continual series of petty actions as he sought to pin the clans in place.

Shaka, of course, had no intention of waiting, and he moved off less than a month after the mission departed. He first inveigled Fynn and Ogle and a party of armed natives from Port Natal into joining him, by pretending he was only after a few cattle his half brother Ngwadi had stolen. Fynn, noting that Shaka had 20,000 warriors with him, was not taken in, but decided he had better accompany the impi if only to act as a restraining influence. Shaka then announced he intended to raid the amaMpondo under Faku along the lower St. John's River and the Tembus further inland. Moving south rapidly, he halted on the Umzimkulu River. Here he divided his forces, sending one division under Mdlaka to the left to tackle the amaMpondo in the coastal region and the other under Manyundela to the right to hit the Tembus inland. Ogle and the armed natives went with Mdlaka, while Fynn stayed behind with Shaka, who, at Fynn's urgent insistence, at the last moment ordered his generals not to become embroiled with any European force.

Word of the Zulu advance flashed south. The amaMpondo scattered into brush country upstream, and Mdlaka's force shot past them as far as the Umtata River, destroying the empty kraals as it swept through. The inland division smashed into the Tembus and destroyed them, although Manyundela himself was killed in the battle. Mdlaka's force then turned about and started north again, passing through ama-Mpondo country just as that wretched clan was recongregating. It was sent flying again, and Mdlaka rejoined Shaka with thousands of captured cattle. Shaka granted Mdlaka's regiments the headring, and ordered a celebration that lasted until the inland division rejoined. Despite the 10,000 head of Tembu cattle it drove in, Shaka executed several hundred warriors for having lost Manyundela, and then, continually urged by Fynn to quit the area before the full weight of British wrath was released, ordered an expedition against Soshangane in the area bordering Delagoa Bay far to the north. The army was stunned. It had just completed a successful campaign farther south than it had ever been before, and now, instead of the season's rest at its home kraals that it expected, with an opportunity to exploit the newly won headrings, it was ordered off against a tough enemy farther north than it had ever been before. For the first time in his career Shaka had overreached himself, but there was no open sign of his error as the warriors sullenly started on the long road back.

The story of Shaka's advance, garbled and magnified, reached General Bourke at Grahamstown, and he at once sent out a Major Dundas with a company of Imperial troops and a few mounted Boers to repel what appeared to be an invasion of the Cape Colony. By the time Dundas reached the Umtata, the last Zulu was long gone, but the area was in such a turmoil that Dundas could get no proper information. Casting about on the lower Umtata, he heard that the Tembus were being threatened farther inland, so he veered west and on the twentieth of July sighted and attacked a large Bantu force and knocked them helter-skelter out of the area, although he did not have sufficient weight to destroy them. Then, satisfied that he had scotched the Zulu threat, he retreated.

He had, of course, beaten the remnants of the emaNgwaneni, who under Matiwane had just emerged from their stormy career among the Sutu clans of the inland plateau. Matiwane rallied his battered forces and sought a fresh haven a few miles away. It was not to be found.

Bourke, after dispatching Dundas, sent for reinforcements, and in August (when Shaka was already back at kwaDukuza and impatiently awaiting the return of his mission) sent out Lieutenant Colonel Somerset with 200 Imperial cavalry, 800 mounted Boers, and an estimated 18,000 Tembu allies. Somerset in his turn found the emaNgwaneni on the twenty-sixth of August and in two days wiped them out. Matiwane himself escaped with a few retainers, and started the long trek back to his homeland and his death.

Shaka's mission, in the meantime, had not fared well. The *Elizabeth and Susan* reached Algoa Bay on the fourth of May, and King at once sent news of his arrival to Capetown. He then had his grant notarized, and the Europeans scattered to sample the primitive amenities of Port Elizabeth and to search for decent clothing. Isaacs, sunburnt and bearded, was again down to a tattered pair of duck trousers and the wreck of a straw hat. He stayed on the schooner to ride herd on the Zulu members of the mission, who at once started to grow restless.

Sotobe and Mbozamboza were expecting an immediate audience of King George and a swift return to their waiting master; Mbozamboza, in fact, was not even to await the outcome of the negotiations but was to report at once on the mission's reception and King George's attitude toward the frontier clans. The realities of civilized diplomacy were understandably upsetting.

Word presently came from Capetown that the mission was to be entertained at government expense. Isaacs granted his charges shore leave, where an introduction to gin soon compounded their frustration and despair. Sotobe tried to run away several times, and Isaacs, fearing what might happen to Fynn and the others if Shaka's ambassador returned with the tale of such a rebuff, restrained him with difficulty. Then Jakot, totally irresponsible, caused fresh troubles by informing Sotobe that no such person as King George existed; this was simply the name of a mountain. (No one knew where he acquired this misinformation, but oddly enough a mountain was so named shortly thereafter.)

After three solid months of waiting, a Major Cloete, commanding the troops at Port Elizabeth, finally visited the schooner and interviewed the inDunas. Lieutenant King was temporarily absent, and Sotobe was subjected to a hostile and insulting interrogation that made it clear Cloete regarded him as little better than a spy. Isaacs was forced to interpret for this interview, since Jakot as usual proved incompetent. Sotobe defended himself with simple dignity against implications that since Shaka could not read, he was ignorant of the contents of the missive he had signed; that Sotobe himself was not actually a chieftain; that Shaka had not sent him, and that he was in reality taking orders from King. Cloete then went on to outline a series of complicated hypothetical situations, designed to determine if Sotobe would proceed to Capetown without King, until Sotobe finally took the stand that all he wanted was to return to Shaka as speedily as possible, and in King's company.

Isaacs, alarmed at the effect Sotobe's report must inevitably have on Shaka, was vastly relieved by King's sudden return, whereupon Cloete subsided into an embarrassed silence. Isaacs' indignation was natural; the performance had been "an insignificant display of paltry authority and power . . . but little becoming the dignity of a British officer. What could have called for such an attempt to confound two or three unlettered people on an especial mission from their king . . . I know not, but I have no hesitation in declaring unequivocally that it redounded but little to the credit of the officer who was the King's organ." Since Cloete, however, was undoubtedly aware of the Zulu advance and of Bourke's correspondence (which Isaacs apparently was not), the suspicion that the mission was simply an attempt to lull the government into a false sense of security was quite understandable.

The long official silence from Capetown was finally broken on the second of August, when H.M.S. *Helicon* suddenly arrived at Port Elizabeth with gifts for Shaka from the government and orders to take the mission back to Port Natal. Since the government was now using force to repel what it thought to be the Zulu army, it did not wish to meet the ambassadors after all. Sotobe flatly refused to go back unless King or Isaacs went with him to help explain his lengthy absence. King therefore decided to return in H.M.S. *Helicon*, and since he did not wish to be separated from his schooner, nor Isaacs from him, Isaacs took passage in the *Elizabeth and Susan*. Farewell also decided to return.

The two ships arrived off Port Natal on the seventeenth of August, and King, seasick and depressed over the failure of his mission, transferred to his schooner and accidentally grounded her—without serious damage—after transiting the bar. The warship waited for news outside. The other settlers were waiting for them, and the errant Hottentot Michael drowned while attempting to swim out to the ship, regretted by no one. The returning party then got ashore, and Fynn briefed them on recent events; the entire Zulu army was off to the north to strike Soshangane. This news was transmitted to H.M.S. *Helicon*, which left at once for Algoa Bay. King now permitted himself the luxury of collapsing.

Isaacs spent the day getting the horses and supplies off the *Elizabeth and Susan*, and returned to King's hut in the evening. He saw at once that more than seasickness and exhaustion ailed his friend. King, in fact, was dying of a liver ailment.

Isaacs now had to supervise the report to Shaka. Calling Jakot and Sotobe as witnesses that he had not removed anything from the sealed gift chest, he opened it and spread out the government's presents. Sotobe had been hoping that these would be of a quality that might make up in part for his lengthy absence and diplomatic failure, but both he and Isaacs saw at once that the gifts would only enrage Shaka further. In addition to a short length of scarlet broadcloth, the government had seen fit to send only a sheet or two of copper and a few cheap knives. So miserable was the offering that King at once threw in a large mirror and a medicine chest from his own scanty possessions.

Leaving King resting comfortably, Isaacs set off with John Cane and Sotobe on the twenty-fourth of August. Their advance was not cheered by messengers who arrived to urge them on with news of Shaka's towering rage. Isaacs found himself in a quandary as he gradually realized that Sotobe and Jakot were co-ordinating their stories to cast blame on King for having protracted the mission and on Isaacs for having influenced King. He decided to brazen it out, however, and when he arrived, listened silently to Sotobe and then firmly gave his own version of events. Shaka, despite his threats, took no action. He inspected the gifts glumly, demanded to know which were from King and which from the government, and observed that King's were the more valuable.

He then got Isaacs alone in his hut and made him explain, item by item, the contents of the medicine chest. Bewildered by the monarch's increasingly surly comments, he suddenly realized how he had failed him. Shaka had long since lost interest in all the objectives of the mission save one—and Isaacs in the press of all his other worries had completely forgotten it—a bottle of Rowland's Macassar Oil.

Shaka scolded for a while and then announced that John Cane would have to head a second mission, specifically charged with obtaining the hair dressing. Cane voiced the only objection he could think of on the spur of the moment—that he had nothing decent to wear—but Shaka at once furnished him with an old Zulu cloak and sent him back to Port Natal to get ready.

When Isaacs got back to Port Natal, he found King considerably worse. He lingered for a few more days, tended as best they could manage it by Isaacs and Fynn. His last wish was to be reconciled with

Farewell; Isaacs tried to induce him to come, but Farewell only sent a frivolous note. When Isaacs tried to hide it, King got it away from him, scanned it, and said, "I wish I had not read it." He died on September 7, 1828, and was buried by Hatton and the four faithful sailors from the *Mary;* Farewell came to the funeral and apologized to Isaacs and Fynn for his behavior.

John Ross had taken word of King's death to kwaDukuza; he now returned to announce that henceforward Shaka would regard Isaacs as spokesman for the colony (a decision that did little to help the uneasy truce with Farewell), and that Isaacs, Fynn and Farewell were to report to kwaDukuza at once.

The men arrived in the midst of one of the innumerable executions; Isaacs was convinced that Shaka deliberately timed them to coincide with their arrivals. Shaka merely wanted to discuss details of the second mission under Cane; he was taking no chances of missing his Rowland's Macassar Oil and proposed sending an entire herd of cattle and as much ivory as he could scrape up on short notice. Isaacs took the opportunity to secure another land grant from him—about 2,500 square miles covering the same area previously given to Farewell and then again to King. Shaka enjoyed these ceremonies immensely; they obviously pleased his friends and enabled him to participate in the mysterious European rite of appending his scrawl to a document. The contents of the various statements on which he had placed his scribblings meant nothing to him, and just what use Isaacs intended to make of this grant, in view of Farewell's presence at kwaDukuza, he did not state. It was most likely meant to replace King's grant, since, despite some deathbed bequests, he had died intestate.

The party left kwaDukuza on the eighteenth of September, and for a week of intermittent bad weather Isaacs busied himself in preparing the schooner for sea. Then on the twenty-fourth a messenger arrived with awesome tidings. Shaka was dead.

The event was long overdue. Shaka's rule since his mother's death the previous year had passed all bounds of responsibility. The Zulu people, long inured to the slaughter amidst which they lived, were growing restive, and the dread adoration which Shaka had once commanded had long since been replaced by a rule of sheer terror. The incessant executions were no longer regarded as just and inevitable retribution for error, and more and more frequently the intended victims made efforts to save themselves. The kraals in the vicinity of kwaDukuza had already noted the sanctuary that could be found in the kraals at Port Natal, and a small trickle of refugees began to seek shelter under the protection of Fynn, Cane and Ogle.

Shaka had also employed the army most unwisely. It had, at first, built the Zulu nation under his personal direction in battle, and service had come to mean an endless succession of victories and endless streams of looted cattle. The service was no longer so pleasant. The tasks assigned it were now continual, and the objectives so distant and hard that its capabilities were strained to the limit. No one in the army was permitted to marry; Shaka on very rare occasions gave entire regiments permission to don the headring and settle down, but such permission came only when the men were too old to be of further value in the field. The entire youth of the nation was thus held in a state of enforced celibacy, the men in the military formations and the girls in the corresponding female guilds, and the few times that Shaka authorized a regiment to spend a day in ukuHlobonga with a particular female guild did little to relieve the pressure.

He had also stopped leading the army into battle himself—the last occasion had been with Fynn on the Sikhunyana expedition—and not even the indomitable leadership of such men as Mdlaka could keep morale at the pitch the Zulu system required. The current expedition was typical. Weary and disgruntled, over 20,000 warriors passed by their home kraals without pause and started for the north. Shaka stripped the kraals and added every available man to the force, so that none stayed behind but the very young, the very old, and the infirm. Four of his half brothers were sent along: Dingane, who had once hoped to succeed Sigujana, Mhlangana, and the full brothers Mpande and Nzibe. The last was barely twenty, and Mpande, a few years older, was generally regarded as the softest of Senzangakona's brood.

With the army gone, Shaka passed the month of September in typical fashion. He displayed his smelling-out prowess; summoning some three hundred women he asked each one whether or not she owned a cat, and then killed them all regardless of the answer. Most of them had been married to men in one of the headringed regiments then off in the north. He then developed a mild interest in embryology and sliced open a hundred pregnant women to look into the subject. There were still no signs of an open revolt, but there were precious few kraals in Zululand predisposed to stand in the way should one occur.

The intrigue that killed him started in his own family. Mkabayi, full sister to Senzangakona, had been Nandi's devoted crony, and this aging virago nursed the conviction that her royal nephew had poisoned his own mother. While Shaka was absent in the south, she took her suspicions to Dingane and Mhlangana, and urged them to combine with an inDuna named Mbopa, who, as Shaka's head domestic, was continually in his presence. The three men were far from unreceptive, but before they could formulate any plans, Shaka returned, and Din-

gane and Mhlangana were forced to leave on the Soshangane campaign.
Mbopa alone was powerless.

Shaka then added the final straw to the strain on Dingane's patience.
The army had only reached the eGazini kraals (ruled by Mbopa's
father) when Shaka sent an order for all the uDibi boys to return.
These he formed into the *iziNyosi* regiment—"the Bees"—so as to
have at least a bodyguard on hand at his deserted capital, and the army
now had to continue without its transport, shouldering its own assegais, shields, sleeping mats and food. It was too much for the conspirators; Dingane and Mhlangana feigned illness and remained behind
when the army moved on.

They then returned to their kraals, hard by kwaDukuza. Avoiding
Shaka, they sent a herdboy to Mbopa, who casually told Shaka his
brothers were ill and at home. He accepted the news quietly, and the
conspirators breathed easier.

They now urged Mbopa to kill Shaka, but he was unable to nerve
himself to the deed. Then Shaka had a dream; he was dead and Mbopa
serving a new master. He mentioned it to one of the isiGodlo girls in
the morning; she passed it on to Mbopa, who fled in terror to Dingane
and Mhlangana. The three men decided to kill Shaka that very day.

Late in the afternoon of September 22, 1828, a delegation arrived
from the amaMpondo with a gift of crane feathers and otter skins. The
emissaries were somewhat overdue, and Shaka, accompanied by one or
two aged retainers, went to meet them in a small kraal a few yards
from kwaDukuza. Mbopa, in attendance as usual, had a short stabbing
assegai hidden beneath his kaross, and Dingane and Mhlangana concealed themselves behind the low kraal fence. Shaka seated himself and
started to ask the delegation why it was so late, and Dingane motioned
to Mbopa to get rid of the group. Mbopa sprang up and began to
berate the messengers and beat them with a club, and Shaka started to
his feet as the amaMpondo ran out of the cattle pen. Dingane and
Mhlangana vaulted the fence and sank their assegais into Shaka's sides
as he stood there in surprise. Dumfounded, he cried, "Children of my
father, what is wrong?" and then turned and stumbled for the kraal
gate. He fell just beyond it, and the three men closed in to finish him.
At the end his courage and his dignity deserted him, and he died
screaming for mercy and promising to serve his assassins.

The deed was done, but the realization was too overwhelming to
accept at once. The three conspirators fled the scene and all kwaDukuza spent the night quaking in its huts. The gigantic corpse still lay
where it had fallen in the morning; for once, the hyenas had refused to
perform the burial service. The body was hastily bundled into an
oxhide and tumbled into an empty grain pit, which was then filled with

stones. KwaDukuza was later abandoned, and in 1844 became the farm of a Boer immigrant. The exact grave-site was lost, and the founder of the Zulu nation rests today somewhere on Couper Street in the village of Stanger.

Shaka was perhaps forty-one years of age when he died, and he had ruled twelve years. The ancient pattern of Bantu society had passed away in his reign, and with it a Golden Age of Bantu history, in which each of the innumerable clans had still been able to find the space to spin out a pleasant and indolent existence. The upheavals of the last decade had killed two million people and left the landscape dotted with a few mighty nations: the Zulu, the Matabele, the Basuto and the Swazi. The greatest of these was the Zulu, and hundreds of lesser clans had perished or had been swept aside to lead precarious lives among the giants, or to form new and artifical groupings from the debris, which with all hope of self-determination gone eked out half-existences in the shadows of European civilization.

Shaka had not accomplished this by himself, but he had sped the process on its way. He had erected a monolith which towered over the other giants; a quarter of a million strong the Zulus inhabited the coastal strip from the Swazi border on the Pongola River to central Natal, and they ruled from the coast to the Drakensberg mountain range. South of their lands no organized native life existed as far as the Xhosa clans squeezed against the Cape frontier.

The tiny settlement at Port Natal rested in this vacuum, and here Shaka had left the seeds of destruction undisturbed. Alternately irked and bemused, but always aware that the settlers symbolized a power he was unable to fathom, he might have obliterated Port Natal, but he stayed his hand. Now the colony seemed to be on the verge of self-extinction. King was dead, and Farewell and Hatton would soon be dead, and Isaacs and the sailors would soon leave, so that only Fynn and Ogle and Cane and the half-wit Holstead remained of the original group and the settlement's major strength now lay in its kraals, where perhaps a thousand natives had sought protection.

The spark, however, was not to be extinguished. The settlement would become a colony, and in the end it would be Shaka's monolith that tumbled.

DINGANE

THE KING was dead, but as yet there was no king. There was only a triumvirate, and it would have been premature to have wished long life to the men who constituted it.

The conspirators were in a precarious position. Shaka had so dominated the scene that his sudden removal created a vacuum no individual was anxious to fill. The nation had groveled in his presence to such an extent that much of it was incapable of an emotion as rebellious as hatred; personal loyalty to the king had long been submerged in a species of loyalty to the concept of a throne, and as overlord he had inspired no sobriquet but that of "dread." The land was consequently filled with inDunas and petty chieftains who might quite likely resent the idea of his replacement, since only an equal tyrant would justify the debasement they had voluntarily adopted. Other chieftains, leading recently assimilated clans on the periphery of the Zulu influence, were bound to seek retribution for a decade of fire and slaughter as soon as they heard of Shaka's death. To cap the situation, the army was gone, and no chieftain planning to repossess his cattle was likely to be deterred by the sole regiment left at the royal kraal, the iziNyosi, who were utterly inexperienced and much younger than the run of Bantu warriors.

The three assassins, therefore, moved cautiously. Dingane, as the elder half brother, was heir apparent, but at first he made no move to take precedence over Mhlangana. Succession in any event could not be confirmed until the army returned, and both men were content for the nonce to preserve the *status quo* and to leave the administration of the sketchy executive machinery in Mbopa's hands, since he was better acquainted with what had to be done, and because his functioning masked the interregnum with a semblance of continuity. Both men established separate kraals near kwaDukuza and awaited developments.

There was, however, a certain amount of work to be done at once.

The royal kraal was virtually defenseless, so Dingane scraped together
the few hundred men who had not accompanied the expedition and
enrolled them as the *uHlomendini* regiment—"the Homeguards."
These men were *iziYendane,* unaffiliated and despised survivors of the
destroyed clans of Natal, now serving the Zulus as menials and cattle
guards. The two regiments were sent out to collect the royal cattle
from the scores of kraals at which Shaka had quartered them, and as
the herds streamed into kwaDukuza to be divided between the two
new kraals the first signs of tension appeared in the joint rule.

On one point, however, the two men were in complete agreement.
Ngwadi, Nandi's son by the commoner Gendeyana, had led a privi-
leged existence during Shaka's lifetime. Although not in the line of
succession to the Zulu throne, he had been Shaka's maternal half
brother and thus considerably closer to him than the paternal half
brothers who as Senzangakona's sons *were* in the line of succession.
Ngwadi enjoyed a semi-independent status, with his own kraals and
cattle, and he even commanded a small armed force, which had not
been subjected to the draft for the Soshangane expedition. Mbopa was
now sent to destroy him, and did so, but only after a sharp fight in
which the uHlomendini were trounced and in which Ngwadi killed
eight of the iziNyosi before he fell.

The triumvirate also settled a few other holdovers from the Shakan
regime. Ngomane, the chief inDuna, prudently disappeared in the
bush, stayed in hiding for over a year, and only emerged when the
succession had been firmly established. He was not harmed. Nxasonke,
however, a toady so abject that he had killed his seven wives and all
their children when Ngomane a few months previously had accused
them of breaking Nandi's mourning, was followed and slain when he
attempted to flee. Sotobe armed himself and faced the regicides; they
told him they had acted only to halt the incessant carnage, and Sotobe
was satisfied and gave them his support. Nomxamama, official praise-
singer to Shaka, threw himself on the grave, rolled about in a frenzy,
rained curses on the killers, and besought them to deal with him as
they had with his master. They promptly obliged him.

The weeks went by, and there was still no word from the army.
Relations between Dingane and Mhlangana deteriorated. Both men
wooed Mbopa, who secretly threw in with Dingane but retained
Mhlangana's confidence and carried all his plans to his new master. The
climax came one night in October when an assegai whizzed out of the
darkness and wounded Dingane; he wasted no more time and had
Mhlangana murdered the following morning.

What remained of the army began to trickle in a fortnight later. The
expedition had been as disastrous as the last foray to the north, and the

survivors were glad enough to accept Dingane in their relief at escaping Shaka's wrath.

The army, exhausted from the amaMpondo expedition and disgruntled over Shaka's refusal to grant them a season of rest, had continued the march even after the uDibi boys had been recalled, but its mood was sullen, and it began to suffer from mass desertions for the first time in its history. Only Mdlaka's indomitable leadership kept it on the move. The force first visited and destroyed the emaNtshalini clan, for failure to observe Nandi's mourning, and then worked far north, to the present site of Lydenburg, from whence it descended on Soshangane, who was located to the northeast of Delagoa Bay.

By then, two months out, the food supplies were gone and malaria and dysentery had struck. The warriors were reduced to eating strips cut from their shields, and half the force was soon incapable of action. A deserter, moreover, warned Soshangane of the impending attack, and he took his 3,000 warriors into the shelter of a series of rocky caverns. Mdlaka camped before this stronghold one night, intending to attack at dawn, but well before first light Soshangane threw his entire weight against the tip of the Zulu flank and all 30,000 invaders panicked and fled. Mdlaka finally rallied them, but by sunup Soshangane had retreated. The Zulus then gave up and started for home. The remnants of the army that finally reached kwaDukuza owed their lives to a swarm of locusts they encountered on the trail, but even the locusts had their revenge; they followed the Zulus home and devastated Natal for a number of years.

Only Mdlaka himself was inclined to dispute Dingane's accession, and he based his objections not so much on Shaka's murder as on Mhlangana's, since he regarded the latter as a more suitable replacement. Dingane was by now sure enough of his power to have Mdlaka killed, and he was only dissuaded from killing his younger half brother Mpande as well by the pleas of various inDunas, with whom the good-natured youth was popular. Dingane had no more desire than Shaka to leave maturing half brothers scattered about, and in addition to Mpande there still remained of Senzangakona's sons Magwaza, Kolekile and Gqugqu—all striplings who as yet presented no threat. Nzibe, Mpande's full brother, had died of fever on the Soshangane expedition, and his body had been carried home to Zululand for burial.

Dingane was fairly settled by the beginning of 1829, and only Mbopa remained to be dealt with. His loyalty had been complete, and Dingane pensioned him off, settling him in a nearby kraal with gifts of cattle. No Bantu chieftain, however, would long tolerate the presence of a regicide in his immediate vicinity, and some six years later Mbopa was driven away.

The settlers at Port Natal were only dimly aware of these events. They had enjoyed Shaka's protection, and the news of his murder came as a shock which emphasized the realities of their position—a weak handful of Europeans at the mercy of a savage power. They were not only ignorant of Dingane's intentions, but they also feared a civil war even more than the new king himself did. They consequently made haste to put the half-finished Fort Farewell in order, but before they were fairly started, a messenger arrived from Dingane. He reported the facts of the murder, giving the same justification that had been offered Sotobe, and affirming his personal friendship. The settlers thereupon relaxed, but Nathaniel Isaacs determined to leave. He had King's affairs to settle in Capetown, and he felt himself too young to shoulder his late friend's interests in the quarrel with Farewell.

He therefore set about preparing the *Elizabeth and Susan* for sea, and at once clashed with Hatton, who saw no reason to submit himself to Isaacs' orders. Hatton, indeed, had a strong case; he had built the vessel and Isaacs had not, and King had furthermore undoubtedly been in his debt when he died, whereas Isaacs had no valid claim on the estate. Isaacs, however, went to Fynn, who appealed to the sailors over Hatton's head. The decision, oddly enough, was in favor of the boy. Hatton, completely frustrated, promptly sickened and on the second of November, the same day news of Ngwadi's death reached Port Natal, he died.

Before the ship was ready to sail, word came that John Cane, off after Macassar Oil and still unaware of Shaka's death, had reached amaMpondoland, and Henry Ogle returned overland from Grahamstown in the Cape Colony with a Mr. Shaw, sent on a mission to Shaka by Colonel Somerset. Shaw was disconcerted to find Shaka dead, but he stayed on to trade. Isaacs now graciously offered Farewell a passage in what was beginning to look like *his* schooner, and on December 1, 1828, the *Elizabeth and Susan* sailed from Port Natal bound for Algoa Bay and Capetown. She touched on the bar in leaving, as if to remind her passengers of the manner of their arrival in the *Mary* over three years ago.

The voyage to Port Elizabeth at Algoa Bay took twelve days. The sailors soon disclosed why they had opted for Isaacs instead of Hatton; they mutinied. Farewell, sometime officer in the Royal Navy, promptly put the trouble down, assisted by Isaacs, John Ross, Nicolls and M'Koy. The dispute seems to have been primarily verbal; mutiny was a capital offense, but no action was taken after arrival in civilized parts.

Isaacs was now in for another shock. Mr. Francis, the Port Officer, who on the previous visit had seemed to be King's best friend, and who

had granted a sea letter when the *Elizabeth and Susan* sailed with
H.M.S. *Helicon*, now seized the vessel. He gave as grounds the fact
that under her present character she could not obtain a proper register,
and despite Isaacs' ingenious argument that the greater part of her hull
had been built from the wreck of the *Mary*, whose register should
therefore apply, Francis refused to release her. Isaacs' indignation, only
partially held in check by the knowledge that Solomon himself could
hardly have resolved the question of the schooner's ownership, passed
all bounds when Francis sold her and pocketed the price, but there was
no legal objection to such action under the British Registry Act, so
Isaacs abandoned the claim and proceeded to Capetown.

Here he fell ill while preparing a report on Natal for the Governor.
He met with Thompson, one of the founders of the Farewell Trading
Company, and he tried to turn King's effects over to the Orphan
Chamber, but he could not locate the agent for that office. Then,
failing in his attempts to secure an audience with the Governor, and
feeling worse all the time, he gave up the struggle and booked passage
for St. Helena, which he reached on March 5, 1829. He had been gone
for five adventurous years.

He spent eleven months with his relatives, resting and trying to
interest passing ships in the advantages of trading with Natal. His
enthusiasm was so infectious, and St. Helena so dull, that he finally
determined to return himself, signing on as supercargo to a Captain
Page of the American brig *St. Michael*. He sailed on February 18, 1830,
and on the evening of March 30 was once again anchored off Port
Natal.

The following morning Captain Page took four men and set off in
the longboat to sound the bar. He capsized in the surf, one of the
sailors was taken by a shark, and Page and the other two survivors
gained the safety of the keel and finally drifted ashore. Two hours
later Isaacs, still aboard the *St. Michael*, saw five Europeans climb a
sand dune and wave to him, and he knew that at least some of his old
friends were still alive.

The longboat was righted and came out the next morning, and Page
ran the brig into the harbor and anchored. There was a bare ten feet of
water on the bar, and the *St. Michael* naturally scraped her bottom in
passing, a sound to which Isaacs by then must have been accustomed.
John Cane, Henry Ogle and Thomas Holstead were all on hand to
greet him; there were new faces, and there was a long list of news.

To begin with, Farewell was dead. Isaacs had last seen him in Port
Elizabeth the preceding January; Farewell had then gone on to Capetown himself. Here his wife had borne him a son, and he himself had
raised fresh capital—in the form of two and a half tons of beads—and

had interested a few fresh settlers in coming back to Port Natal to trade. By September of 1829 he was back at Port Elizabeth, ready to set out overland for Natal with a wagon train. He had with him a trader named Thackwray and a young naturalist named Walker, who was primarily interested in exploration. John Cane, at last supplied with the Macassar Oil for which the market had disappeared, was also ready to return.

During Farewell's absence in Capetown, amaMpondoland had been subjected to its usual budget of disorders. In March of 1829 Nqetho, a chieftain of the amaQwabe, had quarreled violently with Dingane, and had taken up his people and cattle and fled to the south. He got as far as amaMpondo country, colliding with various clans on the way, and he finally came to a temporary halt in the vicinity of Faku, paramount chieftain in those parts. The unrest his movements caused knocked a number of missionaries loose and sent them scrambling for safety back to Grahamstown. At the amaDola Mission Station a Wesleyan named Shepstone, who had been in the territory for six years, barely escaped with his life. His family included a twelve-year-old son, Theophilus, who was already fluent in the local Xhosa dialect.

Among the travelers who also had to turn back was a party headed for Port Natal, consisting of Andrew Bain and John Burnet Biddulph, who were traveling in company with Henry Francis Fynn's father—also named Henry Francis—and his two sons, Alfred and Francis. The father had decided to move to Port Natal and was taking his two remaining boys with him; a fourth son, William, had already been sent out to locate the wreck of the *Buckbay Packet* and had gone on to join Henry Francis after he found it.

When Farewell started north late in September, the region was quiet again, but Faku, who had seen his land overrun by successive waves of Zulus, Zulu refugees, emaNgwaneni, British troops, and now ama-Qwabe, was gathering sufficient force to drive the new invaders back to the north.

By early November Farewell reached the Umzimvubu River, where Nqetho was camped. Farewell left his wagons in Cane's care some sixteen miles from Nqetho's kraal and then rode on with Thackwray, Walker and eight Hottentot and Zulu servants to visit the chieftain.

It was a rash decision; Farewell was on his way to Dingane, laden with gifts for Nqetho's mortal enemy, and he had with him the son of a Zulu functionary whom the amaQwabe recognized and assumed was a spy. The Europeans nevertheless pitched their tent outside the kraal, and their servants moved into amaQwabe huts for the night. Before Farewell retired, some of his servants told him Nqetho was not to be trusted, and that the atmosphere in the kraal was tense. Long after dark, a Hottentot interpreter named Lynx crept up to his tent and whispered that the amaQwabe were plotting their deaths, but Farewell, who should have known better, called him a coward and went back to sleep. Just before dawn the amaQwabe cut his tent ropes and stabbed the three Europeans to death through the canvas. Lynx had been sitting up in his hut with a loaded musket, and at the first sound he kicked up the others and made a run for the open. Only three of the eight servants got through to Cane's camp; in a running fight Lynx killed three of his pursuers and was himself wounded several times.

Cane grabbed a horse and bolted into the bush with the rest of the servants just as the amaQwabe arrived. When he returned later in the day, he found all his horses and oxen killed and the beads gone. He returned to Grahamstown to re-equip, while Faku fell on Nqetho and drove him out. As soon as he reached Zululand, Dingane had him killed. Cane, Biddulph, Bain and the three Fynns then made their way to Port Natal.

Farewell had practically invited his own death, but his passing was untimely and regrettable. For all his rapaciousness and his occasional chicanery, he deserves most of the credit for founding Port Natal. Aged thirty-eight, he died just too soon to see the fruits of his labors begin to ripen.

With Farewell dead, Cane and Ogle took over what remained of his business, and reapportioned the sizable kraals that were beginning to dot the landscape about the harbor. Henry Francis Fynn continued to trade independently, and first William and then his father and his other two brothers joined him, as did Holstead. Several thousand natives now owed Henry Francis allegiance, and although he never seems to have married into the iziNkumbi clan he founded, at least one brother did. Never a chieftain himself, Francis Fynn took to wife Vundlase, who ruled the clan, and by her he fathered the Charlie Fynn who succeeded Vundlase in 1882.

Isaacs decided to join the Fynns and set out to visit Dingane, who had moved his kraal from kwaDukuza to a new location 150 miles inland at emGungundhlovu, in the heart of the original Zulu territory. Henry Francis Fynn accompanied him; on their way they stopped off to visit Jakot, now rich in lands and cattle but as illogical as ever. Jakot was beginning to sour on Europeans. In Shaka's time his linguistic accomplishments brought him fame and honour, but when Dingane continued to send for him at every appearance of a white skin, he began to find his role irksome. Just before Shaka's death he had accompanied Sotobe's unsuccessful mission to Port Elizabeth, and in March of 1829 Dingane sent him north to Delagoa Bay with two English explorers named Cowie and Green, who had traversed amaMpondoland just before Nqetho's revolt. Both men had died of fever, and Jakot had been in terror of capture as a runaway slave, and he now wanted peace to enjoy his kraal.

Dingane received Isaacs and Fynn courteously and was enthusiastic about the prospects of trade. Profiting from their experience with Shaka, the two young men brought royal gifts along, and Dingane responded with a quantity of ivory. He had ideas of his own; he wanted Fynn to become King of Natal and to act as his agent at Port Natal, and he was vexed with Cane and Ogle for having appropriated Farewell's cattle; these had been gifts from Shaka and should have reverted to the royal herds when Farewell died. Fynn gently turned down the suggestion he enter Dingane's service, and he promised to see what he could do about the cattle. Both men were pleased with Dingane's attitude, although Isaacs failed to mention the translation of the new Zulu name he acquired on this visit. He was now *Dambuza um-Thabathi*—"He Who Takes Things."

The prospects indeed looked bright, for Dingane was a fresh wind in Zululand. Perhaps thirty years old, he was tall, broad and magnificently muscled, with the enormous thighs that characterized the House of Senzangakona. When his life became sedentary—as it did the instant he ascended the throne—he started to run to fat and developed a paunch that thereafter was his most noticeable feature. He bore himself with an alert and regal air, missing nothing, and giving evidence of a high order of intelligence.

His life for the past twelve years had provided opportunities to develop a number of interesting qualities. He had participated in all of Shaka's campaigns in the amaWombe regiment, and he was thus familiar with the best techniques of Bantu warfare. As Shaka's next eldest half brother he had spent the entire reign in the role of heir apparent, a peculiarly dangerous post in Bantu society, and in this case made even more conspicuous by Shaka's announced policy to sire no heirs. That Dingane survived is more a tribute to his own self-effacement than to Shaka's brotherly affections. The long training in self-control, coupled with his intelligence, gave promise of a fruitful reign, and Dingane had, so to speak, entered office on a platform of peace and prosperity.

It seemed at first as if this policy were sincere. The army was allowed to scatter to its home kraals, and a number of regiments were permitted to don the headring. The senseless slaughter at the court stopped, people breathed easily again, and the thick fog of fear that lay over the land thinned perceptibly.

Dingane's reign, however, proved to be disappointing almost from the outset. His only interest was self-indulgence, as if to make up for

the lean years, and within the primitive and rather austere opportunities provided by Zulu society he achieved something very close to
debauchery. He was a glutton with an enormous capacity for the
wholesome fare of his people, and beyond gloating over the royal
herds as they were driven past for his inspection, only the isiGodlo
occupied his attention. He cut Shaka's 1,200 "sisters" back to 300 girls,
whose dress he designed and personally supervised. He developed and
participated in the incessant dancing, and spent the bulk of his time
isolated in the seraglio. The precise nature of his activity in this field is
not known; like Shaka he never fathered a recorded child, but since
there is no evidence that he suffered from his predecessor's impotency,
he was most likely sterile. He built a mound of earth by the isiGodlo
wall so that he could peer over and supervise the remainder of the
kraal without leaving the royal preserve; it is all that remains of em-
Gungundhlovu today.

Dingane was also bone-lazy, and unable to separate considerations of
national policy from his personal affairs. The laziness extended to his
mental activity; it compounded the national inability to exercise any
degree of foresight, and it injected an element of caprice into his
decisions that made him even more unpredictable than Shaka, who had
at least acted within a rough framework of logic. Dingane was merely
treacherous.

The army was not left alone for long. Dingane first amalgamated the
remnants of the broken Shakan regiments into the *iziBawu*, and then
went on to create a half-dozen regiments of his own. He waged few
major campaigns, but he was quick to resort to a military solution for
even minor policy matters, and his troops were rarely idle. Although
the blind slaughter of Shaka's court had stopped, executions were still
frequent, and the atmosphere was soon as foreboding as it had ever
been.

Clear evidence of these failings, however, still lay in the future, and
Isaacs threw himself into his partnership with the Fynns with enthusiasm. He had brought a stand of twenty muskets with him; some of these
he rashly gave Dingane, and the rest he used to equip a small body of
Port Natal natives which he hoped to train as a standing force. (One of
his trainees promptly blew an arm off a comrade.) Henry Francis
Fynn's interminable wanderings, moreover, had finally provided him
with a profitable arrangement which he hoped to exploit through the
St. Michael, since Captain Page promised to return after sailing with a
first load of ivory. The foothills of the Drakensberg were still swarming with Bushmen who had been driven out of the coastal strip, and
Fynn stumbled onto a small Bantu clan deep in the interior which had
learned the use of the Bushman's poisoned arrow. The clan turned to

elephant hunting, camping beside each kill until the meat was gone and then moving on to the next. It was thus in a position to provide a small trickle of ivory, and Fynn secured from them a promise not to trade with anyone else. Ivory was still Natal's most valuable export, but it was hard to come by without the direct intervention of the Zulu king, since elephant hunting with assegais was dangerous to the point of lunacy, and digging traps involved more labor than the meat was worth to the natives.

Other traders began to drift north through the coastal strip. Biddulph got through at last, and was soon trading with two men named Oughton and Collis, and old and new hoped for fresh settlers. Biddulph and his partners, however, decided to return to Grahamstown in September after a two months' stay, since Fynn's virtual monopoly had shut them out and they needed more trade goods.

Cane was also due for another trip, this time on Dingane's behalf. The king had nothing particular in mind, except perhaps to advertise his own importance, but it occurred to him that an offer of friendship and peaceful intentions would be repaid with gifts. Emulating Shaka, he therefore made Cane his emissary and assigned seven Zulus to accompany him, mainly to insure that bearers would be on hand for the presents he expected. When Cane requested an interpreter, Dingane naturally sent for Jakot.

Jakot was furious. He blamed Cane for this latest interruption of his peaceful kraal life, and quarreled with him bitterly all the way to Grahamstown, which the party reached on the twenty-first of November. Cane dutifully delivered his message to the Civil Commissioner, sold the four tusks Dingane had given him, bought a few presents, and then left before he had even gotten a reply. His object was to get back north before the rivers rose, which would have barred travel for several months, but his abrupt turnabout gave further ammunition to the irate Jakot.

Grahamstown was abubble with rumor about Port Natal. A number of local merchants were interested in trade, and Biddulph, Collis and Oughton were questioned closely. They reported favorably on the trade opportunities, but complained about the monopoly Isaacs and the Fynns had established. Cane, for different reasons, helped to blacken Isaacs' reputation. The settlers were anxious to see the Union Jack flying over the bay, which would have given them the protection of Imperial troops as well as the advantages of law, order and regularized commerce, so Cane, in an effort to flag official interest, slyly reported that Isaacs was arming the natives and that the American brig on which he had returned was due back with settlers from the United States. The tale indeed stirred interest, and there was some mild talk of sending a party of troops to Port Natal. Jakot, who had been talking to some disgruntled local natives, heard the talk, and with his genius for illogical deduction reached several erroneous conclusions.

By March 10, 1831, Cane was back at Port Natal. He had been gone six months, his kraal needed attention, and he saw no reason to make the long trip to emGungundhlovu to report to Dingane in person, especially as he had no message to deliver. He consequently busied himself with his domestic affairs and sent his presents on to Dingane in Jakot's care. This was foolhardy, and Jakot made the most of his opportunity.

His report to Dingane was lurid, alarming and convincing. He blamed the continual unrest in amaMpondoland on the presence of missionaries, whom he described as the entering wedge of European domination. He accused the Cape Government of a deliberate advance up the coastal strip, and announced an army was even then on its way to attack the Zulu nation. And for all of this John Cane, peacefully tending his kraal, was somehow to blame.

The story was eked out with sufficient detail to convince Dingane of its accuracy. He called out a regiment and sent it down to wipe out Cane's kraal. The impi arrived before dawn on the eighteenth of April, and Cane fled to the bush while his kraal was burned and his cattle lifted. The other settlers fled as well; for the first time in seven years the Zulus were attacking a European and not even the Fynns waited long enough to ask questions. In a few days Dingane sent messengers to inform the others his quarrel was with Cane alone, so Henry Francis Fynn, the best linguist, took one of his brothers and visited the king. He brought with him the largest load of gifts that had ever gone to the Zulu capital; it required the services of eighty porters and included eleven muskets.

To Fynn's astonishment, he found that Jakot's tales had caused an acute panic. Dingane had not only mustered the entire army but had even persuaded the Portuguese to send him a company of forty colored soldiers from Lourenço Marques.

Fynn's eloquence and his gifts lowered the tension, but the chain of misunderstandings was not yet complete. As the party was returning to Port Natal, a chieftain, aware of the crisis but not the *démarche*, warned Fynn that Dingane was about to attack the harbor. The settlers scattered again, and Sotobe, set long ago by Shaka to watch them, jumped to the conclusion that they were absconding with the royal cattle to which Dingane had laid claim. He sent an impi to recover the herds, and the Fynns barely got away with their lives. Francis Fynn was actually trampled on in the dark, Henry Francis's infant son was killed, and he himself only got away by taking to the sea and swimming to a rocky outcrop across an inlet.

The recurrent crises were too much for Nathaniel Isaacs, who was also somewhat disturbed by the interpretation Grahamstown had placed on his activities. The *St. Michael* was again at Port Natal; on the twenty-fourth of June Isaacs boarded her and sailed away, to play no further part in the history of Natal. Still only twenty-three years of age, he ranks with Farewell, King and Fynn as a founder, and he did as much as any of them to stir up interest overseas. He closed his diary with his departure and dropped into limbo, leaving only brief glimpses behind. He started a trading company in England, but he could not break himself to office routine or life in civilized society. He then spent the rest of his life trading in West Africa. For many years he lived alone on a plantation in Sierra Leone, exporting arrowroot, and the last trace of him was recorded in 1864 when he visited relatives in England. He is supposed to have died alone on an island in the Gulf of Guinea.

As the months passed and Jakot's invasion failed to materialize, Dingane gradually realized the truth. He sent messengers after the scattered settlers asking them to return, and Cane, whose carelessness had caused it all, took his life in his hands and visited the royal kraal. By January of 1832 the air was clear and the settlers back in place. Dingane, now well aware that Jakot was the source of the trouble, asked Cane to kill him, so Ogle, nothing loath, sought him out and shot him down. Cattle thieving had brought him to Robben's Island and launched him on his career, and cattle thieving undid him; the final straw had been added to Dingane's patience when Jakot tried to cut a few head out of a royal herd.

Although the immediate cause of friction was gone, the settlement was again on the verge of extinction. Dingane had actually sent an impi to attack the Europeans, something Shaka had never done, and the odd air of trust that marked the early days was gone forever. The settlers were down to John Cane, Henry Ogle, the hapless, good-natured Holstead and the four Fynns, and a youth of nineteen named Richard Phillip King who had arrived in 1828 as a servant to Cowie and Green. All of these men were on edge, and not one was willing to invest any effort in a homestead that might be raided at any moment. The Fynns had even moved some distance to the south, and all of the settlers lived in rude huts and lean-tos inferior to the carefully constructed Bantu huts. Rachel still lived nearby in splendid isolation.

The settlement was now saved by the work that King, Farewell, Isaacs and even Cane had done in the past. Time and again they had extolled the virtues of Natal; their accounts had circulated in Port Elizabeth and Grahamstown and Capetown and as far away as London, and there were merchants, traders, farmers and hunters in all these places seeking fresh frontiers. The first of them started to arrive in 1832, and nine of them joined the settlers before the year was out. They included the three Cawood brothers—religious devouts who held daily services and thereby provoked Henry Francis Fynn, who feared the Zulus might misinterpret a lay liturgy that closely resembled the ritual used to doctor an impi for a military expedition!

Three arrivals were temporary visitors. Dr. Andrew Smith and a Lieutenant Edie came all the way from the Cape to make an official check on the petitions Isaacs and Farewell had left there. They were accompanied by William Berg, a frontier Boer and the first true farmer to visit Natal. Dr. Smith was enchanted with what he saw, and his report was so lyrical that a large number of Cape citizens petitioned the Crown to occupy Natal. Berg submitted no written report, but he carried back the tale of a wondrous farming country—fertile, well watered and well nigh vacant. There were urgent reasons why the Boers should listen to such an account that year, and the story spread like a grass fire.

The settlement's growth continued in 1833, despite a temporary setback in April. Dingane sent an impi against the amaMpondo, which worked its way south far inland along the Drakensberg foothills, and somewhere on a riverbank it found a party of eight colored hunters from the Cape Colony. It killed seven of them and carried off one youth as a prisoner. Rumors of this incident reached Port Natal, where it was assumed that the party attacked had been that of the Cawood brothers, who had been hunting in the area. The settlers attacked the impi on its return, killing over 200 of the Zulus, who did not fight back. The entire settlement then bolted again, since it had suddenly occurred to them what Dingane's reaction might be. They could have spared themselves the trouble; Dingane released the prisoner, killed the impi's leader, and blinded the scouts who had failed to perceive the civilized character of their victims. The Cawoods, however, had enough and left for good.

Settlers continued to trickle in during 1834. Hunters predominated, but the trade was growing difficult. The traders purchased their ivory, hides, cattle and grain with beads, and they were now being undercut both by the Portuguese and by hordes of American whalers, who had recently appeared in the Indian Ocean. These ships landed parties along hundreds of miles of the coast to replenish water and purchase meat and corn. They had no objections to purchasing ivory as well, since it took up remarkably little space, and they paid for their purchases with an inexhaustible supply of trade beads which knocked the bottom out of the market. Before the year was out the Fynns gave up the struggle and left to take up civil posts in the Cape Colony.

Henry Francis Fynn became interpreter to Sir Benjamin D'Urban, Governor of the Cape Colony. After a series of posts as British Resident and Diplomatic Agent with various clans, he returned to Natal as a magistrate in 1852. He died in 1861, in a house on the Bluff near the site of his original campsite. By far the most capable of the early settlers, he had never been given an acre of land by the government of the colony he helped to found.

As the winter of 1834 drew to a close, a party of visitors arrived whose numbers almost doubled the population. Twenty-one men and a woman in fourteen wagons, led by Petrus Lafras Uys, pitched a camp at the mouth of the Mvoti River. Boers, they were courteously welcomed by the settlers, whose enthusiasm grew as the newcomers explained their mission.

They constituted one of a number of *kommissie trekke*, sent out by the farmers of the Cape Colony frontier to explore the lands to the north. Other groups from Graaff Reinet and Colesberg had crossed the Orange River and skirted Mshweshwe's Basutos to view the depopulated inland plateau; they themselves, from Uitenhage and Grahamstown, had traversed the coastal strip to see the land Berg had spoken of in such glowing terms, and to judge if there was room here for some of the thousands of Boers who had lately decided to quit the Cape Colony and British rule. That the land was good they could see at once, and there remained only the question of ownership.

Gerbrantzer's lesson of 1705 was forgotten. The Bantu viewed the land as an entailed property that belonged to the clan. A chieftain might dispose of the right to live on the land, but he could not dispose of the land itself, nor were his arrangements binding on his successor. The European mind in general could not grasp this concept and regarded a land transaction as a permanent exchange of real property. The Bantu view insured European encroachment and the European view future strife, and Uys's kommissie trek had already been given a hint of its nature. Uys had first inspected the region just beyond the Great Fish River, and Hintza, a Xhosa chieftain, had magnanimously given him permission to settle on his northern borders. When Uys reached the area, he found it occupied by the amaMpondo, whose chieftain Faku with equal generosity gave him permission to settle in Hintza's domain.

The Zulus, however, were sufficiently powerful to speak for a vast and empty region on their borders. Dingane had withdrawn all his garrisons after the Cawood scare, and the great arc of Natal to the south of the Tugela River and to the west of its tributary the Buffalo stood empty. The settlers suggested that Uys apply himself to Dingane, and Uys sent Richard King to speak for him. Dingane listened with interest, but suggested the trek leaders appear in person. Uys was down with fever and the rest of the men had fanned out to explore the countryside. Uys finally sent his younger brother Johannes, but by the time he reached the Tugela the river was in flood and he was unable to cross. There were Zulus on the far bank, and Johannes Uys shouted his identity and his mission, and eventually he returned to Port Natal to tell his brother that the land was indeed vacant and that Dingane had given the Boers permission to settle it. Uys's party then departed, sped on its lumbering way by a report that another Kaffir war had broken out on the frontier near their homes. As the Boers moved south through amaMpondoland, an Englishman was riding north to Port Natal, driven by a sense of personal urgency so strong that he had left his wagons to catch up with him as best they could. The contemporary world was about to burst on Port Natal.

1835 was a critical year for southern Africa. There had been no radical change in the borders of the Cape Colony for the preceding sixty years, nor in the nature of the forces that kept the frontier in a precarious equilibrium. The Bantu had checked the Boer drift to the east in the 1770's, but the internal pressures behind that drift now came to a head and culminated in the eruption of the Great Trek. The first parties of what would eventually total some 14,000 Boers disposed of their homesteads, packed their household goods in ox-drawn wagons, gathered their herds, and quietly moved north out of the Cape Colony and away from British rule. They crossed the Orange River and picked their way through the Griqua settlements that lay beyond; then, skirting the Basuto, they moved out across the inland plateau that had been depopulated by the Mfecane. Only the Matabele, lying at the center of a fresh circle of destruction, opposed them, and they struck Mzilikazi so hard that he retreated north of the Matopo Range and his tribe was lost to history for fifty years. The trekkers crossed the Vaal and carried their civilization as far north as the Limpopo River, and sizable numbers of them turned east, descended the passes of the Drakensberg Range and entered Natal—thus bypassing the jammed bottleneck at the southern end of the coastal strip. In less than a year they effectively destroyed the boundaries that had confined European civilization to a narrow belt at the southern tip of the continent, and when their movements petered out a decade later, the outlines of the modern Republic of South Africa had been formed. In the end they failed to achieve their immediate purpose, for they drew British administration, reluctantly but inexorably, after them.

In 1778 Joachim van Plettenberg, Governor of the Cape Colony, finally visited his eastern frontier. His visit was long overdue, for the United Chartered East India Company no longer had any idea where the frontier actually was, nor knew what manner of folk lived there. His arrival more or less coincided with the Boer-Bantu clash on the Great Fish River, and he was thus able to fix his colony's boundary on the middle reaches of that stream. He was also able to meet with a people who had been beyond the effective reach of the East India Company's administration for a full century, and he returned to Cape-town with a clear and somewhat disturbing picture of the civilization which they had developed for themselves.

This new civilization suited the frontier Boers admirably. It was a simple and practical life in which a minimum of labor returned a harvest that satisfied their modest needs. The *lekker lewe*—"the sweet life"—was carefully attuned to the ecological demands of one of the most isolated regions on the face of the earth, already beyond the control of a Capetown which in its turn lay three months' sail from Europe. The frontier Boers asked only to be left in their isolation, and to be allowed to administer to their lives as they saw fit. What had disturbed Van Plettenberg was the patent knowledge that not one of the three basic requirements for the lekker lewe could be met without increasing difficulty in the future.

The first requirement was continuing access to ample farmland. All land in the Cape Colony nominally belonged to the company, which demanded an annual quit-rent of £5 for each holding. No real effort had ever been made to enforce this demand except in the immediate vicinity of Capetown, with the net result that each adult Boer was convinced that his birthright included a farm, for which he was pre-pared to pay £5 per annum at the most—if a strenuous effort were made to collect. Every Boer family produced a number of sons who regarded themselves as adult at the age of sixteen, and Boers thought of farms as roughly circular holdings of at least 6,000 acres (and prefer-ably two or three times that size), far enough removed from all neigh-bors to prevent strife over undefined boundaries. Each Boer was not truly satisfied until he possessed two such farms, one for winter graz-ing and another for summer, and a single Boer couple, therefore, within a span of 25 years, could quite easily generate a demand for something like 100,000 acres. Africa was big, but it could not be sub-jected to such demands indefinitely, and the collision with the Bantu had effectively scotched the previous solution to this problem. Vast reaches of the Cape Colony were still vacant, so that nothing like an acute land hunger developed, but the Boers began to feel themselves increasingly crowded.

The second requirement for the lekker lewe was cheap labor, and although the problem appeared quite simple to the Boer—a matter of black and white, in fact—his approach to its supply made difficulties for even the sketchiest of European administrations. Few Boer holdings on the frontier were farmed either intensively or scientifically, and the demands made on farm labor were neither heavy nor complicated. The Boer, however, refused to participate in farm labor himself, and he was content to oversee the minimal labor that was performed by the natives. As long as this labor was provided, and the natives performed it on the Boer terms, no one was particularly concerned with the nature of the contractual relationship between the two parties. Outright slavery was still legal, and in the western Cape Colony there were decided differences between slaves and indentured servants, but these differences tended to merge on the frontier. The natives worked, and their wants were satisfied, and if they became lazy or insubordinate or tried to run away, they were beaten. They had at best only a dim idea of what their relationship to their masters actually was, and they tended to equate it with their relationship to a kraal head, which they understood perfectly. There was no legal apparatus to which they could appeal, nor, within the settled areas, any organized tribal life for them to fall back on. This state of affairs was naturally satisfactory to the Boers, who looked on any attempt to change it as a threat to the lekker lewe. There were, quite naturally, abuses of this system, but in the light of the times they were minor abuses, and in the light of the frontier they were not abuses at all. Very few Boers were sadists or tyrants, and if they exploited their indentured servants, they undoubtedly treated their slaves better than those held in bondage in numerous contemporary societies.

The third requirement was physical security. The natural dispersion of the Boer farms, and the lack of a surplus male population, barred standing military forces and made each homestead an easy mark for marauders. The problem was minimal within the Cape Colony, where the major threat stemmed from wandering Hottentots and the few Bushman bands that still survived. The labor policy itself tended to eliminate wandering natives, and as early as 1819 the British came to the aid of the farmers with pass laws to pin the natives to the farms. The Bushmen were simply hunted down, except for infant children, who were captured and raised for domestic service.

On the frontier, however, the Boers were confronted with strong tribal organizations just across the border. Both societies measured wealth in cattle, and theft and countertheft insured continual strife. Border law sanctioned making good a theft from the cattle of the nearest kraal to which the spoor led, and commando riders expected to be paid in cattle. No administration, and certainly not the parsimonious company, could afford sufficient troops to keep Boers in and Bantu out; and Boer, Bantu and official grievances flourished. After one flare-up in 1793 a discouraged official noted that the itemized losses submitted by the local farmers totaled exactly eight times the number of cattle the same men had just reported for tax returns.

Between Van Plettenberg's visit in 1778 and the start of the Great Trek in 1835 the frontier was subjected to five separate administrations. The first four of these—the expiring company, the first British occupation, the short-lived Batavian Republic, and the second and permanent British occupation—were generally sympathetic to the frontier Boers and tried to grapple with their problems. In each case, moreover, the administration at Capetown, influenced by a surrounding belt of settled Boers, served as a buffer between the wilder spirits on the frontier and the ultimate seat of authority in The Hague or London. There was, however, a feeling among the frontier Boers that *no* government understood them, and by the time a reform administration took over in London in 1825, this resentment had started to crystallize into hostility.

The process started when the border closed in 1778. Never really intense, the slight pressure nevertheless sufficed to dot the eastern Cape Colony with a series of small villages: Port Elizabeth and Uitenhage, Graaff Reinet and Colesberg, Somerset, Cradock and Grahamstown. When the British came, these settlements served as administrative centers and brought the restive Boers more and more within the reach of new regulations. There was a rising at Swellendam as early as 1795, perilously close to Capetown, and another one in the frontier village of Graaff Reinet. The friction, rooted in company policies which seemingly allowed the Bantu to raid at will but interfered with Boer counterraids, passed in the company's demise, but succeeding administrations did little to reassure the sullen farmers.

The strongest blow at the lekker lewe was struck by the introduction of a fundamental concept of British justice—the equality of all mankind before the bar of law. In 1806, the year the British came to stay, slavery and the slave trade were still legal throughout the Empire, but the trade was abolished in 1807 and the movement for complete emancipation was growing. The Boers might not like this movement, but they could understand it, and since in the loose master-servant relationship they favored, slavery was largely a matter of semantics, they could even accept emancipation provided they were compensated for their losses. What they could not understand, and would never accept, was the concept that their servants were their legal equals, and that they as masters might be brought to book on charges of maltreatment.

The situation was inflamed by an influx of missionaries. Some of these newcomers, to whom equality and freedom were not words but banners, displayed more zeal than common sense. A few of the early arrivals married raw Hottentots from the bush, and the very real work that most of them performed in civilizing large numbers of semisavages was overlooked in the complaint that by drawing the floating population into their mission stations they were simply creating a labor shortage.

Circuit judges were sent to the frontier in 1811, and some of the missionaries made immediate use of this new weapon to fight for the rights of their black charges. One missionary alone was responsible for the arrests of over twenty Boers on charges of murder and maltreatment. Most of his accusations evaporated in the cold light of evidence, but the very fact that a man could be forced to leave his family unprotected while he traveled to a distant court to defend himself against the capricious charge of an irresponsible Hottentot was deeply disturbing. One dazed Boer arrested in such a case could only mutter, "My God, is this a way to treat a Christian?" The year 1812 was known as the Black Circuit.

In 1815 a recalcitrant farmer named Frederic Bezuidenhout precipitated a crisis. He had ignored the repeated summonses of a Graaff Reinet court, and a party of Hottentot soldiers under a British lieutenant was finally sent to bring him in. Bezuidenhout retired to a cave and opened fire, and the Hottentots finally shot him down. This was too much for the immediate neighborhood, which not only revolted but also sought aid from a Bantu chieftain over the border. The rebellion was quelled and five of the ringleaders were hanged at Slagter's Nek, but the incident rankled for a century. Bezuidenhout's friends and relatives had gotten remarkably little support from the other Boers in the district, many of whom actually helped to hunt the rebels down, but the Boers who came out for law and order had not expected the executions. The hangings were botched, some of the ropes broke and the grim ceremony had to be repeated.

The first mass British immigration started in 1820, when several thousand settlers were brought into the southeast part of the Cape Colony. The majority started as farmers but soon wound up as artisans in the towns, and the land pinch they caused sent the restless Boers north to the banks of the Orange River. A few farmers crossed, settling in a belt recently ravaged by half-breed banditti and only recently stabilized by the Griquas and the mission stations. The mass of Boers held fast in the Cape Colony. In 1825 the situation was still stable, and although the seeds of a host of grievances had been planted, good will and sense might still have scotched a crop of tares.

Then, for a decade, the blows fell thick and fast. The new administration held to the old boundaries, and the threat of land hunger rose again. A move to auction the remaining Crown lands caused consternation, as did an abrupt repeal of the pass laws. Then the long-awaited Emancipation Act went through, and the orderly transition that had been promised failed to materialize. Compensation was less than half of what had been promised, and it was payable only in London, which no frontier Boer had ever seen. To top it all off the Boers were subjected to an incessant barrage of unjustifiable odium, and while they were all but ignorant of the outside world, they were extraordinarily sensitive to public opinion. They knew their own world intimately, how to live in it and how to deal with its inhabitants, and they smarted under abuse from outsiders. Missionaries, Capetown officials and casual travelers were apt to write them off as semicivilized brutes and born troublemakers, and the calumnies filtered back to them from far places which had the power to decide their future although they had no voice there themselves.

By 1834 they were ready to go. There were almost as many specific reasons for wanting to leave as there were Boers involved, but the common thread was the conviction that the lekker lewe could only be established beyond the reach of the British Crown. It was a secession rather than a revolt, and had Bantu or Griqua held the line of the Orange River with a tenth of the tenacity the Xhosa displayed on the Great Fish River, there would have been a revolt instead of a trek. In the event, the line was not held, and the road to the north was open. The mechanics of trekking were common knowledge, and the few artifacts of a Boer household could be packed in a wagon as easily as the rude homesteads could be sold or abandoned. The one form of wealth that had any significance could be driven alongside the wagons.

The kommissie trekke went out in 1834 and returned with favorable reports from Natal and the lands to the north of the Orange and the Vaal just as a fresh Kaffir War sharpened all the old complaints on the border. The first party, under Louis Trigardt, moved out in November of 1835, and the Great Trek was under way. There was no hurried exodus, but a cautious, planned movement, as family after family reached its own decision. The stream, in fact, did not reach sizable proportions until 1837, when the failure to compensate for the emancipated slaves and fresh grievances rising from the settlement of the Kaffir War embittered still more farmers. There was also a tendency to wait to see how the first trek parties fared, and especially to see what action the British would take. They took none; the Cape of Good

Hope Punishment Act subjected all British citizens—including trek-king Boers—to the provisions of the Cape criminal law, but since no means existed to exercise that law north of the Orange River, or to bring wanderers back to an area where it was operative, the act was a dead letter, although nominally effective as far north as the twenty-fifth parallel.

Trigardt, with less than a dozen families, was as great an individualist as Van Rensberg, who followed on his heels with ten. Both men led their groups straight north across the Vaal River; Van Rensberg's party eventually wandered off and disappeared, while Trigardt settled near the Zoutpansberg Range. After a promising start, his people found the area too isolated for survival; they might do without tea, coffee and sugar, and they might conserve their lead, but powder was irreplace-able and not even the most austere Boer household could survive with-out that. Trigardt tried to open a trade with the Portuguese at Delagoa Bay, but no one there could translate his scrawled attempts to write Afrikaans, which had come a long way from High Dutch. The per-plexed Governor finally sent guides and invited the party down to the coastal region. Trigardt accepted, manhandled his wagons down the escarpment of the Drakensberg Range, and settled in a fever district. In 1839 Trigardt's son with 26 women and children, all that survived of the original party, were evacuated by sea to Port Natal.

The parties that followed came in greater strength and moved with more caution. Early in 1836 Hendrik Potgieter and Sarel Cilliers led some 65 families across the Orange River; Paul Kruger, age ten, was in Cilliers' party. By the end of the year they were still south of the Vet River. They had made their peace with Mshweshwe and Sikonyela, son of the terrible Mantatisi, who now ruled the baTlokwa, but in October Mzilikazi's Matabele, 20,000 strong, attacked their encamp-ment at Vegkop. Forty Boer rifles beat off the attack, but the Matabele took all their cattle with them, and Potgieter had to fall back to Basuto territory, where Gerrit Maritz joined him with a hundred families.

The cattle had to be recovered, and the Matabele checked. Potgieter and Maritz now led 107 Boers and 40 Griquas north in January of 1837. Mzilikazi could field 20,000 men and more, but on the open veld infantry could not compete with mounted men determined to press an attack. The Matabele lost 400 men, and the victorious Boers retired with over 7,000 head of cattle.

Piet Retief trekked in April of 1837 with 120 families, followed by Piet Uys with another large party. All these groups came together in June on the Vet River and tried to work out their future, but the task was hopeless. Individualism had been carried to its extreme; the leaders were barely able to regulate the men in their own treks, and attempts to reconcile the major groups foundered on innumerable and frequently petty differences. A measure of civil and military authority was grudgingly granted to Retief, who spent months riding from laager to laager in a hopeless search for unity. Retief and Maritz sided against Uys and Potgieter, and even these groupings were ridden by dissension. Retief and Uys wanted to push on to Natal, Potgieter wished to settle north of the Vaal River, and Maritz favored the high veld. There was endless bickering over the direction the treks should take, over who was to lead, about what form of government should be adopted, and to whom and in what manner clerical status might be granted. Fresh treks arrived and added to the clamor, and by September 4,000 people had left the Cape Colony and were milling about on the veld and a final attempt to organize them at Tafelkop had failed.

A split in what had bravely been named the United Laagers was now inevitable, and there was to be no unified Boer political power north of the Orange River. Retief decided to push on to Natal with whoever would follow his lead, and by October he stood at the edge of the plateau, staring down the jagged scarp of the Drakensberg Range into western Natal hundreds of feet below. Even as he looked, a party of Sikonyela's baTlokwa climbed over the rim from Natal and moved off across the veld, driving a mass of cattle they had raided from the Zulus. The raiders were mounted and carried firearms, they wore tattered European clothing, and they used a trick they had learned from the Bushmen to move the unwilling beasts up the precarious rocky trails; they smeared fresh manure ahead of the herd to con the leading beasts into thinking others had passed that way before.

Retief had fifty wagons with him and he expected more. He took fifteen men and hurried on to Port Natal, 200 miles away, to confer with the settlers and to treat with Dingane for permission to settle on the periphery of the Zulu domain. His wagons rattled down through the passes and camped on the small streams in the foothills of the Drakensberg Range to wait for his word before fanning out into the rich lands below them.

Behind him, Uys and Potgieter held together just long enough to carry out the long-delayed punitive expedition against the Matabele. The January commando had simply recovered the Boer cattle; now it was time to sweep Mzilikazi out of the path of the Great Trek. Since neither Boer would serve under the other, the 135 men who accompanied them rode in two companies, and they ran into the Matabele forces beyond the valley of the Marico River. The fighting lasted for nine days, and in the end the Matabele streamed away to the north and abandoned the inland plateau. Their defeat once and for all convinced the Boers—who had not lost a man—that no native power could withstand them. They might lose isolated clashes in the future, but black Africa was theirs for the taking, as far as they wanted to go.

The settlement at Port Natal that Retief reached in November still bore a superficial resemblance to the one which Uys's kommissie trek left three years before, but there had been profound changes. The group still consisted of less than fifty settlers, with no European women, and perhaps 3,000 natives living in the nearby kraals owed allegiance to the senior traders. Only one man had bothered to build anything like a substantial house, and the settlers lived in what amounted to total anarchy. A political spirit had quickened, however, and the group was beginning to think in communal terms. This quickening—and the changes it was about to produce—was largely due to the rider Uys had passed as he returned to the Cape Colony late in 1834.

Allen Francis Gardiner was born in 1794, and while still a boy gave evidence of the traits that were to drive him through his strenuous life to his bizarre death. Deeply religious, he was consumed with curiosity about the far places of the earth, and he was ridden by a restless energy that made idleness torture. He chose a naval career, and the hard life and the constant travel suited him exactly. By the age of forty he was a married captain with three small children, and in May of 1834 he was temporarily in England. Then his wife died, and on her deathbed he swore to devote the rest of his life to bringing the Gospel to primitive peoples. By August he was on his way to Port Natal, determined to start with the Zulus.

It would be interesting to know what led him to this choice; Isaacs had not yet published his account of Shaka's people, and very few people in England could have been aware of their existence. Gardiner may have encountered James Saunder King, at that time the only man from Port Natal who had ever visited England, or the Church Missionary Society, which backed him, may have recommended the Zulus as among the most unenlightened of savage folk. Gardiner belonged to that brand of single-minded zealot to whom salvation through Christ was so simple and clear that he could not imagine a mentality that would not accept it at once. From the instant he left England, he sped on his chosen task with a drive that verged on madness. He reached Grahamstown hours before the Sixth Kaffir War broke out and plunged at once into Xhosa territory with a few wagons, a Polish gentleman he had encountered on the voyage to Capetown, and a young interpreter named George Cyrus. When flooded rivers stalled his wagons, he left them with his Polish friend and forged on with his interpreter. He lost one horse to quicksand on the Umzimkulu River, another drowned, and for a period he lived on a cheese rind and a small packet of damp sugar.

In the end he left even Cyrus to catch up as best he could, and on December 29, 1834, he reached Port Natal in a state of exhaustion. James Collis, the most substantial trader, greeted him, but was unable to detain him for more than two days. Gardiner borrowed a wagon and started at once for emGungundhlovu, with Cyrus pounding after him. The Umgeni River was in flood, so he abandoned the wagon, and the flooded Tugela separated him from all but a single horse, which he shared with Cyrus. Unable to wait for the guides Dingane sent out, he blundered off the trail, and he finally reached the royal kraal with much of the country behind him in an uproar and the Europeans convinced he would never be seen again.

His reception was by no means cordial. He had outstripped his presents, which soured Dingane at the outset, and his very presence brought to mind Jakot's prophecy that the doom of the Zulu nation would start with a single missionary. Gardiner tried to bypass the inDunas and deal directly with the king, and he spoke of a King William, tending to confirm Jakot's claim that there had never been a King George. When Dingane finally granted Gardiner an audience, he was unable to explain to the unimpressed monarch what he hoped to do for his people. All Gardiner wanted was a hut and permission to start preaching, but Dingane, who grasped only that this urgent personality was not a trader, was unable to fit him into any comprehensible category. He claimed to be a teacher, but he refused to teach musketry, and questioning him about his subject matter touched off tirades about the nature and penalty of sin, the power and omniscience of God, and the awful day of account. Dingane let him stew in his hopes for two months, and then packed him back to Port Natal.

Stunned by this refusal, Gardiner brightened when some of the settlers met him with a petition to conduct services for *them*. Looking about, he saw close to fifty Europeans and over three thousand natives who were as much in need of the word of God as the inhabitants of the royal kraal. As usual, he lost no time. The petition was dated March fourteenth, and the next day he preached to thirteen of the settlers. By the nineteenth he had selected a site for his mission on the ridge overlooking the bay and had christened it Berea, and on the twentieth the settlers all signed a document of title in his favor. On the twenty-fourth he preached to six hundred natives, and on the twenty-fifth he opened a native school with six pupils.

A month later he gave further impetus to the communal spirit. Shaka until his death and Dingane until recently had ignored the natives at Port Natal. The settlers were men of consequence who had every right to form their own households, and these early kraals had coalesced around detribalized natives Farewell and Fynn had flushed out of the bush. In recent years, however, a trickle of refugees had started to flow in from Zululand itself—men who were running away from the ire of the king and who sought sanctuary at the Port. Dingane was now threatening to come after such refugees, and Gardiner saw that the apathetic attitude of the settlers toward permanent construction was largely due to these threats. He called a meeting and suggested that Dingane be pacified by a treaty promising that no more refugees would be accepted. The response was enthusiastic, and the men sent Gardiner back to emGungundhlovu to negotiate.

Gardiner did his best, but Dingane's views on contractual obligations put him in an untenable ethical situation at the outset. In return for a full pardon for the natives already at the Port, Gardiner offered to bring future refugees back to the king personally. Dingane accepted, but on the next day asked to have a recent runaway exempted from the pardon. Gardiner agreed with misgivings that were confirmed a few days later when Dingane tried to get a large party exempted. Gardiner now put his foot down, pointing out that his ability to catch future refugees depended on the good will of the natives already at the Port, who would hardly co-operate if they doubted the king's promises concerning their own security. He also mentioned that he had already dispatched a messenger with the text of the treaty, and were the king to change the terms now he would be placed in a bad light. Dingane backed down reluctantly.

Gardiner used the opportunity to plead his own cause, and now got a grudging permission to return to teach the word of God. He made another futile attempt to explain to Dingane and his inDunas just what he intended to teach, but he was sufficiently chastened to keep to general moral principles, divorced from the detailed theological material for which, he now realized, the Zulus were far from ready.

Gardiner was given an immediate opportunity to try out his treaty. On his way back to Port Natal he stopped at a kraal from which a high-ranking adulteress has just fled with two servants and three young children. Gardiner soon rounded up the three adults, as well as the man whose exemption he had allowed. He brought them back to Dingane, but his diplomatic zeal was dampened by the time he turned them over to the king. He had started to give religious instruction to his prisoners; they had been receptive, and he was now horror-stricken to realize that what might have been his first converts were shortly to suffer impalement. Gardiner had still not grasped the moral nature of the man with whom he was dealing, but he was about to have a lesson. He appealed to the king's magnanimity and requested a full pardon for all the prisoners, but the reaction to this suggestion was so decided that he hastily settled on a plea for their bare lives. Dingane then promised not to kill them, but merely to confine them, and Gardiner was still naïve enough to reflect that the confinement would probably be for life. He visited the prisoners the next day, and was shocked to discover they were being starved to death. Dingane topped off this performance by demanding the three children as well or—had they escaped—the head-man of the kraal at which they had been quartered. Gardiner had no choice but to comply, and the grim errand was a severe strain on his conscience. The children had *not* escaped, but the headman was related to them and besought Gardiner to take him instead. Gardiner refused, and before he got the children back to Dingane (carefully shielding them from knowledge of what lay ahead), he met a messenger who informed him that the first batch had been slain as soon as he was gone. Gardiner was by now sufficiently in touch with reality to request Dingane to kill future prisoners out of hand instead of starving them to death.

By June Gardiner was back at Port Natal, supervising his small community at Berea. It was midwinter, hunting was at a temporary standstill, and a high percentage of the settlers were actually at the bay. Collis's simple building and Gardiner's school and his services were the first civilized touches the settlement had ever seen, and they sparked a desire for further amenities. On June 23, 1835, most of the settlers gathered and quite spontaneously decided to form a proper township. They laid out a proper street plan, allotted lands for public functions, and forbade the erection of any more Kaffir huts. They named the new township D'Urban, in honor of the Governor of the Cape Colony, and almost immediately dropped the apostrophe. Of the original settlers, only John Cane and Henry Ogle participated. Gardiner's Polish friend was elected treasurer, although he was off on a visit to the Cape Colony and was lost at sea before he could return, and when pledges were collected to start a town fund, someone signed for Henry Francis Fynn, although he was at Grahamstown and unlikely to return. Rachel, still living nearby, was not consulted.

Three days later Thomas Holstead arrived with news that Dingane had ordered him out of Zululand and had ruled that no kraal was to give him food. No more Europeans except Gardiner were to be per-mitted to enter. Gardiner left at once for emGungundhlovu to see what the trouble was.

Dingane had a legitimate complaint; the traders were not living up to their end of the bargain. Holstead had enticed two servants away from a kraal just before the treaty was concluded, and then had the gall to visit the very kraal from which he had taken them. The headman quite naturally killed the two servants. Other traders were smuggling young girls out in their wagons, and while Dingane could not prove this charge, he did have a list of 25 recent refugees he wanted Gardiner to round up and return. Gardiner accepted the list, but pointed out that he had no real authority over the Europeans and that he would soon have difficulties if he took a strong line. Dingane would not accept this reasoning. Port Natal was still Zulu territory, and he wanted an agent there to cope with the Europeans he had permitted to settle at the bay. He now appointed Gardiner a chieftain and stated he would permit no further traders to enter Zululand unless they secured permission from Gardiner.

Dingane had made roughly the same suggestion to Henry Francis Fynn a few years before, and Fynn had wisely turned it down. Gardiner rashly accepted. Dingane's arguments struck him as reasonable, and the new township of Durban was as godless as Zululand and for all its fine intentions had no effective political machinery. Gardiner knew he could never rule in Dingane's name, however, and he decided to return to the Cape Colony to ask Sir Benjamin D'Urban to take the area over as a colony and to appoint proper officials.

He left with his usual speed, and got far down into amaMpondo country before a native war turned him around and sent him back to Durban. Here he reprovisioned and struck off inland for the Drakensberg Range. The day after he left, on September twenty-fifth, a messenger brought him word that Collis was dead; a Hottentot had inadvertently fired a musket into 1,500 pounds of gunpowder in the trader's store. The explosion cost Durban its most progressive citizen, his infant son, and its only modern house. Gardiner moved south through the foothills, skirting the fighting, and at Grahamstown learned that Sir Benjamin was at Port Elizabeth. He rode through the night to reach him on the third of December, and reported on his treaty, his appointment, and on the new township.

Sir Benjamin was pleased and flattered, and he wrote Dingane to confirm the treaty, promising to send an official to govern the settlers. He did not, however, have anyone to send at the moment, nor would he officially annex Natal. Gardiner decided the problem could only be settled in London, and promptly set off for Capetown, where he rushed aboard a ship just clearing for England. By February 20, 1836, he was back in Falmouth, characteristically landing in the pilot boat to save a night.

A Select Committee of the House of Commons was sitting to consider the treatment of aborigines in the British colonies, which was just the audience Gardiner wanted. Natal was not yet a colony, nor any form of British territory, but that stopped neither the missionary nor the committee. Gardiner was out to present the strongest case he could, and in his testimony presented the settlers in a scandalous and immoral light. There was no one from Natal to gainsay him, and the net result was that when the Cape of Good Hope Punishment Act, aimed at the frontier Boers, was passed in August, its provisions were deliberately extended to include the English settlers at Durban. Well satisfied, Gardiner spent the rest of the year writing a book about his experiences, getting married a second time, and rounding up help for his missionary endeavors. The Church Missionary Society continued its support, but disapproved of his entry into politics.

By May of 1837 he was back in Durban with his new wife and the three children of his first marriage. The eldest, a girl of twelve, died just before his arrival, so that his first act on his return to Berea was to dig a grave for his first-born. By July the Reverend Francis Owen had joined him with his wife, his sister, and a Welsh serving girl named Jane Williams. There had been changes at Durban in Gardiner's absence, and his status had suffered.

Even as Gardiner was leaving in 1836, a steady trickle of settlers had started to reach Durban. The very ship that took Sir Benjamin's letter to Dingane carried three American missionaries, later joined by three more, who among them started a string of four mission stations, two to the south of Durban and two in Zululand itself. Owen was placed in emGungundhlovu, but was able to do little more than hold his place, in momentary fear of annihilation. Among the settlers who arrived in May was a blacksmith, the town's first independent businessman, and the total population was growing too large for the prevailing state of anarchy. There was still no political leadership, and of the elected Town Committee only Cane and Ogle were still on hand. Crises were handled at mass meetings, where an ex-paymaster of the 85th Regiment of Foot named Alexander Biggar seemed to have had as much influence as anyone.

In June of 1836, while Gardiner was testifying in London, Alexander Biggar's son Robert took a hunting party into Zululand. Two of his natives kidnaped some Zulus, Dingane again stopped entry, and to appease him the settlers voted renewed allegiance to Gardiner's treaty and sent a strong party under Cane to help Dingane on an expedition against the Swazi chieftain Sopusa. Cane's firearms won an easy victory, and the 15,000 head of cattle he brought back restored good relations.

Dingane now demanded the services of a full hundred settlers for an expedition against Mzilikazi, and the settlers were only able to avoid the levy by beginning to sell the Zulus the firearms for which they were clamoring. After a few sales at steep prices, Dingane accused a party of hunting in a prohibited area and removed eight guns by force. The hunters now avoided Zululand, and an uneasy impasse prevailed until the month before Gardiner returned. Then two small clans bolted out of Zululand and sought refuge at the bay, and Dingane threatened to attack the settlement.

The settlers reacted vigorously. They appointed Alexander Biggar commandant, organized themselves and most of the natives at the bay into a body of troops, collected supplies, and commenced an imposing stockade. Dingane backed down completely, sending a conciliatory message of good will and friendship—in which he named Gardiner as author of the policy denying entry to Zululand. The unwitting captain returned in the midst of these preparations to find sentiment at Durban heavily against him.

He called a meeting on the first of June and announced that he had been appointed a justice of the peace under the Punishment Act, with authority over the Europeans but not over the natives. He also posted his first proclamation, prohibiting gun-running into Zululand. This was too much for the settlers, who knew that gun-running was perfectly legal—if somewhat shortsighted—and who were also aware that Gardiner had no police powers whatsoever. They had also taken a quite natural personal dislike to him, since reports from Dingane, Capetown and London all confirmed the fact that he regarded them as a set of unprincipled scoundrels who would have to be checked with a firm hand. The uproar was so great that he had to leave the area and settle some twenty miles to the north, from whence he could do little but bombard Capetown with scandalized accounts of the settlers' conduct.

The settlers had just cause for complaint. They were by now far too numerous to continue as a collection of independent campers in a nominal city that had no buildings and in which nothing could be bought except by barter. Any vessel that put in could sell whatever trash it carried at exorbitant prices, and the entire settlement could hardly have produced a collective set of decent clothing. Such staples as tea, sugar and flour were simply unknown. The British government was apparently unwilling to provide any assistance beyond Gardiner's worthless appointment as a magistrate, and the settlers began to seek help elsewhere. They now looked forward to the long-awaited arrival of the emigrant Boers.

It was this situation which Piet Retief met when he rode into Durban with fifteen followers on October 20, 1837. The settlers welcomed him formally, and announced their intention of co-operating with the Boers.

Despite the amity and the enthusiasm, the ingredients for a truly chaotic situation were at hand. Natal—and Durban—clearly belonged to Dingane, and every European in it was there on his sufferance. The British government regarded Natal as a part of Independent Kaffraria, in which Dingane, as a duly constituted chieftain, had every right to rule. It refused to annex Natal, but it regarded all Europeans in Natal—Boer and Briton—as British subjects under British law and justice. It then freely admitted that it could not enforce that view beyond the borders of the Cape Colony, and it was even then telling Gardiner that anything he undertook would be at his own expense and without official backing. The Britons would have acknowledged British rule if Britain had deigned to exercise it, but the Boers were violently opposed to any such acknowledgment and would most likely fight if the claim were enforced. And these two groups—Boer and Briton—now proposed to make common cause. Durban, lately Port Natal, might yet become Port Holland.

Retief was glad to accept the proffered co-operation. The Britons wanted an orderly township under an administration that would interfere with them as little as possible. Retief foresaw an independent farming republic, and since Durban was the natural port for Natal, the Britons would serve to service those communal facilities the Boers lacked and were disinclined to develop. Retief's first order of business was to get Dingane's permission for the Boers to enter Natal, and he left at once for emGungundhlovu, which he reached on the sixth of November.

Since Shaka and then Dingane had already signed documents ceding major and overlapping portions of Natal to Farewell, Fynn, Isaacs, Collis and Gardiner, and since Uys had brought back a garbled oral permission, Retief expected no difficulties. Accustomed all his life to dealing with the docile Cape Kaffirs, he proceeded openly and carelessly, and made no effort to understand Dingane. The Zulu monarch was in a state of deadly fear, and he had no intention of allowing an armed European folk who had beaten the Matabele—something the Zulus had tried to do and failed—to settle in numbers on his borders. Jakot's prophecies were true after all, and each succeeding day proved their validity. Gardiner had been followed by the Americans, and Owen was camped within eyesight of the royal kraal, spouting arrant nonsense to whomever would listen. (This well-meaning but ineffectual missionary was now grappling with the problems posed by his linguistic deficiencies and his audience's literal-mindedness. His first sermon on God caused hoots of derision, until he discovered the Zulus thought he was talking about King George, and an attempt to explain the immortality of the soul and the blood of the Lord led to a riot.) Gardiner's treaty had not stemmed the refugee flow, and all Dingane's efforts to equip his people with firearms were brought to naught; he could not even get powder for the few poor guns he had. Then the settlers had produced a large military force at short notice, scaring him out of his wits, and now here were Retief and his men, mounted on the fearsome horses and telling tales of the destruction of Mzilikazi. For all Dingane knew, they were the forerunners of the army from the south that Jakot had foretold would come to destroy the Zulu nation.

Retief knew this background in general terms, but he drew no conclusions from it. He rode into emGungundhlovu with a half-dozen men, and after a few days of ceremonies in which Dingane did his best to impress the Boers, the two men met formally. Retief made his request for the vacant territory; Dingane countered with an accusation that the Boers had already stolen 300 head of his cattle. This had been Sikonyela, who was wont to cover his depredations by posing as a Boer, and when Retief pointed this out, Dingane promised him the land if Retief would prove his innocence by recovering the cattle. Retief gladly accepted, and left for Durban to report his progress.

Before he left, Dingane sent orders to an inDuna named Sigwebana, who lived on the trail to Durban, to murder Retief as he passed. Sigwebana wanted no part of this plan, so he gathered up his clan and started for Durban as a refugee. He dawdled too long, Dingane learned of his defection, and sent an impi which caught him on the north bank of the Tugela River. Sigwebana got away, but he lost 600 followers, and no European learned of the reason for his flight for weeks afterward.

From Durban Retief sent messengers to the wagons camped at the foot of the passes. The waiting Boers exploded in a paroxysm of joy, sent word back to the high veld that Natal was about to be opened, and began to edge down to the lowlands. Hundreds of additional wagons rumbled down through the passes, and by the time Retief reached them, there were over a thousand wagons camped in little laagers of two and three families along the upper Tugela River and its tributaries, the Blaauwkrans and Bushmans Rivers. These premature movements were reported to Dingane, who naturally interpreted them as confirmation of the invasion he was expecting.

Retief now rode to Sikonyela's territory, lured him into his camp by a trick, handcuffed him, and ransomed him for all his cattle—700 head—in addition to his horses and guns. Auctioning off the excess, he drove the 300 head of Zulu cattle back to emGungundhlovu, accompanied by a commando of 69 Boers and a number of Hottentot servants. Thomas Holstead went along as interpreter. The Boers arrived at Dingane's kraal in high spirits; the end of their long journey was in sight and the Promised Land was all but theirs, and riding in such strength, they feared no power in black Africa. A commando only half as strong again had broken the Matabele.

With his mind on the land, Retief ignored the portents, and Dingane's usual amicability lulled him further. Durban had taken to the bush again when the impi came after Sigwebana, and Owen, in mortal terror of his life, was holding on to his mission station with a courage born of despair. He had seen 3,000 additional warriors march into the kraal, and his wagons had been searched for firearms, but not even the increasing insolence of the Zulus warned him of Dingane's true intentions. Perhaps the coolest member of his household was William Wood, the thirteen-year-old son of Collis's former partner, a fluent Zulu speaker who had accompanied Cane's expedition against Sopusa. Owen frequently used him as an interpreter, and the boy was sharp enough to soften the missionary's blunt comments when he thought they might cause trouble.

Retief paraded his strength, galloping his men around the kraal and firing from the saddle. Hoping only to impress Dingane, he drove the monarch's anxiety into open panic by harping on the Boer victory over the Matabele and boasting of how he had stripped Sikonyela of his cattle, horses and guns without firing a shot. Dingane made a last effort to have the captured horses and guns turned over to him, Retief refused, and the die was cast.

On February 4, 1838, Dingane put his mark on the document Retief had drafted (in English, oddly enough), ceding Natal from the Umzimvubu River to the Tugela, from the mountains to the sea, and specifically including Durban, to Retief as Governor of the emigrant Boers. Retief put the document in his leather hunting pouch and made preparations to depart.

On the morning of February sixth Dingane invited all the Boers and their servants to a farewell dance. The Boers breakfasted, stacked their arms by their saddle packs at the entrance to the kraal, and strolled into the cattle pen. When they had seated themselves in a group in the center, and had refused a second meal, the dance started. It was the usual display of native pomp, with massed regiments stamping and chanting, rattling their assegais against their great oxhide shields, and swirling through the intricate drill maneuvers. When the dance was at its height, Dingane suddenly leaped to his feet and screamed, *"Bambani abaThakathi!* (Kill the wizards!)"

The dancers swept forward and additional thousands of warriors poured out of the huts surrounding the pen and vaulted over the low barrier. Each unarmed Boer, before he could rise, was seized by a group of Zulus and dragged out of the kraal to the neighboring hill of execution, where Retief was held fast and forced to witness the scene as each Boer in his turn was impaled and had his skull smashed by knobkerries, until they were all dead and tossed out on the hillside, and then Retief himself was slain. Not a gun was fired, and only one or two of the Boers had sufficient time to get so much as a pocketknife out with which to defend himself. Thomas Holstead, original settler, for all his addled wits managed to kill two warriors before he was overpowered and dragged off with the others.

Just before the massacre Dingane sent a messenger to tell Owen not to be alarmed; he was simply going to kill all the Boers. (William Wood had told Owen and Retief himself the same story the day before.) That hapless cleric was thus a horrified witness of the entire episode, since both cattle pen and hillside were visible from his doorway. When the killing was done, Dingane sent a second messenger to reassure him, and when Owen expressed his blazing indignation as forcibly as he could, young Wood dropped all pretense of accurate interpretation and asked the messenger to thank the king for his politeness.

What Dingane hoped to accomplish is still not clear. He seems to have thought he could drive the Boers out without disturbing his relations with the settlers at Durban. He had, of course, stirred up a hornet's nest and signed the eventual death warrant of his nation.

The news of the massacre was carried to Durban by Owen's party, which the jeering warriors molested but allowed to pass. Alexander Biggar, whose colored son George was camped with the Boers, sent Dick King upcountry afoot to warn the laagers. A few hours after the massacre Dingane sent out three regiments to attack the Boer families waiting below the Drakensberg Range, and King arrived too late. The wagons were scattered on the banks of a score of mountain streams, and in addition to the seventy men who had accompanied Retief dozens of others were away hunting or searching out farmsites. What followed was seared into the Boer soul as no other event in their history. The impis fell on the defenseless clusters of wagons in the predawn blackness of a moonless night, and 41 men, 56 women, 185 children and some 250 Hottentot servants perished in the ferocious onslaughts. Isolated knots of people, alerted by their dogs or by the noise of a neighboring attack, rallied to beat off the warriors, with women and small sleepy children manhandling the heavy guns. One man, out to quiet his howling dogs, was overrun by a charge and had to fight his way back to his family; another rode out bravely to rescue the family powder supply from a nearby wagon.

Individual tragedies were submerged in the mass horror. Adriaan Russouw's young child recovered from thirty stab wounds to find his parents and four brothers and sisters dead; Piet du Pré, out hunting, returned to find his wife and seven children slaughtered, and one infant lost a father in the Retief massacre and his mother and all ten brothers and sisters in a blood-soaked wagon. The Zulu ferocity went far beyond the usual slash to open the belly. One man found the corpse of his three-day-old child flung on the hacked-off breasts of its mother, a woman at term was ripped open and her embryo was smashed against a wagon wheel, and a returning hunter was caught, killed and castrated and left with his genitals stuffed in his mouth. When a Boer village eventually arose in the area, it was simply called *Weenen*—Weeping.

The slaughter in the foothills had been carried out by three regiments, which returned to Zululand driving 10,000 head of cattle ahead of them. Then, for the moment, Dingane rested.

The panic in the surviving Boer laagers was acute but only temporary. The wagons were filled with desperately wounded people and scores of young orphans who were unable to fend for themselves. Most of the stock had been driven off, and many of the wagons had been immobilized with the draft oxen killed. There was momentary talk of abandoning Natal and returning to the high veld, but this soon died out. Natal was too fair a land to be abandoned without a struggle, and a grim determination to seek revenge set in. Despite the grievous losses, less than a twelfth of the Natal Boers had perished, and reinforcements were arriving daily. Retief's place was more or less filled by Gerrit Maritz, who had arrived just before Retief left for emGungundhlovu (and who had gallantly offered to replace him as the more expendable were Dingane to prove treacherous), and Piet Uys and Hendrik Potgieter with their fighting men were soon at hand. The Boers coalesced into three large laagers and sent a patrol to Durban to arrange a joint attack on Dingane.

Although not as yet directly threatened, the bay area was also in an uproar. Owen and his party were in from Zululand, Gardiner brought his family down from Tongaat, and the American missionaries were straggling in from their stations. A brig, the *Mary*, had just arrived with a lay assistant for Owen, and the missionaries moved aboard or sought shelter on Salisbury Island.

The settlers, still fired with their previous martial ardor, organized their own expedition under John Cane without waiting for Boer cooperation. In addition to a handful of Europeans, the party included 2,000 men from Fynn's iziNkumbi clan. Early in March it struck at the kraals near Kranz Kop, whose men were away in the general Zulu mobilization, and without fighting, Cane brought 4,000 head of cattle and 500 Zulu women and children back to Durban.

The Boers in the meantime dispatched their own commando. An enormous force of over 350 men rode out under Uys and Potgieter, its effectiveness hampered by the fact that the two leaders were barely on speaking terms. The commando crossed the Buffalo River, and on the eleventh of April flushed a small party of Zulu scouts which led them into broken country near eThaleni. The two Boer leaders made unco-ordinated attacks on the main Zulu force that was waiting there; Potgieter launched a cautious charge to the left which was beaten off, and then, unable to make proper use of his mounted strength, he prudently left the fight. Uys charged to the right, broke the left horn of the Zulu impi, and took off in pursuit of the survivors, only to find himself cut off by Potgieter's retreat. He bunched his men and blasted an exit through the surrounding ring of Zulus, but eight Boers were dragged down in the run for the open. Uys himself broke through, and then stopped to sharpen the flint in his gun. An assegai wounded him mortally, he slipped from his horse, and two men tried to help him away. The Zulus were closing in again, and Uys ordered his men to put him down and leave him. They did so, and had gained perhaps a hundred yards when they looked back. The first Zulus were just coming up to Uys, and he was seen trying to lift his head. This was too much for his son, Dirk Cornelius, a boy of fourteen. He wheeled his pony and charged back, killing three Zulus before he fell across his father.

Potgieter, again enmeshed in the political bickering that plagued the laagers, was accused of responsibility for this defeat, and in disgust took his men back to the high veld. The defeat of what was soon known as the *Vlug Kommando*—the commando that ran away—had not resulted in serious losses, but it had been defeat in a fair fight of one of the largest forces the Boers could assemble, and they now marked time and rested.

The Vlug Kommando returned to the laagers on April twelfth; on the seventeenth a second force left Durban to attack Dingane. Cane was well aware that his initial foray had merely inflamed the Zulus, and Robert Biggar had just returned from a trip to Capetown to hear of his half brother George's death in the foothills. Seventeen settlers and over eight hundred natives now moved out to cross the Tugela River and invade Zululand. Henry Ogle was not along, but he sent a large unit from his kraals, which had recently quarreled with the iziNkumbi. This force ran into a major Zulu impi nominally under Mpande, Dingane's younger half brother, and over six hundred of the Port Natal natives died when the iziNkumbi refused to support Ogle's warriors. Sigwebana, recent refugee from Dingane's wrath, was slain, and all but four of the Europeans died on the field, including Robert Biggar and John Cane, who now reaped the whirlwind he had sown with his earlier cavalier treatment of Jakot and Dingane. Henry Ogle was now the last of Farewell's original party, which had reached Port Natal fourteen years ago.

Durban had now attacked Dingane and had been repulsed, and retribution would be swift. A coasting vessel, the *Comet*, was in the harbor, and Gardiner, Owen, all the American missionaries but one, together with all their families and all the settlers save a half-dozen who decided to take their chances on Salisbury Island or in the bush, sought refuge aboard her. The Zulu impi appeared on the Berea on the twenty-fourth of April, and for a week ransacked the settlement and hunted down the natives who had not fled. Among the families watching from the crowded deck of the *Comet* was that of Robert Dunn, who had recently reached Durban. Dunn's father had been killed on the beach, but his wife, his five-year-old son John, and John's three younger sisters had reached the safety of the *Comet*. Like William Wood and Theophilus Shepstone, young John Dunn had been raised by native nurses and played with native children, and he was equally facile in English and Zulu.

The *Comet* sailed away on the eleventh of May, leaving Ogle, Alexander Biggar and a few others behind. The Zulu impi retired beyond the Tugela River, and a species of peace settled over Natal for a few months. Most of the refugees, including the Dunns and the American missionaries, trickled back to Natal, but Gardiner never returned. Every hand in Natal was against him, and his stations on the Berea and at Tongaat lay in ruins. For the thirteen years that remained to him he ranged the earth in a series of ever more hopeless missions to primitive peoples. He failed in Chile and he failed spectacularly in Papua, and in 1851 he went to Tierra del Fuego, where a forlorn band of naked and freezing Indians lived on the perpetual verge of extinction. Gardiner's zeal as usual outstripped his capacity, and his party landed without any gunpowder. Two relief vessels failed to reach him, and, the last of his party, he finally starved to death. The final entry in his journal read, "I neither hunger nor thirst, though five days without food—marvellous loving kindness to me a sinner."

There was no essential change in the position of Bantu, Boer or Briton during the winter months of 1838. By June the Boers were in two main laagers with a strength of about 640 men, 3,200 women and children and over 1,200 native servants. Dingane attacked one of the laagers in August, making off with most of the cattle, and the Boers were forced back on the main laager, where close to 4,000 people were living in cramped, muddy misery. Sickness broke out and struck at man and beast, and the political squabbling continued unabated. Gerrit Maritz died in September, and then, with the Boer fortunes at their lowest ebb, the tide turned. Andries Pretorius of Graaff Reinet was on the way with sixty men and a cannon, and he bade the United Laagers prepare for the long-awaited punitive expedition against Dingane. By late November he had reached the camp, and he moved out at once with a commando of 464 men. There were wagons enough to form a strong laager at night, and the best horses and draft oxen that still survived. And, for once, a major commando was under a single commandant. The expedition had barely cleared the camp before ominous tidings arrived from Durban. There were British troops at the bay, and the message announcing their arrival included an order to Pretorius to stand fast. Stephanus Maritz, Gerrit's brother, decided to hold it for his return.

The troops had been bound to come. Sir Benjamin D'Urban had done everything in his power to stop the trekking, but the Boers continued to leave. He himself had won their sympathy, but they no longer trusted the Colonial Office which controlled him. Even the Colonial Office was far from hostile, and the main objection it held to the trekking lay not in the population loss but in the fear of fresh native unrest that the Boers would inevitably stir up beyond the borders. The one solution, annexation of the territories into which the Boers were moving, was unacceptable to London, which intended to rely on the worthless Punishment Act to control Crown subjects beyond the frontier.

The trekking continued, and in January of 1838 D'Urban was replaced by Sir George Napier, who was at once flooded with reports of fighting, cattle theft and of ex-slaves forced to trek against their will. (Napier sent after such trek parties as were still within reach to check this last story, but over half the Hottentots elected to remain with their old masters.) When the main stream of trekkers seemed to be congregating in Natal, and news of the Retief massacre and its consequences arrived, Napier first forbade any traffic in arms to Natal and then in desperation requested permission to occupy Durban. The Colonial Office relented; Napier might send troops, whose commanding officer would hold a commission under the Punishment Act, but he could not annex. Napier sent Major Samuel Charters, Royal Artillery, with eighty men of the 72nd Highlanders and a few fieldpieces. The expedition was not a vindictive one. Charters was ordered to keep the peace and succor the needy, of whom there seemed to be a growing number.

The troops arrived by sea on the third of December, 1838. Charters found that the Boers had annexed the settlement in May (as Port Natal—they would never refer to it as Durban) and had appointed Alexander Biggar as Landdrost. They intended to govern Natal as a republic, and when a Boer with some legal experience had arrived in the upcountry laagers, they had drawn up a constitution. Charters ignored these moves, distributed such supplies as he had, and sent orders to all to stand fast and not to move against Dingane. He was too late by a few days; the Boer commando was gone when his message arrived, and Alexander Biggar, with a few Europeans and seventy Natal natives, had already left Durban to join them. Charters could only wait for the commando's return.

In the absence of a proper fort, Charters seized Robert Dunn's store, ran up a flag, and then stopped the sale of gunpowder to the Boers. There was little else to do at the moment, and he was not unwelcome, since the Britons preferred Imperial annexation to Boer rule, and with the Zulus still unchecked any troops were welcome.

On Charters' small staff, serving as interpreter, was the twenty-two-year-old recently married son of the Wesleyan missionary who had been run off the amaDola Mission Station in amaMpondoland when Nqetho blundered into the area. Theophilus Shepstone had left his bride behind and, despite the inconvenience of an ulcerated throat, was taking the measure of Natal and adding a mastery of Zulu to his already fluent command of Xhosa. He did not care for the Boers, and he did not particularly care for the Bantu, and he was through and through a conservative and an Imperialist, and something of a prig to boot. He was, however, painstaking and thorough, and whatever he may have thought of the Bantu did not prevent him from learning everything he could about them, from the nuances of their complex speech to the intricacies of their even more complex politics. His Zulu speech never quite lost its Xhosa accent, and in his search for knowledge in the undocumented annals of Bantu history he soaked up large masses of misinformation.

While Charters was waiting at Durban, Pretorius rode off into Zulu-land. There were to be no mistakes with this commando, and Pretorius exercised all his redoubtable skill as a fighter. His mounted men would fight in the traditional Boer pattern, but bearing in mind the broken country ahead of him, Pretorius sacrificed his speed of advance and took a wagon train along, so that nightly defensive laagers might be formed. This was no mere cattle raid; every man was determined to see the Zulu power broken, and the faint-hearted deserted in the first few days to slink back to the laagers—where they were placed under arrest or sent back to rejoin the commando.

The commando crossed the Tugela and the Klip Rivers, naming the Biggarsberg Range in passing. By Sunday, December ninth, they were camped on the banks of the Waschbankspruit, and Sarel Cilliers, who was acting as chaplain, proposed a vow that if God would grant them a victory, they would build Him a church and forever after celebrate the anniversary as a Day of Deliverance. All the Englishmen joined in the vow, and only five Boers abstained, fearing the Lord's vengeance if their posterity should break the promise.

Pretorius took his men across the Buffalo River, skirmishing with light Zulu patrols, and avoiding the obvious traps that had ensnared Uys and Potgieter. The main Zulu force was obviously lurking in the vicinity, but it refused to come to grips. On Saturday, December fifteenth, the commando crossed the Ncome River, and Pretorius laagered for the camp in which the Boers always remained on Sundays. He found a position of exceptional strength on the steep left bank, where a small stream entered the main channel from a deep donga, forming a wide, high point. The wagons laagered on the point, so that no access was possible from the two sides on the banks of the Ncome and the donga. Each disselboom was run under the bed of the wagon ahead and lashed into place, the wheels were covered with rawhide shields, and lanterns were hung from the long whipstocks, which were angled out from the wagon beds. Short ladders gave rapid access to the beds, and ample supplies of powder and piles of bullets were placed in each wagon and between the wheels. The draft oxen and the horses were bedded down in the laager.

The Boers slept fitfully, while their Hottentot servants kept the watch. Rising in the first gray light, they peered out of their stronghold into the hot stillness of a summer morning. As the light strengthened, they got the shock of their lives. "All Zululand" was out there, rank on rank of warriors silently sitting and watching the camp, something over 12,000 of them.

Even as the Boers grabbed for their guns and manned the wagons, the entire horde rose to its feet as one man and charged. The first earsplitting volley thundered out, and the battle site was instantly hidden in a cloud of rolling, greasy smoke, through which the bounding forms of the Zulus could be dimly seen.

The strength of the position was soon apparent; the mass of the charging enemy was hemmed between the banks, and the press grew intolerable as the regiments strove to reach the wagons. There was no room to hurl an assegai, no room to wield shield or knobkerrie, and hundreds were trampled as the impi was compressed into a target at which it was hardly necessary to aim. It was only necessary to fire and reload and fire again at the black mass that seethed out of the smoke. The Boers poured powder down the hot barrels, spat out a bullet from a stock held in their mouths, thumped the butt against a wagon bed to set the charge, primed, cocked and fired. A vast column of smoke rose to a tremendous height in the windless sky.

The fight might have lasted two hours—if there were watches in the laager no one bothered to look. Pretorius finally sensed a change in the tempo of the continual charges. The press seemed to be thinner and less certain; mounds of bodies impeded the survivors, and scores of

Zulus had slipped off the banks and were floundering in the water. Not a single Zulu had gotten within ten yards of the wagons. Pretorius gave rapid orders; two of the wagons were unlashed and rolled aside and the Boers, mounted and yelling, poured out of the opening. The regiments broke and fled, and in their flight they lost the cohesion on which their power was based. For the rest of that long day small parties of Boers chased dwindling groups of Zulus, shooting them as long as their bullets lasted, firing pebbles when the bullets were gone, and riding them down when the powder was finally exhausted. Hundreds of Zulus took refuge in the river, hiding in the shallows with only their nostrils showing, or wading away under the pathetic shelter of their shields. The Boers ranged the banks, flushing them out and picking them off one by one. The commando only reassembled in the dusk, in exhausted exultation.

More than 3,000 Zulus had died, and among the bodies "heaped like pumpkins on a rich soil" lay Kolekile and Magwaza, two of Senzangakona's extensive progeny. Not a Boer had been killed in the laager, and only four had been wounded in the pursuit, Pretorius among them. In the confusion of the sally he had grabbed a half-broken horse instead of his own, and the brute threw him when he fired at a Zulu. He managed to kill his opponent with his own assegai in a hand-to-hand struggle, but not before his left hand was stabbed so severely that he had to use a sling for months. The Ncome was ever after known as the Blood River.

The commando pushed on to emGungundhlovu, where Dingane fired the isiGodlo before he fled to the north. There had been something like a riot over who would carry the tidings of victory back to the United Laagers; sixty Boers left at once, and deserters were now slipping away by twos and threes. The bulk of the commando stayed in hand, however, for the Boers were out over 15,000 head of cattle since their arrival in Natal, and they intended to make good their losses at the expense of the Zulu herds.

The Boers found the rotting remains of Retief and his men on the slope below the hill of slaughter. The bones were collected and buried, and Retief's skeleton was identified from scraps of clothing that still clung to it. His leather hunting pouch was still intact, and among his papers lay the deed Dingane had signed almost a year before ceding Natal to the Boers. Pretorius reported his arrival at emGungundhlovu on a blank piece of paper from the same hunting pouch.

Two days after Christmas the Boers tried to recover their cattle, which the Zulus had driven off somewhere to the north. A captured deserter offered to guide them, and 300 Boers rode out, together with Alexander Biggar and his Natal natives. Pretorius stayed behind.

The cattle were found soon enough, but the deserter led the Boers on into a trap formed by the bulk of the surviving Zulu forces. They had placed their main weight between the Boers and the royal kraal, but the Boers, mounted and in open country, cut through the ring on the far side, drove the cattle across the White Umfolozi River, moved upstream and recrossed to the south, and eventually rejoined Pretorius with 5,000 head of cattle. The Zulus dogged them during the long hot day, charging at the confusion at the river crossings. Six of the Boers died, Alexander Biggar was killed, and most of his natives had been shot down by Boers who mistook them for Zulus. Pretorius stayed three more days, fired the rest of the kraal, and by early 1839 was back at the United Laagers. This was the *Wen Kommando*.

The fortunes of the Natal Boers had now turned, and the population in the cramped laagers burst out and spilled down into Central Natal. The Zulu army was largely intact, and quantities of Boer cattle, horses and even guns were scattered at every kraal in Zululand, but Dingane would think twice before he attacked again, and the final settlement could wait. The British troops were still camped at Durban, but while Charters insisted on regarding the Boers as Crown subjects, he was under definite orders not to annex, and the trek Boers were now pouring into Natal in such numbers that the future of the republic they hoped to found seemed assured. These unresolved problems would be dealt with eventually, but they posed no immediate threat, and for a few short months the future was bright and golden.

The majority of the Boers now congregated at a site, some fifty-odd miles inland from Durban on Natal's central plateau, which they had picked for the capital of "The Free Province of New Holland in South East Africa." It was an odd choice, closer to the Zulus across the Tugela than Durban was, fifteen or twenty miles from the nearest supply of firewood, and situated in a hot hollow dominated by the surrounding ridges. The Boers laid out their new town, hardly more than a pretentious laager, and christened it Pietermaritzburg in memory of Piet Retief and Gerrit Maritz. They auctioned off plots, called "erven," for payment against deeds which were never delivered, and a ramshackle collection of mud-daubed cabins soon arose. Water from a nearby stream was led into the town's streets in irrigation ditches, and the settlement was soon noted for mud, odors and the packs of wild dogs that roamed the streets.

The Boers thought it was beautiful. It lay in good farming country, and it was far removed from the reach of British seapower. Its inhabitants had lived for close to four years in their wagons; countless miles of veld, innumerable rivers, and a dozen mountain passes lay behind them, and all were conscious of the hundreds of lonely graves scattered on the high veld, in the foothills of the Drakensberg, and at emGun-gundhlovu. It was time to re-establish the lekker lewe, and they fell to the task with a will.

The Zulus were also quiescent. Dingane set about rebuilding emGun-gundhlovu, and he waited for the next move. He was still determined to evict the Boers, and still unable to find any weapon but treachery.

The British also left the Boers in peace. Major Charters departed Durban, taking Shepstone with him and leaving a Captain Jervis behind with the troops. Jervis faced a difficult task, which he carried out well. Far too weak to take a high hand with the Boers, he was only able to exert an influence on the immediate vicinity of Durban, and even here he left as much of the local administration as he could in the hands of the officials the Boers had appointed. Some of these, like Morehead the harbormaster, were Britons, and while relations were generally cordial among the Boers, the British settlers at the bay, and the British troops, not all newcomers were welcome. The Boers were determined to regu-late the character of their republic, and they examined the religious beliefs of all new arrivals before permitting them to land. Some of the more lawless settlers were hounded unmercifully; Ogle at one point was actually arrested for traveling without a permit. He took the incident philosophically; he had been arrested for the same offense in the Cape Colony long before he joined Farewell.

The seat of Boer rule was a Volksraad in Pietermaritzburg, which Pretorius led. An excellent military leader, he proved a failure in civil rule, and his only trump card lay in his threat to resign. The Volksraad was long on argumentation, correspondence and high-flown proclama-tions, but lamentably short on practical results. There was little or no ready cash in the country, and the treasury was born, lived and died empty.

In March Jervis tried to patch up a peace with Dingane. He sent a deputation of Durban Boers who extracted 300 head of cattle, 52 mus-kets and 43 saddles from the recalcitrant ruler. The next few months were uneventful; trek Boers continued to arrive and busied themselves with farming and the construction of Pietermaritzburg, and a number of trading vessels visited Durban. The *Eleanor*, owned by Capetown Boers, was hailed as the first commercial tie with the Cape Colony (she was unfortunately wrecked on a subsequent voyage), and the *Mazeppa* brought back one of the American missionaries and then in July landed the survivors of Louis Trigardt's party of pioneer trekkers from Dela-goa Bay. In the same month a druggist and a hatter landed.

In September Dingane attempted to salvage his battered military reputation with a major—and successful—expedition against the Swazi, but in preparing for the invasion he unwittingly touched off the final round in his struggle with the Boers. He sent messengers to all his military kraals ordering his regiments to assemble, and the summons reached his younger half brother Mpande coupled with a rumor that Dingane intended to kill him. Mpande pleaded illness and begged off, thus crystallizing whatever intentions Dingane may have had. He now sent Mpande a peremptory command to appear at emGungundhlovu, and Mpande fled south across the Tugela River with 17,000 followers.

It was one of the few decisive acts of his long life. Mpande was intelligent and more capable than either Shaka or Dingane of relating cause to effect; he had an almost European sense of honour and he always held to his word. He would, in fact, have been more successful in a European society than he was in his own, where he was almost totally ineffectual and constantly ignored by his own relatives, inDunas and subjects. That he was never assassinated was more a tribute to his amiability than to his powers, and he was tolerated as a leader simply because he rarely interfered with his subjects and because his commands could be ignored with impunity. Any change would have been for the worse. The mass of Zulus who now accompanied him were not motivated by obedience but merely wished to get beyond Dingane's reach.

The news of his coming threw the Boers into consternation, but a passing hunter visited him and heard his story. He then induced Mpande to accompany him to Pietermaritzburg, and on the fifteenth of October he appeared before the Volksraad. The Boers were delighted with his conduct and his attitude. In return for permission to settle south of the Tugela River he offered to comply with any Boer demands. A fortnight later a deputation visited him at his new kraal and installed him as "Reigning Prince of the Emigrant Zulus," with suzerainty over all the natives in Natal. Mpande promised not to wage war, to stop smellings-out, and to submit his eventual choice of a successor to the Volksraad for approval. His subjects showed the visitors what they thought of the new prince by murdering under their eyes an inDuna he had just appointed.

The British garrison withdrew from Durban on the twenty-fourth of December. There was peace in the land, and the infant republic seemed fit to rule itself and to work out satisfactory arrangements with the tribes on its borders. Jervis had done what he could, and official opinion in Capetown and even in London was veering to the decision to recognize the new state. Jervis made a farewell speech to wish the Republicans good luck, and left the impression that his departure meant the end of British interest in Natal. Then, almost at once, the actions of the Free Province of New Holland in South East Africa began to insure the speedy return of the British Crown.

The Boers hoisted their own flag over Durban as soon as the British were gone, and the Volksraad put a cherished project into effect. The British had been a political threat, but the Zulus were still a physical one. Dingane could never be trusted, and 5,000 head of Boer cattle were still penned into Zulu kraals. Repeated demands for their return had produced only a few hundred head, and the Boers now sent a demand for 19,000. Dingane countered by sending 200 oxen and two inDunas, Dambuza and Khambazana, to negotiate what he felt was an unreasonable demand.

The Boers were past reason. They arrested the ambassadors on the charge of complicity in the Retief massacre, recounted late claims and raised their demand to 40,000 cattle, and mustered a commando of 350 men who rode into Zululand under Pretorius on January 21, 1840. The commando took Mpande along as a hostage, and a large impi from the forces which had crossed the Tugela River with him was placed under Nongalaza, the inDuna who had defeated John Cane's expedition.

The two columns marched along parallel routes. The Boers encountered a few minor chieftains, who promptly came over to them, and on the twenty-ninth of January they reached the site of the Blood River battle. The ground on the point where the laager stood was literally white with bones, and Pretorius picked this spot to execute the two Zulu inDunas, whom he had brought along in chains. The Zulus died well. Dambuza freely admitted his part in the massacre and tried to protect Khambazana, who scorned such aid. Mpande's testimony convicted them out of hand, and when Pretorius made an effort to convert them, Dambuza replied that he only knew one master—Dingane—and if a still higher one existed He could only approve of his faithful conduct. His last request was to be shot by men and not by half-grown boys, and this was granted.

The following day Nongalaza sent word that he had met Dingane's forces and defeated them in a bloody fight attended by great losses on both sides, and that Dingane was fleeing to the north. The Boers took off in pursuit, but missed him, and then fanned out to sweep up all the cattle they could find. There was none to gainsay them, and they stripped kraal after kraal, ranging far and wide through Zululand. Nongalaza's men brought in still more, and when the commando returned to Pietermaritzburg, it was driving more than 36,000 head. It also brought in more than 1,000 "orphaned" Zulu apprentices who were put to domestic service.

Mpande was left behind. On the tenth of February on the banks of the Black Umfolozi River, the Boers had proclaimed him King of the Zulus. The bill for the ceremony was an additional 8,000 head of cattle, and lesser chieftains accused of withholding loot were charged still another 8,000 head. This was aptly named the *Beeste Kommando*, and the more than 60,000 cattle the Zulus had now lost since the Boer retaliations started comprised an appreciable percentage of the nation's stock.

Dingane murdered his unsuccessful general, and then crossed the Pongola River to the north, entering Nyawo territory. A few thousand Zulus were still with him, but his people wished to return to the promised peace of Mpande's reign, and his following gradually drained away. He was finally killed by a small party of Nyawos, who had sought advice from the neighboring Swazis. One of the men who killed him died a centenarian in 1911; the assassins had piled three large stones on his grave and the site was rediscovered in 1947.

The British were gone, apparently for good, the Zulus had been defeated and their army had been dispersed, and there was abundant land and cattle and cheap labor for all the Boers. They spread over the face of Natal and settled down to enjoy the existence in search of which they had quitted the Cape Colony five years before. The ingredients of the lekker lewe were available in undreamed-of quantities, but the national genius for discord manifested itself at once. Domestic politics remained chaotic. Pretorius, still only commandant, was opposed when he reached for the presidency, and the office remained vacant. Taxes were voted but rarely collected, and the civil service was virtually nonexistent. The masses of Zulu cattle, and even the land itself, proved insufficient to meet the swollen claims that now poured in. The year of 1840 passed in happy and growing clamor.

Sir George Napier, in the meantime, was also facing problems. Basically sympathetic, he hoped for a solution that would allow the Boers to depart in peace, but he could not, unfortunately, abandon his jurisdiction over them simply because they had moved north of the Orange River. The Colonial Office continued to feel a responsibility for their actions and would do so until they had established a stable government of their own—something they were apparently incapable of. And their activity against the peoples of Independent Kaffraria inevitably caused repercussions against the sensitive borders of the Cape Colony. Napier had withdrawn Jervis's detachment not because he meant to abandon Natal but because he knew the force was too small to do more than antagonize the Boers. He was more than half-inclined to write off Natal when news of the Beeste Kommando arrived, with the account of an attack on a peaceful chieftain (for all his treachery Dingane had signed a peace treaty with the British before Jervis left), the rapacious looting of the Zulu cattle, and above all the kidnaped apprentices. In June Napier received summary instructions to reoccupy Durban, and he was still attempting to get them reversed when a fresh Boer offense sealed the fate of the republic.

The Boer farms from the outset had started to suffer from counter-raids, first from the looted Zulus and then from parties of Bushmen who still inhabited the fastnesses of the Drakensberg Range in large numbers. In December of 1840 Pretorius assembled 200 men and swept south along the Drakensberg Range to quell this nuisance. He had no very clear idea of who the villains were, but the spoor he was following led him to the amaBaca, a small clan of professional thieves under a chieftain named Ncapaai, who stemmed from the party Nqetho had led out of Dingane's reach. Pretorius wiped out the clan, collected such cattle as he could find, and trotted back to Pietermaritzburg while news of his excursion flashed south. By the time it reached the British in the Cape Colony, it sounded like a full-fledged attack on the tense clans packed to the north of the border, and in the suddenly inflamed atmosphere Napier's attempts to reach a settlement were broken off.

Worse was to follow. Dread of the Zulu impis had kept the great arc of Natal clear of survivors of the clans Shaka had smashed. When news of Dingane's death spread, thousands of refugees moved back from their exile in the south or on the high veld to settle at their old kraal sites. Boer families, given farms in the general handout, arrived to find hordes of returning natives busily erecting their huts and cattle pens. In August of 1841, moved to distraction, the Volksraad voted to gather the entire influx and move it off to a specific area in the south. Only five families would be permitted to remain on each Boer farm to insure a handy labor supply. The move might have succeeded had the Volksraad thought to inform Faku, paramount chieftain of the amaMpondo, of the precise boundaries of the new reserve. In the event, Faku naturally thought the entire body of refugees was simply being driven into his own tribal lands, and he complained vigorously to the British. Almost simultaneously news reached Capetown of the arrival of an American trading brig at Durban. The commercial community attacked the authorities just as the border situation was again slipping out of hand. Napier could do no more. The nearest Imperial troops to Durban were at a small fort in amaMpondoland, and Napier ordered the commander, Captain Thomas Charlton Smith, to abandon the outpost and to occupy Durban.

Smith set out with two companies of the 27th Foot, a few artillerymen, a detachment of Royal Engineers, and a few men from the Cape Mounted Rifles. Commanding 263 men in all, and accompanied by 250 servants and dependents, with his supplies in 60 wagons, each drawn by 10 oxen, he left his fort on the first of April, 1842, and started a difficult journey of over 150 miles. His wagons were drastically undermanned—the Boers would have used eighteen oxen on each wagon and driven spare teams alongside—and the country was so broken that he kept to the beach unless rocky outcrops drove him inland. He crossed 122 rivers, some so wide and deep at the mouth that he had to detour miles inland to the nearest drift, and if the wagons could at least move on the beaches, the sand got into the men's boots and cut the leather and their feet to ribbons impartially. The regimental surgeon delivered two officers' wives a few days after the march commenced.

The task ahead of Smith was immense, and would call for political skill as well as military experience. His regimental career, typical for the times, had fitted him well for such work. Unable to afford the purchase of a step up in rank, he was now well into middle age, a stolid, dependable officer to whom long service (as a junior officer he had fought at Waterloo) had given something of a flair for administration. Short on imagination and temper, he was prudent and methodical, and while still far south of Natal he sent a messenger ahead to Durban to find out if he could count on the support of the British ivory traders. The settlers, whose position had been deteriorating, assured him he could.

The Volksraad had been stunned by Napier's announcement in December of 1841 that the British would resist the seizure of Faku's lands, and by the storms the Beeste Kommando and the Ncapaai raid had whipped up. Pretorius was censured for his conduct, and the nagging problem of land claims was almost forgotten in political recriminations. The Volksraad was powerless to stave off British intervention, and endless and indecisive debates were broken only long enough to send Napier a series of piteous letters, in which the long story of Boer injustices was eloquently summarized and capped with a final plea to be left in what passed for peace with them. As a determination to fight off any British attempt to annex Natal grew, the British traders at Durban fell under a cloud of suspicion. The Volksraad refused to sell them land in the new settlements, and the common cause enforced by the Zulu threat was now broken. The traders' only hope for a share of the land they had settled a decade before the Boer arrival now lay in the speedy return of Crown authority.

The Boers could only prepare to fight, and their determination to do so was strengthened in March when a small trading vessel, the *Brazilia*, arrived in Durban. She had been sent out by an enterprising Dutch firm to capture a trade monopoly with the new republic, and when her supercargo, Johan Smellekamp, landed, he made a curious discovery. The Boers by now regarded themselves as indigenous, but they still spoke a corrupt Dutch, and insofar as they still felt ties to a European motherland, that country was Holland. Utterly ignorant of contemporary European politics, they still regarded Holland as one of the great kingdoms of the continent, and they saw no reason why an alliance with Holland should not serve as an effective check to the British. Smellekamp in his turn saw no reason to disillusion them, and he painted a glowing picture of a Holland swept with sympathy for its long-lost sons and ready to come to their aid. He sold his cargo at excellent prices, and then traveled to Pietermaritzburg, where the citizens detached his oxen and drew his wagon through the muddy streets themselves. The Volksraad saw in him the solution to most of its problems, with *de jure* recognition in the offing, and it promptly drafted a treaty of friendship and trade with the Netherlands. When Smellekamp signed, casually adding the phrase "subject to His Majesty's approval," the Boers gave him funds and sped him on his way overland to Capetown to attend to ratification. He was naturally arrested even before he reached that city, but the British finally released him and packed him off to Holland.

Captain Smith, therefore, leading his weary column into Durban on the fourth of May, was met by a nervous contingent of British settlers and found the Boers ready to fight. Passing through the almost deserted Boer settlement at Congella on the shores of the bay, Smith moved on to the northern shore, covering the settlement of Durban a mile or so inland, and erected his camp. As soon as Smith went by, Pretorius moved back and occupied Congella. Smith built a triangular earthen fort with a stockade, placing his howitzer and two fieldpieces in the corners, and gave every indication that he regarded his sojourn as permanent.

The Volksraad was in despair, and Pretorius, whose armed strength gradually drew ahead of Smith's as Boer after Boer rode in, made repeated efforts to get him to leave. (Smith's bugler, who kept a lively journal, described Pretorius: "He is about six feet high and has a belly on him like the bass drum.") Smith was not hostile, but he made it quite clear that he regarded the Boers as British subjects, and when Pretorius mentioned the treaty with Holland, he merely snorted. When Smith rode out at the head of a hundred men to display his force, Pretorius met him with an equal force and told him he would stand fast until he received instructions from the Volksraad. Smith thought he meant to disperse his commando, and a few days later, when armed Boers rode through his camp and jeered at the British soldiers, he threatened to clear the Boers out of Congella.

Two trading vessels, the *Pilot* and the *Mazeppa*, arrived a few days later, bringing Smith two more fieldpieces and sorely needed supplies. Pretorius, fearing that Smith's strength would grow if more supplies were landed, finally decided on a showdown and ran off most of the English draft oxen. Smith could still fight, but he could no longer move, and his patience was at an end. Late on the night of May twenty-third, in brilliant moonlight, he led his troops south along the bay shore to attack Congella. He took a fieldpiece with him, and he loaded his howitzer into a scow with instructions to bombard the Boer encampment from the bay. Pretorius was not to be taken in by such maneuvers; he scattered his men through the mangrove trees bordering the bay and opened a devastating fire at point-blank range when the British were abreast of him. The troops formed up and attempted to reply with volley fire, but the battle was already lost. The oxen broke out of the artillery traces and stampeded, the scow with the howitzer grounded too far offshore to help, the Boers were invisible in the trees, and Smith had to order a retreat. He got his command back to the fort with 20 dead and 31 wounded, and made what reply he could to the peppering fire the Boers kept up till dawn. Pretorius lost one man.

Smith was now besieged, with close to 500 people jammed into a crowded laager, low on food and with no good water. There was no relief in sight, but Smith never considered surrender. Under a flag of truce he buried his dead and gathered his wounded and set about making his plight known.

Most of the British settlers had taken refuge on the two trading vessels in the bay, and Smith sent George Cato out to the *Mazeppa* to wake up Dick King. King listened to Smith's proposition, agreed to it at once, took a sixteen-year-old Zulu retainer named Ndongeni, and rowed to Salisbury Island with two saddles and a single set of stirrups, towing two horses in the water behind him. He landed, saddled up, crossed the island and waded across the narrow channel to the mainland, and set off at once for Grahamstown, 600 miles to the south.

Dick King was now twenty-nine years old, and he had been in Natal since 1828. He spoke fluent Zulu, and had borne a charmed life for all those fourteen years. He had visited Dingane first with Gardiner and then with Owen, and he had crossed Natal afoot and alone immediately after the Retief massacre to participate in the defense of the laagers. He had been one of the four Europeans to escape from John Cane's ill-fated expedition, and he was now off on his most important mission. Pretorius heard of his escape at once and sent a party after him; King stopped long enough to ask a friendly Zulu to obliterate his spoor and rode on, traveling by night and slipping past the Boer pickets at the river drifts south of the bay. He finished in ten days a trip that usually took well over three weeks; a blacksmith found him in a state of collapse on a racetrack on the outskirts of Grahamstown and helped him into town. Ndongeni, no horseman and assigned the saddle without stirrups, stayed with King until the skin had been chafed from his bare legs, when King had to order him back. Ndongeni waited until his legs had healed and then walked home; he was later given a piece of land near Durban and died there in 1911. King also returned to Durban and became successively a butcher, a farmer and a mill owner. He died in 1871 and his mounted statue today dominates the city's waterfront.

King's tidings settled the fate of Republican Natal. The emigrant farmers were now open rebels who had attacked Her Majesty's forces. The only troops in Grahamstown, a company of the 27th Foot, were packed into a small coasting vessel named the *Conch* and started for Durban while messengers set out for Capetown to round up heavier reinforcements.

Smith continued to hold out. Only half the stores had been landed from his two ships and still lay on the beach outside the fort. Pretorius, irked by King's escape, attacked the next morning. Smith beat him off, but Pretorius captured the stores and then ferried his men out in small boats and took the two ships. A convoy of 56 wagons with 25 captives started for Pietermaritzburg.

Pretorius now offered to return the two ships if Smith would use them to evacuate his troops. Smith, stalling for time, finally arranged to have all his women and children transferred to the *Mazeppa*. The siege dragged on; Smith was down to quarter rations and Pretorius, with 600 men, had no powder to spare for a major attack.

The Boers had taken the officers off the ships, but had posted no guard. On the tenth of June Christopher Cato mustered the twelve crewmen still on the *Mazeppa*, lined his bulwarks with hammocks and mattresses, put the seven women and eighteen children aboard to work, cut his cable and took the ninety-ton schooner to sea. The Boers blazed away at her as she passed the Bluff, but Cato worked her safely over the bar and took departure for Delagoa Bay, where he hoped to find one of the ubiquitous frigates of the Royal Navy. Smith, with two appeals for help under way, was vastly encouraged and hung on.

The tiny *Conch* entered the harbor a fortnight later, and the same evening the frigate H.M.S. *Southampton* anchored outside the bar with five companies of the 25th Foot. Pretorius made a last effort to rush the fort and then prepared to receive the inevitable landing. It came in the morning, and as soon as the troops were fairly ashore, Pretorius retired to the bush. The siege, 34 days long, was raised that afternoon.

Colonel Josias Cloete, commanding the 25th Foot, was as little inclined to listen to talk of Boer independence as Smith had been. He snapped up what supplies he could find and, to make good the draft oxen Smith had lost, ordered the local natives to bring in teams from the nearest Boer homesteads. Mpande, suddenly realizing that the British had concluded a treaty with Dingane predating his own arrangements with the Boers, had qualms about his status, which depended on the Volksraad, and magnanimously offered to call out his regiments to attack Pietermaritzburg. Cloete curtly told him to sit tight.

Pietermaritzburg was in an uproar. The support from the high veld evaporated, and half the Volksraad, unwilling to be connected with a surrender, drifted away. News of Mpande's offer gave a strong impetus to those departing, and not even Pretorius, still hoping for support from the King of Holland, could rally them. Cloete finally rode up to the Boer capital and announced his terms: the Volksraad would submit to the Queen, all prisoners and captured property would be released, and a few Boers, wanted for looting the *Mazeppa*, would be handed over. The Boers reluctantly agreed.

The 25th Foot was wanted in Afghanistan, so Cloete presently departed, leaving Smith, now promoted to Major, at Durban with a garrison of 350 men and eight guns. The Volksraad was still trying to control the Republicans, although its authority was shattered, and Smith, furious at the mess the Boers had left behind, still had nothing to fall back on but the inadequate Cape of Good Hope Punishment Act. His orderly mind was obsessed with stolen Crown property; he eventually got most of his oxen back, but the few muskets Pretorius could round up were broken and there was little left of the *Mazeppa* loot but a pile of empty crates.

Larger problems also boiled over. The local natives had shown great enthusiasm in carrying out Cloete's rash order to bring in draft oxen, and the Boers were counterraiding kraals and British settlers. Mpande suddenly drove his American missionaries out and eradicated one or two small kraals that had shown signs of a mass conversion, and he only retired when a Boer patrol trounced a small party of Zulus. Above all, and long since past any hope of reasonable solution, was the land problem. A dozen claimants wrangled over every farm, most of which were vacant except for the returning natives who were happily oblivious of the overlapping grants. Smith held to Cloete's edict—pending a final settlement of Natal's status, black and white would hold what they had acutally occupied when the troops arrived. Smith grappled with all these problems while officialdom in London and Capetown considered the future of Natal. In addition to his civil labors, which he discharged with credit, Major Smith also had to cope with military correspondence. In view of the ease with which Colonel Cloete had dispersed the Boers, Smith's superiors wished to know, how had he managed to get himself bottled up by such a motl'ey gang of opponents? Smith told them at some length.

While Smith administered to Durban, and the ineffectual Volksraad tried to control the bulk of Natal's Boer population, the slow process of colonial administration continued. Sir George Napier in Capetown might ask the Colonial Office in London a question, but the answer would not be in his hands for six months, even if it left England the day his dispatch arrived. In August of 1842, for example, the Colonial Office ordered Napier to withdraw the garrison from Natal, but since this order was sent long before news of Smith's siege reached London Napier disregarded it, reported recent events, and settled back to await an answer. Sent in December of 1842, it was not ready for promulgation in Capetown until May 12, 1843, when Napier announced that Her Majesty Queen Victoria intended to adopt Natal as one of her colonies. The Honourable Henry Cloete, a Capetown barrister and brother to Colonel Josias Cloete, was appointed High Commissioner and sent on to Natal to prepare the groundwork. Cloete was skilled and polished, of Dutch extraction and already known favorably to members of the Volksraad. He arrived in Durban on the fifth of June.

The Republic of Natal was far from defunct. It was still exercising a species of *de facto* authority, and it hoped to extract the most favorable terms it could from the Crown. Colonies ranged from advanced societies with almost total control over domestic legislation to primitive areas where officials appointed by London wielded autocratic powers. Much would depend on Cloete's report, and the Volksraad was even in sudden high hopes of seeing the Queen's decision reversed. A month before Cloete arrived, the *Brazilia* had appeared off Durban with Smellekamp aboard. Smith refused to allow anyone to land and shooed the vessel off to Delagoa Bay, but a rumor swept through Natal that Dutch warships were in the offing and about to run the British out of Natal.

Cloete's first problem was not with the Boers but with Major Smith, who had not been informed of the High Commissioner's status through his own channels and consequently refused to provide the escort Cloete wanted to visit Pietermaritzburg. Cloete thereupon rode up alone, to find the town boiling. The Landdrost seemed friendly, and a large number of citizens were obviously willing to co-operate but were being intimidated by wilder spirits who put their faith in Smellekamp and who had already sent for help to the high veld. Cloete explained his mission to a large gathering, but the gavel was taken out of his hands by a group that read a long list of complaints and appealed to the meeting not to recognize Cloete's authority. The High Commissioner called a special meeting of the Volksraad for the seventh of August and left in disgust.

Back in Durban, he sent for reinforcements and attempted to

straighten out his relationship with Major Smith. When 200 reinforcements arrived with an authorization to send them on to Pietermaritzburg, Smith again refused, this time on the grounds that the force was totally inadequate. Cloete, momentarily stymied, was rescued by a letter from the Volksraad assuring his personal safety and asking him to come alone. When he arrived, he found the Boers sullen and angry, but at least willing to negotiate.

The meeting with the Volksraad was turbulent. A party of 200 Boers had arrived from the veld, and under the peculiar provisions of the republic were now represented in the Volksraad. The outsiders were less amenable to reason than the Natal Boers, but a letter from Smellekamp had cut the heart out of the resistance movement. The King of Holland had no intention of provoking Great Britain, whose writ, under the Cape Punishment Act, ran to 25° South latitude. The Boers were on their own.

Cloete could not make himself heard in the Volksraad, and he finally retired to his quarters to await the decision. A delegation of irate Boer wives helped him pass the time; they barged into his room and demanded a voice in the negotiations. Their husbands had already evicted them from the Volksraad, and Cloete, more scandalized by their appearance on the political scene than by their views, threw them out.

A deputation from the Volksraad visited Cloete in the evening. Twenty-four out of twenty-five were ready to accept the British annexation. Cloete was exultant; he reported his success at once and recommended the colony assume the boundaries specified in the Zulu grant to Piet Retief. Most of the men from the high veld left, but the remainder were so troublesome that Cloete called Major Smith up from Durban. The Major for once co-operated, and on the thirty-first of August ran the Union Jack up over his camp, Fort Napier, perched on a hillside overlooking the hollow in which the town lay.

With the Boers finally in line, Cloete set out to learn as much as he could about the new colony. Late in September he visited Mpande, taking Ogle and a few other settlers in lieu of the escort Smith again failed to provide. Mpande was particularly eager to please Cloete, since he held his throne from the Volksraad and he wanted to be in the good graces of the new administration. He arranged an enormous and interminable dance, which bored Cloete unutterably, and when Mpande dared mention the presents which were customarily given on a state visit, Cloete stared him down. No treaty, no presents, and Cloete was not ready to sign anything. He first wanted to see St. Lucia Bay, and although it was obvious that the area could never be turned into a commercial harbor, Cloete insisted Mpande cede it to the British. He then made Mpande promise that the Zulus would remain north of the

Tugela and east of its tributary, the Buffalo, and on the fifth of October he finally signed a treaty. Mpande breathed easier, and Cloete reported with some satisfaction that the British now controlled every possible harbor from Capetown around the African coast to Delagoa Bay.

Cloete now returned to Durban and gave his attention to the land problem. Although only 365 emigrant Boer families were living in Natal, and most of these were in townships, no less than 760 individuals had submitted claims—most of them more than one. A Commandant Rudolph, who had done little farming but a considerable amount of commando riding, laid claim to forty farms totaling 400,000 acres; Pretorius himself wanted ten farms. A Mr. Aspeling in Capetown, who had never been in Natal, outdid them all by claiming 3,500 square miles. He had married Farewell's widow and based his claim on Shaka's original grant. Since Farewell had signed the claim over to his financial backers, an identical claim was submitted by their successors. Cloete ruthlessly disallowed all these claims and gave some 200 families who were able to prove they had occupied the land for at least a year farms of 6,000 acres each. Smaller grants were made to families that had been farming for less than a year, and the rest could whistle or return to the high veld. At the beginning of 1844 Cloete inspected the northern section of Natal, and at the end of April he rode off to Capetown, leaving Major Smith as Commandant of Natal.

Cloete, now thoroughly familiar with the geography, population and problems of Natal, made his report. The final decision came back from London in February of 1845. Despite Cloete's recommendations for a considerable degree of autonomy, Natal was to be annexed to the Cape Colony as a district, with legislative power in the hands of the Governor and the Executive Council in Capetown, and ultimate judicial power in the Supreme Court of the Cape Colony. Natal would have a lieutenant governor, and an executive council of five members, and municipalities might control local taxation.

This was cold comfort for the Boers, and it meant the end of the lekker lewe in Natal. The Great Trek was ten years old, and the Crown had already caught up with them. The struggle and sacrifice for Natal had all gone for nought, and they could only submit or pack up and trek again.

The new colony was poor, far-off and unimportant, and there were no volunteers for the new civil list. Cape Colony combed through the more able junior members of its own list, and Martin West, a forty-one-year-old Anglo-Indian then serving as Resident Magistrate at Grahamstown, was appointed the first Lieutenant Governor. Theophilus Shepstone, now a government agent at Fort Peddie, was put on the Executive Council as Diplomatic Agent with the Africans in Natal, and the new officials began to congregate in Natal.

In August Major Smith was relieved by a lieutenant colonel and a new regiment, and Martin West finally arrived in December. He reached Pietermaritzburg on the twelfth, and Natal commenced its career as a British colony.

MPANE

B Y THE beginning of 1846 Natal was finally able to look
forward to a long period of peace. The colony was
firmly under British administration, and Zululand was under a pliant
monarch. The ethnic composition of the colony, however, was still
in a state of flux.

There were perhaps 3,000 Europeans in the land: the small but growing group of British settlers at Durban, a few Boers and British settlers
and officials at Pietermaritzburg, and some 400 Boer families scattered
about on inland farms. There had been many more Boer families,
but they had started to leave in 1842 when they saw that the British
meant to stay, and by 1848 there would be less than a hundred left.
These survivors had abandoned the old dream of the lekker lewe and
were now resigned to accepting the amenities of British rule. A very
few, obstinate to the end and unwilling to face further trekking, made
a last despairing effort to avoid the inevitable and announced the formation of the Klip River Republic in upcountry Natal. Its declaration
of independence was the sole public act of its existence, and its policy
was to evade all contact with the scandalized officials who came to
order it out of existence. Scarcely more than a gesture, it soon collapsed.

The native population was already large and it was still growing.
When the trekkers arrived in 1837, there had been fewer than 3,000
natives in Natal, most of whom lived in the kraals around Port Natal.
By the time Martin West arrived at Pietermaritzburg, over 40,000
refugees had returned from their exile in the south or on the high veld,
and more thousands were arriving every month. They came singly and
in family groups and in tiny clans, instinctively seeking the ancestral
grounds from which Shaka had driven them, and they spread out over
the face of the land in hundreds of small kraals which had little or no
political connection with one another. These kraals were seeded in and

about the European homesteads like so much loose gunpowder, and the infant government of Natal had neither a policy to control them nor the power to enforce a policy were one adopted. It had only the post of Diplomatic Agent to the Natives to cope with the problem.

There was also a continual trickle of refugees from Zululand itself, periodically swelled by a large population mass expelled by one of the recurrent crises in the affairs of that nation. Mpande brought out 17,000 followers when he fled into Natal in 1838, and many of these people remained behind when he returned to Zululand. In 1843 he took the precaution of murdering Gqugqu, his younger half brother and the only other surviving son of Senzangakona. He thus upset a delicate political balance, and Gqugqu's aunt, Mawa, bolted for the safety of Natal with so many thousands of adherents that the southeast corner of Zululand was virtually depopulated. "Mawa's Flight" passed into Zulu history as one of the events on which the nation hung its chronology.

In 1848 Langalibalele—"the Glaring Sun"—was driven out with his entire amaHlubi clan and also sought refuge in Natal. The amaHlubi were a Basuto strain, related to the clan that had sheltered Dingiswayo during his exile, and they now found a new home in the foothills of the Drakensberg Range, where they served as a buffer between the low veld farms and the Bushmen who still infested the heights.

By the mid-1850's there were 150,000 "Natal Kaffirs" packed into the colony—the number would eventually reach a quarter of a million —and somehow room had to be found for all of them. The refugee stream from Zululand was finally choked off in 1856 by a regulation requiring each new arrival to work three years for a European master before he could settle in a kraal of his own choosing.

Natal would need a large European population if it were ever to become a civilized colony, and it was obvious that the ivory trade would not attract further settlers. Elephants, in fact, were already scarce. The government therefore took immediate steps to encourage the immigration of farmers, artisans and merchants. Karl Marx was even then writing *Das Kapital* in London, and the industrial conditions that spurred him on insured a large crop of potential emigrants. The problem was to find them, to organize them, and to bring them to Natal, and the government turned to land speculators. Between 1848 and 1851 over 3,000 Englishmen were brought out by a few entrepreneurs who stood to make large profits in the process. These men bought up enormous tracts of land from the government, at prices ranging from a penny to a shilling an acre. They drummed up initial capital by charging resident natives rent in the form of a hut tax— cattle were too hard to count, and since the kraals averaged a hut for each wife, the number of huts was an excellent indication of the kraal head's prosperity. They then printed extravagant brochures describing the virtues of Natal and omitting all reference to the disadvantages of pioneering in a totally undeveloped country, and offered a small farm and a passage out for two people for what looked like a bargain price.

The early arrivals had no idea of what actually awaited them, and only the fact that retreat was impossible held many of them in Natal. Scores left anyway, to return to England or to go on to the gold fields in Australia, but by 1851 the tide had turned. The passage out was a grim experience, and few captains cared to risk their keels on the notorious sand bar that guarded the bay. They anchored in the open roadstead, transferred cargo and passengers in baskets to crude lighters, battened down the hatches, and ran the lighters in through the surf. As many as not would capsize. It was a fit climax to an interminable voyage jammed into a wet steerage, and the new immigrant waded ashore from the lighter to catch his breath on the bare, sandy beach of his new home. If he was lucky, an agent of the company that sold him the passage might be on hand with practical advice on how to reach whatever township he was headed for, and if he had funds, he might be able to rent an ox wagon.

It was sink or swim with a vengeance, and most of the newcomers swam. They hacked new townships out of the bush, which either flourished or stagnated, depending on whether or not competent artisans were at hand and on luck in the nature of the surrounding farmlands. Natal was verdant, but the very lushness was deceptive; large stretches of pasture were rank and sour, and the subtropical growth of the lowlands choked farm after coastal farm.

Boer families saved many of the new arrivals. A thousand tricks of the land—how to clear and farm it, how to cope with the natives and with the frequently dangerous fauna—were all part and parcel of their heritage, and they passed their skills on freely and with good will. Pietermaritzburg, symbol of the lost hopes of the Republic of Natal, took on the aspects of a boom town as hundreds of settlers armed only with determination passed through on the way to their new homes. The population was small, and a man's very presence in Natal was sufficient to open most doors. People helped one another, and they learned about the land and wove the fabric of their new society at the same time.

There was hardly any economy. The farms had to reach a level of bare sustenance before they could think about any form of trade but barter, and there were as yet no markets nor even more than the rudiments of a transportation net. The first regular communication between Durban and Pietermaritzburg was by native runner, and even a weekly stagecoach lay over a decade in the future. As soon as farmers could feed themselves, they began to think about export crops; and tobacco, flax, pawpaws, red bananas, pineapples, arrowroot, coffee and tea all had their exponents. Most of these experiments failed, either through agricultural difficulties or because the market was undercut by another colony elsewhere. The first success came with cotton, and for a time Natal slowly moved toward something very like the plantation system of the American South.

Willing immigrants soon began to build up more than the lekker lewe that had sufficed the Boers. For fifty years, however, the greatest single obstacle to Natal's economic growth was the wretched sand bar that blocked Durban's harbor. Water over the shifting sands varied from less than three feet to never more than twelve; scores of early residents remembered wading from the Point to the Bluff, and only the clumsy box lighters or the smallest of coasting craft could chance the entry. Scheme after scheme was adopted, and an endless series of moles and breakwaters washed away as fast as the fortunes and reputations that had backed them. The solution was not found until shortly before the turn of the century, when solid breakwaters narrowed the channel and a combination of tidal scour and dredging finally insured free passage for seagoing vessels. Within a decade Durban turned into a major port and overtook the provincial capital of Pietermaritzburg.

Over the years a colonial society developed in Natal. Pietermaritzburg grew from a muddy village into a proper town, and Durban pulled itself together and shed its chaotic infancy. A score of villages dotted the rolling landscape, serving several thousand agricultural Britons and a thin sprinkling of Boers. All travel was by horse, and what commerce there was moved in ox wagons. Almost all manual labor was performed by inefficient help drawn from the thousands upon thousands of Natal Kaffirs.

Most of these settlers farmed or traded or tended stores for fifty years or ten years and then died and were forgotten by all but their immediate families. A half dozen or so left marks of various significance on history, and their stories can stand for the others.

James Rorke was typical of the early settlers. An Irish regiment had landed at Mossel Bay in 1821 to fight in some forgotten clash with the Kaffirs, and two brothers and a cousin named Rorke were serving in the ranks. One of the brothers stayed in the Cape Colony after his service expired—or he may have simply deserted—and there he married and there his son James was born in 1827. James in his turn served as a civilian attached to the commissariat in the Seventh Kaffir War in 1846, and in the course of that year he arrived in Durban. He married, and a year or so later he drifted upcountry with his wife. In 1849 he acquired a 3,000-acre farm on the right bank of the Buffalo River.

It was a pleasant location. A hunting trail from the outpost settlement of Helpmakaar, twelve miles to the southwest, crossed the river into Zululand on his farm. The trail skirted the northern flank of a nameless, rocky mountain just before it reached the river, and Rorke made his homestead a quarter of a mile from the riverbank, between the trail and the lower terrace of the mountain. He built a thatched house out of stones and homemade bricks, but he was neither an architect nor much of a hand as a builder. For some reason he had an aversion to inside doors, and of the eleven rooms in his house, five communicated only with the outside. The remaining six rooms were split into two isolated suites, and five of the rooms were windowless. It was a typical structure for that time and place, and from his veranda under the extended thatch Rorke could look down over a small rocky ledge, past his vegetable garden, and up the broad valley of the Buffalo, although the river itself was invisible from his house. Ten miles to the east in Zululand he could see the mountains of the Nqutu Range. One of these invariably drew the eye. It was no higher than the others behind it, but it was isolated on a terminal spur, and it had a compelling shape, something like a crouching sphinx. The Zulus called it Isandhlwana, from a fancied resemblance to the second stomach of a ruminant.

The Buffalo River at this point was broad and smooth, although there were turbulent stretches immediately above and below the farm. Except in spate, it was rarely higher than a man's chest, and because it was the most convenient crossing point for miles in either direction, Rorke knocked down the banks to make a proper ford. The trail gradually turned into a dirt road as hunters and traders and natives passed to and fro, and the ford was named Rorke's Drift. Rorke got on well with the Zulus in the kraals beyond his drift, and he eventually built a small store to which they came for trade goods. They had trouble pronouncing "Rorke" and called him Jimu, and the vicinity of the drift was known to them as kwaJimu.

Rorke continued to farm and to trade, and he became a field cornet in a small group of local militia that called itself the Buffalo Border Guard. He died about 1875, and his farm passed to a Swedish missionary named Otto Witt, who moved his wife and infant children into Rorke's house. Witt left the house alone, but he turned the storehouse into a neat stone chapel, and he replaced Rorke's cattle pen, little more than a circle of large boulders, with a stout rectangular wall of breast-high stone. He also named the mountain behind him the Oskarberg, in honour of Sweden's king.

John Robert Dunn's origins were also unexceptionable. His father was an Englishman who came to Algoa Bay to trade in 1820 when he was twenty-four years old; there he married Ann Biggar and after a decade or so removed to Port Natal. He was a loose, unprincipled man, greatly given to drink, and he fathered five children. His only son was born in 1833—whether at Algoa Bay or Port Natal is uncertain—and John passed a carefree childhood playing with the children of the Zulu refugees squatting on his father's homestead in the isolated brush of the Berea. When Dingane sacked the settlement in 1838, the family sought refuge on the *Comet,* and when that scare passed, Robert Newton Dunn returned to the bush to trade in ivory and to dispense rude medicine to his neighbors. He took his son on long expeditions to trade with the native clans, and in 1847, aged fourteen, John Dunn saw his father trampled to death by an elephant. The boy shot his first tusker several months later, and in 1853 with his friend George Cato killed the last elephant to be seen in the vicinity of Durban.

Ann Dunn took her family back to Port Elizabeth, where the daughters eventually married, but she soon returned to Port Natal with John and in 1851 she herself died. John Dunn, now eighteen, was on his own. He was a large, powerful youth, quiet, amiable and unambitious. He could read and write but was largely uneducated, and he had no skills beyond a native command of Zulu and an uncanny way with a rifle. He had grown up too far apart from normal society to mix easily, and farming in any event did not appeal to him. He earned his first pennies guiding hunting parties for the officers stationed at Durban, but this was hardly sufficient to support him, so he took a job as a transport rider, convoying a few wagons to Potchefstroom in the Transvaal on behalf of a local merchant. When he returned after the better part of a year, the merchant refused to pay him, claiming that under the Roman-Dutch law of the colony no contract with a minor was binding. Thoroughly disgusted, Dunn crossed the Tugela River into Zululand and drifted aimlessly for a year or so, living off game bartered to the local kraals. He took with him Catherine Pierce, the fifteen-year-old daughter of his father's European assistant and a Cape Colony native woman. Catherine's elder brother Paul had already run off to Zululand with an Irish ruffian named Tim Dupré, and the two renegades lived with native women in huts at the Lower Drift of the Tugela, claiming Mpande had empowered them to collect a toll from all who used the ford.

In 1854 Dunn met Captain Joshua Walmsley, who lived on the Nonoti River. From here, as Border Agent, he kept an eye on the Lower Drift of the Tugela and the traffic to and from Zululand, reporting to the Diplomatic Agent to the Natives in Pietermaritzburg.

Walmsley took Dunn on as an assistant, using the youth's knowledge of Zululand and its people to eke out his own sources of information. Dunn enjoyed the work, which gave him some status in Zululand, where he was known as "Jantoni." Walmsley's childless French wife, Maria, was lonely and unburdened by the prejudices of the other colonists, and she accepted Dunn's relationship with Catherine Pierce. The youth also had time to attend to his finances. Buying a team of trained oxen from a passing officer, he traded it for two unbroken teams and trained them himself, repeating the process until he had acquired a sizable sum. He might in time have put his irregular liaison behind him, as scores of others had done, and gone on to comparative wealth as a respected trader, but Catherine by now had given him colored children, and his loyalty to her proved stronger than any call from the society which had rejected him. His future lay along another road.

James Rorke and John Dunn were settlers; Theophilus Shepstone was an official. Natal was a backwater, and the men who were posted there were largely young and inexperienced—culls, in fact, from the civil service list of the Cape Colony. Shepstone was only twenty-eight in 1845, but as Diplomatic Agent to the Natives he soon overshadowed his colleagues in the official circles of Pietermaritzburg. He was admirably suited to his work, but his rise was due even more to the fact that his area of responsibility encompassed the major problem facing Natal, and he was patently the only man in the colony who could cope with it.

The presence of the Natal Kaffirs put the administration in an unenviable position. Nowhere else in southern Africa was European civilization in such danger of being swamped in a black flood, and nowhere else were the means to staunch the flood so limited. The imbalance between European and native was considerably less in the Cape Colony, where civilizing influences had been at work on the natives for almost two centuries. When the Great Trek leached 12,000 of the most intransigent Boers out of the European community, the Cape began to move rapidly toward political and civil—if not cultural— equality. On the high veld, the trek Boers were now in the process of evolving two independent states in the Orange River Sovereignty and in the Transvaal, and they were able to deal with the natives as they saw fit. The entire area had been largely depopulated by the Mfecane and the Matabele ravages, and the Matabele had now moved on to the north. Except for Mshweshwe and his Basuto in their mountain fastnesses, what was left of native life on the high veld could not withstand the Boers, who were able to drive organized clans off the lands they wanted, retaining only a few families of squatters on each farm to provide labor.

Neither solution was possible in Natal. The natives were far too numerous, too disorganized and too primitive to leave as they were, and the colony had neither the means, the will nor the room to drive them away. The colonists, moreover, were of two minds; the thousands of kraals constituted a very real danger to the scattered European homesteads, but a growing number of the inhabitants of these very kraals were wanted for farm and domestic labor.

The Natal Kaffirs, however, provided only a thin trickle of workers. The native had his own ideas about the lekker lewe, which for him was based on a kraal life where he could support himself with a small herd of cattle and the labor of as many wives as he could afford. He saw no reason to spend hard years away from his comfortable home, working long hours for little pay at what he in any event regarded as woman's work, so that when he did come in to work he was generally lazy and inefficient, and he was apt to leave suddenly as soon as he had accumulated sufficient cash for his immediate needs.

A solution would have to be found within the geographical limits of the colony. What made one even remotely possible was the fact that the bulk of the settlers were of English stock, amenable to a reasonable framework of law. While most of them looked down on the natives with varying degrees of contempt, exasperation, fear and disgust, very few of them suffered from a pathological hatred.

Major Smith had foreseen the problem when the influx of Shakan refugees had started in his time; Henry Cloete had described it in detail and had proposed a solution based on native reserves. Theophilus Shepstone now adopted Cloete's basic plan and set to work. At his instigation the administration of Natal provided a total of 1,168,000 acres, and Shepstone divided the land into eight major reserves and started to move the bulk of the Natal Kaffirs into their new homes.

Shepstone brought to his thankless task a profound knowledge of the Nguni Bantu. He spoke Xhosa and Zulu with native fluency—and the still-evolving Afrikaans of the Boers as well—and his knowledge of native custom and usage went far beyond a mere linguistic prowess. He was able to do something that very few of even the most devoted missionaries could do—he could think in native terms and see the complex world of European civilization through Bantu eyes. He admired and—what was much rarer—respected native civilization, and he had enormous pity for that culture in its struggle against the continual European encroachment. These were qualities that had turned many a missionary into a Bantophile, but Shepstone retained a curious detachment to the end of his days. His pity verged on sympathy, but it never extended to affection, and his correspondence on native problems at times sounded rather like that of an entomologist engrossed in a colony of ants. He was also patronizing. Unable to credit Shaka with sufficient invention to have developed his military innovations by himself, he adopted and spread the canard that he at some time had lived in the Cape Colony, where he had picked up his military ideas while watching European troops at drill.

Shepstone was a large man, with a broad, impassive face, and he cultivated a ponderous dignity that cowed every native—and most of the Europeans—whom he encountered. A chieftain, summoned to an inDaba, could expect no casual encounter. Shepstone would be seated on a thronelike chair, and from his shaded eminence would parley with the man squatting in the dusty sunlight before him. Shepstone would listen gravely, take snuff in native fashion, nod sagely. When he spoke, his rhetoric was that of a tribal elder and his allusions those of a Bantu savant. His edicts were delivered with the awesome finality of the Judgment Seat, and no matter how petty the agenda had been, a native who had consulted with Shepstone knew that he had been in a Conference.

He was shrewd, infinitely patient, laborious, courageous—and ambitious. He had the temperament of a trained diplomat and he was inordinately fond of secrecy. His department was small, and he shared neither his plans nor his responsibilities. He deliberately fostered the notion that his province was an arcane one in which none might interfere. He trusted only his immediate family, and that only partially, and when he finally left his post after more than thirty years, he was followed first by a brother and then by a son.

His fame soon extended beyond Natal. Capetown and London sought his advice, and from an apparently subordinate position in a minor colony his influence helped to shape native policy throughout southern Africa and even beyond. He was an Imperialist to the core, but despite his devotion to the policies of a homeland he had not seen since he was three, he remained a Natalian, and he identified himself with the colony's population as few appointed officials of his time were able to do.

There was only an insinuation, no more, that some natives had correctly judged what lay behind that pompous exterior. His native name was "Somtseu." Shepstone had been an avid sportsman in his youth, but on his first visit to Port Natal with Major Charters in 1838 he had stumbled onto an elephant in the thick bush on the Berea. The irate beast almost killed him, and the shock was so great that he would never face an elephant again, not even a tame one behind bars. To give him the name, as the Zulus then did, of a famed Xhosa hunter skirted the verge of sarcasm.

Shepstone's reserves varied in size—one of them ran to 400,000 acres. They were carefully chosen to interfere as little as possible with the existing clusters of farms. They separated traditionally hostile clans, and they also served as buffers. Natives were packed into vacancies to the south where they formed a belt between Natal and amaMpondo-land, others were spotted along the Tugela and Buffalo Rivers between Zululand and the European settlements, and clans like the amaHlubi were posted in the Drakensberg foothills to occupy the Bushmen and to guard the passes against the Sutu peoples of the high veld. In all, Shepstone moved some 80,000 Natal Kaffirs about on the complicated ethnic chessboard of Natal, and only twice in three decades did he have to resort to force.

His original plan envisaged reserves under the control of European magistrates and mission stations. Each reserve would have a native police force under European officers, and there were to be schools to teach agricultural and mechanical skills. The reserves would not only control the natives and keep the peace, but would civilize the clans as well.

Shepstone saw almost at once that his scheme was too grandiose for Natal's finances. There was barely sufficient cash to staff his own small office, and hardly a penny left for the reserves. Qualified magistrates were scarce, and even reliable border agents were hard to come by. Most of the candidates were untrained settlers who agreed to accept the post for the prestige it afforded; few were versed in law, and fewer still spoke Zulu. Many, like James Rorke, were simply the only settler in the vicinity. Some 150 natives were eventually organized into a rough police force, without proper arms or uniforms or training, and without the hoped-for European officers, and they served as little more than interpreters and messengers for the magistrates.

Shepstone issued most of the orders to the chieftains himself, trusting that the pure force of his personality and the often questionable authority of the chieftain would then insure that the order was carried out. Since these orders frequently involved dislodging a large clan and all its worldly goods from an area it did not wish to leave and moving it several score miles to a new area it did not wish to enter, both the personality and the trust were audacious.

The schools, the training and the civilization were only dreams, and Shepstone abandoned them. Control was paramount, and since it was not to be had in a European framework, Shepstone fell back on native authority. Native law was unwritten, but it was astonishingly uniform from clan to clan, and, hammered out by generations of tribal elders, it was acceptable to all the kraals. Despite a strong element of witchcraft, it recognized trial procedures, the right of limited appeal, and standardized punishments for misdemeanors. Shepstone now confirmed the authority of the hereditary chieftains where such figures still existed, and then pasted new clans together from the bits and pieces of the disintegrated units and appointed new chieftains to rule these creations. When all the Natal Kaffirs had been incorporated into a tribal framework, he took a major step. He recognized the unwritten native law of the kraals, debriding it of such atrocities as smelling-out and capital punishment for most offenses, and he authorized the chieftains to administer this law, with a right of appeal through him as Paramount Chieftain under the Crown to the Executive Council of Natal.

The concept was revolutionary, and it led to immediate opposition. Never before had the British Crown been asked to condone the existence of an alien legal code in one of its colonies, and the adoption of Shepstone's system meant that the Natal Kaffir could never stand before the bar of British justice as the legal equal of his European neighbor. Native law had never been codified, it was filled with inconsistencies, and it recognized such principles as polygamy and the native concepts of land tenure. Henry Cloete, who as Recorder of Natal now presided over a single-judge court in Pietermaritzburg, objected strenuously, and the fight grew so acrimonious that for a time no social event in the capital could be graced by the wives of both the Diplomatic Agent to the Natives and the Recorder of Natal. Shepstone won the battle, and the blessings of the Colonial Office in London, because the Roman-Dutch law of the Europeans simply could not be applied to the Natal Kaffirs. An attempt to treat bigamy as a crime, or to interfere with the native form of primogeniture, would have reduced all the kraals to chaos.

The Ordinance of June 23, 1849, abrogated Roman-Dutch law for the Natal Kaffirs and substituted Native Customary Law. The next year the Lieutenant Governor of Natal was proclaimed Supreme Chief of the native population, *vice* the Zulu monarch, who was thus barred from exercising any control over, or even communicating with, the natives who until then had still been his nominal subjects. A framework of control over the natives had now been achieved, at the price of almost all hope of ever civilizing them, and the framework could be adjusted as necessary in language every Natal Kaffir understood. Hearken to Shepstone on November 25, 1850, substituting capital punishment for the native system of cattle fines in cases of murder:

Hear ye and listen with both ears. Whereas from your youth up you have been taught to consider a man's life to be the property of the Supreme Chief, and that it is unlawful to destroy such life without his consent, and whereas the Supreme Chief of this district is the Lieutenant-Governor, representing the Queen of England, and whereas several lives have been destroyed without trial, and without his knowledge or consent:

Know ye, therefore, all Chiefs, Petty Chieftains, Heads of Kraals, and Common People, *a man's life has no price: no cattle can pay for it.* He who intentionally kills another, whether for Witchcraft or otherwise, shall die himself; and whether he be a Chief, a Petty Chieftain, or Head of a Kraal, who kills another, he shall follow his murdered brother; his children shall be fatherless and his wives widows, and his cattle and all other property shall become forfeited.

Let this be proclaimed in every kraal and on every hill, so that none may say "I knew it not."

It was this rule which led to the first opposition to Shepstone, and the ugly little incident, soon forgotten, was to have an unfortunate sequel years later. A refugee chieftain named Matyana had been settled with his clan on a reserve in the Klip River division, and in 1850 he killed his uncle and two cousins. Because of his youth and the relatively short time he had been in the colony, Shepstone forbore to invoke a severe penalty, and merely cautioned him, fining his clan 500 head of cattle. In 1858, however, a witch doctor smelled out an umThakathi, and Matyana had him beaten so severely that he died. Shepstone thereupon sent for him, and Matyana scattered his following amongst the neighboring clans and fled into Zululand with a large party of armed retainers.

Shepstone was infuriated and sent a handful of regular troops and mounted volunteers to bring him back. To eke out the force, he ordered Langalibalele to arm some of his mounted amaHlubi, and he placed these warriors under the command of his brother, John Wesley Shepstone. "Misjan" was almost as fluent in Zulu as his brother, but hardly his match in character. Matyana's clan was passive, and the European troops soon disbanded, but John Shepstone took the amaHlubi on to the border of Zululand and called for Matyana to attend an inDaba. Matyana knew and respected Misjan, but he was still suspicious, and he appeared with his retainers armed. This was grossly disrespectful, and Shepstone chided him and arranged for a second parley which all participants would attend unarmed. Matyana complied, but Shepstone was determined to arrest him. He concealed a pistol in each coat pocket, and his wife placed a shotgun under the leopard skin on which he was seated. He also arranged for the amaHlubi, waiting nearby, to ride in between Matyana's men and their arms, stacked several hundred yards away, when he gave a signal.

The parley started in good order, but as soon as Shepstone gave his signal and the amaHlubi started to move, Matyana sprang clean over the men squatting behind him and tried to escape. Shepstone pulled out a pistol and fired at him, wounding one of his inDunas, and a general melee developed. Before it was over, Shepstone had received a slight wound from an assegai and the delighted amaHlubi had slain some thirty of Matyana's followers. Matyana himself escaped and settled among the rugged Malakata Hills on the left bank of the Buffalo River, ten miles south of Rorke's Drift.

Opposition to Shepstone's work came not only from official circles and disgruntled natives but also from the settlers themselves. There were, naturally, objections to the size and location of the reserves, but the most vociferous complaint was that the reserves made it too easy for the Natal Kaffirs to avoid work on European farms. A commission studied the problem in 1852, and Shepstone came under fire from irate landowners, who included George Christopher Cato, now serving, among other functions, as the first American consul in Durban. The commission deprecated a system which "dried up the source whereby an abundant and continuous supply of Kaffir labour for wages might have been secured" and went on to make a series of impractical and contradictory recommendations without spelling out how any of them might be implemented. Shepstone sat out the storm with his customary imperturbability, and continued precisely as before. The major result was that his title was changed to Secretary for Native Affairs. The attacks on the reserve system continued, however, and at one point Shepstone announced his readiness to take 50,000 Natal Kaffirs south to a strip of land Faku had just ceded to Natal (it was infested with Bushmen) and there to rule over them personally. Nothing came of this scheme, although Shepstone was much smitten with it at the time. The same group of landowners in 1860 attempted to solve their labor problem by importing Indian workers on an indenture system. By that time the sugar-cane industry was well established and the demand for labor had risen sharply. The Indians worked well, and when their service was over they sent for their families and settled in Natal. The labor market was thus secured at the cost of still another ingredient in the seething ethnic cauldron of the colony.

Within a decade of Shepstone's appointment, his system was in effect and working well, and none could gainsay him in native affairs. In 1864 he succeeded in creating the Natal Native Trust to control the reserves in trust for the native population, thereby improving the security of their tenure. He was still uneasy, however, since the reserves were crowded and their population growing. The settlers regarded the reserves as far too large already, although by Boer standards, with winter and summer farms of 6,000 acres apiece, they would have supported less than a hundred families, and that only for the first generation.

In the same year Shepstone introduced a system of exemption from native law, to shelter the small group of natives who had been detribalized and civilized by missionary endeavors. It was a hard bridge to cross, but any Natal Kaffir who was property-holding, monogamous and literate might petition the Lieutenant Governor to be brought under Roman-Dutch law. If the petition were accepted, he was still not the exact legal or political equal of a European, but his basic civil rights and obligations were the same. Not a single application was received through the first twelve years of this system; between 1876 and 1880, when Misjan held the post, 149 exemptions were granted.

In 1865 the franchise was granted to exempted natives. They had to be residents of Natal for twelve years, to hold their exemptions for seven, and to produce recommendations from three Europeans and a magistrate. The impulse was liberal, but in 1905 it was discovered that exactly three natives of Natal and Zululand had been granted the franchise in forty years.

Beyond all other names, that of John William Colenso, D.D., first Bishop of Natal, is inextricably woven into the history of the colony and the story of the Zulu people. He came to Natal in 1854, and his restless personality soon catapulted him into the center of the storm that rent the Anglican Communion in the second half of the nineteenth century. The role he played in this controversy cost him much of the influence he needed in his fight for the cause of Zulu justice, and before his death he was to see the fall of the pagan nation he had championed. To the Zulus he was always *Sobantu*, "the Father of the People."

In order to follow his career in Natal it will be necessary to examine the structure of the Church of England. In the early years of the reign of Queen Victoria, perhaps 70 per cent of the predominantly Protestant population of England belonged, at least nominally, to the established Church of the realm. The balance was either Roman Catholic or adhered to one of the Nonconformist, or dissenting, sects, of which the Methodists were perhaps the strongest. The ministry of the Church of England was actually independent of its congregations, being confirmed in its livings by the various patrons who had them at their disposal, and while it looked to its bishops for doctrinal guidance and the day-to-day administration of its dioceses, its ultimate authority stemmed from Parliament and the Crown. The final court for church law actually lay in a civil body, the Judicial Committee of the Privy Council. The situation was far from satisfactory, and it became intolerable when the Reform Bill of 1832 opened Parliament to Roman

Catholics, to members of dissenting sects, and even to non-Christians and atheists.

The situation in overseas colonies, territories, and dependencies was as varied as the administrative systems that governed such areas. Bishoprics were established as needed and manned by men who were chosen in England and sent out holding letters patent from the Crown. If a territory possessed an elected legislature, and was thus self-govern-ing, the final court of appeal for the diocese in property matters was vested in the supreme civil judicial body; if it were only a Crown colony governed by appointed officials, the appeal went back to the Judicial Committee in London. If a territory advanced from a Crown colony to self-government, the situation of the clergy appointed in the earlier phase was confused, and the lines of jurisdiction were, perhaps fortunately, rarely put to a test.

The Church of England in any event displayed little missionary zeal, and the primary function of the overseas dioceses was to care for the emigrant Anglican flock and not to convert the indigenous heathen. The private Society for the Promotion of Christian Knowledge and the related but chartered Society for the Propagation of the Gospel in Foreign Parts (by which originally had been meant Ireland, Wales and the highlands of Scotland) had been founded in 1699 and 1701, respec-tively, and they worked to provide an orthodox clergy and to finance their work in overseas posts. Such evangelicals as had not gone over to the dissenting sects were backed by later organizations, of which the London Missionary Society, which had financed Captain Gardiner, was the largest.

The Church of England was generally tolerant, as it had to be to shelter so large a proportion of a diverse nation, and its pulpits spanned a spectrum from Anglo-Catholicism at the one end to evangelical and unitarian movements at the other. It was largely Erastian until well into the nineteenth century, with a complacent clergy that tended to look on the ministry much as it did on the army and the civil service—a respectable governmental living in which good connections and senior-ity would insure a comfortable career.

The Church of England had separated from the Church of Rome in the reign of Henry VIII as the result of a personal political impasse, and while the Anglican faith had since gone its own way, its trappings retained an external resemblance to Roman Catholic practice. The bulk of the population had no understanding of theological niceties, but it entertained a lively fear of Romanism, in which it discerned a fancied threat of foreign political domination. Both the Low Church and the dissenting sects drew much of their strength from this fear, which also hampered the Church's efforts to gain control of its own destinies. The people could still be rallied by a cry of "No popery!" They were liable to judge popery by externals, and they had on frequent occasions rioted in the streets over such matters as clerical garb, plain chant, altar decorations and even church architecture. They preferred to leave religious control in the hands of a Parliament that was amenable to popular will rather than in the hands of the High Church prelates who might desert Canterbury for Rome.

Like all state churches, England's was from time to time convulsed by large and complex movements. Each of them was comprised of theological, political, social and personal factors, and none of them lends itself to a simple retelling. All of them, however, left their marks on the landscape of English history, and three of them must be mentioned in this narrative.

The Industrial Revolution had by the accession of Queen Victoria created a large and bitterly distressed proletariat huddled in the slums of the new urban centers. The Church of England had been organized to cope with many rural parishes and a smaller number of well-to-do urban congregations, and it had neither the machinery, the personnel nor the imagination to adjust to the new social structure. It was, by and large, leagued with the very forces that had created the slums, and what effort it expended on the working classes went to a totally inadequate alleviation of immediate miseries. It made no effort to attack or to modify the system which was responsible for the slums, and it consequently lost almost all touch with the great masses of people who inhabited them. Most of those who still sought religious solace found it in the dissenting sects, and since the depressed classes provided many of the emigrants who populated the colonies, the overseas congregations generally displayed little sympathy for the High Church party.

In 1833 a new movement revitalized the Church of England. Stung by the implications of the Reform Bill, a small group of young High Church clergymen at Oxford struck out at Erastianism and clerical complacency in a series of tracts which called for a redefinition of the Anglican faith. This was the Oxford Movement, and its Tractarians rallied the High Church to a new sense of dedication, but the very urgency of their crusade pulled them away from a population and a segment of newly aroused clergy which was already suspicious of the High Church emphasis on ritual and Anglo-Catholic doctrine. John Henry Newman and some of the other leaders of the Oxford Movement were eventually received into the Church of Rome, and the Church of England was left with a High Church and a Low Church party, each with a sensitivity that left little room for toleration of the other.

At much the same time the advance of scientific methodology caught the Church unprepared. The Bible was generally regarded as the literal word of God until well into the nineteenth century, and the Old Testament was taken at face value. In 1654 Archbishop Ussher had even worked out the exact date of the Creation—March 23, 4004 B.C.— and the implications of new discoveries went largely unnoticed. By the end of the eighteenth century, however, paleontological and archeological findings were in hand that were clearly inconsistent with Biblical accounts of Creation and the Deluge, and new methods of historiography had produced startling results when applied to the New Testament. In 1830 Charles Lyell, the leading geologist of his day, started to publish material which established the true antiquity of the earth, and more than Archbishop Ussher's chronology was swept into the dustbin. Large portions of the Old Testament were quite suddenly reduced, apparently, to the level of myth or legend, and what seemed to be true of the Old might be true of the New as well. A Higher Criticism that treated scripture as a carelessly written text by various unknown authors was an attack on the very divinity of Christ, and while such attacks threatened the evangelical groups, with their emphasis on a fundamental gospel, the menace to the High Church was even greater. More and more men were exposed to a scientific education, and for many it grew harder and harder to accept the Bible as the literal word of God. The Low Church unitarian elements, already uneasy over a High Church view of the Trinity which emphasized Christ's divinity at the expense of His manhood, had little difficulty in adopting the thesis that the Bible simply *contained* the Word of God, but this was too large a step for the evangelicals and the High Church party. Men were faced with what appeared to be a choice between two mutually exclusive gospels, and when one had been chosen, the other either appeared to be heretical or outraged human intelligence. The speculative Darwinian disclosures over the origin of species and the descent of man provided perhaps the most notorious battlefields for the warfare that now commenced, but they were far from the first clashes and by no means the most serious.

John William Colenso was born on January 24, 1814, at St. Austell in Cornwall. He was the eldest of four children. His father was a luckless mining agent, and his mother, who died when he was about fifteen, belonged to a dissenting sect. While he was still a child, his father lost the entire family holdings in a tin mine that the sea flooded, and Colenso soon realized that he would soon be responsible for contributing to the care of his family and for making his own way in life.

Little is known of his childhood, but a remarkable letter survives

which he wrote to an aunt when he was only sixteen. He mentioned
that he could not recall a time when he had not been aware of eternity
and the danger threatening the soul, and he added that he had known
for at least two years that he would devote his life to God. This
showed a precociousness not unusual in his day, but Colenso went on
to mention that while he realized his beliefs made him a dissenter, he
had decided to remain in the Church of England because only there
would he find the independence to preach as he saw fit—in a dissenting
sect he would be at the mercy of his congregation!

By the time he was seventeen, he was teaching as an assistant in a
school in Dartmouth, and thinking of Cambridge. He could have no
career without a university education, but what money he earned was
already going to his family. Cambridge would be an expense for which
no funds were at hand, and it would interfere with the education of his
younger brother, who would someday be able to share the burden he
himself had already shouldered. Penniless, he turned to an uncle to beg
the loan of £20 to see him through his first year. The uncle's financial
position was little better than Colenso's, but he promised £33 for the
second year if someone else would underwrite the first. An aunt came
to the rescue, and in September of 1832 he matriculated at St. John's.

He was a tall, gaunt youth, forced to deny himself every indulgence
and not a few necessities. He worked hard. He proved to be a first-rate
classical scholar, with an odd flair for mathematics. His mind was
logical and ruled by common sense. He was quick and confident, with
little time to waste, and he found it difficult to suffer those of lesser
intelligence, so that only the deliberate exercise of his great personal
charm saved him from making enemies. Neither social background nor
economic status impressed him, and his friendships were firm and
lasting.

He had, of course, seriously overestimated his ability to stretch £20,
and his studies were interrupted by time-consuming efforts to ward off
starvation. In his first year he edited translations from Horace and
annotations on the Gospel of St. Matthew for publication, and he then
translated Plato's "Apology of Socrates" himself. An examination prize
of £20 eased the pressure but was still not sufficient to clear the way.
By his second year he was in difficulties. He was on the verge of seeking out pupils to tutor, but his own tutor would not hear of it and prevailed on his aunt to help him again. By the end of the second year he
had won a number of additional prizes and had also written a mathematical textbook. In 1837 he was elected a Fellow of St. John's, and for
the first time he could breathe easily.

In 1839 he was admitted to Deacon's Orders by the Bishop of Ely,
and two months later he went to Harrow as a mathematical tutor. The

organization of the school was peculiar: each master operated a house which was his personal property, maintaining the overhead and taking his profits from the fees paid in by the pupils who boarded with him. The headmaster supervised the academic routine and set the tone for the school as a whole. The man who preceded Colenso in his house had retired with a fortune, and Colenso, seriously overextending himself, bought the property with great expectations. His two-year sojourn, however, was an unmitigated disaster. His advent coincided with that of a new headmaster under whom the school's reputation disintegrated, and Colenso's house, heavily mortgaged and virtually uninsured, burned down. In addition to suffering the loss of all his personal property, he had to make good on his students' possessions and even their furniture. His bankers would help him no further, a friend provided a large loan, and by 1842, aged twenty-eight, he was back at Cambridge owing more than £6,500. It was an enormous sum for the time and a well-nigh crushing one in the light of personal prospects.

He now took on pupils in mathematics, earning about £800 a year. His interest payments alone ran to £550 and he faced bleak years of a frustrating existence. He had, moreover, encountered a most unusual girl just after his return to Cambridge, and although he became engaged almost immediately, he was in no position to think of marriage. His one hope was his mathematics book, which might be adopted as a standard text.

Sarah Frances Bunyon, born in 1816, was blessed with an intellect that matched Colenso's. It was not an age in which a female could hope for much in the way of formal education, and what schooling was provided was mainly intended to develop the social graces. Frances Bunyon nevertheless spoke Greek and Latin, French and German, and she had somehow acquired a thorough grounding in metaphysics. In effect a dissenter, she had not yet left the Church of England, and although shy and retiring, she had already been in touch with leading figures of the Low Church party. Chief among these was Frederick Denison Maurice, who had been raised a Unitarian but who deliberately joined the Church of England because he felt that a national church was a necessity, and that it had an obligation to purify and elevate the mind of the nation. He was one of the very few theologians to protest the economic system that produced the Industrial Revolution, and he was widely regarded as little more than a muddle-minded mystic. It took courage for a layman, and even more for a clergyman, to admit to being a Maurician, but Frances Bunyon did so proudly, and Colenso, largely through her influence, shortly counted himself one as well.

By 1846 Colenso's efforts had reduced his debt to manageable proportions, and he finally felt free to marry. Maurice himself performed the ceremony, and Colenso took his bride to the parish living of Forncett St. Mary in Norfolk. For the next six years he devoted himself to a parish of 300 souls in a primitive farming community, and there his two sons and two daughters were born. The death from tuberculosis of his younger brother, Thomas, just as the education Colenso had helped to finance was completed, was a heavy blow, and in addition to the payments he was making on his debt, he was still contributing to the care of his father. Then, late in 1852, Robert Gray, the first Bishop of Capetown, visited Forncett St. Mary and asked Colenso to accept the newly created diocese of Natal.

It was a strange choice. Gray, born in 1809, had gone out to Capetown in 1847. The Cape Colony then had no self-governing legislature, so Gray took his oath of obedience to the Archbishop of Canterbury, and he carried a Royal Mandate in the form of letters patent from the Queen. On his arrival he found a diocese of over 250,000 square miles, with boundaries resting on distant hills and rivers that few Europeans had ever seen, served by a total of thirteen Anglican clergymen and one catechist. He had practically no money and he was in poor health; he had survived a brush with tuberculosis and had never fully recovered from the effects of an incident at Eton, when a turbulent mob of schoolmates emerging from a classroom had trampled him underfoot. Gray was as High Church as Colenso was Low, and his exhausting efforts to organize his unwieldy see, to provide it with clergymen and to raise funds for its management were marred by continual clashes with Low Church colonists who regarded him with deep suspicion. The isolated Anglican priests scattered across his vast territories had failed to dent the mountain of work that had to be done, and most of them were Erastian and unacceptable to their new bishop, who displayed an arbitrary and hostile attitude toward his subordinates. Within three months Gray had suffered a nervous breakdown, but he recovered and continued to hack away manfully at the problems that beset him. He was a hard worker, an intelligent man with great personal charm, and he knew exactly what he wanted, which was an independent High Church diocese ruled by a clerical synod in southern Africa. The majority of his Anglican adherents had no intention of seeing the control of their churches pass to a High Church body with no civil barrier between it and Rome, and they resisted every move he made in this direction. By 1852 he saw that the task was too large for one man, and he returned to England to seek the creation of two new dioceses, Grahamstown and Natal. The two new bishoprics would not only reduce his own see to a more reasonable size, but would presumably provide him with firm allies in the form of two additional bishops.

The work in England was strenuous. The technical difficulties in establishing the new dioceses were enormous, Gray had to undertake a major fund-raising campaign as well, and candidates for colonial bishoprics were not easily found. Within a month Gray suffered another breakdown, and he spent some time recovering. During his convalescence he was unable to attend to all of his business, and one of the matters he perforce let slide was an even cursory investigation of the background and credentials of the man who had been recommended to him for the bishopric of Natal.

Gray had met Colenso, and the two men took an instant liking to each other. The Colensos were deeply interested in missionary work, and the idea of evangelizing the Zulus appealed to them. The meeting must have been short, and the conversation devoted almost entirely to work among the heathen, for Gray overlooked entirely the fact that Colenso would also be responsible for the Anglican congregations in Natal. Colenso was both a Low Churchman and a Maurician, and even his bishop was regarded as somewhat heretical, and a moment's reflection should have shown Gray that he would never find the ally he was seeking in the rector of Forncett St. Mary.

Even as the offer was extended, Colenso gave clear warning of his sympathies. Maurice, whose theological commentaries spanned a wide range, had just been hounded out of his professorships at King's College, London, as the result of his published views on the dogma of eternal punishment. Colenso had just published a volume of apparently innocuous sermons. At the height of the controversy he dedicated his book to his friend, going out of his way to acknowledge Maurice's influence on his own thinking. Even Maurice was dismayed by this rash act, fearing it would set Colenso at war with the English bishops. He expressed his gratitude and uneasiness in a letter, adding:

> Nevertheless, I do so thoroughly and inwardly believe that courage is the quality most needed in a Bishop, especially in a missionary Bishop, that I did at the same time give hearty thanks to God that He had bestowed such a measure of it upon you.

The honour of a bishopric was great, but the offer was not to be taken up lightly. It meant exile from home and exchanging the comforts of a placid English parish for a lifetime of hard work in a raw, backwater colony. Frances Colenso had little desire to go; her sister had married the Bishop of Borneo and lost five children in six years. At least Colenso's finances were at long last in order; his mathematics textbook was now standard in schools and had earned him £2,400, and the next few generations of English schoolchildren would learn their arithmetic from his manual. Colenso asked for six months to consider, and then, in April of 1853, announced his willingness to go. On St. Andrew's Day, the thirtieth of November, he was consecrated in the parish church of Lambeth, and the Bishops of Capetown, Oxford, London, Lincoln, Adelaide and Guiana joined the Archbishop of Canterbury in the laying on of hands. Henceforth he would sign himself "John W. Natal."

Colenso and Bishop Armstrong of Grahamstown, consecrated at the same time, drew letters patent from the Queen, for neither of their respective dioceses was ruled by a self-governing legislature. Gray was also granted new ones, giving him authority as bishop of the now reduced diocese of Capetown and at the same time naming him Metropolitan of South Africa. He wanted the designation of Metropolitan to insure his leadership over the new dioceses, but constitutional government had been established in the Cape Colony the previous year, which affected the validity of his new letters. Great Britain had never claimed the authority to issue such a commission to a bishop whose diocese lay in a country that had been granted responsible government, but no one questioned the anomaly at the time.

A fortnight later Colenso sailed for a whirlwind tour of Natal. Bishop Gray's party was on the same vessel, but despite the close quarters and the extended voyage the initial rapport continued. Gray was a sensitive man whose landscape was littered with unpleasant realities to which he was apt to react violently, but he had an enormous capacity for self-delusion and he now managed to ignore the implications of the Maurice dedication and the significant trend of Colenso's conversation.

Once in Natal, Colenso rode almost continuously, visiting many of the settlements and native reserves. He interviewed scores of officials and chieftains, and from Theophilus Shepstone to Langalibalele he liked the people he met, as they liked him. The tour was short but informative, and by May of 1854 he was back in England, where he published *Ten Weeks in Natal* and then set out to crisscross the country, lecturing and preaching to raise the money he needed. There was little public interest in southern Africa, and the war in the Crimea had dried most of the usual springs, but he managed to raise over £11,000, counting the profits from his book.

In March of 1855 he sailed with his family, and by September, when his last daughter was born, he had already started to construct his mission station at Bishopstowe, some six miles out of Pietermaritzburg and facing a table-topped mountain that he and his wife learned to love. He named the site *Ekukanyeni*—"the Home of Light"—and he was thrilled when the natives responded by naming the small kraal that grew there *Esibaneni*—"the Place of the Torch"—that had been kindled at his light.

Almost his first problem was the language. No Zulu grammar existed at the time, but he soon published one in England. He followed this with an elementary manual and bilingual reading texts, and went on to translate the New Testament, portions of the Old, and the greater part of the Book of Common Prayer. Within five years he had brought out a dictionary with over 10,000 entries. It was a remarkable achievement, and more so in the light of his other labors, and his work has stood the test of time. His orthography was close to that officially adopted a half-century later and his manuals are still used by students.

Colenso now entered a period of seven years of unremitting toil, marked by progress in establishing his mission and by the deterioration of his relations with Gray. The mission work advanced in the face of continual financial difficulties. Colenso had appointed a farm manager at the Bishopstowe site after his visitation, and during his absence the man had obligated most of the available funds for a series of impractical projects. The small congregations of Natal could provide little ready cash, and the Society for the Propagation of the Gospel kept a close and galling control over the sums they made available. Colenso nevertheless managed to build a number of churches, to open a school at Bishopstowe for the sons of Natal Kaffir chieftains, and to start a printing press staffed with Bantu workers. His educational efforts had the full support of Theophilus Shepstone, who saw in Bishopstowe the institution which might train the future leaders of his native reserves.

Ecclesiastical progress was less satisfactory. St. Peter's Cathedral was completed in Pietermaritzburg and St. Paul's in Durban. The latter congregation viewed Colenso with grave initial suspicion, purely because Gray had chosen him, and Colenso, who was apt to regard the doctrinal implications of church administration as relatively unimportant, found it humorous that he, a Maurician, should be suspected of papist leanings.

The situation in Pietermaritzburg was marked by more serious difficulties. Gray's representative in Natal since 1849 had been James Green, an extreme High Churchman with rigid convictions. He had been one of the few people not smitten with Colenso's charm during his visitation, and when Colenso returned to England, he wrote Green suggesting he might perhaps be more happily employed in the Cape Colony. Green took this broad hint to resign to Gray, who tried to gloss over the fundamental differences between the two men. The Bishop of Capetown was still blinding himself to Colenso's true colors, but he was not so blind as to remove from the scene a man on whom he could rely implicitly. Colenso made the best of the situation, and

Green was appointed Dean of St. Peter's. The two men worked in harness until 1858, when Green refused to recommend a candidate for ordination because of what he regarded as heretical views on the sacrament of baptism. Colenso overrode him and not only ordained the candidate but went on to preach three sermons setting forth his views in unmistakable language. Green retaliated by presenting Colenso to Gray for heresy, and Gray, although privately disturbed by Colenso's doctrinal tack, was forced to back his fellow bishop and to admonish Green. From that time on the break between Colenso and Green was open; Green took his accustomed seat in the choir at services, but he refused to communicate with Colenso or to participate in the services. The candidate, Walton, later repaid Colenso by turning into one of his bitter foes.

Colenso's ecclesiastical and mission duties were heavy, and Green's opposition and the lack of funds made them no easier. Frequent services and the administration of parish churches several days' hard riding apart took endless time, and the teaching load and the Zulu translations demanded still more. The tall, gaunt man on a great black horse named "Pen"—short for Pentateuch—was a familiar figure on the rough roads of Natal. Colenso nevertheless found time during these years to devote to a major theological work. His Low Church views had not been fully formulated when he arrived in Natal, and his subsequent study had carried him Lower than ever before. His attitude toward scripture changed most of all. In translating the Old Testament into Zulu he had used William Ngidi, an intelligent convert, to help in the difficult task of rendering the text into colloquial Zulu. In the process he had been forced, sentence by sentence, to explain the material to a rational, questioning and mature mind quite untrammeled by any previous instruction. In the light of his own knowledge of geology alone he found he could no longer insist on the veracity of such accounts as that of a universal deluge, and he was now led to examine the entire Pentateuch and the Book of Joshua with a mathematician's eye and a view of reducing popular superstition concerning the literal inspiration of the Bible. Starting with an exhaustive attack on statistical exaggerations and contradictions, he went on to a constructive investigation of the Pentateuch and came to the conclusion that it was actually the work of several authors writing at different times. Such conclusions, which would hardly cause a ripple of comment today, were inflammatory in 1860. In December of 1861, when the balance of this work was done, he published a commentary on St. Paul's Epistle to the Romans in which he attacked orthodox views on atonement and eternal punishment. The article served to alert the citadels of reaction, and the eyes of the High Church began to focus upon him.

In May of 1862 he returned to England for an extended visit, bringing his family with him. Financial considerations concerning his mission work would have justified a visit in any event, but the reaction to his commentary on St. Paul, the approaching publication of his Pentateuchal studies, and the political implications of Gray's concurrent visit demanded his own presence. The last three years had seen a final rupture between the Bishops of Capetown and Natal, and Colenso was of half a mind to abandon his diocese altogether, to move into Zululand to devote his full energies to missionary work.

The atmosphere was already tense when Colenso reached England. The Darwinian controversy was then at its height, and a collection of iconoclastic essays published at Oxford in 1860 had exacerbated High Church emotions still further. The climate was hardly propitious for a fresh attack, and Colenso now committed a major blunder. His work spanned seven volumes, which were to appear at intervals through 1878. The bulk of his devastating analysis of factual errors lay in the first volume, which now appeared some months before the next volume was ready to go to press. Read out of the context of the entire study, the first volume appeared to many to be little more than an attempt to destroy the Bible.

Colenso was fully aware that his material would meet with opposition, and, careful scholar though he was, he had a small boy's delight in shocking others. He could hardly, however, have foreseen the ferocity of the storm that now broke over his head. The few friends who still stood by him quailed before the blast, and the isolated voices who felt he at least had a right to publish his opinions—Matthew Arnold among them—thought it a pity he had not published in Latin. Even Maurice broke with him, and Gray called on the English bishops to bar their pulpits to him. Frances Colenso's own mother refused to write her, and John William Colenso stood accused on every side of heresy, moral degradation, intellectual dishonesty and even plagiarism.

In February of 1863 the English bishops sent him a round robin calling on him to resign, and when he refused to do so, his trial for heresy was a foregone conclusion. Since he had taken his oath of canonical obedience to Gray, he could only be tried in Capetown. Gray was only too happy to oblige, but he proved miserably unsuited for the task. He was determined to eliminate Colenso from the African scene, seeing in him not only a heretic but also the major obstacle to his own goal of establishing an independent Anglican church free of the Erastian shackles of the mother church. He arranged the trial in some haste and with no regard for legal niceties, so far forgetting his judicial responsibilities as to furnish the accusers with some of Colenso's private correspondence to him.

The trial of the Bishop of Natal for erroneous teaching opened in Capetown on November 17, 1863. Colenso, still in England, was represented by proxy in the person of Dr. Wilhelm Bleek (he who had coined the term "Bantu"), who simply protested the legality of the proceedings and reserved the right of appeal. The Bishop was charged with holding improper views on atonement and eternal punishment, with denying that the Bible was the Word of God, and with asserting that it only contained the Word of God. He was accused of maintaining that the Bible was inspired only as other books are inspired, and of having questioned the authenticity of portions of the Old Testament. He was also charged with denying the absolute perfection of Christ by suggesting that Jesus was ignorant and in error over the authorship of the Pentateuch. He was also accused of disparaging the Book of Common Prayer and of inciting his clergy to disobedience. The Bishops of Capetown, Grahamstown and the Orange Free State first met in synod to declare the Faith of the Church on the points at issue, and then met as a court to find Colenso guilty on all counts and to sentence him to deprivation. Gray allowed a fortnight for a personal appeal to the Archbishop of Canterbury (rather than to the ecclesiastical Court of Arches—thus implying that there was no legal appeal to the court he had instituted in Capetown) and then gave Colenso four months to retract, failing which the diocese of Natal would be declared vacant.

Gray's conduct had been headstrong, and elements of public opinion now began to veer to Colenso. Much of the Natal laity rallied to his side, mainly out of opposition to Gray, and such influential newspapers as the London *Times* spoke out in his favor. Waiting until Gray declared the Natal see vacant in April of 1864, Colenso presented his petition to the Queen to set aside the Capetown sentence, and the Judicial Committee of the Privy Council, sitting as a civil rather than an ecclesiastical court, delivered its verdict on March 20, 1865. Bishop Gray's sentence was declared null and void in law.

The decision ignored the doctrinal issues and concerned itself solely with civil rights. It held that Bishop Gray's letters patent of December, 1853, were invalid, thus invalidating his coercive authority as Metropolitan, so that Colenso's oath of canonical obedience conferred no jurisdiction on Gray by which he could impose on him a sentence of deprivation.

While the decision cut the ground out from under Gray and freed Colenso from any question of his control, it also brought to light an unfortunate factor in Colenso's own status. When the instrument which had created the Legislative Council of Natal had been drafted, the usual clause by which the Crown reserved the right of legislation by Order in Council had been omitted, apparently by an oversight.

The Judicial Committee now took the view that Natal had *not* been a Crown Colony but had in fact possessed an independent legislature in 1853 when Colenso's own letters patent had been issued. If this were the case, Natal itself could have granted diocesan status in 1853, and Colenso's letters patent, issued by the Queen, were themselves of questionable validity.

The situation was confusing, and it did not lend itself to a neat legal resolution. Gray had no personal power over Colenso, although as Metropolitan he still had a considerable voice in Natal. Colenso's own status was in doubt, and would take some time to clarify. He now decided to return to Natal to resume his functions, and by November of 1865 he was back at Bishopstowe. Delegations of settlers in Durban and Pietermaritzburg presented him with addresses of welcome, but he was under no illusions about the bitter struggle that still lay ahead.

Dean Green had not been idle. There was a small but influential party of High Church laity in Pietermaritzburg, which now had physical possession of St. Peter's, and Colenso's financial resources, including his bishop's stipend and the contributions from the S.P.G. and the S.P.C.K., stemmed from English bodies which backed Bishop Gray. With the control of their salaries in Bishop Gray's hands, very few of the Natal clergy were in a position to declare for Colenso, no matter what their personal feelings were. Colenso's first problem was to regain access to his cathedral. The doors had been locked and the communion plate removed, and Colenso was obliged to apply to the Supreme Court of Natal for an interdict to restrain Green. His legal right was clear, and the court complied, but Green still held the post of Colonial Chaplain and also had vested rights in St. Peter's. Colenso was unable to evict him completely, and in the future Green held services at nine o'clock while Colenso held his at eleven and in the evening, maintaining his position by a prompt resort to legal aid whenever Green overstepped himself. To regain his stipend Colenso successfully sued Gladstone and the other trustees of the Colonial Bishoprics' Fund. His existence, however, was now tied to a sterile controversy which nullified much of his effectiveness. His funds were more limited than ever, and he hardly dared leave St. Peter's unattended for a single Sunday, so that most of his diocese went unvisited.

Gray continued his efforts to dislodge him, and on January 7, 1866, Green read out his sentence of the Greater Excommunication from the altar steps of St. Peter's, in conformance with which Colenso was "to be taken of the whole multitude of the faithful, as an heathen man and a publican." The move had no effect on Colenso, only making Gray look foolish, but it served to add to his difficulties in Pietermaritzburg, where society was soon split into two camps. Most of the officials, who were all too frequently involved in the dispute through their positions, did their best to remain neutral, although the Shepstones were openly partisan to Colenso.

Since Gray could not evict Colenso, he tried to solve his problem by appointing another bishop, but it was not until 1869 that he managed to install one. There were a number of legal obstacles, and very few candidates cared to assume the formidable burden the new bishopric would obviously entail. The first choice withdrew, but William Macrorie finally accepted the post. Gray had hoped for a Royal Mandate, which would allow his man to challenge Colenso with the backing of the Church at home, but he was unable to secure this, nor could he get Macrorie consecrated in England. In January of 1869, Macrorie was finally consecrated in Capetown as Bishop of Maritzburg; Gray had not dared to take a title from any place that existed in law in the diocese of Natal, and Maritzburg, the colloquial abbreviation for Pietermaritzburg, was as close to the wind as he could sail.

The battle raged for years. Macrorie had hardly been consecrated before Bishop Twells of the Free State was charged in a criminal warrant with pederasty and fled the country in disguise. This was a bitter blow to Gray, since Twells had been one of the three bishops who had condemned Colenso, and he had also assisted at Macrorie's consecration. Green, on the other hand, was reconfirmed as Colonial Chaplain, and a key phrase was removed from a judgment rendered in England whereby Colenso hoped to bar him from St. Peter's. It later developed that the phrase had been removed at Gray's instigation by two of the three judges involved, after judgment had been rendered but before it was published, and still another thread was added to the tangled legal skein of Anglican affairs in southern Africa. By now hardly any of the principals knew where they stood. Various church and civil courts and bodies in England, the Cape Colony and Natal had issued so many opinions, judgments, verdicts and assorted legal instruments with ill-defined jurisdictions and frequently imperfect wordings that the basic issues had long since been lost in a maze of legal technicalities.

Robert Gray died on the first of September, 1872, and much of the bitterness and personal rancor passed from the strife. At the height of the dispute Green's small son had slipped from a wagon and was crushed under a wheel before his mother's horrified eyes. Colenso had then written an unanswered note of sympathy, and years later Green admitted how touched he had been, adding that he had never failed to remember Colenso in his prayers. Pietermaritzburg was by now used to the notoriety of its overlapping bishoprics, and Colenso was a famous tourist attraction. Few visitors failed to attend one of his sermons, usually leaving disappointed not only by his failure to shock them but also by his delivery. His sermons were long, and frequently dull and complicated, and he read through them rapidly in a high-pitched voice, holding the sheets close to his nearsighted eyes. Macrorie proved to be a mild and inoffensive man, with little desire to continue the battle. The two bishops nodded to each other in the street, but otherwise ignored the presence of a rival, and Colenso continued to carry out his duties as best he could.

Beyond the Tugela River lay Zululand, which faced its own problems in the years that Natal was growing. The colony had tacitly dropped the suzerainty over Mpande it had inherited from the Volksraad, and the native kingdom had been permitted to go its own way. The boundary line of the Tugela and the Buffalo Rivers was clear and firm, and it remained remarkably free of the friction which characterized other demarcations between European and native communities. The Zulus, for the first time since Senzangakona's days, were not beset by pressures from within or without, and the natural resilience of the people soon effected a complete recovery from the blows inflicted by the Boers.

Mpande ruled the country from his royal kraal at Nodwengu on the White Umfolozi River. He exercised little direct influence on domestic affairs, but he made a satisfactory figurehead, carrying out the required functions of a Zulu king. He performed the routine ceremonies, dispensed justice in the cases that were brought to his attention, and as the iNtangas came of age, he enrolled them in regiments. Before a decade of his reign had passed he had nominal command of more warriors than Shaka had ever fielded.

His private life followed the pattern Dingane had set. He took full advantage of the amenities offered by the throne, and he grew so fat that in his later years he could not walk and had to be drawn about his kraal by two retainers, seated in a small cart. His interest in his isi-Godlo was as high as Dingane's had been, but Mpande for a change was fertile. He sired 23 sons and a number of daughters.

It was customary for a Zulu of rank to marry a commoner while he was still young. His first-born son, therefore, was not normally his heir; that honour was reserved for the eldest son of his Great Wife, whom he would choose later. Mpande, however, did not follow the normal pattern, and his failure to do so brought him personal tragedy and disaster to his people. He took his first wife about 1825. Her name was Ngqumbhazi, and she was the daughter of a chieftain named Manzini. She had already been married and had an adolescent son, but her husband died and Shaka married her off to Mpande. Such a move, whereby Mpande was expected to "raise seed" for the dead husband, was traditional, and Shaka's choice of his own half brother was a signal honour, but Ngqumbhazi's son, who could hardly have been much younger than his new stepfather, objected, and Shaka had him killed. At the same time Shaka ordered Mpande to marry a woman named Monase; she too had a half-grown son, and he too was killed at Shaka's order. Mpande thus found himself at the age of twenty-one or so married to two childless widows, the first of whom was a chieftain's daughter.

Mpande's first child of his own, by Mgqumbhazi, was a son born about 1827 whom he named Cetshwayo—"the Slandered One." Shortly thereafter Monase bore a son whom he named Mbulazi, in honour of Shaka's friend, Henry Francis Fynn. Both these children were less than two years old when Shaka was killed, and by the time they were twelve or so, Dingane had been killed as well, and their father sat on the Zulu throne.

Mpande married a number of other wives, but he married solely as his fancy struck him and he never took an official Great Wife. He had a total of three sons by Mgqumbhazi, and four sons and three daughters by Monase, and neither he nor any member of the Zulu nation could say with certainty who the heir to the throne was. Cetshwayo was the king's eldest son, and he was the eldest son of the highest-ranking wife, but since his mother was the *first* wife, she could not be the Great Wife, and Cetshwayo was presumably not the heir. Monase, on the other hand, was outranked by the first wife, and had never been declared the Great Wife, but Mpande obviously regarded her as his favorite wife and he treated her eldest son as his favorite child. Until Mpande took a Great Wife, therefore, Mbulazi's claim to the throne was as good as Cetshwayo's.

The situation was impossible, and even Mpande realized that the two women and their respective broods could not be housed in the same kraal. He consequently moved Ngqumbhazi and her children forty miles south to a kraal on the Umhlatuzi River, and Monase and *her* children forty miles north to a kraal on the Black Umfolozi. This solution only postponed the inevitable explosion.

The administrative structure of a Bantu clan was not adapted to the rule of an extensive territory. Based on the personal power of a chieftain who depended on runners and oral messages for his communications, it was centralized at the royal kraal, and only a supremely aggressive personality, such as Shaka had been, could enforce the rule in distant parts. When a lazy man inherited the throne, the central power at once began to pass to strong inDunas in the outlying regions. This process now commenced, and while Mpande was allowed to survive for the sake of peace, various chieftains began to exercise an independence that would have been unthinkable in Shaka's day. As Cetshwayo and Mbulazi grew to manhood, two factions began to coalesce about them. Neither youth at first had need to resort to intrigue, and their respective parties only took gradual shape as the surrounding kraals, with an eye to the future, cast their lot with the nearest potential heir. The factions were finally firm enough to be referred to by name: Cetshwayo's, the *uSuthu*, and Mbulazi's, the *iziGqoza*. By accident of geography as much as anything else, the uSuthu were three times as numerous as the rival iziGqoza.

Mpande continued to form his regiments, and Cetshwayo was duly enrolled in the *uThulwana*, Mbulazi in the *amaShishi*. Some years after the uThulwana were formed, Mpande launched the only military campaign of his reign. He had no positive goal in mind, but the uThulwana wanted experience, and the south was blocked by the British and the west by Boers. The impi therefore raided Swaziland, to the north, in a bloodless foray so mild that even the date has been lost, and the expedition was labeled the *Fund' uThulwana*—"Teach the uThulwana." The amaSwazi prudently retired to the mountains until the impi was gone, and they later sent Mpande a hundred head of cattle to show they held no ill feelings. They had driven the bulk of their herds into the Transvaal until the danger was gone, and they discharged their obligations to the Boers by handing over a number of captured Tonga children to be trained as servants.

Cetshwayo ran true to Senzangakona's line. He was tall and muscular, with finely chiseled features and a regal air. He inherited the royal tendency to fat, but he led an active life and managed to avoid the gross obesity which had overtaken his father and Dingane, his uncle. Sensitive and intelligent, he displayed a considerably better grasp of political reality than his father had done. He could, however, only deal with immediate situations, and the complexities of European civilization were too great for him to extrapolate with certainty. He grew to manhood during a time of Zulu troubles, and he had an innate suspicion of Europeans and especially of Boers. He was deeply imbued with the vanished glories of the Shakan era, and bitterly aware of the contrast between the prestige the Zulus had then enjoyed and the sorry pass his father had brought them to. His attitude toward his father is difficult to judge. He had a distinct element of filial respect, and he never attacked his father directly, but he displayed an open contempt for the manner in which his father chose to rule, and he was utterly ruthless when his own rights of succession were at stake.

Matters came to a head in 1856, when Cetshwayo was close to thirty. Mpande had still not chosen a Great Wife, and even were he to do so at this late date, the leader of the uSuthu would hardly acknowledge an infant three decades his junior as heir apparent. The choice would have to lie between Mbulazi and Cetshwayo.

Each faction mustered the regiments in its own district, and Mbulazi saw at once that his position was critical. His iziGqoza numbered a bare 7,000, while Cetshwayo commanded close to 20,000 uSuthu warriors. He consequently gathered the entire iziGqoza faction—upwards of 30,000 men, women and children—and raced south to the mouth of the Tugela River, with the startled Cetshwayo close on his heels.

The move was born of desperation. Mbulazi knew a fight was inevitable, and although he commanded tough, older Zulus from a rocky, thorn-strewn country, he was heavily outnumbered. He now hoped for a measure of support from the government of Natal and, failing that, to place his adherents within the reach of safety if the fight went against him. He also had Mpande's support for what little it was worth; his father had dispatched the one or two regiments whose loyalty he still commanded to his aid, and no less than six of Mpande's sons, including three of Monase's, were aligned with the iziGqoza.

Natal watched the crisis with growing alarm. Frightened Zulu refugees slipped across the Tugela during the last days of November, and two British traders, Waugh and Rathbone, abandoned an enormous herd of cattle they had been driving toward the Lower Drift and fled to safety. The river was rising, but nothing stood between the Lower Drift and the city of Durban should the victors take it into their heads to sack the harbor, as Dingane had done twenty years before.

Over 20,000 dependents were huddled on the banks of a small stream that tumbled down a ravine into the Tugela River by the 'Ndondakusuka kraal, at the spot where John Cane lost his life on his ill-fated expedition. The iziGqoza impi was posted just beyond them, passively awaiting the advance of the uSuthu forces, who were still some miles away. Mbulazi and two of his brothers now crossed the river to confer with Walmsley, who had been drinking and was in a panic at the thought of what was coming. Shepstone was on his way from Pietermaritzburg, and Walmsley declined to involve the administration and sent the Zulus back. At the last minute he gave John Dunn permission to accompany them, perhaps with some vague idea that he could stave off a battle. Dunn took a small party of the mounted natives who served Walmsley as a police force and joined the iziGqoza.

Dunn had no business in Zululand, and had Shepstone arrived a day earlier he would never have permitted him to cross. He hardly had official status, but he was a European in Walmsley's pay, and his presence with the few armed Natal Kaffirs who accompanied him placed Natal squarely on the side of the iziGqoza. His force was far too feeble to serve as a peacemaker or to affect the outcome, and he himself was sure to be drawn into the fight.

The uSuthu arrived on December 2, 1856. Cetshwayo led the center, while his younger half brother Uhamu led one wing and a Boer named Christian Groening, who had somehow attached himself to Cetshwayo, led the other. Dunn urged Mbulazi to move his impi inland, to avoid being pinned against the river, but the iziGqoza cause was lost before the battle started. A puff of wind lifted Mbulazi's ostrich plume out of his headdress and cast it on the ground, and his appalled warriors awaited the onslaught in dumb terror. Dunn rode forward to scout, and watched a black thread crest the line of a distant hill and thicken into a tide that darkened the slopes. He waited until the last moment, fired a few shots, and then retired through the ranks of the iziGqoza as a short and violent battle started. By the time he reached the riverbank, the fighting was over and the slaughter of the dependents had started.

During the next hour the killing reached a peak that Africa had probably never witnessed before. Dunn fought his way through a crowd of hysterical women who offered him their babies, past masses of children and aged men and women caught between the maddened uSuthu and the flooding river. He stripped at the water's edge and plunged in, carrying his rifle and holding on to the tail of the big white horse he had borrowed from Walmsley. A small punt rescued him in midstream, and the crew beat off other frantic swimmers who had chosen the river and who now threatened to swamp the boat. Not a single survivor of the battle, nor any of the dependents, were spared ashore. The entire iziGqoza faction perished, including all six of Mpande's sons. Thousands of bodies littered the sands at the mouth of the Tugela, and they washed up on the coast for weeks afterward as far south as Durban. The stream at 'Ndondakusuka was marked for decades by a great white smear of skeletons, and was forever after known as the *Mathambo*—"the Place of Bones."

One of the few survivors was an infant girl that Walmsley fished out of the river. Maria Walmsley adopted the child and raised it as her own. She learned to speak French and to play the piano, and when she reached maturity, she married a Zulu and moved into his kraal. The Walmsleys, heartbroken, could only demand a high lobola, to insure her a good status in her new life.

Cetshwayo withdrew with his victorious uSuthu, and the immediate danger of a raid into Natal passed. There remained the problem of the cattle which Waugh and Rathbone had abandoned and which Cetshwayo had taken with him. The traders had influence in Pietermaritzburg and they threatened to sue the government, claiming that Dunn's interference had occasioned the loss. Henry Francis Fynn, now back in

Natal and serving as a magistrate, made an effort to recover them, but he was unable to meet with Cetshwayo. Dunn then offered to go himself.

It was a brave move that verged on rashness. Dunn's support of the iziGqoza had been quite open, and there was nothing to hinder Cetshwayo had he chosen to kill him out of hand. Dunn, however, wanted the £250 reward that had been offered for the cattle, and unless he could make his peace with Cetshwayo, Zululand would be closed to him forever. He slipped across the Tugela with a wagon and a half-dozen retainers, leaving them at Eshowe and pushing on with his headman to Mpande's kraal. The king was pathetically glad to see him, grateful for Dunn's support at 'Ndondakusuka and eager for detailed news of the battle in which so many of his sons had died.

Dunn then went on to Cetshwayo's kraal, sending his headman to announce his arrival. The meeting was tense, although Cetshwayo proved to be magnanimous and friendlier than his inDunas. Dunn disarmed them by greeting Cetshwayo with the royal salute of "Bayede!" and heaping praise on the conduct of the uThulwana. When he left three days later, he had the cattle, and he had won Cetshwayo's respect as well.

A few months later Cetshwayo invited him to return and settle in Zululand. The offer was unusual, and Dunn's status was to differ from that of the score or so of traders and mission workers whose presence in the land was tolerated. Cetshwayo was determined to succeed his father, and after his victory over Mbulazi no rival dared raise his voice. He now felt the need for an official adviser who might guide him in his relations with the two European civilizations that flanked the kingdom he hoped to rule. His father had paid craven fealty first to the Boers of the Natal Republic—who now threatened Zululand from the Transvaal—and then to the British who had replaced the Boers in Natal. Mpande was patently incapable of fending off either power, and Cetshwayo, throned or not, would brook no incursions. Dunn, a European, would presumably understand the workings of both powers, and he could read such diplomatic messages as found their way to his kraal and draft the replies.

The idea was sound, but Cetshwayo could hardly be blamed for his failure to see that the very qualities that made Dunn attractive to him at the same time barred him from any future influence in Natal. Neither his liaison with Catherine Pierce nor his lack of education appeared an obstacle to Cetshwayo, who naturally was unable to judge how seriously such social stigmas would impede his acceptance in European circles. He offered Dunn a large tract of country along the coast north of the Tugela, with the full rights of a chieftain, and

Dunn accepted with delight. The land had been thinly populated since Mawa's flight, but it abounded in game, and hunting was his passion. He brought in Catherine and her children, building for her a crude mud hut that was the first of a series of increasingly imposing residences. For the first few years he spent most of his time hunting, but he enjoyed the favor of both Mpande and Cetshwayo, and he gradually acquired adherents and cattle. Within a decade he was wealthy, and he ruled over kraals with a population of more than 10,000 Zulus.

Over Catherine's futile protests, he began to take Zulu wives, paying lobola for them and settling them in new homesteads when they clashed with Catherine. The total was never established, but at his death 49 wives and 116 children figured in his will.

He soon attained a position in Zululand that made him a power in the land. Cetshwayo sent for him on every occasion, and he exercised a considerable force for moderation at the Zulu court. The men in his kraals were exempt from the regimental call-ups, and although he was far too astute to build an independent military force of his own, which might have become a factor in Zulu politics, he maintained a small band of retainers armed with rifles. He aped the life of the English landed gentry, driving expensive carriages with carefully matched teams. He set a good table, serving a favorite mixture of champagne and claret to the numerous sportsmen who visited him. He visited Natal freely, putting up at the Royal Hotel in Durban, and if no single drawing room in the colony would receive him, his life was the scandalized envy of most of the male population.

Colenso despised him, but Shepstone, who treated him with a cold civility, found him fairly useful. Dunn would have liked to deal with the Secretary for Native Affairs as an equal—one foreign minister to another, as it were—but Shepstone never gave him the chance. Shepstone used him as an informant, playing on the British citizenship which Dunn never quite dared to renounce.

Cetshwayo now entered a period during which he exercised practical control of much of the kingdom. He was content to await his father's natural death, keeping a wary eye on his still-numerous half brothers, and acting to consolidate his position when he felt it was necessary and he could afford to do so. No one dared to counter him, but each half brother and every distant chieftain was still a potential rival. The strongest of these dwelt in the north: Uhamu, who had fought with him at 'Ndondakusuka, Umnyamana, and a distant cousin named Mapita. They were too weak to attack Cetshwayo but too strong to be destroyed; Mpande allowed them to continue in semi-independence, and Cetshwayo could only watch them and wonder.

Lesser fry to the south were in greater danger. Mpande sneaked Monase's last surviving son, Mkungo, across the Tugela, where with Shepstone's blessings he was entered in Colenso's school at Ekukanyeni. Two other youngsters, Sikhota and Sikhungu, also found shelter in Natal. Mpande, still unwilling to confirm Cetshwayo's position as heir apparent with his official sanction, then began to show marked attention to still another wife, Nomantshali, without reckoning the possible cost to her children. Cetshwayo stood it until 1860, and then sent an impi to wipe her out. She and her daughters died, but her two eldest sons, Mtonga and Mgidhlana, escaped to the Transvaal and sought refuge with the Boers. This left the youngest, Mpoyana, barely twelve years old. He got away from his mother's kraal just as the uSuthu impi arrived, but was hunted down in the White Umfolozi valley and taken to Mpande's kraal at Nodwengu. The king was seated in his cattle pen when the party of warriors entered with their captive. He rose to greet his son, and before his eyes the uSuthu picked the lad up and hurled him against a hut so violently that he arose bleeding from the ear. He was killed on the spot, weeping and protesting that one so young could never dispute the succession.

Cetshwayo was still not satisfied. The refugees in Natal he ignored, but Mtonga in the Transvaal had been Mpande's favorite, and he was mature and agile. The leader of the uSuthu could not rest easy until he had scotched him, and he now commenced a dangerous three-cornered game he was ill equipped to play. In order to follow the subsequent events, it will be necessary to look briefly at the fortunes of the trek Boers after they left Natal.

After his defeat in the Vlug Kommando in 1838, Potgieter had taken his people back to the high veld and had settled at Rustenburg, far across the Vaal River. Here he encountered the same difficulties that had once beset Trigardt; he was deep inland and too isolated from the minimal commerce he needed to survive. In 1845 he shifted eastward to the Lydenburg district, where friendly relations with the Portuguese at Delagoa Bay promised him a chance of eventual access to the sea. He was still far to the north, with the Swazi nation between him and Zululand, and he had moved into an area inhabited by a miscellany of clans too weak to oppose him. The strongest of these were the baPedi (connected to the clan whose four-breasted chieftainess had killed Zwide), and their heir apparent was a young man named Sekukuni. Like most trekker republics, that of Lydenburg had an ineffectual government and no clear idea of its own boundaries. Its Volksraad, however, wanted at least a nominal claim to the land it occupied, so over Potgieter's protests it sent a deputation to the Swazi king to negotiate a sale. The delegation returned with a treaty in which the Swazi king sold the Lydenburg Republic all the land north of the twenty-sixth parallel of southern latitude, south of the Olifants River, and inland from the sea to the Elands River. The price was a hundred head of cattle, fifty to be delivered within the month, and the balance within two years. Very little of this territory belonged to the ama-Swazi—some was claimed by Portugal and the rest was occupied by other clans.

Late in 1847 Andries Pretorius led the bulk of the Natal Boers back to the high veld. Sir Harry Smith, Governor of the Cape Colony, met him in Natal just as he was going and tried to induce him to stay. Failing to stop him, on February 3, 1848, he annexed all the territory between the Orange and the Vaal Rivers as the Orange River Sovereignty. Pretorius was enraged. He had led his people out of the Cape Colony to get away from the British; he had beaten off the Matabele and then entered Natal; there he had fought the British as well as the Zulus, and now he found the inexorable Crown established over his latest refuge. He called up 400 men and drove the British administrator out of Bloemfontein, and breathed defiance until the British returned in August and defeated him at Boomplaats. He was now outlawed, and he took his people north of the Vaal, into the area Potgieter had lately vacated.

There the matter rested for four years. The most intransigent of the trek Boers were now all north of the Vaal, beyond British rule if not beyond British claims, and they were soon engaged in the depressing strife that accompanied all their attempts to govern themselves. The Orange River Sovereignty, on the other hand, was under British administration, which many of the trek Boers, weary of the years of wandering, now welcomed. Those who were still intractable moved north of the Vaal, and those that remained were soon joined by many of their Cape Colony brethren, who had long been reconciled to Crown rule. While trek Boers were thus in the majority both in the Orange River Sovereignty and north of the Vaal River, there was a decided difference in the temper of the two areas.

English policy in these years had finally veered. It had long fluctuated with every succeeding administration, but it now took a permanent set which reflected the rising influence of the middle classes. It was, in fact, a business policy which was no longer willing to see money spent on philanthropic projects in distant parts far beyond British borders. On February 17, 1852, British commissioners signed the Sand River Convention, and the trek Boers north of the Vaal were finally released from their unwanted status as British subjects and were at long last free to go their own way. Two years later the Orange

River Sovereignty was abandoned as well, and the territory became the
Orange Free State.

The subsequent history of these two areas is long and complicated.
There were for a time four separate republics north of the Vaal, until a
single—although hardly stable—government was formed in 1860. This
South African Republic, usually referred to as the Transvaal, was
marked even more than the Orange Free State by a large and ill-
defined territory, a scattered and individualistic population, and a weak
and disputatious central government. Border wars, native disturbances
and civil strife proliferated, and both areas slowly sank into a poverty-
stricken impotence. The story is of importance to the history of the
present Republic of South Africa, but it is not germane to the history
of the Zulu nation, and we shall confine our attention to the area of the
Transvaal that abutted on Zululand.

In the treaty which he had signed with Mpande in 1843, Cloete had
defined the line of the Tugela and the Buffalo Rivers as the boundary
between Natal and Zululand. There had been no mention of Zululand's
other boundaries, nor had the Sand River Convention defined the area
of Boer independence in any other terms than "beyond the Vaal
River." There was, as a result, no firm boundary between Zululand and
the Lydenburg Republic, and about 1847 a Boer named Cornelius van
Rooyen, with a few companions, obtained permission from Mpande to
settle near the headwaters of the Buffalo River on the Zulu side. He
was thus out of Natal, in a verdant area sparsely settled with Zulus, and
about 1855 he moved to secure his tenure. In return for the usual
hundred head of cattle, Mpande put his mark on a carelessly worded
title ceding Van Rooyen the long wedge of land between the Buffalo
and the Blood Rivers, and the line then ran across country from the
headwaters of the Blood River to a point on the Pongola River, which
was generally accepted as the northern boundary of Zululand and to
the north of which the Boers had also been moving toward the sea.
This was the Utrecht District, which was now united to Potgieter's
Lydenburg Republic, and it was to this area that Mtonga and his
brother fled.

Cetshwayo wanted Mtonga back at any price, and the Boers always
wanted land. Although he was not in a position to speak for the Zulu
nation—and even had he been, he had no right to alienate tribal land—
Cetshwayo now offered the Boers of the Utrecht District a large strip
of territory in return for the surrender of the fugitives, and the offer
was accepted with alacrity. At the end of March, 1861, Marthinus
Pretorius, son of Andries and President of the South African Republic,
which had by now absorbed the Lydenburg Republic, signed the
Treaty of Waaihoek, changing the border between Zululand and the

Transvaal. The northern end still lay at the same point on the Pongola River, but the southern end was advanced from the headwaters of the Blood River to a point far down the Buffalo River, near Rorke's Drift. Cetshwayo for his part agreed not to harm Mtonga or his brother, and for good measure promised to leave his father in peace and not to cause bloodshed in Zululand or across its borders. Mpande, for the consideration of 25 cows, a bull and a saddled horse, confirmed the transaction.

Theophilus Shepstone watched these transactions with growing alarm. The first decade of his activity had been devoted to the Natal Kaffirs, who were now more or less in hand, and until the fight at 'Ndondakusuka, Cetshwayo had not been a factor in his dealings with the complacent Mpande. After 1856, however, Mpande lost what little control he enjoyed, and Shepstone was faced with the problem of winning Cetshwayo's amity. Without it Natal would face a large and hostile native kingdom on its northern border, and unless the amity extended to a measure of control as well, Zululand might quite likely embroil itself with the Transvaal. The idea was anathema to Shepstone, whose policies also included the aim of cutting the various Boer republics off from access to the sea. The day of reckoning might be decades away, but he knew that Zululand could not be permitted to survive indefinitely as an independent power, and when it fell, it must go to Natal and not to the Transvaal Boers.

Cetshwayo was hardly aware of such long-range designs on the kingdom he had not yet inherited, but he was fully conscious of the hostility between Natal and the Transvaal, and he was in an excellent position to play one off against the other. He had no intention of giving either of his European neighbors control of Zululand, but he wanted the support of both to secure his own precarious position and he knew that both sides were eager to cultivate his friendship. Even with Mtonga safely tucked away in a guarded kraal, there were still a number of possible claimants. Uhamu was unassailable in the north, Mkungo was at Bishopstowe, and still two more half brothers were somewhere in Natal. There was a rumor afoot that Mpande intended to divide his kingdom amongst all his sons, a thought that drove Cetshwayo to distraction, and there was nothing to balance the growing Boer influence on his northern border. Cetshwayo turned to Natal.

He had lately acquired a number of Basuto ponies, and some of his warriors could now ride. In July, three months after the Treaty of Waaihoek, a rumor swept Natal that a Zulu impi was about to raid Bishopstowe to kidnap Mkungo. The story was firm enough to move volunteer troops to the border, and a sudden alarm forced Colenso and his family to evacuate their home in the middle of the night and seek shelter in Pietermaritzburg. He broke up the school and hid Mkungo in a nearby kraal, and because he was about to leave for England, he did not reconvene the school.

Shepstone now retrieved Natal's position by a master stroke. He entered Zululand with his son Henrique and a few retainers and traveled straight to Mpande's kraal at Nodwengu. Here he offered to *beka* Cetshwayo—to proclaim him heir apparent in the name of the Queen. Mpande accepted and sent for Cetshwayo, who came accompanied by John Dunn and his own inDunas. Cetshwayo was overjoyed; such a proclamation not only implied the support of Natal, but would also shore up his position in Zululand itself. Only his own inDunas hung back. They saw no need for Natal's blessing on their chieftain; it appeared to them to be a gratuitous intrusion into their domestic affairs, and Shepstone, for all his prestige, was a European and a commoner with no royal right to proclaim heirs apparent. One of Shepstone's inDunas had, furthermore, been caught wandering about Mpande's isiGodlo, a transgression which merited instant death, and for a while Shepstone's position looked grim. There was a stormy inDaba, at which Mpande for once exerted himself and Shepstone summoned every rhetorical device at his command. The impasse was finally solved by investing Shepstone with the spirit of Shaka, a dubious device even by Bantu standards, and Cetshwayo was duly proclaimed in the position he had fought for so long. John Dunn, assuming from Mpande and Cetshwayo that the matter was settled, wandered off before the final session, and Shepstone never forgave him for leaving him and his young son in what he chose to regard as mortal danger.

Shepstone was not content to leave well enough alone. His journey would easily have won Cetshwayo's friendship, but he now tried for the control he would eventually need as well. He boldly picked up the long-dormant suzerainty of the Republic of Natal over Zululand, and made a patronizing speech in which he cautioned Cetshwayo to conduct himself properly in the future, warning him that he would tolerate no injustice in his rule. The implication was that Cetshwayo was only the heir on Shepstone's sufferance, and while the attitude might have impressed a Natal Kaffir, it left a bad taste at an independent court. Cetshwayo could only sit and listen.

The next few years were quiet, marred only by a smallpox epidemic that ravaged the country in 1863. Then, in 1864, Mtonga fled to Natal. Cetshwayo had scrupulously adhered to his promise not to harm him, but Mtonga could hardly have found life restful within reach of his ruthless relative. Shepstone received him warmly, as a useful pawn for future combinations, and he blandly refused Cetshwayo's demand that he be returned. Pretorius, however, rightly fearing that Cetshwayo would now repudiate the Treaty of Waaihoek, took immediate steps to beacon off the border. Under one of the quirks of Boer politics, he had been serving as President of the Orange Free State as well as of the Transvaal Republic, and he had been occupied of late with internal revolts and a clash with Mshweshwe's Basuto. He now proceeded to Zululand, and with a delegation of Boers personally rode the length of the new line, accompanied by a Zulu chieftain named Sihayo, who lived across from Rorke's Drift at the southern end of the line. To prevent any misunderstandings, Pretorius insisted that the Zulus place the first stone in each pile before his men built up the beacon. Shepstone, usually so well informed, did not learn about the beacons for more than twelve years.

In October of 1872 Mpande died of the infirmities of age—the last of Senzangakona's sons and the only one of the twelve who reached maturity to die peacefully in his own kraal. The last years of his life had been fruitful ones for the nation, and the old monarch in his lassitude had been granted affection if not respect. A peace of 32 years had been broken only by the fight at 'Ndondakusuka, the kraals were flourishing, and the cattle had long since made good the losses from the Boer depredations. All the men between twenty and sixty years of age were enrolled in regiments which could be mobilized in a few days, and the nation was more powerful than it had ever been before.

Cetshwayo was now about forty-five years old and at last free to reign as king. He made, however, no immediate move to mount the throne that was rightfully his. By normal Bantu usage, the head inDuna of a dead chieftain could proclaim the eldest son of the Great Wife the new ruler, and the entire population of the clan would be at hand to accept or reject the choice. The transfer of power was in any event a critical moment for the heir, who might be opposed on the spot by anyone who felt he had a better claim, or who simply felt stronger, and for Cetshwayo the tension was enormously heightened by the sheer size of his domain and his inability to sound the temper of distant parts.

His troubles started even before Mpande was dead. Moved, apparently, only by filial devotion, Mtonga slipped out of Natal and sped to Nodwengu to visit his dying father. With Cetshwayo's spies on his heels, and frantic messengers from Shepstone searching for him as well, the elusive rival then raced to the Transvaal Republic, leaving Cetshwayo precisely where he had been in 1863 and all his troubles with the border Boers for naught.

Cetshwayo's claim to the throne was pre-eminent, but his uSuthu were by no means the only nor even the strongest faction in Zululand. Uhamu and Umnyamana in the north were still unknown factors, and even though Uhamu had fought beside his half brother at 'Ndondaku-suka, he had since been given strong reasons to mistrust Cetshwayo. He dwelt in the area affected by the Treaty of Waaihoek, which Cetshwayo had long since repudiated. Mpande had eventually with-drawn his approval as well, probably at Cetshwayo's instigation, and had returned the purchase price to Pretorius. The dispute, however, by now far surpassed a simple question of whether or not a treaty concerning a beaconed line was valid. There had been few Boers and fewer Zulus in the disputed territory in 1861, but it was now dotted with scores of kraals and dozens of Boer homesteads. Each homestead had come to its own terms with the nearest kraals, and there were tacit agreements, verbal agreements and written agreements, some of them graced by payment of sorts and others not. Some of the written agree-ments were illegible, or if legible so vaguely worded as to be meaning-less, and others bore signatures and marks, Boer and Zulu, that could not be identified. Many had come to the attention of neither Mpande nor Cetshwayo, nor even of Uhamu, the chieftain most directly con-cerned. Mpande himself had followed the outlines of Cetshwayo's game, and, unable to oppose him openly, had been sly enough to stir up trouble by roiling the already chaotic border situation.

Mapita had also brought his regiments to Cetshwayo in 1856, but he had since died and had been succeeded by his daring and resolute son Usibebu. This chieftain had so far managed to avoid declaring for any candidate; he commanded the strongest faction of all, and his kraals would follow him whichever way he chose to go.

To add to Cetshwayo's other worries, a rumor now sprang up that Mbulazi had not really been killed at 'Ndondakusuka, but had been living secretly in Natal since 1856 and was now about to enter Zulu-land as a British candidate for the throne. Cetshwayo had ordered him flayed alive and crucified on an anthill after the battle, but the story of his impending return spread like a grass fire.

There was still a period of grace during the protracted funeral ar-rangements, and Cetshwayo took immediate steps to strengthen his position. Apparently ignoring the vacant throne, he sent for John Dunn a few days after Mpande's death and announced his intention of raiding the amaSwazi. Dunn talked him out of this project, using the argument that the amaSwazi were equipped with firearms and the Zulus were not, and Cetshwayo promptly bade him procure guns in Natal. Dunn went to Shepstone and urged Cetshwayo's case, pointing out that a few guns would not add appreciably to the power of the Zulu nation, but they would enormously strengthen the uSuthu and thus reduce the chances of civil strife over the succession. Shepstone

agreed, and Dunn returned with 150 rifles, with another hundred coming later. When it eventually became apparent that several thousand
Zulus were armed with rifles, Dunn was naturally accused of gunrun-
ning. He denied the charges hotly, and, while he undoubtedly
smuggled in several score for use as gifts, the bulk of the charges were
probably unjust. Most of the guns came in through Delagoa Bay, as did
those that went to the amaSwazi, for the Portuguese had fewer
scruples than the British.

With Mkungo and possibly Mbulazi in Natal, Mtonga in the Transvaal, with both European powers eying the disputed territory and
mistrustful of each other, and with Uhamu's and Umnyamana's loyalty
uncertain, Cetshwayo saw that the only solution to his problems lay in
choosing one of his European neighbors as a protector. If the decision
was hard to reach, the choice was easy. In February of 1873 Dunn
accompanied Zulu messengers who asked Shepstone to "establish what
is wanting among the Zulu people, for he knows all about it and
occupies the position of father to the King's children." The only written account of this oral request stems from Shepstone, who was not
above embellishing such items, and it ends with the highly suspect
request that Natal occupy the disputed territory to insure peace between Zululand and the Transvaal. Shepstone, always eager to check
the Boers, had lately broached this very idea himself, seeing in the
border district a safety valve for his always overcrowded reserves.

Nothing could have pleased the Secretary of Native Affairs more
than this invitation to crown the King of the Zulus in the name of
England's Queen, and he made elaborate preparations to comply. He
sent his son Henrique as far afield as Capetown to purchase suitable
gifts, and the master tailor of the Natal garrison, working with ostrich
plumes, scarlet dye, and contributions from the wardrobe of a traveling opera company, turned out a robe and a tinsel crown of imposing
regality. He also collected an enormous marquee and a pair of carved
oak office chairs. When he entered Zululand late in July, his escort
included over one hundred men of the Victoria Mounted Rifles, the
Alexandra Mounted Rifles and the Richmond Mounted Rifles, and the
Durban Volunteer Artillery brought both its cannon. The artillery had
splendid uniforms, but no horses, and the fieldpieces were towed behind ox wagons. There was also a brass band.

By early August the various factions had started to converge on the
royal seat at Mahlabatini, accompanied by all the regiments from their
respective districts, much of the population, and all of the royal cattle.
Progress was slow, and the groups killed time by hunting as they
sought out news of the other groups.

John Dunn had purchased the finest barouche to be had in Durban, equipped it with four of his best grays, and presented it to Cetshwayo as a royal carriage. He also hired a photographer. Then, just as the uSuthu were about to start, Dunn's eldest son fell seriously ill and he informed Cetshwayo he could not leave the bedside. Cetshwayo at once sent his own witch doctors and a large black ox which was ritually slaughtered in front of Dunn's house. His disgusted protests were stilled when the boy rallied at once and demanded to be carried to the door to witness the ceremony.

The cavalcade finally got under way, traveling a few miles each day and camping in a sprawling bivouac at night. Cetshwayo slept in a tent which Dunn provided, and he rode for a part of each day in the carriage. Dunn was barely able to restrain him from racing ahead; the grays were much faster than the decrepit nags the inDunas were riding, and Dunn was suspected of wanting to spirit Cetshwayo away in order to clear the path for a British candidate. All the game was flushed and slaughtered, and it never returned to the level of the past.

The uSuthu reached the royal valley a few days before the northern factions, and Dunn discovered that no one had any idea of what was to be done. There were no plans, and because there were no precedents, no one was willing to make any suggestions.

On the final morning Dunn rode forward with Cetshwayo and his inDunas, with all the uSuthu regiments strung out behind them in a vast half-circle. Cetshwayo was considerably more confident than Dunn, who noted that the warriors carried drill sticks instead of assegais. Presently they encountered Uhamu and Umnyamana with their warriors, and, off to the side and slightly behind, Usibebu with his impi. The three factions cautiously drew together, and when Usibebu's men suddenly broke into a run to close the distance, the uSuthu grew nervous and began to huddle into a military formation. Dunn urged Cetshwayo to send messengers to stop Usibebu, and the impi finally slowed. The three chieftains at last met in the center to greet one another, and the tension broke at once. The others had come in peace, and within minutes Cetshwayo's succession to the throne was finally certain.

The same slow procedure now started again. Shepstone had barely crossed the border, and the closer he came the higher the tension mounted. His armed escort had been noted, and despite the denial he sent ahead, the entire Zulu nation was ready to believe that he had Mbulazi with him. The pressure served to unify the factions, and when Shepstone was still a day or two away, Masipula, the aged inDuna who had served first Dingane and then Mpande as prime minister, proclaimed Cetshwayo king. That same night he told Dunn that his work was finished, and he died before the morning, but his proclamation had in effect solved the problem that brought Shepstone to Zululand, and his presence was now redundant.

Cetshwayo balked at meeting Somtseu, but he did not quite dare to break off. He first called for a delay of four days to bury Masipula, and he then began to shift his camp from day to day; this spot was unsuitable, that one inauspicious. Shepstone, his dignity and his patience alike at an end, was forced to shift as well, finally finding himself on the site of one of Cetshwayo's recent encampments, which offal and muddied water made most distasteful. Dunn was at last able to arrange a meeting, and Cetshwayo submitted to what followed.

On September 1, 1873, in the presence of a vast concourse, Shepstone placed his toy crown on Cetshwayo's headring and proclaimed him king of the Zulu nation in the name of Queen Victoria. Still wearing Shaka's ghostly mantle, he then assumed an authority that was not rightfully his, and proclaimed the principles by which he expected Cetshwayo to reign.

On this of all days, Shepstone chose to work through an interpreter. The assembled chieftains of the nation were informed that the indiscriminate shedding of blood in the land would cease. In the future no Zulu would be condemned to death without an open trial and the public examination of witnesses, and if condemned he would have the right of appeal to the king. No Zulu's life was to be taken without the knowledge and consent of the king, and for minor crimes the loss of property was to be substituted for the punishment of death. The material was delivered in the form of a series of rhetorical questions, to which the chieftains could only reply with the customary "*Vuma!* (We agree!)"

It was an audacious performance, the climax of Shepstone's distinguished career in Bantu politics. Shepstone was attempting nothing less than the application of the Native Customary Law of Natal to the independent kingdom of Zululand, which, in the eyes of the British government, was thus reduced to the level of one of Shepstone's own Natal Kaffir reserves. He had delivered a similar admonishment a decade earlier; Cetshwayo then had little choice but to listen, but he was now surrounded by the full might of his kingdom, and Shepstone had no hold over him beyond the control he could establish by the sheer weight of his personality. That was still a considerable force, however, and Cetshwayo again listened in silence. In private, however, he raged at being treated like a child.

He had not the slightest intention of adopting Shepstone's guidelines, which would have constituted a serious impediment to the exercise of his royal prerogatives, nor was he taken in by the ceremony Shepstone had designed with such care. He saw the ludicrous crown for the gimcrack bauble it was, and he was not mollified by the tawdry gifts that Henrique had picked up in Capetown. He had been accorded the royal salute of "Bayede!" by Uhamu and Usibebu, and this was worth more than the seventeen rounds fired by the Durban Volunteer Artillery. Under the circumstances, it was probably just as well that he did not know that royalty was entitled to twenty-one rounds; even an ambassador rated nineteen.

Cetshwayo then discussed another matter. Neither the Natal reserves nor the growing stream of Indian labor could cope with the expanding demands of the sugar-cane industry, and the diamond fields and the gold mines on the high veld were draining off much of the labor that was available. The Zulus themselves would provide no recruits, but the amaTonga, a subordinate tribe in the fever-ridden lands around St. Lucia Bay, were willing to work. John Dunn offered to convoy contract labor parties across Zululand to Natal for a salary of £300 a year and his expenses. Shepstone would only promise to recommend the appointment to the Legislative Council, a suggestion which annoyed Cetshwayo, who regarded the choice as a domestic decision involving one of his own inDunas. In the event, Dunn was confirmed in the post, but Shepstone was uneasy about the influence he obviously commanded at the Zulu court, and he made it clear in writing that he would never recognize Dunn as an independent power in Zululand.

Then Shepstone and his escort left, and before the Secretary of Native Affairs was back across the Tugela, the first Zulu had been killed. A petty chieftain stole a supply of chlorodyne from the coronation presents; he was caught, convicted out of hand by the nearest inDunas, and executed with a knobkerrie.

Cetshwayo established his royal kraal at Ulundi, on the gentle slopes that rose from the broad valley of the White Umfolozi, and settled down to review his cattle. There were over 100,000 of them, and Dunn grew inexpressibly bored as the endless herds streamed past. Within the year more than half were dead. A few cows brought lung sickness to the review, and the disease spread through the land when the herds returned to their local kraals. The nation's cattle never recovered from this blow, and Cetshwayo's royal vanity accomplished what the greed of the trek Boers had failed to do.

The coronation was over, and Cetshwayo ruled a united nation which was, on the whole loyal and happy to see him replace his father. Except for the quarrel with the border Boers, Zululand had no enemies without nor any problems of domestic significance. Shepstone returned to Natal deeply impressed with Cetshwayo: he was intelligent and forceful; his attitude was respectful, and he was infinitely more sophisticated than his father had been.

In 1816 Shaka had started to forge the Zulu nation, and in 1873, 57 years later, his nephew came to the throne of the most powerful nation in all of black Africa. The omens were auspicious, but before the year was out, events had been set in train which in six short years would destroy the kingdom. The first act was over.

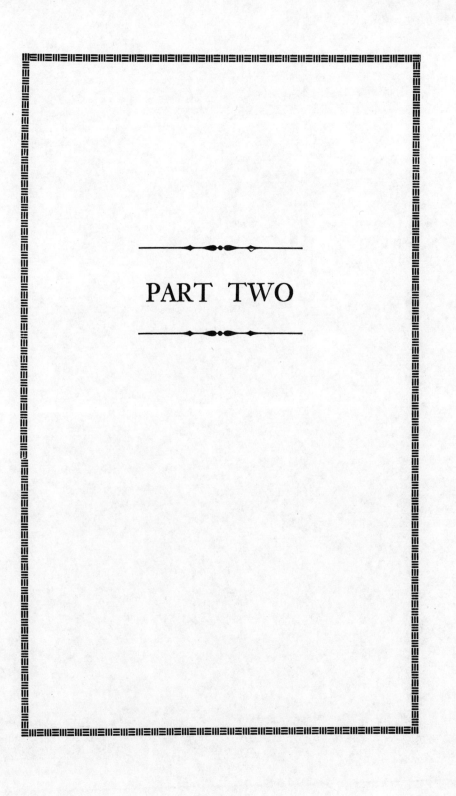

PART TWO

CONFEDERATION

WHEN Theophilus Shepstone returned to Natal in September of 1873, his reputation was brighter than ever. His work on the Natal reserves had by now spanned almost thirty years, marred only by the all-but-forgotten Matyana incident, and he had capped his service by entering Zululand on invitation to crown the absolute monarch of the most powerful independent native kingdom in southern Africa. No one dared question such a man, and certainly not the new Lieutenant Governor, Sir Benjamin Chilley Campbell Pine, who was chiefly noted for the continual rumors of concubinage that gathered in his wake. A nod from the powerful Secretary for Native Affairs could make or break a career in Natal, and it was high honour to be counted one of his friends—the more so because he had few if any intimates.

The Colensos numbered themselves among the fortunate few. Shepstone, born a Wesleyan, had joined the Church of England on his marriage, and bishop and bureaucrat were in accord on most issues. Their mutual respect had grown with the years; Colenso found in Shepstone one of the few colonial officials with a genuine empathy for the Bantu civilization to which both men had given so much of their working lives, and Shepstone's position was sufficiently secure to enable him to provide the Bishop with a warm and generous support that made up for many of the official slights to which the family was subjected. Colenso invariably stopped at the Shepstone household each Sunday on his way to take the late morning service at St. Peter's, and he had reason to feel he knew the taciturn and reserved Secretary as well as any man in Natal.

These ties extended to the children. There were a half-dozen Shepstone sons and two daughters, much of an age with the Colenso brood, and they formed part of the small circle with which Robert and Francis Ernst Colenso rode and hunted until they left to be educated in England.

Another close friend was Henry Charles Harford, the son of an army captain who lived in the colony. Harford and the Colenso boys shared a passion for natural history, and Harford went so far as to become proficient in Zulu, as were all the Colenso children, before he too returned to England and a military career. Neither Robert nor Frank Colenso had received the classical polish their father had before his own matriculation, and there was some doubt as to their ability to meet English academic standards. Robert, however, returned to Natal as a doctor, and Frank as a lawyer.

Harriet, the eldest daughter, was known as Harry to the family and uDhlwedhlwe—"the Staff"—of her father—to the natives. "Devoid of original sin," she was utterly loyal to her parents and soon shouldered her share of the teaching burden at Ekukanyeni, as did Agnes, the youngest sister, who at twenty was the best linguist and towered even over her tall father. Frances Ellen, known as Fanny, was twenty-four in 1873; she had spent several years in England and already bore the marks of the tuberculosis that would eventually kill her. The girls were fiercely partisan, with enormous capacities for work, but it was Harriet who had the greatest share of John W. Colenso's clear intellect and balanced judgment. Frances Ellen, aware, perhaps, of the brevity of the time allotted her, was more impatient and frequently allowed her emotions to tinge her writing.

The family's notoriety, its English social standards, and its intellectual interests cut it off from the social life of the colony, but most new arrivals from England found their way to Bishopstowe, and the best of them, including many of the officers from the garrison forces at Pietermaritzburg, became steady visitors. For at least one of them Fanny Colenso was as great an attraction as her famous father.

Anthony William Durnford was born in Ireland in 1830 to an Army family which had sent generations of its sons into the service. By the time he was eighteen he had been educated in Germany and had passed through the Royal Military Academy at Woolwich to take his place as a second lieutenant in the Corps of Royal Engineers, in which his father was then serving as a captain. He spent a few years in England and Scotland, and in 1851 he came to the fort at Trincomalee in Ceylon.

It was one of scores of tiny, isolated posts in which much of England's Army was frittered away, but Durnford's Corps stood him in good stead in the next five years. Colonies usually lacked competent civil engineers, and Durnford was soon appointed Assistant Commis-

sioner of Roads and Civil Engineer for Ceylon. He had a tendency to
act without considering consequences—he was a heavy gambler and
until he quit, a heavy loser—and on the strength of his appointment he
married the daughter of a retired lieutenant colonel. It was a rash act in
an age when military professionals married very late in life if they
married at all, and low pay, long tours in primitive posts, and the lack
of pensions all contributed to the aphorism, "Captains may marry,
majors should marry, colonels must marry." Both Durnford and his
father defied convention by marrying as lieutenants, and Durnford,
with an unhappy alliance on his hands, eventually paid the price. He
left Ceylon in 1856 and for ten years moved through a series of postings that took him to Malta, England, Gibraltar and then back to
England. He thus missed service in both the Crimea and the Sepoy
Rebellion, in either or both of which virtually all his contemporaries
were blooded.

An infant son born in Ceylon died in Malta, a daughter born in
Malta in 1857 survived, and another daughter born in England in 1859
died the following year. Durnford gambled harder than ever in Gibraltar, and, back in England in 1864, his wife sought solace for her
troubles elsewhere. There was a carefully hushed scandal, Durnford's
wife was put aside, and the family never mentioned her again. Divorce
was out of the question; not even the aggrieved party could hold a
Queen's commission, and Durnford covered the situation by taking his
future postings abroad, as others had done before him, while his family
raised his daughter. He sailed for China in 1865, but he suffered a
nervous breakdown en route and Lieutenant Colonel Charles George
Gordon, already famous as "Chinese," who was embarked on the same
vessel, landed him in Trincomalee and nursed him back to health. He
spent five more years in England with light duties and one in Ireland,
where a railroad accident almost cost him his life. In 1871, a forty-one-
year-old captain who had never seen active service, he arrived in
Capetown. A year later he was a major and had been posted to Natal
just in time to accompany Shepstone on his coronation mission into
Zululand.

Natal suited Durnford admirably, and his letters home were enthusiastic. His father was by now a major general; his brother Edward
Congreve Langley Durnford, a captain in the Royal Marine Artillery.
The family name was already well known in Natal, where Point Durnford honored a distant relative who had served Captain Owen as a
midshipman, and Uncle George Durnford, now a retired colonel, had
led the grenadier company of the 27th Foot ashore from the *Conch* to
rescue Captain Smith from the Boers under Pretorius. Durnford was
enchanted with the country, enchanted with colonials, and above all

enchanted with the Bantu. "They are fine men," he wrote home, "very naked and all that sort of thing, but thoroughly good fellows."

He was a tall, balding man, with handsome and sunburnt features, intelligent eyes, and a famous mustache that dangled below his collarbones. His religious views and his attitude toward the natives soon made him welcome at the Colenso household, and Fanny's eyes burned brighter than ever when he came.

Theophilus Shepstone was occupied in Zululand from July until September of 1873, and it was not until his return to Pietermaritzburg that he was able to devote his attention to the problem of Langalibalele, the hereditary chieftain of the amaHlubi.

These Zulu refugees were kin to the Basuto, whose territories on the high veld abutted their own reserve in the Drakensberg Range. They were generally regarded as better fighting stock, and as decidedly more unruly, than the run of Natal Kaffirs, and Langalibalele, as a hereditary rather than an appointed chieftain, was relatively independent of governmental support in ruling his clan. He was located in an area where many of the remaining trek Boers had settled, and the local magistrate was inclined to take a more serious view of his capricious attitude than might have been the case elsewhere in the colony.

It was, therefore, a matter of concern to the government that the amaHlubi were acquiring firearms. Hardly a single Natal Kaffir had any real need for a gun; the game had long since disappeared from the reserves and interclan warfare was naturally forbidden. The amaHlubi, it was true, had been set to guard certain passes of the Drakensberg Range against Bushman raids, but these descents were no longer the problem they had been a quarter of a century ago, and in a colony with 16,000 Europeans and over 300,000 Natal Kaffirs, armed natives were a natural source of alarm.

Natal did not forbid the possession of firearms, but it discouraged them. An ordinance made it illegal to own an unregistered firearm, and the Natal Kaffirs soon learned that registration was equivalent to confiscation. Guns brought in were either retained indefinitely or rendered useless before return.

For the last few years the young men of the amaHlubi had been slipping away to the diamond fields on the high veld, where miners were offering a gun in place of a season's wages. These firearms were naturally not being registered when the men returned to Natal, and the resident magistrate, alarmed by the reports of paid informants, finally ordered Langalibalele to enforce the ordinance. The chieftain's sympathies lay with his clansmen, and, chieftain or not, he had no real power to force them to comply. He was a dissolute old ruffian; he wanted no trouble with either his men or the administration, and he adopted a typically native solution—he temporized. He pleaded first ignorance and then ill health, and when the messages ordering him to report in person to the magistrate became insistent he simply ignored them. A final summons came in the name of Sir Benjamin Pine, who as Lieutenant Governor held the position of Supreme Native Chieftain, and while Pine's native messengers suffered no hurt, hands were laid on them and they were severely jostled and insulted.

To Shepstone such conduct was tantamount to rebellion, and he promised to come to fetch Langalibalele in person. Before he could make good on his threat, he was called into Zululand, and Langalibalele, still hoping his troubles would simply evaporate, was sufficiently alarmed to sound out a few neighboring Basuto chieftains. Basutoland was now Crown territory as well as Natal, and the Governor of the Cape Colony administered it as High Commissioner, but some of the Basuto clans promised to shelter the amaHlubi if they came that way. Langalibalele waited only long enough into October to make certain that Shepstone was in earnest, which he certainly was, and he then distributed a portion of his cattle for safekeeping among the neighboring amaPutini, left his elderly clansmen hidden in caves in the Drakensberg Range, and struck out with the bulk of his clan and his cattle for the high veld.

Shepstone was in a cold fury. If the treatment of the messengers had been a personal affront that verged on rebellion, the flight was treason. It was a dubious interpretation; Langalibalele was hardly a British subject in the accepted sense of the word, although bound to observe Crown terms as long as he occupied Crown land. No law denied him the right to emigrate if he chose, although the Governor of the Cape Colony could of course deny him entrance to Basutoland. Shepstone, however, could hardly afford to let him go, or depend on the Governor to turn him back. If Langalibalele got out of Natal with 10,000 amaHlubi, his act of defiance might well destroy Shepstone's precarious control over the other hereditary chieftains and bring the entire reserve system crashing down in ruin, and the clan's arrival in the Cape Colony would in any event lead to a most unwelcome probe. Shepstone simply had to stop him.

The expedition to do so was placed under the command of Lieutenant Colonel Milles; it consisted of two companies of his 75th Foot, several score colonial volunteers, and 8,000 Natal Kaffir levies who had been drafted and placed under the command of Zulu-speaking colonists. Major Durnford was appointed Chief of Staff, and the force proceeded to the amaHlubi reserve, where it paused long enough to make certain that Langalibalele was committed to Bushman's River Pass for his escape attempt.

Milles now drafted a plan. Two light forces were to move up to the high veld through the passes immediately adjacent to Bushman's River Pass, and were then to converge on the narrow mouth of that pass, blocking all egress and forcing Langalibalele back into the arms of the troops waiting below. The light forces, one consisting of 500 Natal Kaffirs and the other of 25 mounted baTlokwa and 55 European volunteers, were to leave on the second of November and to be in place on the following day, when Sir Benjamin Pine planned to issue a proclamation giving the amaHlubi three days in which to surrender. Milles gave Durnford command of the mixed party, and, in view of the planned announcement, Pine impressed on him the importance of not firing the first shot—if it came to shooting.

The plan was sounder than the staff work. Very little was known about the passes of the Drakensberg, and the Natal Kaffirs set out in search of a nonexistent one and never reached the top. Durnford's pass—Giant's Castle—at least existed, but he was sadly misinformed about the distance he would have to travel to reach it, and the pass itself called for skilled mountaineering.

Durnford hurried off to inspect his command. The baTlokwa were under a young inDuna named Hlubi, and seventeen of them were armed with an assortment of muzzle-loading flintlocks and percussion pieces. The remainder carried assegais, and a mission native, Elijah Kambula, was on hand to interpret. Durnford's personal leadership was strong enough to survive transmittal through an interpreter; he treated the baTlokwa like soldiers, and they responded in kind.

The Europeans consisted of a contingent from the Richmond Mounted Rifles and the Karkloof Troop of the Natal Carbineers. Captain Charles Barter of the Karkloof Troop was the senior officer, a rather unsoldierly rector's son who was popular with the rank and file. The senior N.C.O. was a Sergeant Clarke, much looked to as a source of military information by virtue of long service in the regular forces. The volunteers were smartly uniformed and armed with the Terry breech-loading carbine.

Durnford set out at dusk on the second of November, and at once came face to face with the difference between his regular troops and the volunteers of the Karkloof Troop. He had carefully ordered Barter to have each man carry rations for three days and forty rounds of ammunition, but when the column got under way, the rations and the ammunition were all on pack horses. These wandered off in the middle of the night; Durnford sent a party to scout for them, but neither pack horses nor searchers turned up until the expedition was over.

In the morning Durnford asked the baTlokwa to share their meat, biscuits and rum with the Europeans, and pushed on toward Giant's

Castle Pass. The steep trail led up through wild and broken country, where the horses had to be led along narrow ledges skirting tumbled rocks and threading the edges of frequent cliffs. Some of the men became exhausted and had to fall out. In the course of the day Durnford's horse, Chieftain, slipped and dragged him backwards over the lip of a cliff. Chieftain fetched up uninjured at the foot, but Durnford bounced off the rock face and was brought up by a tree limb that snagged his left armpit. His head was severely cut, his shoulder was dislocated, and two ribs were broken. It looked like the end of the expedition, but the thought of turning back never crossed Durnford's mind. A professional soldier for 25 years, he had never commanded troops in action before, and he was determined to carry out his orders and to set a proper example for the volunteers. He had himself bound up as best his men could manage—no one could set his shoulder and his left arm was useless—and as soon as he could stand, he ordered the advance continued.

By dusk he was fairly into the pass itself, a deep gash in the escarpment like a tumbled staircase of rock. Durnford was close to delirium from pain and exhaustion, and he called a halt to rest. The path was too steep to lie level, and the men pushed a few rocks together to form a bench and padded them with grass. Before he dozed off in the bitter cold, he dictated and signed orders sending a half-dozen baTlokwa on ahead so that at least a part of his command would be at the head of Bushman's River Pass at the agreed time.

He awoke at moonrise, before midnight, gathered his command and pressed on. The path grew too steep for walking, Durnford's injuries had stiffened, and he could barely stand. For a while he had himself carried, but his men were almost as exhausted as he was. He finally contrived a sling from a blanket; two men tugged at each end while he leaned back in the bight with two men pushing. Thus, a few steps at a time, he worked his way to the crest. Here, at four in the morning, he met one of his baTlokwa, who reported that all was still quiet at the head of Bushman's River Pass, twelve miles away, although a few of the lead amaHlubi were just beginning to emerge. Durnford mounted, and led his baTlokwa and the thirty-odd Europeans who were still with him on to the pass.

Bushman's River Pass terminates in a saucer-shaped depression a quarter of a mile across, and the first of the amaHlubi cattle, with perhaps a hundred herders, were there as Durnford arrived. More cattle and more herders, most of them armed, were visible below, and Durnford posted his men across the depression and sent six of his baTlokwa to drive the herd back into the pass. He gave his men, rationless since dawn 'the preceding day, permission to catch and slaughter a beast, and when he tried to pay for it, Barter told him the Natal Kaffirs customarily fed government troops free of charge.

The incident did nothing to lessen the sullen hostility of the herders, and presently the baTlokwa returned and reported the amaHlubi in the pass would not permit the herd to descend. Durnford now rode out with Kambula and gathered the herders already in the basin together. He announced Pine's proclamation, and suggested the herders inform the remainder of the clan no hurt would come to them if they would return to their location. The herdsmen thanked him and moved toward the pass to comply, but more and more men came slipping out of the pass to join those already in the basin. Durnford now ordered the newcomers back, and a spokesman finally replied that they would only descend if Durnford and his force preceded them, as they feared being shot at. When Durnford curtly refused, he was at once threatened by a few of the warriors and he would have been killed had not an inDuna arrived and intervened. This was Mabuhle, and he knocked down the men who had shaken assegais at Durnford or pointed guns at him, and begged him to leave before his men got out of hand. Durnford retired to consider his position.

AmaHlubi by twos and threes were still emerging from the pass, and those in the basin were drifting to the cover of rocky spurs along the sides. Durnford had already sent for help, for the stragglers presumably collecting at the head of Giant's Castle Pass and for proper reinforcements from the main force below, but it was now clear that he might have to hold with the forces in hand for some time to come. He at once moved into a strong defensive position, sending the baTlokwa to cover on one side of the trail and half the Karkloof Troop on the other. With the head of the pass in a crossfire, he shook the balance of the volunteers into a line across the trail itself and sent a final six men to cover the only exit from the basin, a notch in the rim where a spring fed one of the sources of the Orange River. The men had no sooner reached their posts than Barter, in charge of the exit, cantered back to inform a thunderstruck Durnford that the Carbineers could not be relied on and a retreat was advisable.

The amaHlubi were milling around the nervous volunteers planted across the trail. Regular troops might have stuck it, but the young, cold, hungry and inexperienced volunteers needed positive leadership, and the font of their military information, Drill-Instructor Clarke, chose this moment to lose his head. He rode in and out among the men babbling that they were surrounded and would all be massacred. Durnford and Kambula cleared the amaHlubi away from the troopers by themselves, but Barter was clearly right, and the men were on the verge of breaking. Durnford called out dramatically, "Will no one stand by me?" and when only three men responded he ordered the rest to retire at a walk.

Two of the three, Bond and Potterill, offered to ride down among the amaHlubi to show the others there was no cause for alarm, but Durnford refused the offer. The third volunteer was Robert Erskine, the son of the Colonial Secretary, who had spent most of the preceding night tending Durnford as he tried to rest. The volunteers started to turn, and someone later remembered Clarke hoarsely yelling, "Form fours!" when one of the baTlokwa cried out that the amaHlubi were about to fire. There was a single shot—almost everyone remembered it as a single shot, although none could say who fired it—and then a ragged volley. Bond and Potterill fell dead on the spot, Erskine's horse reared, his saddle turned, and he fell under the flashing assegais, and the Karkloof Troop broke and ran. One of the baTlokwa slipped off his mount, and Elijah Kambula's horse was cut down. Durnford stopped to help him up on Chieftain, but Kambula was shot through the head and Durnford himself was stabbed twice, once in the side and again with a second, serious thrust through the elbow of his useless left arm. He managed to work his revolver free, shot down two of his assailants, and rode to safety with the reins loose on Chieftain's neck.

Hlubi rallied his baTlokwa just beyond the rim, and Durnford used them to check the pursuit when it got too close, but the amaHlubi followed him the twelve miles to Giant's Castle Pass. Here he found Lieutenant Parkinson with twelve stragglers, and here he finally caught up with his errant command. Weeping with rage and frustration, he berated them, and held the baTlokwa up as examples of proper soldiers. At the first sight of the pursuing amaHlubi, however, the volunteers bolted down the pass like so many rabbits. Durnford turned to ride back alone, but the baTlokwa, despite his inability to communicate since Kambula's death, divined his intention and caught his bridle, and he suffered himself to be led down the pass. Only four of the amaHlubi followed them down; the baTlokwa ambushed the lead man and found he had been firing pebbles from his antiquated flintlock.

Durnford reached the main camp after midnight. Learning that a large party had been sent to his aid, he set out again the same night with a small escort to head it off. His shoulder had been set and his wounds bound, but he still had two broken ribs and the assegai thrust in his elbow had severed a nerve, and he had permanently lost the use of his forearm and hand. For the rest of his life he kept the withered limb thrust into the front of his tunic. He did not report sick once in the days that followed.

The defeat was a more serious disaster than the casualty list indicated. Langalibalele had gotten clean away, and Shepstone had failed.

Natives had defied the administration, resorted to arms, killed three Europeans and successfully decamped. If the 300,000 Natal Kaffirs chose to follow the amaHlubi lead, the colony might be snuffed out in a twinkling. The fear that gripped Natal was natural and acute, and it accounted for much of what followed.

The bulk of the amaHlubi were gone, but close to a thousand old men and women with hundreds of young children were holed up in caves and ravines on the reserve. Adjacent to them lived 5,000 amaPutini, who had accepted amaHlubi cattle for safekeeping and had taken back a few clanswomen who had married into the amaHlubi but were too old to migrate. For this aid and comfort Shepstone now declared the amaPutini guilty of treason, although they had taken no part in the move and had followed the instructions of their local magistrate at every turn. The expedition moved in to subdue and chastise both clans; the men burned all the kraals and confiscated 8,000 head of amaPutini cattle. Every native found was taken prisoner, and over 200 amaHlubi were killed when fire, smoke and artillery fire drove them out of their caves. The survivors broke up, making their way to other reserves to seek shelter, and over 500 prisoners were assigned to private farmers for labor in virtual slavery.

The colony's search for a scapegoat was as short as it was inevitable. Durnford had not been in the colony long enough to make many friends, and his official report on the conduct of the volunteers who had accompanied Shepstone into Zululand had already alienated many colonists. His account of Bushman's River Pass had nothing good to say of anyone but the three volunteers who had been killed and the baTlokwa. His views on natives and their treatment had also done little to endear him to Natal, and the newspapers were soon filled with abusive letters. It was left to Colenso and a lone editor, Sanderson of the *Natal Colonist,* to defend him.

Durnford was still unaware of the feeling against him, and still actively campaigning. Two days after his descent from the plateau he rode into Pietermaritzburg and back—fifty miles each way—and a fortnight later he took a force of regular troops up through Bushman's River Pass to see if it was still occupied. It was not. Durnford buried his five companions, and he also buried and erected a cairn over the two amaHlubi he had shot. The services were conducted by the Reverend George Smith, minister of St. John's church in Weston. Something of a fire-eater and a rabid High Churchman, he had barricaded his church as a refuge for his parishioners and had then ridden off with the Karkloof Troop.

Colenso, meanwhile, followed the campaign through the newspapers and through private correspondence. He was, at first, thoroughly in accord with the proceedings; Langalibalele had obviously been guilty of a still-undetermined measure of resistance, and the amaHlubi had certainly fired on European troops. Colenso's trusted friend, Shepstone, was in charge of the activity, so there was clearly no cause for alarm.

The first signs of irregularities came from letters which the newspapers now started to publish. They had been written by enthusiastic colonists who had been present at what could only be described as atrocities: prisoners shot and stabbed by native levies after they had surrendered or had been dragged out of hiding places. Colenso was not the man to let such evidence pass—he had even chided Durnford for speaking of "avenging his losses"—and he now questioned his friend closely. Durnford admitted that such incidents had occurred, adding that except for the use of artillery against some of the caves Imperial forces had not been involved. He, of course, personally deplored such acts.

Now thoroughly aroused, Colenso waited until Shepstone had returned to Pietermaritzburg, and then took him to task about the atrocities and the plight of the amaPutini. To his astonishment and despair, he found Shepstone prepared to vindicate and defend every act, and in a few truculent sentences he made clear to the Bishop the fundamental differences in their characters. Colenso saw at once that he had mistaken this man for years, even as Gray had once mistaken him, and that the ruthless vindictive official who now confronted him had always been present. He had never realized it before only because he had never seen Shepstone opposed. The break was sudden, complete and permanent, and Colenso returned to Bishopstowe more alone than he had ever been before.

Langalibalele had transited Bushman's River Pass two days before the brush with Durnford. He wandered about the high veld for six weeks, staying just beyond the reach of a large pursuing force from Natal and dodging other forces from the Cape Colony, Basutoland and British Kaffraria. On the eleventh of December, when most of the amaHlubi cattle had already been captured, a son of Mshweshwe betrayed him with four of his sons into the hands of the Cape Colony column. Mabuhle was captured as well, but slipped out of his handcuffs and sought refuge in Zululand. Langalibalele was turned over to the party from Natal, laden with chains, and led back to Pietermaritzburg. In January of 1874 he was tried on charges of murder, treason and rebellion.

Few more disgraceful farces have ever been staged in a British courtroom. Theophilus Shepstone, wishing to avoid the tiresome formalities of a trial in Roman-Dutch law, tried the case on Native Customary Law. "It is only by the fiction of considering Sir B. Pine a Native 'whose ignorance and habits unfit him for civilized life' that a crime against him is brought within Native Law at all," a reviewer later commented. Native Law had never been designed to cope with a European courtroom, so Shepstone was able to organize the court as he saw fit and to invent procedure that suited him. Pine sat as Supreme Chieftain, assisted by Shepstone, four European magistrates and six appointed native chieftains. The prosecution was entrusted to John Wesley Shepstone, and Langalibalele was not represented by counsel.

Colenso sent what comfort he could to the prisoner. Langalibalele meant "the Glaring Sun," and when an eclipse was due, the Bishop sent word that it was a perfectly natural phenomenon, not to be taken as an omen of personal disaster. He also tried, and failed, to find a man willing to defend the chieftain.

The court opened and at once proceeded to discard Native Law, which even if not codified followed an age-old trial procedure. John Shepstone presented the charges, and called on the prisoner to plead. The accused admitted some of the factual content of the specifications, but maintained that the conclusions the prosecution had drawn from events were wrong. This was construed as a plea of guilty, the six native "judges" were then called upon for comment and proceeded to abuse the prisoner. One called him a dog who had bitten his master, another stated that his conduct caused all men, European and native, to lift their hands in amazement, and still another concurred in all that had been said and refrained from additional comment to avoid taking the court's time. The native members then pronounced him guilty.

The trial was in effect over, but Shepstone decided to prolong the exhibition and devoted a second day after judgment had been rendered to "taking evidence." By the end of the second day Colenso had finally prevailed upon a lawyer to represent Langalibalele, and Pine graciously assented. The Resident Magistrate, however, would not permit him to confer with his client, so the lawyer withdrew. Pine then sentenced Langalibalele to life imprisonment on Robben's Island. His sons and inDunas drew long sentences as well, and the amaHlubi and amaPutini were ordered dispersed. The sentence, unknown in the Native Customary Law under which the trial had allegedly been held, was not only harsh but actually illegal, since Natal had no right to transport convicts to the jurisdiction of another colony.

The sentence was universally acclaimed in Natal as a model of justice tempered by Christian mercy. Not a single voice was raised against the trial or its outcome except that of John William Colenso, and for the first time in his life the Bishop of Natal found himself utterly alone in a fight. He was sixty years old and worn down by crushing labors, he had no financial resources, his legal position was still embattled and precarious and he had just lost the comfort of a highly valued friendship that had supported him for all his twenty years in Natal. Not one of these considerations made a particle of difference to him, and he now concentrated all his energies into a supreme effort to secure justice for Langalibalele and the dispersed clans.

He started by taking over the legal defense himself. Pine, vaguely uneasy over what was occurring, granted an appeal against the sentence to the Executive Council of Natal. There was, of course, no hope of the council allowing the appeal, but the attempt gave Colenso the opportunity to get a proper defense on record. This he did with his usual care and thoroughness, commenting exhaustively on the events of the campaign and on the "evidence" produced at the trial and bringing into the open what he considered a significant point.

One of the main charges against Langalibalele concerned his treatment of Pine's messengers, and Colenso's quick eye had noticed three fleeting references to John Shepstone, Matyana and a hidden pistol. Since John Shepstone had conducted the examination in which these points were mentioned, they had naturally been glossed over. Colenso now ferreted out the sixteen-year-old story of John Shepstone's treachery, sending for witnesses to Zululand, and stressing the fact that Langalibalele had been a deeply impressed witness of the incident. Colenso offered the material as extenuating circumstances, but the Executive Council, of which Theophilus Shepstone was a member, disallowed the appeal and the case, now including Colenso's defense, was referred to the Colonial Office.

In London there was immediate talk of a Royal Commission, and Pine, now thoroughly alarmed, sent Shepstone to England to stave off an investigation. Colenso went as well, since there was nothing more he could do in Natal for Langalibalele, the amaHlubi or the amaPutini. The two clans were in pitiable condition. They had lost their land, their cattle and their very blankets, and in acute want wandered about in search of shelter. So many had been arrested that in lieu of jail sentences the Executive Council had approved a bill directing prisoners to be assigned to private individuals for three years of compulsory labor.

Durnford, now a lieutenant colonel and the Assistant Colonial Engineer, found the atmosphere in Pietermaritzburg so distasteful that he soon moved to a rude camp at Fort Napier outside the city. His Army reputation was unblemished, but Natal was not ready to forgive him; society shunned him, and his favorite dog was poisoned. He remained cheerful throughout the storm, writing home about the fancied recovery of his arm, which he must have known he would never use again.

The Army granted him a disability pension of £100 per annum; on his death it was discovered that he had never drawn a penny of it.

He had unofficially adopted the destitute amaPutini, whom he now set out to rehabilitate. He had been given the ridiculous task of sealing the Natal Kaffirs into the colony by destroying the passes over the Drakensberg Range, so he hired ninety amaPutini and marched them upcountry in a loose formation, and he was promptly accused of "drilling" Natal Kaffirs. In bitter cold he quarried cliffs across the passes at their narrowest points, so that cattle could no longer be driven through, and when the work was done, he brought his men back. By August he had succeeded in obtaining a pardon for the tribe, which freed them from the onus of living as outlaws but still left them stripped of land and possessions and close to £20,000 worth of cattle.

One problem Durnford did have, about which he could do little but suffer in silence. He was forty-four years old and had not seen his wife in a decade; she lived somewhere in England and had no contact with Durnford's relatives, who were raising their sixteen-year-old daughter. He now fell deeply in love with Frances Ellen Colenso, and she with him. Their respective positions and the mores of the time locked them into a vise of convention from which only the death of Frances Tranchell Durnford could free them, and she was to survive them both. Fanny Colenso was just twenty-five, a frail and beautiful girl whose parents, aware of her plight, for all their love could do nothing to help her. Natal was a small provincial colony, thriving on tittle-tattle, and narrow-minded gossips were as plentiful as people who hated Durnford and the Colensos, but so closely did the two guard their pathetic secret that no breath of scandal ever arose. When Durnford was killed in 1879, Fanny Colenso carried the secret to her own grave in 1887. Some hint of her feelings escaped into her impassioned defense of Durnford after his death—under a pseudonym she published a eulogistic biographical sketch—and in a country which had never known, or had forgotten, that Durnford was ever married, the legend arose that the two had been engaged.

Natal's Bishop and her Secretary for Native Affairs had meanwhile reached London, where Colenso's arrival stirred the usual ripple of alarm in High Church circles. He was, however, far too busy for theological sparring, and barring a squabble or two over what pulpits he might preach from, he caused little stir.

The man both Shepstone and Colenso had traveled to London to meet was Henry Howard Molyneux Herbert, the Fourth Earl of Carnarvon, who had just assumed office as Secretary of State for the Colonies in Disraeli's new ministry. He had been Undersecretary in 1858 and 1859 under Bulwer-Lytton, and he had been secretary for eight months in the Earl of Derby's 1866 cabinet. Still only thirty-five years old, he had then introduced the bill that led to the confederation of the North American provinces, a notable colonial milestone. He was a conscientious, well-informed and able official whose public career had started with a speech to the Society for the Prevention of Cruelty to Animals (of which his father was president) when he was seven. He was also ambitious, obstinate and sensitive to criticism. His colleagues called him "Twitters."

Colenso was concerned solely with the cause of justice for a wronged native chieftain; Shepstone with somewhat broader questions of native policy. These were provincial viewpoints, but the supplicants had now brought their cases to London, and, seen from Whitehall, all of southern Africa was but a single colonial conglomerate in an array that girdled the globe. Carnarvon could still discern the injustice done to Langalibalele and act to correct it, but at the same time the very distance put the incident and the locale in a fresh perspective.

The Colonial Office in 1874 was not inclined to overlook Natal's conduct in the Langalibalele Rebellion, and Carnarvon's concern went far beyond the simple question of justice that had called Colenso to London. Natal's fitness to manage her own affairs, and especially her ability to formulate and administer a native policy, were just then under anxious scrutiny, and Carnarvon was approaching a decision that was to set all of southern Africa in halting movement along the road that led to modern times.

England's policy toward her colonies had not so much veered as it had developed, and an Imperial process, of political evolution and territorial integration, was by now well advanced. Early in the century humanitarianism had been able to dictate much of colonial policy, but when the mercantile classes had risen to power, a stringent economy dominated decisions. The humanitarianism still ran strong, but it was compromised at every turn by insufficient financial support. Too rigid an economy, however, defeated its own aims. Starveling colonies required Imperial troops to defend them and Imperial diplomacy to extricate them from their perpetual troubles with their neighbors. They were an incessant administrative headache and a continuing drain on the Exchequer. It was obvious that contiguous groupings of such territories might profitably be replaced by single political entities considerably stronger than the sum of their parts and able to keep order in their own houses. In addition to Canada, movements toward unification had been capped with success in such diverse areas as Australia and the Leeward Islands, and it was in comparison with these examples that southern Africa by 1874 seemed overripe for similar progress.

Only confederation could give her a unified native policy, and only a unified native policy would permit further political development.

The project was commendable and audacious, but the obstacles were truly formidable, and not even Carnarvon sensed their magnitude when, by the end of the year, he determined to proceed. To begin with, his ambitions greatly exceeded the power of his office; he represented the Imperial factor to scores of thousands of colonists and several million natives, but his cabinet post was a minor one, and the exigencies of the British budget wrote as much colonial history as the Colonial Office did. Secondly, the territories he proposed to invite to join one another differed greatly and were in many cases mutually antagonistic.

When Carnarvon had last left the Colonial Office in 1867, the entire land had been a primitive agricultural area in the grip of a severe economic depression. There was neither private industy nor public transport, and the imminent opening of the Suez Canal threatened to destroy what scant advantage Capetown enjoyed as the Halfway House on the route to India. Two British colonies, two Boer republics and an ill-defined clutch of native kingdoms filled the southern part of the continent, and the future promised little hope for change. In October of 1867 a hunter named John O'Reilly passed to a Boer named Schalk van Niekerk, who farmed near the junction of the Orange and the Vaal Rivers, a pretty pebble some children named Jacobz had found, but Carnarvon could hardly have heard of the stone or guessed its significance before he left office.

The stone, however, had immeasurably altered the scene that greeted him on his return. The first trickle of mineral wealth and the new ideas and attitudes that followed in its wake had finally snapped the last lingering ties with the eighteenth century, and all the individual territories had been affected.

The Cape Colony was the largest, the strongest and the most advanced of them all. It had been governed under a constitution since 1854, first by a governor appointed in England assisted by a locally elected bicameral parliament, and, since responsible government had been granted in 1872, under an elected Prime Minister, John Charles Molteno. Theoretical racial equality prevailed, in that the constitution made no mention of color and no literacy test was required, but the franchise was limited to those who dwelt in immovable structures worth at least £25, which excluded those who lived in grass huts. The Governor, Sir Henry Barkly, was thus the link between the Colonial Office and the Prime Minister of the Cape, an Imperial ambassador whose relationship with his host government had neither been clearly defined by law nor fully explored in practice. Barkly was at the same time the High Commissioner for those British territories which did not enjoy self-government, and in practice this executive function was difficult to separate from his advisory function.

The Cape Colony was split into a relatively settled and relatively sophisticated Western Province, in which Boer and Briton generally saw eye to eye, and a turbulent Eastern Province with an urban British population centered on Grahamstown and several other small settlements, and a rural Boer population. This frontier province had borne the brunt of the Kaffir Wars with the Bantu clans of the coastal strip; in 1866 it finally absorbed British Kaffraria and was now beginning to grope toward a precarious stability with its border along the Great Kei River. This placed the Gaikas in Ciskei, and beyond lay the Transkei and a wilderness of Xhosa tribal remnants that stretched 200 miles to Natal's southern border on the Umzimkulu River. Here lay Gcalekaland, Fingoland, Tambookieland, Mpondoland and the frankly labeled Nomansland, which would presently become Griqualand East.

The Britons of the Eastern Province wanted complete separation from the Western Province, because they resented a border policy that was controlled by distant Capetown. In this they were opposed by their own Boer Midlanders, who had no desire to see control pass to urban Britons, East or West, and by the Britons of the Western Province, who did not wish to lose their parliamentary support. Molteno held power by grace of a strong element of Western Boer support; he was thus responsive to Boer sentiment both in the Cape Colony and without, and he was implacably opposed to separation. He had not yet been consulted, but he would also be opposed to the idea of confederation, because he needed every penny of the still scanty Cape revenues at home and did not wish the fiscal responsibility for the less developed territories elsewhere.

Political stability evaporated north of the Orange River, which gave the Cape Colony one of the few firm natural boundaries in all Africa. For 600 unnavigable miles inland from the Atlantic Ocean, to the confluence of the Vaal River, it skirted the south of vast empty regions with names like Damaraland, Great Namaqualand and Bondlezwaart's Territory. Here lay the Kalahari Desert—the Great Thirstland with its surviving Bushmen—and here dwelt Koranna, baTlapin and Bechuana clans.

The Orange Free State occupied the great inland plateau bounded by the Drakensberg Range and the Orange and the Vaal Rivers. It was occupied by a thin sprinkling of Boers, most of whom had close ties with the Cape Boers who had not trekked. Independent since the Bloemfontein Convention of 1854, the Orange Free State was governed by an elected Volksraad under President Jan Hendrik Brand, who in

1864 entered what eventually stretched to a quarter of a century in office. The irascible Barkly, quarreling with him over control of the diamond fields and bested by him in diplomacy, rhetoric and especially control of temper, summed him up neatly in a letter to Carnarvon: "President Brand of the Free State is still a member of the Cape Bar, and might be recommended to me for Chief Justice. His father is the Speaker of the Cape Assembly, his wife is an Englishwoman, and his eldest son is now studying at the Middle Temple, and yet he can declare war on me tomorrow."

The Orange Free State operated on the continual brink of financial collapse, but it might have enjoyed a settled existence behind excellent natural boundaries had it not been for the presence of two exasperating peoples whom neither natural nor man-made boundaries could contain.

Mshweshwe's Basutos spilled out of the southeast mountains of the Free State and, in constant need of arable land, raided and settled at will beyond the easily forded Caledon River. Of all the Bantu chieftains, Mshweshwe alone had divined the secret of European military superiority: neither gun nor horse, but their use in combination. He consequently collected firearms assiduously, including a few artillery pieces, and he turned his people into a nation of horse thieves. When the long-suffering Free Staters rode out on commando, they had to cope with upwards of 7,000 warriors mounted on tough ponies and armed with musket or war axe, with a capital on Thaba Bosiu that Brand found as impregnable as Matiwane had almost fifty years before. A Captain Ward tried to separate Boer from Basuto with a surveyed line in 1849, but Mshweshwe, whose political astuteness included an utter lack of scruple, broke promise after promise to observe it. He would raid until the Free State was driven to retaliate; facing defeat he would then beg for British intercession and promise to behave. Brand finally gathered his forces and smashed him in 1868, but the postwar situation was so chaotic that the participants could no longer arrange a viable peace. Mshweshwe made a last despairing appeal for the Queen's protection, and Wodehouse, the High Commissioner, finally exceeded his instructions and annexed Basutoland to the Crown. The Colonial Office gave unhappy approval, and Mshweshwe, before dying in 1870 at the age of eighty-four, had the satisfaction of seeing his people safely into the Imperial fold. They were well out of what lay ahead.

The Orange Free State's problem of determining where its western border lay was enormously complicated by the Griqua people, who sprawled across the lower valley of the Vaal. These were the self-styled Baastards, a semicivilized folk descended from early Dutch settlers and long-vanished Cape Hottentot clans. They had moved north of the Orange River long before the Boers began to trek, and they were loosely organized into family groupings answering to hereditary chieftains, to which a few neighboring Bantu clans had attached themselves. The largest of these groupings thought of themselves as independent states, but few of them possessed adequate executive machinery, or even clear title to their domain. There was, for example, a large Griqua holding named Philippolis stretched along the northern bank of the Orange River east of the Vaal. Philippolis had a law, or perhaps just a tradition, against selling land to non-Griquas, but when the Boers began to trek, Philippolis Griquas sold and leased farms to them. After 1854 the British abandoned responsibility for events north of the Orange, and the new Orange Free State naturally confirmed its burgers in the farms they occupied. Grey, the High Commissioner, eventually felt a pang of responsibility for the Griquas, and he offered their leader, Adam Kok III, the empty Nomansland in the coastal strip. Kok accepted, and led some 2,000 followers on a two-year trek to his new home, where he founded Griqualand East and its capital of Kokstad, and before he went, he offered to sell the Free State the remnants of Philippolis.

The Free State decided to make the gesture of purchasing the land to forestall future claims, although it already had a fairly valid title to much of the area. The sale, completed in December of 1862, tacitly confirmed the validity of the prior Griqua claims, and, because both the Orange Free State and the agent who negotiated the sale for Kok were greedy, it led to untold future sorrow.

In 1857 one Cornelis Kok made over his land on both sides of the lower Vaal to Adam Kok, who added them to Philippolis. Three years later Adam Kok passed Cornelis Kok's lands to Nicolaas Waterboer, who owned enormous tracts west of the Vaal. When Adam Kok sold Philippolis, his agent inserted the phrase "and the lands of the late Cornelis Kok" into the bill of sale simply to run up the price, and the Free State, with no idea of what lands were really involved, accepted merely to acquire more land. By 1863, therefore, both Nicolaas Waterboer and the Orange Free State had claims in good faith to certain areas on the eastern side of the lower Vaal.

The Transvaal simply did not have any borders, except for a stretch of the upper Vaal shared with the Orange Free State. Under President Marthinus Wessel Pretorius, it extended to wherever Transvaal Boers drifted, until someone protested. Even the Vaal only protected the Free State, for Transvaal Boers had moved down its western bank through baTlapin lands and into Griqua country, so that Nicolaas Waterboer was not only beset with the Free State claims east of the Vaal but with Transvaal claims west of the Vaal as well.

At this point a Cape Colony lawyer named David Arnot decided to take a hand. He was frankly a gambler, but he was also motivated by sound British patriotism. He was convinced that the vast unexplored reaches of the African interior would someday be of enormous importance, and he was determined to preserve a road to the north for future British expansion. Griqualand West was the gateway to this road, and it would be shut tightly if the Free State gobbled up Waterboer, or if he fell victim to the Transvaal Boers. Arnot therefore went to him and offered to represent him, and Waterboer gratefully accepted.

Arnot now began a patient legal battle which stretched over the next eight years. He set out to establish legal claims to all the lands to which Waterboer had even a vestige of a right, including areas in which no Griqua had lived for years and which the Free State occupied and administered. The Free State refused to discuss the lands east of the Vaal, but it offered to negotiate or bargain over claims to the west. There were fewer than 150 farms involved, and the desultory case over a few thousand sunburnt acres might have droned on for years, but for the Jacobz children and the pretty bauble they found on the west bank of the Vaal River. The argument came to life with a bang.

Diamonds could not have been discovered in a more unfortunate location. The first finds were in territory claimed by both Waterboer and by the Transvaal; subsequent finds were in areas claimed by Waterboer and the Orange Free State. Scores and then hundreds and then thousands of enthusiastic diggers began to pour in from all over the world. They soon exhausted the alluvial deposits along the Vaal River, and they then settled down in cheerful anarchy to serious mining in the far richer deposits where Kimberley stands today.

Despite a recent gold strike at Tati, the finances of the Transvaal were desperate. Pretorius, never at his best in the world of diplomacy, had recently failed to float a public loan of £300, and he now saw salvation in the diamond fields. He took immediate steps to place them within his borders; in 1868 he annexed the entire interior of Africa westward to Lake Ngami by proclamation, and for good measure he gave himself an outlet to the Indian Ocean by annexing a strip to the east through Portuguese territory. Outraged protests from the Cape Governor, the Portuguese, and missionaries with the affected clans were so vociferous that he hastily dropped the measure and tried a new tack. Ignoring the vexatious question of ownership, he granted a long-term diamond-digging monopoly to three personal friends. The diggers retaliated by declaring an independent republic themselves and electing an ex-sailor of the Royal Navy as president. Wodehouse had already left for home and Barkly, his replacement, had not yet arrived, and an interim governor sent an observer north of the Orange River armed with the ineffectual provisions of the moribund Punishment

Act. Barkly arrived at the end of 1870 to find British neutrality well-nigh destroyed, and Brand slyly demanding foreign arbitration.

No foreign power would be permitted to decide questions in a British sphere of influence, but an impartial judge was clearly needed. Barkly appointed Robert William Keate, the Lieutenant Governor of Natal, and persuaded Pretorius but not Brand to abide by his decision. The Keate award of 1871 went hard against the Transvaal, pushing its boundary far back up the western bank of the Vaal, not only out of Waterboer's territory but past baTlapin lands as well. At the same time it established Waterboer's northeast corner, thus vindicating the whole of Arnot's claims. Waterboer now requested British protection, and Barkly at once annexed the whole of Griqualand West, diamond fields and all, to the British Crown.

The Transvaal had suffered a stinging setback, but it had little cause for ire. It had never held a claim to the diamondiferous ground east of the Vaal, and its burgers had drifted down along the west bank farther than they had any right to carry their government. Such resentment as the Transvaalers felt they expended on their President, who was turned out of office.

The Free State, however, was appalled. Its burgers had seen first Basutoland and then the wealth of Kimberley pass to Great Britain, and in each case after the Crown had gratuitously intervened on behalf of the Free State's antagonist. Britain in both cases had acted reluctantly and in the interests of a minority, but the net result put her in a bad light. There was extreme indignation and a deep bitterness, and it was not limited to the Boers of the Free State. The feeling ran almost as deep as it had at the time of the Great Trek, and it helped to drive a wedge between Briton and Boer. Even a payment of £90,000 (which the Colonial Office charged to Griqualand West) did little to soothe ruffled feelings, and anti-British feeling stiffened.

There were, however, compensations. The annexation of Basutoland had removed a vexation from the Free State's shoulders, and it had given her both a steady supply of labor and a market for her produce. The removal of the diamond fields had also been a blessing in disguise, for the 7,000 and more foreign diggers would inevitably have swamped the Free State electorate and its minimal executive machinery, and the market provided by Griqualand West was better than the one in Basutoland.

Natives seeking employment streamed into the diamond fields from all over southern Africa. What had always been a rural frontier problem was suddenly an urban one, and all at once there was a landless black proletariat. The new class focused attention on new problems. There were Bantu working for Europeans in every nook and cranny of southern Africa, and from all quarters there arose a cry for reliable sources of labor. When a Bantu could not satisfy such needs as basic sustenance or the artificial ones created by taxes or a desire for European goods, he could only bridge the gap by the sale of his labor. Such pressures would bring him out of his kraal for a season or two, but the insatiable demands of the diamond fields sucked in workers from the Cape to the Zambesi. A gun was the only European artifact that would bring a native 500 miles afoot for a season's work, and it was in firearms that the diamond fields paid their labor. A growing trickle of armed natives fanned out from Griqualand West, traversing the Free State and the Transvaal, and dropping down into Natal, and petty chieftains far and wide found young men of their kraals fondling cheap muskets and breathing a new and a hard defiance. The military strength these men contributed to the clans was negligible, for a native armed with a smoothbore flintlock and with an uncertain ammunition supply was much less of a threat than the same man armed with an assegai, but the defiance was far from negligible. The grievances were real as well. A disparate proportion of the land and a hugely disparate proportion of the water were controlled by an expanding European population, and a native population that grew even faster faced starvation. When the Free State and the Transvaal Boers tried to stop and disarm these returning workers, they banded together and traveled in groups somewhat too large for Boer comfort. If the Jacobz children had set in train the events that led to Kimberley, they had the Langalibalele Rebellion to answer for as well.

The grandeur and simplicity of Carnarvon's dream dulled his perspicacity, and his moves, although well intentioned and apparently sensible, brought him no closer to his goal. If even two of the various territories could be cajoled or bludgeoned into some sort of confederation, the rest must inevitably follow, and the economic and social blessings of union would transform the land. Carnarvon planned his campaign with care, and his first step was unusual.

James Anthony Froude, born in 1818, was a disciple of Thomas Carlyle's, and the author of a dramatic if somewhat slipshod history of England. He had a proven ability to absorb and organize masses of documentary material, he had a keen appreciation of the flow of English history, and he had few preconceived notions about southern Africa. Carnarvon called him into the Colonial Office, gave him access to all the files, and asked him for his advice. Froude confirmed Carnarvon's opinion that confederation was imperative, and he also convinced the Secretary that the Boers, and especially the Orange Free State, had been unjustly dealt with. This was a fresh breeze indeed in Whitehall, and had Carnarvon acted with more care, or had he been spared even slightly the pressure of events that lay ahead, he might have succeeded. In his eagerness to start, however, he now moved too fast.

He sent Froude to Capetown to preach confederation, and at the same time he wrote Barkly a mild but firm manifesto on the subject, taking his acquiesence for granted and proposing a conference for all interested parties. He had failed, however, to impress on Froude the unofficial nature of his visit, and he had not clarified the historian's status to either Barkly or Molteno. He had also failed to consider his timing. Molteno was engrossed in the domestic policies of the Cape Colony, and he regarded confederation as a high road to economic ruin. He had Barkly's complete sympathy, and the two men consequently gave Froude a frosty reception. The historian, correctly assessing Barkly and Molteno as major obstacles to Carnarvon's project, attended a dinner given by their political opponents on the very night of his arrival and proceeded to attack them in ringing terms. He then embarked on a tour of the Cape Colony, Natal and the Free State, whipping up a political storm against Molteno and implying that he spoke with Imperial sanction. Carnarvon, more shocked by Barkly's stand than by Froude's activity, rebuked the Governor and called on him either to co-operate or to resign. Barkly refused to do either, Molteno weathered the storm, and Froude finally returned to England with the Cape Colony further than ever from confederation.

If the Cape Colony could not be undermined, Griqualand West and Natal were amenable to a more direct assault. Under the irascible Southey, Griqualand West was sliding toward civil chaos, and its political form was still so raw that it could be counted on to do London's bidding.

This left Natal. That unhappy colony, vaguely aware that it had transgressed in the Langalibalele Rebellion, but unable to see the precise error of its ways, was about to meet with retribution. Natal was ruled by a Lieutenant Governor, who was assisted by a Legislative Council. Since the five members of the council appointed by the Lieutenant Governor were outnumbered by thirteen elected members, Natal enjoyed a large measure of autonomy, and London could not easily impose its will. Carnarvon now determined to change this situation, partially as a punishment for misconduct, but also to insure future compliance in the matter of confederation. The Queen could theoretically alter or even annul a granted colonial constitution, but Carnarvon chose the gentler course of having the council surrender its own autonomy, by voting an increase in the appointed members until the elected members were outnumbered.

Sir Benjamin Pine, sixty-seven years old in 1875, had been a colonial administrator since 1848, when he had served as temporary governor of

Sierra Leone and had distinguished himself on a military campaign. Very few colonial officials had a chance to display military prowess, and Pine's bravery tended to obscure his weaknesses as an administrator. From Sierra Leone he went on to Natal, where he had been Lieutenant Governor at the time of Shepstone's trouble with Matyana; in 1856 he was knighted and went to the Gold Coast, and from 1859 until 1873 he was in the West Indies, first as Lieutenant Governor of St. Christopher and then as the first Governor of the recently federated Leeward Islands. Back in Natal, he had virtually allowed Shepstone to rule in his name as he coasted toward retirement, and he was now made to a pay a scapegoat's price. It would obviously take no mean skill to induce the Legislative Council to commit political suicide, and the mediocre Pine was patently not equal to the task. Carnarvon applied to the War Office for the loan of a particular major general and replaced Pine, whose governing days were at an end, with the most glamorous administrator a dazzled colony had ever awaited.

Major General Sir Garnet Joseph Wolseley, G.C.M.G., K.C.B., enjoyed an immense reputation for success. He was far and away the youngest general officer in the British Army, having reached that exalted rank before he was forty. He was firmly identified with reform, and he combined a high order of common sense and devastating self-confidence with a remarkable degree of tart intolerance. His opponents were many and highly placed, and both luck and political friendship had been needed to save his career. He left a lasting imprint on the British Army and his two abrupt forays into southern Africa affected the history of Natal and the fate of the Zulu nation. His career is worth detailed examination.

Wolseley was born in 1833 to an impoverished Army family residing near Dublin. His grandfather had squandered a fortune in a crack cavalry regiment and had been forced to sell his commission after marrying a beautiful but penniless woman. He took holy orders and sired fourteen children, of whom the fifth, Sir Garnet's father, also entered the Army. Without any means, he stagnated in West Indies garrisons and died when Garnet was seven. When the boy reached the age of eighteen in 1852, he was given a commission without purchase, in recognition of his father's services.

Wolseley joined the 80th Foot, then stationed in India, because he could not afford duty in England. He arrived in Calcutta on the day the bells were tolling the death of the Duke of Wellington, and, finding his regiment had been sent to Burma, hurried on to Rangoon. Like so many colonial wars, the Second Burmese War consisted of a series of confused petty skirmishes aimed at chastening an obstreperous native leader—this one was named Meeah-Toon—and within a few months Wolseley had seen his first, and very nearly his last, action. He led a party of troops against a log stockade and received a stone bullet in his thigh that invalided him home and affected his gait for the rest of his life. He also carried back the first stirrings of impatience with an organization that forced him to fight in a steaming jungle clad in a scarlet jacket buttoned tightly to his chin and wearing white buckskin gloves.

Back in Ireland, Wolseley was promoted lieutenant and transferred to the 90th Light Infantry. Barely a year later he was on his way to the Crimea, in command of troops armed with the smoothbore flintlock "Brown Bess," as the new Enfield rifles had all been requisitioned to equip preceding drafts. Ashore in the Crimea, Wolseley was soon taken off regimental duties and turned loose as an assistant engineer. He was also promoted captain. Disgusted with the chaotic administration and antiquated equipment of his own forces, he noted with surprise that the faintly ridiculous French, fighting alongside the British, were better equipped in every respect and led by officers in whom common sense outweighed a blind adherence to outmoded techniques. He developed something of an obsession about transport facilities.

During the spring and summer of 1855 he suffered three slight wounds, and in August a bursting shell drove a piece of wood through his wrist, tore away part of the shin of his sound leg, and sent a stone through his face that destroyed the vision in one eye. He was about to return home to have the eye attended to when he was offered a tempting staff slot with the Light Division. He stayed through a second Crimean winter and finally rejoined his regiment at Aldershot in the fall of 1856.

In April of 1857 the 90th Light Infantry embarked in H.M. Troopship *Transit* for passage to China, where there had been diplomatic difficulties. Wolseley was resigned to a boring voyage in a foul, crowded transport, but there were to be diversions. Anchored off the Isle of Wight on the first night, a receding tide settled the vessel on her own anchor and one of the flukes pierced her bottom. After repairs and a second start, a storm caught her in the Bay of Biscay and sprang her masts, forcing her into Corunna for a refit. Finally under way again, she rounded the Cape of Good Hope and made it to the middle of the Indian Ocean before a cyclone struck her. Battered, leaking and waterlogged, with the end of the nightmare voyage finally in sight, she limped into Banca Straits off Sumatra, ran onto a rock, and tore her bottom out. The troops spent a harrowing night in ranks on the tilted decks, with the vessel threatening to slide off her perch every instant, before dawn disclosed a barren coral reef nearby on which all hands landed safely. Despite the dubious future, no one was sorry to see the

Transit sink. The boats had all been saved, and the men transferred to a neighboring island, where a questing gunboat found them ten days later. The Sepoy Rebellion had broken out in the meantime, and the regiment was now ordered to India. Wolseley reached Calcutta again, via Singapore, 133 days out from England.

He served throughout the Rebellion in a variety of active duties, leading the first storming party into besieged Lucknow and gaining first a brevet majority and then a brevet to lieutenant colonel. With the final embers stamped out in India, he was able to join the long-delayed expedition to China, where he served on the staff while Peking was captured. By the spring of 1861 he was back in England.

He was twenty-seven and a lieutenant colonel, and to date he had not spent a penny on his promotions. Had he chosen to sell out, he might have realized £8,000 on his commission. In nine years he had participated in four campaigns, he had been wounded five times, and had been mentioned in dispatches nine times. He had decided opinions on all phases of equipping, training and managing a contemporary army, and he had a solid reputation for gallantry, resource and initiative. It was a long way from an Irish boyhood with no expectations, and his career had barely started.

In December of 1861 the *Trent* affair alarmed England sufficiently for her to reinforce her Canadian garrisons. Wolseley was sent out with a staff billet, but by the time he had landed in Boston to proceed overland to Montreal, the danger had been averted. Canada was quiescent, but the raging Civil War proved an irresistible attraction, and Wolseley put in for six weeks' leave with the avowed intention of meeting General Lee. The battle of Antietam put an end to his plan to meet him in Washington, so, bribing a Federal officer with a good cigar and a fisherman with a golden sovereign, Wolseley crossed the Potomac and made his way to the headquarters of the Army of Northern Virginia. He was enormously impressed by Lee and Stonewall Jackson, and the ragged aspect of the Confederate troops did not for an instant blur the magnificence of their fighting qualities in his eyes. Wolseley described the trip anonymously in an English magazine, and was pleased both by the £40 he received for his first literary effort and the comment it inspired. American commentary was equally spirited; Wolseley had also been impressed by Abraham Lincoln and General Grant, and with splendid judgment but poor tact had showered his compliments along both banks of the Potomac.

In 1865 he was promoted full colonel, and the following May had a brief flurry of activity when an army of 12,000 Irish Fenians crossed the Niagara River to capture Fort Erie. Canadian militia dispersed them before Wolseley reached the scene with regular troops, and scandalized Federal forces helped to round up the adventurers. In 1868 he snatched two months' leave and hurried to England to get married.

In 1869 he got his first independent command. Louis Riel captured Fort Garry, at the site of the infant village of Winnipeg, and proclaimed a republic. So remote and thinly settled was the area that the government might have ignored him, had he not executed a man who tried to release some imprisoned settlers. Wolseley was given command of the 60th Rifles, some Canadian militia and four six-pounder guns. His task was to take the force 1,200 miles through an unexplored wilderness, restore the flag at Fort Garry and get back out, all between May, when the ice melted on Lake Superior, and the October freeze. The job demanded detailed staff planning down to the last ounce of food to be carried, considerable flexibility and a high order of personal leadership over independent backwoods guides and troops, who with canoe and tumpline served as their own transport. Wolseley met all demands brilliantly and retook Fort Garry without a fight. Riel scampered off into the bush, to be hanged after a second rebellion sixteen years later.

The Red River Expedition earned Wolseley a K.C.M.G., and he returned to London with every right to expect fresh and important employment. To his astonishment he was placed on half pay, frequently the prelude to ignominious semiretirement. He had been hoist on his own literary petard.

Much as the young Churchill was driven twenty years later by the boredom of Indian garrison duty to remedy a defective education, so did Wolseley turn to omniverous reading during his sojourn in Canada. The process had the same effect of introducing him to the power of the pen. His article on the Civil War and a book on the China Expedition published the same year were received well enough, but in 1869 Wolseley broke precedent with his *Soldier's Pocket Book*, an optimistically entitled compendium of 400 closely printed pages which was addressed to officers as well as enlisted men and crammed with practical advice and information for active duty and conduct in the field. Such a vade mecum was sorely needed, but Wolseley used its pages to air his opinions about a number of touchy subjects, notably the professional fitness of the contemporary officers' corps. His half-pay status was a direct result of his temerity.

He was rescued from the sidelines by Edward Cardwell, since 1868 Secretary for War in Gladstone's cabinet, who was about to institute needed Army reforms, and who saw in Wolseley an obvious ally. The Cardwell Reforms, which radically altered the structure of the British Army between 1870 and 1873, were a belated response to the deficiencies revealed by the Crimean War, spurred on by the fate that had overtaken the French Army in 1870. Previous secretaries had tinkered with the totally inadequate medical and supply services, but in 1870 Britain's Army was still unfit for a major European war. Led by a dependable if unimaginative and inadequately trained officer corps that the purchase system linked to the wealthier classes, 171,000 well-disciplined troops were organized into 141 battalions, half of which served overseas. Little more than a world-wide colonial police force, the Army had no strategic reserve and no body of ex-servicemen in civil life to form one from, since long-term enlistments kept men in the ranks until they were past military age.

Cardwell first attacked purchase, which had outgrown its late-eighteenth-century abuses, when commissions had been purchased for five-year-old children, and had settled into a peculiar semiefficiency in which everyone at least knew where he stood. In theory, one purchased a vacant commission from the Exchequer for a price ranging from £450 in a line regiment to £1,260 in the Household Cavalry; a few initial commissions went free to deserving candidates, and a very few men were promoted from the ranks. Each step thereafter had to be purchased, part of the price being offset by the sale of the current step to the next comer. Since no one could purchase out of turn, the semirich were as well off as the very rich. A lieutenant colonel of a line regiment could look forward to a retirement financed by the sale of a commission officially worth about £4,500, and vacancies were fairly steady as lieutenant colonels retired. Since higher ranks were chosen and not sold and general officers thus had no commissions to sell when they retired, few lieutenant colonels were willing to block promotions by hanging around long enough to be "caught in a brevet." Commissions vacated by death on active service were filled without purchase, which was hard on widows and orphans and led to the toast: "To a bloody war and a sickly season." As the Earl of Cardigan put it, at Balaclava he had "carried £10,000 on the point of his sword."

The major abuse was a system of kickbacks, by which an officer hurried the formation of a vacancy by paying an additional unofficial sum to the man ahead of him. These sums more than doubled the value of the commissions, and the command of a crack cavalry regiment cost a young fortune; £15,000 was common, and the Earl of Cardigan had drastically understated the value of his saber, since it was common knowledge that he had paid in excess of £35,000 for the 15th Hussars. There was also a considerable amount of lateral movement between regiments, frequently to escape overseas postings in undesirable areas, and it was not unknown for a regiment to take up a collection to induce its lieutenant colonel to retire, or for a lieutenant colonel about to retire to cast about for a regiment more affluent than his own into which he could exchange.

There was enormous Army resistance to the abolition of purchase; the Duke of Wellington had been firmly in favor of it. The opposition was openly based on the prospect of the lower social classes that might be admitted to the service, but privately founded in the fear of losing the highly unofficial sums that all the officers had invested. Even when Cardwell promised to reimburse the actual value of each commission, a sum that eventually totaled more than £8,000,000, Army resistance defeated the bill, and Cardwell had to resort to a Royal Warrant to abolish purchase.

He was less successful with a reform of the rank structure. The Guards regiments enjoyed a higher rank than the rest of the army, so that lieutenants were promoted to "lieutenant and captain" and then "captain and lieutenant colonel" before reaching the rank of major. The Life Guards, although not the Royal Horse Guards, enjoyed a dual rank at "major and lieutenant colonel," and even the guardsmen in these regiments outranked the men in the line regiments. These prerogatives were sacrosanct, and they survived Cardwell's attacks.

His Army Enlistment Act decreed a service term of twelve years, six with the colours and six in reserve, which made a start toward establishing an authorized reserve of 60,000 men. The most radical reform, however, came with the Localization Act of 1873, establishing seventy brigade areas to each of which were attached two linked battalions, one to serve overseas while the other replenished losses and trained up by recruiting from a depot in the brigade area. The system broke down almost at once, since by 1879 there were 82 battalions overseas and only 59 at home. Each fresh alarm from a distant corner of the Empire increased the imbalance, and battalions ordered overseas made good their war establishment by raiding other battalions and leaching out the experienced N.C.O.'s. Many of the home battalions existed in name only, and overseas drafts were filled with last-minute enlistments.

Wolseley had been in the thick of the reform fight. Assigned to the Adjutant General's department, where he reviewed courts-martial, he actually served as Cardwell's military mentor, adding his professional knowledge to the civilian's political skill. His reward came in August of 1873, when King Koffee of Kumasi sent his Ashanti into the Gold Coast Protectorate to harry the Fanti, attack Elmina and worry missionaries and sundry Europeans. The Earl of Kimberley decided to quell him, and Wolseley was given the job.

The Gold Coast was a sickly bed of smoldering problems. British occupation was limited to a few coastal toeholds, and the military garrison consisted of the colored troops of the West India Regiment and a few naval scrapings. The climate was so bad that 108 out of the 130 Europeans ashore were bedridden. Wolseley was given civil as well as military authority, a combination that appealed to him mightily, and he decided on a novel campaign. Kumasi lay 110 miles inland behind the Prah River, and the climate was only bearable from the beginning of December to the end of February. Wolseley landed at the Gold Coast Castle at the beginning of October with 35 hand-picked officers and no troops. Raising a few unreliable units from the coastal natives, he built a road inland to the Prah and then called for three battalions of regulars, who arrived in mid-December. By the end of the month he started his dash inland, housing his precious troops in prepared camps and fending off Ashanti resistance along a road that was little more than a tunnel pushed through the rain forest. At the end of January he blasted the spirit out of King Koffee's army in a sharp fire-fight at Amoaful, six days later he burned Kumasi, and by the beginning of March he was on his way back to England. It was a brilliant campaign, soundly conceived and ably executed. The hand-picked specialists, many former colleagues from the Red River, were dubbed the "Ashanti Ring" and the phrase, "Everything's Sir Garnet," passed temporarily into the language.

Wolseley's economy and his common-sense approach endeared him as much to politicians as his military achievements endeared him to the public, and he was a natural choice for the delicate task of inducing Natal to surrender her independence. Success, however, had gone to his head, and he displayed many of the unpleasant personal traits that had once attended George Brinton McClellan's too-sudden elevation. He was of the opinion that only soldiers were capable of resolving great complexities, either military or civil, and he was privately convinced that his own qualifications for such activity were pre-eminent. He had actually digested very little of the great masses of print he had devoured, and Sir William Gilbert was to prick him neatly as the "very model of a Modern Major-General." Obsequiousness itself to aristocracy, he had an abrasive scorn for civilians, and especially the politicians and newspapermen who had made him. The latter he referred to in his *Pocket Book* as the "newly-invented curse of armies" and a "race of drones," not even excepting the famous Henry Morton Stanley, whom he grudgingly admitted having seen at Amoaful giving yeoman service in the front lines with a rifle. (Stanley paid him back in coin by pointing out that half the Ashanti Ring was making anonymous money on the side scribbling for the dailies, and even chided Wolseley himself for scoring a beat by sending a special steamer to England simply to announce his intended movements—at a cost of £7,000.)

If the Gold Coast had been an almost purely military problem, Natal was a political one. For all his overweening self-confidence, Wolseley was apprehensive. He knew very little about southern Africa and less about its politics, and his mission was ticklish. Before he left London, he was carefully briefed by Carnarvon, and also by Shepstone, who was more firmly entrenched than ever. Shepstone had successfully foisted the onus of the Langalibalele trial onto Pine, who had sent him to London to plead his case, and when he returned to Natal it was with the dispatches informing Pine that Wolseley was to replace him. His survival was based not only on his overwhelming knowledge of native affairs, which made him appear indispensable, but also on his accord with Carnarvon's confederation schemes. Froude was still digesting the Colonial Office files, and Wolseley went out armed with the rudiments of each man's thinking.

He planned his trip as carefully as his military campaigns. His staff included the brilliant Pomeroy-Colley, Major Butler, Henry Brackenbury and other veterans of the Ashanti Ring, soon to be known as the "Wolseley Ring," and he spent the long March days on the passage out poring over Blue Books. Before he reached Capetown, he had formed a solid estimate of the situation, and from Madeira he cabled Carnarvon for the two items Natal would infallibly request: a larger Imperial garrison to counter the Zulu threat, and a loan of £1,000,000 for a railroad to the interior before the Transvaal drove a line to Delagoa Bay. The hapless Pretorius had eventually been succeeded by the Reverend Thomas François Burgers, who was even then in Europe raising an inadequate loan at usurious rates, and Burgers had left General Petrus Joubert behind as Acting President. Carnarvon granted the troops freely, but he had already been to Parliament once that year for a loan for the Fiji Islands, and he did not care to repeat the experience.

Wolseley landed at Capetown, where he met Barkly, Molteno and Lieutenant General Sir Arthur Cunynghame, known as "War Horse," who commanded the troops in southern Africa. Molteno was furious, because the returning Shepstone had brought him the news that an enactment of his Parliament had been repealed, with Langalibalele to be released from Robben's Island and given the run of the Cape Colony, and his ire stiffened his resistance to all suggestions from Carnarvon. Wolseley was to predict correctly that confederation was a forlorn hope as long as Molteno was in office. Cunynghame was also much put out, because he had had every right to expect the post that Wolseley now held, and Wolseley's attempts to soothe his ruffled feelings were hardly helped by his previous insistence to Carnarvon that his military command was not to be subordinated to Cunynghame. Leaving the sticky atmosphere of Capetown, he pressed on to Durban by warship and to Pietermaritzburg in a bone-jolting brake.

He was sworn in immediately and plunged into his assignment with an aggressive energy that left Natal gaping. Sir Benjamin Pine, unwilling to face the patent end of his comfortable career, was hanging on and complaining pathetically that the Colonial Office was still addressing dispatches to him. Wolseley unceremoniously packed him into the limbo of retirement, and then spotted his staff in strategic executive offices. Accustomed to stringent military accountings, they made short work of confusion and mismanagement and soon infused an unwonted zeal and punctuality into the lackadaisical administration.

Wolseley never lost sight of his main objective. For the sake of his own reputation he hoped to succeed without calling for help, but he candidly admitted at once that he had the threat of coercive Imperial legislation in his pocket. There was, furthermore, a likely war shaping up again in Burma, and Wolseley, with his eye on the command of the inevitable expedition, wanted to be out of Natal by November.

He neatly side-stepped the thorny question of Natal's parallel bishops. "I will ask both of them to dinner," he confided to a friend, "and go to neither of their services." He was civility itself to the Colensos, until Harriet staggered him by her relentless dinner-table campaign for justice for the amaHlubi. Langalibalele remained in exile, and the sum appropriated for amaPutini restitution remained undistributed. Wolseley, "that mighty man of war," as Mrs. Colenso styled him, dismissed the languishing chieftain with a feeble bon mot: "I call him 'Longbelly,' for I never can spell his infernal barbarian cognomen." With Shepstone at the new governor's elbow at every step, the Colensos had reason to grieve.

Wolseley shrewdly depended on the very rawness of the colonists to help his political campaign. He was the pampered darling of the distant, glittering and unattainable world of London high society, and for a brief instant he opened its doors to the starvelings of Natal. Armed with a cargo of champagne purchased in Capetown, of a brand so inferior he disdained it himself, he gave a series of balls to which almost everybody in Natal who owned a frock coat and a colored tie was invited. Levees with 600 guests cast even Prince Alfred's visit a decade earlier into the shade, and every yard of silk and every pair of white gloves in Natal was bought out. When the Duke of Manchester sent out his son armed with a letter from the Prince of Wales and seeking employment as an A.D.C. (Wolseley had skillfully avoided him in London), Lord Mandeville was set to work correcting invitation cards.

Wolseley professed to find the work distasteful. He had characterized the *haut monde* of Capetown as "a collection of housemaids with their greengrocer admirers in attendance upon them. Only fancy having to make love to such a set for months to come." In Pietermaritzburg, complaining to his wife that his hand was still clammy from the pump-handle work, he found the women "plain, with yellow-green complexions: they look like cockatoos with dirty plumage."

The political mission was settled by May. Despite suborned newspapers and stunned legislators, Wolseley failed to reduce the number of elected members below the number of appointed members, but his compromise bill to bring the number of appointed members up to the number of elected members passed, aided by the fortuitous absence of two members of the opposition and the momentary confusion of his major opponent, who voted the wrong way. With the Governor casting the deciding vote in deadlock, it was victory of sorts. Enormously relieved, he made way in August for the able Sir Henry Bulwer and sailed away in search of fresh laurels.

His last months in Natal had been devoted to confederation. He sent Butler to the Free State and Pomeroy-Colley to the Transvaal to sound Boer temper for Carnarvon. Joubert, perhaps suspecting that Wolseley was capable of annexing the Transvaal out of hand, saved the South African Republic for two years by tantalizing Pomeroy-Colley with soft words that sent Carnarvon's hopes soaring. Froude had landed in Capetown and he visited Wolseley on his tour. He wanted Wolseley to chair the confederation conference he still hoped to convene in Africa, but Molteno's resistance scotched that plan and Carnarvon, still hopeful, announced that a preliminary conference would be held in London.

It met in August of 1876. Carnarvon chaired it himself, with Wolseley (the Burmese expedition having fallen through) as vice-chairman. Froude represented Griqualand West, and Brand came for the Orange Free State, although he walked out as soon as confederation was mentioned. Shepstone had come to London again to represent Natal; Molteno happened to be in London but refused to appear even as a witness. The Transvaal was not represented.

The conference was not even able to discuss confederation, and Carnarvon's policy had reached an impasse. He was powerless to move against Molteno, but he could move against Barkly, and Froude now made what seemed to be a brilliant suggestion. On October 13, 1876, Carnarvon wrote to Sir Bartle Frere and urged him to go out to the Cape as Governor.

The choice was indeed impressive. Henry Bartle Edward Frere had been born in 1815 and had entered the Bombay civil service in 1834 after attending Haileybury. Irked by the prospect of a long sea voyage via the Cape of Good Hope, he proceeded to Malta, where in a month he picked up sufficient Arabic to "scold his way through Egypt." He then took passage to Alexandria in a Greek barkentine, pushed up the Nile, and struck out across the desert on a camel. He crossed the Red Sea in an open boat, visited Jidda while crossing Arabia, and sailed from Mocha in an Arab dhow. His arrival in Bombay was so unusual that he had difficulty in proving his identity.

In a year he spoke Hindustani, Marathi and Gujarti and was a collector at Poona. By 1842 he was Secretary to the Governor of Bombay and had married his daughter. In 1850 he became Governor of Scinde. His direction was firm, his manner mild and conciliatory. A man of enormous integrity, he had a powerful sense of the civilizing responsibility of the British Raj, and he labored incessantly to improve the lot of his charges. Land reform, roads, municipal buildings, civic organizations, hospitals and schools marked his progress. He had remarkable trust in properly trained native officials, and whenever possible he staffed his innovations with Indians. Returning from home leave in May of 1857, he found India aflame with the Sepoy Rebellion. He hurried to the Scinde, already asmolder, and instead of calling for help dispatched all the troops at his command to the centers of the revolt. With less than 200 European troops, at a time when still-loyal Sepoy regiments were being disarmed and disbanded, he raised fresh native levies and used them to stamp out the few sparks in his territory, turning captured leaders over to native courts for trial.

In 1859 he received the thanks of both houses of Parliament and a Companionship of the Bath; in 1862 he became Governor of Bombay. He governed for five years during a frenzied speculation touched off by the failure of Confederate cotton to reach the world market; before the end of his term in 1866 the price of Indian cotton collapsed and with it the Bank of Bombay. Frere had been a director, and had foreseen but could not forestall the crash, which was caused by a defective charter. He returned to England in 1867 to join the Indian Council, and in 1872 he visited Zanzibar to negotiate an antislavery treaty with the Sultan. By 1876 he was a Grand Commander of the Bath, a baronet and a member of the Privy Council. He was still a poor man, and was hoping to retire.

Frere was a man of exceptional ability who unquestionably had the stature to carry union into effect, but his talents did not readily lend themselves to the southern African scene. India's millions, topped with a proportionally small but still numerous class of educated natives, had been governed by a professional corps of trained civil servants. Most Englishmen in India were somehow connected with the task of civil or military administration, and distance from London gave this corps a degree of autonomy that the Cape had never enjoyed, even in the days of sail. Frere's skills had been developed in an atmosphere of benevolent autocracy; he was prepared to assume responsibility for major policies, and he had the confidence to act without a tedious wait for approval from London. His success had furthermore been based in large measure on the enthusiastic support of the leaders of the people he had been appointed to govern. He had never had to cope with the political capriciousness of an elected prime minister, nor to deal with natives lacking civilized leaders, who could hope for no civil service post higher than interpreter.

The Cape post was a thankless one, with prestige and prerogatives too low to attract a leading proconsul of Empire. Carnarvon entreated Frere to accept for two years to preside over union and to remain as the first Governor General. Deprecating the present salary of £5,000, he added an immediate representation allowance of £2,000 and suggested £10,000 for the rank of Governor General. There was also the plain hint of a peerage, and to increase his status Frere was also to be High Commissioner of Native Affairs for South Africa, giving him a strong voice in Natal, Griqualand West, Basutoland and the Transkei, as well as in the Cape. The offer was tempting, and by mid-April of 1877 Frere was in Capetown.

He was still getting settled, sixteen days later, when he received the news that Theophilus Shepstone had annexed the Transvaal on the twelfth of April.

Frere had known that some such action might be in the wind, but it had not been of his making. The annexation was the second result of the impasse Carnarvon had reached after his abortive conference in London in August of 1876.

The South African Republic was only legally a nation state. The commerce of its small scattered settlements was largely in the hands of perhaps a thousand English settlers, while some 6,500 Boer families dwelt on the sprawling farms that petered out at ill-defined boundaries. Boer and Briton lived in amity, without racial bitterness, and if the Dutch stock controlled the rude governmental machinery, British influence was strong—and vociferous. The Boer ran to a parochial self-rule; he was passionately political but far too individualistic to submit to majority rule. The Transvaal was a true but a feeble democracy, and the law did not run powerfully. The President was a well-meaning predikant, who spent his personal wealth freely on his state, but plagued by the vagaries of his people, chronic ill-health and a hopeless press of problems, he brought his country to the verge of chaos. When the Reverend François Burgers was elected, over 300 Boers registered their protest at the scandal of heresy which had tainted his clerical career by trekking beyond what passed for the borders, and those that remained withheld the trust he needed. In speech and thought and dress he was more European than Boer, and when he put his profile on a new coinage his people were shocked.

The Transvaal had a dream. If it could drive a railroad from Pretoria east to the sea, it could win a true economic independence from the long arms of British commerce that forever barred its access to the world markets. Delagoa Bay would replace Durban and Capetown, and the high veld would bloom. Railroads, however, cost money, which was a notoriously short commodity in a state where the Postmaster General eventually had to take his salary in stamps and the Surveyor General in land, and the mid-1870's were poor times to raise capital abroad. There was little faith in foreign investments, less faith in speculative railroads, and least faith of all in the Transvaal's ability to repay. Burgers tried. His government was already being kept afloat by secret loans from the Cape Commercial Bank, and when the directors refused to increase a debt that was already disastrously high and secured by dubious collateral, Burgers fled to Europe and secured a loan in Holland at a ruinous rate. The shares in his venture were virtually unsalable, the rail line had never even been surveyed, and Burgers used his initial payments to purchase rolling stock in order to bolster public confidence. The loan was secured with 3,000,000 acres of public land, and when the first installment was due, Burgers was forced to meet it out of the capital. He returned to the Transvaal with less cash than he had started with, to find the baPedi chieftain Sekukuni surging out of his cramped quarters and already astride the projected rail line and a portion of the pledged lands to boot.

Burgers called out a commando, enlisted Swazi allies, and set out to wage war. The campaign was a fiasco. The Boers, brave fighters in defense of their own farms, saw no reason to risk their lives or their horses fighting for a state cause, and Sekukuni beat off their half-hearted attacks. The commando expected its pay in looted cattle, and since the baPedi had prudently removed their herds, the Boers confiscated the few that their native allies had captured. The Swazis quit in a dangerous huff, and the commando retreated. Sekukuni's initial success sent a wave of defiance welling through all of black southern Africa, and the Transvaal was decried on all sides. Alleged atrocities by a few mercenaries under a Prussian adventurer added to the uproar.

The Colonial Office had followed these events with interest. Carnarvon was determined to stop Boer access to the sea. International arbitration under Marshal MacMahon of France had placed Delagoa Bay firmly in Portuguese hands, and the Colonial Office had neither the cash to buy it nor the temerity to approach Parliament. The answer was obviously annexation, which would join the Transvaal to Natal and Griqualand West in a northeast union with which the relatively stable Orange Free State and the Cape would have to come to terms. England, however, could hardly cap its long vacillating history in southern Africa by gratuitously snuffing out the independence of a sovereign state, however misguided, and annexation would only be possible if it were the freely expressed desire of the population.

Carnarvon's ears were alert to just such sounds, and they were not lacking in the long months of 1876. The Transvaal Britons urged just this course in newspapers, letters and petitions, and the directors of the Cape Commercial Bank, scenting rescue from their dilemma, worked toward the same goal. Many responsible Boers, tired of their antic Volksraad, were not averse to the idea, and there were no means to sound the temper of the high-veld Boers, who had not yet coalesced around their most able leader, Paul Kruger. The old cries of Boer slavers and cruelty were raised anew, and they went largely unanswered. When the Sekukuni imbroglio focused attention on native disturbances throughout southern Africa, Carnarvon found his opening.

Sir Theophilus Shepstone, K.C.M.G., had been knighted upon his arrival in London at the beginning of August, 1876, and throughout the confederation conference he had been a tower of strength and a restraining influence on Carnarvon. He conferred with Wolseley, Froude and Brand, and he tried to induce Molteno to attend the sessions. He counseled against precipitous action in the Transvaal, and he advised that negotiations with that unhappy state should be put in the hands of Sir Henry Bulwer, currently governing in Natal and longing for release from his duties in time to visit his dying father in England. Shepstone was touring in Wales when he saw in a newspaper an excited telegram from Barkly painting a lurid picture of the defeat of the Sekukuni commando. He hurried back to London, to find Carnarvon galvanized. The leading authority on native affairs was suddenly bathed in a new light. Speaking fluent Afrikaans and known to thousands of Boers, it seemed to Carnarvon that his ability to influence the Transvaalers must equal his proven ability with the Natal Kaffirs and the Zulus. On the twenty-third of September, on a day's notice and much to his astonishment, Shepstone sailed for Capetown. Among his papers was an unsigned copy of a secret Royal Commission and ringing in his ears were last-minute instructions from Carnarvon the gist of which is not clear to this day. The two taken together empowered him to proceed to Pretoria and to run up the British flag, providing he felt he had the consent of the population.

The written charter hedged his power by clearly stating that the consent of the Transvaalers was mandatory, and it further required him to submit his proclamation to Barkly—then in his final weeks before Frere replaced him—for approval. The last sentence then gave him permission to annex without referral if "the circumstances of the case are such as in your opinion make it necessary to issue a Proclamation forthwith." This was carte blanche.

At precisely what point Shepstone decided to proceed with annexation is shrouded in mystery, but somewhere on the four weeks' voyage the impassive administrator of native affairs entered on a new and, for him, disastrous role. Ignorant of the most elementary principles of finance, of framing laws to govern Europeans, and above all, ignorant of the character of the high-veld Boer, he saw his ancient dream of benign rule over a personal kingdom at last within his grasp, and with the natives replaced by Europeans to boot. He shut his eyes and ears to all sights and sounds save those that fitted his delusion, and slowly and implacably assumed a role for which he was entirely unfitted.

Both Shepstone's vessel and the transport bringing a reinforcing battalion hard on his heels were wrecked on Dassen Island, but Shepstone reached Capetown safely to learn that Sekukuni had not followed up his initial advantage and that the crisis that had triggered Carnarvon was even then passing. Annexation demanded a crisis, and if Sekukuni would not provide one, Cetshwayo would. For the next few months Shepstone cut a sorry figure.

He first proceeded to Natal, and then paused for ten weeks of cautious backing and filling. A Wolseley—and for all his bombast Sir Garnet was a remarkably clear-headed man of direct action—would have pressed straight on to Pretoria and taken over, but Shepstone now tarried for several reasons. Neither the original of his secret commission with the Queen's signature nor the extra battalion of the 3d Buffs, which Barkly was holding at Capetown, had yet arrived, and Shepstone was not the man to move without the one in his pocket and the other on the Transvaal border. An even more important reason was the effect his move might have on the unpredictable mind of the Zulu king.

Cetshwayo ruled from month to month with no firm policy. The increasing number of altercations with Boer farmers drifting into the disputed area behind the Blood River irked him, Swazi cattle in Transvaal territory north of the Pongola River tempted him, Shepstone's personality and a vague sense of the consequences were he to disturb the peace of Natal intimidated him, and the restless vigor of his unblooded regiments kept him considering opportunities for the long-overdue washing of the spears that custom demanded of his reign. Beyond these formless pressures no rudder steered the Zulu ship of state. Through the occasional exchange of messengers, Cetshwayo maintained a species of contact with Sekukuni and with native chieftains as far afield as the Transkei and Basutoland, and he was reasonably well informed about major events and attitudes. The links, however, were far too sketchy to maintain anything like a co-ordinated plan of action, and in the utter absence of written records not even their purport can be traced. Cetshwayo, for example, may have urged Sekukuni to attack the Boers, or Sekukuni may have urged Cetshwayo to threaten the Swazis, or both may have occurred. The subject at any rate seems to have been discussed, and action by either party would have pleased the other. For fifteen years Shepstone had resolutely vetoed any demonstration by the Zulus, but he now ardently desired them to bring pressure on the Transvaalers and their subject Swazis in order to increase the justification for his contemplated annexation. He had not the slightest intention of permitting a general outbreak, and since his control over Cetshwayo, while successful to date, was largely based on the personal image he had managed to project, it was imperative for him to sound the Zulu's temper and to insure that his own movements and the alarming concentration of troops in Natal were not misinterpreted.

There was fog in the press and fog in official correspondence, and even Bulwer, who was unusually impervious to cries of havoc, was uneasy about the Zulus. At this critical juncture, with his career dependent as never before on an exact knowledge of the temper of the royal kraal, Shepstone cast aside a lifetime's social prejudice and sent for John Dunn. The message crossed that drifting hunter's trail on one of his periodic visits to Durban to buy guns and replenish his ammunition; Shepstone hurried down from Pietermaritzburg but missed him, and Dunn returned to Cetshwayo's kraal and stayed there while Shepstone drummed his fingers and wondered if his letter had ever reached him. He then interviewed another trader who had been visiting Uhamu near the disputed territory, but the results were meager: the Zulus most likely would not attack the Swazis, and they didn't like the Boers. Just before Christmas Shepstone finally saw a detailed letter Dunn had sent to a friend in Natal, which indicated that Cetshwayo was determined not to yield the disputed territory, but had no intentions of making an attack on either the Swazis or the Boers. This was disappointing news, but Shepstone had waited long enough.

On the twenty-seventh of December, accompanied by 24 members of the Natal Mounted Police and a staff of eight civilians, Shepstone set out for Pretoria. He took four weeks to get there, and he stopped to talk with every shop and hotel keeper along the way. With Sekukuni quiescent and Cetshwayo biding his time, the Transvaal's frozen credit and the prevailing financial distress formed the most visible crisis, and

Shepstone's journals and correspondence sound as if he had embarked on a special survey for the Bank of England. Intent on his instructions not to annex without the consent of the population, he listened to an interminable stream of conversation that obviously favored a change of government. He was welcomed on every hand because he was a famous man and in many cases an old friend, and if the purpose of his visit was not quite clear, he was obviously a representative of the Crown, which stood for stability and order and increased commerce. He failed to talk to a single high-veld Boer, and he thus missed the important point that the only change the fiercely independent farmers who formed the bulk of the population wanted was the replacement of the odious Burgers.

The President, facing an imminent election he was bound to lose, and the population of Pretoria, largely Englishmen or long-unpaid Transvaal civil servants, welcomed Shepstone warmly. He started out to use Wolseley's "sherry and champagne" tactics, a role he was ill adapted for, and when Paul Kruger gratuitously warned him not to tamper with the Republic's independence, he lapsed into the devastating silence that had always served him so well with the Bantu. Visiting Boer politicans were shunted to his staff, which included a son-in-law financially involved in the Natal railroad schemes and thus resolutely opposed to the Delagoa Bay line, and Rider Haggard, the future novelist, who was violently prejudiced against Boers. Burgers knew what was coming, and Shepstone informed him he would stay his hand if the President would carry out necessary reforms. Burgers, however, could do nothing with his noisy and recalcitrant Volksraad. It postponed to May the presidential election, refused to sign a peace treaty with Sekukuni, installed Kruger in the hastily created post of vice-president, batted down most of the proposed reforms, and then disbanded. Shepstone discussed the proclamation of annexation with Burgers, as well as the formal note of protest Burgers would present, and on April 12, 1877, the Queen's flag floated over Pretoria.

Initial congratulations poured in from every side. Shepstone, still listening to his selected voices, was convinced his act was justified and that he had won a signal victory for confederation. He had in reality wrecked it, and marred the final stages of his own career. Disillusion was not long in coming; the Transvaalers, happy enough to see Burgers go, had no desire to see him replaced by such a centralized autocrat as Shepstone soon proved to be, the appalled Orange Free State feared for its own independence and wanted nothing more to do with confederation, and a wave of protest swept even the western Cape. Shepstone shortly had his hands full with the administration of the Transvaal, and he hardly had time to note the death of confederation.

Burgers was pensioned off—there is clear evidence that the Colonial Office felt obligated to him—and all the former civil servants except Kruger agreed to stay on. Shepstone was at first inclined to dismiss the political strength of a man who combed his greasy locks at the dinner table and used his napkin for a handkerchief; he found Kruger's threat to travel to London to protest to Carnarvon amusing until Kruger actually managed to scrape the money together. When Carnarvon fell back on Shepstone's position and claimed that the sentiment of the country was in favor of annexation, Kruger did what Shepstone should have done in the first place; he circulated petitions and proved that the bulk of the population was opposed to life under a British government.

All of Shepstone's failings were now exposed in a pitiless light. Accustomed to running a small governmental department on an annual appropriation, he ran through a large Crown grant without accomplishing any reforms or providing for future revenues. His accounts were so dilatory and bizarre that he soon had a London official at his elbow to control him, and his bent for rule by executive fiat destroyed any chance for rapport between the Boers and the Crown. Kruger bided his time, and the influence of Sir Theophilus Shepstone, K.C.M.G., sometime Secretary for Natal Affairs in Natal, slowly began to fade from the scene of Zululand.

Frere in the meantime was settling into his work in Capetown. The terms of his commission gave him no clear-cut authority outside the Cape Colony, and Shepstone in particular was independent of him. Frere privately thought his act of annexation was premature, but he supported Shepstone as best he could, and the two were in continual and amicable correspondence. Frere saw, long before Shepstone, the financial reefs toward which the new administration was drifting, and he tactfully kept Carnarvon apprised of the dangers. He also took steps to fortify Simons Bay and he tried unsuccessfully to induce Carnarvon to annex the great wastelands of Namaqualand and Damaraland.

In August he decided to visit Shepstone in Pretoria, using the opportunity to see the eastern Cape and Natal for himself. The native unrest disturbed him considerably, and it was difficult to judge the merits of each fresh dispute from the distant and settled atmosphere of Capetown. The slow increase of tension on all sides reminded him uncomfortably of India in the years preceding the Sepoy Rebellion, and he was convinced that the greatest barrier to confederation was the lack of any unified native land policy. Much of the resistance to the objective he had been sent out to attain obviously stemmed from each area's fear that in union it would lose the independence it needed to cope with a particular local situation, and unless Frere could somehow lance the pressure the golden advantages of confederation would never be apparent.

He sailed to Port Elizabeth and moved on through Grahamstown to Kingwilliamstown, the last Cape Colony settlement in the Ciskei. He found the frontier in the grip of an acute war scare, and at this point the pressure of events took over his movements and effectively removed him from the road to confederation. He would be seven months in Kingwilliamstown, living in barracks with the officers of the 1st Battalion of the 24th Regiment, and it would be an eventful year and a half before he would finally see Shepstone in Pretoria.

Kingwilliamstown lay between the Great Fish River, which in the 1770's had suddenly become the boundary between the Bantu pressing down from the north and the advancing fringe of Boer civilization, and the Kei River, to which this frontier had been pushed in a century of constant turmoil. The area between the two rivers was inhabited by a mixed population of English settlers and Boer farmers, with a heavy admixture of German immigrants who had been refugees in England when they had formed a German Legion to fight in the Crimean War. Trained too late for use, many of them accepted land in British Kaffraria as a reward for their services. Jammed in amongst these settlers lived the Gaikas, under a lame and alcoholic chieftain named Sandili. These were British subjects, but just across the Kei River dwelt two semi-independent tribes, the coastal Gcalekas under Kreli and the Fingoes farther inland.

The Fingoes were governmental favorites, praised for their industry and progress. Originally mixed refugees from the Shakan deluge, they had once been Gcaleka slaves and were even now emplaced on land taken from Kreli. The best frontier officials had worked with them, and their loyalty to the Crown was based on gratitude and an acute fear of their former masters. Kreli's Gcalekas had been neglected and were regarded as indolent troublemakers. An overworked British Resident, Colonel Eustace, represented the Crown, but he had to live in a native hut and did not even have the services of a paid clerk.

Both Ciskei and Transkei were greatly overcrowded with Europeans, natives and cattle, and the land was overgrazed and failing. A ruinous drought had brought the frail native economy to the edge of collapse, and complaints of trespass and cattle theft were unending. Frere entered the Transkei to confer with Eustace, but Kreli, whose father, Hinza, had been shot under a flag of truce, refused to come when summoned. Frere retired to Kingwilliamstown, the Gcalekas sought relief at the expense of the Fingoes, and events took their natural course.

John X. Merriman, the Cape Commissioner of Crown Lands, and

Charles Brownlee, the Cape Secretary for Native Affairs, were both in Kingwilliamstown. Able, intelligent men, they owed their loyalty to Molteno, and they found Frere's presence confining. Sir Bartle had placed direction of operations against the Gcalekas under Sir Arthur Cunynghame, but the bulk of the available troops were Fingo levies, colonial volunteers and several hundred men of the Frontier Armed & Mounted Police, an overworked and underpaid standing body of troops under Commandant Charles Duncan Griffith, an old soldier who had fought against both Sandili and Kreli twenty years before and who had helped to track Langalibalele down in Basutoland in 1873.

In October the Gcalekas attacked the Fingoes, the settlers and scattered units of the F.A.&M.P. indiscriminately; Cunynghame and Griffith moved their forces into the Transkei; there were a few sharp fights; and by the end of the month Kreli had fled north of the Bashee River with his forces, leaving 720 dead behind. The volunteers burned the Gcaleka kraals, lifted 13,000 of their cattle and returned to Ciskei as settlers began to move into the deserted lands.

The campaign had been short and apparently decisive, but it was no sooner over than Merriman began to quarrel with Frere. The two Cape officials felt that colonial forces were better fitted to wage native war than Imperial forces, and they resented the control Cunynghame had exercised over the F.A. & M.P. and the colonial volunteers. Molteno was shortly drawn to the defense of his ministers, and even as they bickered, Kreli and his men came streaming back across the Bashee and Sandili's Gaikas rose to join them. The Gcalekas were independent, but Sandili was a British subject and his Gaika rebels were to be shot on sight; the settlers fled to hastily laagered dorps and the various forces started the arduous task of flushing small bands of ill-armed natives out of the great patches of impenetrable bush that dotted the arid hills.

Frere now had a full-fledged Kaffir War—the Ninth—on his hands, and Merriman was still making trouble. He had elevated Griffith to the post of Commandant General of the colonial forces, created a separate commissariat, and had announced his intention of operating independently of Cunynghame.

Molteno first tried to induce Frere to return to Capetown, and then, in January of 1878, came himself to Kingwilliamstown. A series of unsatisfactory interviews ensued. Molteno, the elected official, was insistent on the prerogatives of colonial independence; Frere, used to the order and dispatch of competent administrative procedures, was disgusted by the haphazard staffing of the sketchy Cape Colony structure and horrified by what he regarded as sheer lunacy on Merriman's part. Molteno finally lost his temper and threatened to resign; to his utter amazement Frere called his bluff and, when he retracted, dismissed him anyway. Gordon Sprigg, a member of the Legislative Assembly, left his family and farm near Kingwilliamstown at Frere's bidding (his cattle were lifted hours later by raiding Gaikas) and dutifully undertook to form a new ministry.

Frere's action had been considerably more precipitate and of a more dubious legality than had Shepstone's. The dismissal was virtually unique in British constitutional annals; the relationship between appointed Governor and elected Prime Minister had never been clearly defined, and if nothing in Frere's charter empowered him to remove the people's choice in the name of the Crown, neither was there anything to hinder him. The high-handed action, viewed askance in London, received the approval of the Cape, since Sprigg was popular and the dragging war had weakened Molteno's image too much to allow him to kindle a flame on the altar of colonial independence.

There were other changes as well. Carnarvon, discouraged by the disappearance of all hope of confederation, abruptly resigned. He was replaced by Sir Michael Hicks Beach, whose attention was almost immediately engaged by events in Afghanistan and a growing crisis with Russia. Frere was left without his sponsor, and with southern Africa no longer at the top of the Colonial Office agenda, the close attention previously paid to his activity lessened.

Sir Arthur Cunynghame, who was anathema even to the officials who supported Frere, was also recalled. His place was taken by Lieutenant General the Honourable Sir Frederic Augustus Thesiger, C.B., who arrived in Kingwilliamstown on March 4, 1878, and quietly assumed command of the Imperial forces in South Africa.

The Thesiger family, of yeoman Saxon stock, moved to England from the vicinity of Dresden in the middle of the eighteenth century, and the General's father, after a short stint as a midshipman, embarked on a legal career in 1818. His progress was distinguished. After successive service as Solicitor General and Attorney General he attained the highest judicial post in the land and in 1858, aged sixty-four, was appointed Lord High Chancellor and raised to the peerage as the First Baron Chelmsford. His active career continued until 1868, when Lord Derby retired. Disraeli wanted a stronger orator for parliamentary battles, and rather summarily set Chelmsford aside.

Frederic Augustus Thesiger was born on May 31, 1827. He was the eldest of seven children, and by the time he was sixteen, his father was already applying to the Duke of Wellington for a vacancy in the Grenadier Guards. The waiting list proved to be too long, and in December of 1844 Thesiger was gazetted to the Rifle Brigade, then in Halifax. The lad bided his time, however, and a year later he had purchased an exchange and was on his way back to London as ensign and lieutenant. In 1850 he was promoted lieutenant and captain, and in 1852 started a tour as A.D.C. to the Viceroy of Ireland.

In May of 1855 he reached the Crimea, where he saw both troop and staff duty and was promoted brevet major in November. Following two more years in England, he reached India in June of 1858, where as captain and lieutenant colonel he participated in the last stages of the Sepoy Rebellion. From 1861 until 1863 he was on staff duty in Bombay, and for the next five years he commanded the 95th Regiment in India. In 1866 he had married the daughter of an Indian Army general, and in 1868 he first accompanied Sir Robert Napier's staff on the Abyssinian campaign to chastise the Emperor Theodore, and then served for a few months as A.D.C. to Queen Victoria. He then returned to India as Adjutant General, and finally came back to England in March of 1874.

He first commanded troops at Shorncliffe, where Sir John Moore had trained the Light Division for the Peninsular campaign, and then took command at Aldershot. In March of 1877 he was promoted to major general, antedated to November of 1868. His career had been varied, light on action and heavy with peacetime staff duties, but Thesiger was as well qualified for his profession as the run of his contemporaries.

He was a tall and lanky man, with handsome intelligent features half hidden behind the thick bush of a rounded spade beard. He was known to the Army as a competent and reliable officer, well thought of at Horse Guards and Windsor, a man who would never come to mind for a particular job by virtue of special talents, but one who once chosen would be quite reliable. In only one respect was he regarded as above the average; he was known as a perfect gentleman and a model of considerate tact.

It was a peculiar factor to be noted, and it was not based on any exaggerated observance of protocol. Thesiger was neither a dandy nor a high liver, and he was in fact a teetotaler. His contacts with others were marked with an essential decency that left a vivid impression and drew an intense loyalty from his staff. His decisions were quick but never obstinately held, and he was more apt to be accused of vacillation than procrastination. He was also capable of sharp, and even stinging rebukes, but they were never the result of choleric outbursts and he issued them only when he felt they were truly deserved and the fault was still warm.

Unlike Wolseley, he believed military operations and politics were distinct fields, which were best not vested in one man. He saw himself as the military arm of the political administration, and he devoted himself to attaining the military objectives set before him without questioning their genesis. Wolseley's superior in tact and insight, he left far fewer enemies in his wake, but he utterly lacked Sir Garnet's fire and impetuous drive. He cultivated a reserve so intense that he appeared wooden and colorless to all save a few intimates, and a letter to his expectant bride as he left for Abyssinia is perhaps characteristic:

I am afraid if anyone saw me writing these lines, they would not believe that I was an Adjutant General proceeding to join an army in the field—I feel more like a schoolboy leaving home the second time, when the novelty of the new life has vanished and nothing remains but the miseries of the moment. It is, of course, when alone, that I feel as I have written; I do not let the outside world penetrate into my secret thoughts.

The call to finish a sputtering native war on the eastern Cape frontier was not one to arouse enthusiasm in the breast of a British general. Many officers had broken their teeth on the problem of using European troops to apply pressure to mosquitolike clouds of Bantu who never presented a firm target and melted into the features of a crevice-ridden landscape. Clear-cut victories were out of the question, and potential disaster lurked in every patch of impenetrable bush. "Yours, my dear Thesiger, is a command of great danger to your reputation," wrote a retired Kaffir-fighter in a rambling letter filled with misinformation about the location of Gaikas and Gcalekas a generation ago and much sage advice about patrol jackets and waterproof sheets. A general blooded in the Eighth Kaffir War wrote his successor in the Ninth Kaffir War: "At present, I would presume to say, if it is proposed tormenting the Caffres by destroying their huts, this can only be done with safety with judicious skirmishing thro' the bush, and never appearing within shot in the open. The Caffres will retire before you, but when the huts are destroyed you must then retire. Your rear and perhaps your flanks will be attacked."

By early February Thesiger was aboard a mail steamer en route for Capetown, and taking stock of the additions to his command. A detachment of 190 men scraped together from Cardwell's new depots and destined to reinforce battalions already serving in South Africa drew his attention, and he lost no time in pointing out to His Royal Highness the Duke of Cambridge that over 60 per cent of these men had less than four months' service, had never fired a musketry course and had not even been dismissed recruit's drill.

If Thesiger was exasperated by the quality of the recruits, he found some consolation in the dining salon, where two remarkable officers assigned to his staff were already embarked. Lieutenant Colonel Henry Evelyn Wood, V.C., C.B., and Major Redvers Henry Buller were widely known as staunch fighters and protégés of Sir Garnet Wolseley.

Evelyn Wood, a short lumpy man with mournful eyes and an un-kempt mustache, was physically unprepossessing. Something of a hypochondriac, he showed an alarming tendency to catch whatever ailments were current, and between bouts of genuine illness he suffered from a continual series of psychosomatic complaints. His military record, however, belied his medical history.

Born in 1838, he ran away from school in disgust over an unjust caning and entered the Royal Navy as a midshipman when barely fourteen. Three years later, a seasoned salt of sixteen, he went ashore with the Naval Brigade in the Crimea. For nine months he toiled and fought on a diet of raw salt pork, rotten biscuit and rum, and when the British assaulted the Redan in June of 1855 he arose from a sickbed to which dysentery and delirium had confined him for a fortnight to take his place in the storming column. He could barely walk, and a sailor trotted alongside to keep him in the saddle of his pony. The attack was a failure, and only two men of the entire column got through the abatis and up to the Russian embankment. They were Wood and his sailor-nurse, now struggling with a storming ladder meant for eight grown men. The sailor was killed and Wood was shot through the elbow. Somehow he crawled back to camp and remained conscious just long enough to argue a busy surgeon out of amputating his arm. A year later, with the aid of a mirror, he took his pocketknife and grimly dug eight bone splinters out of an abscess that had never healed.

Invalided home, he was offered an Army commission and reported to the 13th Light Dragoons in Ireland for training. The body of the regiment was still in the Crimea, and within a month the Commander in Chief of the British Army was writing the officer commanding the depot, ordering him to instruct Cornet Wood *not* to write Lord Har-dinge directly in future, but to go through proper channels. He added that Cornet Wood's wishes to return to the Crimea had been noted, but "Lord Hardinge has always understood it takes more than twenty-four days to make a perfect cavalry officer, which time it appears Mr. Wood has been at the depot."

In January of 1857 he started back for the Crimea and got as far as Scutari before typhoid and pneumonia laid him low. He became deliri-ous, lost all his hair and did not recognize his mother when she arrived to take over his nursing. After a long convalescence during which bedsores ate his hips away to the bone, he rejoined his regiment, but the fighting was over.

Back in Ireland he grew desperate. Cavalry life was more expensive than he had anticipated, and his raging thirst for action was unslaked. He was about to join the Foreign Legion when the Sepoy Rebellion broke out, so he exchanged into the 17th Lancers and squeaked aboard their transport just as it weighed anchor. Mastering Hindustani, he spent the long, hot summer of 1858 assigned to a column mopping up the large bands of mutineers who still roamed the countryside. Administrative duties robbed him of sleep for days at a stretch after the interminable marches were over, and fever, sunstroke and exhaustion crippled him time and again. His only concession was bed-rest in semiconscious delirium until he was able to crawl into a saddle again. Neuralgia and bad teeth puffed his face out till his eyes shut, and to add to his other difficulties he tried on a dare to ride a giraffe in a Nawab's private zoo. He slipped and the beast stepped on his face, mashing his nose and cutting his cheeks through to the teeth. For the next three days he accompanied his troops on a stretcher. Still only a twenty-year-old lieutenant, he next raised an irregular cavalry regiment, and then won a Victoria Cross by attacking a gang of bandits at heavy odds to rescue a kidnaped native merchant.

Back from India, he was stationed first in Ireland and then at Aldershot, and in a vain search for active duty and to reduce his costs transferred from the 17th Lancers to the 73d Foot and then to the 17th Foot. He abstained from one favorable exchange when an officer in the new regiment, who had been commissioned in the field in the Crimea, appealed to him not to block his promotion by coming into the regiment. By 1873 he was a brevet lieutenant colonel in the 90th Light Infantry, a graduate of the Staff College, and to have something to fall back on if he ever left the service, he had qualified as a barrister. When he married, he made his wife swear never to stand in the way of active service. She never did.

Wolseley asked for him for the Ashanti campaign and put him to work raising a regiment from the coastal tribes, using material that was substandard even by irregular standards. Wood as usual worked himself to the verge of a breakdown doing the work of ten men. He helped drive the road inland through the swamps and jungle and accompanied the subsequent advance. The retreating Ashantis, skirmishing incessantly from the jungle, left a decapitated sacrifice every few yards along the trail. Wood was finally struck down by a slug hammered from a nail, fired at point-blank range from a few yards off the trail. The surgeon exploring the wound stopped in dismay when his probe reached the pericardium; Wood was given up for lost. Wolseley bade him a tearful farewell, and he was carried back to the hospital. A few days later, feeling about as well as he ever did, Wood walked out of the hospital in disgust and rejoined his unit at the head of the road, having staggered all night through a torrential downpour on the greasy mud track. The slug never did show up.

Buller, born in 1839, had enjoyed a quieter career. Expelled from

Harrow, he entered Eton, and at sixteen had a scarifying experience. Coming home to Devon for the Christmas holidays, his tubercular mother met him in the railroad station at Exeter and suffered a hemorrhage just as his train pulled in. She could not be moved, and for two days the distraught boy tended her on a screened-off bench in the busy terminal before she died in his arms. At nineteen he was gazetted to the 60th Rifles, where his muscular figure, impassive bearing and habit of speaking in sudden final pronouncements earned him the nickname of "the Judge." He arrived in India too late for the fighting, but saw some skirmishing on the China expedition in 1860, there encountering Garnet Wolseley for the first time. He later refused to wear the campaign medal, on the ground that the war had been unjustified.

The next year he was in Canada, where a fatherly colonel took the hard-drinking youth in tow and set him on the road to professional qualification. Assigned to Wolseley for the Red River expedition after a half-dozen years of stagnation, his solid grit and determination caught Sir Garnet's attention. He passed through the Staff College by dint of sheer application, and Wolseley made him the head of the Intelligence Department on the Ashanti campaign. He stopped a slug at Essaman which failed to penetrate his skin, and he was wounded at Ordashu.

Buller was archetypical of the British field grade officer of the second half of the nineteenth century. It was a time when a career officer still needed few qualifications to follow the military trade beyond outstanding personal courage and the ability to conform with the contemporary concept of a gentleman. Buller was pre-eminent on both counts, and his courage verged on sheer rashness. He may have known the meaning of the word fear, but there is no evidence that he ever let it influence his conduct and he had no tolerance for it in others. His horsemanship was superb and his magnificent endurance let him ride most men into the ground.

He also possessed a very high order of personal leadership. He based his command on the pure force of his personality; he was stern without unjust harshness, and his demands were high but never more than he was giving himself. His enthusiasm was infectious, and he was one of the few Imperial officers who could squeeze out of irregular volunteers the performance and reliability expected of professional troops. He was, in fact, one of that small and fabled band of leaders men cheerfully follow to hell.

There were, unfortunately, serious flaws in his talents, and although the authorities were vouchsafed a glimpse of them at a critical moment in 1879, they passed unnoticed and their full import did not become apparent for another twenty years. His drinking was not yet a problem, but he had a terrible temper and his treatment of civilians was even brusquer than Wolseley's. He had threatened to horsewhip correspondents on the Gold Coast who filed copy that displeased him, and he once rose and kicked out of a mess tent a reporter who said he would read personal mail in search of a story. His leadership, moreover, so bright and sure when he rode at the head of a troop, simply did not extend beyond the range of his own voice. His powers of administration and organization were low, his grasp of strategy even lower. He was vociferous rather than articulate, and his positive manner masked the fact that what he said and wrote was not always what he actually had in mind. He was also indecisive. He made a superb major, a mediocre colonel, and an abysmally poor general.

Once at Kingwilliamstown, Thesiger set to work to get his command in hand. He left all political considerations in the hands of Sir Bartle Frere, and devoted himself to repairing the damages Cunynghame and Merriman's quarrel had inflicted on his military forces. "I was sorry to find on my arrival at this station yesterday, that I should not have the benefit of your advice and experience," he wrote immediately on his arrival to the charmed Commandant General Griffith. "My great object will be to assist the Colony in every way that lies in my power," he went on, adding, "I am most anxious to give the Colonial troops every help that they may require." This was a refreshing breeze indeed, and his division of Ciskei and Transkei into well-defined military districts, with Imperial troops and colonial volunteers alike assigned definite objectives, was greeted with enthusiasm. Equally friendly and flattering letters had gone to other officers, who under his watchful eye continued to operate with a large measure of autonomy.

The center of unrest was in the Perie Bush north of Kingwilliamstown, rough hilly ground covered with extensive patches of shrub so thick that visibility was restricted to a few feet. Gcalekas, armed with assegais and an assortment of antiquated firearms, drove their cattle into these patches whenever they were threatened, so that Thesiger's problem was limited to flushing them out and attacking them with artillery when they made a run for the next patch. It was exasperating work, largely profitless until Sandili or Kreli were killed or captured, when the tribes would collapse. It was only dangerous when troops approached the edges of the bush patches and came under fire from hidden natives; once in the bush themselves they were relatively safe.

The operations at least served to season the troops. The 1st Battalion of the 24th, the 2nd Warwickshire (in 1881 it became the South Wales Borderers), consisted of men with 21 years' service; they had been stationed in India and Gibraltar and had been in South Africa since 1874.

Old stagers, they had long since adapted themselves to the requirements of the country, and they looked with disdain on their 2nd Battalion, men with less than six years' service who had been stationed in England since 1873 and had only arrived in South Africa in March, brought up to strength with the raw recruits Thesiger had objected to. Many of their veteran N.C.O.'s had been transferred before they left England to staff Cardwell's depots, and what little training the men had received had taught them to fight shoulder to shoulder under the steadying influence of their company officers. Bush fighting was new and unsettling work. The instant a man entered a patch, his comrades were lost to sight, his officers disappeared, and he was suddenly and horribly alone in a tangled growth through which he could barely hack his way, subject to sudden shots that exploded under his very feet from natives he could not see until he literally stepped on them.

In one such action Thesiger set his guns on a nearby hill and ordered a company of the 24th to drive the Gcalekas out of a valley bush patch. The company formed an extended line and cautiously entered the undergrowth. Thesiger waited for three hours, restlessly scanning the periphery for the first sign of an emerging foe. He finally heard a single shot and saw a sudden commotion; a wounded private stumbled out, and the entire company, which had not penetrated more than a few yards, scrambled back in confusion to accompany their comrade to the rear. Thesiger sent for the company officers and vented his feelings before ordering the company back in. This time they broke through, and a small band of natives broke cover to scurry like so many quail for the next patch, while the seven-pounder muzzle-loaders loosed a few futile shells.

Buller was in his element commanding the Frontier Light Horse, a sterling body of over 200 volunteers raised the previous year at Kingwilliamstown. The troop started out in black corduroy uniforms with double red stripes down the breeches and a red puggree wound around a slouch hat, but they were soon accepting any man who could ride and shoot in his own clothes, simply adding a strip of red flannel to whatever hat he was wearing.

Wood, a hard taskmaster, was doing equally well with a roving command, and he was as usual plagued with fevers that ranged up to 104°. At one point he assembled a set of symptoms which even he found bizarre; the glands in his groin, armpits and neck swelled up, his skin peeled off "like a mummy," and chilblainlike openings appeared on his hands. Nothing daunted, he paid four Hottentots £2 to carry him to the nearest doctor, who put him to bed. A fortnight later he was again spending all day in the saddle.

Thesiger rode from one command to the next, meeting and assessing the colonial and Imperial officers who bore the brunt of the fighting. In addition to Commandant General Griffith, he liked Rupert de la Tour Lonsdale, a thirty-year-old ex-Imperial officer who invariably popped up at the first sign of a fight, leading a batch of Fingo levies, all thoroughly seasoned bush fighters. Colonel Richard Thomas Glyn, commanding the 24th Regiment, was a short, grouchy officer, inclined to need urging and forever at odds with his own officers and superiors, but he had good subordinates. Brevet Lieutenant Colonel Henry Burmester Pulleine commanded the old hands of the 1st Battalion, and had found time to raise an irregular force from the idle railroad workers who plagued the small settlements. A rough crowd of disreputable drinkers, they were soon christened "Pulleine's Lambs" and their commanding officer had his hands full. Brevet Lieutenant Colonel Henry James Degacher, commanding the 2nd Battalion, was an energetic officer and a gifted sketcher; his younger brother William commanded a company in the 1st Battalion. There was another set of brothers in the 24th Regiment, whose father had served at Waterloo. The Bromheads stemmed from Auburn in Lincoln, and they had sent their sons to the 2nd Warwickshire since 1756. Brevet Major Charles James Bromhead, a veteran of nineteen years' service, was a brilliant staff officer and a charter member of Wolseley's Ashanti Ring, who was currently on detached service in London. His younger brother Gonville was thirty-three years old and was entering his twelfth year of service. He commanded "B" Company of the 2nd Battalion. The future of his career was in considerable doubt. He had been hard of hearing for many years, and by now was virtually stone deaf. It was a serious defect; the only hearing aid of the time was an ear trumpet that no Army officer could use, and Bromhead, if he wished to continue, had no choice but to try to hide his ailment. He missed commands at drill and could do little in the field; he was moody and avoided his men, who naturally disliked him. His superiors, taking pity on him, tried to postpone the inevitable by giving "B" Company assignments that would not tax their handicapped commander, and the disgusted men usually found themselves on detached duty guarding supply dumps. In "G" Company of the 2nd Battalion Lieutenant Charles D'Aguilar Pope pointed out to Thesiger Private William Griffiths, who in 1867 had been one of five men of the regiment awarded the Victoria Cross for taking a small gig in through a thundering storm-lashed surf to Little Andaman Island to rescue a detachment imperiled by natives.

Thesiger's artillery, "N" Battery of the 5th Brigade, was under Major Arthur Harness, R.A. The forty-year-old son of a retired general, he had served many years in India, and was still unmarried. A thoroughly competent if unimaginative officer, he devoted his entire existence to the six brass seven-pounder muzzle-loaders and the 124 men of his command, and he cared little about his surroundings except insofar as they provided him with targets.

By the end of May Gcaleka resistance had petered out, and Sandili was hiding in a cave. He was known to ride a white horse, and every captured mount was eagerly inspected to see if one stirrup was shorter than the other. At the end of the month he was mortally wounded in a skirmish with Lonsdale's Fingoes; he lingered six days and then died. The body was recovered, and the heart went out of the Gaikas.

Thesiger had acquitted himself well, and he had shown a distinct flair for handling mixed, prickly groups of colonial volunteers, native levies and Imperial troops. The colonial officers found him easy to work with, and he was lavish in his thanks. The Imperial troops were equally content; there was a tendency in Kaffir warfare for units to be broken up into small parcels and strung out all over the landscape, with handfuls of men eventually getting reattached to other groups far from their parent units. Thesiger had patiently sorted out these orphans and reassembled the Imperial companies, leaving them under their own officers. Even the Navy was thankful; Cunynghame had commandeered all their landing forces to form a Naval Brigade equipped with Gatling guns, and Thesiger had sent the sailors back to their short-handed ships.

By the first of July the General was back in Capetown to confer with Frere. He reported the end of the war to the Duke of Cambridge, and thanked him for the dispatch with which he had sent out six requested staff officers. He apologized for in a sense having brought them out under false pretenses, now that the fighting was over, and he trusted the Duke would not object to his retaining them for the nonce, at least until he had been able to talk the situation over with Sir Bartle Frere. The reason he gave was ominous: "It is still, however, more than probable that active steps will have to be taken to check the arrogance of Cetywayo, Chief of the Zulus."

THE COMING OF THE WAR

G ENERAL THESIGER's matter-of-fact acceptance in July of
1878 of the probability of a war with the Zulu nation
did not stem from the results of his own observations. He was simply
accepting the opinion of his duly constituted political superior, Sir
Bartle Frere, and because it would be his job to wage that war, he
had no sooner brought the Ninth Kaffir War to a successful conclusion
than he dutifully began to prepare for such an eventuality.

A man of exceptionally broad vision, Sir Bartle Frere was one of the
very few to whom all of southern Africa was a single arena in which
no event was an isolated phenomenon. Almost from the day of his
arrival, for example, he had seen that the twin problems that beset
every territory, European underpopulation and native overpopulation,
were in every case the result of a faulty land policy, and the Ninth
Kaffir War had shown him that there was no essential difference between the land policies of the Boer republics and those of the British
colonies.

Well-watered, grassy flatlands were essential to native and European
pastoralists alike. Despite the enormous size of the country, suitable
pasturage was limited; steep mountain ranges and arid desert ate up
vast tracts, and great stretches of potentially fertile flatland were at
best only usable when water trickled through the stony riverbeds.
Winter pasturage was even more limited, and during the frequent
years of drought the scarcity of land became critical.

The distribution of these vital flatlands had been inequitable in every
territory in southern Africa. Boer and Briton had taken the best of
them, in the course of two centuries of steady encroachment backed
by force of arms, and in the process they had crowded hundreds of
thousands of natives into marginal areas where primitive agricultural
procedures had compounded the ever-present threat of drought. There
had been even more injustice in the distribution of the water, and
native land frequently depended on sources which were reserved for

adjacent European tracts and to which the native cattle were denied access. Beneath the interminable raid and counterraid for cattle was visible a far deadlier struggle for the land itself, and by the 1870's the imbalance had produced an explosive situation which the next drought might spark off.

Only in Natal had any land been set aside for the natives, where 300,000 Natal Kaffirs were crammed into reserves totaling 2,000,000 acres while perhaps 16,000 Europeans held title to another 10,000,000 acres. Despite this gross imbalance, even Natal suffered from the prevailing scarcity of land. A short-lived gold boom and the plain signs of mineral wealth and the coming railroads had long since put much of the European acreage into the hands of speculators, who rented over 5,000,000 acres of it to native squatters and waited for the inevitable rise in land prices. Natal's roads bustled with ox-drawn commerce while its farms stagnated, and with no free farms to offer immigrants, the government lured only 45 settlers in 1874.

The Transvaal had never set any land aside for its native clans, simply assuming that Africa was large enough to absorb them if they were forced to move. It had then spent its millions of acres like so much paper money, giving titles to thousands of unsurveyed and unoccupied farms to its burgers for the asking, and pledging millions of additional acres as collateral for loans. Shepstone faced not only mountainous debts and a population that objected to taxes, but also the absence of the one form of wealth which would pacify his new British subjects and finance his administration.

Only a centralized government could cope with such evils, and Frere's problem was to stave off the continual warfare caused by the scarcity of land long enough to achieve confederation. Severe drought in 1876 and 1877 and the annexation of the Transvaal now focused his attention on Zululand. Despite the absence of European settlers, this kingdom suffered from the same land shortage as the other territories. Many of the well-watered sections were hilly and stony, other grassy slopes and elevated flats were infected with the lung sickness and redwater fever that had ravaged the Zulu herds after Cetshwayo's coronation, and the tsetse fly barred broad belts to settlement. Primitive agriculture made inefficient use of what remained, and the population of perhaps a third of a million Zulus was thickly clustered about such centers as the royal kraal at Ulundi while other sections were deserted. The drought of 1877 and the winter months thus sent a wave of pressure surging against the fertile lands between the headwaters of the Buffalo and the Pongola Rivers, which had been a subject of dispute with the Transvaal since 1861.

Confederation, which Frere was more than ever determined to achieve, would inevitably have to include Zululand. There was room within union for any number of subjugated native clans, which might still retain their tribal civilization with a large degree of autonomy, but an utterly independent savage nation, with a standing army of 40,000 warriors, regulated only by the whim of an uncivilized monarch, whose frontiers marched for 200 miles with European territories, was unthinkable. Whether or not Cetshwayo had any intention of sending that army rampaging into Natal or the Transvaal was irrelevant; the point was that he could, at a score of undefended crossings. Zululand was singularly impervious to civilizing forces, and it would eventually have to be disarmed and either annexed or made to accept the guidance of a British Resident. The question was not whether such steps would ultimately be necessary, but only of the manner and timing of their occurrence, and either course ran a high risk of war.

Frere's intellect could easily accept these facts as inevitable, and he could thus consider the contingency of a preventive war while lesser minds still grappled with the question of whether or not a clash would ever be necessary. He was now subjected to strong pressures which with increasing momentum led him along the path of war, until in the end the necessity of destroying the Zulu power became an obsession with him.

The forces that influenced him are plain enough. There was, to begin with, the ground swell of restlessness that drought, cattle disease and the lack of land sent rippling across southern Africa. The Gaikas and Gcalekas were exhausted, but disorganized clans in Griqualand West were already in a rough and tumble, a Basuto faction under Morosi was in open conflict, Korannas and baTlapin of the western Transvaal were in arms, and Sekukuni's defiant bePedi were still unvanquished. Cetshwayo had never provided direct support or positive guidance for these quarrelsome clans, but they unquestionably drew a spiritual fire from the example of the Zulu nation. Scores of wandering visitors and emissaries from the kraals of Zululand kept hundreds of native firesides in the Transvaal, the Free State and the Cape spellbound with the vision of an armed and defiant black nation, staunchly resisting the encroachment of Boer and Briton alike. None dared touch them, and the washing of their spears was still to come.

These subversive comings and goings were constant and real, but they were too formless to justify a war. The pressure that Frere felt from the Transvaal was far stronger and much more clearly defined.

Theophilus Shepstone's grip on the Transvaal was loosening. His administration was financially too weak to take any positive action, and the high-veld Boers, whom he had so disastrously misread, were beginning to harden against the Crown. The very factors that rankled the native clans—drought, cattle disease and lack of land—were also goad-ing the Boers, and Shepstone could promise no relief.

Paul Kruger was slowly emerging as the leader of this movement. Without an official position in the administration, his people neverthe-less turned to him. He was prepared to counsel moderation until he had overwhelming evidence of Boer solidarity, and then he was willing to think of himself as the Vice-President of the South African Repub-lic, the post to which a still-independent Volksraad had elected him.

When Carnarvon had claimed that public sentiment favored annexa-tion, Kruger had returned to the Transvaal and over Shepstone's op-position collected petitions which showed less than 600 Boers in favor of the Crown and some 6,600 opposed. Since Shepstone had given the total population as less than 8,000, this was proof enough for Kruger and he again traveled to London. Hicks Beach received him coldly and gave him no satisfaction, although he did urge on Shepstone the neces-sity of granting a liberal constitution and the desirability of naming the delegates to a conference for that purpose before Kruger should re-turn. Shepstone, however, continued to keep the leading Boers at arm's length and cast about for other measures that would bring solvency to his administration and win him the allegiance of the Boers.

His salvation clearly lay in the overthrow of the Zulu nation. The Transvaal claims in the disputed territories contained sufficient land to satisfy all Boer claimants and enough left over to pay off his debts. With Cetshwayo humbled, Sekukuni would undoubtedly fall as well, stopping a major drain on his treasury and releasing his citizens from their main native threats. Hut taxes and marriage fees on the submis-sive clans would then remove most of the tax burden from the Euro-peans and win him the Boer support he needed.

Too stiff-necked to liberalize his regime or to admit the Boers to his confidence, Shepstone sought to win popular support by adopting such isolated elements of the Boer policy as might strengthen his own posi-tion. The net result was an abrupt *volte face;* after more than fifteen years of supporting Zulu aspirations in the disputed territories, during which he had more or less allied himself with Cetshwayo in opposition to the Transvaal, he now suddenly threw the considerable weight of his influence and prestige into the other side of the scales and blindly and recklessly backed the dubious cause of the frontier Boers.

In October of 1877 he visited the Zulu inDunas on the Blood River. He still thought the Zulu case was valid, and he had, apparently, hopes of personally negotiating a settlement favorable to the Transvaal. He was due for several distinct shocks. Cetshwayo had been somewhat alarmed by the influx of troops in the vicinity of the disputed area on the eve of the annexation. Unable to fathom the tangled motives that led to that event, he greeted it with initial enthusiasm. He was under the impression that his friend Somtseu was entering the Transvaal as a conqueror, and he gathered an impi near the border and offered to attack. The frontier Boers, already pressed by drought and increasing friction with border Zulu factions, scurried back into laager, and several of their deserted farms were burned. Shepstone ordered Cetshwayo to retire, and it gradually dawned on the Zulu king that the man whom for fifteen years he had regarded as the embodiment of the Crown in Natal now spoke with the voice of the Transvaal Boers. The change would have bewildered more sophisticated statesmen than an untutored black monarch. Shepstone had not merely switched his allegiance from the British settlers of Natal to the hated *amaBunu*, he had somehow taken the Crown with him and placed the Transvaal on the same level as Natal. Cetshwayo had always looked to the Crown for relief in the border dispute with the Transvaal. He had applied for arbitration no less than eighteen times between 1861 and 1876, and in 1869 his father had even offered to cede most of the area to Natal to place a buffer between Zululand and the Transvaal. Nothing had ever come of these applications, although in Keate's time arbitration had fallen through only after the Transvaal had failed to produce its documentation before a committee.

When Shepstone met the Blood River inDunas he was received with a rude and excited defiance, and for the first time in his career he failed to impose his will on an inDaba. The effect on his temper was predictable. The Boers who accompanied him then pointed out the beacons of the Waaihoek Line, and led him back by the burned farms to the angry refugees clustered in Utrecht.

Frere, while recognizing Shepstone's shortcomings as an administrator, had no reason to suppose that he was also capable of wild error in the one field in which he was a recognized authority—the evaluation of native affairs. He gave serious consideration to the correspondence which now arrived. The Zulu power, Shepstone averred, was the root of evil, and the sooner it were dealt with the better. Referring to his visit to Utrecht, Shepstone wrote:

I then learned for the first time, what has since been proved by evidence the most incontrovertible, overwhelming, and clear, that this boundary line had been formally and mutually agreed upon, and had been formally ratified by the giving and receiving of tokens of thanks, and that the beacons had been built up in the presence of the President and members of the Executive Council of the Republic, in presence of Commissioners from both Panda and Cetshwayo, and that the spot on which every beacon was to stand was indicated by the Zulu Commissioners themselves placing the first stones upon it.

Shepstone promised even further evidence, which he claimed had just been furnished him. These were strong words from a presumably responsible official, and Frere, although the further evidence was not forthcoming, never doubted they were valid.

Cetshwayo, now thoroughly alarmed, sought help in December of 1877. He sent two inDunas to Bishop Colenso, asking him to put the Zulu claim into writing for transmission to Sir Henry Bulwer and to the Queen. John W. Natal injudiciously referred the envoys to his son's law firm. Francis Colenso and his partner, acting from the highest motives and with no thought of recompense, rashly allowed themselves to be appointed "diplomatic agents" before a notary public, to "treat with the British Government on the Boundary question." Shepstone and Bulwer refused to recognize them, and although Carnarvon gave them *de facto* recognition he had them informed that the question would be settled without their help.

Bulwer, in fact, equally impressed by Shepstone's categorical claims, had already offered arbitration to the Zulu king. His message actually crossed Cetshwayo's to Colenso, and the offer was gratefully accepted. Frere, never doubting the Transvaal case, was also enthusiastic. Shepstone had no choice but to accept. He did so with ill grace, since the frontier Boers, chary of any examination of the confused mass of documentation on which their claims rested, were unanimously opposed to the idea.

The Boundary Commission met at Rorke's Drift on March 7, 1878. The President was Michael H. Gallwey, an Irish barrister who had become Attorney General of Natal at the age of thirty-one in 1857. Utterly impartial and imbued with such a deep sense of justice that he was actually offered the presidency of the Orange Free State when Brand died, Gallwey was an excellent choice for the legalistic chore that lay ahead. He was assisted by John Wesley Shepstone, Natal's Acting Secretary for Native Affairs in his brother's absence, whose position and knowledge of the Zulu clans outweighed the disadvantages of his relationship to the leader of one of the plaintiff parties and the native mistrust he had incurred in the Matyana affair. The third member of the Commission was the Colonial Engineer, Lieutenant Colonel William Anthony Durnford, R.E.

Durnford, still in the good graces of the Army although most of Natal was opposed to him, had sailed for England in June of 1876 to seek medical care for his injured arm. A few months at Wildbad with his sixteen-year-old daughter had not helped him, nor had the subsequent posting to the cold damp of Cork. His heart was in far-off Bishopstowe, but when he finally fainted on duty one day and requested a milder climate, the War Office ordered him to Mauritius.

The man who had replaced him in Natal gallantly offered to exchange with him, and a joyful Durnford caught the first transport for Cape-town. Late in March of 1877, on the eve of the annexation, he was back in Pietermaritzburg.

He received a warm welcome from the Colensos, and he found that his successor, who was temporarily on Shepstone's staff in Pretoria, had even retained his horse for him. No one else had been able to ride Chieftain, and Durnford, whose crippled arm forced him to mount from the off side and to ride much of the time with the reins loose on his mount's neck, was happy to get him back.

Disguised in rough civilian clothing with his dispatches sewn in the lining, he set out at once for Pretoria to see what help Shepstone might need. He arrived the day before the annexation, found Shepstone in no danger and his small escort of Natal Mounted Police camped in his garden, and hurried away the same afternoon. Ten miles inside Natal he met a battalion of Imperial troops marching for the border, with no rations and only the ammunition in their pouches. A week later he had rounded up 300 additional troops and two fieldpieces and had then camped, together with supply wagons, a few miles inside the Trans-vaal. Shepstone, who wished to avoid any display of force, sent them back to Natal. Durnford then hurried back to Pietermaritzburg, found himself the senior officer present, and proceeded to organize proper support. He packed the rest of the 80th Regiment upcountry to New-castle—a central location which covered the Transvaal, the Free State and the northern approaches to Zululand—and he mounted a detach-ment of the 24th Regiment on locally purchased horses and sent them after the 80th. He then organized a Transport Corps, and for good measure hunted out Hlubi, the young Basuto chieftain who had served him so faithfully in Bushman's River Pass, and put him in command of a large troop of Mounted Basuto Guides. Armed with the Martini-Henry carbine and riding superbly with only their big toes thrust into rawhide stirrups, they took to soldiering with enthusiasm and were soon known as Durnford's Horse.

In June, with Shepstone apparently secure in Pretoria, he snatched a week to ride down through the disputed territories, from which the Boer refugees were just then streaming.

Of all the imprecise boundaries that grazing cattle had inflicted on southern Africa, that between Zululand and the Transvaal was far and away the vaguest. The area lay north of the point where the subsiding Drakensberg escarpment bore to the west, so that trekking Boers had here spilled into the broad northern entrance to the coastal strip; and the major rivers, instead of separating the two civilizations, cut across their frontier at right angles and facilitated the Boer encroachment.

The Transvaal had published seven maps of the area between 1870 and 1877, showing seven different lines that differed by as much as seventy miles, and no eye had ever squinted at the rolling landscape through a surveyor's transit. There were, actually, three areas involved.

Zulu clans had once lived on either side of the eastward-flowing Pongola, but the lands to the north had been vacated in 1848 when Langalibalele's amaHlubi and the amaPutini had fled to Natal. The amaSwazi, hereditary Zulu enemies, had taken over the area, and the Boers had started to move in as early as 1855, claiming a purchase from the Swazi chieftain for the customary hundred head of cattle. Both Swazi and Zulu denied this sale, but for practical purposes the Pongola was the northern border of Zululand. An outlaw Swazi chieftain who had professed allegiance to Cetshwayo lived on a rocky mountain in these parts, near a flourishing settlement of 140 Germans at Luneberg.

South of the Pongola, along its tributaries, the Pemvane and the Bevane, lay an area of deserted Boer farms and Zulu kraals which had refused to pay Transvaal taxes. The only European settler was a storekeeper named Potter, who lived under Cetshwayo's protection. He did business with all comers, and stoutly flew the Union Jack miles from any territory the Crown claimed.

The Pemvane ran north into the Pongola. Lyn Spruit rose near the Pemvane headwaters and ran south into the Blood River, which continued south until it ran into the Buffalo a few miles above Rorke's Drift. These three rivers, the Pemvane, Lyn Spruit and the Blood, thus formed an almost straight north-south line which, Durnford noted, was the practical boundary between the Boers, who were settled west of the Blood, and the Zulu kraals to the east. This area was the heart of the dispute. The Transvaal claims ran to the Waaihoek Line, which started at Rorke's Drift and angled to the northeast deep into Zululand, until it reached the Pongola. Only one Boer, Cornelius van Rooyen, now lived east of the Blood. He had been friend to Mpande and was now one to Cetshwayo, and he lived in peace with his neighbors. The extreme Zulu claim ignored the Waaihoek Line and took in not only the wedge between the Blood and the Buffalo, with the settlement of Utrecht and perhaps eighty Boer families, but even the lands beyond which extended to the Drakensberg escarpment.

Cetshwayo sent three inDunas to the Boundary Commission, together with a man to act as his "eyes and ears." For the Transvaal appeared Rudolph, the Landdrost of Utrecht; Piet Uys, a farmer in the disputed area who had lost his father and his brother to Dingane's impis in the long-ago Vlug Kommando; and Henrique Shepstone, who was serving on his father's staff in Pretoria. If the Zulu inDunas were confused by finding Somtseu's brother and son sitting as jury and co-plaintiff, the Transvaal delegation made no effort to enlighten them. They referred to themselves as the "Transvaal and Zululand Boundary Commissioners," and, until a scandalized Gallwey moved them, tried to pitch their tents and seat themselves with the Natal party.

The Boundary Commission sat for five weeks, patiently sifting every document and verbal claim that either side could produce. Under Gallwey's inexorable legal scrutiny, the Transvaal case melted away. One vital document turned out to be a patent forgery, others had been altered by unknown hands at unknown dates. Several Zulu signatories could not be identified, or turned out to be commoners of no consequence. The description of the land at issue was often too vague to be matched to the terrain, and in few cases did the detailed memories of the illiterate Zulus correspond with the contents of the agreements to which chieftains had put their mark.

Gallwey's summation was devastating. He had sought to determine the answers to two questions: who had owned the land originally, and had any of it been properly ceded? Not even the Boers questioned the original Zulu ownership, and Gallwey now found that no concession of territory had ever been made by the Zulu nation, and that much of the territory claimed by the Boers had never been occupied by settlers and had always been occupied by the border clans, which had never moved their kraals. The Boers at best had a few agreements to graze cattle on Zulu land, but except in the Utrecht area, where there were no Zulus, they had governed no natives, exacted no rent, collected no taxes and had appointed no officials. They had never established a civil or criminal jurisdiction, and Gallwey recommended that practically the entire Blood River area, including even the settlement of Utrecht, be returned to Zulu jurisdiction.

Durnford did not finish drafting Gallwey's report until the twentieth of June, and no hint of the bombshell it contained leaked out in advance. Cetshwayo had expressed his satisfaction with the proceedings and his readiness to abide by the decision, whatever it was. Frere began to discuss measures for enforcing on the Zulu nation what he assumed would be a verdict favorable to the Transvaal.

The report he received in July shocked him profoundly. Gallwey had placed him on the horns of a dilemma; he could neither reverse the report nor suppress it indefinitely, and if the recommendations were carried out, it could not only mean an open revolt in the Transvaal but, with such a signal victory for the Zulus, could also touch off the general native outbreak he feared was brewing.

For the moment he could gain time by submitting the report to Hicks Beach for approval, since it would be several months before he had an answer in hand. He therefore sent it off to London, pointing out that the report had failed to deal with the area north of the Pongola, and that some provisions would obviously have to be made to protect the Boer families farming in the Blood River territory. At the same time he began to plan for the contingency of war.

He needed, first of all, an accurate estimate of the nature of the enemy and the extent of Natal's military resources. He therefore sent Thesiger, who arrived at Durban on the sixth of August, to commence a survey. Thesiger's job was not yet to plan an invasion, but simply to report what might be needed to carry one out. Within a month his answer was ready.

Thesiger found the colony's defenses in deplorable condition. With over a hundred miles of river border that a Zulu army could cross at a dozen places, no effort had been made to guard the crossings, nor, indeed, would an effort have been practical. There were too many crossings to cover with standing bodies of troops, and Natal had simply relied on native border guards to report movements, trusting that the Imperial garrison battalion, eked out with colonial volunteers, could cope with any impi that crossed. That this was a forlorn hope was obvious. Except for the garrison at Fort Napier and the few score men of the Natal Mounted Police there were no standing troops, and in view of the presence of 300,000 Natal Kaffirs it was patent that a Zulu invasion would lead to an instant and catastrophic conflagration. Thesiger saw at once that the only defense for the colony lay in an invasion of Zululand, where the Zulu army could be destroyed before it commenced an invasion of its own. Since the Zulu forces were infinitely more mobile than any European troops could hope to be, such an invasion would have to consist of several columns advancing from the major crossings, not so much to prevent the Zulus from slipping into the colony behind the invaders as to insure that the Zulus could find and attack one of the columns. It was quite clear to Thesiger that the Zulu military machine was a considerably more dangerous foe than the Gaikas and Gcalekas had been, but he was reasonably certain that it would stand and fight on its home ground and would attack and not evade invading forces. If it did attack, it could be smashed by superior firepower. A war of maneuver was in any event out of the question.

A landing from the sea was also impossible. Thesiger had inspected the coast from H.M.S. *Active* as far as St. Lucia Bay, and he had found only one place where troops or stores might be landed through the surf in rare intervals of good weather. Even there the ships were held four to five miles off the coast by a reef, and the site was too risky for a major undertaking.

There were, in August, insufficient troops in southern Africa to mount an invasion. Even by scraping together the Imperial garrisons from the eastern Cape and Natal, a process that would leave several danger spots perilously unprotected, and by accepting a large influx of colonial volunteers, the columns would be too scanty. At an absolute minimum Thesiger wanted a force of 7,000 native levies raised from the Natal Kaffirs, and he felt that his safety margin would be dangerously low without at least two additional Imperial battalions of infantry and a cavalry force as well. He so reported to Frere, adding that Bulwer would not hear of raising a Natal Kaffir levy on the grounds that there did not appear to be the slightest reason to prepare for an invasion of Zululand, and he forwarded his report to the War Office as well.

Frere forwarded Thesiger's request for reinforcements to the Colonial Office, and repeated it on the ninth of September, adding a request for a score of officers for special assignment on staff and transport duties. Already more than half convinced that a showdown was necessary, he was unable to plan for it until he had either the two additional battalions from Hicks Beach or the Natal Kaffir levy from Bulwer, and neither man showed any signs of giving way.

Frere reached Durban on September 23, 1878. He had intended to visit Pretoria to confer with Shepstone on the boundary award and to supervise Colonel Rowland's projected operation against Sekukuni, but Hicks Beach, uneasy over the tone of reports from Natal, directed him to Pietermaritzburg to acquaint himself with the background of the border dispute. The Boundary Commission's report had only reached the Colonial Office a fortnight earlier, no answer could be expected for over a month, and the problem of how the award was to be announced weighed heavily on Frere's mind.

He now entered a critical period through which it is impossible to trace his true intentions. On the day of his arrival in Durban he for the third time repeated Thesiger's request for reinforcements, and described the Zulus as "out of hand." It is hard to avoid leveling a charge of duplicity against him. The initiative was entirely in his hands from the beginning, and what followed was deliberate and could have only one outcome, but to the very end and beyond he insisted that a war was being forced on him by the Zulu nation. There is little question that by the end of September he had determined on war and was simply seeking the troops and a suitable *casus belli* that the Colonial Office would in retrospect have to accept. He found both by the eleventh of November, and by the sixteenth of November he knew with certainty that hostilities would commence on January 11, 1879. Throughout this entire period he deliberately masked his intentions from the Colonial Office, which, unhappily aware that the situation was deteriorating, could only urge moderation and could not see its way clear to either dictating to or recalling a man of Frere's stature and experience. Hicks Beach, his hands tied by mails which brought his comments to the scene two months after the event, was so pessimistic that, when campaign medals for the Ninth Kaffir War were suggested, he economically recommended waiting so that one medal might be struck to cover any operations in Zululand. In mid-October he informed Frere that the additional officers would be sent, but

Her Majesty's Government are not prepared to comply with a request for a reinforcement of troops. All the information that has hitherto reached them with respect to the position of affairs in Zululand appears to them to justify a confident hope that by the exercise of prudence and by meeting the Zulus in a spirit of forebearance and reasonable compromise, it will be possible to avert the very serious evil of a war with Cetywayo.

It was high time that Frere met with Bulwer, for the Lieutenant Governor's views were diametrically opposed to those of the High Commissioner. Frere was bent on war, but he lacked the means and the excuse to wage it; Bulwer was equally determined to preserve a peace the Zulus had done nothing to threaten, and he did not intend to facilitate Frere's course of action. He was not to be moved by arguments about Shepstone's precarious position or by the needs of confederation, and Frere could make no headway. The impasse was complete, although accompanied by a curious lack of personal rancor. Bulwer was obdurate but dispassionate, Frere too seasoned an official and administrator to attack Bulwer's logic by denigrating the man.

The two clashed almost at once over the question of modifying the boundary decision. The commissioners had assigned the Blood River territory to the Zulus, but had conceded that the Utrecht area Boers would have to be compensated if they did not choose to live under a Zulu regime. Since the British government had promised the Transvaal a secure frontier and protection against native aggression, Frere wanted to leave the settlers under British protection and also wanted compensation from the Zulus for even those farms which had been assigned but never occupied. Bulwer thought this would in effect reverse the award, and he also felt that compensations should come from the Transvaal and not the Zulus, since it had been the South African Republic which had encouraged the encroachments in the first place. In the end Frere had his way. He reported that "Sir H. Bulwer and I, approaching the question by somewhat different roads, agree in the conclusion that we must accept the Commissioners' verdict," but he nevertheless inserted his modifications. He could afford to be generous, since if war came, the award would be largely academic.

An even more fundamental difference between the two men lay in their respective attitudes toward the Zulu nation. When Theophilus Shepstone and his retinue had departed from Zululand in September of 1873, Cetshwayo had settled down in his royal kraal at Ulundi to enjoy his reign in peace. The past five years had been largely uneventful, broken only by a series of minor incidents which Bulwer had accepted as normal to a savage nation, but which Frere now chose to magnify in order to justify invasion. He made his position clear on the twenty-eighth of October:

I can only repeat my own conviction that the continued preservation of peace depends no longer on what the servants of the British Government here may do or abstain from doing, but simply on the caprice of an ignorant and bloodthirsty despot, with an organized force of at least 40,000 armed men at his absolute command.

In 1873 the ignorant and bloodthirsty despot had faced no appreciable internal opposition, nor any dire threat on his borders. Somtseu was his friend, and the Tugela remained inviolate. The amaSwazi and amaTonga were no more than cowed neighbors and abject vassals, and if the Transvaal Boers were irksome, Cetshwayo undoubtedly felt more keenly the clamor of the border inDunas than he did the negligible military threat of the Boers.

The Zulu kraals flourished, and the tenor of daily life differed little from Senzangakona's time. If Cetshwayo lacked Shaka's manic energies, he was both free of Dingane's weak cruelty and the apathy that had marked his father Mpande. Hindered by inexperience and lack of communications from following the nuances of policies that played themselves out beyond his borders, he had, nevertheless, a considerably better grasp of political realities than his predecessors, and within the limits of his background he was reasonable, responsible and forbearing. He enjoyed the loyalty of his people, but his tight grip on the kraals near Ulundi was diluted by distance, until the border clans, amenable to immediate pressures from the Transvaal Boers or Swazi elements north of the Pongola, were forced to act with a semiautonomy to preserve themselves.

Cetshwayo made no effort to change the usages of his people. He accepted and preserved what he had inherited, and the social fabric of the Zulus was still woven on the warp of cattle—now sadly reduced in numbers by lung sickness and drought—and the woof of the military system.

Almost 50,000 men in Zululand were under arms, organized into some 35 regiments. Perhaps 10,000 of these warriors were oldsters surviving from Shaka's and Dingane's times and ranging up to eighty years in age, but over 40,000 men under sixty manned the 26 active corps, and over half of these were thirty or younger. No less than 22 regiments dated from Mpande's reign, and Cetshwayo himself had only called up four regiments. Enlistment was not actually compulsory, but virtually every youth followed his iNtanga into a regiment, and once enrolled he was subject to the full force of Zulu discipline, including the enforced celibacy, until his regiment received royal permission to don the headring. Only eighteen regiments had iKhehla status and wore the isiCoco.

There was no real need for such a force. Cetshwayo unquestionably enjoyed the worried respect he commanded beyond his borders, and the mere existence of the army had forced both Natal and the Transvaal to treat him with greater forbearance than they would have displayed to any other native kingdom. He could not, in any event, have disbanded the army without severe internal disruption, since the warriors enjoyed their status, and the economy could hardly have absorbed a surplus male population of 50,000 men. He only realized gradually that he had a tiger by the tail, and his freedom of action was more and more dominated by the warlike spirit of the regiments.

Twice they caused him trouble. Permission to assume iKhehla status was normally dependent on the display of prowess in battle, but Cetshwayo had been given no opportunity to wash his spears since his coronation, and several regiments were long overdue for the isiCoco. In September of 1876 the *inDlondlo* and the *uDloko* regiments were used to chastise a Tonga kraal, and Cetshwayo gave them permission to marry, directing them to take their wives from a much younger group of female iNtangas called the *inGcugce*. The men were verging on forty, and when they fanned out to seek their brides, they found that the majority of the girls had already given their affections to youths of their own age in other regiments. Complaints poured into Ulundi, Cetshwayo first tried to deal with the cases piecemeal and then issued an order that any inGcugce found living with a man under forty was to be killed and her father's cattle seized. Four or five girls were actually slain in the uproar that followed, while the rest of the girls, under strong parental prodding, hastily sought out older grooms, pretended they were married to the elder brothers of the men they loved, or simply sought refuge in the Transvaal or Natal.

Shepstone was in England, and Bulwer, who had received highly magnified reports of the killing from missionary sources, sent Cetshwayo a chiding message reminding him of the advice Shepstone had given him at his coronation against indiscriminate executions. This was a sore point with the king, who had smarted under the advice and who had always resented Shepstone's implications that he had promised to adhere to the guidance. He had in fact not made any such promises, nor did Bulwer believe that he had, since they would have been impossible for the Crown to enforce. Bulwer, moreover, used as a messenger a refugee Zulu named Mantshonga, a prominent supporter of the Mbulazi faction who was making brazen use of his status as a government messenger to visit his homeland. Cetshwayo was furious, and for once he failed to check out his reply with John Dunn, who was away hunting. The verbal message Mantshonga happily quoted to Bulwer was the most intemperate reply that had ever been received from Ulundi:

Did I ever tell Somtseu I would not kill? Did he tell the white people I made such an arrangement? Because if he did so he deceived them. I do kill; but do not consider that I have done anything yet in the way of killing. Why do the white people start at nothing? I have not yet begun; I have yet to kill; it is the custom of our nation and I shall not depart from it. Why does the Governor of Natal speak to me about my laws? Do I go to Natal and dictate to him about his laws? I shall not agree to any laws or rules from Natal, and by doing so throw the large kraal which I govern into the water. My people will not listen unless they are killed; and while wishing to be friends with the English I do not agree to give my people over to be governed by laws sent to me by them. Have I not asked the English to allow me to wash my spears since the death of my father Mpande, and they have kept playing with me all this time, treating me like a child? Go back and tell the English that I shall now act on my own account, and if they wish me to agree to their laws, I shall leave and become a wanderer; but before I go it will be seen, as I shall not go without having acted. Go back and tell the white people this, and let them hear it well. The Governor of Natal and I are in like positions: he is Governor of Natal, and I am Governor here.

Bulwer, although privately alarmed at the tone, recognized the cause of this flash of temper, took the message in good part, and let the matter drop. In January of 1878 Cetshwayo himself reported another outbreak. The army had gathered at Ulundi for the important First Fruits ceremony, and his own uThulwana regiment was quartered near the much younger inGobamakhosi. A young iNtanga had been incorporated into the uThulwana to eke it out, and the inGobamakhosi, some of whom had lost inGcugce fiancées to older warriors, resented the youthful draft's assumption of the prerogatives of their elder colleagues. A stick fight broke out, both regiments went for their assegais, and the battle raged through and wrecked John Dunn's camp, leaving over sixty bodies strewn among his tents and wagons. No messenger from the king could get near the scene, as the inGobamakhosi were attacking every man wearing the isiCoco, and the uThulwana every man without one. When the imperturbable Dunn returned in the evening, he made his servants clean up his camp, wiping the blood off his saltcellar and Worcestershire sauce bottle before he sat down to his evening meal. Uhamu, Cetshwayo's brother and the inDuna of the uThulwana, was outraged and demanded the death of Sigcwelegcwele, the leader of the inGobamakhosi. When he did not get it, he led his regiment back to the Transvaal border in a huff, while Sigcwelegcwele sought shelter in the south. Cetshwayo, uneasy at the thought of losing Uhamu's allegiance, and disturbed by continual rumors that Sigcwelegcwele was an umThakathi who traveled about in the shape of a baboon, decided to kill him after all. He sent for him and posted an impi to ambush him en route, but Dunn warned him of the danger and Sigcwelegcwele finally bought his safety with a large cattle fine.

Although Bulwer had taken both incidents in his stride, they had been reported to him in greatly exaggerated form by several of the missionaries whose stations dotted Zululand. Gardiner and Owen had been followed by several score of dedicated men who had moved into Zululand to bring the Gospel to the heathen. The Americans and Germans had been active, and by 1878 over a dozen tiny mission stations were still in existence, manned principally by Norwegians or High Church Anglicans. A Bishop Schreuder had started the Norwegian stations in 1851, and he was joined two years later by Sivert Samuelson, a lay worker who was trained as a carpenter. In 1857 Samuelson decided to cast his lot in with the Anglicans and joined Colenso, who put him to work in Natal with one of his own deacons, a Scot born in 1831 named Robert Robertson. After Robertson was ordained in 1860, he founded a mission station at kwaMagwaza, south of Ulundi. His wife was crushed to death by a millstone that fell out of an overturning wagon the following year, and Samuelson then joined him for a while. Robertson, however, was too High Church to stay in harness with Colenso, and in 1864 he left to found three more stations of his own. Samuelson also moved on to start a station ten miles from Rorke's Drift, where Witt was at work in Natal. Another Norwegian, Oftebro, had been in Zululand since 1849 and worked out of Eshowe—then spelled *Ekowe*.

Colenso's battles with the church authorities at home led to the appointment of a missionary bishop of Zululand in 1870. Wilkinson took over kwaMagwaza in 1870 and stayed until ill health forced him out in 1877. Although Cetshwayo trusted Sobantu above all other church workers, Wilkinson and Robertson would have nothing to do with him and ignored him completely. Only the gentle Samuelsons were able to maintain good relations with all.

Cetshwayo had ambivalent feelings toward the missionaries. Most of them had been admitted to the country by his father, and with one or two he became close friends. As a young man, for example, he had led his victorious uSuthu faction back from the slaughter at 'Ndondaku-suka, and, passing the Samuelson station, had heard that Mrs. Samuelson was seriously ill. He at once stopped the victory chants of his warriors, and led his impi and the captured cattle on a long detour around the homestead so as not to disturb her. He also had a high regard for Schreuder and Oftebro, but Wilkinson and especially Robertson he tolerated only because they had entered the country armed with letters of introduction from the Lieutenant Governor of Natal. He knew that Robertson maligned him repeatedly in anonymous letters to the Natal press, and that all events in Zululand would be reported in the worst possible light. He was unable to follow Colenso's theological struggles, and could not comprehend Sobantu's waning influence on events in Natal.

Although several of the missionaries were thus welcome as friends, Cetshwayo both regretted and resisted their attempts to evangelize his subjects. He could understand teachers; on occasion he expressed a mild desire to learn to read, and he eventually learned to scrawl his name. The intricacies of the Gospel, however, were beyond him, and since there was no place in his kraal society or regiments for a pacific Christian, he regarded a converted Zulu as a spoiled Zulu. The mission stations collected pathetic handfuls of converts, but they were invariably either misfits who were unable to retain their place in kraal life or simply refugees from Zulu justice. Missionaries like Samuelson could understand the situation and were content to salvage such souls as they could while they worked to ameliorate the lot of the heathen. Men like Robertson, however, burned with the same fires that had driven Gardiner, and they regarded Cetshwayo and his entire regime as a blight which for the sake of the Gospel and simple humanity should be swept aside at the earliest moment. It was, perhaps, the old question of the end justifying the means, and Samuelson and Robertson were divided by the same attitudes that separated Bulwer and Frere.

The Crown had scrupulously avoided intervening in Zulu affairs on behalf of the missionaries, and it had never promised them protection. Most of them had implicit faith in their personal relations with the king. Robertson's camp felt no such assurance; they held out bravely enough, but were alarmed by every passing hunting party and swayed by every rumor. It had been one of Robertson's wild reports that had sent the Colensos scurrying out of Bishopstowe in the middle of the night to seek shelter in Pietermaritzburg in 1861, and he attributed every violent death in Zululand to the despotic nature of Cetshwayo's reign. Such men had no comprehension of Zulu society or the nature of the throne; one missionary had even called Cetshwayo a liar to his face in front of his inDunas. In August of 1877, at the height of the alarm on the Transvaal border, most of them left Zululand, and they added their voices to the war party in Natal.

In point of fact no missionary had ever been harmed or even threatened, nor was a single abandoned mission station destroyed by the Zulus during the war. The converts, however, were frequently threatened, and three of them were actually killed. Two of the killings had nothing to do with the victims' conversions—one, indeed, had relapsed. They were refugees from kraal justice who were captured and thrown into crocodile pools. The third, however, was a true martyr. One of Oftebro's converts named Maqamsela had been warned by his inDuna to avoid the mission station. He appealed to Cetshwayo, received a noncommittal reply, and moved there anyway. In March of 1877 a party of warriors waylaid him on his way home from services and assegaied him after he had received permission to pray. Bulwer took no notice, and not even Shepstone cared to recommend intervention, since there was no evidence that the murder had been instigated by the king.

In the course of 1878 several of the Zulu border inDunas involved the kingdom with its neighbors. The first of these was Mbilini, a claimant to the Swazi throne his brother Umbandeni occupied. Mbilini offered allegiance to Cetshwayo, who, hoping to strengthen his claim to a corner of the disputed area, carelessly accepted. When Mbilini turned out to be a freebooter who raided Zulu and Swazi kraals and Boer homesteads indiscriminately, Cetshwayo suddenly found himself responsible for his actions. The Boers north of the Pongola demanded his extradition, Cetshwayo demurred, but sent a peace offering of a hundred head of cattle, which was accepted. When Mbilini continued his depredations, Cetshwayo disavowed him completely, and gave the Boers permission to kill him. A commando attacked his lair on the Tafelberg, but Mbilini, with only nineteen followers, beat it off.

In July of 1878 a more serious incident occurred. An inDuna named Sihayo lived in a rocky gorge a few miles from Rorke's Drift. His Great Wife Kaqwelebana and another wife had started affairs with younger lovers, and while Sihayo was absent at Ulundi, Kaqwelebana's eldest son Mehlokazulu discovered what was going on. He conferred at once with his uncle, Sihayo's brother Zuluhlenga, and three of his own brothers, Bhekuzulu, Nkumbikazulu and Shenkwana, and the family conclave decided that the Great Wife should be killed at once. They attacked her hut that same night, wounding Kaqwelebana, but both erring women and their lovers escaped to Natal, where they sought shelter at the kraals of two of the native border guards a few miles from the crossing.

Such situations had occurred in the past, and Mehlokazulu was not unduly worried. Zulu refugees who escaped to Natal became Natal Kaffirs and were lost to Zulu justice, but until Bulwer put a stop to the practice in 1875, refugee wives were regarded as chattel goods and like straying cattle were returned by the Crown on demand. In February of 1877 a party of Zulus had crossed the Tugela to kidnap a refugee girl, and Bulwer had merely informed Cetshwayo of this lawless act on the part of his subjects. The king had thanked him, and asked to be informed if such an act were repeated. The Crown frequently crossed the Tugela in pursuit of fleeing Natal Kaffirs—just as John Shepstone had gone after Matyana—and on one occasion Cetshwayo had even delivered a Zulu named Jolwana, who had killed a European trader, to Natal for trial. Jolwana had been returned, with the message that as a Zulu subject he could not be tried in Natal, so that Mehlokazulu expected no serious repercussions when he decided to go after the refugees.

He crossed the Tugela with his uncle, found his father's younger wife, dragged her back across the river and turned her over to a party of his supporters. They looped a rawhide line around her neck, pulled the ends tight, and then struck the back of her head with a knobkerrie. Her lover was left unharmed in Natal, and the border guard did not even bother to report the incident.

A few days later Mehlokazulu located his mother, who was resting at the kraal of a border guard named Maziyana. Early the following morning he led a mounted party of thirty men up to the kraal, while fifty more afoot covered the rear. His uncle and his three brothers accompanied him. Maziyana was inclined to remonstrate, but he subsided when he saw the size of the escort. He watched in silence while Kaqwelebana was dragged through the ford to a waiting impi which shot her to death. Her lover also was left untouched.

Both raids were now reported. This was too much for the patience of even the long-suffering Bulwer, who reported the matter to Cetshwayo and requested the extradition of Mehlokazulu, his uncle and his three brothers, for trial in Natal. Bulwer did not believe that the acts had been committed with the consent or even the knowledge of the king, and his note, while forcible, was couched as a request rather than a demand.

Cetshwayo acknowledged the message, admitting that the men should be punished, but he deprecated the seriousness of the offense. The women were clearly guilty in Zulu law, and they and their lovers deserved to die. Mehlokazulu had scrupulously refrained from killing them on Natal soil, and he had harmed neither the border guards nor the paramours, whose status as Natal Kaffirs he had recognized. The king then turned to John Dunn, who suggested offering a fine. Cetshwayo accepted the advice, and, most likely because it was all the cash he had at Ulundi, sent Bulwer £50, adding that the request to surrender the men would have to be placed before the inDunas. Bulwer rejected the money. Knowing what the inDunas' decision would be, however, he was toying with the idea of a stiff cattle fine, on the order of 5,000 head, when Frere took the matter out of his hands.

Still one more border incident occurred before Frere arrived in Natal. Wolseley had ordered certain roads to be built leading down to the drifts of the Tugela, and as part of his survey Thesiger wanted them inspected. A surveyor named Smith, who worked for the Colonial Engineer, started to inspect the road leading from Greytown to Fort Buckingham, and, because the border kraals had been alarmed by troop movements near the river, he was ordered to proceed alone. This he did, taking with him only a trader named Deighton. The two men were spotted by a small party of Zulus, who shouted across the river to ask what the men were doing and if they were connected with the troops. The men ignored the calls, and then started to inspect the drift itself, reaching a small island near the Zulu shore, which at the current low water was practically part of Zululand. The warriors splashed through the shallows and detained the men for an hour, trying to find out what they wanted. Neither man was injured, although someone in the party made them turn out their pockets and then stole their pipes and handkerchiefs. A passing inDuna returned their horses and ordered them to be released. Only Deighton bothered to make a report.

Bulwer regarded nothing that had happened as more than the normal incidents to be expected in a colony with an uncivilized kingdom on its borders. There had been a remarkable freedom from serious disturbances, and Cetshwayo had given no evidence at all of intent to invade and had in the main responded satisfactorily to the spirit of all exchanges. Bulwer was, therefore, astonished when Frere took an extremely serious view of all that had passed and insisted on regarding the Zulu nation as a high and immediate threat to the safety of Natal.

There was little change in the situation in October. Early in the month Mbilini made a raid on nearby Swazi kraals and killed four or five men. The First Baron Chelmsford died, and on the twenty-sixth General Thesiger learned that he had succeeded to the title. His relations with Bulwer were civil but stiff, and he could not understand why his efforts to prepare an invasion force, fully backed by the High Commissioner, should be frustrated by the Lieutenant Governor of Natal.

Early in November Frere finally received Hicks Beach's answer to his request for reinforcements. There were to be no additional Imperial battalions. Armed with this evidence that Natal would be responsible for defending itself with resources already in hand, Frere returned to the attack. On the eleventh of November, with great reluctance, Bulwer agreed to allow the new Lord Chelmsford to raise a levy of 7,000 Natal Kaffirs, and the General, who already had detailed plans for their training and employment, reported at once that he was now ready to enter Zululand, "should such a measure become necessary." It was all Frere needed.

On the sixteenth of November Bulwer informed Cetshwayo that the boundary decision would be announced at the Lower Drift of the Tugela on the eleventh of December. A large bluff overlooks the Lower Drift, and below it, between steep green banks, the broad river bends to the left to flow, a few miles farther on, over a large sandbank into the Indian Ocean. Garrison troops had erected a stout earthenwork fort atop the bluff in early November, and on the twenty-fourth it had been occupied by the 170 sailors and marines of the Naval Brigade, who had marched up from Durban. Chelmsford had again culled the landing forces from the ships of the South African Squadron, and they had brought with them two breech-loading fieldpieces and their Gatling guns.

Three principal inDunas, eleven subordinate chieftains, forty retainers and John Dunn arrived at the drift on the appointed day. The drought had broken and all the rivers were full, and the men were brought across in boats. Two large fig trees stand on a small ledge below the bluff, by the road that leads out of the drift, and here the inDunas met the party from Natal. John Wesley Shepstone, Charles Brownlee, Henry Francis Fynn (who had succeeded his father as the Umsinga magistrate) and Colonel Forestier Walker of the Scots Guards, Frere's Assistant Military Secretary, had been camped there for two days. The sun was broiling and a large tent fly had been hoisted into the trees and spread to provide shade, but the Naval Brigade and a score of volunteers from the Stanger Mounted Rifles, who made the inDunas uneasy, were soon dismissed.

At eleven o'clock John Shepstone started to read the award in English, while H. Bernard Fynney, a border agent who used his fluent Zulu to dabble in ethnology, translated sentence by sentence. The inDunas would memorize it at a single hearing; it was the customary mode of diplomatic exchange with the natives and even lengthy messages got through with reasonable accuracy. There were copies in English and Zulu for the record, which John Dunn, the only literate person to whom the Zulu king had ready access, retained.

Frere had subverted the report of the Boundary Commission, but even with his modifications the Zulu claims were largely upheld, and the inDunas received the award with qualified satisfaction. The sovereignty of the Zulu nation over the Blood River territory was recognized, but it was then nullified by the recognition of Boer residential rights. Those that left were to be compensated by the Zulus; those that chose to stay would have their protection guaranteed by the Crown, with a British Resident at Utrecht to enforce it.

The inDunas made preparations to depart, but Shepstone presented them with a bullock and bade them reassemble after a noon meal. An hour later he began to read to them a 4,000-word document which Frere had drafted some time earlier with Gallwey's help, to which they listened for three hours in growing consternation. It was a rambling ultimatum, in Theophilus Shepstone's rhetorical Zulu style, in which a number of demands were mixed with passages that purported to justify them. Stripped of its verbosity, it called on Cetshwayo to meet three demands within twenty days:

1) Sihayo's brother and his three sons were to be surrendered for trial by the Natal courts.

2) A fine of 500 head of cattle was to be paid for Mehlokazulu's outrages, and for Cetshwayo's delay in acceding to Natal's previous request for his surrender.

3) A further fine of 100 head of cattle was to be paid for the offense committed against Smith and Deighton.

Ten further demands were to be met within thirty days:

1) Mbilini, and others to be named thereafter, were to be surrendered for trial by the Transvaal courts.

2) Shepstone's advice at the coronation was to be adhered to; no Zulu was to be executed without an open trial before the inDunas, with the right of appeal to the king.

3) The Zulu army was to disband, and the men were to be permitted to return to their homes.

4) The current Zulu military system was to be abandoned, and new regulations concerning the maintenance of armed men and the defense of the realm would be worked out between the Great Council and British representatives.

5) Every Zulu was to be free to marry on reaching maturity.

6) All missionaries and converts who had fled Zululand in 1877 were to be permitted to return to their mission stations.

7) All missionaries were to be free to teach as they pleased, and all Zulus who cared to attend were to do so without let or hindrance.

8) A British diplomatic resident was to reside in Zululand to enforce these provisions.

9) Any dispute involving a European was to be heard in public in the presence of the king and of the British resident.

10) No sentence of expulsion from Zululand was to be carried out until the British resident had approved it.

The powers delegated to Sir Bartle Frere were considerable and only loosely defined. They unquestionably gave him the right to resort to military force to settle any internal question that might arise, and they also gave him the right to deal with contiguous non-Crown territories on local issues. The document he had now issued, however, went far beyond such steps. The terms of his ultimatum, as he well knew, were completely unworkable; they were not so much a call for reform as an outline of the shape of the administration he intended to impose on Zululand by force. Without clear authority, without sufficient justification and in the teeth of the repeated and strongly expressed desires of the Colonial Office, he had committed Her Majesty's Government to an invasion of an independent country.

Frere's dispatches to Hicks Beach held hints aplenty of his attitude toward the Zulu military machine—"celibate man-destroying gladiators" was the least of his phrases—but he did not send the draft of the ultimatum to London until five days after it had been delivered to the inDunas. "I really can't control him without a telegraph, I don't know that I could with one," Hicks Beach had complained as early as mid-November. "I feel it as likely as not that he is at war with the Zulus at the present moment." He had finally issued a flat veto on the war, which reached Frere two days after he had issued his ultimatum, but he had then relented and sent the two requested battalions "to assist the local Government as far as possible in providing for the protection of the settlers in the present emergency, and not to furnish the means for any aggressive operations not directly connected with the defence of Her Majesty's possessions and subjects." The strictures, like the veto, arrived too late.

Frere had presented Hicks Beach with an expensive *fait accompli*. Recognizing the impossibility of the terms he read for the first time on January 2, 1879, the Colonial Secretary knew that the invasion would be a fortnight old before his reply could reach Frere. There was nothing he could do but hope that the campaign would be mercifully short, and his strongest reproach lay in his caustic comment on the reactions of his colleagues: "I may observe that the communications which had previously been received from you had not entirely prepared them for the course which you have now deemed it necessary to take."

If every European witness of the scene recognized the ultimatum for the death knell of Zulu independence, the inDunas seemed to have missed the point. They had not been prepared for what was coming, and, already burdened with the details of the lengthy boundary award, were apparently unable to grasp the significance of the demands or the implications of a failure to comply. Fastening on the order to surrender Mehlokazulu and the cattle fine, they pointed out that the rivers were in flood and the cattle could not be collected in twenty days. To the rest, their reaction was indignation rather than alarm. They were not impressed by the Naval Brigade or by the Stanger Mounted Rifles, and they took natural exception to a message which implied that the Zulus were longing for liberation from a cruel and oppressive tyrant. "Have the Zulus complained?" growled one of them. Shepstone would allow no discussion, and the meeting was over.

The inDunas departed for Ulundi, but their progress was slow. The rivers were full, and they loitered at each kraal on the way to tell the story of the inDaba. They were, in truth, fearful of reporting to Cetshwayo, and it was two weeks before they reached Ulundi.

The tidings traveled with greater speed than the bearers. John Dunn had recognized the ultimatum for what it was. His way of life had trapped him, and his position was critical. The war could have only one outcome; if he cast his lot with the Zulus, he would be branded a traitor; and if he fought with the British, he was probably through forever in Zululand. His one chance was to stand aside, which Cetshwayo would understand even if half the inDunas already regarded him as little better than a spy.

As soon as he reached his camp a few miles north of the Lower Drift, he sent the import of the ultimatum on to Ulundi by his own messengers. The Great Council met at Ulundi, but there was no wild excitement, nor even a sense of urgency. No Zulu inDuna had any comprehension of the awful might of the Crown, and while some, Cetshwayo among them, regarded the prospect of war as an unnecessary calamity, not one anticipated total and inevitable defeat. They had lived their lives surrounded by the Zulu warriors in their thousands, and they had seen nothing of the British Army but the few companies that had moved along the border roads. They were not impressed by firearms, because thousands of Zulus possessed them, and they were too uncivilized to realize that the bulk of them were cheap trade flintlocks—"Birmingham gas-pipes"—of more danger to the owner than anyone else.

There was, thus, no serious discussion of disbanding the army, nor of meeting the other demands that struck at the independence of the kingdom. The slow deliberations revolved around the first three demands alone. The inDunas regarded the crisis as a personal matter between Cetshwayo and the Crown, and felt that he should settle it himself. The king was willing enough to surrender Mehlokazulu and the cattle, but Mehlokazulu commanded a company of the inGoba-makhosi, and the regiment would not hear of it. The cattle were a further complication; surrender of the men *and* a fine seemed like a double punishment, and 600 head could not be easily shaken out of the complex system of herd ownership.

On the eighteenth of December Dunn sent Chelmsford a message from the king. He had agreed to the surrender of the men and to the cattle fines as well, but he begged that no action be taken should the twenty days expire before the cattle arrived. The rivers were in flood, and the cattle would first have to be collected from Sihayo's people and then brought to Ulundi. Mehlokazulu and his brothers had been sent for, but the messengers had not yet reached his kraals; indeed, the inDunas from the Lower Drift had not yet reached Ulundi. The other demands were still before the council. Frere termed the answer a "piti-ful evasion" and announced that the word of the government had been given and could not now be altered. The troops would enter Zululand at the end of twenty days, but they would not advance until the full thirty days had expired.

Dunn could wait no longer, and at Christmas he rode down to the Lower Drift to see Chelmsford. He found, as he had feared, that Chelmsford intended to invade and to advance when the time came, and that he would not be permitted to remain neutral. He returned to his homestead, rounded up 2,000 of his people and 3,000 head of cattle and brought them down to the Lower Drift on the thirtieth, where the Naval Brigade spent two days ferrying them across the Tugela. They had already transported H.M.S. *Tenedos'* bower anchor to the Zulu shore, stretched a cable across, and used it to haul the punts they had constructed back and forth. The Zulu regiments were all collected at Ulundi for the First Fruits ceremony, and there was no interference.

Chelmsford had promised to feed Dunn's people, but he merely settled them some distance to the south of the Tugela, after disarming them and passing Dunn's rifles out to the native police. Dunn, dis-gusted, was forced to slaughter his own cattle to feed his retainers, but he soon sent wagons to Durban for grain and then started to sell his cattle to the commissariat, at prices that assuaged his feelings.

On January 4, 1879, Frere placed the further enforcement of all demands in Lord Chelmsford's hands. On the eleventh of January he published the following notification:

The British forces are crossing into Zululand to exact from Cetywayo reparation for violations of British territory committed by the sons of Sirayo and others; and to enforce compliance with the promises, made by Cetywayo at his coronation, for the better government of his people.

The British Government has no quarrel with the Zulu people. All Zulus who come in unarmed, or who lay down their arms, will be provided for till the troubles of their country are over; and will then, if they please, be allowed to return to their own land; but all who do not so submit will be dealt with as enemies.

When the war is finished, the British Government will make the best arrangements in its power for the future good government of the Zulus in their own country, in peace and quietness, and will not permit the killing and oppression they have suffered from Cetywayo to continue.

H. B. E. Frere
High Commissioner

The war had begun.

PREPARATIONS

Early on the morning of Saturday, January 11, 1879, Lord Chelmsford was a reasonably confident, if somewhat exhausted, general. No less than 16,800 men, deployed in five widely separated columns, were amenable to his orders; he had over 2,000,000 rounds of ammunition available; there were ample stores in his depots; and to keep the columns supplied as they advanced, they would be accompanied by 113 two-wheeled carts, 612 wagons and 7,626 commissariat oxen, horses and mules, while several hundred additional wagons worked stores up to the border along roads in Natal that were guarded by eight detached companies of Imperial infantry. In the light of what he had found on his arrival just five months earlier, it was a very creditable military showing, but it had not been easy to accomplish. There had been no help from the War Office until the last-minute arrival of the two additional battalions. Bulwer had fought him every inch of the way, and only in the last two months had he been permitted to take any active steps to implement his early planning.

Chelmsford lost no time after his arrival in August. While he was still investigating Natal's resources and surveying the coast of Zululand, he put H. Bernard Fynney to work on a detailed report of the Zulu army. Fynney had his faults as a border agent, but he had been collecting just such information for years as a hobby, and he soon produced a few packed pages that outlined in precise detail how the Zulu forces were raised, armed, drilled, officered, organized, fed and doctored. He described how they marched and how the tactics of the chest, the horns and the loins worked. To this succinct compendium he added a complete list of the Zulu regiments, giving for each one the Zulu name and its translation, who had raised it, the name of the commanding inDuna, the headquarters kraal, a complete description of its distinctive uniform, a close estimate of the number of warriors and their average age. Chelmsford, much impressed, threw in the best map

292

of Zululand Durnford could produce and published the whole in Pietermaritzburg in November. When Fynney sent him a list of over a hundred of the chief Zulu inDunas, giving each man's father, age, regiment, clan and residence, together with a brief estimate of his strength, character and political leanings, Chelmsford promptly published a second edition of his pamphlet, and when his forces entered Zululand, every company commander had a copy in his kit. No expeditionary force had ever started a native war so well informed about its enemy.

Chelmsford also sought advice in other quarters, interviewing most of the men in Natal who had a reputation for knowing something about Zululand. It was an engaging trick; he was a good listener, and the men he questioned were flattered and went away with a good impression. His own impressions he kept largely to himself. Except for Bulwer, and, of course, Colenso, he found the colonists ready enough for the risks of war. The standing menace of the Zulu army, which even Colenso privately admitted existed, and the lack of means to do anything about it had kept the colony from serious consideration of a war for years. The Europeans had gotten along well with their Natal Kaffirs, and they had avoided any major friction with their neighbors across the Tugela. Now that the Crown was at last prepared to act, they were cheerful. The war meant the end of the Zulu menace, pleasant excitement and excellent business prospects. There had always been a tendency to belittle the Zulu power, with talk of marching from one end of the country to the other with two hundred redcoats, and because the best-known inDunas were those caught between two fires in the borderlands, there was a feeling, which even Fynney shared, that Cetshwayo might not be able to rally his people.

At the end of November Chelmsford had one interview he later had reason to remember. Paul Kruger landed in Durban on his way to Pretoria after his second trip to London, and he stopped at Pietermaritzburg to see Frere. A minister of the Dutch Reformed Church brought him to see Chelmsford, and recorded the interview. As a boy of twelve, Kruger had been in the wagon laager at Vegkop when 33 Boers under Potgieter and Sarel Cilliers had beaten off a Matabele impi. With the decisive Boer victory over the Zulus at Blood River in mind as well, he emphasized to Chelmsford the need for distant scouting to locate the mobile impis, and warned him of the vital necessity of laagering his wagons every night. Chelmsford agreed heartily in principle, if not in detail. There had been 400 Boers armed with muzzle-loaders in the Blood River commando, and they had traveled lightly, with their scanty rations in a score of wagons. Chelmsford's columns would have more than three times as many breechloaders, not to mention artillery, and even the experienced Kruger had little idea of the hundreds of wagons and the vast amount of impedimenta that a British expeditionary force needed to sustain itself in the field. Small British detachments would laager as a matter of course, but the campsites of the main columns would be scouted for miles about, and would have scores of pickets and cavalry vedettes flung out at night. It would take hours to laager the hundreds of unwieldy wagons and to unlaager in the morning, and at main camps the troops would entrench, using a wagon laager only to form a protective kraal for the draft oxen.

Once Chelmsford had decided that Natal's only practical defense lay in an invasion, his plans took rapid shape. The prolonged nuisance of the Ninth Kaffir War had taught him that the first blow in native warfare must be a heavy one, and he correctly saw that the only effective manner of impressing a victory on the unsophisticated Zulu minds would be to smash their army and capture their king. A single heavy column might easily push through to Ulundi, but it would solve nothing by merely occupying the royal kraal. If it were too massive it would never be attacked by the Zulus, who might then decide to evade it to descend on a defenseless Natal. He therefore decided to strike out straight for Ulundi with *three* columns, entering Zululand from the principal crossings. The first column would cross at the Lower Drift of the Tugela and head north through John Dunn's territories along a well-defined track that led to Eshowe, the second would move northeast from Rorke's Drift on the Buffalo, and the third would move southeast from the disputed territories around the headwaters of the Blood River. A fourth column would be kept in reserve at the Middle Drift of the Tugela below Kranz Kop, where Smith and Deighton had been molested. It would guard the most direct route from Ulundi to Pietermaritzburg against the danger of a Zulu counterinvasion, and it could later be committed as events dictated. Colonel Rowlands' force, still in the Transvaal, formed a fifth column which might become available later. The main Zulu forces would almost certainly attack one of the invading prongs, which was exactly what Chelmsford wanted them to do, and as the columns converged on Ulundi from three sides, there would be an ever-lessening danger of an impi slipping through to raid Natal.

Frere had even modified the timing of his ultimatum to help Chelmsford's plan. Mid-January was harvest time in Zululand; there would be little food in the country and the people would presumably be busy gathering the crops and disinclined to break away for fighting. It was a miscalculation, however; the rains had been late and the harvest was not ready. Chelmsford had also forgotten the First Fruits ceremony, which Cetshwayo held on schedule, so that all the regiments were fully mobilized at Ulundi before the invasion started. The women would attend to the harvest when it came, and the grain pits and cattle herds could feed the nation in the meantime.

The concept of the invasion was sound, and it met as adequately as possible the twin objectives of defeating the Zulus and defending Natal. On a sprawling scale, Chelmsford had quite unconsciously adopted the Zulus' own tactics, with a chest at Rorke's Drift, a right horn at the Lower Drift of the Tugela and a left horn at the head-waters of the Blood, and the loins in reserve at the Middle Drift. As if tacitly confirming this plagiarism, he made the chest his strongest force and decided to accompany the central force when it crossed at Rorke's Drift.

Chelmsford shared with every loyal subject of the Crown an implicit faith in the steady, aimed fire of the disciplined Imperial battalions. They were the heart of any campaign, and he now had eight of them: both battalions of the 24th Regiment and the 90th Regiment, the single-battalion 99th Regiment and odd battalions of the 3d, the 4th and the 13th Regiments. The single-battalion 80th Regiment, with which Rowlands had failed to subdue the elusive Sekukuni in October, was by January camped at Luneberg. Within easy call, it guarded against a Zulu outbreak to the north of the Pongola, but the need to watch the baPedi and the increasingly restless Transvaal Boers held it out of the invasion.

Each Imperial battalion had eight lettered companies of ninety to a hundred men apiece. Most of the colonels and many of the majors were veterans of the Crimea and the Sepoy Rebellion; the company officers and the men had seen action at Peking and the Taku Forts, in Abyssinia and New Zealand, in Burma and on a score of forgotten Indian battlefields. Five of the battalions had fought in the Ninth Kaffir War. These were the redcoats, the professional infantry of the line, who earned a shilling a day and, with stoppages for rations and cleaning gear and other sundries, were lucky to net a penny. The Army had come a long way since the Crimea. It no longer recruited in the gutters and the jails, and there was machinery to unload worthless incorrigibles, but most of the men were barely literate, amenities were primitive, and the choice of an enlisted career was still something of a last resort. Unemployment and Jack Frost were the best recruiters, and the Army still used the lash in the field. Serious crime was rare, however, and the men existed in the tight encapsulated world of their own battalions, with few contacts with the civil communities about them.

Their business was fighting, and they were very good at it. Even the raw recruits Chelmsford had complained about on his transport were veterans now. They had fought in the Perie Bush and slept in the open for a year, in the great bell tents that held eighteen men like the spokes of a wheel when they were near their regimental luggage, but more often wrapped in a greatcoat or a blanket under rain or the stars. Universally mustached and mostly bearded, they were lean and hard and tanned, in fine fettle and with few complaints. The country was healthy, and the itching pepper-tick bites were a small price to pay for the absence of malarial mosquitoes.

The men regarded themselves as well fed. The two staples were bread and meat, eked out by tea, coffee, preserved potatoes and rice, with whatever fresh vegetables the country might provide. Salt beef and pork came packed in barrels, but a battalion on the march usually drove slaughter beeves along and killed what it needed. Field bakery wagons accompanied the troops but usually stayed in the main camps; on the march the men were issued hardtack biscuits. The men received a half a gill of rum a day, and the officers consumed great quantities of porter, which came in stout black bottles with patent stoppers. Natal's standard tipple was gin, available at every public house. It came in rectangular bottles and was known as "squareface"; the Zulus called it "the Queen's tears."

The uniforms were still impractical, but they were considerably more comfortable than they had been in the Crimea. The line regiments wore single-breasted red tunics, with blue trousers which in the field were usually stuffed into heavy ammunition boots shod with iron heels. Each regiment strove to erect its own façade on this common base, varying the facing colors of cuffs and collars and adopting their own buttons, badges and buckles. The 24th Regiment wore grass-green facings; they lost them in a uniform modification in 1881 and agitated for twenty years until they got them back. The universal headgear was a light cork sun helmet covered with white canvas, with the regimental badge affixed in front. It afforded protection from the tropical sun and kept rain from dripping down the back of the collar, but the low brim restricted vision and the drooping nape made it difficult to fire from a prone position. During a campaign the men wore a single uniform until it was in patched rags and ribbons, and a mass replacement was issued only when nudity threatened.

Accouterments had finally received some professional attention in 1868, and ammunition pouches, knapsack, mess tin, waterbottle, greatcoat, blanket and spare boots had been strapped and buckled into a complicated unit. Properly worn, the ammunition pouches were in front, a haversack for rations and loose gear on the hip, and everything else behind, where the various items stretched from the ears to well below the hips. The equipment cut into the small of the back and banged into the buttocks on the march, and on campaign the men carried the pouches and a haversack and slung everything else into a company wagon. Fully accoutered, with rifle, seventy rounds of ammunition and two days' rations, each man carried 57 pounds.

The Army was equipped with an excellent single-shot breech-loading rifle. The Model 1871 Martini-Henry fired a black-powder .45 caliber center-fire Boxer cartridge of thin rolled brass, with a heavy lead slug weighing 480 grains, paper-wrapped at the base to prevent its melting in its passage down the bore. The breechblock was hinged at the rear and dropped to expose the chamber when the lever behind the trigger guard was depressed, flipping out the expended case. A fresh round was laid atop the grooved block and thumbed home, and the piece was cocked when the lever was raised. There was no safety.

Henry Peabody, an American, had invented the action in 1862. Failing to sell it to the Union forces, he passed it to Friedrich von Martini, a Swiss gunsmith who improved the action and removed Peabody's external hammer. Von Martini in turn sold the patent to the British, who coupled it with a polygon rifling system invented by Alexander Henry of Edinburgh and issued it to replace the earlier Sniders.

The action was simple and sturdy, and in trained hands the rifle was accurate to a thousand yards and more. Battalion volley fire against massed targets frequently opened at 600 to 800 yards, and even an average marksman could score hits at 300 or 400 yards. The soft lead slug was a man-stopper that smashed bone and cartilage and left wicked wounds. The gun was not pleasant to fire. The 83 grains of powder made its ten pounds kick viciously, especially when the bore was foul, and a few rounds bruised shoulders, and nosebleed was not uncommon. Despite the protection of a wooden forestock, prolonged firing soon made the barrel too hot to touch, and old stagers soon learned to sew wet cowhide covers, hair and all, around the balance, cutting a hole for the rear leaf sight after the skin had dried and shrunk.

The men carried no arms except for the rifle and the old triangular bayonet they called the "lunger." Their cartridges came in paper packets of ten rounds; each man carried four packets in the leather ammunition pouches on his belt, ten loose rounds in a small canvas expense pouch and two additional packets tucked into his knapsack. If an alarm was sounded in camp, he would grab his rifle and belt and fall in with fifty rounds; on the march he carried the full seventy. Very few battles ever called for the expenditure of seventy—or even fifty—rounds, but additional ammunition always accompanied the troops. Sturdy wooden boxes held 600 rounds; they were two feet long, seven inches wide and nine inches deep, they weighed eighty pounds full and were equipped with rope handles at either end. The lids were held down by two strong copper bands, each secured with nine stout screws. A battalion on the march carried a regimental reserve of almost fifty of these boxes, packed into two special wagons or three carts, enough to provide thirty extra rounds for each man. Enough boxes to provide a field reserve of 480 rounds for every man moved with the supply train from main camp to main camp on extended campaigns.

The uniforms the officers wore resembled those of their men, although officers of the Royal Artillery, Royal Engineers and those on staff or various detached duties frequently wore a dark-blue Norfolk jacket in the field. The officers carried privately owned swords and center-fire double-action .45 caliber revolvers, mostly made by Adams or Webley. Optional binoculars were beginning to replace telescopes; and haversacks held maps, cartridges and loose gear. Each officer in the field was permitted forty pounds of personal clothing, which he generally stowed in the pillow of a sleeping bag that rolled up to form a handy waterproof valise. The remainder of his equipment was packed into a large bullock trunk, which stayed behind at the advanced depot.

The officers of each battalion were a close-knit band, who messed together, played together, and fought together. With rare exceptions the company grades were bachelors, and frequently only the colonel was married. Such a group might stay together for years with few changes occurring. There was little room for friction, and strife was rare. The only outcasts were the men with honorary commissions like Quartermasters James Pullen of the 1st Battalion and Edward Bloomfield of the 2nd Battalion of the 24th Regiment. Essentially supply clerks, they had, like the riding masters in cavalry squadrons, been raised to their present positions after long service in the ranks of other regiments. They might look forward to promotion to honorary lieutenant, and even honorary major, but like the lieutenants of hospital orderlies they were not full members of the regimental messes and only dined with their colleagues on Guest Night.

The regimental basis of the British Army was unique, and the officers used it to build up an *esprit de corps* that no service in the world could match. The appeal was never for the sake of Empire or the Crown or the service; it was always for the sake of the regiment, and the men always met it. The badges, the facings and the buttons were important, as were the regimental marches, the nicknames and the traditions. As in the Zulu army, there were units in the British Army that were best not quartered too close together. The 1st and the 2nd Battalions of the 24th Regiment, for example, were barely on speaking terms, and certain regimental feuds were notorious. Other regiments were traditional friends, a condition which usually stemmed from shoulder-to-shoulder service in a long-ago battle, and the officers were honorary members of each other's messes.

The soul of every battalion resided in the Colours. Each battalion of infantry of the line carried two gold-fringed silken standards: a Sovereign's Colour of the Union Jack charged with the Crown and the regimental title, and a Regimental Colour that matched the color of the facings and bore the regimental crest and the battle honors. They had originally served to rally units disorganized in the shock of battle, and in 1879, for the last time, they were still being taken into action. They were carried cased on the march and kept in the guard tent in camp, uncased only on Guest Night in the mess, at special ceremonies when one Colour at a time was trooped to show it to the men, and in battle. Battalions might carry their Colours for half a century and more, and when the worn fabric was hopelessly frayed, they laid them up in the regimental cathedral and were issued new ones. The loss of a Colour was a disgrace felt so keenly that officers and men would unhesitatingly risk their lives to save what Rudyard Kipling once described as something looking like "the lining of a brick-layer's hat on a chewed toothpick."

The 24th Regiment had suffered singularly ill luck with its Colours. In 1806 the 1st Battalion had participated in the expedition to capture Capetown. In 1810 it embarked in five transports to attack Mauritius, and French warships found the convoy. Two transports with the colonel and four companies were captured after an all-day fight, but the Colours and the regimental records were dropped over the side before the French boarded. In 1849 the 24th, then a single-battalion regiment, fought in the battle of Chillianwallah in the second Sikh War. While attacking the center of the enemy line through a swampy forest, Lieutenant Phillips was hit and fell into a pool with the Queen's Colour. Private Connolly saw him fall, fished out the Colour, ripped it off the broken staff and wrapped it around his body under his tunic. He then returned to the charge, but was killed and later buried, with thirteen officers and 224 other men, by a working detail that failed to notice what he was carrying. Soldiers' graves were not marked, and the Colour was never recovered. The officer carrying the Regimental Colour was killed as well, but another private brought it safely into camp.

The Queen's Colour was replaced in 1850. The regiment returned to England in 1861 after fifteen years in India; a 2nd Battalion had been raised in 1858 and was then in Mauritius. By 1866 the Queen's Colour of the 1st Battalion was so frayed that a new one was again issued, which Richard Glyn and Wilsone Black received on parade on the Curragh in Ireland from Lady Wodehouse. The two battalions, utter strangers, met for the first time early in 1878 at Kingwilliamstown, and all four Colours were now in Natal.

The Imperial battalions would form the hard core of the columns, but they were far too scanty in numbers to invade Zululand by themselves. Chelmsford did not have a single Imperial cavalry troop in all southern Africa, and the columns would be blind without scores of daily mounted patrols. There would also be ceaseless demands for small detachments: to man pickets, vedettes and outposts, to guard camps and stores and drifts, to reconnoiter in force, and to escort wagon trains. If these demands were levied on the Imperial battalions, the anvil on which the Zulu army was to be shattered would shortly melt away. As the prospects of war shifted from a possibility to a virtual certainty, however, a peculiar colonial phenomenon began to manifest itself. With hardly more than a nod of encouragement from the authorities, irregular volunteer units mushroomed into existence and were gratefully incorporated into the British forces.

The military requirements of the frontier colonies of southern Africa fluctuated from month to month, and no government on earth could have met in full the continual demands of the colonists for local garrison forces. As British subjects they felt entitled to protection, but with the best will in the world, which they did not possess, they could not have borne the expense of a tenth of what they demanded. The Crown acknowledged the claim to protection, but it was disturbed by the excessive demands and truly horrified by the expense of what it was grudgingly forced to provide. The British Army was designed to wage continental warfare, and it was ill adapted for the native wars which formed the bulk of its work. The responsibilities of Empire eroded its strength and frittered the battalions away in distant, expensive squabbles, and the Crown was continually prodding the colonies both to reduce the squabbling and to assume more of the burden of their own defense. This was, in fact, the primary motivation of the drive for confederation, and no corner of the Empire constituted a greater drain on the Imperial treasury than southern Africa.

Driven by stark necessity, the colonists had taken a few faltering steps short of forming regular standing forces, but they still turned to the Crown in every crisis. What little they had done was modeled on the practical system evolved by the Boers, who did not look to a central government for help but regarded the defense of their homesteads as a normal farming chore. They had no use for the concept of a professional soldier, because every male Boer past the age of puberty was a soldier as well as a farmer. They fought, when they felt they had to, in their everyday clothing, riding their own horses and carrying the rifles which seldom left their hands. When a commando was called out, each man came as he was, ready to fight and bringing such rations as he felt he might need. He accepted military direction from a commandant chosen for his experience, and the commandant limited himself to military direction because each man still governed his own affairs and no supplementary body of regulations was necessary. Discipline, in the European sense, was unknown and unnecessary, because each man knew what to do and did it. When the work was finished, the men dispersed at once.

For a large number of reasons, the European colonist was incapable of such a simple approach to soldiering. Socially and politically more sophisticated, he regarded warfare as the province of a trained professional, and, especially if he were urbanized, his commitments were too binding to allow him to go off campaigning on a day's notice. When he did go, he demanded considerably more in the way of a military atmosphere, with uniforms, drilled movements, a closely ordered rank structure, an arcane vocabulary and a central government to foot the bill. To the European mentality, there could be no military effectiveness without rigid discipline, which called for some people to give orders and for others to take them and carry them out. The European, however, was no more willing than his Boer neighbor to place himself under the irksome petty supervision of a fellow settler. He still regarded enlisted service in the regular forces as only a notch above life in the gutter, and he could be induced to volunteer his services only to an informal group that engendered prestige. The net result was small volunteer units with grandiose names, little training, and precarious discipline.

An early Natal ordinance made all adult males liable for service on call, and although frequently modified, the law remained essentially in effect. The first unit was formed in January of 1855 as the Pietermaritzburg Irregular Horse, and since recruiting was equally successful in other areas as well, the name was changed to the Royal Natal Carbineers within three weeks. A loose organization with elected officers, the Carbineers provided their own uniforms and mounts and drew firearms and ammunition from the government. They met quarterly for drill but were rarely in action, although frequently called out to impress balking Natal Kaffirs and to guard the Tugela and Buffalo Drifts against raids which never materialized.

Recruiting was casual and local; the Carbineers remained based on Pietermaritzburg, and similar autonomous units were spawned in other localities. Some, like the Royal Durban Rangers and the Umgeni Rangers, withered away from a lack of recruits, but in 1878 there were Mounted Rifle troops from Alexandra, Ixopo, Isipongo, Durban, Newcastle, Stanger and Victoria, as well as the Natal Hussars and the Buffalo Border Guard. The Royal Durban Rifles and the Maritzburg Rifles were infantry units—merchants, clerks and civil servants who had banded together for local defense. Some of the cavalry units had been with Theophilus Shepstone at Cetshwayo's coronation, others had participated in the Langalibalele Rebellion.

The men in the cavalry units were mostly established settlers: superb horsemen and crack shots with years of experience in the country. Two of Shepstone's sons were enrolled; Theophilus Junior, a lawyer known as "Offy," captained the 32 men of the Carbineers, and William led 35 men of the Durban Mounted Rifles. All told, the volunteer units mustered 660 colonists, but less than half of them were available for the coming campaign. The 240 infantry volunteers failed to muster, and the Ixopo Mounted Rifles were kept on the Umzimkulu River in southern Natal to watch Kokstad, where the Griquas were out of hand. The Isipongo Mounted Rifles stayed in Natal, patrolling the Tugela River, and other volunteers were ill or otherwise occupied. The units that answered Chelmsford's call provided only 290 mounted men for service in Zululand.

Natal's irregular units were backed by a small standing body of quasi-military police. The conduct of the volunteers in Bushman's River Pass had convinced Sir Benjamin Pine that the irregulars were a weak reed, and in December of 1873, at the height of the Langalibalele Rebellion, he advertised for a man willing to organize a permanent body of mounted men. John G. Dartnell, a Sepoy Rebellion veteran who had sold out an Imperial commission as a major in 1869 to try his hand at farming in Natal, was about to return to England, but he answered Pine's call, spent a fortnight in Kingwilliamstown to observe the Frontier Armed and Mounted Police, and returned to Pietermaritzburg with a former sergeant of the Cape Mounted Rifles named "Puffy" Stean. The first man was enrolled in the Natal Mounted Police on March 12, 1874.

The early years were not easy. The colony had little money to spare for equipment, and the original recruits had to be drawn from the flotsam and jetsam of the colony—deserted merchant seamen, paid-off soldiers, and social failures of all ages and physical descriptions. Dartnell was dubious at first, but Puffy Stean knew his work and left a lasting impression on the corps. He broke or drove off the hard cases, chasing one or two off the drill field and out of the unit with his sword, while Dartnell battled the Executive Council for funds. The early brown corduroy uniforms stank so badly in wet weather that the men were known as "the Snuffs," and it was years before the commissariat was on a sound footing. The terms of service were far from attractive. The men were paid 5s. 6d. a day—a laborer could earn as much—and out of this sum not only had to provide their own uniforms and board but also had to pay back an advance for their horses and military equipment. They also had to locate and prepare their own food, find their own quarters and pay for the forage for their horses, and they could look forward to little or nothing in the way of promotion or retirement benefits. Despite the obstacles, the Mounted Police flourished, and gradually began to enlist a better stamp of men directly from England. By 1878 they were 110 strong, well trained, self-reliant and disciplined. Scattered in small posts all over the colony, they aided the magistrates and caught cattle thieves and gunrunners, riding patrol year in and year out. They were delighted to be drafted; the Crown took over the expense of rationing them and for the first time in their corporate existence the men were all out of debt.

Even with the welcome addition of the Natal Mounted Police, Chelmsford had less than 400 mounted men, and he now cast about to the other territories. The results were gratifying. Roughly the same process had occurred in the Cape Colony and the Transvaal as in Natal, and several large bodies of mounted volunteers that had been formed to fight in Griqualand West in the Ninth Kaffir War and against Sekukuni were still in existence and willing to serve in Zululand. Baker's Horse, 236 strong, rode up from the Cape Colony, and Buller brought in 216 of his superb Frontier Light Horse from the unsuccessful campaign against Sekukuni.

Frederick Augustus Weatherley, a Canadian who was farming and gold mining in the Transvaal, brought down 61 men of his Border Horse. After service as a young man in the Austrian cavalry he had obtained a commission in the 4th Light Dragoons and had charged with the Light Brigade at Balaklava. Exchanging into the 6th Dragoons, he fought in the Sepoy Rebellion and had been a close friend to Bartle Frere in India. Under something of a cloud after a regimental tiff, he finally sold out and acquired property near Lydenburg. He had been on both expeditions against Sekukuni, and had raised the Border Horse as lancers for the second one. He had just divorced his wife, and both his sons, one a boy of fourteen, were serving in his unit.

Friedrich Schermbrucker, a civic-minded officer in the old German Legion, had been farming in the eastern Cape Colony since 1858. Appointed Military Commandant for his district, he had fought well in the Ninth Kaffir War. He now collected 42 of his German neighbors, equipped them as infantry, named them the Kaffrarian Vanguard and brought them to Natal. Chelmsford sent him to guard his compatriots in the Luneberg area, and eventually mounted the unit.

One final reinforcement came from an unexpected source. After the conclusion of the Ninth Kaffir War Colonel Wood had marched several companies of the 90th Regiment, together with Harness's artillery battery and Buller's Frontier Light Horse, north through the coastal strip to Natal, crossing 122 unbridged rivers on the way. He paused for a full month in the vicinity of Kokstad to eye the sullen ama-Mpondo, who were thinking of attacking the amaBaca. With the help of a Mrs. Jenkins, a missionary's widow who lived alone with the ama-Mpondo and treated them like naughty children, he averted the attack and in September brought his thoroughly bored troops to Pietermar-itzburg. Chelmsford sent him to Utrecht, from whence the Frontier Light Horse went on to the Transvaal, leaving Wood with a handful of men to guard the disputed territories. When Cetshwayo asked the German settlers to leave Luneberg, Wood split his tiny force to garri-son the town. He also rode alone through the kraals on the fringes of the disputed territories, facing down petty chieftains on the verge of attacking the isolated Boer homesteads to the west. His health for the moment was better than usual; in addition to visiting all his pickets twice a night, he was spending two hours every evening playing polo or lawn tennis, which he had just discovered. In mid-November Bartle Frere asked him to try to induce the Utrecht Boers to provide a force for the invasion. He naturally met with a cold reception; Andries Pre-torius was barely civil, and the Boers would do nothing until Paul Kruger was back from London with their independence. At this junc-ture Piet Uys stepped forward. He farmed on Balte Spruit in the Blood River Territory, and had been one of the Transvaal delegates to the Boundary Commission. He was bitterly opposed to the annexation, and probably knew that the boundary decision would go against the Boers, but he had a long memory and more reason to hate the Zulus than even his neighbors did. It had been his elder brother, Dirk Cornelius, then only fourteen, who had charged back into one of Dingane's impis to die by his mortally wounded father on the Vlug Kommando in 1838. Piet Uys now equipped forty of his relatives and neighbors, among them a fifteen-year-old son, at his own expense and placed himself at Chelmsford's disposal. His motive was patriotism and he refused to accept a penny of pay.

With well over 1,000 mounted volunteers available, Chelmsford felt he could meet the majority of his scouting needs. He felt less easy about the weight of his infantry. Split amongst the columns, the Im-perial battalions would barely provide adequate firepower to cope with the main Zulu army should it attack any one column. There would be no reserve for the inevitable demands for small detachments, and the equivalent of a full battalion had already been bled away by the need to garrison the lines of communications in Natal. One company of the 99th was to be left in Durban and another would have to garrison Fort Pearson at the Lower Drift of the Tugela. A company of the 2nd Battalion of the 24th Regiment would have to be left at Greytown to guard the road to the Middle Drift of the Tugela and no less than four companies of the same battalion would be needed to man the main supply depot for the Central Column at Helpmakaar and the crossing twelve miles below at Rorke's Drift. The 88th Regiment was unavailable in the Cape Colony, but an odd company, wild Irishmen of the Connaught Rangers, would garrison Fort Napier at Pietermaritzburg. There were no more Imperial forces to be had, and no further major units could be shaken out of the colonists. The 300,000 Natal Kaffirs were the only untapped source of manpower left.

There had been native allies fighting beside Europeans since Van Riebeeck's day, but they were generally of dubious value. Called out in disorganized mobs, and rarely equipped with firearms, they could be used to charge a greatly inferior foe or to mop up a beaten one, but they were of little value in defense. Difficult to maneuver, they were never properly trained, because they were rarely assembled until just before the fighting started. Dartnell had hoped to enroll Natal Kaffirs in the Mounted Police, but the colonists would not hear of it, and except for Durnford's work with Hlubi and his Basutos no attempt had ever been made to arm or drill the natives in Natal. Chelmsford, however, had seen Lonsdale's superior Fingoes in the Perie Bush, and he was half convinced that something might be made of native units if they were properly taken in hand.

A fortnight after his arrival in Natal he received a memorandum from Durnford, who proposed to raise no less than 7,000 Natal Kaffirs with European officers and noncommissioned officers. His scheme had been worked out with care; it called for proper training and laid great emphasis on the caliber of the Europeans selected to lead these troops. Chelmsford was delighted and at once requested Bulwer's permission to proceed, but the horrified Lieutenant Governor vetoed the project. He saw no need for such a body of troops, and he feared the colony's reaction were he to arm so many of the Natal Kaffirs. When Hicks Beach initially refused to provide Imperial reinforcements, a Natal Native Contingent became a necessity, and Frere finally wore Bulwer down in mid-November.

Chelmsford at once ordered Durnford to proceed, intending to give him over-all command of the force. His staff objected, however, because Durnford was somewhat junior for so large a command (his brevet as colonel did not arrive until December), and as a Royal Engineer he had never commanded any force in action larger than the party he took into Bushman's River Pass. Chelmsford, therefore, reversed himself, making the three proposed regiments independent of one another. He gave Durnford command of the 1st Regiment of the NNC, with three battalions of 1,000 natives each, and gave the second and third two-battalion regiments to Major Shapland Graves, seconded from the 3d Regiment, and to Rupert Lonsdale, fresh from his Fingo command in the Perie Bush.

The seven battalion commanders for the NNC were all experienced Imperial officers, or mature colonials who had served as commandants on commando, but close to 300 Europeans were needed as company-grade and noncommissioned officers, and these were harder to find. They would need at least a smattering of Zulu, if anything were to be made of their troops, as well as past experience in handling native laborers. The best class in the colony was already serving in the mounted volunteer units, and what was left was unprepossessing. It consisted, roughly, of men who could not afford a horse or a gun—a few clerks, foreign construction workers and plain drifters. They were taken because no one else was available, and they effectively sabotaged Durnford's scheme. Pulleine's Lambs, for example, were drafted to a man as noncommissioned officers, put in immediate contact with the native platoons, and entrusted with the job of transmitting orders from the company officers to the troops. They were totally unfitted for the work. Their number included illiterates known only by such names as "Kentish John" and "Bully Karl," and their Zulu was limited to a few degrading obscenities. Pulleine had raised the Lambs in the early stages of the Ninth Kaffir War from discharged road workers simply to keep them out of jail, and he had regretted the act ever since. He had located a hard-bitten Irish contractor named Hamilton-Browne, known as "Maori Browne" from service in a volunteer unit in New Zealand, and had charged him with keeping the Lambs occupied and away from the towns. Hamilton-Browne was now given command of the 1st Battalion of Lonsdale's 3d Regiment of the NNC, and he ruined it. He had little use for his sixty noncommissioned officers and absolutely none for the 1,200 natives under his command, whom he consistently referred to as "niggers," even in official correspondence.

Economy played further havoc. Durnford hoped to issue red tunics and white canvas trousers to all the men, not only to raise their own morale and to impress the enemy, but also to permit the British forces to distinguish between the Zulus and their native allies. He also planned to arm them all with firearms. The uniform was now cut back to a red rag tied about the head, and only one man in ten was given a firearm, breech-loading rifles alternating with the older Sniders and muzzle-loading percussion Enfields. The rest were armed with the light throwing assegais, knobkerries and shields they had brought from their kraals when the district magistrates drafted them and delivered them to the training camps.

Each man with a firearm was given five rounds of ammunition, and a halfhearted effort was made to teach the troops to drill, load and fire. The results were ludicrous. The Natal Kaffirs, with the natural dignity of their native garb grotesquely set off by discarded bits and pieces of European uniform, were barely able to form a straight line, and only knew that their efforts made them the butt of their leaders' scorn and hilarity. Tactics were out of the question, and there was no musketry instruction or target practice worthy of the name. Even the company officers shunned the vicinity of their units when the men were firing; Hamilton-Browne refused to issue further ammunition when the five rounds were gone and took up the Martini-Henrys as soon as he could. The drill of the N.C.O.'s was in any event little better than that of their charges. Chelmsford had purchased horses and mounted them all, but the best steeds had gone to the volunteer cavalry units and there was little left but broken-down plough horses and other nags that had seen better days. The horses were gun-shy, and many of the N.C.O.'s were riding for the first time in their lives, so that the Natal Kaffirs had a few no doubt welcome opportunities to laugh themselves.

Lonsdale's regiment was ruined before it was born, but he had one good man on his staff. Henry Harford, the childhood playmate of the Colenso boys, was back in Natal as a lieutenant of the 99th Regiment. He had resigned his position as adjutant to come out several months before his regiment was detailed to the Cape, and because he was virtually unique among Imperial officers in that he spoke fluent Zulu, Chelmsford posted him to Lonsdale, who did not. Harford was delighted. The position gave him an extra ten shillings a day, and there were old friends in the NNC. He found a servant named Jim who had worked for his father, and, on Lonsdale's staff, Mkungo, the last of Monase's sons and Cetshwayo's half brother, who had fled to Natal in 1856 and had been educated at Bishopstowe. Mkungo was too obese to take the field, and his assignment had been made in hopes of sowing dissension among the Zulu inDunas who had not forgotten Mbulazi. As a substitute his son was serving in the ranks. Harford, a teetotaller, was popular with the colonial officers, who were inclined to be sensitive about patronizing regulars. He was an enthusiastic amateur naturalist, with a distressing habit of using the scanty supply of gin to preserve his specimens, but when the troops of the 3d Regiment of the NNC were required to do anything en masse, it was usually Harford who explained what was wanted and coaxed them along.

Harford's cabin mate on the voyage out was a tall, thin lantern-jawed lieutenant, Horace Lockwood Smith-Dorrien, only twenty years old but already adjutant of the 95th Regiment, Chelmsford's old command in India. The General had asked for him by name, and when his commanding officer refused to release him, Smith-Dorrien wired

the Commander in Chief directly, stating his willingness to go. He had
gotten telegraphic orders the same afternoon. He spoke no Zulu, and
Chelmsford put him in the Transport Service and set him to working
stores up from Greytown through Helpmakaar to Rorke's Drift,
where he soon added a post-graduate course in the care of oxen to his
Sandhurst education.

The training camps of the NNC bustled with activity. Lonsdale,
returning from a visit to headquarters to report on his progress, failed
to inform Harford, his adjutant, that Chelmsford intended making a
formal inspection. His pony "Dot" then stumbled and threw him so
heavily that he was still unconscious when the General arrived. Lonsdale did not recover from his concussion until a week after the invasion started, and Chelmsford posted Major Wilsone Black of the 24th
to replace him.

Durnford's 1st Regiment received better attention. He was by now
well acquainted with the various clans of Natal Kaffirs, and many of
the men in the ranks knew him of old. He was also able to select his
officers personally, and even to snag the best men left for his noncommissioned officers. Among them was a gigantic and improvident
young Swiss named Schiess, who had been working as an unskilled
laborer in Natal. He had served in Bourbaki's army in the Franco-
Prussian War and was quickly accepted for service in the NNC. Durnford had two months before the invasion, and he made the most of
them. By January his men were able to drill, and they had a modicum
of trust in their officers, which the 3d Regiment did not.

Durnford did not stop with his infantry regiment. He organized 270
of his best natives into three companies of Natal Native Pioneers,
equipped them with pickaxes and shovels and armed them as well.
They were the pick of the entire levy, and Durnford somehow managed to find them the uniforms he had hoped to issue to all.

Hlubi's baTlokwa horsemen were not forgotten. Many of the Natal
clans owned horses, and the baTlokwa were soon joined by mounted
groups from the native reserves. Sikali brought in 150, Jantji 50, and
Mafunzi 75. There was a mission station at Edendale near Pietermaritzburg, and John Zulu, brother of Langalibalele, rode into Durnford's
camp at the head of over a hundred horsemen—splendidly mounted,
accoutered and uniformed at their own expense. Durnford promptly
issued them all Martini-Henry carbines. Simeon Kambula, the son of his
interpreter Elijah, who had been shot as Durnford tried to rescue him
in Bushman's River Pass, was a sergeant in the ranks. The men were all
devout Christians, who rose every morning before the rest of the camp
to hold their services and sing hymns. George Shepstone, still another

of Theophilus Shepstone's six sons, was on Durnford's staff, and was given a large command of native horse.

Chelmsford had assembled the Imperial battalions and the colonial volunteers and had raised the Natal Native Contingent. He had collected his stores, filled his depots, equipped and trained the volunteers and native levies, organized his columns and marched the men to the invasion points, attending to the voluminous administrative detail the work had involved, including constant friction with the civil administration of Natal, all in sixty days. Despite the labor this task had entailed, more than half his time had been devoted to surmounting an obstacle which continually threatened to stall the entire campaign—transport. From the outset he ran into a series of problems which, no matter what care and effort he devoted to their solution, simply spawned fresh problems. More and more of his time was given to these problems, they grew more numerous and complex hourly, they interacted on each other and proliferated, and in the end what time Chelmsford could give to the other aspects of his campaign had to be snatched from the interminable question of transport. The Transport Service swelled beyond belief; officers from fashionable regiments seconded to the campaign found themselves hiring oxen, buying oxen, caring for sick oxen and inevitably burying dead oxen, and before the campaign was over a major general was assigned to transport and even he was limited to the oxen not yet in Zululand.

Ulundi lay less than 75 miles from the three invasion points, and the country, while rolling and seamed with small rivers and dongas, was generally open. A mounted man could reach Ulundi from the Tugela in a long day's hard riding, a Zulu impi or a Boer commando in two or three days' travel. Even unopposed, however, a British infantry battalion would take the better part of a fortnight to get in and out, and Chelmsford, of course, expected no such rapid progress. He would have to feel his way with wagons along unsurveyed tracks from camp to camp, continually probing for the main Zulu force and consolidating the territory behind him. He would have to fight numerous skirmishes and, he hoped, several pitched battles. He estimated that his campaign would last no less than six weeks at best, and more likely something over two months, and he planned his supply requirements accordingly.

With what the men carried on their backs, a British battalion with access to water could survive two or three days and fight one pitched battle. It would then be helpless. The light camping equipment for a battalion weighed nine tons, the regimental reserve of ammunition weighed two tons, and the ninety tents alone weighed over four tons when dry and more like five and a half tons when wet. Each battalion also consumed well over a ton of foodstuffs every day, not to mention a ton and a half of firewood, which was scarce on the open veld. In rough figures, therefore, Chelmsford had to be ready to move something like 1,500 tons of equipment, ammunition and rations as far as Ulundi to keep his four columns supplied for even six weeks.

This was an enormous load for the primitive transport of the area, and the more closely he inspected the problem, the worse it got. Driving slaughter beeves and using captured cattle would reduce the load of rations, but artillery and its ammunition, rocket batteries, camp kitchens and bakeries, engineering equipment and medical stores, and signal companies and shoeing smithies would run the total up still higher. Wagon transport meant hundreds of drivers and thousands of draft animals, who would not only require rations and equipment for themselves, but who would also slow the advance of the columns to a crawl, thus increasing the continuing need for daily rations for everybody. To top it off, the wagon transport was far from self-sustaining and would have to carry a proportion of its own fodder; if unable to graze, an ox or mule team could easily consume in a week all it could draw in a wagon. Even a single column of 4,000 men could not possibly exist for six weeks sustained by integral wagon transport, and the columns would have to halt at each camp long enough for the transport to build up a reserve by continual trips back to the Natal border before they could move to the next site. The deeper the columns advanced into Zululand, the longer the lines of communication would grow, with ever longer and more perilous trips for the wagons and increasing demands for escorts. Colonel Rowlands' small force had been turned back more by a simple lack of water than by any action of Sekukuni, and Chelmsford had every reason to pray for an early and a decisive battle.

It was a situation that every military commander operating in a primitive area had faced before him, and in one fashion or another it had always been solved. Chelmsford had seen at first hand the chaos of the Crimea, where a stupefying lack of foresight had prevented the supply of a small army never more than a few miles from the sea, and he was conversant with the details of Wolseley's two classic campaigns, in which meticulous planning had enabled expeditions to survive in virtual isolation. His columns in Zululand would differ in degree but not in kind.

The commerce of the world of 1879 moved quickly and smoothly over the sea lanes, where steam had been known for fifty years, and in civilized parts over the expanding railway net which had already been forty years in the making. Beyond the railheads and the seaports of less fortunate countries all short-haul public and private transportation and all agriculture depended on the beast of burden, and the vast, throbbing structure of the Industrial Age rested on countless thousands of horses, mules and oxen.

The English were the finest horse masters in the world, and if the draft animal made a precarious perch for the industrial structure, they were determined to make it as firm a base as possible. Surfaced roads, bridges and tunnels stitched the countryside together, and an enormous amount of time, money and creative energy had been devoted to horses and their appurtenances. The results of this activity were notable, and the management of horseflesh verged on a science. Thirty years before, all Europe knew and marveled at the schedule of the "Quicksilver" coach of the Devonport Mail—240 miles in 24 hours—and at the wealth of a country that could devote an average of better than a horse a mile just to keep one daily coach moving up and down the line at such a rate. The nine tons of camping equipment a battalion needed could be moved on English roads by four two-wheeled carts and five wagons drawn by thirty-three English horses, and three of the wagons and twelve of the horses were needed for the tentage alone.

No one expected such service in southern Africa, where the magnificent Clydesdales, Percherons and Shires of the English countryside were unknown. Coastal shipping connected a half-dozen ports afflicted with sand bars, open roadsteads or poor holding ground, and except for a rail line stretching out from Capetown toward the diamond fields, only a few lines of track connected such cities as Capetown and Durban with their immediate suburbs. Beyond the settlements there were virtually no roads or bridges at all, and since ox teams and wagons broke down surface vegetation and soil crusts, transport riders rarely followed the exact path of their predecessors. The tracks connecting the settlements were thus five and ten miles broad and wandered at will through cultivated areas, to the great indignation of the settlers. The tracks drew together in mountain passes or at the innumerable drifts, where a shallow river bed and low banks permitted a crossing. Traffic soon reduced the vicinity of most drifts to a quagmire, and even light rains might force a driver to camp for a week or so until the drift was once more clear. Not until 1870 did Natal limit the width of roads and permit farmers to specify particular fields where travelers might outspan for the night.

All commerce moved in ox-drawn wagons which resembled the Conestoga prairie schooners of the American plains. The Boers had trekked in these wagons, and with slight body modifications they were still in use for transport. They were long and narrow, eighteen feet by six, and the great rear wheels, shod with half an inch of iron, spanned six feet and were fixed to a solid axle. The smaller front wheels turned on a pivoted axle, and a heavy top of doubled canvas was spread over wooden hoops fastened to the high sides. The wagons were pegged and wedged and lashed together, not only because nails were scarce but also because, a dozen times on a journey, the wagon might have to be broken down and manhandled over obstacles the oxen could not surmount.

A full span of oxen ran from fourteen to eighteen beasts. Less than ten were rarely yoked, for while they might still move the wagon with a ton of goods aboard, they would be stopped by the slightest rise. On steep hills and at drifts where the wheels sank into mud or sand, double spans were needed, and up to forty oxen might be needed to breast the mountain passes. The beasts were yoked two and two, each in his assigned place, with the strongest pair on the disselboom, from which a stout leather or chain *trek tow* led forward between the rest to the oldest and most experienced pair in the lead. The driver carried a long whip and rode on a box seat or walked alongside. There were no reins, and a *voorlooper*, usually a native boy, strode in advance to guide the team.

Two breeds of oxen had developed over the years—short compact beasts of great endurance that were used for long hauls on flat terrain, and a tall breed of enormous strength for sandy country and the steep mountain tracks. The teams were matched in color; the Boers preferred red-and-white or black-and-white animals and had an aversion to white or slate-gray oxen. Every adult Boer owned such a span, and he was not secure in his manhood until he had it. The owner of a wagon and a trained team was a person of consequence; he had a roof and a livelihood, and all Africa was his to choose a home from.

Within the limitations imposed by their digestive tracts, such spans did excellent work. An ox required eight hours a day to graze, and a further eight hours to rest while the results of his grazing passed through his multiple stomachs and was regurgitated as cud for a second leisurely mastication. This left eight hours a day for work, during which a full, fresh span might move more than a ton of goods at a steady three miles an hour along a level road. If the team was kept spanned for the full eight hours, it would need several days to recover from the experience, and the teams were usually outspanned for a couple of hours at midday. Under ideal conditions, this meant that a wagon might move as much as eighteen miles in a day, but since there were hardly eighteen miles of surfaced level road in all of southern Africa, few wagons ever covered more than ten miles a day. A stony track, a sandy drift, or a rainstorm might reduce progress to three or four miles, or even stop it entirely. A broken disselboom or a snapped trek tow would cost a full day, and a smashed wheel or a broken wooden axle might take a week to repair. The wagons could hold up to four tons, but no one ever loaded more than one, since the wagons might have to be unloaded and reloaded several times a day in bad country.

This was the basic material with which Chelmsford would have to work, a far cry from the customary transport of his homeland, and the problems were just beginning. English shipping could bring the wealth of the civilized world to Durban, where the irksome bar necessitated transshipping to lighters but hardly interfered with the movements of goods by rail to the outskirts of Pietermaritzburg. Passable roads led on from there up through the arc of settlements all the way to the Transvaal, but the commercial traffic had been heavy and the pasturage in the vicinity of the roads was played out. Another good road forded the Umgeni River north of Durban and led through Verulam and Stanger to the Lower Drift of the Tugela. A sketchy system of roads led down from the main arc to the upper Tugela Drifts—through Greytown to the Middle Drift and through the two or three houses of Helpmakaar to Rorke's Drift on the Buffalo. The Blood River territory was crisscrossed with old hunting and trading tracks, and everything Chelmsford needed could be brought to the borders of Zululand without excessive difficulties.

The problems began in earnest at the border. The Lower Drift could not be forded except at dead low water in the dry season, and even Rorke's Drift was impassable to foot and mounted traffic after a heavy rain. Flat-bottomed punts, pulling themselves along permanently anchored cables, could ferry a company of men or a wagon span across at a time, but the crossings would be slow and vulnerable and would have to be guarded by permanent garrisons. The banks would be cut to a muddy welter, and would need continual repairs. Once into Zululand, the situation deteriorated completely. There were no roads at all in Cetshwayo's domain, and the native tracks that led from one kraal to the next kept to a particular valley or skirted a particular hill and by no means implied the existence of a well-defined trail or even a worn spot in the grass. Traders had taken their wagons into Zululand for decades; they knew the country and picked their way across it as the fit seized them, but none could say if several score of wagons could proceed from any one point to another. A donga that a mounted man would hardly notice might take a wagon a day to cross, and a single boulder that a man on foot ignored might block all wheeled traffic. Ten wagons crossing at once could ruin a drift that had been used for years, and until every foot of a contemplated route had been inspected by a man thinking in terms of wagon transport, Chelmsford could hardly hazard even a rough estimate of the time he would need to reach Ulundi.

New problems arose in convoy. A wagon with a full span of oxen stretched for almost forty yards, and it needed sixty yards in column. Thirty wagons stretched a full mile, and if the teams had to be doubled at a drift or a donga, the wagons would bunch and the first to pass could not proceed until the last had been brought through. A wagon column strung out on a narrow road presented a target that a full battalion could hardly guard, and a few dozen wagons following one another's tracks would rut and destroy a road in short order. In open country, therefore, the wagons proceeded five and six abreast in choking clouds of dust so that a single breakdown did not stop the column, and the train would be easier to guard.

Chelmsford's initial estimates called for six or seven hundred wagons to accompany the columns, with another two or three hundred to keep supplies in Natal moving to the border. Not until mid-November was he able to take steps to acquire the transport, and it was only then that the magnitude of the task he had undertaken began to press upon him. The British Army, 30,000 strong, had landed in the Crimea with 21 wagons; Chelmsford was thinking of close to a thousand for an expeditionary force half the size.

The British government might condone an inefficiently conducted campaign, it might overlook a lost battle or two, but not under any circumstances nor for any reason would it tolerate an expensive campaign. The War Office remained inviolate in the military sphere only so long as its expenditures remained within its estimates; the Colonial Office might dictate policy to an Empire if it did not request additional funds. The instant the expenses rose, the full weight of parliamentary displeasure descended on the War Office and the Colonial Office and was rapidly passed to the hapless commanders in the field. A trained span of oxen cost more than £300, and with a good wagon the price might range as high as £500. Chelmsford might need a thousand wagons and teams, in addition to hundreds of oxen for replacements and slaughter beeves, which cost about £17 apiece. He thus faced an initial outlay for transport alone that might verge on half a million pounds, without even considering pay and rations for the driver. It would, true, be only a temporary investment, since the transport could be resold after the campaign, but between the inevitable attrition and the obvious fact that he would be buying in a seller's market and selling in a buyer's market he would be lucky to recover half his outlay.

Chelmsford began to buy transport in November. Prices rose at once, and it became apparent that Natal did not possess nearly enough transport for his purposes. Despite the primitive nature of its economy, Natal depended heavily on wagons and transport riders who carried goods from Durban to the Transvaal, and long before Christmas

Chelmsford controlled two thirds of the colony's wagon teams. Officers in civilian clothing fanned out to the Cape Colony, the Orange Free State and the Transvaal in search of oxen and horses. Word of their mission invariably preceded them, owners were reluctant to sell, and prices soared. The officers bought what they could, hired native drivers and voorloopers, and started the wagons toward Natal.

The first of the purchased teams began to arrive in December, and Chelmsford found that there was not enough pasturage in the vicinity of the supply depots to graze the spans that had already been collected. Oxen began to starve, and Chelmsford began to rent farms, at exorbitant prices. Once a sick herd had been grazed on a farm, the land was unfit for years afterwards, and scores of infected farms stood vacant. Other farms had been savagely overgrazed, until the land was hammered and exhausted. Officers fresh from England pressed into transport duties rented both in their ignorance, and the fresh teams were turned loose to graze in pastures saturated with lung sickness, redwater fever and quarter evil. An unscrupulous settler offered Smith-Dorrien a fat fee to rent a notoriously unhealthy farm; Smith-Dorrien threw him out of his tent and was later disgusted to learn that a superior officer had taken the place after all.

The attrition was harrowing. Teams were infected and started to die, and when they were moved, they tainted still fresh farms. The native drivers had little concern for the spans, and the transport officers assigned to supervise them were inexperienced and overworked. Oxen were driven eight hours and more a day with heavy loads on poor grazing and began to die. They were driven through light showers and kept in yoke without being thoroughly dried; the hide on their shoulders not only chafed but peeled off in strips. Native drivers built campfires and bedded down under wagons loaded with ammunition, officers urged teams into high drifts and drowned them, or outspanned in dongas and watched the oxen swept away in flash floods. When everything else failed, they kept the oxen yoked in thunderstorms and lost entire spans when lightning struck the iron trek tows. By January, before the campaign started, almost a third of the transport coming in was being lost monthly.

Chelmsford turned to mules. A team of eight cost less than £200 and could draw almost as much as an ox team, but the mules could not be grazed and consumed 120 pounds of fodder a day, all of which they had to carry with them. Chelmsford eventually acquired over 5,000 mules, but not before one of his transport officers in desperation had traveled all the way to America to buy 400 in Texas.

In December, at Wood's suggestion, Chelmsford stopped buying oxen and started to hire them. Far more owners were willing to rent than to sell, and the rate of acquisition increased. The savings were illusionary. Span and wagon came for £90 a month, and if the owner hired out as driver, the team was assured of decent treatment, but many of the teams took over a month to get from their homes to Natal, and the Crown had to pay for any beasts that died.

By January there was sufficient transport for the columns to start, but the problems never ended. Time and again troop movements were stalled for want of transport, and purchase and hire continued. Chelmsford farmed the work out to contractors, freeing many of his officers but adding additional middlemen who had to be paid. Before the campaign was ended, Chelmsford was to have over 27,000 oxen on his establishment at one time, with over 2,500 vehicles of various descriptions. The War Office exceeded its normal expenditures by more than £4,000,000, and the lion's share had gone to transport.

The last volunteers came in. John Robinson Royston, sixteen years old, was the son of a civil engineer in Durban. Still in high school, he slipped out of his home one night carrying a hunting rifle, crossed the Umgeni, and joined a British camp. His irate father came after him in the morning, but the boy pleaded so hard to be allowed to remain that his father gave him a pony and his blessings. Royston joined the Isipongo Mounted Rifles. George Mossop, also sixteen, had run away from his Greytown home two years earlier to join a party of Boer hunters in the Transvaal. Mounted on a Basuto pony he had purchased from a native for £3 and named "Warrior," he now rode down through Utrecht and, half starved, joined Wood's camp on Balte Spruit. Buller asked him if he could shoot, and took him into the Frontier Light Horse.

Throughout December units were moving to their assigned positions, and by early January the columns were taking shape. The 24th Regiment marched out of Pietermaritzburg for Helpmakaar, Colours flying and the band playing "I'm Leaving Thee in Sorrow, Annie," a tune to which many a Confederate regiment had marched off to war. Durnford paid a last visit to Bishopstowe, where an anguished Colenso and his family were powerless to stem what they were convinced was an unjust and totally unnecessary war. The Bishop's last words to his friend were "God bless you. Do what is right." Durnford then marched the 1st Regiment of the NNC, Sikali's Native Horse and a rocket battery to the Middle Drift of the Tugela. The 90th Regiment and the 1st Battalion of the 13th were long since with Wood at Balte Spruit, with a battery of six seven-pounders, the Frontier Light Horse, Weatherley's Border Horse, Uys's burgers, and 500 disaffected Zulus from the disputed territories, whom Wood had formed into two infantry battalions under a colonial named White and Major William Knox Leet of the 13th Regiment.

The 99th Regiment and the 2nd Battalion of the 3d Regiment joined Colonel Pearson at the Lower Drift of the Tugela, where the Naval Brigade had been waiting since early December. The Natal Hussars came in, to join the Mounted Rifles from Durban, Alexandra, Stanger, Victoria and Isipongo, and the small mounted troop of soldiers from the 24th under Lieutenant Carrington that Durnford had raised in 1877. With the 2nd Regiment of the NNC and over 600 wagon drivers, Pearson had 4,750 men camped on the flats below the knoll.

Colonel Glyn's Central Column assembled at Helpmakaar and then marched down to the sprawling camp around Otto Witt's mission station at Rorke's Drift. Chelmsford had commandeered both buildings, turning Witt's little stone church into a storehouse and the thatched mud house James Rorke had built so long ago into a hospital. Witt was an odd missionary, unpopular in Zululand, where Cetshwayo had forbidden him the country, and more unpopular in Natal, where the colonists resented the wildly inaccurate stories he gave to the English newspapers. He had now sent his wife and three small children off in a wagon to Pietermaritzburg, and was camped in a tent near his house and ruined gardens.

Lieutenant Colonel Arthur Harness with six guns of "N" Battery of the 5th Artillery Brigade was camped on ground below the mission station, near the 3d Regiment of the NNC. The Natal Carbineers, the Newcastle Mounted Rifles and the Buffalo Border Guard were camped together, and a welter of transport, hospital wagons, field bakeries, veterinarians and engineers covered the grassy slopes below the Oskarberg. The Natal Mounted Police were late joining; camping after dark on the way to Helpmakaar, they had turned their horses loose through a gate into what someone assumed was an enclosed paddock. The rest of the pasture was unfenced, and it was a week before all the men found their horses.

Several units would remain when the column left Rorke's Drift. "B" Company of the 2nd Battalion of the 24th was assigned as a permanent garrison. The men were disgruntled, and inclined to blame Lieutenant Bromhead, whose notorious deafness had in all probability been responsible for the assignment. Smith-Dorrien, still busy with transport duties, had established a wagon repair facility. He messed with Bromhead and Lieutenant John Rouse Merriott Chard, a thirty-two-year-old Royal Engineer from Devon who had served in Bermuda and was still waiting for his first promotion after eleven years of service. Chard was in charge of the punts and the banks of the drift a quarter of a mile beyond the mission station. He commanded no troops but depended on the services of a few native laborers and ferrymen under a civilian named Daniells. Surgeon Major James Henry Reynolds, a thirty-five-year-old Irishman who had served in the Perie Bush, was in charge of the hospital, with a single private to help him as hospital orderly. The Reverend George Smith, who had helped Durnford bury his dead in Bushman's River Pass, was there as well. A tall man with a great red beard, he had been appointed Chaplain to the Volunteers and was invariably clad in a tattered alpaca ecclesiastical frock, which had long since turned green with age. His general gullibility and unquenchable enthusiasm for military life afforded the other officers a measure of relief from the hardships of the field.

The three quasi officers of the Commissariat and Transport Department messed separately. Assistant Commissary Walter Alphonsus Dunne, a twenty-six-year-old Irishman, was in charge of the stores, although Acting Commissariat Officer James Langley Dalton was older and more experienced. Almost fifty, he had enlisted in the 85th Regiment in 1849 and had settled in Natal after being pensioned off as a sergeant major in 1870. Acting Storekeeper Louis Alexander Byrne, just twenty-two, had barely started his career. The stone church, once Rorke's store, was again filled with goods, stuffed with scores of stout copper-banded biscuit boxes and hundreds of bags of mealies.

The tension mounted as the eleventh of January drew near, hardly dampened by the incessant rains. The sentries along the river had watched the green hills of Zululand for weeks; lifeless and dotted with deserted kraals, they stretched away into the wet distance and merged with the skyline of the Nqutu Range. There was no word from Cetshwayo. Chelmsford had established his headquarters at Helpmakaar, where two corrugated-iron storage sheds had been added to the few houses of the settlement. The traffic along the twelve miles of muddy, rutted track down through the hills to Rorke's Drift was heavy; Chelmsford and his staff moved down on the tenth, and the word was passed to the units that the crossing would commence in the morning. A sutler named Stewart brought in two wagons from Greytown loaded with gin and cigars and did a thriving business on the last afternoon. The men looked to their horses, rifles, accouterments and tack, and there was a last-minute flurry of letter writing. The skies were clearing, and the sun set at seven. It was dark by seven thirty, and the men turned in early. Except for staff officers busy with final preparations, the camp was soon quiet.

Shaka's empire, which had lasted for fifty years and was still incomparably the most powerful native state in Africa, was about to be put to a test which had been inevitable since the far-off day the first European in Farewell's party had waded ashore in Port Natal.

INVASION

EVEILLE AT Rorke's Drift sounded at two on the morning of Saturday, January 11, 1879. It was an hour earlier than expected; someone had looted Stewart's wagons after dark and as soon as the men paraded, their officers began to inspect their haversacks for cigars and their water bottles for gin. They found nothing, and Chelmsford told Stewart he would have his wagons pitched into the river if he had not cleared off by daybreak. The skies had clouded while the search was in progress, and by four thirty a thick fog and a drizzling rain had all but choked out the first light of a chill dawn as the men began to move down to the river.

Lieutenant Colonel Harness took his six guns to a small knoll, from which he could see nothing, to cover the crossing, and the first companies of the 24th Regiment embarked in the two punts. Chelmsford was eager to get some weight across the river as soon as possible, and the mounted volunteers and the Natal Native Contingent were to wade across. Lieutenant Harford, scouting a few hundred yards upstream, discovered a second drift which looked feasible, and Chelmsford at once directed Major John Cecil Russell to take the cavalry and Cooper's 2nd Battalion of the 3d Regiment, NNC, to the new crossing while the Natal Mounted Police and Hamilton-Browne's 1st Battalion crossed near the punts. Cooper's Natal Kaffirs had brought their own witch doctor along, and he felt that the invasion of the ancestral homeland called for a speech. The battalion settled on its haunches to listen attentively while he launched into a long harangue, and he was still recounting the early history of the Zulu nation when Harford cut him off and got the men moving again. In the meantime, the first man of the column to set foot in Zululand had splashed across—Charles Norris-Newman, a garrulous but competent ex-Imperial officer now serving as special correspondent for the London *Standard*, and the only English journalist then in Natal. Known as "Noggs," he had attached

319

himself to Lonsdale's staff, and he proudly wore the badge of the NNC, a red rag twisted into a puggree about his sun helmet.

The mounted men were soon across and spurred on to the low ridge beyond the flats at the edge of the Buffalo. Dismounting, they established a ragged line of vedettes on the rising ground and settled down to guard the crossing. Several men went astray in the fog, wandering off into the hills and staying lost until a hot early morning sun burned off the mist and enabled them to find their units.

The water in the drift was neck-deep and the current was swift. Zulu-fashion, the men of the NNC locked arms and rushed the river, the force of those behind sustaining those in front who lost their footing. Cooper's battalion crossed without loss, but several of Hamilton-Browne's Natal Kaffirs were swept away and drowned. How many, he could not say, for he had never bothered to count his command.

By six thirty the NNC had joined the mounted volunteers on the ridge, and the 24th Regiment had started to establish a long, sprawling camp on the Zulu bank of the river. The chilly dawn gave way to a sweltering noon, and the men on the ridge sat in the shade of their horses, or propped borrowed Natal Kaffir shields on assegais thrust in the ground, and watched through the long afternoon as the punts began to bring the transport across.

As soon as the infantry was safely over, Chelmsford set out with a strong mounted escort to ride north on the eastern side of the Buffalo. He had not seen Colonel Wood since October, and the two men had arranged to meet halfway between their respective lines of advance. Wood, who had brought his column from Balte Spruit across the Blood River the previous day, had established a laagered camp at Bemba's Kop on Lyn Spruit and he had set out at two thirty that morning with Major Buller and the Frontier Light Horse. The two parties met shortly after nine, ten miles north of Rorke's Drift. The conference lasted for three hours, while the Frontier Light Horse rounded up a large herd of cattle grazing near the meeting site. Chelmsford did not realize it, but these were the cattle Sihayo had collected from his district to pay his fine. Two or three unarmed herders were captured as well; Chelmsford carefully explained to them that he had crossed in force and then let them go, hoping they would carry the news to Ulundi. Wood, somewhat prematurely, had been raiding Zulu cattle since the second of January. He had already taken 2,000 from Seketwayo, the strongest inDuna on his line of advance, whom he hoped to disaffect from the Zulu cause. Seketwayo might have his cattle back if he brought his men in and disarmed them, but the herd was too large to graze in the vicinity of Wood's own transport oxen, so Wood sent it to the Transvaal. Seketwayo, fearful because the herd contained a large number of

(*above*) Henry Francis Fynn (1803–61), Shaka's friend 'Mbulazi', taken about 1855; (*below*) Sir Henry Bartle Edward Frere (1815–84)

(*above*) John Wesley Shepstone, 'Somtseu's' brother 'Misjan'; (*below*) Sir Henry Ernest Bulwer, Lieutenant-Governor of Natal 1875–80

(*above*) Theophilus Shepstone (1817–93), 'Somtseu', as Secretary for Native Affairs in the late 1850s; (*below*) Anthony William Durnford (1830–79), about 1875

(*above*) Sir Theophilus Shepstone, K.C.M.G., 'Somtseu', as Administrator of the Transvaal in 1878; (*below*) Langalibalele, the chieftain of the amalHlubi at the time of his trial in 187

(*left*) John Colenso, D.D. (1814–83), 'Sobantu', in 1864; (*right*) Garnet Wolseley (1833–1913)

(*below left*) John Dunn, 'The White Chief of Zululand', about 1878; (*below right*) John Dunn (1833–95), 'Jantoni', as a young hunter soon after his move to Zululand in the late 1850s

(*above*) Teignmouth Melvill, v.c. (1842–79), Lieutenant and Adjutant, 1st/24th. Killed attempting to save the Queen's Colour at Isandhlwana: (*below*) Cetshwayo (1827–84), aboard the steamer *Natal* on his way to captivity in Capetown in 1879

(*above*) Nevill Josiah Aylmer Coghill, v.c. (1852–79), Lieutenant, 1st/24th and A.D.C. to Colonel Glyn. Killed going to Melvill's rescue; (*below*) Cetshwayo in 1881 at Oude Moulen

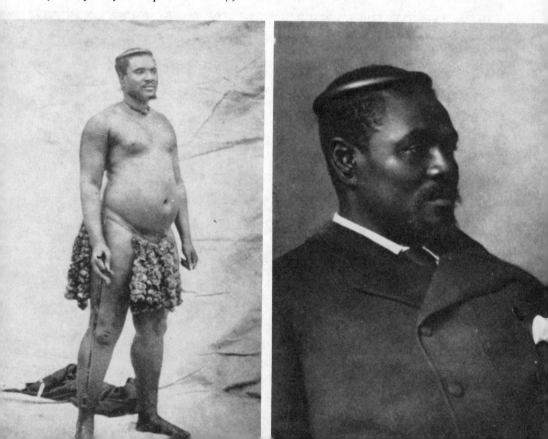

(*above*) Henry Evelyn Wood, v.c.
(1838–1919); (*below*) Three officers of the
1st/24th killed at Isandhlwana. C. W.
Cavaye, Lieutenant, 'A' Company;
F. P. Porteous, Lieutenant, 'E' Company;
W. Degacher, Captain, 'G' Company, commanding the battalion on January 22nd, 1879

(*above*) Frederic Augustus Thesiger,
2nd Baron Chelmsford (1827–1905), in 1878,
at the outset of the Zulu campaign; (*below*)
Redvers Henry Buller, v.c. (1839–1908),
taken in the early 1880s

(*above*) John Rouse Merriott Chard, v.c.
(1847–97), Lieutenant, Royal Engineers;
(*below*) John Williams Fielding, v.c.
(1858–1931), enlisted in the 2nd/24th in
1877 under the name of John Williams

(*above*) Gonville S. Bromhead, v.c.
1845–91), Lieutenant, 'B' Company
2nd/24th Regiment; (*below*) Napoleon
Eugène Louis Jean Joseph Buonaparte, the
Prince Imperial (1856–79). From a
photograph taken in Natal a few weeks
before his death

Troops in Bushman's River Pass in 1873 during the Langalibalele Rebellion

Cetshwayo's coronation on September 1st, 1873. Henrique Shepstone at the king's left shoulder. Theophilus Shepstone seated, in diplomatic uniform. George Shepstone holds an umbrella over his father. Anthony Durnford (in cocked hat) directly behind Theophilus. Four of John Dunn's wives in his wagon behind the group.

John Wesley Shepstone reads Sir Bartle Frere's ultimatum to the Zulus on December 11th, 1878, at the Lower Drift of the Tugela

The Zulu indunas who received Frere's ultimatum at the Lower Drift. From left to right, the first three in the front row are Uvumandaba, Umandhuli and Ugebula

Lord Chelmsford and his staff, January 1879. (Standing) Bvt.-Maj. Matthew Gosset, 54th Regiment; Lt. A. Berkeley Milne, R.N.; (seated) Commander H. J. F. Campbell, R.N.; Lord Chelmsford; Lt.-Col. John North Crealock, 95th Regiment

The Alexandra Mounted Rifles in the 1870s—no two uniforms alike. The rifles are Sniders

The Buffalo Border Guard in the field in 1879

Mehlokazulu ka Sihayo—the ostensible cause of the ultimatum. After Ulundi he surrendered under a false name, was recognized and sent to Pietermaritzburg. No charges were pressed, and he was subsequently released.

Zulu warriors in war regalia. Several regiments are represented

Natal Kaffirs from Captain Barton's 4th Battalion of the Natal Native Contingent. Most of the men are armed with Martini-Henrys

Natal Kaffirs, unidentified unit of the Natal Native Contingent. Each man has the distinguishing red rag drawn over his isiCoco

Fort Pearson and the tents of the Naval Brigade, above the Lower Drift of the Tugela

The punt in operation at the Lower Drift of the Tugela, by Ultimatum Tree. Fort Tenedos on the Zulu shore. The tree, a national monument, was still standing in 1986

A company of the 99th Regiment crosses the Tugela at the Lower Drift on January 12th, 1879

Why progress was slow—a typical drift. Pearson's 400 wagons are forced to cross the Inyoni one at a time

The Amatikulu Drift on the coastal road. The Natal Native Pioneer Corps (resting on either side) has 'improved' it by clearing the brush and knocking down the banks

May 21st, 1879. Drury-Lowe leads a strong force back to Isandhlwana. In the foreground, bodies of men and slaughtered oxen on the site of Durnford's last stand

The wreckage of the wagon park in the Saddle. The cavalry beyond is searching through the tent areas

A sentry of the 2/24th guards the Saddle at the site of the wagon park on May 21st, 1879, while Drury-Lowe's cavalry searches the battlefield beyond

Fugitive's Drift on the Buffalo River from the Natal side. On January 22nd, 1879, the river was in flood and the rocks were under rushing water. The stone cross in the foreground was erected by Sir Bartle Frere to mark the spot where Coghill and Melvill fell royal beasts belonging to Cetshwayo, could not make up his mind to defect.

Wood's column presented Chelmsford with a problem. It was too far away for him to control, and he could not co-ordinate its movements with Colonel Glyn's Central Column until both had converged on the march to Ulundi. In the meantime, he was forced to give Wood latitude to act as he saw fit, asking him to demonstrate so as to draw pressure away from the Central Column. Wood was happy to oblige. He had collected six weeks' worth of rations for his column at Balte Spruit by purchasing in the Transvaal—Chelmsford had rations for only a fortnight at Rorke's Drift—and the spies he had hired in the border kraals and sent all the way to Ulundi informed him that the main Zulu impi was still at the royal kraal but would soon attack the Central Column.

Chelmsford returned to his camp in the course of the afternoon to find Colonel Durnford, who had ridden in from his own camp at Kranz Kop, waiting to see him. Durnford's column was another problem. It consisted entirely of native troops, and although they had been considerably better trained than the other native units, and Durnford had grabbed the pick of the Europeans for his officers, including a high percentage of Zulu speakers, it was too weak to enter Zululand by itself before the main enemy impi had been located. Chelmsford had also decided that it was poorly placed. He had only built up his three main columns by paring to the bone the troops guarding his lines of communication in Natal. He had a company of Imperial infantry at Greytown and four at Helpmakaar, and he was now concerned about the fifty-mile section of road between these two settlements, which lay on his main line between Pietermaritzburg and Rorke's Drift. The road crossed the Mooi River and the upper Tugela at deep, sandy drifts, and at Umsinga near Sand Spruit it was only five miles from a point on the Buffalo that the Zulus might easily cross. The Umsinga District, moreover, was a Natal Kaffir location, a natural Zulu target and an area that would provide few armed colonists to defend a laager if the Zulus invaded. Chelmsford had therefore decided to break up Durnford's column, and had already ordered him to move two of his three battalions to Umsinga. He could not yet bring himself to leave the Middle Drift uncovered, however, so he canceled his original orders and told Durnford that only one battalion was to be moved to Umsinga in a few days' time, after Pearson's Right Column and Glyn's Central Column had advanced to their first objectives, thus lessening the danger of an attack on the Middle Drift. The move was to be made when Chelmsford sent the word, and at the same time Durnford was to bring his Natal Native Horse and the Rocket Battery that constituted his only artillery all the way to Rorke's Drift to join Glyn. Durnford's column was thus to remain at Kranz Kop for the nonce, and Chelmsford gave him permission to make short, defensive strikes across the Tugela if he became aware of small groups of Zulus in the vicinity of the Middle Drift.

Durnford was intelligent and aggressive, but Chelmsford was hesitant about entrusting him with the degree of independence he granted Wood. Impulsive and overly eager to act on his own whenever he got the chance, Durnford was quick to accept heavy responsibilities. These were qualities that frequently led fortunate men to greatness, but they had also foundered many a lesser figure. Durnford's service reputation was good, but he had given his superiors a few uneasy moments in the past. A cooler head might have avoided the fiasco in Bushman's River Pass, and Colonel Hassard, the Colonial Engineer in the Cape Colony, had been greatly perturbed by Durnford's reckless expenditures in raising his various units.

Durnford had no sooner returned to his column at Kranz Kop than he gave further evidence of his penchant for independent action. He found a letter for him from Bishop Schreuder, who had long since moved to the safety of Natal, but who still received visits from an occasional Zulu refugee from his former mission station. One of these brought him a rumor that the main Zulu impi intended to attack Natal by the Middle Drift of the Tugela; he passed the story to Durnford, and Durnford characteristically wasted no time. He alerted his command, and sent a hurried note to Chelmsford that he intended to cross the Tugela the following morning to take up a favorable defensive position. He had actually marched his command down to the riverbank in the cold predawn darkness on the fourteenth, when a messenger, pounding through the mist, reached him with Chelmsford's reply:

Dear Durnford;

Unless you carry out the instructions I give you, it will be my unpleasant duty to remove you from your command, and to substitute another officer for the command of No. 2 Column. When a column is acting SEPA-RATELY in an *enemy's country* I am quite ready to give its commander every latitude, and would certainly expect him to disobey any orders he might receive from me, if information which he obtained showed that it would be injurious to the interests of the column under his command. Your neglecting to obey my instructions in the present instance has no excuse. You have simply received information in a letter from Bishop Schroeder, which may or may not be true and which you have no means of verifying. If movements ordered are to be delayed because report hints at a chance of an invasion of Natal, it will be impossible for me to carry out my plan of campaign. I trust you will understand this plain speaking and not give me any further occasion to write in a style which is distasteful to me.

Chelmsford did not refer to the incident again, but it bothered him. Two days later he finally made up his mind about the disposition of Durnford's column. Two battalions were to be left at the Middle Drift, one moved to Umsinga, and the Natal Native Horse and the Rocket Battery, with three companies of infantry, were to move to Rorke's Drift. Durnford himself was to accompany the Horse, and would thus be subordinated to Glyn and directly under the General's eye. It was a worse blow than the stinging written rebuke, and it removed the dejected Durnford from any chance for independent command.

In the meantime, there was work for the Central Column. Chelmsford had picked Isipezi Hill, near Matyana's stronghold 22 miles into Zululand, as the site for the first of the fortified camps he intended to establish on the track to Ulundi. One or two intermediate camps would be necessary as well, and it was now apparent that it would be several days before the column could even leave the new camp on the Zulu side of Rorke's Drift. The track to Ulundi no sooner crossed the first ridge than it descended to the valley of the Bashee River, a small tributary of the Buffalo, and the lower Bashee ran through marshlands, with two swamps on the track into which the wagons sank to their beds. A corduroy surface would have to be built on a solid roadbed before the transport could cross the Bashee, and Lieutenant Francis Hartwell Macdowel, Royal Engineers, with four of his own men and Nolan's company of the Natal Native Pioneer Corps, began to plan the job. Macdowel was actually serving under Lieutenant Chard, who was responsible for the punts at Rorke's Drift, but since the company of Royal Engineers slated to accompany the Central Column had only recently reached Natal and was still marching upcountry, Chard had detached Macdowel to assist Glyn.

Before Macdowel's men could go to work in the Bashee valley, there was a job for the troops. A small spruit lay beyond the Bashee, emerging from a narrow gorge with high, rocky sides. Sihayo was at Ulundi with his son Mehlokazulu, but several of his other sons, with a strong party of personal retainers, were still living at his kraal deep within this gorge. His cattle, goats and sheep were grazing in the Bashee valley, and since his kraal threatened the track and Sihayo himself was one of the ostensible causes of the war, Chelmsford decided to capture his cattle and burn his kraal.

The entire force paraded on Sunday the twelfth of January at three thirty in the morning. Commandant Lonsdale was still recovering from his concussion, and Major Wilsone Black of the 24th had taken over the 3d Regiment, NNC, of which Hamilton-Browne's 1st Battalion was to lead the attack. Captain Degacher was to back him with four

companies of the 1st/24th, and the whole of the cavalry was to scout
ahead under Lieutenant Colonel John Cecil Russell. Cooper's 2nd/3d,
NNC, and the rest of the 24th were to stay in reserve.

As the troops approached the gorge, the herders drove the cattle
into the entrance and gave the alarm. The mouth of the gorge was
choked with boulders, and several scores of Zulus were posted behind
the rocks and in caves and crevices high on the sides of the ravine.
Many of them were armed with rifles, and they opened a heavy and
largely inaccurate fire on the advancing troops. Glyn sent a few companies out to flank the position, shook the NNC into a line and posted
the Imperial infantry behind it, and then ordered Hamilton-Browne to
attack the gorge.

Hamilton-Browne had little confidence in the bulk of his battalion,
but he had hopes for three of his companies. In January of 1878, when
the inGobamakhosi had attacked the young draft incorporated into the
uThulwana regiment at the First Fruits ceremony, over 300 men of the
young draft, the inDlu-yengwe, had fled to Natal under their iNtanga
leader, Mvubi. They had been drafted in November with the Natal
Kaffirs and they now formed Companies 8, 9 and 10 of Hamilton-
Browne's battalion. Infinitely better warriors than the Natal Kaffirs,
whom they despised, they were eager to revenge themselves on their
former compatriots, particularly the inGobamakhosi, a wing of which
Mehlokazulu led. Hamilton-Browne, whose strong prejudices were inflamed more by cowardice than by color, was quite willing to let them
try. His 9th Company was guarding the camp and the 10th was off
with a flanking party, but the 8th Company, with Mvubi himself and
led by Captains O. E. Murray and Duncombe, the only fluent Zulu
speaker in the battalion, was in the center of the line.

The fire died down as the attackers approached the mouth of the
gorge, and a Zulu voice cried out, asking by whose orders they came.
Duncombe thundered back, "By the orders of the Great White
Queen!" and was answered by a renewed fire and a cascade of heavy
boulders rolled down the slopes. One of the bounding stones grazed
Major Wilsone Black, who broke into his shrill native Gaelic as Hamilton-Browne ordered his battalion to charge. Mvubi's Zulus followed
him readily, but the other companies hung back, and when their European officers started to belabor them they turned to run. They found
the Imperial infantry behind them, and, with their retreat barred by a
line of bayonets, they reluctantly began to advance.

There was a short, sharp melee among the boulders, and then Sihayo's retainers broke and fled into the depths of the gorge, leaving
twenty dead behind. Two of Mvubi's Zulus had been killed, Lieutenant Purvis had been shot through the arm and Corporal Mayer behind

the knee, and Corporal Schiess, in the thick of the fight, had been
struck by a lunging assegai which ripped his boot open and slashed his
calf. They were joined in the ambulance for the trip back to the
hospital at Rorke's Drift by two wounded survivors of Sihayo's party,
one with a thigh broken by a rifle bullet. Chelmsford intended to
release them as soon as they were recovered.

The flanking party drove in another group of Zulus with no loss to
themselves. Among the dozen Zulu dead they found Sihayo's son
Nkumbikazulu, named in the warrant for the surrender of Mehlokazulu. There was no further resistance, and the force advanced into the
gorge, capturing the livestock and firing Sihayo's kraal.

Lieutenant Harford had done well in his first action. He had given
Hamilton-Browne a scare by dropping to his hands and knees as the
attack started, but when the battalion commander rushed to his side he
found Harford intent on transferring a rare beetle to a small tin box.
He had helped to stem the faltering Natal Kaffirs, kicking several of
their European N.C.O.'s out of the shelter of some rocks, and had then
spotted a half-dozen Zulus firing from a cave entrance far up the side
of the gorge. He stripped off his revolver belt, sword, spurs and
courier bag, grabbed a Martini-Henry carbine and a handful of cartridges, and clambered up after them. The Zulu in the mouth of the
cave was dead when he arrived, but a man behind him thrust a muzzle-
loader in Harford's face and pulled the trigger. The cap snapped, but
the gun missed fire. Some of the Zulus started to scramble down and
the rest fled into the cave. Harford, an abominable marksman, stood up
and fired six shots at the retreating Zulus but only wounded one; he
then threw down his carbine and called into the cave. Startled to be
addressed in fluent Zulu, the men emerged and surrendered, and Harford turned his four prisoners over to Chelmsford.

The force was drenched by a terrific thunderstorm on the way back
to the camp. Passing a deserted kraal, Lieutenant Nevill Josiah Aylmer
Coghill, 1st/24th, saw a bedraggled chicken and took after it with a
whoop. His horse slipped and Coghill fell heavily, wrenching his knee
so badly that he could barely stand. He had been Cunynghame's aide
and had returned to England with him, coming back to Natal to rejoin
his regiment. Since the 24th had a full roster of officers, Chelmsford
had attached him to Colonel Glyn as an extra A.D.C. Despite the pain,
he refused to return to Rorke's Drift, and since his duties were light,
Glyn let him stay with the column.

It would take at least a week for Macdowel's men to finish the
roadbed. Chelmsford gave the troops the Monday off to rest and to
dry their equipment, and Tuesday morning the engineers moved to a
small camp in the Bashee valley and started work. A few companies of

the 24th went along as a guard, and Hamilton-Browne's battalion moved to the camp to provide additional labor, a task not at all to their liking.

There was little to do until the road was finished. On the fifteenth Lieutenant Colonel Russell led a reconnaissance all the way to Isipezi Hill, but encountered no Zulus. The track was passable beyond the Bashee, with good water and wood at a camping site ten miles beyond Rorke's Drift at Isandhlwana. Dongas and small gullies would slow the transport and the artillery along the track, but they would not stop it, and Chelmsford decided to make his next intermediate stop at Isandhlwana.

John Cecil Russell had been a brevet major, an equerry to the Prince of Wales and a member of the Wolseley Ring who had accompanied the Ashanti expedition while seconded from his regiment, the 12th Lancers. Despite his high social position, he was unpopular with the men, and possibly because of their lack of enthusiasm Chelmsford found his scouting inclined to be careless. Wanting Major Dartnell for a command with the Natal Native Contingent, Chelmsford had removed him from his cavalry command, but the Natal Mounted Police had virtually mutinied, refusing to serve under an Imperial officer. Chelmsford had been forced to transfer Dartnell to his own staff, leaving him in over-all command of the cavalry, and he had given Russell a local promotion, but the men were barely satisfied. In addition to the quasi-official Natal Mounted Police and the volunteer units, the cavalry included almost a hundred Mounted Infantry under Lieutenant Edward Stevenson Browne, 1st/24th, descendants of the force Durnford had raised under Lieutenant Carrington of the same regiment in 1877. The men had been scraped together from every Imperial infantry battalion in the command and mounted on local horses— grooms, cooks, bandsmen and privates who claimed familiarity with horses. They carried Martini-Henry rifles instead of carbines, their horsemanship was dubious, and their uniforms varied and tattered, as they were forever missing the periodic distributions made to their parent components, but they were Imperial troops and considerably more reliable than the somewhat independent colonials.

The orders to move went out to Durnford on the sixteenth, and he started on the morning of the seventeenth. Leaving the 1st and 3d Battalions at the Middle Drift, he dropped the 2nd Battalion at Umsinga and pushed on by forced marches to Rorke's Drift. The drifts at the Mooi River and the upper Tugela were in flood, and a man had to swim the river at night to rouse the punts, but Durnford brought the exhausted men still with him into Rorke's Drift after dark on the twentieth, and let his men sleep while he sent a messenger up the track to report to Chelmsford and to ask for instructions. There were none for the moment, so Durnford moved across the river and settled into the camp the column had just quitted for Isandhlwana.

Durnford had retained "C," "D" and "E" Companies of the 1st/3d, NNC, well-drilled Natal Kaffirs from Sikali's reserve. He also had 250 men of the Natal Native Horse—five troops of fifty men apiece drawn from Sikali's men, Hlubi's baTlokwa Basutos, Jantzi's tribe and the Edendale Mission. The men were all superb riders, who thrust their big toes into rawhide thong stirrups and guided their tough ponies with their bare heels. They were armed with the Westley-Richards carbine, a complicated but light and serviceable capping breechloader developed in 1858 and known as the "monkey-tail" from the long, curved lever which actuated the breechblock. Passable marksmen when dismounted, the natives had a tendency to hold their pieces at arm's length and fire them like pistols when riding. The men of the Edendale Horse, led by Lieutenant Nathaniel Newnham-Davis of the 3d Regiment (the Buffs), were booted and spurred, and armed with the Martini-Henry carbine. As civilized Christians, they held themselves somewhat apart from the rest of the native cavalry, but their request to be issued the same rations as the European volunteers, instead of the unslaughtered beeves and mealie meal of the NNC, had been turned down. Only Lieutenant Raw's troop were baTlokwas, a Basuto strain, but the entire contingent was known as "Durnford's Basutos," because Hlubi's mounted men had been used as early as 1866 and the Basutos were ineradicably associated with Durnford from the action in Bushman's River Pass.

The Rocket Battery consisted of a bombardier and eight soldiers detailed from the 24th Regiment, under Brevet Major Francis Broadfoot Russell of the Royal Artillery. Hale's patent rockets were exasperating weapons. The shells were oblong steel cases a foot long and three inches in diameter, fired by hand-lit fuses from light metal troughs resting on flimsy bipods. The exhaust nozzles were set at an angle, but despite the spin-stabilization the six-pound shells were notoriously inaccurate and incapable of hitting anything but large masses at short ranges. The rockets made a hideous shrieking noise in flight, emitting a thick trail of white smoke punctuated by fat yellow sparks, and they were chiefly valued for their psychological effect on unsophisticated opponents. Russell rode a horse, but his men were mounted on the spare pack mules that carried the battery.

Glyn's entire column had moved on by the time Durnford reached the Zulu side of the Buffalo. The troops which had been encamped on the Bashee reached Isandhlwana by noon, and Major Cornelius Francis Clery, Glyn's principal staff officer, started to lay out the new camp.

Despite the encouragement of the bands, the main force moving up from the first camp took all day to cover the eight miles; there were over a hundred wagons to bring up, and the track across the small spruit beyond the Bashee collapsed early in the day. When darkness fell, thirty wagons were still waiting to be dragged through, and several companies of the 24th camped beside them for the night.

The track to Ulundi rose from the wet lowlands of the Bashee valley and crested a broad, smooth saddle between the high southern end of Isandhlwana to the left and a large stony koppie to the right. Ahead lay a level rectangular plain four miles across, stretching eight miles east to Matyana's stronghold in the Nkandhla Range, with Isipezi Hill on the skyline just to the north of it. The right of the plain was bounded by the Malakata and Inhlazatye Hills, with broken country beyond them that ran down to the valley of the Buffalo. The river itself was invisible from Isandhlwana, but the green hills of Natal rose beyond it, and, looking back from the saddle, eight miles away to the west, the Oskarberg hid all sign of the mission station nestled on its far flank.

The Nqutu Range lay to the left, rising from a plateau that lay several hundred feet over the plain. This plateau, seamed with deep ravines, terminated in a sharp escarpment that ran along the left side of the plain, and several steep ravines notched the rim to give access to the plain below. The largest of these ravines opened just beyond a large conical koppie that rose from the plain a mile and a half in front of Isandhlwana. The mountain itself lay north and south, and a broad spur ran from its low northern end up to the plateau 1,500 yards away; the top of Isandhlwana was little higher than the plateau, so that a man standing on its summit had a somewhat better view of the plain, but could see little more of the Nqutu plateau than he could from the base.

A wide, shallow donga, through which a small stream trickled, angled across the plain a mile away, between Isandhlwana and the conical koppie. The open ground in front of Isandhlwana fell gently away to the donga, and here Clery laid out the camp, in the shadow of the mountain. Lonsdale, still suffering from the effects of his concussion, had rejoined, and he took his two NNC battalions off the track to the left, even with the northern end of Isandhlwana. The 2nd Battalion, 24th, followed him, with Harness and his artillery and the mounted units, just to the left of the track, behind. The 1st Battalion, 24th, camped just to the right of the track, on the slopes of the stony koppie, and Chelmsford placed his staff tents in the center behind the 2nd/24th. Each unit placed its horse lines and regimental transport behind its own tentage, and the main wagon park was established off the track on the saddle itself, just behind the camp of the mounted men. Each unit dressed its tents on its neighbor, and the whole camp stretched for 800 yards clear across the eastern slopes of Isandhlwana and the saddle.

It was the best campsite for miles about. There was wood in the valleys behind and water in the donga ahead, and if the ground was stony, the surface rubble was small enough to scrape aside, so that the tents could be pitched on bare and level ground. The view of the approaches was as good as could be expected in a hilly country, and there was no cover for an attacking force within a mile and a half of the camp. An impi charging the camp would be visible for fifteen or twenty minutes in every direction save one before it could close, and a picket posted at the head of the spur where it joined the plateau would cover the single blind approach. The defensive position was strong; the troops could form in a solid phalanx on the open ground in front of the tentage or even behind the regimental transport and the horse lines and, with the precipitous slopes of Isandhlwana protecting their rear, could beat off any attack mounted on the front or the flanks of the camp. The site was dominated by the edge of the Nqutu escarpment, but this was no failing in the face of a foe that lacked artillery, nor was the slight bare eminence of the stony koppie a particular peril.

Chelmsford had issued a profusion of field regulations before the campaign started, covering in considerable detail every phase of camp and march discipline. The very first of these orders dealt with laagering the camps, specifying how the wagons were to be used if entrenchments were not dug, and making clear his intention of turning every halting place into a defensible position. It was clear from context, however, that the oxen were his main concern, and that large bodies of troops might fight in the open. No campsite of the Central Column had been fortified yet, however, and a few of the officers, especially the colonials, were beginning to comment. Piet Uys's brother had visited Chelmsford on the sixteenth on his way to join Colonel Wood and, noting the unlaagered camp sprawled along the Buffalo, had repeated Kruger's advice almost verbatim. He had lost his father and his brother through underestimating the Zulus, he added impressively, failing to mention Potgieter's lack of support and its role in the defeat of the Vlug Kommando.

The danger of an attack on a camp of the Central Column was increasing with each passing day, but no steps were now taken to fortify the new site at the foot of Isandhlwana. The omission loomed much larger in hindsight than it did at the time. Putting one or two hundred loaded wagons end to end in a rectangle or a circle was a hideously complicated task; the oxen could not back their wagons, which with their fixed rear axles were hard to maneuver in tight corners. Fifty men could barely wrestle a loaded wagon into place, and attempting to move several wagons back and forth at once in confined quarters invariably led to snarled trek tows and hopeless confusion, and imposed fresh burdens on the oxen during the hours they needed to graze and rest. The number of wagons available, moreover, was never static, as small convoys were forever coming and going, moving stores up from the depots in Natal. Laagered wagons might have to be pulled out of the line at any time, and the use of laagers at the main camps would have led to endless delay.

The alternative was entrenchment, but even a shallow ditch around the tent area alone would have stretched for over a mile; only the native Pioneer Corps carried a few shovels, and the ground in any event was too stony to dig. The field regulations were quietly forgotten, and no one feared the result of any attack that might be launched on a camp sheltering the better part of two Imperial battalions. As long as the troops had sufficient warning to form, each company in two ranks, the front one kneeling and the rear standing, the crashing volleys of rifle fire would provide all the protection needed.

Chelmsford was not a fool, and he was well aware that he was running a calculated risk. The size of his columns and the ponderous nature of the oxen transport had slowed him to a crawl; he had not the means for a campaign of more than two or three months, and he had to get on to Ulundi. Turning every halting place into a Zulu-proof bastion would have immobilized him, and the Central Column alone still had almost eighty miles to cover before it reached the royal kraal. His risk was justified only as long as his scouting arrangements afforded him adequate notice of an impending attack; he had placed his faith on the infantry and he could not afford to be surprised. As at his first camp, he ringed this one with a circle of infantry outposts flung out a mile and more, beyond the stony koppie, beyond the big donga and almost up to the conical koppie, and far up the spur to the lip of the Nqutu plateau. The circle contracted at night, but it still ringed Isandhlwana and the stony koppie, and a strong detached picket of the NNC remained on the spur to guard the approach from the plateau. The camp awoke long before dawn and fell in on the parade areas in front of the tents, standing to arms until the sun rose and the day's work began. The quartermasters stood by the wagons with the regimental reserve of ammunition and mustered the drummer boys, one to a company, who were waiting to carry haversacks filled with the ten-round paper packets to the ranks. The drummer boys were a tough lot; soldiers' orphans and the like as young as ten years of age, they could hardly remember a life outside the barracks and they looked forward to regular enlistment when they reached seventeen.

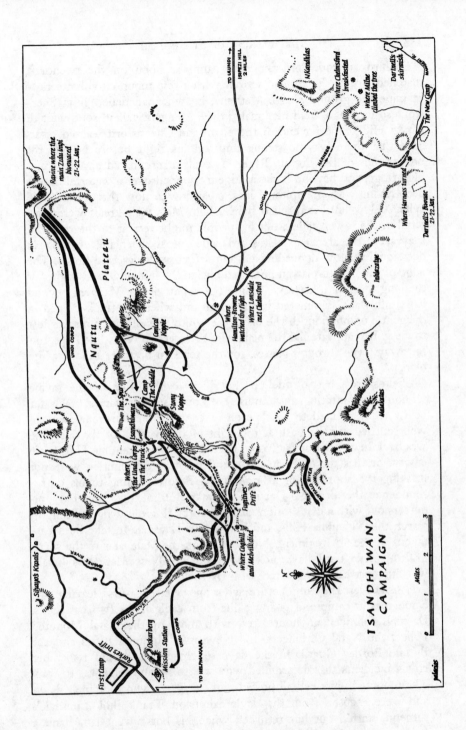

ISANDHLWANA
CAMPAIGN

Miles

0   1   2   3

N

Chelmsford rode into the new camp at noon on the twentieth, snatched a quick lunch, and set out with a few mounted volunteers to examine the ground ahead. Matyana, he who had defied John Shepstone so long ago, held his kraals in the Mangeni valley, southwest of Isipezi Hill at the far end of the plain, and Chelmsford wanted assurance that there was no strong impi on his right before he left the borderlands of the Buffalo River. The plain terminated abruptly in a high ridge, and beyond it the Mangeni dropped over a waterfall into a deep ravine with precipitous sides, emerging to flow through a broad valley below until it reached the Buffalo. Matyana's kraals were scattered in the lower valley, but his people might retreat to the ravine if they were threatened. Chelmsford rode across the plain, crossing an occasional shallow donga and passing a few small deserted kraals. The edge of the Nqutu plateau bordered him to the left, and to his right lay the long mass of Inhlazatye, hiding the valley of the Mangeni beyond it. Isandhlwana shimmered in the haze, and when the track dipped in the gentle undulations of the plain, the white blur of the camp was lost to view. It reappeared as the plain rose to meet the Nkandhla Hills, too far away, even through glasses, for the tents to be more than a white blob.

Chelmsford's party rode up the ridge to the edge of the ravine without encountering any Zulus. He could see Matyana's kraals far below; they seemed to be deserted except for an occasional woman who scuttled for the bush at the sight of the patrol. By six thirty he was back in camp, but far from satisfied that the Nkandhla Hills were empty, or that the Malakata Hills and Inhlazatye Mountain were not masking the approach of a large force. Before turning to his correspondence, he ordered Dartnell to take 150 of the mounted volunteers out with a day's rations at four thirty the following morning to search the Nkandhla Hills, and he ordered Lonsdale to take both battalions of the 3d Regiment, NNC, through the Malakatas to the south of Inhlazatye until he struck the Mangeni above Matyana's kraals, working upstream until he met with Dartnell.

Lonsdale left the camp before dawn on the twenty-first, leaving two companies in camp and taking eight from each of his two battalions. Dartnell followed an hour later, with most of the Natal Mounted Police, the Natal Carbineers, the Newcastle Mounted Rifles and the Buffalo Border Guard. In the days to come men would remember trivial incidents that determined who was to go and who was to stay. The mounted units had all posted night vedettes who rode in at dawn and were excused from the day's excursion. Frank Bull, Lonsdale's surgeon, started out but returned when his horse went lame, and a trooper in the Natal Mounted Police named Parsons accidentally fired his revolver and was thrown when his horse shied. Young John Clarke had just reached the camp from a night vedette, but he was ordered to replace Parsons because his horse was so fresh.

Lonsdale was soon in rough thorn country south of Inhlazatye. Cooper's battalion moved along the crest of the ridge, while Hamilton-Browne pushed up the valley, searching deserted kraals and capturing small numbers of goats and cattle. A few women, found near the kraals, were enticed in by promising them their goats back. They stated that the men had all left long ago to muster at Ulundi, and when asked where the army was now, simply pointed vaguely in the direction of the royal kraal. Hamilton-Browne found two unarmed warriors who had deserted the main impi at Ulundi a week ago to visit their sick mother; he roughed them up severely but could get little more out of them. They simply indicated the same direction the women had, adding that the army had no doubt left Ulundi by now and would probably attack in two days, when the moon would be new.

By four in the afternoon Lonsdale had emerged from the hills. He was seven miles from Isandhlwana and he could see Dartnell's force resting on a hillside of the Nkandhlas three miles ahead of him. His natives were only fed once a day and had received no rations since the preceding noon; his European N.C.O.'s were afoot and exhausted, with tempers frayed from scrambling about in the thorns. He detached two companies under Captain O. E. Murray to start the captured cattle back to camp, and let his men rest while Lieutenant Harford rode on ahead to confer with Dartnell.

Harford was back in an hour. Dartnell intended to remain where he was for the night, and he wanted Lonsdale to join him. He had taken his force to the edge of the ravine and had then split it, sending Captain Theophilus Shepstone, Jr., to his right with the Natal Carbineers to comb the northern slopes of Inhlazatye while Lonsdale was still to the south of it, and he had then taken forty troopers of the Natal Mounted Police across the Mangeni. Almost at once he had found several hundred Zulus in the hills before Isipezi, where the plain rose to join the far end of the Nqutu escarpment. He had retired across the Mangeni and rejoined Shepstone, and then sent three officers back to Isandhlwana to ask Chelmsford for a small reinforcement and for permission to attack in the morning.

Hamilton-Browne protested vigorously, pointing out that the Natal Kaffirs had neither food, blankets nor ammunition, and that the European N.C.O.'s were patently unfit to lead the men into what might be a heavy action on a second rationless day. Their orders were to return to camp, and they could just reach it by dark if they left at once. Lonsdale, eager for battle, would not listen to him and chivvied the force to its feet to join Dartnell. Several of the officers attempted to argue with him, and two of them, Lieutenants Samuel Avery and Frank Holcroft, left their companies and rode off to return to camp without orders. They were followed by several of the European N.C.O.'s and another officer or two, and a few of the natives quietly slipped away as well.

The rest of the officers got the troops moving across the intervening ridges, and settled down on an eastern slope near Dartnell's men for a cold and hungry night. Shortly before dusk a party reached the bivouac area with blankets and rations on pack horses and a note from Chelmsford giving Dartnell permission to attack at his discretion on the morrow. This Dartnell was willing to do, but as the light began to fail, he saw small parties of Zulus begin to slip over the crest of the next ridge three miles to the east and settle down for the night. They had been reinforced and now numbered over 1,500 warriors. Dartnell pushed a mounted patrol into the valley, which paused while a few scouts galloped to within 800 yards of the impi. The Zulus rose at once, and two horns raced out to surround the patrol, which immediately retired. The impi was too large for Dartnell's force to handle, and he sent a second message back across the plain through the gathering dusk asking Chelmsford to send out several companies of infantry for the attack he planned in the morning.

Chelmsford had also been busy during the day. After Lonsdale and Dartnell had left the camp, the rest of the wagons and their guard from the 2nd/24th came in over the saddle, and the troops in camp started to unload the wagons that had arrived the previous day, so that they could be sent back to Rorke's Drift on the morrow for additional rations.

Shortly after breakfast Chelmsford sent Lieutenant Browne out with a small party of the Mounted Infantry to scout the approaches to Isipezi Hill again. The track to Ulundi crossed the Mangeni a mile to the north of the gorge in the Nkandhla Hills, which Dartnell was investigating, and two miles further along, in open country, skirted the northern slopes of Isipezi. Colonel Wood's spies had reported that the main Zulu impi would leave Ulundi on the seventeenth to attack the Central Column, and if this were so it should be drawing close to Isipezi by the twentieth. It was virtually certain that the impi would stick to the track until it reached Isipezi, but its movements in the final stages of its approach to the Central Column could not be predicted, and Chelmsford could not afford to let it slip past his scouts. The Zulus would hardly be foolish enough to stick to the track all the way to the camp, attacking across eight miles of a perfectly bare plain, and from Isipezi, ten miles from the camp, they could either swing north onto the Nqutu plateau or south to pass through Matyana's stronghold, picking up his retainers and then approaching the camp behind the shelter of Inhlazatye and the Malakatas. Either approach would bring them within a mile or two of the camp unseen unless the scouts caught them, and Chelmsford needed continual information from the Nqutu plateau, from Isipezi Hill, and from behind the barrier formed by Inhlazatye and the ridge to the west of the gorge.

Sihayo's brother Gamdana lived in the Malakatas, a few miles south of the camp. He had few retainers and was sixty-eight years old, and when his brother's kraals were attacked, he hastened to submit. He first sent messengers to his old friend Henry Francis Fynn II, who was Magistrate at Umsinga, and when the Central Column reached Isandhlwana he approached Chelmsford directly. The General was willing to let him remain in his kraal providing he surrendered his firearms, but he was furious to learn that Fynn had been negotiating a surrender on his own, without bothering to notify him. He sent a letter to Fynn, ordering him to report to him immediately, and on the forenoon of the twenty-first rode to Gamdana's kraal to visit the man himself. Gamdana was gone—all his people had taken to the bush that morning when Lonsdale's regiment passed through the area—but he followed Chelmsford back to the camp and met him after lunch, promising to send his firearms in the following morning. Fynn also arrived, somewhat startled by the turn of events but willing to accommodate the military. Sir Henry Bulwer had resolutely refused to declare martial law in Natal, and Chelmsford had experienced difficulties in getting the local civil administration to cooperate with him. Fynn had naturally assumed he was within his rights in accepting the surrender, but he now agreed to remain with Chelmsford as an interpreter and political adviser.

Lieutenant Browne returned to camp early in the afternoon. He had seen several large parties of Zulus near the track in the vicinity of Isipezi Hill and had exchanged a few shots with a group of forty warriors, but there had been no sign of the main impi. Isipezi Hill was clear, and even if the main impi had gotten that far, it had certainly not swung to the south, or there would have been news from Dartnell and Lonsdale.

There remained the Nqutu plateau, and Chelmsford decided to reconnoiter it himself. Taking his staff and a small mounted escort, he rode up the spur to the vedettes posted on a small knoll at the edge of the plateau. They had seen nothing, but the surface of the plateau undulated far more than the plain below, and their view was imperfect. Small ridges and slopes bordering the ravines which seamed the plateau blocked a clear sight of the distance, and a man riding out to the north or the east was lost to view after a mile or so.

A final vedette had been posted on another knoll on the edge of the plateau two miles to the east, just beyond the ravine that notched the rim behind the conical koppie. The knoll was slightly lower than the one at the head of the spur and it suffered from the same barriers to visibility, but from its summit another mile or so of the pleateau was open to sight, and no one could approach within five miles of the camp along the plateau without being seen from this farthest outpost. Chelmsford reached the vedette shortly after three o'clock in the afternoon, to find that these men had seen no sign of the enemy either. Just as he was preparing to leave, however, a party of mounted Zulus suddenly rode into view on a ridge a mile away. There were fourteen of them, and they reined in when they saw the vedette. A moment later they turned and disappeared, and the plateau was bare again. Chelmsford descended to the plain by the ravine behind the conical koppie and started back to the camp.

As he approached the track, he fell in with Brevet Major Matthew Gosset and Captain Ernest Henry Buller of his personal staff, who had ridden out with Dartnell that morning. With the Honourable William Drummond, the son of Lord Strathallen, a Natal civil servant acting as Chelmsford's intelligence officer, they had ridden back with Dartnell's request for reinforcements after his first encounter with the Zulus. Chelmsford was irked by the request, and turned it down. Dartnell had been sent on a reconnaissance in force with most of the mounted men, and he should have returned the cavalry to the camp by evening. The main impi had apparently not yet reached Isipezi, according to Browne, but the several hundred Zulus Dartnell had seen, those Browne had encountered, and the fourteen Chelmsford had seen himself on the plateau indicated that it was drawing near. Chelmsford wanted a battle, but he wanted to be attacked with his force in camp and not strung out on a line of march. If the track ahead was clear, he would move to Isipezi and accept the battle there; if the impi arrived before he could move, he would accept it in his strong defensive position at Isandhlwana. Dartnell had overstepped his orders by remaining where he was, and it was too late in the day to order him to return before dark. Chelmsford was forced to accept his decision, and he sent the blankets and rations Dartnell had requested out on four pack horses with an escort of mounted infantry under Lieutenant Walsh. He also gave Dartnell permission to attack the force opposing him in the morning; if it proved too strong for him, he was mobile enough to elude it and return to the camp.

Dartnell's second messenger did not reach the camp until one thirty in the morning. He had been overtaken by darkness on the plain and had been slowed to a walk, and Chelmsford was asleep when he arrived. The second message reported the presence of more than 2,000 Zulus in front of Dartnell, near the track in the Nkandhlas and two or three miles past Isipezi Hill. The information altered the situation radically. Such a force obviously contained more than Matyana's estimated 700 retainers, and it could only mean that the overdue main impi had finally reached the vicinity of Isipezi Hill, probably sometime during the preceding afternoon after Browne had left. The impi could not have slipped past Dartnell to the south of Inhlazatye, and Chelmsford himself had inspected the Nqutu plateau for a distance of five miles from the camp. The impi must therefore be somewhere in the vicinity of the head of the plain, and Dartnell, with 200 mounted men and Lonsdale's 1,400 Natal Kaffirs, was too weak to oppose it and might be in a serious scrape and unable to extricate himself if the impi found him the next day. Chelmsford decided to march to his relief at once, arriving at daybreak with a force strong enough to give battle if necessary. He would have to split the Central Column, and he made quick calculations. The reinforcement for Dartnell would be in greater danger than the force left in the camp; it would in all likelihood intercept the main impi before it reached the camp and thus be in action first, and it would have to fight in the open and not in the defensive position at the camp. There were five companies of the 1st/24th Regiment in the camp and seven of the 2nd/24th; two 1st Battalion companies were at Helpmakaar and one still farther back in Natal, and "B" Company of the 2nd Battalion was at Rorke's Drift. He would take the 2nd Battalion out with him and leave the 1st Battalion under Colonel Pulleine in the camp. Lieutenant Pope's "G" Company of the 2nd Battalion was on outpost duty that day, so he would leave it behind as well. That would give him six companies to reinforce Dartnell and leave Pulleine six to guard the camp.

Colonel Harness had six guns in his battery; he could bring four and leave one section of two guns under Brevet Major Stuart Smith in camp. There were a number of shallow dongas with sharp banks running across the plain and they would probably slow the guns; the Natal Native Pioneer Corps company could march with the advance guard to cut down the banks and ease the passage of the guns.

Dartnell had made contact south of Isipezi Hill, and the Zulus in front of him might be only a screen to hide the main impi if it chose to move up to the Nqutu plateau. It would be necessary to scout Isipezi Hill again, and Russell could take out the Mounted Infantry to ride on to the hill while Chelmsford accompanied Colonel Glyn and the 2nd Battalion to join Dartnell. That would still leave Pulleine over a hundred mounted men from the Natal Mounted Police and the volunteers for his vedettes around the camp. To eke out his force he would also have almost 600 Natal Kaffirs, the four companies Lonsdale had left behind and the two that had returned the previous evening with the captured cattle.

He issued his orders to Brevet Lieutenant Colonel John North Crealock, his military secretary, and reveille sounded a few minutes later. Candles soon illuminated the tents and the fires were stirred up, the orders passed down through the officers, and the men began to assemble their gear. Chelmsford then remembered Durnford, waiting on the Zulu bank of Rorke's Drift with 250 mounted natives, 300 native infantry and the rocket battery. The drift would be in no immediate danger. Major Spalding had Bromhead's "B" Company of the 2nd Battalion, and "D" Company of the 1st Battalion had been ordered down from Helpmakaar and should be there by now. He also had close to 300 Natal Kaffirs under a colonial named Stephenson, unattached to any regiment of the NNC and simply used to guard the Buffalo border. Chelmsford ordered Crealock to move Durnford up to the camp, and Crealock scribbled a short note which he sent back to the camp at the drift by an officer messenger:

22nd, Wednesday, 2 A.M.
You are to march to this camp *at once* with all the force you have with you of No. 2 Column.

Major Bengough's Battalion is to move to Rorke's Drift as ordered yesterday.

2–24th Artillery and mounted men with the General and Colonel Glyn move off at once to attack a Zulu force about ten miles distant.

J. N. C.

Fifty wagons were due to return to Rorke's Drift in the course of the day, and Chelmsford canceled the movement to spare Pulleine the necessity of providing an escort. He missed Pulleine in the bustle, but he gave his orders to Crealock, who passed them on orally. The cavalry vedettes were to be kept advanced, but the line of infantry outposts was to be drawn in closer. Pulleine was to remain in the camp and defend it if he were attacked. He was also to keep a wagon with the regimental reserve of ammunition for the 2nd Battalion ready to follow Glyn in case the reinforcement should be engaged. There was no amplification, nor was one required, and Chelmsford did not even trouble to ask Crealock what orders he had transmitted until long after he had quitted the camp. Pulleine still controlled 600 Imperial infantrymen, and when Durnford arrived, there would be over 1,700 armed men in the camp. Chelmsford hardly had to spell out in detail to an officer with 24 years' service how to use such a force if he were attacked.

The reinforcement was on the march by three thirty, moving out across the darkness of the plain. The night had been moonless and misty, and the first faint light came as the column was passing the conical koppie. The mist began to clear with the dawn, but the day was dull and the sky heavily overcast. A few patches of sky appeared as the day advanced, letting a thin watery sunlight shine through at intervals, but the day stayed dark. An eclipse of the sun, of two-thirds totality, was due to occur at one o'clock in the afternoon, but even those who were then unoccupied failed to notice the event.

Chelmsford and his personal staff rode on ahead to find Dartnell and to learn what changes had occurred since the message that had been dispatched at dusk the night before. They found him at six o'clock, still holding his ridge, with the men long awake and under arms. The slope ahead, on which Zulu campfires had been visible throughout the night, was now bare, with only a few straggling warriors still slipping over the crest. The long-awaited main impi was still unlocated.

Dartnell had passed a restless night. Neither the rations nor the blankets sent out the night before had sufficed for the entire force, and the hungry and chilled men had settled down to sleep on the bare ground in hollow square, with the officers in the center, and each man's arm looped through the reins of his saddled horse. Lonsdale's Natal Kaffirs, who had not been fed since noon Monday, formed a similar ragged square a few yards away, with the Europeans also in the center. The officers of the NNC did not carry rifles, and the N.C.O.'s, who were afoot, had for the most part left theirs in the camp. Hamilton-Browne prudently took up all the firearms that had been issued to his Natal Kaffirs and distributed them to his Europeans before he settled down for the night. It was just as well. Long after midnight a chance noise in the brush stampeded one side of his square through the Europeans sleeping in the center. The clustered horses broke the force of the route, and Mvubi's Zulus on the far side of the square stood fast and stemmed the torrent with their shields and assegais. Hamilton-Browne, awakened when his horse trampled him, grabbed a knobkerrie and with his other officers clubbed the terrorized natives back into a semblance of their original formation, but all chance of rest was gone. Norris-Newman, also stepped on by horses, moved in disgust to Dartnell's square, where the men were awake and ready to repel an attack. The noise gradually died down, but Lonsdale's square broke once again before daylight. The officers were awake this time and stopped the stampede before it was well under way.

The ridge on which the Zulus had slept lay just to the west of the Mangeni gorge and several miles south of the track from Isandhlwana to Ulundi. Chelmsford now set out to comb the area thoroughly, in hopes of finding the main impi. Glyn was still several miles behind, and Chelmsford sent word back for him to take the infantry and the guns to the north of the ridge while Dartnell took the mounted men around to the south. Lonsdale's Natal Kaffirs were launched at the ridge itself.

The infantry was slow, but the artillery was even slower. Harness was plagued by innumerable small dongas and could not keep up. Glyn detached two of his six companies to escort him and continued his advance. The Zulus had reoccupied the crest of their ridge in some force as the sun rose, but they retired before the reluctant advance of the NNC. They were just crossing the rocky valley behind when Dartnell entered it from the south, and the mounted men plowed into them and left thirty dead Zulus sprawled over the rocks, while the rest scrambled to the safety of the next ridge or sought shelter amongst the boulders. Lonsdale's battalions came over the crest of the first ridge, and Cooper's men dropped into the valley to help flush the Zulus out of their hiding places, killing another fifty or so, while Hamilton-Browne prepared to follow. Lieutenant Harford distinguished himself again, crawling into a narrow crevice to kill two Zulus and capture a third, while Captain Theophilus Shepstone, Jr., of the Natal Carbineers, chased Matyana himself for three miles until the harried chieftan slipped off his horse and slid down a krantz to get away.

Chelmsford and his staff had ridden north to join Glyn before the skirmish started. The infantry arrived too late to participate, but small bodies of Zulus were still retreating to the east and Chelmsford ordered a general advance to drive them all over the Mangeni.

By nine thirty the last Zulu was out of sight and the firing had died out. Chelmsford ordered a halt for breakfast and sent for Hamilton-Browne. The main impi was certainly not between Isipezi Hill and Matyana's stronghold, and over half the Central Column was now on the Mangeni. Chelmsford had decided to site his next camp in the broad valley below Dartnell's bivouac, where a loop of the Mangeni provided water, and he now wished to order Pulleine to strike the main camp and march to join him. When Hamilton-Browne came up, he ordered him to return to the camp to help with the move, brushing aside any Zulus that might have crossed the plain to scout the camp. Hamilton-Browne had the grace to refuse the proffered breakfast in front of his starving men, and as he was moving off, a mounted messenger arrived with a note signed by Pulleine:

Staff Officer—Report just come in that the Zulus are advancing in force from left front of the camp. 8.5 A.M.

The message was puzzling. The force referred to must have been on the Nqutu plateau, but Pulleine indicated no emergency and would presumably have stated so if he thought it were the main impi. It must therefore be a strong advance party, and it shed no further light on the mystery of the location of the main impi. Chelmsford was not alarmed, and two factors made him treat the news, as well as any other message that might reach him from the camp, with only casual concern. The force he had left in the camp was quite sufficient to beat off any attack the Zulus could mount, even an unlikely attack by the main impi, and any news he received from the camp would be close to two hours old. It would take him a good three hours to reassemble the advanced units and march them back to camp, and the troops would arrive almost five hours after whatever message calling them back had been sent, by which time the situation would have resolved itself one way or another. Chelmsford was trying to move the Central Column forward, and he did not regard Glyn's force as a reconnaissance from the camp. He already thought of it as the main force, and his objective was to bring Pulleine forward to join Glyn as soon as he could do so in safety and not to return Glyn to the camp.

As a courtesy to the Naval Brigade Chelmsford had a naval officer on his staff, and Lieutenant Berkeley Milne carried a telescope far more powerful than the Army's binoculars. Chelmsford sent him to a neighboring knoll from which Isandhlwana was visible, and Milne climbed a low tree and spent a long time gazing at the distant camp. The tents were only a white blur, and no individual figures could be distinguished. Milne finally reported that he thought the oxen had been moved closer to the camp, but that everything else appeared normal.

Reassured, Chelmsford continued with his plans. Hamilton-Browne was sent off, with final orders to search through the maze of small dongas as he crossed the plain, and Harness was ordered to break off his laborious advance after the infantry and to bring his guns south to the new campsite. Brevet Major Stuart Smith had come along for the ride, leaving the two guns in camp in charge of Lieutenant Curling, and Chelmsford sent him back with Captain Alan Gardner, his staff transport officer, to order Pulleine to strike the tents of Glyn's force and send them on with rations for seven days. Glyn's advancing infantry in the meantime had passed the ridge on which Chelmsford was breakfasting, but the retiring parties of Zulus showed no signs of allowing him to close the long gap between them. After a mile or so Glyn broke off and retraced his steps. Still farther north, Russell and the Mounted Infantry had disappeared in the direction of Isipezi Hill.

By noon the forces with Chelmsford were scattered over several miles of hilly country, with the various units frequently out of sight of each other. Chelmsford himself had ridden south to the new campsite, and Harness had topped the last ridge, where Dartnell had bivouaced, and was resting for a moment before moving down into the valley. By twelve thirty both Chelmsford and Harness were aware that the troops left in the camp under Pulleine were engaged in some sort of action. Harness on the ridge could make out several bodies of Zulus on the edge of the Nqutu plateau, and Chelmsford was just questioning a few prisoners taken in Dartnell's skirmish, who claimed that the main impi was due that day from Ulundi, when they all caught the unmistakable sound of cannon fire from the two guns left in the camp. "There! Do you hear that? There is fighting at the camp!" exclaimed the prisoners, and Chelmsford spurred up the slope with his staff and the men leveled their glasses on the camp. The tents were clearly visible, and they could see the small bright flashes of a few shells exploding against the face of the Nqutu escarpment. There seemed to be figures moving about through the tent area, and after a while the cannonade died out. Satisfied that if an attack had occurred it had been beaten off, Chelmsford descended to the valley.

All was quiet for a while. Dartnell's men had offsaddled and were resting after their exertions of the morning, and Commandant Cooper's 2nd Battalion of the NNC finished poking about among the rocks at the scene of the morning's skirmish and moved to join them at a leisurely pace. Lonsdale himself had decided to ride back to Isandhlwana to insure that the rations and blankets for his exhausted men were hurried along; the regular quartermasters were apt to overlook the needs of the Natal Kaffirs.

Harness had also heard the firing that attracted Chelmsford's attention. An intervening rise on the plain blocked his view of the camp itself, but he too had seen the shells bursting on the Nqutu escarpment, and he had wondered about the action. All was soon quiet, however, and he ordered his battery to fall in and prepared to descend to the new camp. Glancing back, he saw a large body of natives some five miles off, directly between him and the rise that blocked his view of the camp. This was obviously Hamilton-Browne's battalion, but instead of moving toward Isandhlwana it seemed to be returning, and even as he watched, a European officer detached himself from the body and came toward him at a gallop. Harness ordered his trumpeter to dismount and asked Captain Church, commanding one of the two companies of escorting infantry, to go and meet the messenger. Church was back in fifteen minutes with a startling message from Hamilton-Browne: "For God's sake come back with all your men; the camp is surrounded and must be taken unless helped."

Harness at once turned his guns around and started for Isandhlwana.

Major Gosset had ridden over from where the General was inspecting his new campsite, and Harness asked him to carry the tidings to Chelmsford. Gosset had actually seen the camp a little while before, when all appeared to be normal, and, knowing Chelmsford's views on the adequacy of the defending force and his intention to move the column forward, he tried to discourage Harness from returning. Harness was not to be stopped, however, so Gosset rode back to Chelmsford, leaving Captain Develin, who had brought the message from Hamilton-Browne, with the guns. Gosset caught up with the battery before it had covered a mile. Harness was to carry out his orders and move to the new campsite. The bouncing gun carriages and the limbers slowed to a walk, and once again the battery turned around.

There is strong evidence indicating that Gosset never gave this message to Chelmsford directly, and it is virtually certain that if he even delivered it to Crealock or one of the other staff officers, he did not deliver Hamilton-Browne's verbatim wording. Whatever word reached Chelmsford simply seemed to be another report of the action he had witnessed himself.

Hamilton-Browne had been having a hard day. He left Chelmsford shortly after ten to start back on the long twelve miles to the camp. The day was hot despite the cloud cover, and the plain was baking. His command was on the verge of collapse: it had not eaten for two days and had spent the preceding day in a fatiguing scramble among the rough thorn valleys. It had stampeded twice during a cold and sleepless night, and Mvubi's Zulus had wounded a number of the men in stopping the routes. It had then participated in the charge up the ridge before Chelmsford called it out of action, and the men were now played out. The European N.C.O.'s, afoot and wearing heavy boots, were in even worse condition than the troops, and they were using kicks and curses to keep the sullen Natal Kaffirs moving along. Hamilton-Browne and his adjutant, Lieutenant Campbell, were riding in advance, and while still eight miles from the camp, they saw two Zulus resting in the shade of a large rock several hundred yards ahead. They gave chase; Campbell shot his quarry while Hamilton-Browne rode his down and captured him. The prisoner was a young boy who had been sent, he said, from the main impi on the Nqutu plateau to see if there were any troops among the hills at the far end of the plain. He added that there were twelve full regiments, perhaps 20,000 men, in the impi.

Hamilton-Browne scribbled a note, told Campbell to have it sent to Chelmsford at once, and then rode on ahead to inspect the camp, still five miles ahead. He was in low ground and the heat haze made the distance quiver, but the camp was visible and seemed to be quiet. While he was watching, two Natal Kaffirs laden with haversacks approached him. They belonged to one of the two companies he had left in camp the preceding day, and they were bearing rations sent out that morning by one of his officers. They also carried a lighthearted note from Edgar Anstey and James Patrick Daly, Lieutenants of the 1st/24th. They had visited Hamilton-Browne's tent the night before, they wrote, and had found a good dinner spoiling. They had eaten it for him, and were sending him two bottles of whisky in return.

Hamilton-Browne returned to his command and distributed the food to the Europeans. He then got his men to their feet and started them for the camp again. A mile or so along, with the scene clearing more and more with every yard, he saw the shell bursts on the Nqutu plateau that had attracted Harness's and Chelmsford's attention. He wrote out a second note and gave it to Sergeant Turner with orders to find Chelmsford. At the same time the first messenger, Lieutenant Pohl, returned. He had not been able to find the General, but he had given the note to an officer who promised to deliver it.

The low ground below the tents was not visible, but it was quite clear that a major attack from the Nqutu plateau was developing on the left of the camp. Large masses of Zulus were pouring over the lip of the escarpment and others were streaming down the spur to the north of the mountain. Hamilton-Browne started his men up again, moving them forward to his own left so as to approach the right of the camp, still four or five miles away. The Natal Kaffirs, however, had by now seen their dread foes in the distance and refused to budge. Even Mvubi's Zulus were unable to move them more than a few hundred yards, so Hamilton-Browne let them sit and spurred forward to watch. All alone, less than four miles from the camp, he saw the black mass on the left of the camp lap forward and race across the plain in front of him, until it extended far beyond the right of the camp and even the stony koppie. More Zulus were pouring down the escarpment on his own right, behind the conical koppie and as far back into the plain as he himself was, and Hamilton-Browne bethought himself of his battalion. He rode back and formed his men into a ring, dismounting the European officers and hiding them in the middle. He sent Captain Develin back with his last desperate warning and started to retreat. A mile farther along, in some low ground halfway between Isandhlwana and the new campsite, he came to a slight rise. His men were played out, and presumably one of his three messengers had reached Chelmsford, who would no doubt be coming to the aid of the camp shortly. Several bodies of Zulus had swept across the plain behind him, passing within a mile of the Natal Kaffirs, and Hamilton-Browne was finally at a loss. He could not advance, and there was no sense in retreating any farther. The 1st Battalion of the 3d Regiment of the Natal Native Contingent sat down to await events.

Lieutenant Colonel Russell had been detached early in the morning to have another look at the critical vicinity of Isipezi Hill. He had continued along the Ulundi track with his Mounted Infantry when Glyn took his infantry off to the southeast, and the scene of the morning's activity, six or seven miles behind him, was soon hidden by the rolling foothills. He found Isipezi Hill occupied in some force, with large detached bodies of Zulus drifting northwest toward the eastern end of the Nqutu plateau, but he extricated his small command without a fight and around noon started back along the track. He had offsaddled his command to rest his horses, about five miles north of the new campsite, when Lieutenant Pohl reached him with Hamilton-Browne's first message. Russell had no idea where Chelmsford might be, but he started to cast about in his immediate vicinity, and while he was still waiting for his scouts to return, Sergeant Turner rode up with Hamilton-Browne's second message. The gist of the two notes indicated a heavy attack on the camp, so Russell sent both men back to Hamilton-Browne and rode south to find Chelmsford himself.

Neither of these two messages, which Russell probably delivered as one and which must have reached the General about the time that Gosset's watered-down version of Hamilton-Browne's third message reached his staff, alarmed Chelmsford. They all obviously referred to the same incident, and Chelmsford himself had inspected the camp after it had occurred. Pulleine had quite obviously been in some kind of an action, but it was all over now. Chelmsford nevertheless decided to return to the camp to find out what happened. The Zulus were in force on the Nqutu plateau, and if the main impi had actually slipped past the advanced section, it would not be prudent to move Pulleine up to the new campsite, leaving the main impi between the Central Column and Natal. He decided to take Russell's Mounted Infantry as an escort in case he encountered any Zulus on the plain, leaving Dartnell, Glyn and Harness at the new campsite.

Chelmsford and his staff rode north to regain the track and to pick up Russell's men, passing Harness moving on to the new campsite, where Glyn's infantry was also beginning to arrive. Their pace was slow; the horses had been moving since early morning and the heat was intense. The Mounted Infantry joined them and they started to move along the track. A mounted messenger reached them with a laconic note from Pulleine, answering Chelmsford's order to strike the camp, which he had dispatched four hours earlier by Captain Gardner:

Staff Officer. Heavy firing to the left of our camp. Cannot move camp at present.

The message confirmed what was already known, and changed nothing. A little later a second messenger delivered a note to Major Clery:

Heavy firing near left of camp. [George] Shepstone has come in for reinforcements and reports that Zulus are falling back. The whole force at camp turned out and fighting about one mile to left flank.

Clery did not bother to hand the note to the General. The reference to Shepstone indicated that Durnford had reached the camp, and the tenor of the message again confirmed what the staff already knew.

A few miles farther on, Chelmsford came across Hamilton-Browne's battalion, still perched on its rise and waiting for relief. As soon as he saw the General, Hamilton-Browne sent a rider over to announce that the camp had been taken and that there was a large party of Zulus between him and Isandhlwana. The camp was not visible from the low ground, and Chelmsford, whose opinion of the 3d Battalion, 1st Regiment, NNC, was not high, simply did not believe him. He ordered Hamilton-Browne to fall in behind the Mounted Infantry, and continued his advance.

It was three thirty, and the camp was still five miles away, when a stumbling figure was seen leading a lethargic horse over the plain. It was Commandant Rupert Lonsdale, and as soon as he could catch his breath he gasped out the unbelievable truth. The Zulus were in possession of the camp, and of all the force that had been left in Isandhlwana that morning, not one soul there was still alive.

Lonsdale had started back toward the camp after Dartnell's morning skirmish. He was a fat man, and far from well; he was barely over his concussion and had been nagged with a low fever for weeks. The preceding day's scouting, the sleepless bivouac and the morning's skirmish, coming on top of weeks of grinding labor, had brought him to the verge of a breakdown, and he was in critical need of rest before facing the morrow's problem of moving the NNC to the new camp.

His pony Dot was hardly in better condition. She had been ridden hard on short rations for several days, and that morning had already carried Lonsdale's weight for several hours at fast paces over hilly country. When the track emerged from the foothills, Dot sighted Isandhlwana across the plain, with the white smear of tenting at its base. She broke into an easy jog, slowing to a walk on the gentle rises, and Lonsdale, marking her eagerness to reach the camp, gave the horse her head. He tugged at his sweat-soaked corduroy jacket and sank into a stuporous relaxation.

Lonsdale's mind was a thousand miles away as Dot approached the camp, and he was dimly aware of a seemingly normal bustle among the tents. Even a black figure that rose beside his horse and fired a gun at him failed to shake him completely out of his reverie. Taking the man for one of his own ill-trained Natal Kaffirs, Lonsdale simply snarled at him and rode on. Dot entered the tent area and slowed, looking for her own picket rope in the horse lines.

A Zulu holding a blood-smeared assegai and wearing a torn red tunic emerged from a tent. Lonsdale gaped at him, trying to grasp the significance of the incongruous apparition. The last clouds cleared from his numbed brain. Speechless, he twisted in his saddle and stared about.

The only figures moving in the camp were Zulu warriors. There were thousands of them milling about, and scores had pulled on bloody red tunics of the 24th Regiment or had clapped white sun helmets over their heads. As far through the camp as Lonsdale could see, the ground was littered with hundreds of bodies, black and white. They lay in mounds through the camp and were draped over the wagons behind. Every European belly had been slashed open from sternum to groin, and blood and entrails were spattered on the tents and lay in wet puddles on the rocky ground. He had ridden in to the tent area through windrows of dead Natal Kaffirs. Galvanized, he snatched at his reins.

He reckoned without the horse. Dot, close to food and rest, had no intention of leaving the horse lines, and she laid her ears back. Zulus were beginning to look up all around, and Lonsdale knew he was a bare hairbreadth from death. He twisted Dot's head around savagely and sank his spurs into her flanks as hard as he could. The horse gave in and broke into a shambling trot, while Lonsdale continued to spur and flailed away with the ends of his reins. He moved back out of the camp at an agonizing crawl, acutely aware of his bulk as a shower of assegais flashed over his bent back and bullets whistled past his head. He got out of the camp unscathed, and Dot moved a few hundred yards more before she sank to her knees. Lonsdale slithered off her back, got to his feet, threw the reins over her head and dragged at her until she lurched to her feet and followed him. No one came in pursuit, but Lonsdale did not stop to rest until he had put a mile between himself and the camp. It took him almost two hours to cover the five miles of level plain before he met Chelmsford.

The news was shocking, but not yet catastrophic. Lonsdale had few details—only that the camp had fallen and many had been slain. It was inconceivable that the entire force had been wiped out, and surely a part of it had been able to fall back on Rorke's Drift.

Chelmsford's position was perilous. He was caught in the open with a small escort, the rest of his force scattered five miles behind him; it was late in the day and the main impi was somewhere close in front. His immediate concern was to retake the camp, if that were possible, and he sent Gosset pounding back to the new campsite to order Glyn to abandon the new camp and to return with his entire force at his best speed. He then formed the Natal Kaffirs into line, stiffened them with the Mounted Infantry on their flanks, and advanced to within three miles of the camp. He then sent the Mounted Infantry forward to reconnoiter. They were back within the hour to report that thousands of Zulus were still in the camp and swarming like ants over the plain and up the spur to the Nqutu plateau. They were burning the tents and looting the stores, and dragging away all manner of booty as they retired.

Gosset did not reach the new bivouac area until four, and it was after six before Glyn was back with the infantry and the guns. The men had been marching with full packs for over twelve hours, and the grim tidings that Gosset had given Glyn and one or two of the staff officers had filtered down through the ranks. The men were limping and stumbling as they came in, and frankly incredulous. Chelmsford, his heart sinking, made a short speech. He told them the camp had been taken and the road to Rorke's Drift was probably cut off as well. He announced his intention of retaking the camp, and the men responded with cheers. Reassured, Chelmsford formed his lines. With the four guns in the center, the Imperial infantry on either side, a battalion of the NNC beyond them and Dartnell with the mounted volunteers on the extreme left and Russell with the Mounted Infantry on the right, they moved forward.

As the force approached the wide donga, four figures armed with spears moved forward out of the dusk. Russell's men fired a volley, one of the figures dropped, and the other three cast their weapons aside and ran forward, waving their arms. They were Natal Kaffirs from one of the companies left in the camp; they had played dead during the fight and, apparently being taken for fallen comrades by the victors, had escaped injury. Now one had been killed and another wounded by the volley, and the incident did little to hearten Lonsdale's regiment as the men rejoined.

The western sky had cleared. Sunset was just after seven, but long before that Isandhlwana cast its lengthening shadow far out over the plain, concealing the horror at its base. By the time the line had reached the donga a mile outside the camp, the daylight was gone. The stony koppie, the saddle and the mountain were dark masses outlined against the afterglow. Scores of wagons could be seen jumbled together on the saddle, and at the northern end of Isandhlwana a few

Zulus retreating to the Nqutu plateau were silhouetted against the sky. Harness unlimbered at the edge of the donga and sent four rounds of shrapnel into the mass of wagons; it was long range for the muzzle-loaders and the fuses glowed for an interminable time before the shells burst on the crest of the saddle.

The troops had been advancing through a sprinkling of dead Zulus, which thickened as they neared the donga. The men crossed the shallow watercourse, empty except for thousands of expended cartridge cases, and halted on the far side. Major Wilsone Black picked three companies of infantry, fixed bayonets and moved off into the darkness. The balance of the force closed in and the 1st/3d, NNC, spent and quaking with fear, balked again, but Hamilton-Browne grabbed their inDuna by his headring and threatened to blow out his brains if his men did not move. After a while there was a single volley from the darkness ahead, a moment's silence, and then the sound of cheering. The Zulus were gone, and Wilsone Black had carried the stony koppie.

It was pitch black when the troops finally reached a relatively clear area on the saddle and bivouacked in a sprawling ring. The men had been stumbling over bodies, already stiff and cold, for the last few hundred yards of their advance, feeling their way along through scores of slaughtered oxen and horses and a great profusion of wagons and littered stores. There were bodies in the bivouac area as well, and the troopers of the Natal Mounted Police grimly rolled four of them out of the way before settling down to wait out the night.

There was no sign of the main impi. A few Zulus, drunk on brandy looted from the stores, were found wandering on the saddle as the men advanced and were killed with the bayonet. One Zulu, armed with a gun and obviously besotted, was perched somewhere high on the flank of Isandhlwana. He babbled and sang through the night, occasionally firing his piece, and much ammunition was expended on him to no effect. Solitary campfires could be seen amongst the hills for miles about, but none so grouped as to indicate the presence of a large force.

Many of the men wanted to visit the camp area, but Chelmsford would not permit it. Trooper Scott of the Natal Carbineers wanted to look for his brother, the officer in charge of the Carbineers left in the camp that morning; Trooper Clarke had left his spurs in his tent when he was called out to replace Parsons. Both men tried to slip off, but Dartnell turned them back. George Shepstone had arrived with Durnford, and his brother Offy was sick with worry. He shook hands with so many of his troopers, bidding them farewell and muttering that they would never see the sun rise again, that the men began to lose confidence in him. Henry James Degacher and Alfred Godwin Godwin-Austen of the 2nd/24th both had younger brothers in the companies left in the camp.

The Natal Kaffirs were past caring what happened to them, and by twos and threes began to slip down the saddle to melt into the night. Harford noticed them going and somehow reasoned them into returning to the bivouac, where Chelmsford posted sentries to hold them in place, a little removed from the main ring. Toward morning they bolted again, scared by a noise from the plain, but as they rushed in on the main force the men, already sleepless and alert, rose to their knees from their resting places and stopped them.

The sky cleared toward midnight and the stars came out. Captain Hallam Parr, on Glyn's staff, set about searching the wagons for rations. He found a load of bread and tinned meat, and called for messengers from each unit to distribute it. When the infantry and the mounted men had been fed, he called over to the Natal Kaffir bivouac, and the Europeans came over to get food for their men. An officer appeared in the darkness and asked for rations for six or seven of his comrades, and when Hallam Parr asked for his haversack, the man said he had forgotten it. Hallam Parr told him to hold out his hat, and the man answered stiffly, "Sir, I must object to your suggestion. I should prefer to go without my rations than carry them in my hat."

The Commander in Chief was numbed with fatigue and depression. It was beyond belief that all in the camp had perished, but he knew not how many had survived or where they had gone. No more did he know where the main Zulu impi was—it was only apparent, with awful certainty, where it had been at noon. It had certainly not returned along the track, and it might be resting on the Nqutu plateau or in the Bashee valley ahead. It might even have entered Natal to try for Pietermaritzburg or some other unsuspecting settlement, and there was nothing to stop it and no hope of overtaking it. The Central Column, in any event, had been shattered, with part of Durnford's column as well, and all the agonizing months of struggle that had gone into planning and mounting the campaign were now set at nought. His immediate problem was to extricate the remnants of the Central Column in the morning, to join up with whatever forces had gathered at Rorke's Drift or Helpmakaar. Beyond that there was nothing on which he could base a plan. He had stripped Natal to mount the campaign, and even if Wood and Pearson were safe, he would need massive reinforcements from England before he could consider re-entering Zululand. The transport problem alone was sickening. He had left close to 2,000 oxen in the camp, the entire transport for the Central Column and almost fifty teams drawn from the Natal lines as well, and their carcasses surrounded his bivouac. The night was endless, no one slept and each man was alone with his thoughts and acutely aware of the tall, somber figure that paced back and forth through the lines.

Henry Francis Fynn II was resting by one of the groups near the looted wagon park. Long after the bivouac was quiet, he heard a soft groan from the darkness ahead. It was a Zulu voice, and Fynn called back and asked who it was. The man was a warrior of the uThulwana, who in his ignorance after the battle had tried to slake his thirst with a great draft from a jug of carbolic acid he had found in the veterinary's wagon. He was dying, but before he expired he told Fynn the story of the battle.

Then a final blow fell. As the restless horses and the men gradually settled and the bivouac grew still, a few sharp ears near the crest of the saddle caught the faint, distant sputter of prolonged musketry. The sound was hard to place in the hills, but the elusive popping was continual and obviously involved scores of rifles. Staring eyes roved the encircling night, but there was nothing to see in the dark hills. Then, seven miles to the west, the unmistakable outline of the Oskarberg sprang out of the darkness, outlined by a red glare behind it. The mission station at Rorke's Drift was burning.

ISANDHLWANA

As COLONEL GLYN's force started to march out of the camp at Isandhlwana at three thirty on the morning of Wednesday, the twenty-second of January, a solitary horseman slipped out of the camp across the saddle and started back along the track to Rorke's Drift. Lieutenant Horace Smith-Dorrien was carrying Crealock's order to Colonel Durnford to bring his force up to the camp, and he forged ahead bravely in the misty night. It was a long ride in total darkness, over ten miles by the wandering track, but Smith-Dorrien was carrying an important dispatch and he was further fortified by the valor of ignorance—it did not occur to him until the following day that there might have been Zulus about.

The horizon was already light when he reached Durnford's camp on the Zulu side of Rorke's Drift. Durnford had just left with Lieutenant Newnham-Davis and the forty men of the Edendale contingent to ride to Helpmakaar, where he hoped to secure a few wagons for his force, so Smith-Dorrien gave the message to Captain George Shepstone, Durnford's political agent and interpreter, and Shepstone sent Lieutenant Henderson after Durnford. The colonel returned at once, ordered his force to fall in, and moved out along the track. The five troops of the Natal Native Horse, 250 men in all, led the way, followed by the rocket battery and the three companies of the 1st Battalion, 1st Regiment, NNC. A half-dozen wagons, with Durnford's reserve ammunition and a few rations, paused long enough to pack up the tents and then followed.

Smith-Dorrien saw them off, and then splashed through the drift and rode on to the mission station for breakfast. The camp seemed almost deserted after the activity of the preceding fortnight. Lieutenant Gonville Bromhead was still there with his luckless "B" Company, as were 300 Natal Kaffirs under a colonial volunteer, Captain Stephenson, and a few European N.C.O.'s. Stephenson's men were not attached to any of the regular battalions of the Natal Native Contingent; they were simply spare Natal Kaffirs assigned in bulk to guard the Buffalo River border, and they were even more poorly equipped, trained and led than the NNC. There were no other units stationed at Rorke's Drift, although "B" and "D" Companies of the 1st/24th were ten miles back at Helpmakaar. One of these companies had been ordered to move down to the mission station; it was now two days overdue and Major Henry Spalding, in charge of this section of the lines of communication and the senior officer at the mission station, was beginning to fret.

Smith-Dorrien ate breakfast with the other officers and passed on the news from the Central Column, especially that the General and Colonel Glyn had moved out and a big fight was expected. Lieutenant Chard pricked up his ears. His work with the punts was undemanding and boring, and there was little chance of seeing any action at the drift. Under the pretext of wanting to confer with Lieutenant Macdowel, he asked Major Spalding for permission to ride up to Isandhlwana, received it, and left shortly after breakfast.

Smith-Dorrien puttered about in his tent for a while, and then supervised the erection of the large gallows structure he intended to use for stretching rawhide cut from dead oxen to replace the trek tows that were forever breaking. Around 8:00 A.M. he prepared to return to Isandhlwana, since fifty of the hundred wagons he had left there were due to return to Rorke's Drift as soon as the camp could spare an escort. He remembered he was short of ammunition for his revolver, the only arm he carried, so just before he rode off, he sought out "Gonny" Bromhead to borrow a few rounds. Bromhead was also low, but he finally gave his friend eleven cartridges, and Smith-Dorrien started back for Isandhlwana, reaching the camp a little after ten, hard on Durnford's heels.

It had been a busy morning for Pulleine after Chelmsford left. The last of the departing troops were away by four thirty, and Pulleine began to arrange his outposts for the day. Lieutenant Pope, with "G" Company of the 2nd/24th, was posted 1,500 yards in front of the camp, with his men in groups of fours strung out for almost a thousand yards along the wide donga. Pope took the right of the line, where Lieutenant Anstey with a small party from "F" Company of the 1st Battalion was working on the track where it crossed the lip of the donga. Pope chatted with Anstey for a moment; he was lonely and missed his terrier "Pip," which he had left with Surgeon Reynolds back at the mission station. Lieutenant Frederick Godwin-Austen, Pope's second-in-command, took the left of the line. Godwin-Austen had an unusual distinction. One brother, Alfred Godwin, was a captain in the same battalion, but another, Henry Haversham, had surveyed some hitherto unmapped regions of the Himalayas, and the second-highest mountain in the world was to bear his family name.

Pope's right was bent back to face the Malakatas and cover the stony koppie, and his left joined two companies of the NNC, who continued the line along the front of the camp and the foot of the spur. A third company of the NNC was posted on the mound at the lip of the escarpment, where the spur joined it. A small mounted vedette of mounted men loitered in front of them, watching the empty plateau. The vedette that had occupied the second hillock, two miles farther along the rim beyond the conical koppie and the ravine that notched the edge of the plateau, where Chelmsford had seen the fourteen mounted Zulus the previous afternoon, had been withdrawn.

The call for breakfast sounded about seven thirty, and the men took their mess kits and congregated around the field kitchens the company cooks had set up behind each unit's tent area. Before the meal was well under way, a mounted man galloped down the spur from the advanced vedette and reported that a large body of Zulus was advancing from the northeast across the Nqutu plateau. Lieutenant Teignmouth Melvill, the adjutant of the 1st Battalion, ordered his bugler to sound "Fall In," and then to add "Column Call," applying the order to everybody in the camp. The breakfast lines dissolved, the men grabbed their rifles and accouterments and scurried to the parade grounds in front of their tents, struggling into their shoulder straps and buckling their heavy belts as they ran. Pope brought in "G" Company and Anstey his detachment, and the two NNC companies along the front of the camp came in as well. The company on the mound stayed where it was, as did the mounted vedette in front of it. The 1st Battalion band fell in behind the lines to act as stretcher-bearers—all except Private Bickley, who was posted in the officer's mess tent to guard the uneaten breakfasts. Quartermasters Pullen and Bloomfield reported to their ammunition wagons and counted the drummer boys, and Pulleine sent a messenger racing after Chelmsford, long out of sight across the plain, with the message the General received while he was having breakfast.

Within ten minutes the entire force was arrayed in two lines stretched across the front of the camp, with the flanks refused to cover the Malakatas and the spur. The line was ragged, with gaps between the units left by the force that had departed that morning, and the company commanders jockeyed their men back and forth to even the interstices. There were five companies of the NNC in camp, in addition to the one at the head of the spur, but they played no part in the front line of defense. Their function was to pursue defeated Zulus and to scout, and they were now held bunched in front of the exact center of the camp, several hundred yards behind the Imperial companies. There was, in fact, a tendency to ignore them, and so little notice was taken of them during the morning that no one was later certain which company had been on the plateau and which left in camp.

There was no further word from the vedette on the plateau for over an hour. Then a few Zulus appeared on the edge of the escarpment, on the hillock where the vedette had been the previous day. They were almost three miles from the camp and two from the vedette covering the head of the spur, and they inspected the scene below them before they disappeared. A second messenger came down from the vedette to report that the Zulus had been in three columns; two had retired to the northeast and disappeared in the rolling ground and the third was moving to the northwest.

Lieutenant Chard had reached the camp while the men were under arms, and he considered this last message. If the third column of Zulus was moving northwest, it might cross the Nqutu plateau far to the north of Isandhlwana, ford the Bashee near Sihayo's kraals, and then turn south. He decided to return to Rorke's Drift after all. A few miles back down the track he encountered Durnford, spurring on with his mounted natives while his infantry lagged behind with the rocket battery. Chard passed him the news from the camp, as well as his fear that the Zulus might have a "dash at the drift," and Durnford used him to pass his orders to the troops behind. Captain Russell was to take Captain Nourse's "D" Company with his rocket battery and to hurry on as fast as he could, detaching Captain Stafford and "E" Company to escort the wagons. "C" Company, under Lieutenants Black and Lister, was to come on as well. All hands were to keep a sharp lookout to their left. Chard passed the orders on and continued, meeting Smith-Dorrien on *his* ride back to the camp before he himself got back to the punts. A few minutes later Stafford detached Lieutenant Wallie Erskine with sixteen men to stay with the wagons, and with the rest of "E" Company hurried after the others.

Durnford reached the saddle shortly after ten and cantered into the camp, past the wagons on the left and the guard tent on the right. The men were still under arms in front of the camp, and the first man he encountered beyond the guard tent was Paul Brickhill, Colonel Glyn's interpreter, who had not accompanied the force that left in the morning. Brickhill was leading eight Zulus out of the camp to the south.

Durnford, who remembered Brickhill from the sittings of the Boundary Commission the preceding year, greeted him warmly and asked him what he was doing. Brickhill explained that the Zulus were some of Gamdana's retainers, who in accordance with the arrangement Chelmsford had made were just surrendering eleven old muskets. They now wished to return to their kraals, to round up the cattle Lonsdale had scattered in his sweep through the Malakatas the preceding day.

Durnford let them pass, and rode on to find Pulleine. The two men greeted each other, and Pulleine then outlined the situation, enumerated the forces in the camp, and passed on the tenor of Chelmsford's orders. The two men of course knew each other, and the meeting was perfectly civil and the conversation normal. The situation was nevertheless somewhat delicate. Durnford was more than four years senior to Pulleine, who was still only a substantive major, and as a matter of normal military routine the command of the camp had now devolved on the new arrival. Chelmsford's order to Durnford, as penned by Crealock, had not specifically mentioned a change of command, although both Chelmsford and Crealock knew perfectly well that Durnford was the senior. In all probability the point had never crossed the General's mind; he had simply intended to add Durnford's strength to that of the camp, and both men were equally capable of exercising the command until Glyn or Chelmsford returned or the force in camp marched out to join them. The major force in the camp, moreover, was Pulleine's own battalion, which he would of course continue to command even if he were to come under Durnford's direction.

Durnford had no desire to throw his weight around under such circumstances—Engineers were somewhat sensitive to such nuances— but the initiative was plainly his. Since the last report had indicated that the Zulus were retiring, Durnford suggested dismissing the men to finish their interrupted meal, with the proviso that they keep their accouterments on. His own infantry was beginning to arrive, and, worried about the small escort with his wagons, he ordered Lieutenant Vause to take his troop of fifty native horsemen back to implement the guard. Durnford and Pulleine then snatched their own belated breakfasts.

Twenty minutes later they had emerged from the mess tent, and almost immediately Lieutenant James Adendorff rode down from the vedette on the plateau with a message.

Adendorff is a shadowy figure, whose movements during these days are shrouded in obscurity. Little is known about him, except that he was a colonist. He was probably not a landowner, or he would have joined one of the volunteer groups, and he was probably more than a drifter, because someone gave him a commission in the Natal Native Contingent. He seems to have been attached to Lonsdale's 3d Regiment, but no one now remembers in which battalion he was, or in which company he served. There is evidence, however, that he was attached to Hamilton-Browne's battalion, and a plain hint that he may have been one of the officers who quietly decamped to follow Avery and Holcroft back to the camp the preceding evening when Lonsdale moved on to join Dartnell in the presence of the enemy impi. If this were so, he might have had difficulty in explaining his unauthorized departure, and he may have been making amends, in anticipation of trouble when Hamilton-Browne returned, by volunteering for the vedette on the plateau and then offering to take the message to Pulleine. The oral report he delivered, in any event, concerned the movements of the Zulus on the plateau, and he apparently had not seen them himself, because his details were so confused that Pulleine sent another officer of the NNC, Lieutenant Higginson, up to the plateau to clarify the report.

While Durnford and Pulleine were waiting for Higginson to return, Durnford ordered Lieutenants Charles Raw and Roberts to take their troops of Native Horse up to the plateau to scout it thoroughly. Captain Barton, Durnford's general staff officer, was to accompany Roberts and scout to the northwest in search of the Zulu column that had been reported moving in that direction, and Captain George Shepstone was to accompany Raw on a search to the northeast for the two columns that had been reported as retiring that way. As they trotted up the spur, they passed Higginson on his way down, with a written note from the commander of the vedette, which he started to hand to Pulleine. Pulleine ordered him to hand it to Durnford, and Durnford announced that the Zulus were retiring along the plateau to the east and would have to be followed up.

Raw and Roberts had reached the head of the spur and disappeared from sight on the plateau. Firing broke out almost immediately; the Zulus Adendorff had tried to report had evidently come quite close to the vedette before they had turned. Durnford reached a decision.

Chelmsford's orders, transmitted to Pulleine through Crealock, had been to stay in the camp and defend it, and Durnford had inherited these orders with the command of the camp. He nevertheless decided to make a sortie, using the forces he himself had brought, and he plainly felt that if Pulleine remained in the camp with his original force, the spirit of the General's orders would be met. With Chelmsford's reprimand fresh in his mind, Durnford might be expected to think twice before risking a fresh venture into independent command. He *had* thought twice, but the situation had clearly changed since the General had issued his orders. It now called for action.

The camp had noted the sound of Dartnell's distant skirmish, and everyone—Chelmsford himself, Pulleine and now Durnford—was quite convinced that the main Zulu impi lay somewhere along the track ahead. After seeing the fourteen mounted Zulus the preceding afternoon, Chelmsford had intended to scout the Nqutu plateau, but

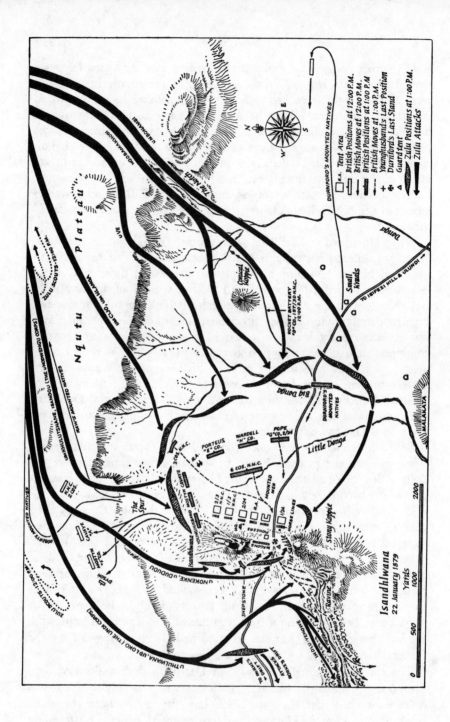

Isandhlwana
22 January 1879

Legend:
- R.A. Tent Area
- British Positions at 12:00 P.M.
- British Moves at 12:00 P.M.
- British Positions at 1:00 P.M
- British Moves at 1:00 P.M.
- Younghusband's Last Position
- Durnford's Last Stand
- Guard Tent
- Zulu Positions at 1:00 P.M.
- Zulu Attacks

Yards
0   500   1000   2000

Map labels:
- Nqutu Plateau
- The North
- UVE
- UMCIJO, UM.HLANA
- Conical Koppie
- Zulu Scouts—12:00 P.M.
- UMKHULUTSHANE, ISANGOU (THE UNOKHENGU CORPS)
- RAW'S MOUNTED NATIVES
- ROBERTS MOUNTED NATIVES
- ZULU SCOUTS—12:00 P.M.
- U THULWANA, UDLOKO (THE UNDI CORPS)
- KAC. 2 GS.
- The Spur
- CAVAYE "A"
- M.BO.CO.
- DYSON
- Isandhlwana
- U NOKENKE UDUDU
- SHEPSTONE
- TO DRIFT
- ROURKES DRIFT
- ATTACKS TOWARDS
- INDLU-YENGE
- TO DRIFTS
- The FUGITIVES ROUTE
- Ravine
- WAGONS
- MASOPHO
- 2/3 N.N.C.
- PORTEUS "E" CO.
- 2 GS. N.N.C.
- R.A.
- WARDELL "H" CO.
- POPE "G" CO. 2/24
- 6 COS. N.N.C.
- MOUNTED MEN
- CAVAYE
- YOUNGHUSBAND
- 2/3, 1/3, 2/24, H.Q., R.A.
- PIONEERS
- HORSE LINES
- Stony Koppie
- Little Donga
- DURNFORD'S MOUNTED NATIVES
- Big Donga
- ROCKET BATTERY "D" CO., IST/30 N.N.C. 12:00 P.M.
- Small Kraals
- TO ISIPEZI HILL & ULUNDI
- DURNFORD'S MOUNTED NATIVES
- MALAKATA
- Donga
- N E W S (compass rose)

he had not gotten around to it, and there was now a large force of Zulus on the plateau apparently retreating to the east and consequently threatening the left rear of the forces the General had with him. Durnford decided to prevent the Zulus on the plateau from rejoining the main impi; Shepstone and Raw with Roberts in support would drive them along the plateau, while he himself with the balance of the mounted natives and the rocket battery would ride out across the plain. If Shepstone managed to drive the Zulus over the edge, he would catch them in the open; if they eluded Shepstone, he would still beat them to the far end of the plateau and could interpose his forces between them and Chelmsford's left rear.

It was an admirable plan, but it was unfortunately based on a totally erroneous conception of the number of Zulus on the plateau. Durnford announced it to Pulleine, and asked for two companies of the 24th Regiment to accompany him. Pulleine demurred; he frankly felt that Durnford was already overstepping Chelmsford's orders, and that the instructions he had received did not warrant stripping the camp even further. Durnford did not insist and prepared to go, and at the last moment Pulleine promised to reinforce him if he became engaged.

Higginson was sent back up to the plateau to find Shepstone, to pass on Durnford's instructions and to tell him to press the attack. The firing had died down, and Raw's troop had apparently lost contact after its first brush.

The camp was in no immediate danger, but the company of the NNC at the head of the spur would clearly be inadequate if the Zulus on the plateau should somehow elude Roberts and Raw. Durnford recommended a stronger outpost, so Pulleine summoned Captain Charles Walter Cavaye and bade him take "A" Company of the 1st/24th up the spur to the rim of the plateau, 1,500 yards from the camp. Cavaye got his men together and marched them up the spur, and when he reached the rim, he extended his company in line to the left of the huddled outpost of the NNC. Remembering the party of Zulus that had been seen retiring to the northwest, he detached a platoon under Lieutenant Edward Dyson and sent him 500 yards farther to the left to watch that direction. Low ridges on the plateau blocked his view. There were no Zulus in sight, Raw's troop was disappearing to the northeast, and Robert's men, finding nothing to the left, were following him.

It was now after eleven o'clock, and Durnford rode out of the camp along the track, crossing the wide donga and setting out across the plain with his force in column behind him. With him rode Lieutenant Henderson with fifty of Sikali's mounted men and Newnham-Davis with the splendid Edendale contingent. Brevet Major Francis Russell followed with the rocket battery, accompanied by Captain Nourse with "D" Company of the 1st Battalion, 3d Regiment, NNC. Captain Stafford was left in camp with "C" Company and most of "E," and the rest of "E" Company, under Lieutenant Wallie Erskine, with Lieutenant Vause and his mounted natives, was still bringing Durnford's wagons up from the Bashee valley.

Durnford kept to the track at first, with the mounted men behind him. Russell, slowed by Nourse's infantry and falling behind, bore to the left to keep closer to the Nqutu plateau and was soon approaching the conical koppie that rose from the plain ahead of the camp. There was no sign of Chelmsford's force in the distance, the plain was empty, and there was no movement along the rim of the plateau to the left.

Higginson in the meantime had located Shepstone and delivered Durnford's instructions. There was no sign of the party of retreating Zulus that had caused the sortie, so Shepstone ordered Raw to spread his men out and search for them to the northeast. Barton took Roberts' troop and began to move to the east along the rim, paralleling Durnford below. The mounted natives fanned out in groups of three and four, searching the hollows and shallow ravines for signs of Zulus.

For a time all was quiet. Then a group of Raw's men saw a few Zulus herding a small group of cattle up a slope some distance ahead. Kicking up their horses, they gave chase. The slope was a full four miles from the head of the spur, and they were soon out of sight of Cavaye's men and of most of their companions. The Zulu herders ran over the crest of the slope and disappeared, and the cattle slowed on the rise and stopped. One of the pursuers cantered up beside them, and in sudden alarm pulled his horse up just in time to prevent a tumble over the edge of a wide, deep ravine that lay just beyond the rise. Then, in astonishment, he stared into the ravine itself. Closely packed and sitting in utter silence, covering the floor of the ravine and perched on the steeply rising sides, stretched as far as the eye could see in both directions, were over 20,000 Zulu warriors. The main impi had finally been located.

As Wood's spies had predicted, it had departed the vicinity of Ulundi on the seventeenth. It had mustered at the great military kraal of Nodwengu, hard by the royal kraal, and there Cetshwayo had given it his final instructions. He knew the initial positions of the columns, but he was ill informed about their subsequent movements and he had no clear plan in mind. He had an army, he had been invaded, and the army was eager to come to grips with the invader, but he was still temporizing and seems to have hoped that a show of his force might somehow free him from the impossible terms of the ultimatum. He accordingly launched the army at the column entering his land from kwaJimu—Rorke's Drift—and, omitting any specific tactical instructions, he simply issued several general strictures. The army was to march slowly, so as not to tire itself, and it was to attack only in daylight. Under no circumstances was it to cross into Natal. He then threw in the extent of his military lore: there would be many civilians with the column, but the soldiers could be identified because they wore red coats.

The impi left Nodwengu late on the seventeenth and bivouacked on the banks of the White Umfolozi that night. There were twelve regiments in all, of varying strength, and some were eked out by fragments of earlier regiments that had long since dwindled away. By Fynney's careful count just before the war, the regiments present totaled 24,400 warriors, but perhaps a tenth of them had not reported for the mustering. They ranged from a handful of *umKhulutshane*, grizzled oldsters in their late sixties who had been formed by Dingane in 1833, now brigaded in the *uNodwengu* corps with the *uDududu* and the *isaNgqu*, to the *uVe*, formed by Cetshwayo in 1875, with 3,500 warriors still in their early twenties.

Many of the regiments were loosely grouped into corps, which took their name from the military kraal at which they had been quartered, or simply from the dominant regiment in the group. The leadership was equally informal. An experienced inDuna led each regiment, and the senior regimental commander guided the corps. A few elder inDunas provided over-all direction, but there was no designated commander in chief. Mnyamana, sixty years old and long famed as Cetshwayo's premier inDuna and in effect the prime minister of Zululand, traveled with the impi, but despite his status he deferred tactically to at least two other inDunas. Mavumengwana, forty years old and originally from the isaNgqu regiment, had been placed in command of the uThulwana by Cetshwayo, who had served in that regiment himself. The uThulwana were now brigaded with the inDlu-yengwe in the *Undi* corps, and Mavumengwana had detached himself from regimental duties to devote his full attention to the direction of the impi. Tshingwayo stemmed from a regiment formed in 1829 and was now in his seventies; too old to fight, he nevertheless marched with the impi and shared the supreme command with Mavumengwana. Dabulamanzi, Cetshwayo's full brother and a roistering fighter now in his dissolute prime at thirty-five, had succeeded to the command of the uThulwana and with it the Undi corps. Other notables were scattered through the impi. Sigcwelegcwele, still breathing fire against the uThulwana, commanded the inGobamakhosi, and Mehlokazulu led a company in his regiment. Usibebu, thirty-five years old, commanded the inDlu-yengwe. He stood high in the king's councils, and had urged submission to the terms of the ultimatum to preserve peace; he had been overridden by the war party and was now loyally prepared to fight.

The impi covered a leisurely nine miles on the eighteenth and a similar distance on the nineteenth, stopping at military kraals both nights. On the twentieth it split into two columns which made long parallel marches, and it spent the night in a hollow just to the north of Isipezi Hill. On the morning of the twenty-first, in fact, when Dartnell and Lonsdale left the camp to reconnoiter, it was exactly where Chelmsford thought it was, but by noon it had moved. The impi would normally have attacked on the twenty-first, but Mavumengwana and Tshingwayo met with Matyana, and found him overbearing, with some idea of disputing the command of the main impi. Partially to get away from him while he was occupied with Dartnell, and also to get closer to the camp under cover, so that they would not have to attack across ten miles of open plain, they moved the main impi up to the Nqutu plateau on the forenoon of the twenty-first, finding the deep ravine running north and south four miles from the head of the spur and bedding the regiments down in the course of the afternoon. The British had come within an ace of discovering the move; Lieutenant Browne had exchanged shots with stragglers from the *uMbonambi* in the rear guard, but assumed his opponents were simply a party of Matyana's retainers, and late in the afternoon Chelmsford himself had seen the mounted Zulu scouts who were screening the movement.

The move had cost an extra day, and there was a new moon due on the afternoon of the twenty-second. The day of a "dead" moon was inauspicious, and the impi, which had already spent a night in the ravine, was prepared to spend the following day and night there as well before giving battle on the morning of the twenty-third. There had been food at the military kraals on the march, and slaughter beeves at Isipezi Hill, but there was no food in the ravine, and at daybreak on the twenty-second detachments from each regiment crept out of their hiding place to scour the small kraals on the plateau for cattle and grain. It was these detachments that had alarmed the camp during breakfast and again after Durnford's arrival, and the cattle which Raw's troop had given chase to were destined for the *umCijo* regiment, which occupied the center of the ravine.

There was a long moment of electric tension as Raw's trooper peered over the lip of the ravine, and the effect on the thousands of Zulus was as profound as it was on the solitary horseman. The impi had been discovered and the fighting would occur on the twenty-second after all; no single warrior needed instructions from an inDuna to realize that. The entire host lumbered to its feet, and the nearest um-

Cijo started to clamber out of the ravine as the horseman, shouting the alarm, turned and fled toward his companions.

The bulk of the umCijo were out of the ravine in short order, milling about in some confusion on the lip, and with them came a small detachment of the uThulwana with Qetuka, the second-in-command of the Undi corps. The rest of the Undi corps and the uDloko regiment, under Dabulamanzi, had been late coming to Isipezi Hill, and it lay in a second ravine a mile behind the large one. Qetuka now took matters into his own hands. Screaming commands, he aligned the umCijo with his detachment of the uThulwana and started them after the retreating horsemen, who were making for Roberts' troop, riding along the edge of the plateau three miles away. The *uNokenke* and the regiments of the uNodwengu corps—the umKhulutshane, the uDududu and the isaNgqu—came boiling out of the ravine to the right of the umCijo and, with hardly a pause to settle their shields on their hands and to heft their assegais, spread their formation and started toward the head of the spur. To the left, the uVe, the inGobamakhosi and the uMbonambi rose and raced forward to take position on the flank of the umCijo.

Mavumengwana and Tshingwayo were resting at the extreme left of the ravine, and they tried to halt the stampede in order to allow a proper formation of the customary squatting semicircle in which the final assignments could be made and from which the classic horns and chest could evolve. They were only able to intercept the Undi corps and the uDloko regiment as Dabulamanzi approached the main ravine; and while they held it back, the direction of the battle passed completely out of their hands.

The ravine lay a good four miles from the head of the spur, and it would be twenty minutes and more before the impi could start its descent to the plain. Shepstone, attracted by the shouting, came up with the fleeing horsemen and saw the entire Zulu host stretching for more than a mile from wing to wing and advancing at the run. There could be no question of what it was, or of the imminent peril to the camp. Several Natal Carbineers from the vedette had ridden forward with Shepstone, and he sent three of them straight for the rim of the plateau with orders to find Durnford on the plain below to warn him. Then, ordering Raw to fall back while hindering the advance as best he could, he took two men and raced for the spur to carry the tidings to the camp himself.

Raw's troop retired slowly, keeping just ahead of the oncoming horde. The men kept up a steady fire, which increased as Roberts' troop joined them, but it was hard to shoot straight from the plunging ponies and it slowed the advance not a whit. Shepstone reached the head of the spur, shouting the alarm to Cavaye and Dyson, and then plunged down the spur and rode for the center of the camp to find Pulleine. He was in his tent and an officer called him out, but Shepstone was utterly out of breath and for the moment could only gasp incoherently and point toward the sound of the firing from the invisible forces on the plateau. While he was gesticulating, Captain Alan Gardner and Major Stuart Smith rode up with the note for Pulleine that Chelmsford had written during his breakfast halt, ordering him to strike the tents and send on the baggage for the men with Dartnell and Glyn. Pulleine read the message aloud, but before he could say anything Shepstone broke in and blurted out his news of the advancing Zulus. Pulleine seemed undecided, but Gardner caught the urgency of Shepstone's warning and urged Pulleine to disregard the order, at least for the moment. Pulleine scribbled a note—"Staff Officer. Heavy firing to the left of our camp. Cannot move camp at present"—and started a horseman across the plain to deliver the note to Chelmsford.

Pulleine then ordered the alarm sounded for the second time that day. All the reports that had reached him during the morning about the Zulus on the plateau had indicated a force of perhaps 400 to 600 Zulus, who had last been reported as retreating. Despite Shepstone's excitement—indeed, perhaps because of it—he seems not to have grasped at once that the full weight of the Zulu army was about to descend on the camp. Nothing else can explain the orders he issued in the next few minutes, or account for those he failed to issue.

Chelmsford had left the camp without qualms, and even before Durnford's arrival there had been an adequate force at hand to beat off any attack, providing that force were properly deployed. The single safe formation would have been a compact mass of troops with the infantry sheltering the useless NNC and the casuals and presenting a solid array of leveled rifles to the Zulu attack. There was room for such a formation behind the wagons and the horse lines, backed against the steep flank of the mountain. It would have been impervious to any onslaught that might have been mounted against its three open sides as long as ammunition lasted, and there were 500,000 rounds in camp. Durnford, however, had effectively removed his entire force from the camp and had furthermore suggested that an Imperial company be posted at the head of the spur. Pulleine still had a quarter of an hour of grace, but instead of retracting "A" Company and grouping the camp's defenders into a tight mass on favorable ground, he proceeded to compound the error by reinforcing Cavaye and scattering his own force still further.

The Zulus were not yet in sight from the camp. All that could be seen was "A" Company firing industriously at invisible targets on the plateau, and the NNC company beside it, already beginning to edge down the spur. Raw's men had reached the head of the spur, and they stood to join their fire to Cavaye's. The men in the camp had formed on their parades, and Pulleine now ordered Captain William Eccles Mostyn to take "F" Company of the 1st/24th to Cavaye's support. Mostyn's company, breathing hard after its fast climb up the spur, fell in between Cavaye and Dyson's platoon. There was no need for orders; the Zulu host was stretched out across the plateau a half-mile away and was coming straight for the rim and the spur. Two regiments, the uNokenke and the uDududu of the uNodwengu corps, had detached themselves from the extreme right of the Zulu line and were sweeping across the front of the infantry 600 yards away, paying no heed to the fire directed at them and heading for the valley at the western end of the plateau that gave access to the back of Isandhlwana. Mostyn realized at once that he could not stem the attack, and prepared to bring the two companies down the spur, contesting the right of way as best he could. The outpost of the NNC had already fled to join the other Natal Kaffirs in the camp below.

There was still no sense of alarm in the camp. Brickhill had overheard Shepstone's conversation with Pulleine and Gardner, and, slightly uneasy, took the precaution of saddling his horse. He then decided to look for a rifle but was unable to find one, so he rode back through the tents and posted himself on the rising ground at the foot of the mountain, where he would have a good view of events. Captain Edward Essex, 75th Regiment, was attached to the Central Column for transport duties. He had little to do until the wagons left to take the baggage to the new camp, and he had been trying to get a letter written all morning. As soon as the first "Fall Out" sounded, he had returned to his tent, but after a while a sergeant came in to tell him that Cavaye's company was firing at something. Essex still had his binoculars slung over his shoulder and he stepped out of his tent to inspect the head of the spur. He did not buckle on his sword, but he did pick up his revolver. He left the unfinished letter on his camp desk. Pope had also taken advantage of the break to bring a somewhat disjointed journal up to date. When the alarm sounded, he too left his writing in his tent and hurried out to join Godwin-Austen on his way to "G" Company on the extreme right of the parade ground. Both men wore monocles, the only officers of the 2nd Warwickshire to do so, and men nodded and smiled at them as they passed. Charlie Pope was gay and likable, and people remembered him wherever the 24th Regiment had traveled.

Gardner for some reason was not satisfied with Pulleine's note; perhaps he thought it too curt. He penned a second one to amplify it:

Heavy firing to the left of camp. Shepstone has come in for reinforcements and reports that the Zulus are falling back. The whole force at camp turned out and fighting about one mile to left flank.

It was a peculiar note. Like Pulleine's, it failed to specify that the main impi had been found, and it is hard to guess where Gardner had gotten the idea that the Zulus were retiring. He may have read too much into the fact that Mostyn and Cavaye were still standing firm, but the wording made little difference in any event. The note was delivered to Crealock or Gossett after Chelmsford had started back but before he reached Hamilton-Browne, and only a verbal résumé was given the General. It is a pity that no one recorded the name of the messenger; he must have had an exciting ride.

The firing from the ridge grew heavier and then stopped. Mostyn and Cavaye had broken off and were retiring on the camp in good order, with the NNC company that had been on outpost duty loping down the spur ahead of them in disarray. Roberts and Raw remained behind for a few moments to pour a last volley or two into the advancing impi. As the two companies reached the flat foot of the spur at the northern end of the camp, Pulleine pulled Captain Reginald Younghusband out of the line on the parade ground and sent him with "C" Company across the corner of the camp to reinforce Mostyn and Cavaye. Younghusband fell in to the left of Dyson, and the three companies came to a halt and aligned themselves 200 yards beyond the northern end of the camp. They covered a front of 600 yards, facing back up the spur down which they had just retreated.

Since Pulleine was now the camp commander, Captain William Degacher succeeded to the command of the 1st/24th, and he turned command of his "E" Company over to Lieutenant Francis Pender Porteous, who with Captain Wardell's "H" Company and Charlie Pope with "G" Company of the 2nd/24th was still on the parade ground 800 yards in front of the tents, with wide gaps left by the absent companies. Pope's right rested on the track, 600 yards behind the wide donga, and Porteous's left was a thousand yards to the north, just past the end of the tents, with a full 300 yards between his left flank and the right of Cavaye's company in the line across the north of the camp. The three companies in front of the camp had evened the gaps; each covered a front of 200 yards with another 200 yards between the companies. The men were arrayed in two lines, several yards apart, with four yards between each man and the rear rank men aligned with the interstices. Pulleine had not retracted the companies. They were stretched perilously thin, with less than 600 men to cover almost a mile of frontage, and Pulleine was about to defend a large amount of unnecessary real estate.

There was a mound a few feet high behind Porteous's left rear, in the gap between his company and Cavaye's, and Stuart Smith took Curling and his two guns to the rise, with a clear field of fire against the front of the Nqutu escarpment.

Neither the Natal Kaffirs nor the mounted volunteers were expected to stand in the line in a defensive fight. The Natal Kaffirs had little firepower and were of dubious reliability, and the mounted men were armed only with carbines without bayonets and were intended only to scout or to pursue a beaten foe. Both groups had been placed in sheltered positions. The mounted men were bunched in the vicinity of the track, 500 yards behind Pope and just in front of the wagon park on the saddle. Six companies of the NNC—four of Lonsdale's 3d Regiment and "C" and "E" Companies of Durnford's 1st—were squatting 300 yards behind Wardell, in the center of the line before the camp. Two NNC companies, more by happenstance than by design, had gotten into an awkward, exposed position. One of Lonsdale's companies had spent the morning on outpost duty, 700 yards to the left front of the camp. It had stayed where it was during the alarms, and when the rest of the troops fell in, it found itself about 200 yards in front of the wide gap between Cavaye and Porteous, inadvertently forming the knuckle between the line of companies to the north of the camp and that stretched across its front. The NNC company that had been on outpost duty at the head of the spur, retreating in a mob beside Cavaye and Mostyn, had joined this group, and their officers had arranged them in a curved line, with their right facing the front of the camp and their left facing back up the spur. Either because they closed the gap in the knuckle and were also covered by the artillery just behind them, or simply because he forgot them, Pulleine ignored them and left them where they were.

Over a hundred men were still milling about in the tents and the wagon park—staff orderlies, bandsmen, grooms and a number of civilian wagon conductors. Bloomfield and Pullen were back in their wagons, the drummer boys at hand, and Surgeon Peter Shepard and his civilian assistant had parked their wagon near the staff tents and were preparing to receive casualties. It was a quarter past noon, and no Zulus were in sight.

Far out across the plain, Durnford and his horsemen had already passed the conical koppie. A slight rise in the plain hid its base, and out of his sight, but still visible from the camp, Russell was just starting to pass between the koppie and the Nqùtu escarpment with his rocket battery and Nourse's escorting Natal Kaffirs. A distant shout from the rim of the plateau attracted Durnford's attention. Trooper Whitelaw of the Natal Carbineers was seen plunging down the steep descent and galloping across the plain toward them. Whitelaw had no sooner delivered Shepstone's warning to Durnford than a sudden shout from his men made the colonel lift his eyes again to the rim of the plateau. For a distance of almost two miles, stretching back to the spur and extending far beyond his own position, the heights were black with Zulus, and, even as he watched, the mass cascaded over the rim and began to pour down onto the plain.

Their numbers seemed endless. To his right, the inGobamakhosi and the uMbonambi reached the level ground and raced across it, wheeling toward the camp as they came. Their stragglers were still dropping from the heights as the fresh mass of the uVe reached the edge and spilled over. To Durnford's left, the umCijo and the *umHlanga* were descending by the conical koppie, boiling down the ravine that notched the rim, and racing around both flanks of the koppie. As the regiments to his left wheeled and began to fan out across the plain, they threatened to cut him off from the camp, and Durnford turned his command and started back, searching for the rocket battery as he went.

He found the remains of it as he passed the base of the conical koppie. Shepstone's other messengers had descended by the ravine and found Russell with the battery directly ahead. Not realizing the full import of the message, Russell started toward the plateau to reinforce Shepstone, and the Carbineer who had found him had no sooner started him toward the mouth of the ravine than the umCijo, 2,500 strong, appeared at the head of it and rolled down to inundate him. Captain Nourse, a mile behind with "D" Company of the 1st Regiment, NNC, made good his escape, bringing his men back to the camp on the run to join the Natal Kaffirs posted at the knuckle, but Russell was caught in the open with his nine men and their mules. He halted and started to set out his tubes, but a ragged volley from the fringes of the onrushing impi stampeded the mules, and two of them hopped on top of a large boulder and would not come down. The men managed to erect one of the tubes, and Russell lit off one rocket, which sizzled away to explode harmlessly against the side of the ravine, and then the horde rolled over the battery. Hardly pausing in their stride, the warriors slashed and stabbed at the mules and the nine dismounted men as they passed, trampling the bodies as they raced on. Russell and six of his men died on the spot; three wounded privates, Grant, Trainer and Johnston, miraculously survived. When all the Zulus had finally passed, they crept across the plain and down through the Malakatas, crossed the Buffalo River and made their way to Helpmakaar.

Durnford had no time to stop. The umCijo and the umHlanga were already between his mounted men and the left of the camp, while farther out across the plain the inGobamakhosi and the uMbonambi, with the uVe behind them, extended across the track and beyond the right of the camp. Durnford formed his men into lines, each firing a volley and then passing through the ranks of the next line as the men reloaded. He was firing into the thick of the inGobamakhosi, fighting the full weight of the left Zulu horn, while the uMbonambi at the extreme tip edged still farther to their left and threatened to outflank him. When he reached the wide donga, he decided to make a stand.

The donga was three or four feet deep and twenty yards across, with a sharp lip facing the plain. The native horsemen dismounted and manned the lip, telling off horseholders to keep their mounts in the shelter of the donga. Crouched in their shelter, Henderson's troop and Newnham-Davis with the Edendale contingent opened a steady aimed fire that first slowed and then halted the left Zulu horn. The warriors squatted and then flung themselves down, and those that carried firearms crept forward to open a heavy but inaccurate fire against the heads peering over the lip ahead.

Durnford strode up and down the donga, his tall body exposed and his withered left arm thrust into the pocket he had sewn in the front of his tunic. He was laughing and praising his men and urging on their fire; one or two tried to pull him down to a more sheltered position, but he eluded their grasp. When the awkward Westley-Richards breeches jammed, the men brought him their pieces, and, holding the gun between his knees, he would clear the jam with his good hand. After a time Captain Bradstreet of the Newcastle Mounted Rifles rode up with thirty of the mounted men posted in front of the saddle, and joined the men holding the donga.

The firing along the entire perimeter of the camp was general by now. The Zulus were all off the plateau, united in a massive line that stretched across the spur, around the 300 Natal Kaffirs at the knuckle and down the front of the camp. The uDududu and the uNokenke had circled far beyond the left of the British line and were advancing through the valley behind Isandhlwana to attack the rear of the saddle, their flank still harried by a few mounted natives from Raw's and Roberts' troops who had stuck with the Zulus when Mostyn brought the three Imperial companies down from the spur. The uVe had been the last regiment to leave the plateau, and was advancing behind the main line, and a few men from the uMbonambi were beginning to slip across the donga far below Durnford, in the hope of outflanking him. The impi was still advancing, but its pace had slowed considerably; here and there a stretch of its frontage had been brought to a halt, and the wave thickened as the warriors in the rear pressed forward. The Zulus had already been running for four and five miles since they left the plateau, and as they closed with the defenders, the artillery and the volleys of rifle fire began to exact a stinging toll.

Back by the ravine in which the impi had bivouacked, Mavumengwana and Tshingwayo had held the Undi corps and the uDloko regiment until they had seen that the rest of the impi could not be stopped. By then it was too late to send the troops they were holding after the main force, so they ordered Dabulamanzi to take these regiments to the western end of the plateau, there swinging to the south and dropping onto the track of Rorke's Drift a mile behind Isandhlwana, to cut off the retreat of any forces that fled across the saddle. The Undi corps and the uDloko set out, passing far to the north of the head of the spur before wheeling left, and playing no part in the battle. When they finally reached the track, they spread out across it for several hundred yards on either side, 5,000 strong, and squatted down to watch.

The battle around the camp was stabilizing. To the north of the tents, Younghusband, Mostyn and Cavaye were directing the massed fire of their three companies into the ranks of the umKhulutshane and the isaNgqu, who had come down the spur and advanced to within two and three hundred yards of the British lines. Within that distance, the fire was too heavy to stand and live, and the warriors had thrown themselves down, creeping and crawling forward between the volleys.

The umCijo were advancing against the knuckle, where the fire was thinner. The 300 Natal Kaffirs had less than thirty rifles amongst them, and they soon expended the five rounds of ammunition they had been issued. The thirty Europeans with them were still firing with carbines and revolvers, and they were backed by about fifty men of the Royal Artillery, who were not actually serving the two guns. The fieldpieces were firing steadily, but doing remarkably little damage; the Zulus had noted the gunners springing back before the lanyards were pulled and threw themselves down at the signal, screaming "*uMoya!* (Air!)" as the shells whistled over their heads. The pressure on the knuckle was heavy, and the Natal Kaffirs were growing restless as the Zulus crept closer.

Porteus, Wardell and Pope were engaged with the umHlanga and the uVe, and the right of Pope's company was supporting Durnford by a long-range fire into the ranks of the stalled inGobamakhosi. The British line in front of the camp was stretched to cover a frontage almost twice as long as that to the north of the camp, and the Zulus had crept closer before the galling fire stopped them. Scores of Zulus dropped at each volley, slain outright or, sorely wounded, creeping under the pathetic shelter of their shields in their last extremity. A

Boer at Blood River forty years before had likened the bodies behind a Zulu charge to ripe pumpkins; Brickhill, farther away, thought of peppercorns as he gazed at the hundreds of Zulus who littered the plain behind the impi.

This was the battle that everyone had wanted, with the savage Zulu power immolating itself on the Imperial volley fire. It was the battle Chelmsford had expected, and it was being fought by officers and men whose organization and training and years of service had been pointed toward just such a fight. Captain Essex, with no assigned post, had joined his friend Cavaye, and he was surprised to note how relaxed the men in the ranks were, despite the climactic tension of the battle. Loading as fast as they could and firing into the dense black masses that pressed in on them, the men were laughing and chatting, and obviously thought they were giving the Zulus an awful hammering.

For a short space of time the battle was static. The firing reached a crescendo, and the immense black wave that lapped around the British line was stopped, with the warriors in their pain and courage murmuring like a gigantic swarm of disturbed bees. Cochrane noted a group of the inGobamakhosi sheltering behind a solitary hut off the track behind the regiment, and Curling limbered up one of the guns and took it to the right to loose a few rounds over the men in the donga. A direct hit reduced the hut to hurtling bodies and wisps of smoking thatch, and Curling brought the gun back to its mate on the knoll. As he passed along the rear of the line before the camp, he noticed that Natal Kaffirs in twos and threes were beginning to slip away from the six companies posted behind Wardell, trotting back through the camp and making for the saddle.

The battle was still going well, but a faint flicker of uneasiness passed over one or two officers. Durnford was one of the first to feel it. His men were firing as steadily as ever, and the inGobamakhosi had gotten no closer, but here and there a man in the line along the lip of the donga had stopped firing and was nudging his neighbor, or had slipped back to search the pockets of the few men who had been killed by head shots and had fallen back into the donga. Others had simply turned and were watching him expectantly. The Natal Native Horse was running out of cartridges.

Several companies of Imperial infantry were low on ammunition as well. Cavaye's men had marched out of the camp with full accouterments and had reached the head of the spur with seventy rounds apiece. The bugle had brought the rest of the men tumbling out of their tents and away from their lunches half-clad, and while they had all been wearing their belts with forty rounds in the pouches, few had brought their haversacks with the extra two packets and some had taken off their expense pouches with the loose ten rounds. The bulk of the men, in other words, had started the fight with only forty or fifty rounds, and Cavaye had now been firing for close to an hour and the rest of the companies for thirty minutes and more.

The company officers were quite aware of this situation, although it hardly worried them. The battalion quartermasters were stationed by the wagons with the regimental reserve—thirty additional rounds for every man—and another 480,000 rounds were packed into wagons parked somewhere on the saddle. Long before the pouches were empty they had sent their messengers, drummer boys and bandsmen, back to the wagons to bring fresh packets up to the firing line.

The tension was considerably higher around the two battalion ammunition wagons than it was on the line. Quartermaster James Pullen was in the 1st Battalion wagon in the regimental transport behind the 1st Battalion camp, and the 1st Battalion camp was at the extreme right of the tent area in front of the stony koppie, south of the track and more than 1,000 yards from any of the five 1st Battalion companies in the firing line. Cavaye's "A" Company, in fact, at the right of the line across the north of the camp, was more than 1,800 yards away. Quartermaster Edward Bloomfield was behind the 2nd Battalion camp in the center of the tent area; he was only responsible for Pope's "G" Company, and "G" Company was 1,100 yards away.

The regimental reserve for each battalion was packed in the heavy wooden ammunition boxes, and the lid of each crate was held down by two copper bands, each fastened with nine large screws. Pullen and Bloomfield had screwdrivers and they undoubtedly started to loosen the screws on at least one of the crates early in the fight, so as to be ready as soon as a request came from the firing line. Six screws had to be removed to raise a lid, and the screws were frequently rusted into the wood and hard to start. Neither man would have been likely to open more than one box at a time; they were careful, methodical soldiers, who by the light of the times had been promoted to a rank considerably higher than their social origins justified. Cartridges were more than ammunition to them, since each and every one would have to be accounted for as expended after the fight. Even the boxes were accountable.

The requests started to come in, and the two quartermasters began to dole out the packets, eying the drummer boys fiercely to make sure they were at the right wagon. Bloomfield was besieged by runners from the line to the north of the camp, who naturally stopped at his wagon because it was the closer, but he sent them all on to Pullen, another 500 yards to the south, because the companies to the north of the camp all belonged to the 1st Battalion. Durnford had sent a few mounted natives back for ammunition almost as soon as he had reached the donga, but their pantomimed requests were refused by both quartermasters. Let the Natal Native Horse draw ammunition from its own regimental reserve; Durnford had surely brought it with him. Since the natives had no idea where the wagons Erskine and Vause had escorted into the camp after the troops had fallen in might be, they finally returned to Durnford empty-handed. Durnford then sent Henderson back, and Henderson had no more luck than his natives had had.

Lieutenant Smith-Dorrien, acutely aware of the situation on the firing line, collected a few camp casuals, grooms and batmen, hunted out the wagon with the field reserve for the 1st Battalion and set out to open several of the crates. There were no extra screwdrivers, and it was slow work. Chelmsford had requisitioned spare ones for this very purpose, but the order was lost somewhere in Natal. The men hacked at the copper bands with axes or thrust bayonets under them and attempted to snap them or prize them up over the screwheads. Smith-Dorrien finally worried one of the boxes open and began to thrust handfuls of the precious packets into the helmets and haversacks that were eagerly held up to him. Bloomfield, working in the regimental reserve wagon nearby, looked up and saw him. He was horrified. "For heaven's sake don't take that, man," he yelled, "for it belongs to our battalion!" Smith-Dorrien snarled back, "Hang it all, you don't want a requisition now, do you?" and continued to dole out the packets.

A trickle was starting out to the companies, but it was not enough. More and more men were coming back in desperation, searching the wagons until they found the familiar crates and pounding the boxes apart with stones when they found them. The fire in the line began to slacken.

Durnford could do nothing. The mounted men had no proper bayonets, only a fitting at the end of the short carbines to which a hunting knife could be attached. The Edendale contingent was still husbanding a few rounds, but the stand in the donga was over. Durnford issued his orders, and the men deserted the lip, found their horses in the donga, and cantered back along the track past Pope's right flank to join the rest of the mounted men in the mouth of the saddle.

The inGobamakhosi and the uMbonambi, freed of the terrible fire from the donga, rose and started forward. Pope's company, its flank now fully exposed, edged back and wheeled to face them. Despite the trickle of ammunition, the fire was slackening everywhere, and the warriors still stretched in the grass around the camp noted the change. Then a great voice cried out in Zulu from the thick of the umCijo regiment. Cetshwayo had many praise names, and, making use of a well-known one earned at 'Ndondakusuka, an unknown warrior shouted, "The 'Little Branch of Leaves That Extinguished the Fire' gave no such order as this!" Thousands of Zulus heard him and took fresh heart. They leaped to their feet and charged forward. The impi had been quiet until now, emitting only a steady humming murmur, but the warriors now stamped their feet and rattled their assegais against their shields, shouting the war cry that had been associated with their king ever since his youth: "uSuthu! uSuthu!"

The sight and the sound were too much for the quavering Natal Kaffirs at the knuckle. They were isolated ahead of the lines, and the fear of the sharp assegais brandished by the advancing warriors was bred in their bones. The umCijo were upon them, and to stay was death. They rose as one man, cast aside their weapons, and fled through the gap between Cavaye and Porteus. A few of their officers tried to stem them, but they were swept aside, and the bulk of the Europeans with them bolted as well. All discipline gone, the disorganized mob streamed back through the tents, sucking the rest of the Natal Kaffirs posted behind Wardell into their wake, making for the saddle and the safety of the track back to Natal.

Stuart Smith saw what was coming and started to limber up. The guns were as precious to the artillery as the Colours were to the infantry, and a captured gun was a disgrace even when the crew died defending it. He started his teams back across the front of the camp, and the fleeing Natal Kaffirs flung themselves on the harnesses and limbers, clinging to the sides like flies while the gunners tried to beat them off. A handful of men from the battery tried to cover the retreat and to plug the gap.

It was hopeless. The Natal Kaffirs had left a hole in the knuckle 300 yards across, and the umCijo came pouring into the gap, with the isaNgqu and the umHlanga behind. Thousands of howling Zulus rushed in, and first Cavaye's company and then Mostyn's was taken in the rear. The men had been formed in two ranks, occupied with the fight on their immediate front and barely aware of the defection of the Natal Kaffirs. Suddenly hundreds of maddened Zulus flung themselves on their backs, and before they could fix bayonets, before many of them could even turn, it was over. Their fire stopped abruptly, and the umKhulutshane in front rose and charged as the umCijo crashed into their rear. There was a brief flurry, and "A" and "F" Companies were blotted out; not a man survived. Cavaye and Mostyn were dead; so were Dyson, and Hamilton-Browne's friends, Anstey and Daly.

On the extreme left of the line, Younghusband with "C" Company was given a moment's grace, and he made the most of it. He got his bayonets fixed and pulled his men straight back, well clear of the slaughter on his right. Behind the tents and the wagons his flank was protected, and with the umKhulutshane and great numbers of the isaNgqu and the umCijo pressing him in front, he retired across the back of the camp, forced up on the slopes of the mountain and rising along a rough ledge until he came to rest on a rocky platform at the southern end of the mountain, a hundred feet over the saddle. His men were almost out of ammunition, and had contested every foot of the way with bayonet and clubbed rifle. Sixty of them reached the platform, and they fought back to back in savage desperation until the last of them had been overwhelmed. A scant few, forced off the platform, died in the turmoil below.

The three companies along the front of the camp lasted little longer. Porteus with "E" Company caught the full brunt of the uVe charging his front, and the umHlanga pouring through the gap carried his left flank away in a swirl of individual redcoats, each the center of a knot of struggling black warriors. Wardell had stretched "H" Company as thin as he dared to cover the front between Porteous and Pope, and the men in his two ranks were almost six yards from their comrades on either hand. His cartridges were gone and his line had no weight. The charge of the uVe burst through the ranks and the momentum carried the fight all the way back to the tents, leaving all of "H" Company dead and scattered between the camp and and the parade ground below.

Pope's "G" Company had already refused its right flank to face the uMbonambi, and his bugler sounded "Retire" as the inGobamakhosi started forward. The men were surrounded long before they could reach the broad flat in the mouth of the saddle, and Zulus who had come through the gap or broken off from the slaughter of Porteous and Wardell caught them in the rear as the advancing regiments overtook them. The men battled their way back along the track, joined by a few survivors from Wardell's right. They died in twos and threes and sixes along the track, and the broken debris of a platoon or so, still led by Charlie Pope and Godwin-Austen, came to a halt in front of the saddle. Within twenty minutes of the time the Natal Kaffirs rose and fled, the entire perimeter was obliterated, and the fight surged into the camp and the saddle.

All organized resistance had ceased, but four or five hundred men in the camp were still alive and fighting. Durnford had reached the saddle just as the knuckle started to go, and he rode toward the center of the camp to find Pulleine. He never reached him, and when he returned to the saddle, the situation had disintegrated. The Zulus were in the upper camp killing the casuals and the survivors of the defense perimeter, and a great mass of refugees was streaming down through the tents and over the saddle. There were no organized units left, only groups of mounted volunteers and a few mounted natives from Henderson's troop, a scattering of men from Pope's company, and camp casuals who had grabbed a gun and joined the fighters. The Edendale contingent had reached the saddle together but had gotten separated from Newnham-Davis, and a few of the men fanned out to search for ammunition. One of them, English-speaking, came across a twelve-year-old drummer boy, who refused to give him any of the cartridges in the wagon that belonged to his battalion. When the native urged the lad to come away with him, since the battle was clearly lost, the boy also refused to leave the wagon he had been set to guard. With Durnford momentarily gone, and unable to locate Newnham-Davis, the Edendale contingent then crossed the saddle and started to retreat under the command of the native sergeant major, Simeon Kambula.

When Durnford returned, he found the uMbonambi and the inGobamakhosi pressing into the mouth of the saddle, and the uNokenke and the uDududu approaching from the back of the mountain. Detachments of the regiments that had come down the back of Isandhlwana had broken off to attack Younghusband before he was forced to retreat, and the rest of them had been slowed by the mounted natives from the plateau, who had stayed with them during their advance. The saddle was still open, and Durnford saw that if he could hold the horns apart for a space, the survivors in the camp might still find safety. He sent a small party to the western flank of the mountain, north of the track, and the men flung themselves down behind boulders to hold back the extremity of the right horn. George Shepstone, who had come down the back of the mountain, took command, and the men continued to fire until their ammunition was gone and the Zulus scrambled in amongst the boulders to finish them off.

Durnford joined the mounted men in front of the saddle to make a stand. He was on rising ground in front of the wagon park, and the men with him, mostly armed with carbines, still had ammunition. They formed a tight circle shoulder to shoulder and began to fire, and Pope's survivors and such casuals as could muster the courage to stay and fight began to struggle toward him. The inGobamakhosi had been mauled by the stand in the donga and had suffered further loss at Pope's hands, and they fell back; but the uMbonambi were still fresh and pressed forward. Durnford had perhaps seventy men with him and while their ammunition lasted, they volleyed into the close-packed ranks that beset them. Mehlokazulu was there with the inGobamakhosi, and he later remembered the tall figure that cried "Fire!" time and again, and the Zulus who dropped as the volleys crashed out. Then the response to the cry of "Fire!" dwindled and died in a spatter of isolated shots, and there was nothing left but the weapons in hand—sword and bayonet, hunting knife and clubbed carbine. The men were still defiant, and the Zulus who sought to close with them died on the bayonets or were clubbed to the ground, but the warriors flung assegais and fired at them until only a few were left. They died in a final charge, with the Zulus hurling their own dead at the bayonets to pull them down and the Europeans fighting with knives and snatched assegais or flinging themselves barehanded on a last opponent before they fell.

The last of the Imperial infantry died a short distance away. They fell one by one, until only Charlie Pope and Godwin-Austen were left, and a half-dozen Zulus rushed forward to finish them. Godwin-Austen was shot through the body, but Pope had saved a few rounds and blazed away at the foremost Zulu, an inDuna from the inGobamakhosi. The shots grazed his neck and his side and wounded him in the leg, but he flung his assegai, and Pope staggered back with the blade sunk in his body. Dropping his revolver, he tried feebly to pluck it out, but the inDuna sprang forward and pressed it home. The warriors, inspecting the bodies, noticed that both men were still wearing their monocles.

Men still survived among the tents and wagons, and as the looting started, groups of Zulus flushed them out and finished them off. Lieutenant Milne's servant, a sailor, put his back to a wagon and defended himself with his cutlass until an assegai pinned him to the wheel. A drummer boy, perhaps he who had spurned the Edendale man's offer, was hanged by his heels to the back of a wagon and had his throat slit. Bloomfield was shot through the head and died over his ammunition boxes, but Pullen, south of the track, jumped to the ground, rallied a few casuals who had not won through to Durnford, and died by the stony koppie trying to push back the extreme tip of the uMbonambi horn.

Captain Younghusband was one of the last to die. When "C" Company's ammunition was gone, he had shaken hands with all his men and stayed to the end of the fight on the rocky platform over the wagon park. He had finally been forced over the edge with three survivors, and the four of them found some cartridges, clambered into an empty wagon, and turned it into a rifle pit. They were rushed, and the three men were killed in the wagon bed, but Younghusband, minus his tunic, got away again and climbed into still another wagon. He was all alone, and the Zulus in his vicinity had stopped fighting, and when he opened fire, they scurried back hastily. He kept firing until all his cartridges were gone, and a few Zulus then tried to close with him. He bayoneted every warrior that laid a hand on the wagon, and he lasted for a long time until a Zulu finally shot him.

Perhaps 400 men, led by the Natal Kaffirs, had gotten over the saddle while Shepstone in the rear and Durnford in front had held the Zulu horns apart. There were ethical considerations involved in leaving a battlefield. No Imperial officer would dream of going while a man for whom he was responsible was still alive, nor would professional soldiers desert their comrades in the ranks. Not a single man from the six Imperial infantry companies had tried to leave the camp; 581 of them had died with 21 of their officers. There came a point, however, when a cause was lost and gallantry could do no more, and a man who had discharged his responsibilities might then seek safety in flight. There was even a term to cover such an eventuality—*sauve qui peut*— and such a point had obviously been reached when the defense collapsed. No such nuances troubled the Europeans in the NNC, or the various casuals and civilians scattered through the camp, but they were very much to the fore in a few professional minds.

Pulleine, for example, made no effort to seek safety on his horse. He witnessed the destruction of the five companies of his battalion from a command post in front of the center of the camp, and when the Zulus began to pour into the tent area, he turned and rode south across the track, behind Durnford and the mounted men, and up to the guard tent of the 1st Battalion. Adjutant Lieutenant Teignmouth Melvill rode with him. Pulleine dismounted and entered the tent. He emerged a moment later with the cased Queen's Colour of the 1st Battalion, gave it to Melvill, and ordered him to take it to a place of safety. The Regimental Colour was with "D" Company at Helpmakaar, and both Colours of the 2nd Battalion were in Glyn's guard tent in the center of the camp, in the thick of the fighting that was raging through the tents. Melvill placed the staff across his saddlebow, saluted, wheeled his horse and plunged into the stream of refugees who were fleeing the camp. Pulleine re-entered his tent, sat down at his field desk, took up a pen and began to write. It may have been a last note for his family—a wife, a son and two daughters. It was more likely a hurried report of the camp's last moments for Chelmsford, but whatever it may have been it was never finished. He was still writing when a Zulu burst into the tent. Pulleine put down his pen and picked up the revolver he had placed on the desk. He fired, wounding the Zulu in the neck, but the man lunged over the desk and sank a stabbing assegai into his chest.

The first refugees to cross the saddle were shocked to see the Undi corps astride the track to Rorke's Drift, barring all flight in that direction. The valley to the north of the track was swarming with uNokenke and uDududu, still engaged with Shepstone and his men, and the only route open was to the south, where the Buffalo River lay three and a half miles away, beyond a nightmare of gullies and broken ground. There was no track, and fleeing men plunged off the saddle and down a steep slope strewn with jagged boulders to the edge of a small stream that had cut a deep gorge in its passage. The stream ran west for a twisting mile before it fell into the marshy bed of the Manzamnyama, a small tributary of the Buffalo, and the dense growth on either bank of the gorge made the passage almost impassable for a horse. Beyond the Manzamnyama the route led over the open shoulder of a hill, dropped down a steep slope on the far side, and was then blocked from the banks of the Buffalo by a final ridge. There was more thick shrubbery growing on the high bank of the river, and the bed, forty yards wide and filled with rocks, was in full flood and brimming over.

The first mass of Natal Kaffirs to start down the slope attracted the attention of the Zulus. The leading wave of the uNokenke and the uDududu followed them down from the saddle, and Dabulamanzi observed the flight and sent the inDlu-yengwe down from the Undi corps to cut into the flight as it reached the Manzamnyama. The Natal Kaffirs were for the most part weaponless and had torn off the red headbands that marked them as invaders. Some tried to work their way back to the Malakatas, hoping for shelter in the small kraals that dotted the area, while others furtively tried to mix with the Zulus and attacked fleeing Europeans. Most of them were discovered and killed, as were the majority of those who reached the river, where the inDlu-yengwe were waiting. By the time the Europeans started to cross the saddle, the bulk of the Natal Kaffirs were dead and hundreds of Zulus were swarming like hornets all the way from the camp to the river.

The limbered guns got through the camp and over the track, losing half the gunners and the fugitives clinging to the horses on the way. Stuart Smith and Curling rode ahead, clearing a path with flashing sabers. The guns started down the slope, slamming and jolting over the rocks and throwing the limbermen from their seats, and when they reached the edge of the gorge they were moving too fast to be stopped. The guns pushed the harnessed horses over the rim and then upset and caught in the shrubbery, and the Zulus speared the horses as they hung down the bank in their traces. Stuart Smith and Curling rode on, with the major nursing an assegai thrust in his arm.

Brickhill was still in the camp when the line dissolved. He met a civilian conductor named Dubois, who was searching for a horse, and decided to leave. He paused on the saddle, and briefly considered joining the group that Pullen was forming, but he saw that the attempt was hopeless and joined the stream of refugees. A riderless horse passed his mount, and he leaned forward to snatch the bridle. A soldier passed him afoot on the slope and Brickhill gave him his spare horse, but the man was shot even as he tried to mount. The slope was alive with Zulus, and Brickhill spurred on to reach the trees by the gorge. Band Sergeant Gamble of the 1st Battalion was stumbling through the boulders, and he begged Brickhill, "For God's sake, give us a lift!" To halt was sheer suicide, and Brickhill replied, "My dear fellow, it's a case of life or death with me," and rode on. A young Zulu sprang up in his path and poised an assegai, then quailed and fled when a burly Natal Kaffir stepped out from behind Brickhill's horse.

Most of the men attempting to flee on foot were killed by the Zulus infesting the rocky slope, but the mounted men reached the edge of the gorge and began to pick their way in single file through the thick growth, looking for a place to cross. A man put his horse at the chasm and jumped, and was crushed to death on the rocks twelve feet below when the horse tripped and fell on him. The file reached a low place in the bank and somehow or other scrambled across, to start down the far side. They passed one of the guns, still caught in the trees, with the dead horses hanging in the ravine. Brickhill found himself behind Melvill, who was still clutching the unwieldy Colour to his saddlebow. The case was half off, the frayed green silk exposed. "Have you seen anything of my sword back there?" he asked Brickhill, who replied that he had not.

The path dipped sharply again, and the line halted as the men edged over one by one. A few men had dismounted to lead their horses down, holding up the line, and Coghill, riding behind, shouted out that this was no place to lead a horse. One of the men called back that it was no place to be riding, either, and slid down the bank. Melvill's horse shot under a tree and a low branch almost unseated him; Brickhill was still behind him and the backlash cost him his coat.

The interpreter had to dismount in the swamps by the Manzamnyama to lead his horse across, and he dropped his spectacles in the marsh. There was no time to search for them, for the valley was swarming with the inDlu-yengwe, and he remounted to cross the shoulder of the hill, finally reaching the flooded river. The rushing waters were dotted with struggling horses and men, all sweeping downstream and rearing out of the torrent in bursts of foam as they struck the submerged rocks. The bank was crowded with men searching for a spot to enter the river; numbers of inDlu-yengwe had reached the bank as well and more were arriving every minute. They were darting in and out of the refugees, spearing men and horses, and even following the fugitives into the river. Two or three hundred had crossed at a drift higher up the river, and were spread out on the Natal bank to meet the men emerging from the water.

Brickhill found an opening in the brush and plunged in, losing his seat as his horse tripped on a boulder. He clutched at the mane to save himself, and swam across, guiding his horse as best he could. He scrambled out on the far bank still holding on, but there was no time to rest. The Zulus were making for him, so he remounted and rode off, not stopping until he reached the Umsinga Mission Station late that night.

Private Williams of the 1st Battalion was Glyn's groom. The colonel had ridden off that morning leaving two of his horses in the camp, and Williams was looking after them. When the fighting started, he joined in with his friend Hough, the colonel's cook, and when the NNC broke, Lieutenant Coghill saw them and ordered them to strike Glyn's tent and load it in a wagon. The two men ran back to the camp and started to comply, but Coghill came by again and stopped them. Hough wandered off, but Williams had prudently saddled one of Glyn's horses, and he now filled his pockets with ammunition from one of the wagons and rode off behind Coghill. He passed Bloomfield, still in his wagon, and the quartermaster asked him to saddle a horse for him, but Williams could not find a bridle and was forced out of the camp as the Zulus entered. He got across the saddle, and on the rocky slope he rode past Gamble, still importuning all who came by for a ride. He caught up with Coghill in time to see a Zulu sink an assegai into the rump of the lieutenant's horse, but Coghill, whose injured knee prevented him from mounting unassisted, dared not stop and rode on. Williams lost Coghill again before he reached the Buffalo, but he got over the river safely and reached Helpmakaar, twelve miles away, late in the evening.

Smith-Dorrien continued to serve out ammunition until the rout became general. Someone had taken his horse, but he caught a broken-kneed old crock and started out of the camp, passing Dubois, who was still looking for a mount. "If I had a horse, I'd ride straight to Maritzburg!" the conductor called after him. Smith-Dorrien made it down the slope, across the gully and up to the bank in good order, firing one of his borrowed cartridges at any Zulu who came too close. He was partially protected by the Edendale contingent, which was retiring in a compact, aggressive band that the Zulus harrying the fugitives avoided. He was protected even more, he noticed, by his blue patrol jacket. Unaware of Cetshwayo's fatuous remark to the impi departing Ulundi, he was later struck by the fact that all five Imperial officers who eventually crossed the Buffalo in safety were wearing dark tunics, and that no one wearing a red coat got away.

Smith-Dorrien dismounted on the bank to look for a path down the steep slope, and a mounted infantryman named Macdonald, who had been assegaied in the arm, asked him for help. Smith-Dorrien fashioned a tourniquet out of his handkerchief and riding crop and started to help the man down the bank, when a voice behind cried out, "Get on, man, the Zulus are on top of you!" He looked up and saw Major Stuart Smith, bleeding profusely and white from the loss of blood, and in the same instant a knot of inDlu-yengwe dropped on them and propelled them into the water. Macdonald, Stuart Smith and Smith-Dorrien's horse all died on the bank, but Smith-Dorrien fell clear. A riderless horse swept by and he grabbed at its tail. Careening off the rocks, he managed to reach the Natal shore, but lost the horse while he was pulling himself out. The Edendale contingent had crossed together, still under the command of Sergeant Major Kambula. Before entering the water, they had dismounted to fire three volleys at the Zulus on the Natal bank, dispersing them for the moment, and after they crossed they stayed for a while to cover the men who were still coming over. Their ammunition was gone, however, and they soon left, still in a body.

Smith-Dorrien started off on foot for the high ground beyond the crossing. He came across a civilian conductor named Hamer, who had been thrown and kicked and could not catch his horse. Smith-Dorrien caught it for him, gave the unarmed Hamer his knife and helped him mount. Hamer promised to catch him another horse, but directly he was up he rode straight off. A group of Zulus behind the Edendale men had spotted Smith-Dorrien by now and they started after him, driving him downstream along the bank. Husbanding the last of the eleven cartridges Bromhead had given him that morning, Smith-Dorrien kept them at bay for the three miles that they followed him. They finally gave up the pursuit, and he struck off cross-country to walk to Helpmakaar, losing the way and striking the road at the Umsinga Mission Station before doubling back. He reached the small laager long after dark, to find Essex, Cochrane, Curling and Gardner, the only other Imperial officers to get away, there before him. He was unscratched but utterly exhausted; in addition to fighting he had ridden thirty miles and walked twenty since he had been awakened before dawn to take the orders to Durnford.

Surgeon Major Shepard got out of the camp just before the ring closed. On the rocky slope he rode past two dismounted Natal Carbineers, Muirhead and Kelly, just as a flung assegai struck Kelly. Muirhead called to him, and he turned back and dismounted, but Kelly was beyond help. As he started to mount again, an assegai caught him and killed him.

Troopers Pearce and Sparks of the Natal Mounted Police started to leave the camp together, but Pearce suddenly turned back to get his bit, which was in his tent. Sparks tried to stop him, but failed. "What a choking off I'll get if the sergeant major sees me riding with a snaffle instead of a regulation bit!" he called back, and disappeared into the fight raging through the camp. Sparks got to the Buffalo River safely, but lost his horse in the water when he crashed into a rock. He swam to the Natal shore and pulled himself out with the help of some reeds. The inDlu-yengwe were spearing survivors along the bank, but to Sparks' amazement he came across a fellow trooper named Kincaid, completely blown, sitting on the bank and calmly draining the water out of his boots. Sparks was unable to rouse him until he caught two saddled horses, and he then prodded his comrade up. Both men reached Helpmakaar.

The Honourable Standish William Prendergast Vereker, twenty-five years old, was the third son of the Viscount Gort. Under primogeniture, there was no room in the nest for younger sons, and little enough room in England if they were not attracted to the Army, the Navy, the Church or the bar. Vereker left Oxford, and for a time thought of becoming a gentleman farmer. Then he embarked for Capetown, and by August of 1878 he had drifted to the Transvaal. The operations against Sekukuni were about to start, and Vereker enlisted under Colonel Redvers Buller as a trooper in the Frontier Light Horse. He did well in the subsequent campaign, and when Lonsdale offered him a commission in the 3d Regiment, NNC, he accepted with alacrity. He had been stationed with the outpost at the head of the spur, and when his company fled, he continued to fight with Raw's troop of mounted natives, down the spur, through the carnage of the upper camp and into the saddle. When the last of the Natal Kaffirs and the mounted natives had gone, Vereker prepared to leave with Raw. He had lost his horse, but Raw snatched one, bridled and saddled, from the refugee stream and led it to his friend. Vereker had already mounted when a dismounted native of the Natal Native Horse rushed up to him and indicated that the horse was his. The Englishman dismounted at once, and with the courtesy of his class handed the reins to the Natal Kaffir. Lieutenant Raw survived; the body of the Honourable Standish Vereker was found in the heap of men who had died with Durnford.

Lieutenant Wallie Erskine with his detachment from Stafford's company of the 1st Regiment, NNC, reached the camp with Lieutenant Vause's troop of Natal Native Horse and Durnford's wagons shortly after the fight had started. Either Durnford or Pulleine seems to have posted Stafford with the outpost at the head of the spur, but Erskine had no sooner reached his company than it retired to join the Natal Kaffirs at the knuckle of the line. Erskine had given his gun to a man in

Stafford's company when Stafford left him behind with the wagons, so he ran back to the camp to get one. He reached the Natal Kaffirs at the knuckle again in time to fire a few shots, and was then carried away when they bolted. He reached the top of the rocky slope, but he was carrying a rifle and his pockets were bulging with cartridges; he had been walking and running since long before dawn, and he was completely winded. Despite the uNokenke and uDududu attacking the fugitives streaming down the slope, he threw away all but five rounds and then sat down on a stone to catch his breath. Some soldiers ran by and the following Zulus caught them and killed them, and while they were throwing them on their backs to disembowel them, Erskine moved on, forgetting his rifle. Just then Stafford rode by, leading a horse, and when Erskine asked him for it he dismounted and gave his own horse to Erskine, mounting the spare himself. Erskine trotted off behind an infantryman, and a Zulu rose from behind a bush and flung an assegai at the soldier, who fell forward with the spear sticking in his shoulder. The Zulu sprang forward, pulled it out and plunged it into the man's heart, crying "uSuthu!" He was left-handed, Erskine noted vaguely, and he just had time to bend over his horse when the same assegai was thrown at him and stuck in his thigh. Another Zulu was coming up, and as Erskine kicked the blade out of his leg a second spear struck his horse and lodged in the shoulder. Still leaning forward, Erskine tugged the blade out and kicked his horse forward. A third Zulu sprang up and fired at him from under the horse's nose; the bullet whistled past his ear. "Who the hell do you think you're firing at?" Erskine asked him crossly in Zulu, and left the astonished warrior staring after him. He reached the edge of the gorge but could find no way across; a score of Zulus were closing in on him, so he shut his eyes and spurred the horse over the edge. He landed safely twelve feet below, found an exit on the far side, and finally reached the river. His horse would not face the water, and Erskine rode up and down looking for an easy entrance. He noticed Durnford's charger Chieftain, with his saddle under his belly, dash up to the bank and spring into the water, to be swept to his death on the rocks below. Lieutenant Cochrane's horse was sliding down the bank, and Erskine's followed Cochrane, but before he could reach deep water, there were five men clinging to the tail. Several of the inDlu-yengwe waded out and stabbed at the men; they fell away and Erskine's horse swam forward. He came out of the water directly under the Edendale men, who asked him to keep his head down, as they were firing at the warriors on the Zulu shore. Erskine edged downstream, emerging by a fight in the shallows between a Zulu and a wounded Natal Kaffir. The Zulu was killed, but others were waiting and as Erskine came out on the bank, a bullet aimed at him killed Dubois, who had found a horse after all. The Zulus gave chase and Erskine rode off, falling in with Cochrane again. By dark both men were at Helpmakaar.

Private Samuel Wassall, 80th Regiment and attached to the Mounted Infantry, reached the river's edge with a group of Zulus close behind his horse. He started to edge into the water and suddenly saw a comrade, Private Westwood, being carried down the stream and obviously drowning. Wassall dismounted and looped his horse's reins to a branch on the Zulu shore. Then he plunged into the water, caught up with Westwood and brought him to shore far below where his horse was tied. He dragged Westwood along the bank back to his mount, untied the reins, walked the horse into the water, and then swam the horse across, keeping Westwood afloat by a grip on his arm. He avoided the Zulus on the Natal bank, and the horse brought both men into Helpmakaar.

Lieutenant Teignmouth Melvill was nearly spent when he reached the river, after a hard ride from the camp. He was still holding the Queen's Colour of the 1st Battalion, and the awkward staff with its torn case had snagged in trees and bushes and slowed him down considerably. His red tunic had attracted continual attention, his sword was lost, and in any event he had no hand free to use his revolver. The inDlu-yengwe swarmed toward the red coat, and he urged his horse into the river at once. The beast sank and Melvill was swept out of the saddle, careening off rock after rock, but still clutching the Colour. He fetched up against a large rock just breaking the surface, to which Lieutenant Higginson, Adjutant of the 2nd/3d, NNC, whose horse had been shot in the river, was also clinging. Higginson grabbed him, and the two men sprawled across the boulder while the rushing current swept over them, and the Zulus on both banks fired at the sodden red jacket. Then they were washed loose from the rock, tumbled through a final stretch of white water, and, more dead than alive, floated into a deep pool below the drift. Melvill was weighted down by his boots, empty scabbard and revolver, and was kicking feebly to keep himself and the heavy Colour staff with its metal lion and crown afloat. Higginson was in no better condition and was unable to help him.

Lieutenant Coghill, in a blue patrol jacket, had reached the Natal shore in safety a few minutes before. He could put no weight on his injured knee, and he had stayed mounted only by a miracle during the fight in the camp and the long, terrible ride to the river. He saw the two men in the water and recognized his battalion's Colour. He instantly put his horse back at the water, but a shot from the Zulu bank

caught the beast in the forehead and Coghill was pitched into the river
as he fell. Despite his useless leg, he managed to reach the two men and
dragged Melvill to the shore, but the staff had finally slipped from
Melvill's weakened grasp and the banner whirled away downstream.
Higginson reached the bank with them. The three men rested for a
few moments, and Higginson wandered off to find some horses. Then
the Zulus saw Melvill's coat and started toward them. A few shots
from somewhere slowed them, and Melvill and Coghill started to
hobble up the steep slope away from the river. Coghill could not walk,
and Melvill was too spent to be of much assistance, but they put their
arms over each other's shoulders and stumbled forward. A hundred
painful yards cost them the last of their strength, and they sank down
with their backs to a large rocky outcropping to await the Zulus climbing after them. Coghill still had his sword and a nickel-plated revolver,
but when Melvill finally pulled out his own sidearm, he found that the
cylinder had fallen out, probably when he was reloading it at the
beginning of his flight. Fynn found it that night in Chelmsford's bivouac
on the forward slope of the saddle.

Higginson found a horse on the ridge, gathered two or three men,
and raced down the slope to the rescue. While still fifty yards away,
with the scene hidden by the jutting rock, he heard the end. There
were a few shots and the sound of a scuffle, and when thirty Zulus
dropped down to the trail he was forced to turn away.

By four o'clock the riverbanks were quiet except for the dull roar of
the water. The last fugitive had appeared on the far bank, to cross or
die, and Sergeant Kambula had taken the Edendale men away. The
inDlu-yengwe had moved upstream; dead men and horses littered both
banks and the shallows, and a few Zulus still worried the thickets,
searching for wounded.

The camp at Isandhlwana was deserted. The orgy of destruction had
spent itself, and the survivors of the impi made preparations to depart.
The last dead defenders were disemboweled, and the Zulus moved
through the camp, dispatching their own desperately wounded with a
merciful thrust under the left armpit. The warriors removed most of
their own dead, dragging them off on strips of canvas torn from the
tents, on shields or piled into wagons. There was no ceremonial burial;
it was just unseemly to leave the dead on the battleground, and the
corpses were dumped into dongas and grain pits in the small neighboring kraals, or piled into huts. Each man took away what he could
carry, but there was little directed activity. One inDuna remembered
the guns, and ordered a party to cut them loose from the limbers and
the dead teams. They were dragged by hand all the way to Ulundi.

The Colours of the 2nd Battalion had been in the guard tent near the center of the camp. Months later one of the staffs turned up in a distant kraal. No trace of the fabric was ever found.

The Zulus departed the camp, consumed by a raging thirst and a great hunger. The spears had been washed at last, and the men were satisfied. They had fought in their great tradition and they did not look beyond the fight; they had cleansing ceremonies to perform and home kraals to visit and the story of the battle to tell to the nation. They fired the camp and they left it, and in their thousands they streamed back to the Nqutu plateau, supporting the hundreds of walking wounded, and there they dispersed. By sunset the mightiest force that black Africa had ever fielded had vanished, and while Chelmsford was still marching back across the plain, only a few befuddled Zulus, drunk on looted liquor, shared the camp with the dead.

There had been almost 1,800 men in the camp at Isandhlwana at noon—950 Europeans and 850 Natal Kaffirs. By late evening 55 of the Europeans were still alive, scattered from the Umsinga Mission Station through Helpmakaar to Rorke's Drift. Perhaps 300 Natal Kaffirs still survived; 470 of their bodies were found in the camp and along the fugitive's trail. The rest had vanished, but scores must have been hunted out of the kraals and crannies and killed far from the field. Six full companies of the 2nd Warwickshire had died without a single survivor—the 24th Regiment had lost 21 officers and 581 men. The Royal Artillery had lost 68 men. The Natal Mounted Police counted 26 dead troopers, the Natal Carbineers 22, the Newcastle Mounted Rifles seven, and the Buffalo Border Guard had lost three men, half the strength it had left in the camp. Of the Europeans who had officered the native units, 84 were slain.

The Zulus had given battle with a high-hearted courage that bullets had not been able to quench, and their losses had been fearful. "An assegai has been thrust into the belly of the nation," Cetshwayo said when the news reached him. "There are not enough tears to mourn for the dead." The uNodwengu regiments had taken the shock of the volleys from the three companies to the north of the camp; the umCijo and the umHlanga had charged into the fire of the line before the camp and had been shelled by the guns; the inGobamakhosi and the uMbonambi had advanced into the fire from the donga and had paid the price Durnford had extracted on the saddle. There was never a count, but over 2,000 Zulus were dead, and scores of them dragged themselves away to die for miles about the camp. Those who could, walked home, to recover or die, and in later years men who visited the kraals were shocked by the fearful wounds warriors had sustained and survived without medical attention.

From the valley which Dartnell had attacked in the morning, through the main killing ground at the camp and down the fugitive's trail to both banks of the Buffalo River, over fifteen miles of the rolling hills, were scattered 3,500 bodies.

The day's toll was not yet over.

THE DEFENSE OF
RORKE'S DRIFT

B Y NINE o'clock on the morning of January 22, 1879, both Lieutenant Chard and then Smith-Dorrien had splashed across Rorke's Drift to ride on to the camp at Isandhlwana, and a lazy morning started for the troops left at Otto Witt's mission station. There was a considerable amount of work to be done around the buildings, but the troops that happened to be stationed there at the moment did not intend to do it. Between the Central Column and Durnford's reinforcements, well over 5,000 men had passed through the site in the last ten days, but except for 36 men in the hospital and a sprinkling of casuals, only the 84 men of Gonville Bromhead's "B" Company, 2nd/24th, and a company of unattached Natal Kaffirs under Captain George Stephenson were left. Neither of these units expected to be there very long. There were five companies of the 2nd Battalion of the 4th, the King's Own Royal Regiment, strung out along the lines of communication back to Greytown, and they were shortly due to relieve "B" Company and the two companies of the 1st/24th at Helpmakaar as the garrison at Rorke's Drift. The three companies of the 24th would then presumably rejoin their respective battalions with the Central Column, and the luckless companies of the 2nd/4th would then have all the time in the world to police the muddied site and to construct the earth-and-stone fort which was to guard the crossing. Chard could not undertake the fort in any event; he had with him only one enlisted man of the Royal Engineers and was responsible only for the two punts and the approaches to the drift.

Bromhead consequently gave his men the morning to themselves, policing only his own tentage on the level ground by the kitchen garden across the track from the front of the Witt residence. Stephenson's company simply idled, as they had been doing ever since they arrived. The only break in the monotony for the Natal Kaffirs was the daily noontime slaughter of two government bullocks for their rations, and neither Stephenson nor his handful of European N.C.O.'s had made any demands on their ill-trained, sullen troops. Stephenson and his charges were not well thought of by "B" Company.

Surgeon Major Reynolds started his morning rounds. With three men from the Army Hospital Corps to help him, and Private Henry Hook, a twenty-eight-year-old Gloucestershire man from "B" Company detailed as a cook, he had established a small field hospital in the ramshackle building Jim Rorke had constructed and which Otto Witt and his wife had made over into a residence. The building, with its stone end-walls, brick side-walls, mud-brick interior partitions, high, small shuttered windows and thatched roof, made a poor residence and an even poorer hospital. The interior was a crazy quilt of rooms, which Reynolds utilized as best he could. He had established a dispensary in an alcove opening onto the veranda, and reserved the two front rooms for dressing stations. His patients were crammed into three rooms and four cubbyholes that surrounded the front rooms and the veranda, and four of these rooms did not communicate with the front of the house but had each their own door to the side or rear of the building. The Witts had a few prized chairs, tables and wardrobes, but few beds, and they had made pathetic little efforts to brighten the drab structure, even putting up wallpaper in the front rooms. There was a wooden privy a few yards to the side, and Hook did his cooking, with the men detailed for the other units, in a small board shanty with a few outside ovens behind the adjacent chapel that was now serving as a storehouse.

The patients were bedded down on straw-stuffed ticking pallets, raised on bricks a few inches off the dirt floor. They came from every unit with the Central Column and stationed on the lines of communication, and they presented a variety of ailments. Only three men were actually wounded; Corporals Mayer and Friederich Schiess, the gigantic, improvident Swiss, were both recovering from leg wounds suffered in the storming of Sihayo's kraal ten days earlier, and one of Sihayo's retainers, shot through the thigh and taken prisoner, was convalescing in a cubbyhole by himself. Four other European N.C.O.'s of the NNC were also patients. The balance of the men were down with assorted fevers or were the victims of wagon accidents and horse falls, and several had been crippled by forced marches in wet boots. There were five soldiers from the 1st/24th and no less than seventeen from the 2nd/24th, including Sergeant Robert Maxfield of "G" Company, in the Witts' best bed and delirious with a raging fever. The four Royal Artillery gunners included Arthur Howard, Colonel Harness's servant, whose fever had subsided, and Bombardier Lewis, whose leg had been injured when a wagon overturned. Troopers Lugg, Green and Hunter of the Natal Mounted Police were in an end room by themselves. The Mounted Police had been in the field in wet weather with poor equipment for a long time before the campaign started; Green and Hunter were almost paralyzed with rheumatism and Harry Lugg, a young immigrant from Bristol, was ambulatory, but his knees were so swollen he could not mount a horse.

Chard was back at the mission station before noon. He had seen no sign of the Zulus to his right on his way back along the track after he passed Durnford and then Smith-Dorrien moving up to the camp, and by the time he had given the news of the camp to Major Spalding, he was no longer worried about the prospects of a Zulu attack on the drift. A faint, distant crackle of musketry started about noon, but although the peak of Isandhlwana was visible from the ground to the north of the mission station, it hid the camp on the far side and nothing was moving on the peaceful hills of Zululand. The firing meant action, but it might mean either a skirmish with the Zulus that had been seen on the Nqutu plateau while Chard was still at the camp, or even that Chelmsford's force had encountered the main impi almost twenty miles away; it was hard to judge the distance and direction of sound in the hills. There was certainly no cause for alarm at the mission station.

The officers ate an early lunch and considered the afternoon. Major Spalding could stand it no longer and decided to ride to Helpmakaar to see for himself what was holding back the company of the 1st/24th that had been due at the mission station two days earlier. There was a moment's discussion to determine who the next senior officer was, and it turned out to be Chard. Reynolds, a surgeon major, could hold no line command. Stephenson as an irregular did not count. Bromhead had purchased an ensign's commission in April of 1867, but he had not been promoted to lieutenant until October of 1871; as a Royal Engineer, Chard had not been subject to purchase and had been commissioned directly as a lieutenant in April of 1868. Although he had been in the Army a year less than Bromhead, therefore, he was actually three and a half years his senior in substantive rank. The question was somewhat academic, because Major Spalding would be back by dusk, and there was no reason for Chard to have to issue orders to Bromhead or to anybody else.

Spalding rode off at two o'clock, and shortly thereafter Chard mounted his horse and rode down to the drift. Sergeant Milne of the 2nd/3d Regiment was supervising six Natal Kaffirs, who were filling ruts and leveling the approaches to the bank, and Mr. Daniells, a civilian, was waiting beside the ox teams for the two punts in case a wagon or a large party of men should wish to cross. The high bank and a small spur of the Oskarberg hid the mission station, 300 yards away from the bank, and across the forty yards of surging, breast-deep water lay the deserted campsite that Durnford had left that morning. Chard wanted to discuss the best place to leave the punts in the event the Zulus ever appeared, and he had just decided that the best solution would be to secure them to the hawsers in midstream when he heard shouting on the far bank. He looked up and saw two horsemen splashing into the drift. They were Lieutenants Vane and James Adendorff of the NNC, and they carried shocking tidings. A gigantic Zulu impi had destroyed the camp at Isandhlwana and killed most of the men there, and a great wing of it was even now heading for Rorke's Drift.

The two men had not ridden to the drift in company. Vane had been in the thick of the fight and had been carried away when the Natal Kaffirs broke and fled. He had paused on the saddle long enough to see which way the fight was going and had finally broken away to join the stream of refugees pouring down to the Buffalo River before the uNokenke and the uDududu came in the back of the saddle to close the ring. On the rocky slope he caught and mounted Surgeon Shepard's horse. In crossing the swamps and the last open shoulder he had been driven to the right by some of the inDlu-yengwe and he had reached the riverbank all alone about two miles upstream from the main crossing. Looking back toward Isandhlwana, he had seen a tremendous mass of Zulus, over 4,000 strong, coming down toward the river from the track, and since they were slightly behind him, he decided to ride on to Rorke's Drift rather than to try to rejoin the other fugitives. The regiments he saw were the Undi corps and the uDloko under Dabulamanzi, who had taken no part in the battle as yet, except to send the inDlu-yengwe forward to harry the fugitives. They had swung wide to the north of Isandhlwana across the Nqutu plateau, dropping across the track to Rorke's Drift a mile behind the saddle, thus forcing the refugees into the broken country below, and they were now coming down to the river to rejoin the inDlu-yengwe. Vane had ridden alone along the Zulu bank for five miles upstream, and had only encountered Adendorff, who rode in from his right to join him, just before he reached Rorke's Drift. Both men were overwrought and had no time for detailed accounts, and Adendorff stated briefly that he had escaped from the camp "by the road" before both men turned their attention to Chard and the others on the Natal bank of the river.

The news was stunning, and Chard was at a momentary loss. Absolutely nothing had been done to fortify the mission station, the buildings were completely open with virtually no natural barriers to protect them and poorly sited to cover each other, and "B" Company could hardly hope to defend the post against a major Zulu attack, even with the help of the casuals and the dubious addition of Stephenson's company. To retreat, however, would be even more dangerous. It would take the better part of an hour to yoke oxen to the few remaining wagons and to load the patients from the hospital, and with "B" Company held back to the pace of the oxen the unburdened Zulu impi would outstrip him long before he reached Helpmakaar, even if he managed to get away before the impi arrived. While he was considering the best course, a man raced down from the mission station with a message from Bromhead; a native had just ridden in with a note announcing the loss of the camp. It came from Captain Essex, who had crossed the river at Fugitive's Drift with Lieutenant Cochrane and had then encountered Captain Gardner on the Natal bank. The three men started to ride to Helpmakaar, but decided to warn the garrison at Rorke's Drift first. Only Gardner had paper and pencil, so Essex dictated the note to him, and Cochrane, who had been on Durnford's staff, gave it to a man in the Edendale contingent who promised to deliver it to the mission station. Essex had fought his way through the inDlu-yengwe with the other refugees, and while he could see that two or three hundred Zulus had crossed the river to attack the fugitives he had not seen, as Vane had, the Undi corps advancing to cross the river farther upstream. His note consequently indicated no danger of an immediate attack.

Chard had by now decided that the safer course was to stand and fight, and he asked Adendorff and Vane to pass his intentions to Bromhead, adding that he would be along directly, as soon as he had filled the two-wheeled water cart and got the tools at the drift, which he would need to entrench, loaded into the wagon. As Adendorff rode off, he called back to Chard that he would stay to assist in the defense.

Bromhead, in the meantime, was in even a greater quandary than Chard had been. Gardner's note indicated that there was no longer any force between the mission station and the main impi, but it did not actually state that an attack was on the way. Bromhead in any event could make no decision until Chard arrived, so he sent a man to fetch him and then started to make preparations to retreat, if that turned out to be Chard's intention. He ordered the tents struck and started to bring up the nearest two wagons to receive the patients from the hospital. The tents came right down—it was merely a matter of kicking out the center pole and dragging the collapsed canvas to one side— but the wagons were full of supplies and they were all parked a considerable distance from the hospital, below the rocky two-foot ledge that ran across the front of the buildings. The men had unloaded them and were wrestling them up over the ledge when Vane and Adendorff arrived with Chard's message. Several of the patients had already been carried out of the hospital, but Bromhead now stopped and waited for Chard to arrive.

According to several men in the camp, Adendorff and Vane then rode on, ostensibly to carry the news to Helpmakaar. Everyone then forgot them and thought no more about them, until several weeks later when word filtered back that both men had been arrested in Pietermaritzburg and were to be tried by court-martial on a charge of desertion in the face of the enemy. There is no evidence that the trial was ever held, but there is a plain hint that the process was quashed because Bromhead was able to identify them as the men who came by Rorke's Drift to warn the garrison. When Chard wrote his official report several days later, however, he identified Adendorff as one of the two men who had ridden up to the drift, and, probably remembering his remark as he rode off, added parenthetically that he stayed to assist in the defense. As a result, Adendorff has usually been added to the list of defenders, although none of the others present who later wrote about it describe his participation, nor did Chard, in a lengthy account that touched in detail on the actions of all the other officers present, mention seeing him after he left the drift. Neither man stopped at Helpmakaar on the way to Pietermaritzburg, and except for the statement that he "came by the road" there is no trace of Adendorff's movements between the time he came down from the outpost on the Nqutu plateau to bring a garbled message to Durnford and the time he joined Vane at Rorke's Drift. The report of the charge of "desertion in the face of the enemy" does not elaborate, and it might refer to leaving his company when Lonsdale moved forward to join Dartnell on the evening of the twenty-first, or to leaving his men in the camp at Isandhlwana. It is at any rate certain that Adendorff departed the camp at Isandhlwana on the twenty-second very early on, long before the Natal Kaffirs, with whom he should have been stationed, broke and fled, for by the time the first Natal Kaffir crossed the saddle, the Undi corps was astride the track, and of the 1,800 men in the camp, not one other person escaped by the road.

Chard reached the mission station a few minutes after Vane and Adendorff rode on, and for a moment the decision to fight or retreat swayed in the balance. It was James Dalton who tipped the scales. A long-time sergeant major, his quasi-military commission gave him the right to speak. He insisted that flight was suicide, and urged using the heavy boxes and sacks crammed in the storehouse to construct fortifications. He was of course right, and Chard decided to stand. Summoning all the men, he issued a stream of orders, and the work began.

The only possible perimeter that would include the hospital was obviously going to stretch the available number of defenders dangerously thin, but there was no other solution. Bromhead set to work to fortify the hospital, while Chard sketched out the perimeter. Dalton began to empty the storehouse, passing out the two-foot-high biscuit boxes, which weighed almost a hundred pounds, and the heavy mealie sacks, which weighed well over a hundred pounds. The boxes were snatched up as soon as they emerged, and the mealie bags began to form a towering pile in front of the storehouse.

The first job was the back of the outpost, which looked out over a shallow ditch, the cooking shanty and the field ovens to the rocky lower terraces of the Oskarberg, 200 yards away. Chard started to construct a wall connecting the rear corner of the hospital with the front corner of the storehouse. The patients had been returned to the hospital and the two empty wagons were standing in the way, so Chard rolled them into the line, running a row of biscuit boxes between their wheels. The mealie bags were piled on the biscuit boxes and across the wagon beds, stuffed into the interstices, and heaped into embrasures on top.

The thatched roof of the storehouse rested on stout stone walls twelve feet high, with no doors or windows opening on the back. A well-built stone cattle kraal, four feet high, abutted onto the northeast front corner of the storehouse, divided in two by a north-south interior partition. Chard blocked up the gates and a side door to the storehouse and incorporated the kraal as it stood in the perimeter.

The back of the station was relatively secure, but the entire front lay wide open, and Chard started a wall that angled forward ten yards from the front west corner of the hospital up to the ledge and then ran across the front of the hospital, the open space between the hospital and the storehouse and then the storehouse itself, finally joining the northwest corner of the kraal. Four feet of biscuit boxes and mealie bags were added to the two feet of the ledge, and the perimeter was complete.

The ledge terminated in a jumble of broken rock in front of the hospital, and a small clump of blue gums and two tall poplars stood in the shrubbery between the ledge and the road below. Witt had started a stone wall bordering the road below his homesite, which would provide excellent cover for Zulus attacking the front wall, but there was no time to pull it down. There was no cover beyond the road, where a kitchen garden separated the track from the main camping ground.

While the work was going on, Chard cantered back to the drift to hurry the men with the tool wagon and the water cart back to the post. The punts were already moored in midstream, and Daniells and Milne offered to man the rafts with a detachment to hold the drift

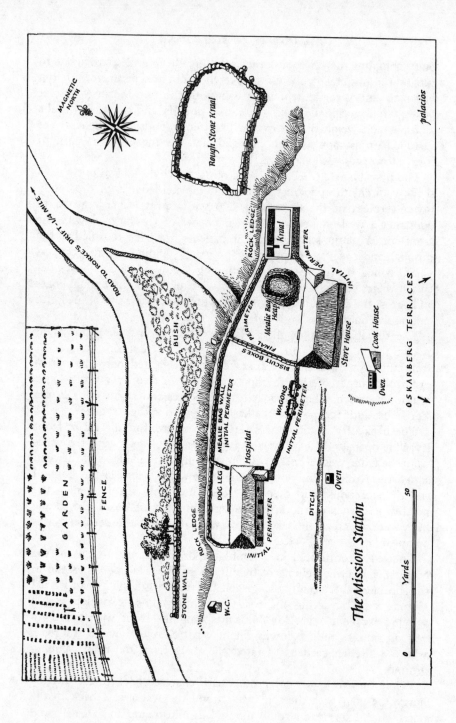

The Mission Station

MAGNETIC NORTH

Rough Stone Kraal

ROAD TO RORKE'S DRIFT—¼ MILE

GARDEN

FENCE

STONE WALL

ROCK LEDGE

W.C.

BUSH

ROCK LEDGE

Kraal

INITIAL PERIMETER

FINAL PERIMETER

Mealie Bag Heap

Store House

Hospital

DOG LEG

MEALIE BAG WALL
INITIAL PERIMETER

BISCUIT BOXES

WAGONS

INITIAL PERIMETER

INITIAL PERIMETER

DITCH

Oven

Oven

Cook House

O S K A R B E R G   T E R R A C E S

Yards

0   50

palacios

itself. The offer was suicidal, as there was no protection from rifle fire or flung assegais, and Chard could in any event ill afford to spare the men. He declined the offer with thanks, and started back. As he approached the station, he heard cheers and found that a European officer with a large troop of Durnford's native horsemen had arrived in a body from Fugitive's Drift and was requesting orders.

Chard never caught his name, but this was beyond cavil Lieutenant Vause, who had been sent back from the camp to escort Lieutenant Wallie Erskine and Durnford's wagons, and who had reached the saddle just before the line in the upper camp collapsed. He had not had time to enter the fight before the first swarm of Natal Kaffirs came rolling toward him, and, apparently assuming that a general rout was in progress, must have gotten his men down to Fugitive's Drift and across to Natal before the uNokenke and the uDududu reached the back of the saddle or the inDlu-yengwe came forward. They had at any rate taken their time in riding over from Fugitive's Drift, since men who got to the crossing long after they did reached Rorke's Drift ahead of them. Chard, much heartened and hardly caring who they were or how they had gotten there, ordered them down to cover the crossing and the open flanks of the Oskarberg, asking them to delay the Zulu advance as long as possible and then to fall back on the post. There were now over 350 men to participate in the defense, and Chard felt that he had a fighting chance to beat off an attack.

A few other survivors of the fight at Isandhlwana also reached Rorke's Drift. A Natal Carbineer rode by, leading a spare horse. Without boots, tunic or a gun, he was utterly exhausted, and he took one look at the preparations for another fight and rode on toward Helpmakaar at once. Troopers Doig and Shannon of the Natal Mounted Police had also gotten out by Fugitive's Drift, and they rode by to see how their comrades were doing. Hunter and Green could not walk, and Lugg could not ride. Too weak to help move the heavy boxes and sacks, Lugg was lashing the split stock of his carbine together with an old rein, and he intended to stay and fight. Doig and Shannon also rode on.

The first layer of boxes was completed and the defensive ring was closed, but the inclusion of the hospital had weakened the perimeter considerably. The front of the structure was covered by the western end of the wall along the front ledge, but the far side, with only a door, and the rear, with three doors and two small windows too high to fire from, formed a part of the perimeter. Three of these side and back rooms, moreover, were cul-de-sacs with their own doors opening to the outside but with no communication to the front of the building. There were patients in each of them who could not be moved elsewhere for lack of time and space, and they could hardly be left where they were undefended. Bromhead picked six men from "B" Company for a harrowing assignment. Taking a haversack filled with cartridges apiece, two men entered each of the three isolated cubbyholes and closed themselves in with the patients. They barricaded the doors with tables or chairs and stuffed rolled straw mattresses into the windows. Then, with pickaxes and bayonets, they attacked the walls and drove loopholes through for themselves and such patients as felt fit enough to handle a rifle.

The 2nd/24th had recruited heavily among the industrial Welsh in Birmingham, and for a variety of reasons many a recruit chose to enlist under an assumed name. The ranks were therefore filled with a confusing number of men named Jones and Williams. There were five of each at Rorke's Drift alone, and four of the Williamses bore the initial "J" and were distinguished on the records only by their regimental serial numbers. Private John Williams (1395) was actually named John Williams Fielding. He was born in 1858, the son of an Abergavenny policeman with eight children, and he took the name Williams when he ran away to enlist so that his father could not trace him. Private John Williams and Private Joseph Williams (1398) took the center room on the side-wall, which held five patients. One of them, Private W. Horrigan of the 1st/24th, was well enough to stand, and the three men barricaded the flimsy door to the outside as best they could and knocked three stones out of the wall for loopholes. There were no other exits from their room.

There were only two patients in the front corner room to the right of the room in which the Williamses were, Gunner Arthur Howard, R.A., and Private Adams of "D" Company, 2nd/24th. Although their room presented a blank wall to the side, a window opened to the front and a door gave onto the inset veranda. The men were both ambulatory, and they barricaded the door and the window and knocked loopholes out to the side.

The rear corner room had a door to the back and connected with the next room along the back, which in turn opened to the interior of the building—the only one of the outside rooms to do so. The only patient in the corner room was the Zulu who had been shot in the thigh at Sihayo's kraal, but there were nine patients in the next room, including a large man named Connolly from "G" Company, 2nd/24th, with a broken femur. Henry Hook posted himself in the corner room with a popular young giant from "B" Company, 2nd/24th, named Thomas Cole, and inevitably known as "Old King." The two men barricaded the back door, using several mealie bags they had carried in, knocked a stone out of the side wall and punched another hole through the bricks of the rear wall. The small crowded rooms were dark and stuffy and Cole suffered from claustrophobia. After a while he could stand the confinement no longer and fled through the building to join the men working on the front barricade, leaving Hook to defend the end two rooms alone.

The next room over, in the center of the back of the building, was a windowless storage compartment with only a single door to the outside. It held a large cupboard with the Witts' spare clothing, and one patient, Private Waters, had been bedded down here. He was ambulatory, and he barricaded the door, which opened outward, and punched a hole through it, more for air than for defense. The next two rooms communicated only with each other and had a single exit, a door to the back of the building. The second of these two rooms was the corner room, lit only by a single high, small window that opened on the yard between the hospital and the storehouse, the only opening in that wall of the hospital. There were seven patients in these two rooms, including the feverish Sergeant Maxfield; and Private Robert Jones (716) and the much older Private William Jones (539) barricaded themselves in, also piling mealie bags against the door. The two front rooms were deserted, and the rest of the patients felt well enough to join the defenders outside the hospital.

Otto Witt was still at the mission station to keep an eye on his property, but he had moved from his house to a tent. Shortly after lunch he set out to scale the Oskarberg with Chaplain George Smith, Surgeon Reynolds and a soldier named Wall. The men hoped to discover the reason for the artillery fire they had heard from the distance, but although the back slopes of Isandhlwana were clearly visible, no movement could be seen. After a while a body of natives suddenly crossed the saddle and disappeared in the low ground on the near side. Smith had a telescope, and the men assumed they were a detachment of the NNC.

Some time later a few horsemen were observed riding toward the post along the Natal bank. Thinking they might be in search of medical assistance, Reynolds descended to find the post alerted by the arrival of first Gardner's note and then Vane and Adendorff. He was shocked to see Vane on Shepard's horse, but there was no time to question him as the arrangements for his patients demanded his immediate attention.

Smith, Witt and Wall remained on the Oskarberg, with a clear view across five or six miles of the Natal bank of the Buffalo, down to a sharp bend which hid Fugitive's Drift. Suddenly they saw the Undi corps, still on the Zulu side near the distant bend.

There were two headringed regiments: the uThulwana, 45 years old and 1,500 strong, and the uDloko, 41 years old and 2,000 strong. A few companies of the uThulwana were missing; they had reached the ravine on the Nqutu plateau well in advance of the rest of the regiment, and they had charged with the umCijo while Mavumengwana and Tshingwayo held back the rest of the Undi corps. The bachelor inDlu-yengwe, 33 years old and numbering over 1,000, had all crossed the river to the Natal shore by now and had reassembled. A few of them had been killed by the fugitives during their flight, and more had fallen to the fire of the Edendale contingent or had drowned in Fugitive's Drift, but their ranks were largely intact. They had been led during the fight by Usibebu, the commander of the uDloko, but Usibebu had been wounded and had turned back, passing the command of his regiment to another inDuna. The inDlu-yengwe moved off upstream, firing into the crevices of the rocky outcroppings to flush out Natal Kaffirs who had escaped earlier, and pausing to set fire to the small kraals and occasional European homesteads that they passed. When they drew abreast of the Undi corps at the bend they paused to rest on a small knoll, while Dabulamanzi, who had brought the uThulwana and the uDloko to the water's edge several miles upstream from Fugitive's Drift, crossed to join them. The current at the bend was swift and treacherous, and the warriors linked arms and edged into the stream until they formed a human chain to the Natal shore. The rest of the warriors crossed in their shelter, and the reunited impi paused on the knoll and took snuff. Then the warriors rose, formed ranks and began to move aimlessly toward the Oskarberg. A party of scouts detached itself and raced ahead, moving toward the western flank of the mountain, and then the three regiments, over 4,000 warriors strong, broke into a flat run to round the flank, led by Dabulamanzi and a corpulent inDuna mounted on white horses. Smith snapped shut his telescope and with Witt and Wall fled down the slope to cry the warning. Harry Lugg later remembered his shout: "Here they come, black as Hell and thick as grass!"

The barricades were going up and Witt, already upset by the ruination of his house and garden, became frantic at the sight of the destruction of his furniture. He asked for an explanation in his broken English, and as he grasped the magnitude of the disaster across the river, he suddenly turned white. His wife and three infant children had left several days earlier in a wagon with a single native retainer to make their way to friends in Durban, and they were now, he knew, at the Umsinga Mission Station. In his excited imagination, nothing stood between them and a bloodthirsty Zulu impi but the Buffalo River and a few miles of open country. Abandoning the last claim to his homestead on the spot, he turned and fled up the track to Helpmakaar to find his family. Chaplain Smith considered going with him, but then discovered that his Natal Kaffir groom had already made off on his horse. He decided to stay to assist the defenders.

The story had a curious sequel. Witt met a native at Umsinga who claimed to have seen the family wagon, and he described in graphic detail to the distraught missionary how his wife and children had been slaughtered by a party of Zulus. A day or two later a Natal Kaffir who had been at Isandhlwana overtook Mrs. Witt, who was far past Umsinga and any possible danger, and he related to her in convincing fashion the death of her husband at Rorke's Drift. Husband and wife, each certain the other was dead, continued on their sorrowful way to Durban, and suddenly encountered each other on the open road on the outskirts of the city. Witt, never popular in Natal, had enough of the colony and soon sailed for England, where he enjoyed a short career as a lecturer who claimed to have been at both Isandhlwana and Rorke's Drift, and he unsuccessfully sued the Crown for £600 for the destruction of his property.

It was four thirty in the afternoon, barely an hour since Vane and Adendorff had ridden up to the drift. The back wall was complete, but a long stretch of the front wall, at the western end in front of the hospital, was only one layer of biscuit boxes high, and two towering piles of mealie bags were still heaped in front of the storehouse. Dalton had set several men to unscrewing ammunition boxes as soon as the first warning arrived, and a dozen of the fifty boxes in the storehouse were open. The men grabbed their rifles and stuffed extra cartridges into their expense pouches. Chard and Bromhead posted the men around the perimeter, mixing the casuals and the ambulatory patients in with "B" Company. Those of Stephenson's Natal Kaffirs who carried rifles manned the walls, and the rest of the company, clutching their assegais, huddled in the cattle kraal. Bromhead ordered the men to fix their bayonets, and then sent Frederick Hitch, a twenty-three-year-old private from Gloucestershire, scrambling up to the ridge pole of the hospital for a clear view of the western flank of the Oskarberg.

Then, with the Zulus still out of sight, the mounted natives who had been posted at the drift and on the flanks of the mountain streamed past the camp, and without a glance at the mission station they fled headlong up the road to Helpmakaar. Lieutenant Vause followed in their wake, reining in long enough to yell that his men would not obey orders before he too disappeared up the road. It was hard to blame the horsemen. They had just witnessed the destruction of a force five times as large as the one at the mission station, and the sight of an advancing impi of 4,000 Zulus was too much for them. Durnford's mounted natives had performed creditably at Isandhlwana—much bet-

ter than anyone had expected—but they had seen enough fighting for
one day.

While Chard was still digesting the implications of this desertion, a
second defection occurred. There were still no Zulus visible, but a
spatter of shots was heard up the road as the fleeing horsemen crossed
the front of the oncoming impi. As Chard himself dryly put it,
"About the same time Captain Stephenson's detachment of the Natal
Native Contingent left us, as did that officer himself." The Natal Kaffirs
simply vaulted over the barricades, fled over the road and across the
fields beyond, and melted into the distant landscape. No one had anticipated much support from this source, but tempers along the barricade
boiled over at the sight of the fleeing European N.C.O.'s. An angry
voice shouted, "Come back here!" and an instant later a shot rang out
and one of Stephenson's sergeants, a foreigner, dropped with a bullet in
his back.

Chard had no time to cope with the incident. At the last instant, his
situation had deteriorated appallingly. He had counted on 350 men to
line the walls when he laid out the perimeter, and now, with the Zulus
on top of him, there were only 140 men left in the post. Over thirty of
them were incapacitated, and only the 81 men of "B" Company
formed a cohesive, dependable unit. There were not nearly enough
men left to man the original perimeter, which stretched for almost 300
yards, and there was no time to effect a change. The hospital would
have to be abandoned, and it would have to be evacuated, somehow,
under fire. Pulling a few men out of the line, he hastily set them to
work running a new line of biscuit boxes and mealie bags straight out
from the western front corner of the storehouse to the front wall
along the ledge, bisecting the post. With the solid stone structure at his
back, the western kraal wall on his right, the new wall on his left and
the wall on the ledge in front, he would have a last redoubt which he
might be able to hold with whatever men could reach the new enclosure.

The working party had barely started the second layer of biscuit
boxes when a shot and a shout from the roof of the hospital announced
the arrival of the Zulus. Hitch slid down from the roof and joined the
men along the front wall, and the inDlu-yengwe burst around the
western flank of the Oskarberg, raced along the lower terraces of the
mountain and turned to charge down at the rear of the post. The first
volley crashed out of the hospital loopholes and from the back of the
cattle kraal and the rear wall, the loading levers were yanked down
and the expended cases tinkled onto the stony ground, and a ripple of
individual shots followed, which suddenly picked up volume as the
uThulwana and the uDloko came into sight and charged at the western

end of the station. There was no cover for the Zulus at the back except for the cooking shanty, the field ovens and the drainage ditch. A number of warriors circled to the eastern end of the cattle kraal, searching for an opening; several score flung themselves into the ditch or crouched behind the structures; and the bulk of the regiment swept back to its left to rejoin the main impi, which had recoiled from the blank side of the hospital and was streaming to the front of the building to find the defenders. The fire along the back wall settled into a steady crackle that pinned the warriors down, and those Zulus who carried rifles retreated to the lower terraces of the mountain, finding niches amongst the boulders from which they returned the fire. Their shooting was wildly inaccurate, and the back wall took little harm, but an occasional bullet struck home in the thick of the men crowded along the front wall, who were now fully engaged in a hand-to-hand melee with the main Zulu force.

The uThulwana and the uDloko had edged around the hospital and extended along the entire front, and a screaming mass of them closed with the men behind the barricades on the ledge. The warriors covered the road, the brush below the ledge was alive with them and Witt's unfinished stone wall was only a ripple in the surging black tide. The frenzied edge of the flood lapped up to the barricade, stabbing and hacking at the smoke-wreathed soldiers above them. For a few moments there was a desperate struggle on the barricade itself, with Zulus standing on the mealie bags and slashing at the defenders, to drop back spitted or shot on the warriors pressing up behind them, and then the tide receded, leaving bloody piles of dead and dying Zulus tumbled along the foot of the ledge and sprawled over the stained mealie bags. Hundreds of warriors crouched below the ledge and behind the stone wall, more hundreds filled the clump of trees and the brush, and knot after howling knot swirled out of the mass to fling itself on the defenders.

The fight flickered and flared along the front wall for an hour with remorseless intensity. Before one rush subsided, another took its place, to be shattered in its turn, and the battle rippled back and forth along the barricade. The defenders stood shoulder to shoulder, crouching to fire as fast as they could load and rising to jab downward with their bayonets when the attackers reached the wall and there was no time to fumble for cartridges. The Zulus dashed forward to clamber over their own dead, but the ledge and the barricade above it were too high to hurdle and they could do little but cling to the front and thrust upward with their assegais, trying to grab the barrels and bayonets that flashed above them, hacking and clawing until they were shot or stabbed and fresh Zulus climbed over them as they fell to continue.

They clutched at the rifles, yanking and wrenching as the owners struggled to insert fresh cartridges in the breeches, and they were smashed down by clubbed butts or blasted loose by muzzles pressed against their naked bodies.

Corporal Schiess was in a raging frenzy. He had bandaged his wounded leg tightly and taken a place in the line at the front wall. He would not accept its shelter, however, and continually stepped up on the mealie bags to get at the Zulus crouching below the ledge. A bullet tore open the instep of his injured leg, but he barely seemed to notice. A Zulu squatting at the foot of the ledge rose and fired at him, so close that the muzzle blast blew his hat off. Schiess sprang up on the wall and sank his bayonet into the warrior and then hopped down to recover his hat, turning just in time to shoot a second Zulu clambering over his companion's body. Before he could reload, a third warrior started up and Schiess again jumped onto the barricade to finish him off with his bayonet.

Dalton moved back and forth along the line with a rifle, meeting the rushes and helping to direct the fire. As one rush receded, he leaned far out over the barricade to shoot at a Zulu seeking shelter below the ledge, and a second warrior crouched beside him raised his rifle. Dalton fired at his man, calling out, "Pot that fellow!" and then dropped his rifle on the mealie bags and fell back with a bullet through his shoulder. Reynolds, with Godwin-Austen's terrier Pip still dancing at his heels, dragged Dalton out of the line to dress his wound.

Young Byrne, who had been working on the inner wall, picked up Dalton's rifle and took his place in the line. Bromhead had also taken a rifle and posted himself behind the line to back it up. Behind him stood "B" Company's drummer, James Keefe, who had already lost his helmet to a chance shot and had tied his handkerchief around the scratch on his head. Corporal Scammell of the NNC had been a patient in the hospital but he had joined the men firing along the front wall. A bullet from the snipers on the Oskarberg caught him in the back, and he had fallen at Byrne's feet moaning for water. Byrne put his rifle down and opened his canteen. He bent over and then fell dead across Scammell, shot through the head.

There was little Chard could do for the moment, so he stepped into the gap the two men had left and picked up Byrne's bloodied rifle to fire at the rushes himself. His shell jacket had no pockets and his belt no pouches, and he soon expended the handful of cartridges he had snatched up. Scammell had pulled himself free of Byrne's body and dragged himself clear. He saw Chard looking for more ammunition and crawled over to hand him packets from his own pouches.

The pressure on the uncompleted barricade at the western end of the front line was relentless. The ledge bulged forward in front of the hospital to within a few feet of the trees, and the single line of biscuit boxes then bent back to meet the far corner of the hospital. Dabulamanzi had dismounted and was directing the attack from below the trees, and the Zulus pressed forward from two sides, fed by constant reserves who had found some shelter around the corner of the building. The defenders, fully exposed, were pinched against the front wings and the inset veranda, firing and thrusting and swinging clubbed rifles at a bristling hedge of assegais. The men filled the narrow strip, leaving no room for lateral movement, and it was impossible to reinforce them during the rushes and difficult to pass fresh ammunition to the hard-pressed men at the far end. Old King Cole fell dead, with a bullet through his head that smashed the bridge of the nose of the man beside him. There was never a letup, and the men were nearing the end of their strength.

More and more Zulus had clambered up to the Oskarberg terraces and their fire grew galling. It had already wounded Scammell and killed Byrne; now Privates Scanlon, Fagan and Chick fell and Corporal William Allan was wounded in the arm. A hammered slug from a muzzle-loader smashed into Hitch's shoulder, inflicting a fearful gash and shattering the shoulder blade to splinters. Hitch fell back and rolled to the center of the yard. When he caught his breath, he crawled over to the wall of the hospital and sat up to rest beside Corporal Allan under the small window that formed the only opening from the interior of the building on that side.

The men along the back wall ignored the struggle behind them and devoted their attention to keeping down the barrage from the terraces. During the initial rush Private Dunbar of "B" Company, firing over one of the wagons built into the wall, had dropped the corpulent inDuna on the white horse, and with eight careful successive shots he killed eight more Zulus. Such expert marksmanship kept the Zulus in the ditch and behind the cooking shanty away from the wall, but it could not cut the increasing fire from the slopes, and an hour and a half after the fight started it became obvious to Chard that he could not hold the front wall much longer. Only a few Zulus had moved past the blank rear of the storehouse to attack the cattle kraal, and a handful of men were holding the eastern end of the post, firing over the kraal walls and from a barricaded door on the far side of the storehouse and a hayloft opening directly above it.

Chaplain Smith had slung a large haversack filled with loose cartridges about his neck. He circled the perimeter incessantly, filling outthrust hands and expense pouches and replenishing his supply from time to time from the open boxes in front of the storehouse. He exhorted the men with wild Biblical phrases, sternly reproving every blasphemy and obscenity his ear caught. The din was deafening, and few voices could be distinguished over the continual crash of the rifles and the clanging of assegai blades on barrels and bayonets. The incessant shouts of "uSuthu!" throbbed from thousands of Zulu throats, now gathered in a unified chant, now rising to a shrieking crescendo during the rushes.

The men crowded against the front of the hospital could hold out no longer, and shortly after six o'clock Chard pulled them back into the yard, bridging the short gap between the front wall and the near front corner of the building with a few boxes and bags. There were no loopholes in the front of the building, and thus no firing to take the Zulus in the flank as they swarmed up on the terrace to attack the new dog-leg barricade. The move shortened the length of the front wall that had to be defended, and it released almost a score of men to add to the reduced perimeter, but it abandoned the front of the building, and with it the two empty front rooms. The main door and the front window had been barricaded, but they were not defended, and when the Zulus broke in, they would have access to the interior door to the two rear rooms which sheltered Hook, nine patients and the wounded Zulu. Hook, alone on his feet, was already defending two loopholes and the door to the back, and he would then have two doors to defend.

The fire from the new dog-leg wall kept the front of the building clear for a while, but it could not reach the back of the inset veranda or the empty, open storage space in the near front corner, and several score of warriors sheltering there now began to attack the front of the building. The men along the front barricade were also beginning to waver. The unending torrent of Zulus was fast eroding their strength, and the fire from the Oskarberg terraces was still striking home behind them. Chard would soon have to abandon the yard completely, to pull his entire force back into the enclosure in front of the storehouse.

The men isolated in the hospital had been struggling to survive an ordeal considerably more perilous than that which their comrades faced outside. When the first attack came, the six hale men at the loopholes added their fire to that of Dunbar and the others along the back wall of the yard, but they had not been able to keep the Zulus away from the building. The loopholes were too far apart, and they made awkward embrasures with limited arcs of fire. Scores of Zulus dashed forward to flatten themselves between the protruding barrels or to crouch beneath them. They grabbed at the barrels as they emerged, destroying the aim, and they thrust and fired into the openings while the rifles were being reloaded. Others attacked the door at the side and the three at the back, hurling themselves at the planks or battering

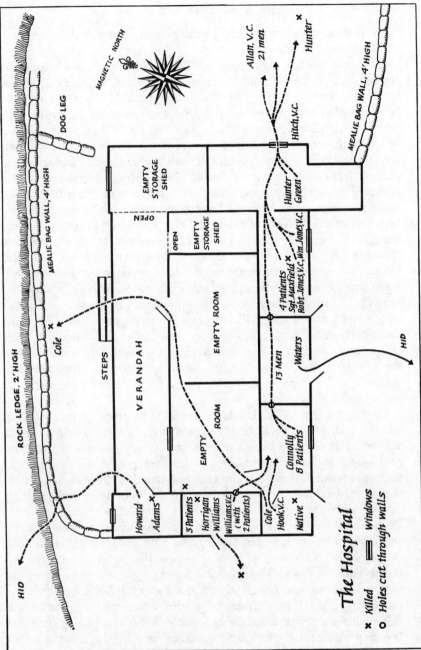

The Hospital

× Killed   ▮ windows
○ Holes cut through walls

away at them with large stones. The fire could not reach them, and one or two of the doors began to give.

Only Arthur Howard, Adams and Private Horrigan were helping on the far side, where hundreds of Zulus were massed, waiting to join the attacks on the front wall. There were four bedridden patients trapped in the small center room as well, and there was no furniture with which to buttress the sagging door. The men could follow the progress of the fight outside, and it was obvious that the front of the building would soon be abandoned. John Williams glanced about, and spied the pickax that had been used to make the loopholes leaning against a corner. He snatched it up and knelt between two of the patients. The space was cramped and he could not swing the pickax properly, but he began to attack the base of the rock-hard partition with short, desperate blows. Joseph Williams and Horrigan stayed at their loopholes, trying to keep the Zulus away from the door between them, and John Williams pounded away at the thick wall, showering the patients with fragments of mud brick and scraping his raw knuckles against the rough surface with every blow. The point broke through at last to the empty front room, and Williams began to enlarge the hole. The outside door behind him was in splinters, the Zulus had redoubled their efforts, and Joseph Williams abandoned his loophole and tried to brace the planks with his body. After long, agonizing minutes the hole appeared to be passable, and John Williams dropped to the dirt floor and wriggled through.

He was too late. The defenders had left the front of the building, and the door to the veranda was already under attack. The only other shelter lay in the two back corner rooms, which opened to the front rooms, and Williams turned and reached through the opening to drag the patients out. The men were weak and could do little to help themselves, and Williams had only worked two of them through the narrow passage when the outside door gave way completely, exposing Joseph Williams to the fury of the Zulus beyond. Somehow he kept his feet and his grip on his rifle, bayoneting the Zulu who had fallen in with the wreck of the door and then springing forward to block the entrance with his body. He fired and lunged forward, stabbing at the nearest warriors, and for a moment the Zulus fell back, giving him a chance to reload. The warriors hung back before his fire, and he was able to loose a few more shots before the Zulus charged again. For a few seconds he fought furiously with only his bayonet, holding back a dozen warriors, and then a black hand closed on his barrel. He wrenched the gun away, but more hands reached forward and yanked him over the pile of Zulu dead that blocked the door. While John Williams, flat on the floor, peered through the opening and the horrified men in the room watched, the Zulus spread-eagled Joseph Williams on his back, pulled away his belt and tore his tunic open. An assegai ripped down through his exposed belly, a dozen blades plunged into his body, and the maddened warriors quartered him and tore the corpse to bloody shreds. Then the Zulus burst into the room, and John Williams saw Horrigan and the last two patients die under the spears before he rose and fled into the back rooms after the two men he had rescued.

The outside door to the corner room had been under attack ever since the fight started. Since Cole fled, Hook had been all alone with the wounded Zulu, trying to defend one loophole on the side wall and another beside the rear door, but the Zulus were firing through whichever opening he was forced to leave unguarded, and the door was beginning to go under the weight of the bodies that smashed against it. Hook decided to retreat to the next room, which contained nine patients. He stopped to take the Zulu with him, but the man indicated that the attackers were his friends, and he preferred to stay where he was. He asked for a knife, and Hook dropped his on the man's pallet and scurried through to the next room, slamming the flimsy partition behind him just as the outside door caved in. He heard the Zulus enter the corner room and converse with the wounded warrior, and then the door to the empty front room opened, the two patients dragged themselves in, and Williams himself followed hard on their heels, shutting the door behind him.

Hook and Williams now had eleven patients with them, and the Zulus had already started to attack the door from the corner room. They would soon be in the front room as well, either breaking in the veranda door or crawling in through the opening Williams had made, and to stay where they were meant extermination for the trapped men. Williams had brought his pickax with him and he wasted no time, clearing the patients away from the blank wall to the next room and again starting to drive a hole through. The Zulus were throwing themselves against the door from the corner room, and Hook set himself to take the impact of the bodies that slammed against it from the far side. Then the slamming stopped and the Zulus began to fire through the wreck of the door. The patients scrambled out of the line of fire, dragging Connolly with them, and a bullet struck the regimental badge on Hook's helmet, sending the headgear spinning and tearing his scalp. For a moment he was dazed, and then he recovered and began to return the fire. His muzzle blast flashed in the gloomy interior, and the explosions in the confined space were thunderous, but the spaced shots sufficed to keep the Zulus back from the doorway in the inner corner.

Williams, able to swing the pickax, had broken through and was already beginning to enlarge the hole. It was growing dark outside, and the gloom in the small chamber thickened. Moments later a wisp of acrid smoke curled under the door to the front room and a sudden blast of heat heralded a new peril. The Zulus outside had succeeded in setting fire to the damp thatch of the roof. Williams peered through his new hole into the next room, the storage compartment in the center of the back wall. It was isolated from the rest of the building, and Private Waters was defending the single door to the outside through the loophole he had made. Williams started to pass the patients through, pushing them into the opening while Waters pulled them the rest of the way. The Zulus had stopped firing through the door to the corner room, and had started to slam it again, and it was on the verge of giving completely. Williams placed Connolly beside the hole, scrambled through, and reached back to pull Connolly after him. He was a heavy man and would not fit, and he screamed in pain as his barely knit thigh bone snapped again. Williams finally managed to work him through, but the splintered door to the corner room had collapsed, and the Zulus were pressing in on Hook. He shot the warrior who tumbled in with the door, spitted the man behind him and thrust him back on his companions. Then he turned and raced for the exit, diving through head first as Williams finally pulled Connolly free.

There were now fourteen men in the center room, and the Zulus were hammering the door to the outside and firing at the hole through which the men had escaped. Waters stayed by the loophole and Hook knelt by the hole in the wall, sending an occasional shot ricocheting off the floor into the room beyond and jabbing with his bayonet at the hands that reached through after him. Williams was already at work on the far wall, seeking for the third time to break out of the trap. There was little time left. The noise of the battle showed that the yard had been abandoned, and the reeds of the roof, thoroughly soaked in the rains of the previous week, were drying out and beginning to blaze. A rosy glow diffused the choking smoke in the room.

It was a long quarter of an hour before Williams finally broke through, and another twenty minutes before the eleven patients were out of the room. When Connolly had been dragged through on his pallet, Hook yelled at Waters to follow him, but Waters refused to leave. The door to the outside had started to sag, but the entire building was now outside the defense perimeter, and Waters preferred the dubious safety of the blazing hospital to the unknown perils of a run in the open. He turned away from his loophole and crawled into the wardrobe at the back of the room, pulling the door shut behind him and burrowing down in the Witts' winter clothing. Hook sent a last shot into the room behind him, stuffed a mattress into the hole and raced for the next opening.

The men were now in the last two rooms, stoutly held by the two Joneses, who had already evacuated a half-dozen patients. A loophole in a small extension of the last room gave them a clear field of fire to cover the outside door. There was no immediate danger from the Zulus, but the final exit from the building was difficult and dangerous. Chard had been forced back from the front ledge and the back wall, and he had fallen back on the enclosure in front of the storehouse, thirty yards from the hospital. The Zulus were pressing around both sides of the abandoned building and lining the deserted barricades, but a heavy fire from the wall Chard had started just as the first attack came was sweeping the yard and keeping the Zulus out of the open space between the two buildings. The refugees from the hospital would have to crawl out of the window in the end room, drop to the ground six feet below, and run, crawl or be carried through the gauntlet to the new barricade, under fire from Zulus on both sides and attacked by the individual warriors who continually braved the fire to dart forward.

The Joneses had gotten their patients out through the window before the yard was abandoned. The window had been too small, and they had knocked the frame out with an ax and enlarged the hole. All the patients had reached the enclosure in safety and the only one left was the delirious Sergeant Maxfield. They had dressed him, but he was thrashing about and they could not induce him to go. When Williams broke through, they left Maxfield and started to help the eleven new patients out of the window.

One by one the men were hoisted to the sill or scrambled up by themselves, surveyed the scene below, and dropped into the flaring night. The prospect before them was enough to make an able man hesitate, let alone the fever-ridden and injured patients, but it was only a question of time before the Zulus broke into every room behind them or before the blazing roof collapsed. As they dropped into the open, their descent was assisted by two men standing below the window. Private Hitch, with one arm hanging useless and weak from pain and shock and loss of blood, gave what help he could, catching those who could not stand on his hip and lowering them gently to the ground with his good arm. Beside him stood Corporal Allan, also severely wounded, who had refused to retreat to the shelter of the new enclosure. Allan was firing at the Zulus who lunged around from the front of the hospital and keeping the space below the window clear.

Nine of the eleven patients who emerged crossed the yard in safety. Trooper Hunter of the Natal Mounted Police was too crippled to walk, and he started to drag himself across on his elbows. He reached the center of the yard before a Zulu vaulted the back wall, darted forward, and sank an assegai into the small of his back. Trooper Green was also unable to walk, and Harry Lugg took him under the shoulders while another man grabbed his knees. They carried him to the barricade, where eager hands pulled them to safety, but a spent bullet had struck Green and wounded him in the thigh. Hook came out toward the last, and Robert Jones hoisted Connolly's inert weight to the window and helped to lower him to the ground outside. Hook picked him up on his back and staggered across the fire-swept yard to the enclosure.

Only Maxfield was left now. The roof was blazing brightly, but Jones turned back and groped his way through the smoke-filled room to find him. He was too late. The Zulus had broken in the rear door and had killed him in his bed. Jones turned back and scrambled out of the window as the roof collapsed behind him, and with Hitch and Allan made his way to the enclosure.

A few men were still alive in other rooms. Gunner Arthur Howard and Private Adams of "D" Company were trapped in the far front corner room, with a door opening directly on the inset veranda. The roof was about to go, and Howard opened the door a crack to peer out. The Zulus on the veranda were all pressed in the far corner, seeking shelter from the storehouse fire, and none was watching behind. Adams refused to leave, so Howard pulled the door open, hurtled out across the veranda and sprang over the mealie bags into the welcome darkness below the ledge. He rolled through the shrubbery, fetching up against four dead horses that the Zulus had killed tethered in the trees. Huddling amongst their legs, he lay still, cautiously pulling a few broken twigs over his body. Zulus running forward hopped over him; a sow ran by and a passing warrior speared it. Presently a bereft piglet appeared, squealing piteously and nuzzling the carcass lying across Howard's legs. The frantic gunner tried to shoo it away, poking at it with a stick, but the shoat would not leave. Howard gave up the effort and concentrated on feigning death. Zulus stepped on him several times. Hours later, when the light of the flaming roof subsided, he wriggled off in the darkness to hide in a clump of bushes several hundred yards away.

When the heat in the hospital became oppressive, Waters opened the door of the wardrobe and peered out. The room was empty, but the back door had been smashed in. The fire had eaten through the thatch, and the rafters were alight, and Waters decided to chance the Zulus after all. He fumbled through the clothing in the wardrobe and finally extracted a large black cloak. Pulling it over his head and his red tunic, he burst out of his hiding place, scurried for the door and ran out of the building. The flickering flames lit up the night, and Waters collided with several Zulus, one of whom stabbed him in the arm, but he reached the ditch by the field ovens and flung himself into it, pulling the cloak completely over him. Zulus waiting to attack the rear of the storehouse were sheltering in the ditch on either hand, but no one paid him any attention. Hardly daring to breathe, he wondered how long it would take for someone to discover him.

The perimeter had contracted to the enclosure in front of the storehouse and the adjacent cattle kraal. The surviving patients and the freshly wounded had been dragged to the front of the building, where Reynolds tended them in the light of the blazing hospital. Several men had climbed onto the sloping roof of the storehouse to fire over the ridgepole at the warriors attacking from the back, and they dislodged the assegais wrapped in flaming bundles of straw that from time to time thudded into the thatch. The biscuit boxes were gone, but two enormous piles of mealie bags still lay in front of the storehouse. Chard pulled a few men back from the walls and set them to rearranging the bags. The men formed a single pile of the bags against the western wall of the kraal, seven or eight feet high, with a scooped-out summit that accommodated the worst of the wounded and fifteen or twenty riflemen to boot.

The pressure on the perimeter increased steadily while the work was going on. With the yard abandoned, the snipers on the Oskarberg had lost their targets along the front wall, and they streamed down to join their comrades. The fall of the hospital released hundreds of additional warriors, who commenced to circle the post, looking for a fresh opening. The back of the storehouse was impervious to attack, and the Zulus gradually concentrated on the cattle kraal, which until now had received little attention. The four-foot walls were solid but they were not topped with mealie-bag embrasures, and the upper bodies of the defenders were fully exposed. An irregular circle of loose boulders which had once served Jim Rorke for a horse pen lay below the cattle kraal, and the warriors sheltered behind the stones and opened a fresh fire on the wall.

The fighting at the far end of the kraal exploded in a series of savage rushes that the defenders were unable to stem. The ground below lay in the shadow, and charge after charge boiled out of the darkness to reach the wall unscathed. Most of the Zulus died at the barricade, but here and there a warrior got over to engage one of the defenders before he was shot or fell under a sideward thrust of a bayonet. The roof of the hospital caved in, the light flared and began to die, and more and more Zulus came over the wall. There was no time to load and they were met with bayonets and clubbed rifles and then the pressure was too great to hold, and the men began to fall back. They retreated slowly, picking up the soldiers along the side walls as they passed them and halting time and again to fire at the Zulus coming over the barricade. For a while they held the low partition that ran across the interior of the kraal, and the Zulu dead carpeted the dirty straw strewn over the floor of the kraal. Then the rushes picked up and hammered away until the defenders were finally driven back over the western wall and completely out of the cattle kraal, into the enclosure in the shadow of the great mealie-bag redoubt. The western wall of the kraal now formed the eastern barricade of the enclosure, and the Zulus now pressed forward on all three sides, pouring into the kraal and crouching behind the shelter of the interior partition. The rushes continued unabated, from inside the cattle kraal, from the front wall on the ledge, and around the hospital and across the yard.

Chard and his men now occupied the last bastion. There could be no further retreat, and if the final walls were breached, there would be no survivors. It was long past ten o'clock and the fight had been raging without pause and with ever-increasing ferocity for more than six hours, but the determined assailants were still coming on as hard as they had at the outset. The ruined interior of the hospital still blazed fitfully, sending up showers of fat red sparks and faintly illuminating the screaming warriors who still pressed forward with unflagging courage.

The defenders were exhausted and their throats were parched; their heads ached and their ears rang with the din and the ceaseless explosions. They remembered curious sounds: the rustling thump of bullets striking the mealie bags and the splintery clangor as they tore into the tinned contents of the boxes. Chaplain Smith was still making his rounds, piling handfuls of cartridges beside the men at the embrasures and shouting his hoarse, homely encouragements. Most of the men had fired several hundred rounds through their scorching barrels, and the fouled pieces kicked brutally, lacerating trigger fingers and pounding shoulders and biceps until they were swollen and raw. Here and there an overheated barrel glowed dully in the dark, cooking off rounds before the men could raise their guns to fire. The breeches jammed unless they were unloaded at once; the heat softened the thin rolled brass, which stuck to the chamber while the extractor tore the iron head off the case, and men dug at the open breeches with their knives to pick out the empties. Despite the protective wooden forestocks, the barrels blistered palms and burned finger tips, and the men wrapped rags around their left hands or sucked at their fingers and tried to fire with one hand, resting the guns on the mealie bags.

The wounded were moaning for water, and the canteens were long since drained. The two-wheeled cart still stood in the yard, and toward midnight Chard led a charge over the western barricade. A group of men boiled up over the wall, firing and stabbing at the Zulus along the back wall and smashing them down with clubbed rifles, while others grabbed at the disselboom and pulled the cart over to the enclosure. It was too large to hoist in, but it drained through a valve and a leathern hose and they led the hose over the wall and slaked their thirst.

Harry Lugg manned an embrasure under the eaves of the store-house, firing at the Zulus who charged across the yard from the ruins of the hospital. A man posted on the ridgepole was shot through the chest and slid helplessly down the thatch to drop in an inert heap onto Lugg. Hands reached out to pull him off, and somebody murmured, "Poor old Brickey," but Brickey opened his eyes and chirped feebly, "Never mind, lads. Better a bullet than an assegai." Brickey had no sooner been dragged away to the shelter of the storehouse than Private Desmond, at the next embrasure, was shot in the left hand. He turned to Lugg and held out his arm, and Lugg tore an old haversack into strips and bound the wound. Desmond turned back to his embrasure and continued to fire.

Surgeon Reynolds extracted the slug and Brickey survived. The doctor had also gotten around to Private Hitch while the light was still good. He picked 36 pieces of his shattered shoulder blade out of his back before he sewed him up. Hitch also survived, but his soldiering days were over.

The men had lost all count of the furious charges and all sense of time. They existed in a slow eternity of noise and smoke and flashes, of straining black faces that rose out of the darkness, danced briefly in the light of the muzzle blasts, and then sank out of their sight. It was long after midnight before the rushes began to subside, long after two o'clock in the morning before the last of them was over. The Zulus had settled down behind every shelter, behind the outbuildings and the bushes, in the ditches and bushes, behind the abandoned barricades and behind piles of their own dead, and hundreds of them maintained a desultory fire against the enclosure as the night wore on. Scores of flung assegais flashed over the walls, scraping across the rocky ground or clattering against the walls of the storehouse. There was no rest for the defenders, except for the occasional man who had dropped across his gun in a stupor.

By four o'clock in the morning the last flicker of light from the hospital was gone, and the Zulu fire finally died with it. Darkness and a strange, uneasy silence settled over the post. Heads ached and bodies were stiff, and the faint whispering noises of the night were drowned in ringing ears, but for the moment there was an end to the fighting. Sunrise was still an hour and a half away.

Chard's position was still perilous. He had started the fight with little more than a hundred effectives; fifteen of his men were dead and two more dying, and Dalton and seven others were severely wounded. There were barely eighty men still on their feet, all of them utterly spent and most of them suffering from burns, cuts, scrapes and minor wounds that sapped their strength still further. They could hardly survive another concerted rush like the one that had opened the fight, and relief was a forlorn hope. Spalding would not be able to split the small garrison at Helpmakaar, the Central Column had ceased to exist, and whatever force Chelmsford had taken out of the camp at Isandhlwana yestermorn had been twenty miles away and more when the attack on the outpost had started, with the victorious Zulu impi between him and Rorke's Drift. The day could only bring further fighting, and the garrison's ammunition was as low as its strength.

The first gray light outlined the distant hills of Zululand, and the dark hulk of the Oskarberg loomed against the sky. The fresh morning air was heavy with the odor of burnt thatch and powder and cloyed with the reek of cold blood. The light formed slowly, and the men, their eyes reddened and their hands and faces black with the greasy residue of the powder smoke, strained to see the battlefield. The impi was gone, and only a few stragglers and wounded warriors were limping painfully around the far flank of the Oskarberg. From the smoldering ruins of Witt's residence, across the yard and in the straw of the kraal, through the bushes below and over the fields beyond the road, hundreds of Zulu dead were scattered in stiffening heaps, the uThulwana bodies with great white shields, green monkeyskin earflaps and ostrich plumes behind their ringed heads, the inDlu-yengwe with white-splashed black shields and cowtail necklaces over their chests and backs, and the uDloko dead with white spots on their red shields and otterskin bands about their ringed heads. Many of the piles still heaved and twitched convulsively, and when the light was certain, a slow crackle of shots began to still them. Shields, assegais and broken guns littered the yard and the barricades; torn uniforms and accouterments and battered cork helmets lay in the bloodied dust and the trodden mealies that had spilt from the slashed bags. The defenders had expended more than 20,000 rounds of ammunition; the spent cases lay in piles along the barricades and littered the yard and the torn paper packets carpeted the debris like snowflakes.

At five o'clock Chard sent a few men out to scout the site. They moved cautiously about the area, collecting firearms and carefully prodding the dead, shooting any that showed signs of life. They poked

Dabulamanzi, Cetshwayo's half brother, who led the Undi Corps to the attack on Rorke's Drift. Picture taken at Cetshwayo's coronation in 1873

The punts of the Buffalo River at Rorke's Drift. The mission station is a quarter of a mile inland to the right

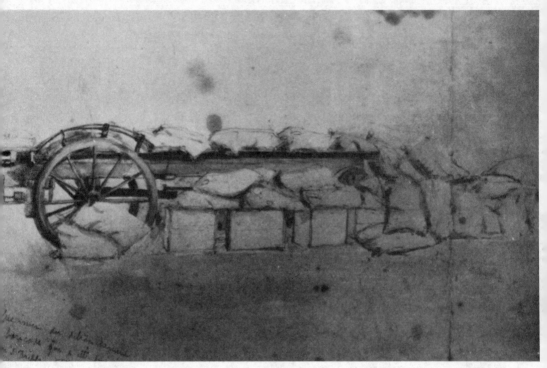

Henry Degacher's sketch of one of the wagons built into the back wall at Rorke's Drift

Rorke's Drift: the mission station before the attack. Witt's house, which served as a hospital, on the right; his chapel, used as a storehouse, on the left

Rorke's Drift a fortnight after the fight, surrounded by the belated stone ramparts. The hospital ruins have been completely dismantled. Note the Oskarberg terraces behind, where the Zulu snipers were posted

Rorke's Drift a fortnight after the fight; the thatch has been pulled off the storehouse and the post circled with a loopholed stone rampart

The men who defended Rorke's Drift. 'B' Company of the 2nd/24th, Lt. Gonville Bromhead at the left. The picture was taken in the coastal area, probably before the campaign started; there are no bamboo trees in the vicinity of Rorke's Drift

Fifty survivors of "B" Company, 2nd/24th. Lt. Bromhead reclining at left end of front row; Godwin-Austen's dog, Pip, leaning against Colour-Sergeant Frank Bourne, D.C.M. Bourne died May 8th, 1945, aged 91, the last survivor of the Rorke's Drift garrison

James Langley Dalton receives the Victoria Cross from Sir Garnet Wolseley at Fort Napier, Pietermaritzburg

A burial party from the 2nd/24th in the vicinity of Rorke's Drift. Probably a posed photograph; the two 'dead' Zulus are wearing European clothing and seem to have assegais tucked under their arms

Helpmakaar and the redoubt built around the corrugated iron sheds after Isandhlwana

Signalling equipment of the 1st/24th Regiment at Helpmakaar

Inside the British square at Gingindhlovu, April 2nd, 1879

The ground covered by the Zulu right wing at Gingindhlovu; Zulu dead in the foreground

Piet Uys and his four sons. On the right is the eldest, during whose rescue at Hlobane Uys met his death

The staff of the Flying Column, in camp on the White Umfolosi before the attack on Ulundi. Three V.C.s left to right in the front row: Lt. Henry Lysons, Evelyn Wood and Redvers Buller. Another V.C., Lord Beresford, second from left at the back

Chard, wearing his V.C., and a group of fellow Engineers in camp towards
the end of the campaign

The field bakery of the Flying Column—a fetish of Evelyn Wood's. The day's product
piled at the left

A group of Uhamu's warriors, who fought for a period with Wood's column

Major Hackett, with two companies of the 90th, sorties from the wagon laager at left to repel the Zulu left horn at Kambula. Artillery in the open firing at the right horn. Wood and his orderly in front of the palisade connecting the redoubt and the cattle laager

Melton Prior's sketch for the Illustrated London News

The donga on the Ityotyosi in which the Prince Imperial was killed. The body was found just below the wooden signboard

The ruins of the kraal on the Ityotyosi at which Carey and the Prince Imperial were attacked

Percy, the horse the Prince Imperial was attempting to mount when the Zulus attacked

June 2nd, 1879, 4 p.m. The uncoffined body of the Prince Imperial, strapped to a gun barrel, leaves Newdigate's camp for Natal. Chaplain Bellard conducting services, Lord Chelmsford as chief mourner standing before his staff at the right, dismounted 17th Lancers in background

June 8th, 1879, Pietermaritzburg. The Prince Imperial's funeral cortege approaching the Roman Catholic chapel. Streets lined with Natal Native Contingent (in uniform for once), and beyond them the 2nd/21st

June 11th, 1879, Durban. The Prince Imperial is taken aboard the tug *Adonis* for transfer to H.M.S. *Boadicea* outside the bar

Major John Fletcher Owen, 10th Battery, 7th Brigade, with the Gatling 124 which he served at the battle of Ulundi. The two Gatlings at Ulundi jammed continuously—the fault of the Boxer cartridges and not of the gun

Lord Chelmsford's final 2nd Division camp, without tents, on the banks of the White Umfolosi on July 1st. The band of the 1st/13th in the immediate foreground

The battle of Ulundi on the Mahlabatini Plain, July 4th, 1879. The infantry on the right face has been marched aside to let the 17th Lancers emerge

Ulundi in flames. The king's kraal burning on the afternoon of July 4th

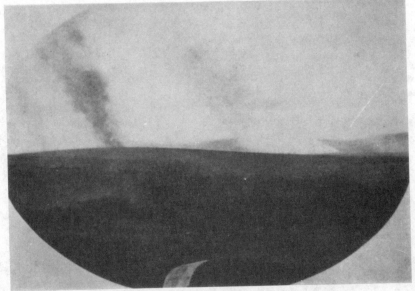

(*above*) The Royal Kraal at Ulundi and (*below*) the 3rd/60th Rifles and mounted officers of the King's Dragoon Guards escort Cetshwayo and several of his wives and attendants into Sir Garnet Wolseley's camp at Ulundi on August 31st, 1879

Port Durnford, September 4th, 1879. Cetshwayo boards a surf-boat for transfer to the *Natal* and captivity at Capetown. The mulecart in which he travelled from Ulundi is behind him; he is wearing a damask tablecloth as a cloak

through the ruins of the hospital, found Maxfield's charred corpse, and the body of the Zulu who wanted to stay. Beyond the far wall they came across the mutilated remains of Joseph Williams, counted fourteen Zulu dead outside his doorway, and marveled at the mute testimony to the fight in the cubbyholes. A sudden movement beyond the poplars caught their attention, and Gunner Arthur Howard, stiff and chilled to the bone but still unscathed, finally rose to his feet. Private Waters cast off his cloak, crawled out of the drainage ditch and thankfully rejoined his companions. A few men dragged the Zulu bodies away from the cooking shanty and began to boil water for tea.

They counted over 370 bodies around the post, and the Zulus were to drag an additional hundred down to the drift on their shields, tumbling the bodies into the river and leaving the bloodied shields on the bank. Scores of bodies turned up for days and weeks afterward, hidden under piles of straw in the cattle kraal, jammed in the crevices of the Oskarberg and lying in the dongas and thickets of the surrounding countryside, where mortally wounded Zulus had dragged themselves off to die in solitude.

Shortly before seven o'clock a Natal Kaffir who lived in the vicinity and was known at the post came in, waving his arms and shouting until he was recognized and allowed to advance. He had no sooner reached the post than the entire impi suddenly reappeared, squatting down in a body beyond rifle range on the western flank of the Oskarberg. Chard called his patrols in, and brought down the men he had set to removing the inflammable thatch on the storehouse. He then scribbled a note to Major Spalding and sent the Natal Kaffir off to Helpmakaar. The weary men took up their rifles and manned the redoubt, watching the impi in silence.

The Zulus were taking snuff and resting. They were equally exhausted, and starving to boot. On the move continually since leaving Ulundi six days earlier, they had consumed their reduced campaign rations during the first two days and had last eaten on Monday, the day before they shifted from Isipezi Hill to the Nqutu plateau. It was now Thursday morning, and the exertions in the last 24 hours had been heroic. Since starting out from their bivouac in the ravine, they had covered twelve miles to Rorke's Drift, mostly at a run, and the inDluyengwe had also fought along the refugees' path and at Fugitive's Drift. The fighting at Rorke's Drift had lasted more than ten hours, much of it in a frantic hand-to-hand struggle and all of it in the teeth of a withering fire that had more than decimated the impi. Hundreds of the survivors were wounded, and they all faced long marches to the nearest food and their distant home kraals. Dabulamanzi could ask no more of them; he had broken the king's express command not to attack in Natal and he had nothing to show for his disobedience but his losses. Only his blood relationship to Cetshwayo would save him from punishment. The spears had been washed, and for the moment there was no desire to renew the fight. After a while the impi rose and trotted off to the drift, swinging wide around the wary outpost into the fields beyond the road.

The men watched them stream by in grateful silence and then settled down to wait. As far as Chard knew, the only relief was at Helpmakaar; the camp at Isandhlwana was gone and he knew nothing of Chelmsford's whereabouts. He put men on the storehouse roof again as lookouts and issued dry biscuits from some of the smashed boxes in the barricades. Sergeant Milne provided a welcome addition to the breakfast. The stores and rations were in great disarray, and the material left in the cooking shanty had disappeared. Milne, however, had come across "B" Company's rum cask, put it in a safe corner and guarded it throughout the fight. Shortly after eight o'clock, the lookouts reported a movement on the road rising from the Bashee valley and dropping down to the drift. A large force had crested the rise, but the figures were too far off to distinguish. At least some of them were natives; shields were visible through binoculars and the rising sun flashed from an occasional assegai.

The tension mounted and all eyes were glued to the road from the drift. There was a sudden exclamation and then a cheer broke out; the men on the roof were grinning and waving a signal flag. A few minutes later Major Francis Russell, with the Mounted Infantry and a few Carbineers and Mounted Police, came galloping up from the drift. The riders waved their hats and cheered the flag stuck into the thatch of the storehouse. The defenders rose behind their barricades, clambered up on the mealie bags and the redoubt and cheered them back to the echo. The men hugged each other and wandered about, exchanging news and inspecting the evidence of the fight. Presently the rest of Chelmsford's force hove into sight, slogging doggedly up the road. Chelmsford spurred forward with his staff and Chard made his report. The General thanked him and his force and the men cheered him again, and Chelmsford sent for several of the defenders to hear the deeds of the night. Private Hook had quietly started to prepare a breakfast for the surviving patients, and someone dragged him off to the General. In an agony of embarrassment at being found in his undershirt and braces and without his tunic, he stood at attention and related the story of the fight in the cubbyholes, while Captain Penn Symonds took it down.

Chelmsford had given no outward sign, but he had been horrified when he saw the outpost. He had been hoping against hope that some of the men from the camp had been able to make their way to Rorke's Drift, and not one was there.

Chelmsford had ordered his troops bivouacked on the saddle at Isandhlwana to fall in at the first hint of dawn. His men had neither rations nor a reserve of ammunition, and the men under Dartnell and Lonsdale had not eaten for two days. There was nothing more to be done in Zululand, and Chelmsford had no wish to expose his discouraged troops to the sights that the full light of day would bring.

The column marched off with Wilsone Black guarding the rear with the Mounted Infantry. One or two officers slipped into the wrecked camp as the light strengthened to search for personal effects. Hamilton-Browne found his two spare horses killed on the picket rope with his Hottentot groom dead between them. His tent had been looted and all that was left was the body of his setter bitch pinned to the ground with an assegai.

As the troops descended to the valley of the Bashee, they saw an impi of more than 3,000 Zulus approaching from their left, climbing out of the valley of the Buffalo. The silent warriors skirted the rear of the column, making no move to close with the troops, and Chelmsford, with insufficient ammunition to offer battle, ordered the march to continue. A Zulu speaker with the rear guard called across to the impi, hardly a hundred yards away, and a warrior of the uThulwana answered the hail.

The depression deepened as the column approached Rorke's Drift. The column of smoke from the smoldering hospital had been visible for most of the march, and none knew what lay ahead. The outpost was not visible from the Zulu shore, and Chelmsford sent Russell ahead to scout. Even before his messenger returned to the drift, the distant cheering wafted the welcome news that the outpost was safe.

The men struggled across the Buffalo, which had subsided during the night, and passed the great heap of bloodstained shields on which the Zulu dead had been dragged to the river. Chelmsford rode on as soon as he had heard the story of the fight. There was still no word from Helpmakaar, and he had to get on to Pietermaritzburg to cope with the panic that was sure to sweep the colony. He took only a small escort and there was a stand-easy for an hour or so, while Glyn's men inspected the battle scene and waited for their cooks to prepare breakfast. Many of the defenders, finally free of the hideous burdens of the night, sought out a corner and fell at once into an exhausted sleep. Some threw themselves down in the dirty straw of the cattle kraal or on the thatch that had been pulled down from the storehouse roof, to discover on awaking that their sleep had been pillowed by dead Zulus.

The sun came out and warmed chilled limbs. A few of the men, too keyed up to rest and too spent to feel the pangs of hunger, simply wandered about and savored the fact that they were still alive. One or two, more imaginative than the rest, were dimly aware that what they had seen and done was in some way unique and deserved to be recorded. Robert Head, for example, had also chosen to enlist under an assumed name, and no one knows what it was, because he signed his correspondence home in his true name. He was not given to letter-writing, but he had a brother who lived in Capetown, and there would never be a better opportunity to write him than on this early morning. Head borrowed the stump of a pencil and began to search for a piece of paper; to his astonishment he found that paper was valuable and not simply to be had for the asking. He finally had to give someone over a day's pay for a piece, and even then it was badly charred, with one edge burned away in a ragged line. It was all he needed, however, so he sat down on a biscuit box and began to write with great concentration:

I now send you these few lines to inform you of what I daresay you will have seen in the paper before you receive this we under Leuit Chard and Broomhead had a nice night of it at Rodke's Drift I call it I never shall forget the same place about as long as I live I daresay the old Fool in command will make a great fuss over our two officers commanding our company in keeping the Zulu Buck back with the private soldier what will he get nothing only he may get the praise of the public Now I shall if God spares me live and see dear old England again I shall find what I say to be true so now as I had to give a shilling for this bit of paper you will only be able to know I am ready and willing to lose my life to win back for our sister battalion 1–/24 renown so kindest love to all I am jolly only short of a [pipe] and bacca

> your loving brother Bob Head

THE FLANKING COLUMNS

COLONEL Charles Knight Pearson, of Her Majesty's 3d Regiment of Foot, commanded the column scheduled to invade Zululand from the Lower Drift of the Tugela. Ulundi lay a hundred miles ahead, via the mission stations at Eshowe and kwaMagwaza, and much of the track traversed hilly, broken ground and crossed a number of major rivers and streams. Durban lay seventy miles behind, at the end of a good road that led through the settlements of Stanger and Verulam, and a telegraph linked Fort Pearson—a stout earthen redoubt on the high knoll overlooking the drift—with Durban and thus with Pietermaritzburg. Pearson's orders were to establish an advanced base at Eshowe, from which to continue his advance to Ulundi. By the time he had gotten his force that far, thirty miles into Zululand, he would be able to co-ordinate his further movements with the Central Column.

The bed of the lower Tugela was broad and even, and, despite a sandbank that pinched the channel, over a hundred yards of open water, too deep to ford at this season of the year, separated Natal from Zululand. If the Zulus were to raid Natal, Durban would be a prime target, but the state of the Lower Drift would shelter the city for several months until the rainy season was over.

Colonel Pearson had a strong force in hand, and his tentage, wagons and supply depots were scattered about the slopes below the fort. In addition to the 2nd Battalion of his own East Kent Regiment, the famous "Buffs," he also had the single-battalion 99th Regiment—the Duke of Edinburgh's Lanarkshire—commanded by Lieutenant Colonel William Welman, and over 200 sailors from the Naval Brigade, many of them veterans of the Perie Bush. Major Graves led 2,256 Natal Kaffirs in two battalions of the 2nd Regiment, Natal Native Contingent, and Captain Beddoes led a company of the Natal Native Pioneer Corps, on which Durnford had lavished such care. The mounted men were under Major Percy Harrow Stanley Barrow, 19th Hussars, a short, slight man with a shock of red hair and a mobile, expressive face. He was a superb cavalryman and one of the youngest men in the British Army to hold a major's command. His 312 men included a detachment of Imperial mounted infantry, the Natal Hussars, and the Mounted Rifles from Durban, Alexandra, Stanger and Victoria.

There were 384 ox wagons with over 620 civilian conductors, drivers and voorloopers, and almost 3,400 transport animals. John Dunn's people and his cattle, camped nearby, added to the press, and hundreds of colonists from Durban and adjacent settlements had ridden to Fort Pearson to visit friends and to watch the excitement, camping wherever there was room to pitch a tent.

The Naval Brigade had brought two seven-pounders to add to the Royal Artillery's two fieldpieces, and it also had a Gatling gun, the proud charge of Midshipman Lewis Cadwallader Coker, who at eighteen was already a veteran of six years of naval service. Invented by an American doctor in 1862, the Gatling was a ten-barreled, hand-cranked machine gun with a prodigious rate of fire, mounted on a light artillery carriage. The doctor's Southern sympathies had delayed the gun's adoption by the Union forces, and the rolled-brass Boxer cartridge hindered its adoption by the British, since the extractors pulled the bases off the cartridges and jammed the barrels. The gun was now going into action with the British Army for the first time, and Coker was determined to prove its worth.

In contrast to the bustle on the Natal side, Zululand was virtually deserted. A few of John Dunn's outlying kraals were visible in the distance, and several groups of Zulu warriors could be seen looting them, until warning shots from the artillery drove them away. The last days before the expiration of the ultimatum were devoted to the construction of a large punt that could transfer a full company or a wagon and team at a time, and to planning a floating pontoon bridge to supplant it later. Shortly after the punt was launched a sailor named Martin fell from its deck and was eaten by a crocodile—the first casualty of the war.

Pearson let the eleventh of January pass quietly and started his crossing early Sunday morning. The Naval Brigade had already dropped a bower anchor from H.M.S. *Tenedos* on the Zulu bank and stretched a hawser across; sliding lizards fastened the punt to the hawser, and first Natal Kaffirs, and then spans of oxen, hauled the punt back and forth, completing a round trip in less than half an hour. The Naval Brigade crossed first, guarding the grassy ridge above the landing while the mounted men trooped ashore, and then leaving the mounted men to cover the infantry.

The bulk of the force was across by Monday evening, including a company of Royal Engineers under Captain Warren Richard Colvin Wynne, which, with the 99th Regiment, was one of the fruits of Hicks Beach's November decision to accede to Frere's request for reinforcements. Wynne had left a wife and three small sons in England to hurry to Natal, and he had only reached Fort Pearson the night before, but as soon as he was across, he started his men to work on a large rectangular fort with high earthen walls, sheltering a storehouse and large enough to contain the entire column in the event of a Zulu attack. The work on the fort continued until the seventeenth, under gray and dripping skies, while the punt worked at the interminable task of ferrying the oxen and wagons across.

Cavalry patrols penetrated ten miles into the countryside without encountering any opposition. Major Barrow stumbled on a dozen warriors who threw down their shields and assegais and tried to run as he pounced on them with the Natal Hussars. He captured five of them; one complained bitterly that 200 mounted men were not fair odds for a dozen men afoot, and he promised them better sport further along.

Fort Tenedos on the Zulu shore was finished by the eighteenth of January, and Pearson made ready to move on. He had left a company of the Naval Brigade and several companies of Natal Kaffirs to garrison Fort Pearson, and he would leave another company of the Naval Brigade and two from the 99th Regiment to hold Fort Tenedos. The Norwegian mission station at Eshowe, 37 miles ahead by the winding track, had been deserted for several months, and Pearson planned to move the bulk of the column that far before co-ordinating his next move with Glyn's 3d Column. The track started out through an undulating grassy countryside, free of bush, and then rose through steep hills covered with shrubbery. It had been pouring for days, the road was bad and the drifts glutinous with mud, and Pearson decided to march in two sections a day apart.

At six in the morning on the eighteenth he left Fort Tenedos with the leading section: five companies of the 2nd/3d Regiment, the Naval Brigade, the 1st/2nd, NNC, all the artillery and the engineers and half the cavalry, accompanied by fifty wagons—2,400 men in all. By two in the afternoon he was camped in high, wet grass on the far side of the Inyoni, a small stream twelve miles above the Tugela, and the last of his wagons was coming up through the drizzle. The Inyoni was little more than a trickle, but it lay in a deep gully with steep sides and only a single double-spanned wagon could cross at a time.

Lieutenant Colonel Welman left Fort Tenedos with the second section the following morning, with four companies of the 99th, the last three of the Buffs, the 2nd/2nd, NNC, and the rest of the cavalry. With eighty wagons it totaled 2,000 men, and it reached the Inyoni before Pearson started to move off with the leading section. By the evening of the nineteenth, Pearson was across the Umsundisi, four miles farther on, and most of Welman's infantry had reached the river as well. The wagons were bunched at the Inyoni, still crossing one by one and coming on as best they could.

A major watercourse with a bad drift, the Amatikulu, lay four miles ahead. Pearson decided to spend the twentieth in camp, to allow the wagons to come on and to give Wynne a chance to improve the drift. The force crossed on the twenty-first, camping several miles beyond in dense bush, which Pearson meticulously scouted before bringing the wagons on. A strong detachment of infantry scouted six miles to the east to inspect a military kraal Cetshwayo had built in 1856 and named *Gingindhlovu* ("He Who Swallowed the Elephant") in honor of his victory at 'Ndondakusuka. The kraal was abandoned except for an aged crone, who had no idea why everyone had left or where they had gone. The troops brought her away and fired the kraal, which they called "Gin-gin-I-love-you."

The morning of the twenty-second dawned hot and clear, and the column marched at five, starting out through low, swampy ground covered with unharvested mealies. A mounted patrol scouted the way, and Wynne's engineers and the Natal Native Pioneers preceded the infantry to repair the road for the wagons behind. The next stream was the Inyezane, four miles beyond the bivouac, and the drift was shallow and firm. Major Barrow found a large level area on the far bank, studded with thick shrubbery, and although Pearson found the bush somewhat too thick for his liking, he decided on a quick halt for breakfast, since there was good water at hand and heavy climbing ahead. The track rose sharply beyond through tumbled hills and a dense forest to the edge of the plateau on which Eshowe was located, and there would be hard work for man and beast on the next march.

Directly ahead lay a steep E-shaped ridge, Majia's Hill, and the track ran up the center spur, separated from the flanking spurs by deep, swampy ravines choked with dense growth. The crest of the ridge was open, and halfway up the center spur, just to the right of the track, was a large, bare knoll. By eight o'clock the troops were all resting over their breakfasts, and the first of the wagons was coming across the drift to outspan on the north bank. A few Zulu scouts appeared near the knoll on the center spur, and Pearson ordered Lieutenant Hart to take his company of the NNC up the track to drive them away. Hart called his men together and started out, but before he could reach the knoll, the Zulus dropped off the center spur, crossed the ravine, and reappeared on the right spur a quarter of a mile away. Nothing loath, Hart left the track and started his men across the ravine in pursuit. He had considerable difficulty in herding them along; the men were reluctant to advance and lost all formation in the tangled growth, none of the officers in his company spoke Zulu and most of his N.C.O.'s were foreign laborers who spoke no English. Breathing heavily, the company finally scrambled out of the ravine and started to re-form on the right spur. Almost immediately a dense mass of Zulus appeared on the crest of the ridge ahead, opened a heavy fire on Hart's men, and started to pour down the spur, obviously headed for the Inyezane, where they could outflank the bivouac and cut into the line of wagons behind. Hart's natives possessed exactly ten firearms, only five of them Martini-Henrys, and they needed no urging in any language to decide on their next move. They plunged back into the ravine, scrambling for the safety of the center spur and the bivouac, while the European officers and a few of the N.C.O.'s made a stand to return the fire. Before they were swept off the spur, Lieutenants Raines and Platterer and six of the men were dead, and Lieutenant Webb and another man were wounded.

Pearson started the nearest troops up the track on the center spur the instant he heard the firing. Lieutenant Lloyd's two guns had just crossed the drift and he reached the knoll hard on Pearson's heels, unlimbering and coming into action even before either Commander Campbell with a hundred men of the Naval Brigade or the two leading companies of the Buffs arrived. The infantry spread out on the knoll and settled down to fire at the Zulus, now strung out along the entire right spur.

The leading warriors had already reached the foot of the spur and turned to their right, disappearing in the thick bush that had worried Pearson, and closing on the wagons. Barrow's cavalry dismounted at the foot of the center spur and turned right to fire on the advancing Zulus. Wynne's engineers had been working on the drift; they dropped their shovels, grabbed their rifles, and doubled through the bivouac to join Barrow. Two more companies of the Buffs, set to guard the wagons, joined him as well, while Coker's sweating sailors manhandled their unwieldy Gatling gun up the track toward the knoll. For ten minutes or so the entire center spur from foot to knoll was wreathed in smoke, twinkling with the red spurts of the fire, and the ear-splitting din of 600 rifles was punctuated by the deep roar of the artillery. Pearson's horse was shot and collapsed, but the Zulu fire was light. The black trickle down the right spur slowed, stopped, and then the Zulus started back. Barrow opened the men on the flat into skirmishing order and started forward through the bush to drive the remnants out.

There was a small kraal to the left of the track on the center spur, high above the knoll near the crest of the ridge, and while the Zulus on the right were under fire, a second mass of warriors had taken possession of it, and still more were moving along the crest behind it to the head of the spur on the left. Commander Campbell now started up the track for the kraal, stoutly supported by Hart's European survivors. The artillery left off hammering the right spur and directed its attention to the kraal, setting it afire. The sailors reached the kraal and occupied it with still another company of the Buffs, and Coker brought his gun up and opened fire as the Zulus abandoned the crest and melted into the countryside beyond. The skirmishers coming up the right spur drove the survivors of the original attack over the crest to join the rest of the retreating impi, and the firing died down.

It was all over in an hour and a half. Two of the Buffs had been killed on the knoll; five more, seven sailors and two of Barrow's mounted men had been wounded. With Hart's original casualties, the total loss was ten men killed and sixteen wounded. The Zulus carried off their own dead, and only one Zulu, wounded in the leg, could be found. He announced that Cetshwayo had given orders to stop the column.

Pearson was feeling quite cocky, and the column was pleased with itself. It had beaten off a heavy attack that had found it in open order, and it had taken the offensive with good results. Even the NNC was elated. Hart's company had broken, true enough, but the NNC was intended for scouting and pursuing a broken foe; no one expected it to stand up to charges.

Pearson had been attacked by a much larger force than he realized. Five full regiments—the headringed *inGulube*, the *iQwa*, the *umXhapho*, the *isinGwegwe* and the *inTsukamngeni*, over 6,000 men under a sixty-year-old inDuna named Umatyiya—had been waiting on Majia Hill to ambush the column at Inyezane drift. The loins had intended a charge down the center spur, while the horns were to race down the flanking spurs, surrounding and destroying the force on the flat. Lieutenant Hart's stand had sprung the trap prematurely, and the artillery and rifle fire from the knoll had broken the left horn before the full attack developed; Campbell had pushed the loins back from the kraal while Barrow was rolling up the left horn and the right horn was still moving into place. About 350 Zulus had been killed, but the impi had retreated intact.

The engineers recovered their shovels and dug a large grave beside the track. The Reverend Robertson read a burial service over the dead while the wounded were placed in wagons. Pearson then marched on at once, not wanting the Zulus to think they had administered a check. Beyond the crest the track led up through hilly country dotted with bush, and early in the afternoon Pearson bivouacked on a ridge near running water. Welman's section was close behind, and the column was strung out over five miles of track.

Pearson reached Eshowe the following morning, on a rising track that for the last six miles was forced into a looping detour by the Hintza Forest. Oftebro's deserted mission station lay on level ground in a magnificent grove of orange trees. His neat brick church with the corrugated iron roof, his school building and his residence were commanded on three sides by low hills a quarter of a mile away, but the view from the high ridge to the south was superb. The Indian Ocean sparkled in the distance, and Fort Pearson's knoll was visible 2,000 feet below and thirty miles away. A fine stream of clear water ran by the church, and none of the buildings had been disturbed, although rank vegetation, harboring a host of puff adders, had covered the ground. Robertson found his wife's grave in the little cemetery behind the church.

Pearson wanted to turn the mission station into a strong base, where he could await word of the location and intentions of the Central Column. The various units pitched their tents around the mission station and dug shelter trenches around them, and the following day Captain Wynne began to trace a proper line of fortifications around all the buildings. Welman's section joined them, and on the twenty-fifth the troops, baking under a hot sun, began to dig at the line Wynne had traced. A convoy of 48 empty wagons, escorted by two companies of the Buffs and two of the 99th, left the fort in the morning to bring up additional supplies from Fort Pearson.

The work continued on the twenty-sixth. The outlines of an angular oblong fort, two hundred yards long and fifty wide, gradually appeared, with walls six feet high over a moat seven feet deep and twenty across, encompassing the buildings. In the evening two native runners arrived from the Lower Drift with a hurried note from Sir Bartle Frere in Pietermaritzburg. The message was ominous and somewhat confusing. It announced that Colonel Durnford's column of natives had been defeated and cut to ribbons, and Durnford himself was dead. There were no further details. Durnford's column, to the best of Pearson's knowledge, was located at the Middle Drift, thirty miles upstream from the Lower Drift. If there was a large Zulu force on the Tugela near the Middle Drift, it might easily get between Pearson and the Lower Drift if, indeed, it did not choose to invade Natal. Pearson began to grow uneasy about his wagon train, and a second messenger, who brought a note from the naval officer commanding Fort Tenedos, did little to quiet him. Lieutenant Kingscote had been attacked the previous night, but despite a heavy fire-fight that lasted an hour, he had lost no men, nor could he discover any Zulu dead in the morning.

There was no further news on the twenty-seventh, but after breakfast on the twenty-eighth a native runner brought a telegram which Chelmsford had sent to Fort Pearson from Pietermaritzburg:

Consider all my instructions as cancelled, and act in whatever manner you think most desirable in the interests of the column under your command. Should you consider the garrison of Eshowe as too far advanced to be fed with safety, you can withdraw it. Hold, however, if possible, the post on the Zulu side of the Lower Tugela. You must be prepared to have the whole Zulu force down upon you. Do away with tents, and let the men take shelter under the wagons which will then be in position for defence and hold so many more supplies.

It was obvious that a major disaster had occurred, but what had happened, or where, was not evident. Pearson had no information on which to base an intelligent decision. He had access to water, and enough ammunition for a major battle, but even with the supplies on the way he would hardly have enough food for a protracted blockade. Eshowe, furthermore, had been picked only as a storage depot because of the buildings, and it had never been considered as a strong defensive position. Wynne was constructing a stout fort, but the ground was commanded on three sides at short range, with ravines and wooded cover to shelter a large impi.

If there was to be no guidance from Chelmsford, Pearson would seek it closer at hand. He called a council of war, explained the situation, and asked for a vote on whether to stay or to withdraw. The officers voted to withdraw, but before the council was over, a messenger reported that Colonel Ely was less than ten miles away, with eighty loaded wagons escorted by three companies of the 99th, two of the Buffs and two of the NNC. The vote was reconsidered, and a decision to stay with a reduced garrison carried by a small majority. A rider went out to hurry Ely on, and by dark he was at Eshowe with 72 of his wagons, having abandoned the rest at the Inyezane drift.

The following afternoon Major Barrow rode out of Eshowe with all the mounted men, and the 2nd Regiment, NNC, marched out behind him. The country was swarming with Zulus; small groups of warriors crowned every rise and crisscrossed the track behind the marchers. They made no move to attack, or even to form an impi, but their presence hurried the men along. Barrow pushed his cavalry and brought his command into Fort Tenedos by midnight. The NNC, left far behind, marched faster and faster, and the long column stretched farther and farther along the track. The leading companies began to trot, and then the column snapped and a disorganized mob of 2,000 natives raced onward, each man making his own way as best he could and ignoring the mounted European officers who tried to reassemble the formation. Darkness overtook them and they left the track to seek shelter in the hills. The first of them reached Fort Tenedos at daybreak, and the last long after dark on the twenty-ninth. The Zulus had stayed their hand.

Pearson now had 1,300 combatant Europeans, and another 400 conductors and native drivers left at Eshowe. On the thirtieth he ran all his wagons inside the completed walls, lining them behind the parapets. The men struck their tents and moved into the fort, camping under the wagons. There was room and to spare, but there was no pasturage for the more than 1,200 draft oxen, and at noon Pearson sent a thousand head of cattle back to Fort Tenedos, escorted by a final company of Natal Kaffirs. The men were back within the hour; the Zulus had attacked them and had captured 900 head of oxen. It was a fearful dent in the transport Chelmsford had collected so laboriously, and while Pearson could still withdraw, he would have to abandon 150 wagons to do so.

Two days later more native runners arrived. They bore private letters to officers, and when the recipients had pieced the information they contained together, something of the outlines of the disaster that had occurred at Isandhlwana could be discerned, although the story was far from clear.

Large parties of Zulus were visible on the neighboring hills by now. They stayed beyond rifle range, and when they were shelled, they simply melted into the distance until the firing stopped. Pearson, with nine companies of Imperial infantry and the Naval Brigade, began to doubt his ability to withdraw. He sent Chelmsford a messenger requesting a reinforcement of seven additional companies.

There was silence for a week. Then, on the sixth of February, a dispatch arrived from the General. He had no reinforcements to send, and he suggested that Pearson retire with part of his force. Pearson replied that he would need at least twenty full wagon teams to do so, and he offered to send back the three companies of the 99th, half his engineers and the bulk of the casuals in return for two companies of the Buffs. Pearson had no clear idea of what was wanted of him, and his messages were crossing those of Chelmsford with great delays between the answers.

The next morning another runner reached the fort. For the first time, sixteen days after the disaster, the men at Eshowe learned the full extent of the catastrophe that had befallen the Central Column. The runner also reported that the road to the Lower Drift was buzzing with Zulu patrols, and that it was much too dangerous to risk a return.

There was silence for another four days, and then a final, frightened runner scurried into Eshowe. Chelmsford would not be able to send a convoy or reinforcements for at least six weeks. Pearson might retire if he could, but he was on his own. Pearson sent his final answer off that afternoon. Unwilling to retire in part or in whole without explicit permission, he announced he would leave Eshowe with the three companies of the 99th, the Naval Brigade and half the engineers on the sixteenth of February if Chelmsford approved. This would leave a force large enough to hold Eshowe and small enough to subsist on the available rations for several months. The messenger slipped out of Eshowe at dusk, but he never reached the Lower Drift.

The days passed, and the loose ring of Zulus on the surrounding hills gradually thickened. No more messengers arrived, and it was obvious that none could be sent. Pearson suddenly realized that he was cut off, and that Eshowe was in a state of siege.

Only Evelyn Wood's column was still at large. He had crossed the Blood River on the tenth of January, conferred with Chelmsford, and then established a camp at Bemba's Kop on Lyn Spruit. Chelmsford had no clear mission for Wood, only asking him to demonstrate in order to hold down the northern Zulus, and since Wood much preferred independent action, the request suited him perfectly. He spent five rain-soaked days in his new camp, using Buller's Frontier Light Horse to scout forty miles afield, and on the seventeenth he started northeast toward the headwaters of the White Umfolozi River.

The northwest corner of Zululand lay in the heart of the disputed territory, far from the royal eye at Ulundi. The land was a rolling plain, studded by isolated chains of table-topped mountains, and the local inDunas controlled a network of semiautonomous clans. The vicissitudes of border life had driven a number of clans onto the table tops with their cattle, and most of the inDunas had held their warriors back from the royal regiments for local defense, so that the area swarmed with small, independent impis. Buller had ranged as far as the Pemvane and the lower Bevane skirmishing with small bands; he had brought in 600 head of cattle but had discovered no major Zulu forces.

One feature of the landscape caught his attention. Ten miles north of the White Umfolozi, and just to the east of the Pemvane, lay Zunguin Mountain, a massive table top that formed the southwest anchor of the Zungi chain of three hills running twenty miles to the northeast. Three miles away across the plain lay the central hill of the chain, Hlobane Mountain, a great lozenge five miles long and a mile across rising a thousand feet above the plain. A perfectly level plateau topped the mountain, surrounded by precipitous rocky cliffs. The southwest end of the plateau came to a point, and more than a hundred feet below lay a smaller triangular plateau, joined to the larger one by a steep, razor-backed ridge. An equally steep ascent, impractical for mounted men, led up for 900 feet to the lower plateau, and aside from the razor-backed ridge the only route to the main plateau was a narrow rocky trail from a terrace at the northeastern end. Several hundred Zulus had settled on the natural fortress of the lower plateau, grazing their cattle on the main plateau, and large numbers of warriors had congregated both on Zunguin and on Hlobane during Buller's raids. Both strongholds would clearly have to be reduced before northern Zululand could be pacified.

Wood reached the White Umfolozi on the twentieth of January and established a stone laager on the southern bank. A petty chieftain named Tinta lived hereabouts, and he promptly surrendered his people when the 4th Column appeared in his domain. Wood sent his clan back to Utrecht with a small infantry escort, and as soon as his wagons were unloaded, started seventy of them back to Balte Spruit to bring up supplies.

Hardly stopping to drop off his baggage, Buller crossed the White Umfolozi and rode north to investigate the Zungi Range. Wood had almost completed the laager in the evening when a messenger arrived from Buller. He had reached Zunguin Mountain in the morning, but an impi of 1,000 Zulus beset him and had driven him back almost to the river before it retired.

Wood finished his camp and at midnight on the twenty-first moved out with his entire force to join Buller, leaving only two companies behind to guard the laager at Tinta's kraal. Marching through the night, he divided his force, sending the Frontier Light Horse on ahead with Piet Uys and his Boers to join Buller's small detachment, and following with the 90th Regiment and his Natal Kaffir Irregulars while the 1st/13th under Colonel Philip Gilbert brought up the rear.

Buller and Wood started to ascend Zunguin long before dawn, and by daybreak were on the plateau, with Gilbert halted to the south of the mountain. The Zulus here were abaQulusi, whose chieftain Msebe dwelt on Hlobane, and when Wood attacked them and captured their cattle, they streamed north across the plateau, scrambled down the northern face, crossed Zunguin Nek, and sought refuge on Hlobane. By early afternoon Wood was on the northern rim, gazing across at a force of 4,000 Zulus drilling on the slopes of Hlobane. By evening he had descended and joined Gilbert.

The column had been under arms for twenty hours. It had marched twelve miles and ascended a steep mountain in the dark, skirmished, marched and countermarched, and then descended the mountain to make camp. Wood decreed a day of rest. At sunset, while the men were supping, they heard the sound of guns far to the south. These were the shells Harness had loosed at the saddle as Chelmsford returned to the wrecked camp at Isandhlwana sixty miles away, and the officers speculated on their meaning. Wood shrugged his shoulders. Artillery fire after dark, he remarked, indicated an unfavorable situation.

At dawn on the twenty-fourth Wood led his men through a thick mist to the north of Zunguin to find the impi he had seen on the twenty-second. As the troops moved along the track skirting the western end of Hlobane, they came under rifle fire from Zulus high on the slopes. Wood took Piet Uys and the 1st/13th off to the right of the track to deal with the snipers. The Boers were reluctant to expose themselves to hidden Zulus, but Wood and Uys led them up to the rocks below the plateau and drove a few Zulus away before descending to rejoin the 90th Regiment on the track. The column had halted for lunch, and Wood was vexed to find that the colonel of the 90th had left his outspanned wagons guarded only by a few unarmed drummer boys while he had taken his men a mile away in extended order to pursue the impi for which they had been searching, which had suddenly appeared on the plain to the north. Some 200 Zulus on Hlobane had seen the untended wagons and were pouring down the slopes to reach them. Wood sent a messenger after Buller, ordering him to take Uys and the Frontier Light Horse after the raiders, and just then a Natal Kaffir rode up to Wood and handed him a note from Captain Gardner announcing the disaster to the Central Column.

The note had an interesting history. It had been Gardner who had thought to warn the garrison at Rorke's Drift when he was barely across Fugitive's Drift himself, and when he finally reached Helpmakaar with Essex and Cochrane that night, he bethought himself of the 4th Column. Gardner had ridden out of the camp at Isandhlwana with Glyn that morning, long before dawn, and he had returned to the camp with a note from Chelmsford just before the Zulu attack. He had fought through the battle, down the refugees' route and across Fugitive's Drift, and by the time he reached Helpmakaar he had covered well over forty miles on horseback since rising. Without dismounting, he now set out for the deserted farm of Dundee, more than twenty miles away on the road to Utrecht. He rode through the dark until his horse foundered. He then located a Boer homestead, woke up the settler, and gave him £20 to ride to Utrecht and from there on to wherever Wood was camped. The Boer set out at once, following the

65 miles of track that led to Utrecht via Newcastle, while Gardner snatched a few hours of sleep. He borrowed a fresh horse at daybreak and started for Utrecht himself, less than forty miles away across the rugged hills and the Doorn Rand that the track skirted. He reached the settlement late on the twenty-third, at the same time that the Boer did. There he found an artilleryman named Cook, who claimed to know where the 4th Column was camped. Cook rode on to Tinta's kraal and then to the camp at Zunguin, passing the note to a mounted Natal Kaffir to deliver to Wood himself. Gardner then returned to Help-makaar.

The impi had retired before the advance of the 90th Regiment, and Buller had dispersed the raid on the wagons. Wood was now operating far ahead of his advanced base, and it was obvious that the invasion of Zululand had been brought to a temporary halt. Reading the note to his men, against the advice of his staff, Wood ordered a retreat to his camp at Tinta's kraal on the White Umfolozi, and when he reached it he considered his position. The site was unsuitable for a long stay; it was open on all sides and without firewood, and he had with him a supply dump of seventy wagonloads with no transport to move it. He had no desire to fall back on Bemba's Kop on Balte Spruit, and he decided to move ten miles upstream to the west, to Kambula Hill. This was in the shadow of the thickly wooded Ngaba ka Hawane, at the headwaters of both the White Umfolozi and the Pemvane, and from there he could watch both Zunguin and Hlobane, fifteen miles to the northeast.

The Boers with Piet Uys had each brought their lightly loaded wagons, and Wood put four tons of supplies in each of them and began a slow retreat. By the twenty-eighth he was across Venter's Drift, and by the thirty-first he had taken a strong position on Kambula Hill. Here he received a message virtually identical to the one Pearson had gotten at Eshowe; he was given complete independence of action and warned that he might have the entire Zulu army on his hands. He replied that he was in a position to receive it, and understood that he was to incur no risk by advancing; he would not move unless it was necessary to do so to save Natal from invasion.

Pearson's column was shut up in Eshowe, the Central Column had been destroyed, and Wood was immobile at Kambula. The long border between Natal and Zululand was undefended, the Zulu nation was fully mobilized and triumphant. There were no reserves in Natal to oppose an impi if Cetshwayo chose to invade, and no reinforcements could be expected from England for more than two months. Shaka's empire, which had existed for fifty years, stood at the very apex of its power. The nadir lay four months away.

AFTERMATH

T HE STUNNING news of the disaster at Isandhlwana sped
along the dirt roads of Natal as fast as pounding hoofs
could carry it. Some 55 Europeans had survived the field, and by late
afternoon on the twenty-second of January the first of them were
stumbling into Helpmakaar. The two or three houses that comprised
the settlement stood at the intersection of the Border Road that par-
alleled the Buffalo River ten miles to the east and the track from Ladysmith, forty miles to the west, that led down to Rorke's Drift. Two
companies of the 1st/24th had established a camp here, centering their
supply dump on a rusty corrugated-iron shed that stood in a low
cleared space, and the first survivor reached the camp an hour or so
after Major Spalding had left for Rorke's Drift with one of the companies. Spalding himself was back by dusk; he had witnessed the fight
at the mission station from afar and, too weak to rescue the beleaguered
garrison, had hastened back to fortify the camp.

There were wagons aplenty, and the men formed a hasty laager
around the shed, eking out the defense with the ubiquitous mealie
bags. Smoke and flames could be seen in the distance, where the Undi
corps had fired the kraals and homesteads along the river, and an attack
appeared imminent. Three of the first arrivals paused only long enough
to gasp out the news before riding on to spread the tidings—Gardner to
the north and Captain Stafford and Lieutenant Newnham-Davis to the
south toward Greytown and Pietermaritzburg. Stafford had commanded "E" Company of Durnford's 1st/1st, NNC, coming up to the
saddle with the baggage wagons just as the route was starting. Newnham-Davis had commanded the Edendale contingent and had been
separated from his men during the retreat to Fugitive's Drift.

It was eighty miles to Pietermaritzburg by the Border Road, which
wound through the hills with two bad drifts at the Tugela and the Mooi
Rivers. The track was dotted with detachments of the 2nd/4th Regi-

ment moving up to Helpmakaar, and the two messengers were stopped time and again. They had little concrete detail to add to the news of the destruction of the camp; they knew nothing of the fate of Glyn's force or of Rorke's Drift. Somehow the news wafted down the road ahead of them, carried by deserting Natal Kaffirs who had struck out for the south from Fugitive's Drift without going by way of Helpmakaar.

The border region scurried into laager as the two messengers whipped their horses on. Settlers congregated on the tiny dorps, and each cluster of houses was barricaded and provisioned. The 2nd/4th entrenched a camp near Sand Spruit, and detachments along the road hurried on. An officer escorting a supply train buried a large quantity of ammunition on a bare hillside before abandoning his wagons and hastening to the next laager; it was several weeks before he was able to return to the site and by then rains had washed away all trace of the digging. The cache was never located.

Stafford and Newnham-Davis reached Pietermaritzburg at seven on Thursday evening, the twenty-fourth of January. Utterly exhausted and semihysterical, they sought out Sir Bartle Frere, who had already received an unconfirmed report. Trooper Charlie Sparks of the Natal Mounted Police—he who had stopped at Rorke's Drift—had ridden cross-country past Helpmakaar before swinging into the Border Road. Stafford and Newnham-Davis were ahead of him, but Sparks had encountered an officer of the 2nd/4th who, with a fresh horse, had beaten them all into town, alerting Bulwer and Frere before he left to rejoin his regiment.

Pietermaritzburg was in an uproar, which the two survivors could do little to still. A disaster had occurred, but its extent was unknown, and by Friday all that Frere and Bulwer had been able to do was to post an official notice confirming the two men's stories. The wildest rumors circulated through the streets, there was talk of mob action against the two officers, and a note from Fynney, reporting that small parties of Zulus had crossed into Natal, fed the flames.

The arrival of Norris-Newman late on Friday afternoon brought the first concrete details. He had left Rorke's Drift on the afternoon of the twenty-third with the first letters from the General and an assortment of personal messages from members of Glyn's force, and Pietermaritzburg now learned that although six companies of the 24th Regiment had perished to a man, Glyn's force was intact, Rorke's Drift and Helpmakaar were safe, and the 2nd/4th was in laager and unharmed.

Norris-Newman, a careful correspondent, had been at pains to compile the most accurate casualty list he could assemble, and the "extra" the Natal *Times* published the same day carried his story. There was

horror at the slaughter of the regular troops and the 28 Imperial officers, all well known to the colony, but 150 European volunteers had
perished as well. The N.C.O.'s of the NNC had been transients and
little more than drifters, but eighty of the dead were Natalians, and
thirty of them, the officers and the men of the Natal Carbineers
and the Newcastle Mounted Rifles, came from the leading families in
the colony.

There was little time for grieving. A blind panic had paralyzed
Natal, and in every mind loomed the vision of an impi headed for
Durban or Pietermaritzburg. The Colonial Secretary, Lieutenant Colonel the Honourable C. B. H. Mitchell, Royal Marine Light Infantry,
was responsible for the defense of the capital, and he took such energetic measures that the populace was convinced the government possessed even more alarming information than it had announced. Mitchell
laid out an enormous laager that encompassed several city blocks, including the courthouse. He barricaded the intersecting streets, blocked
doors and shuttered windows, and loopholed the walls. He mustered
the Maritzburg Rifles, a volunteer infantry unit 78 strong, and issued a
firearm and forty rounds to every male capable of bearing arms. Families for miles about were ordered to set aside bedding and rations and
to fly to the laager if three guns were sounded from Fort Napier. Each
family was to bring two buckets, one for water and the other for night
soil.

The work was well advanced by Sunday, and similar preparations
were in progress in Durban and in every other settlement in the colony. Normal life came to a standstill, and the panic lasted for a full
month before it began to fade. From an excess of exuberance Natal had
passed in a single day to abject fear, and the lighthearted confidence in
the Imperial troops had been replaced by a gross overestimation of the
Zulu power. Not a single Zulu crossed the long river border after
Dabulamanzi led the defeated Undi corps back across the Buffalo, and
the enormous impi that had triumphed at Isandhlwana was scattered
the length and breadth of Zululand for the next two months, resting in
its home kraals.

Lord Chelmsford rode into Pietermaritzburg with his staff on Sunday evening. He had come by Ladysmith and ridden by the Estcourt
road, avoiding the deserted track along the border. He was tired and
discouraged and bitterly sick of southern Africa and the petty incessant political squabbles that had hampered his efforts to fight the Ninth
Kaffir War and to prepare for the invasion of Zululand with a barely
adequate force. The invasion had now come to a disastrous end, the
very safety of the colony was in doubt, and all was confusion and
turmoil. He could do little but regroup his forces to protect Natal

until reinforcements arrived, and he could not even begin to plan the next phase until he learned what reinforcements would be coming. And hanging over his head was the fact that a column under his personal command had suffered a catastrophic defeat at the hands of savage warriors.

The pressures were well-nigh intolerable, and they might easily have shriveled the soul of a weaker man. Chelmsford was not an inspiring leader; he lacked color and dash and he was prone to countermand orders with fresh ones, but he had a considerable reserve of moral strength that manifested itself in a methodical tenacity. He continued to function, and he conducted himself intelligently and with some dignity.

His conscience was absolutely clear. He had taken, he felt, every possible precaution in his preparations for the campaign, and he had marched out of a camp in which he had left an entirely adequate force to defend a fairly strong position—certainly the best site in the area. He had left orders that the camp was to be defended, by which he meant that the troops were to stay *in* the camp to beat off any attack that might develop before he ordered the camp to strike and to join him. The proper tactics to use if an attack did occur were known to the most junior sublieutenant. The senior officer in the camp had been Colonel Durnford, who had reached the camp and received his orders to defend it before an attack had developed. Durnford, however, had chosen to take an appreciable portion of the available strength out of the camp, and when an attack had then developed, it had fallen on a badly scattered and poorly sited force. Whatever had motivated Durnford to leave the camp was irrelevant and could not change the basic fact: Durnford had been the senior officer present and he had disobeyed Chelmsford's orders.

Chelmsford was not vindictive, nor did he feel any need to clear himself by shifting the responsibility to a dead man. The responsibility was already Durnford's and there was no need to spell it out. Neither in his written dispatches nor in his public utterances did Chelmsford make any direct reproach; there was only, by implication, the indirect reproach that the orders had been given to defend the camp.

Before he left Helpmakaar, Chelmsford convened a court of inquiry to collect evidence regarding the loss of the camp. Colonel Hassard, Royal Engineers, and Lieutenant Colonel Law of the Royal Artillery, neither of whom had been attached to the Central Column, were joined by Harness to hear the witnesses. The choice of Harness was unfortunate; when the story of his abortive dash to return to the camp came out it appeared to many that he had been made a member to prevent his testifying as a witness. Chelmsford, however, regarded the loss of the camp as an event in which Glyn's force had played no part, and even if Gosset had allowed him to proceed, Harness could not have reached the camp in time to alter the outcome of the battle.

The court heard Colonel Glyn and Major Clery, the five surviving Imperial officers—Gardner, Essex, Cochrane, Curling and Smith-Dorrien —and Captain Nourse of the 1st/1st, NNC. The evidence was at best fragmentary, since none of the survivors could report more than the swirl of immaterial detail that had passed through his ken. A number of witnesses no farther away than Rorke's Drift were not called, notably Hamilton-Browne, who had witnessed more of the fight than anyone else in Glyn's force, and Raw, who was apparently the only commissioned survivor of the fighting on the Nqutu plateau and the retreat down the spur. The court simply recorded the accounts and rendered no opinion, "as instructions on this point were not given it." Chelmsford, somewhat vexed that more witnesses had not been heard, approved the absence of an opinion, added none of his own, and forwarded the report to London.

He penned his own dispatch to Hicks Beach on the night of the twenty-seventh, after he reached Pietermaritzburg. Chelmsford had not yet seen the report of the court of inquiry, and he frankly admitted that the disaster still seemed incomprehensible to him. He gave a reasonably accurate version of the battle, although he made use of an unfortunate phrase or two, particularly: "It appears that the oxen were yoked to the wagons three hours before the attack took place, so that there was ample time to construct that wagon laager which the Dutch in former days understood so well."

If Chelmsford refrained from pointing a finger of blame at Durnford, his staff was not so reticent. They stated in private conversations that they held Durnford responsible, and even Frere, before he had more facts in hand, referred in a cable to "poor Durnford's misfortune." The gossip flew about the colony, and Natal, with fresh memories of Bushman's River Pass, was willing to believe the worst.

The first references to "poor Durnford" showed the Colenso household in which quarter the wind lay. The Bishop had no liking for the General, but his attitude was based on Chelmsford's role in the genesis of what Colenso felt was an unjustified and unprovoked war on a peaceful nation, and he was not yet prepared to pass judgment on professional military matters. Not so his daughter Frances, who leaped like a tigress to the defense of the reputation of the man to whom she had given her love. All the pent frustrations of her life burst forth, and with burning and implacable animosity she set out to clear Durnford's name and to fix the onus of the defeat on Chelmsford. She soon enlisted the aid of Edward Congreve Langley Durnford, a retired lieutenant colonel of the Royal Marine Artillery, who carried the fight for his brother's reputation to England. Frances was reckless in her accusations, fastening on every chance remark and scrap of rumor to carry her attack; Edward Durnford was somewhat more temperate but equally implacable, and together they hammered on the same themes: Chelmsford had chosen a poor site and had failed to laager his camp, he had failed to scout the Nqutu plateau the day of the attack, and he had allowed the Zulus to lure him away with half his strength. He had ignored repeated warnings that the camp was under attack. Above all, his orders to Durnford to proceed to the camp had not specified that he was to take command on his arrival, and Durnford had in fact not taken the command away from Pulleine but had simply acted as an independent agent with his own force. Durnford had, therefore, not disobeyed any orders which may have been issued to Pulleine, and he was in no way responsible for the defeat.

The indictment sounded impressive, but the points were not telling. Chelmsford needed a temporary camp along the track between Rorke's Drift and Isipezi Hill; Isandhlwana was halfway and handy to wood and water, with clearly visible approaches and strong natural protection at its rear. The Nqutu plateau was masked from the entire length of the track, but even without the picket at the head of the spur an attack from the plateau would have been visible for almost half an hour before it reached the camp. The site was as good as, if not better than, any other for five miles about. Chelmsford had not fortified the camp because it was a temporary one, the ground was too stony to dig, and the wagons were coming and going in such numbers that the effort of a laager would not have been worth the gain. No less than three future actions were to show that the troop strength had been more than sufficient to beat off a major attack without benefit of a wagon laager.

Chelmsford had not scouted the Nqutu plateau because he saw no reason to do so beyond the edge of the escarpment. He was not searching for the impi because he feared an attack on the camp; he *wanted* the impi to attack the camp. He was only searching for the impi because, if it did not attack, he intended to attack it himself. He had certainly not been "lured" out of the camp. He had advanced half his force to a new camp and was preparing to bring the balance up to join him when the attack developed. The Zulu leadership, in any event, had not thought in such sophisticated tactical terms. The impi had been taken up to the Nqutu plateau to get away from Matyana and to prevent him from laying any claim to its command, and, far from having been positioned as bait, Matyana himself did not know where the impi was and was looking for it when Dartnell found him.

Chelmsford had ignored no warnings. Of the half-dozen messages from the camp, only one had actually reached him, and not one as sent had indicated any dire danger. The sole word that the camp was surrounded had come not from the camp but from Hamilton-Browne—no military authority—and this had certainly never reached Chelmsford in the form in which it had been phrased. It would not have alarmed him even if it had. If the form of battle he hoped for had developed, surrounding the camp would not lead to its destruction but to a greater slaughter of the attackers. Chelmsford had left the camp to its own devices and would look on no message as a recall for help; his best arrival time would be four or five hours after the dispatch of any message recalling him, and he had thus never been in a position to influence the outcome of any attack.

And, whether or not the written order to Durnford had included the phrase "take command of the camp" (it had not), Durnford was senior to Pulleine, as Chelmsford knew perfectly well when he issued the order, and the command automatically devolved on him when he arrived. There was no doubt that Durnford himself knew this, for no matter how tactfully he had phrased it, he had influenced the movements of troops under Pulleine's command.

The two viewpoints were based on diametrically opposed concepts. Durnford's defenders saw the camp as the center of the stage, the primary consideration its defense and Chelmsford away in the wings. For Chelmsford, however, the scene had already shifted forward to his new bivouac; it was not he who was away from the camp but the force that was left to defend Isandhlwana that was away from *him*.

For the grieving Colensos all that touched Durnford seemed part of a conspiracy. As Chelmsford's force had prepared to leave the camp to return to Rorke's Drift, a Doctor Thrupp had noticed a gold watch entangled in the scarlet vest of a Royal Engineer uniform on a whiskered corpse near the bivouac. He picked it up and brought it away; he had only met Durnford once and he did not recognize the contorted face in the faint predawn light. It was a full month before it occurred to him that someone might recognize the watch, and even then it did not occur to him that only two Royal Engineer officers had died at Isandhlwana and only one of them was whiskered. The watch bore a peculiar monogram with intertwined, reversed initials, and Thrupp inserted an advertisement in the Natal *Witness* in which a typographical error made the facsimile of the monogram unrecognizable. It was the twenty-second of March, a full month more, before Thrupp, on Frere's advice, brought the watch to Colenso, who recognized it immediately. The dead at Isandhlwana had not yet been buried, and the colony was still filled with rumors of men who had been taken prisoner or who were hiding in Zulu kraals. The watch was more than a me-

mento, it was a death certificate, and only then did Durnford's family go into official mourning.

It was the custom in 1878 for three officers to form a committee of adjustment for the estate of every officer who died on active service; they would call in his bills, auction off his effects to his fellow officers and send the net residue to his family. Durnford's effects were auctioned off at Fort Napier by a committee which had barely known him; the Colensos did not learn of the sale until it was over. All his personal papers were somehow lost. He had left few debts, but when the call went out, a number of dubious bills were presented which totaled more than £370, and the committee paid them all without a murmur. The Colensos, inordinately sensitive from a lifetime of slights, drew their own conclusions.

The news of Isandhlwana traveled to the rest of southern Africa, to England and to the world. Gordon Sprigg, notified by cable at Capetown, had by the twenty-sixth of January embarked the last three companies of the 2nd/4th Regiment, calling out volunteers to take over their guard duties, and was already taking steps to call out sufficient volunteers in Kaffraria to release the bulk of the 88th Regiment from Kingwilliamstown.

By steamer and from Madeira by cable the word went to England. On the eleventh of February, long after he had retired, Hicks Beach was awakened by a messenger who brought him the news. By the following day all England knew, and a wave of horror and shock swept the country, focusing public attention on a situation to which the average Englishman had devoted remarkably little thought. Chelmsford communicated directly with His Royal Highness the Duke of Cambridge, the General Commanding in Chief, but on the local scene he took direction from Sir Bartle Frere. Both Frere and Bulwer communicated with Sir Michael Hicks Beach, the Secretary of State for the Colonies, who was thus, although he did not exercise his prerogatives as firmly as he might have, in a considerably stronger position to control events in southern Africa than was Colonel Stanley, the Secretary of State for War. Hicks Beach loomed large on the horizon of southern Africa, and Stanley loomed large on the Duke's (the Secretary's major function being to pare to the bone that worthy's annual estimates), but both men were simply minor members of the Earl of Beaconsfield's Cabinet, and as Prime Minister, Benjamin Disraeli had more important matters at hand than a war with a native nation few Englishmen had ever heard of. There was a war in Afghanistan, where the Amir had refused to accept a British mission, and the distant fighting in the Khyber Pass was more important than the distant fighting in Zululand, because the Afghan war might embroil England in a general war with Russia. Over the Duke's protests, the Army estimates had been cut even further than usual that year, and the British Army was in no condition to wage a European war. Disraeli, already ailing, took to his bed with the shock, and the Cabinet considered measures.

The government were under considerable fire. They had at their disposal an Imperial Chest of £1,000,000 to cover minor disturbances, and when that sum was expended, they would have to go to Parliament to ask for more. A full quarter of the Chest had disappeared when Frere had airily charged all of the expenses of a petty native brawl in Griqualand West to the Imperial account, and the Zulu War would unquestionably go far beyond the limits of the Chest. There was an immediate reaction against Frere, who had deliberately brought on the war against Cabinet wishes, and against Chelmsford, who held the military command. The public reaction would have to be dealt with, but the Zulus would have to be dealt with first of all.

Chelmsford, conditioned by a lifetime's service to economical operations, held his requests to the minimum. Under the circumstances, he reported, he felt obliged to ask for three infantry battalions, two cavalry regiments, a company of engineers and enough artillerymen to make good Harness's losses. He was also in need of a dozen shoeing-smiths, and two veterinary surgeons would be invaluable. He explained carefully that in addition to the battalion needed to replace the 1st/ 24th, he was asking for two more battalions to replace the 3d Regiment, NNC, which had deserted. He was not, in other words, asking for a larger force; he was only asking to be reinforced to his original strength and he was clearly ready to try again with a force no larger than he had commanded on his first attempt.

There had always been parsimony in peacetime, but the excuse of successive governments had been that they could cope with crisis when it came. The present Cabinet was no exception. In a matter of days the reinforcements were chosen and approved, and within the week the first of them had boarded chartered vessels. Five infantry battalions were to sail from England and another from Ceylon, and the infantry was to be joined by two cavalry regiments from home. Not only were the artillery losses made good, but two additional batteries— 567 men and fifteen guns—were sent as well. There were 379 men from the Royal Engineers, 464 men from the Army Service Corps, 192 from the Army Hospital Corps and the Medical Department, including civilian surgeons and a party of nurses, and detachments from the Ammunition Column, the Ordnance Store Department, the Commissariat and Transport Department, and large drafts to fill the ranks of the units already in the field. Nine veterinary surgeons were sent, instead of the modest two Chelmsford had asked for. In all, 418 officers, 9,996 men, 1,868 horses and 238 wagons were set in motion. The number of Imperial reinforcements far outstripped the total number of Europeans with which Chelmsford had started his campaign.

The newspapers were galvanized; the war had caught them unawares. Accurate information was at a premium, little was known about Zululand and proper names were largely guesswork; Isandhlwana was generally rendered "Sandula" and the Zulu monarch "Cetewayo." There were no maps of the battlefield, and one account was accompanied by a sketch featuring a deep ditch through which the Zulu impi had crept unseen to the center of the camp. The *Standard* had Norris-Newman on the scene, but the other papers were relying on official communiqués and private letters. A horde of "specials" now took passage for the seat of the war, led by Mr. Francis Francis of the *Times*. Several other correspondents were equally well known. Melton Prior of the *Illustrated London News* was a gifted artist who could in short order cram an amazing amount of information onto a sketch pad, which the staff artists in London could then transfer to the pearwood blocks used in printing. (Speed was at a premium, and as many as eight engravers would each take one of the blocks that made up a full page illustration, with a specialist to cut water effects and another to bridge the interstices after the blocks were bolted together.) Prior worked for his sponsors for a quarter of a century, through the Boer War, and only managed to spend one year in England. The pace he set himself cost him his marriage, and the *Illustrated London News* still cherishes the khaki sun helmet, size six and seven-eighths, that he wore on the Zulu campaign and accidentally left in the office on a visit in 1896. Archibald Forbes, a short Scot with a great bow-wave of a mustache, was the pride of the *Daily News*. After an unsuccessful sojourn at the University of Aberdeen, he served as a trooper in the 1st (Royal) Dragoons and then bought out, soon becoming editor of the *London Scotsman*. In 1870 he went off to cover the Franco-Prussian War for the *Morning Advertiser*, switching to the *Daily News* to report the Carlist War in Spain, the Russo-Turkish War and assorted fighting in the Balkans and Afghanistan. He was on intimate terms with half the general staffs of Europe, and he had long since passed from straight reporting to highly opinionated criticisms of generals, battles and campaigns. Intense and dramatic, good stories were more important to him than facts, and his popular books bore such titles as *Glimpses Through the Cannon-smoke* and *Barracks, Bivouacs and Battles*. In 1900 he died in a feverish delirium in the arms of his editor, and his last words were "Those guns, man, don't you see those guns? I tell you the brave fellows will be mowed down like grass!" It had not yet occurred to the

Daily News that Forbes had never covered a British campaign before and that his cocksure carping style was likely to cause more friction than it did when he applied it to Russians and Serbs.

There was joyful chaos in the regimental mess rooms. None of the units was ready for overseas duty; there were families to resettle, debts to pay, equipment to purchase, and ranks to fill. Few of the junior officers had been on active service before, and the military outfitters did a thriving business on a cash basis. "When gentlemen are going out as you are, sir, it is always a case of ready money," said one tailor; and a bootmaker shook his head over Isandhlwana with: "Sad business, sir, very sad. We lost three customers by it." White's in Aldershot was filled with piles of freshly purchased buckets, pillows, canteens, valises, collapsible tubs, water filter bags, tables, chairs and bedsteads, all to be painted with the owner's name, rank and regiment and most of it perfectly useless on campaign.

The men in the depots were issued new boots and tunics, and the sickly were weeded out and turned over to a woebegone lieutenant or two under orders to remain behind. The battalions went out at full war strength, 900 men on the dot, but only at the expense of exposing the deficiencies of the Cardwell system. Great drafts of raw recruits were snatched from other units—young, untrained short-service youths who knew neither each other nor their new regiments and who were strangers to their officers—and the depot battalions were crippled still further.

The battalions converged on the transports waiting at Portsmouth and Southampton from depots all over England. They came by train through the driving sleet from Shorncliff, from Aldershot, from Leeds and from Manchester and went into temporary camps: the 2nd Battalion of the Royal Scots Fusiliers, the Rutlandshire Regiment, the 3d Battalion of the King's Royal Rifle Corps, Princess Louise's Argyllshire Highlanders and the 94th Regiment—one of the only two nameless regiments in the Army.

The 17th Lancers, "Bingham's Dandies," were alerted at Leeds. Lieutenant Colonel Thomas Gonne accidentally shot himself supervising N.C.O.'s pistol practice the day the orders came, and Colonel Drury Curzon Drury Lowe was hastily gazetted back to take command. Some 65 men were plucked from other regiments, and by the twenty-fourth of February they were aboard the transports, 622 strong with 422 of their own horses. Lieutenant John Brown, the adjutant, and Quartermaster John Berryman, V.C., had both charged with the regiment at Balaklava as sergeants. The 1st (The King's) Dragoon Guards came down from Manchester 649 strong; the regiment had last seen action in China in 1860, and of the officers only the colonel had been on active service before.

By the first week in March the Duke of Cambridge had inspected all the departing units and the country settled back with an air of once again having done its duty by the Army. Little additional information had arrived from Natal; the colony appeared to be safe for the moment and there was nothing to be done but to await the outcome of events. The government now turned to face the considerable political pressure that had been building up for the last four weeks.

Her Majesty's loyal opposition did not intend to allow such a ready-made opportunity to slip by, and Isandhlwana in fact marked a turning point in South African policy. The disaster touched off a nationwide debate, in which the public sought a scapegoat for a lost battle and Parliament a scapegoat for a bankrupt policy. The fire mounted and the government trembled, and the Cabinet met on the seventh of March.

Disraeli, always sensitive to the temper of the House, was aware of the danger but refused to accede to a majority decision to recall Sir Bartle Frere. Whatever Frere and Chelmsford had done between them, they had been sent out as representatives of Cabinet policy, and what-ever Disraeli's private opinions of the two were, he refused to with-draw his official confidence. The result was a weak compromise, and the following day a stinging censure of the High Commissioner was published, terminating in a statement that his future actions would no doubt prevent a recurrence of any cause for complaint. He had not been justified, the censure claimed, in sending Cetshwayo an ultimatum without the full knowledge and sanction of the government, and noth-ing in his own communications justified the precipitousness of his action. Hicks Beach added a private letter urging him not to resign.

The censure was fully deserved, but the manner of its issue was not. The government had saved itself by tossing Frere to the wolves, and while they were in a position to answer at once any attack from Parliament or the press, Frere could not reply until two months and more had elapsed. Frere might continue to function, but his voice was now stripped of the authority he might have retained had the censure been private and the request to retain his post public. His power to shape policy was gone. Confederation was dead—it had died at Isan-dhlwana—and it was only for the sake of confederation that Frere had ever consented to accept the post.

The news reached him at a critical time. On the fifteenth of March, just as the first reinforcements were arriving in Natal, Frere finally set out for the Transvaal, where he was now more than six months over-due, and where Sir Theophilus Shepstone, K.C.M.G., sometime Secretary for Native Affairs of the colony of Natal and the first British Administrator of the Transvaal, had come to the end of his active career. The first bright, chancy days of the annexation, when understanding and energetic measures might still have secured the Boer population to the Crown, had passed, and the ensuing months had been squandered as well. Land reform, taxes, finances and native unrest had all been pressing problems that should have been dealt with at once. Somtseu had done little or nothing, and instead of native unrest the Transvaal now faced European unrest and the very real threat of a Boer rising. A quick grant of local autonomy in the form of a liberal constitution might have saved the situation, but Shepstone was incapable of conceiving or drafting such a document or of allowing others to do so for him. His answer to all criticism was complete withdrawal and massive inactivity; as a result, his finances were chaotic and Boer tempers flared unchecked. In January of 1879, just as Chelmsford's invasion was starting, he received word that his presence was desired in England by the Colonial Office. It was tantamount to recall, but to save his face he was allowed to depart on leave and Colonel Owen Lanyon was appointed Acting Administrator, to be confirmed two months later. Shepstone had reached Utrecht by the twenty-second of January, and there, late on the twenty-third, Captain Gardner found him on his own journey to Wood's column and told him there was little doubt but that his son George had fallen at Isandhlwana.

By March Frere's presence was desperately needed in the Transvaal. Kruger and Joubert were waiting in a camp thirty miles outside Pretoria with 1,500 armed and angry Boers. They wanted full independence for the Transvaal, and Frere was barely able to pacify them by promises of self-government within confederation, the use of their own language in the administration, and recognition of their beloved flag. Frere talked fast and earnestly, and the Boer leaders, under an impression that he had promised more than he actually had, ordered the camp to disband. Hours later the dispatch with the censure reached Frere; had it come a day earlier he might have had a revolt on his hands. He rode on to Pretoria to meet with Lanyon, and did not return to Natal.

Chelmsford, in the meantime, was preparing to renew the struggle, but a letter he penned on the ninth of February to the Secretary of State for War on an administrative matter soon returned to haunt him.

I consider it my duty to lay before you my opinion that it is very desirable, in view of future contingencies, that an officer of the rank of Major-General should be sent out to South Africa without delay.
In June 1878 I mentioned privately to His Royal Highness the Field-

Marshal Commander-in-Chief, that the strain of prolonged anxiety, physical and mental, was even then telling on me. What I felt then, I feel still more now.

His Excellency, Sir Bartle Frere, concurs in this representation and points out to me that the officer selected should be fitted to succeed him in the position of High Commissioner.

In making this representation I need not assure you that it will be my earnest desire to carry on my duties for Her Majesty's service up to the fullest extent of my powers.

Chelmsford
Lieut-General

The letter was published in England on the seventeenth of March and was widely and incorrectly interpreted as a request for relief. It triggered an explosion in the press, which was still hunting for a scapegoat and was undecided between Chelmsford and Durnford. With more indignation than attention to grammar, the *Standard* intoned: "No such appeal to the Authorities in England for dismissal from a position to which Lord Chelmsford felt himself unequal had ever before been addressed to them by a General in the field commanding Her Majesty's troops."

The accusation was quite unfair. Chelmsford was depressed and discouraged when he wrote; he had already requested reinforcements but had as yet not even heard how the news of Isandhlwana had been received in England. He was in the midst of a serious quarrel with Sir Henry Bulwer which took up much of the time he needed for his military problems, and he had no one to relieve him of the burden. He was a substantive major general with the local rank of lieutenant general, and the next senior man to him in southern Africa was Glyn, who had been a colonel since 1872. Strickland had been a deputy commissary general since 1870; he had a colonel's prerogatives but could not succeed to a line command, and he was fully occupied with transport duties in Natal. Chelmsford, therefore, with an eye to his health simply wanted a qualified second-in-command who could succeed him if necessary and who could at the same time take the more onerous administrative duties off his hands. Frere, concurring, had stipulated that the officer also be qualified to succeed him as well—a not unreasonable request since the rank was more than adequate for the post.

Chelmsford did not know it, but no less than four subordinate major generals were on their way to join him when his request arrived. He followed the first letter with a more clearly worded private note to the Duke of Cambridge, but the damage had been done, and the public image of Chelmsford as a man who would welcome recall as the result of Isandhlwana gained wide currency. As late as mid-May, almost three weeks after the Cabinet had decided to supersede him, he was still explaining to the Duke: "The idea of resigning whilst there was work in the Field to be done, never entered my head."

There was little military activity in the weeks following Isandhlwana. Life in the wet little laagers that dotted the roads was far from pleasant. The survivors of the Central Column had escaped with only the shirts on their backs. "I am obliged to let my beard grow, I regret to say," Harness wrote home from Helpmakaar, "for Ketshwayo has both my razors." He was commanding two companies of the 1st/24th, the bulk of the Natal Mounted Police, some Royal Engineers and his remaining four guns. He had lost half his men and all his transport and records, Stuart Smith was dead and Curling had suffered a nervous breakdown, and Harness despaired of ever reconstituting the unit that had been his whole world. The camp was built in a depression and entrenched with mealie bags, the grain began to rot and sprout in the rains and the cramped garrison slept in the mire. Fever struck, many sickened, a number died, and an addled doctor was soon caring for more than forty patients, with no medical supplies at hand.

The only activity was at Rorke's Drift, where the troubles of the 3d Regiment, NNC, had not ended on the twenty-third of January. The sullen Natal Kaffirs had been largely ignored during the day Glyn's force returned from Zululand and they had occupied themselves searching for food and killing such wounded Zulus as they could find in the vicinity. As night drew on, Lonsdale was ordered to keep his men outside the mission station and to furnish the pickets as well. This was an utter impossibility; it was now Thursday night, and the Natal Kaffirs had not been fed properly since Monday. In the intervening three days they had been herded, kicked and beaten from Isandhlwana to Matyana's stronghold and all the way back to Rorke's Drift, and had been held in line only at gunpoint. They now congregated in the crannies of the Oskarberg and refused to muster, and in the end Lonsdale and a few of the officers posted the pickets themselves.

Chelmsford had ordered Lonsdale and Cooper to Helpmakaar, leaving Hamilton-Browne in charge of the 3d Regiment. Before he went, the General asked him what should be done with the Natal Kaffirs, and Hamilton-Browne in disgust urged him to disband the lot. Chelmsford had only wanted an opinion and rode on without making a reply, and as soon as he was gone, Hamilton-Browne took it upon himself to end that unhappy unit's existence. He called the men together, berated them for the last time through Duncombe and sent them packing. He then formed the European N.C.O.'s into a mounted patrol which became the nucleus of three troops known as the Natal Horse.

Hamilton-Browne now eked out the government rations of the garrison by raiding and burning the small kraals for miles along the Zulu bank of the Buffalo. Few natives were safe in his presence. Having contributed to the ruination of whatever value the 3d Regiment, NNC, might have possessed, he now proceeded to wreak brutal vengeance on Zulu and Natal Kaffir alike. The kraals he ravaged were denuded of warriors, and he tortured the few scouts he found in search of information. Smith-Dorrien had ridden into Rorke's Drift from Helpmakaar the morning after Isandhlwana, and was shocked to find two Natal Kaffirs hanged from the gallows he had erected to stretch riems. He never discovered who they were or who had hanged them— they may have been men from Stephenson's batch who had joined Dabulamanzi and had been recognized by the garrison the following morning—but the gallows was used again. Several days later Hamilton-Browne rode down a young Zulu who had twisted a red rag about his head in the hope of being taken for a member of the NNC while he scouted Rorke's Drift from the Natal shore. Without a trial, Hamilton-Browne pronounced him a spy and cheerfully hanged him from the same structure. His raids continued for a space, but presently he was ordered to the Cape Colony to recruit Hottentots for Lonsdale's Mounted Rifles, and the Buffalo saw him no more.

On the fourth of February Major Wilsone Black led a small patrol out of Rorke's Drift to visit Fugitive's Drift. Scouts came across the bodies of Melvill and Coghill a half-mile from the river, and the Reverend George Smith read a burial service over a grave dug in the shelter of the rock under which they had died. The patrol then descended to the banks, still littered with dead horses and men. The river had gone down three feet since the fighting, and the rocky shallows lay exposed. A quarter of a mile below the drift a Colour case lay in a quiet pool, and Captain Harber, now of the Natal Horse, found the Queen's Colour of the 1st/24th a few yards beyond. The silk was in shreds, but the gilt lion and crown still surmounted the battered staff. The patrol bore it in triumph back to Rorke's Drift, and the men left their dinners to line the walls and cheer. Black handed the Colour to Colonel Glyn, who received it in tears. As a young officer thirteen years before, he had accepted it for the Battalion on the Curragh in Ireland. It was taken to Helpmakaar the next day and turned over to the 1st Battalion companies posted there. When the battalion returned to England, Queen Victoria sent for the Colour and placed a small wreath of silver immortelles about the crown. Despite its tattered condition it remained in service; the 1st Battalion carried it across the Rhine in December of 1918, and in March of 1933, after 67 years of use, it was finally laid up in the regimental chapel in the cathedral at Brecon.

Over a month later, on the fourteenth of March, Major Black led a patrol of 27 men to the field of Isandhlwana. A few Zulus from the neighboring kraals scurried away as the men posted vedettes and proceeded to inspect the field. More than seven weeks had passed since the battle, but all still lay where it had fallen. The Zulus had burned some of the tents and cut the others away, but the bare poles still stood. They had dragged many of the wagons away but over a hundred still stood behind the skeletons of their ox teams. A few of the bodies were identified but no one was buried; some were already skeletons and others so deliquescent they could not be approached. There was no trace of the Colours of the 2nd Battalion, but months later the bare staff of the Queen's Colour was found in a deserted kraal deep in Zululand. Officers, assuming that the standard itself had been taken to Ulundi, questioned some Zulus in the vicinity. The puzzled natives listened to the description of the Colour and replied that they had seen no such strange object; they added that they doubted it had been taken to the royal kraal, as Cetshwayo would never wear anything that gaudy.

The men poked through the debris that littered the field, and the incredible profusion of paper scattered about caught their attention— books, letters, cheques, photographs, newspapers, journals and company records. All unbroken rifles and all ammunition had been taken away, and every box of stores had been broken into. The spilled grain by the wagons had started to sprout, in some cases growing through and covering the bodies. The patrol left the field to follow the refugee route down to Fugitive's Drift. The dead artillery teams were still hanging down the face of the ravine, but the two guns had been cut loose and dragged away. Stuart Smith was lying on the edge of the river; the ground was softer here and they buried him where he had fallen.

Chelmsford, in the meantime, could do nothing to renew the invasion of Zululand until he heard what reinforcements were on the way. He could only wait, with such patience as he might muster, while fresh European volunteers dribbled into Natal from the Cape Colony and the Transvaal and while his transport officers struggled to scrape together the last available ox teams and what wagons could still be found. The problems were considerably worse than they had been in November and December of 1878; Chelmsford already controlled two-thirds of Natal's transport and had virtually crippled the colony's economy. Prices had risen steeply with the demand, fresh farms had been infected with cattle sickness, and with fall coming on suitable pasturage was hard to find. The rains and the heavy traffic had ruined the roads, and the sum of transport needed promised to be higher than ever before. Isandhlwana, Eshowe and the loss to disease, ill usage and rations had already cost more than 3,500 animals.

Mounted volunteers were the least of the problems, although there were few more to be found in Natal. The N.C.O.'s of the disbanded 3d Regiment, NNC, mounted at Rorke's Drift in the days following Isandhlwana, were formed into three troops of the Natal Horse totaling 140 men under De Burgh, Cooke and Bettington. The 42 men of Schermbrucker's Kaffrarian Vanguard were mounted, and the Frontier Light Horse began to recruit again, reaching sufficient strength to spawn a new unit 138 strong called the Natal Light Horse. This was placed under an ex-Imperial captain named Watt Whalley, who had started his career in the 17th Lancers and had then been wounded in the Sepoy Rebellion, in China, and in Abyssinia. He then joined the Papal Zouaves in time to be wounded in the Franco-Prussian War, commanded a regiment in the Carlist War (which he survived unscathed), and had reached southern Africa in time to be wounded again in the Ninth Kaffir War.

Lonsdale recruited 236 Mounted Rifles in the Cape Colony in February and March, including Hottentot volunteers; and a Captain Baker, late of the Ceylon Rifles, raised another 236 in the vicinity of Port Elizabeth. Colonel Ignatius Ferreira, an ex-Imperial officer, raised 115 mounted men in the Transvaal, and although no more Boers came forth to join Piet Uys and his gallant forty, a commandant named Pieter Raaf began enlisting Hottentots and such Europeans as he could find in the vicinity of Kimberley. When he rode into Zululand at the head of his 138 Transvaal Rangers, an officer of the Frontier Light Horse remarked that "a more forbidding lot of mixed Hottentots and the scum of the Diamond Fields was never collected together outside a prison wall." A mounted man with a gun was grist for the mill, and Buller happily added the Rangers to his command.

Fresh Natal Kaffir volunteers came forward as well. The five troops that had been with Durnford, each a distinct ethnic unit, had returned to their clans to recruit. The Edendale Mission fielded 128 men, now known as the Natal Native Horse and under Captain Cochrane, and Theophilus Shepstone, Jr., rode off to recruit in the Orange Free State and returned with 180 of Hlubi's baTlokwa. Jantji sent 68 mounted men, Mafunzi 73 and the amaNgwani 37 mounted scouts. All in all, 560 mounted natives armed with breech-loading carbines joined the more than 850 fresh colonial volunteers.

One further reinforcement fell into Chelmsford's net. On the twenty-first of February the General was riding back to Durban from a visit to Fort Pearson, when he encountered a smart gig driving north. John Dunn, the unhappy occupant, had been dreading this meeting, but it could be put off no longer. Chelmsford dismounted and joined him in the gig for a serious talk. Dunn was well aware that the war could only have one outcome, and he naturally hoped to return to Zululand when the fighting was over. He was desperately trying to maintain a precarious neutrality, and neither he nor his adherents had as yet done any fighting. To declare for the Zulus would make him a traitor, and whatever his way of life had been, he was a loyal Englishman at heart, but if he openly joined Chelmsford he might never be able to return to Zululand, and there was no room for him in the English society of Natal. Chelmsford now forced him off his fence. Dunn's domain lay between the Lower Drift of the Tugela and Eshowe, and communications with Pearson had broken down. Chelmsford needed reliable scouts who knew the countryside, and Dunn reluctantly promised to raise them. Chelmsford was sufficiently sympathetic to his problem not to force him to accept an official post, but before the column to relieve Eshowe finally got under way, the pressure had increased, and when the troops entered Zululand, John Dunn marched at the head of 244 armed retainers, officially listed as the Chief of Intelligence.

Sir Henry Bulwer proclaimed Wednesday, the twelfth of March, a Day of Humiliation and Prayer. The first shock had worn off, the panic was lifting, and the colony was looking forward to the arrival of the reinforcements. The populace dutifully flocked to its churches, and in most of them it heard a pious memorial service for the sons of Natal who had died at Isandhlwana, with an added tribute to the Imperial soldiery that had fallen as well. No such sermon was preached in the Cathedral of St. Peter in Pietermaritzburg. Like Amos of old, John William Colenso castigated his congregation for a people who had forgotten mercy and turned from righteousness. Calmly and dispassionately he traced the causes of the war, hammering home the full sense of guilt that he as a European and a Christian felt. He then mourned with them and with the thousands of grieving Zulu families the deaths of their sons. It was a memorable sermon, and perhaps the bravest act of a courageous lifetime. To Natal's credit, the colonists remembered it with pride.

Chelmsford had been having difficulties with Bulwer ever since his arrival in Natal, and they flared into open argument as the time for Frere's departure drew near. It seemed clear to the General that Natal was not shouldering its full share of a war that could only benefit the colony, and the implacable figure of the Lieutenant Governor stood in the path of every effort Chelmsford made to draw additional strength from Natal. The removal of the Zulu threat was to be accomplished by Imperial gold and Imperial blood, and the colony had contributed only a small number of mounted volunteers, over half of whom were simply transient residents and most of whom Bulwer was now holding back in Natal. It had made available only limited transport and produce, for which it charged high prices, and, above all, it had released only a small fraction of the teeming Natal Kaffirs. Chelmsford wanted martial law so that he might commandeer the produce and the transport, and, despite the unsatisfactory performance of the Natal Native Contingent to date, he envisaged a useful role for the colony's non-European population. Under the impression that the 3d Regiment, NNC, had simply deserted, he wanted it ordered back to the ranks. He also wanted nothing less than a mass invasion of Zululand by scores of thousands of Natal Kaffirs armed with their native weapons; he had no illusions about their ability to vanquish Zulu impis, but they might tie down the enemy regiments and erode his strength while his own forces won through to Ulundi. Bulwer, however, saw Natal as something more than a warehouse of military assets for the Imperial forces. The initial effort had already brought the colony's economy to the verge of a breakdown, and Bulwer was determined to prevent a collapse. Transport and produce were in short supply, and Chelmsford would have to compete for them in the open market. Above all, he was horrified by the General's plans for the Natal Kaffirs, and he refused point-blank to countenance any such schemes. No colonist wanted large masses of Natal Kaffirs armed or moved off their reserves; to do so might upset the precarious system that Shepstone had built over the years, and Natal Kaffirs raiding into Zululand would inevitably draw the Zulu ire as no European invasion could ever do. Bulwer was prepared to make available several thousand Natal Kaffirs for labor in the colony, and he would permit the existing units of the NNC to fill their ranks, but that was all. After a thorough investigation he satisfied himself that the 3d Regiment had in fact been disbanded and had not deserted as charged, and he refused to order it to reassemble.

Bulwer's attitude appeared as little short of deliberate obstruction to Chelmsford, and without Frere's astute tact to move the Lieutenant Governor, his efforts to build a reserve of supplies and transport were brought to a virtual standstill. The impasse degenerated into a sterile and acrimonious correspondence. Complaints to the Colonial Office were hopeless; no answer could be expected for over two months, and Chelmsford was facing problems that demanded an immediate solution. He made the best he could of the situation, but the price was high. Expenditures soared, and every planned movement had to wait until the transport had been collected. His reputation, already besmirched, might have been retrieved by fast, decisive movements, but even after the reinforcements arrived, the weeks passed slowly with little movement, and England's patience was running out. The public image of Chelmsford as a dilatory dawdler gradually took shape, while his progress was tied to the precious and exasperating oxen.

The 3d Regiment was gone for good, but there remained the three battalions of Durnford's 1st Regiment and the two of Major Graves' 2nd Regiment. Chelmsford now dropped the regimental structure and established the five battalions as independent units. Shapland Graves had taken command of the 2nd Regiment on the march to Eshowe, turning his 1st Battalion over to Captain Geoffry Barton. Chelmsford confirmed the original battalion commanders, and made an effort to arm the NNC properly. Barton's men, now the 4th Battalion, all received Martini-Henrys, and Captain Charles Cherry's 3d Battalion, busy constructing Fort Cherry in the vicinity of Umsinga, Sniders and muzzle-loaders.

One immediate military problem pressed on Chelmsford while he waited for his reinforcements. Pearson, flung thirty miles into Zululand like an isolated pawn, could neither advance nor retreat and was doing remarkably little good where he was. Chelmsford did not doubt his ability to beat off an attack, and he was in no immediate danger, but there were 1,400 European troops and 460 natives in Eshowe, communications had broken down and no one knew how long their rations could last. On clear days the edge of the plateau was visible from the Lower Drift, although the site of the fort could not be seen. The intervening country was broken by watercourses and bad tracks, and the distance was too great for a large force to cover in one day. Chelmsford wanted an advanced coastal base, but until he actually saw the site of the fort, he would not be certain if it should be placed there or sited elsewhere. Pearson was far too weak in transport to extricate himself, and what little he had would slow him to a snail's pace if he tried to get out. In any event, a relief column would have to go in to get him out and to bring up adequate supplies for the advanced base, and by the tenth of February Chelmsford was at the Lower Drift to investigate the possibilities. They were most unpromising, and he abandoned the project at once. The small garrisons at Fort Pearson and at Fort Tenedos across the river were needed to guard the vital road to Durban, and there were no troops to spare. Pearson would have to await the arrival of the reinforcements from England.

Life for the garrison at Eshowe swiftly slid into a strange routine of semisiege. Never closely invested, and rarely under the fire of more than an occasional sniper, the troops lived in the mild anticipation of an attack that never came. By the end of January the church and the three buildings that comprised the mission station had been surrounded by an oblong fortification. There was abundant labor and little to interfere with the work, and under Captain Wynne's direction the defenses flourished. The fort and the moat were finished, with a drawbridge leading to a main gate. A loopholed palisade of thick logs surmounted the parapet, the four fieldpieces and the Gatling gun were revetted and wire entanglements and an abatis ringed the position. Much of the moat was filled with sharpened stakes, and the firing lanes were posted with distance markers.

Mounted patrols roamed the neighboring hills in the daytime, and the men were free to come and go in the vicinity of the fort. The remaining oxen went out to graze each morning, with a company of infantry to support the herdsmen, and the flock ranged farther and farther afield as the nearby pasturage was used. The pickets came in at night and the horses and cattle were bedded in the moat, while the men slept under the wagons that had been brought into the fort. An occasional patrol skirmished with small parties of Zulus—one or two of the mounted men were lost in this fashion—and the artillery loosed warning shots at any warriors who showed themselves on the hills. There was bathing in the spring betwixt times, organized games in the afternoons, and the two regimental bands played in the evenings. Mr. Robertson lectured on Zulu history.

Pearson cut the ration issue and estimated that he could hold out until early April. The food was adequate but the diet monotonous, and late in February the garrison searched the effects of the mounted men who had returned to the Lower Drift and auctioned off their finds. Tobacco, cocoa, condensed milk, bottles of pickles and curry powder and a large ham went for prices only the officers could afford.

There was continual rain and fog every night, and the closely packed men were sleeping on the bare ground without ponchos. Fever and the inevitable dysentery started in February. Norbury, the naval surgeon, had established a hospital in the church, and the straw pallets began to fill. When the medical supplies ran out, he raided the veterinary stores, and was then reduced to experimenting with infusions of bark from nearby trees. To his astonishment, some of them worked very well.

Strengthened patrols of mounted men moved farther afield. They searched for forage and exchanged shots with the ever-present Zulus, who closed in behind as the patrols returned to the fort. Once or twice impis of several thousand men were seen in the distance, but they never closed with the fort. Parties of two or three daring warriors caused more trouble. They cut down the trees at night under which the pickets had sought shade on the preceding day, and they pulled out the distance markers which ringed the fort. The engineers stopped this pastime by planting a large charge of dynamite under a prominent marker, tamped with heavy stones and rigged with a detonating device.

On the first of March Pearson led 400 men out of the fort at two in the morning. He had discovered one of Dabulamanzi's home kraals seven miles to the north and had decided to destroy it. The force groped its way through the dark and came upon the kraal, of forty or fifty huts, at dawn. About fifty startled Zulus bolted into the hills, some clad in red tunics acquired at Isandhlwana, and a few bold souls started a harmless rifle fire at extreme range. After an unsuccessful attempt to catch a prisoner or two, Pearson shelled the refugees and fired the huts, and the force started back. By ten in the morning the foray was over.

The next morning was sunny, and the men in the fort noticed a bright, twinkling glare from the vicinity of the Lower Drift. The first fear that Fort Pearson was afire gave way to great excitement with the realization that a heliograph was at work. Nothing definite could be made of the signals, but every man with a pocket mirror crawled to a vantage point and tried to flash back.

The third of March was intermittently cloudy, but the signals continued and part of a message was finally read: ". . . look out for 1,000 men on the thirteenth, sally out when you see me to . . ." Two days later the complete message was in hand; a column was planning to advance on the thirteenth, and the garrison was to come to meet it on the Inyezane. The next days brought cloudy weather and the garrison tried frantically to acknowledge receipt. A fire balloon failed, as did an enormous paper screen mounted on the skyline. The Zulus were burning grass on the plain and the smoke obscured all efforts. Pearson finally dispatched a runner by a circuitous path, announcing that he had rations till the seventh of April and that he was prepared to march on the thirteenth to meet the relief, but the heliograph then reported that the expedition had been postponed until the first of April. The next day a Captain MacGregor rigged a suitable heliograph. Sighting a long iron tube on Fort Pearson, he mounted a bit of paper at either end of the bore. He then steadied a pocket mirror to catch the sun and reflect it down the tube, assuming that when both bits of paper were illuminated the signals, made by covering and uncovering the mirror by hand, could be read at the Lower Drift. From then on intercommunication was continuous while the sun shone, and Eshowe began to catch up on the news from the outside world after more than a month of isolation.

Private messages were permitted after the official traffic had been cleared. Pearson's wife was expectant, and the first private message from Eshowe was "How is Mrs. Pearson?" The reply started at once, but only "Mrs. Pearson is—" had been received before a cloud bank cut the message off. It was several hours before the anxious colonel was able to get the second half of the reply, "—well and delivered of a baby daughter."

The garrison now started to take an active interest in the campaign. Wynne began to break a straight three-mile road through the Hintza Forest to replace the wandering five miles of the old track, and the men started to overhaul the wagons, which were virtually embedded in the walls of the enclosure. On the tenth of March a native runner arrived from Fort Pearson with an inconsequential message a fortnight old; he claimed that Zulus swarming about the track had forced him far afield to hide in the bush, but it was noticed that he was rested and well fed and that his legs had recently been oiled, so he was arrested.

Two Zulus appeared on the skyline under a white flag on the twenty-third of March. The Reverend Robertson rode out to question them with several officers, and the envoys were then blindfolded and brought into the fort. One had been sent by Cetshwayo to Bishop Schreuder to inquire why the Zulu nation was being attacked; he had returned the answer, "to carry out the terms of the ultimatum," and the king had then sent him on to Eshowe to offer the garrison a safe conduct to the Tugela, providing they would not destroy mealie fields on the march. Dabulamanzi sent the second man to accompany the first, to confirm that the impis would be stayed if the safe conduct were accepted. Pearson regarded the offer as a trick and ignored it, keeping the envoys in irons in the fort.

The excitement mounted as April drew near. The slaughter beeves were long gone, as was all tea, coffee and tobacco, and the men were subsisting on the stringy draft oxen and smoking the used tea leaves. Over a hundred men a day were answering sick call and the hospital was crowded. More than a score had died, including Midshipman Coker, nineteen years old, who to the last had insisted on sleeping in the open beside his beloved Gatling gun. Several of the officers were critically ill with dysentery or enteric fever, including the indefatigable Captain Wynne. In desperation, Surgeon Norbury had sent two Natal Kaffirs to the Lower Drift, and they returned on the twenty-ninth, laden with drugs and English newspapers. A subscription was raised to reward them; they reported that Chelmsford was planning to leave with the rescue column on the first of April, and that Natal Kaffirs along the lower Tugela had called to Zulus across the river that "the cow is just going to calve."

On the second of April the men crowded to vantage points before dawn. For the last two nights they had followed the relief column by its nightly campfires, and they had seen the mounted men scouting along the coastal track known as John Dunn's Road. The advance section of the column had laagered the night before in plain sight twelve miles away, on a grassy, undulating plain just south of the Inyezane six miles downstream from the scene of Pearson's action. The dawn had no sooner brightened than the stillness was broken by the distant boom of artillery, and as the light strengthened, eyes straining through telescopes could discern a major attack on the laager. Black masses of Zulus were pressing in on three sides, and the tide rolled into the edges of the thick clouds of white powder smoke that poured out of the laager before it finally receded. By seven o'clock it was all over, and the faint crackle of musketry, punctuated by the sputter of Gatling guns, had died away. Pearson, ready this day to march out with his entire garrison, flashed his congratulations but stood fast. It would have taken him four hours to reach the scene of the battle by the fifteen miles of track that skirted the broken intervening country.

Chelmsford acknowledged the congratulatory message and replied that he would start for Eshowe the following morning. Pearson should then be ready to abandon the fort completely. The relief started as scheduled, slowed by the presence of a herd of draft oxen for Eshowe's transport, and the need to scout for remnants of the broken impi. At four in the afternoon Pearson could stand it no longer and started down the new road through the Hintza Forest with 500 men. The first person he encountered was the ubiquitous Norris-Newman, who with two other correspondents had spurred ahead of Chelmsford and, spotting the new track, had taken it, leaving his two colleagues dashing eagerly in the wrong direction. "First in Eshowe!" he said, thrusting his arm out. "Proud to shake hands with an Eshowian!" Pearson continued to meet Chelmsford, and Norris-Newman rode into the fort while the garrison lined the ramparts to cheer. Pearson soon returned with the General and his staff and the draft oxen, and the rest of the column continued to arrive until midnight, under a brilliant moon. The 91st Highlanders were the first regiment to come up, marching in past the scraggle of fresh graves by the road with their band playing "The Campbells Are Coming" and Colours uncased. Eshowe, after a siege of ten weeks, had been relieved.

The garrison, weakened by the long stretch on reduced rations and slowed by 119 wagons and 34 sick in twelve ambulances, took a leisurely three days to reach the Tugela. The column passed the wagons Colonel Ely had abandoned, to find the site marked by a sickening stench from the decomposing stores. Beyond was the abandoned bivouac of the impi that had attacked Chelmsford, and nearby the grave of the men who had fallen on the Inyezane on the twenty-second of January. The column paused to replace the hastily erected cross with a more elaborate marker carved by one of the officers. Two of the sick died en route, and the survivors had no sooner crossed the Tugela into Natal than two of the sick officers finally succumbed. They were buried in the small cemetery on the knoll by Fort Pearson, near the nameless graves of a dozen enlisted men, each of which was marked by an iron cross with a small plate reading, "Here Lies a Brave British Soldier." One of the officers was Captain Wynne; he was just thirty-six and left a widow and three young sons, aged five, two, and seven months, behind in England.

The military situation in Natal had changed considerably during the ten weeks of the siege, and much had happened. Chelmsford had returned to Durban on the twentieth of February after his first visit to Fort Pearson to collect transport and rebuild the native levies, and the first reinforcements had reached that city on the sixth of March. H.M.S. *Shah*, returning from an extended commission in the Pacific, heard the news of Isandhlwana while recoaling at St. Helena. Captain Bradshaw took it upon himself to change his orders; he picked up a company of the Connaught Rangers and a field artillery battalion from the island's garrison and steamed for Durban, where he landed 394 of his own men as well to join the Naval Brigade. The 57th Regiment landed from Ceylon on the eleventh of March. H.M.S. *Boadicea* landed 228 sailors on the fifteenth of March, bringing the Naval Brigade up to 863; and the 91st Regiment (Princess Louise's Argyllshire Highlanders) trooped ashore on the seventeenth. On the twentieth six companies of the 3d/60th (The King's Royal Rifle Corps) landed at Durban, and fresh drafts began to arrive almost daily. Brevet Major Charles John Bromhead came late in March and joined his younger brother at Rorke's Drift. The 24th Regiment scraped every man in the depot at Brecon together, tapped other regiments, and recruited in Civil Street, and by the eleventh of April landed 15 officers and 526 men to make good the regiment's losses.

With the arrival of the first six companies of the 3d/60th, Chelmsford finally felt strong enough to mount the Eshowe relief. Pearson had estimated the first week of April as the latest his rations would last, and it was already perilously late. Chelmsford took personal command at Fort Pearson on the twenty-third of March, and by the twenty-eighth all the troops to participate had been ferried across the Tugela and were camping north of Fort Tenedos, in driving rains that put out most of the campfires. The river was in flood and there was still only one punt, which would accommodate only a company of infantry or one wagon and its team at a time.

There were to be two Divisions on the march. Lieutenant Colonel Francis Towry Adeane Law, R.A., commanded an Advance Division to which were assigned two companies of the Buffs, five of the 99th Regiment, the whole of the 91st, and 350 men of the Naval Brigade. Lieutenant Colonel Wykeham Leigh Pemberton, 3d/60th Rifles, commanded the Rear Division with the 57th Regiment and the six companies of his own battalion, now under Lieutenant Colonel Francis Vernon Northey. Pemberton also had 190 sailors and a company of the Royal Marine Light Infantry. The former 2nd Regiment, NNC, now restyled the 4th and 5th Battalions, was split between the divisions. The Royal Navy had also landed two nine-pounder fieldpieces, two 24-pound rocket tubes and two additional Gatling guns, and Major Percy Barrow commanded 70 Mounted Infantry, 130 mounted Natal Kaffirs and had general charge of 150 of John Dunn's scouts as well.

All told, Chelmsford commanded 3,390 armed Europeans and 2,280 Natal Kaffirs, a considerably stronger force than the original 3d Column he had first accompanied into Zululand. The total included a bare fifty European volunteers from Natal. When Bulwer had forbidden any of the Mounted Rifle units to enter Zululand, a number of the men quit their commands in disgust, formed a new unit called the Natal Volunteer Guides, elected Captain Friend Addison of the Stanger Mounted Rifles to lead them, and offered their services to Barrow, who accepted with delight.

One belated volunteer arrived just as the column was ready to start. Bulwer's order had been designed to keep just such boys as the sixteen-year-old John Robinson Royston of the Isipongo Mounted Rifles out of danger, and when his unit paraded at Stanger to pick men for the Volunteer Guides, his services were refused. He promptly deserted and rode north after the departing Guides, reaching the punt at the Lower Drift of the Tugela just as three men came pounding after him with orders for his arrest. Night overtook the party on the ride back to Stanger, and as soon as the escort was asleep, Royston crept off again, reaching the Tugela at four in the morning. The river was in flood, and Royston did not care to wait for the punt's first scheduled crossing. He gave a Natal Kaffir a half-crown to ferry his saddle and kit across later and then plunged into the torrent to swim his horse across himself. Resting on a midstream sand bar until it was light, he finally reached the Zulu shore with dozens of soldiers cheering him on. Addison gave in and enrolled him as a special scout at ten shillings a day.

If Chelmsford had been careful on his first excursion, he was doubly so now. Every cart and wagon in the convoy was to have ammunition boxes in it, the lids of the regimental reserve boxes were all to be unscrewed, and a screwdriver was to be attached to at least one other box in every wagon. The wagons were to from a square laager at night, 130 yards on a side. A shelter trench was to circle the laager nine feet from the wagons, the European troops were to sleep between the trench and the wagons, and the Natal Kaffirs, the horses and the draft oxen were to bed down in the laager itself. All hands would rise at four in the morning to stand to arms, and no bugle call but the alarm was ever to be sounded. A picket of a dozen men would be placed a half-mile in front of each laager face every night, and native scouts would be pushed out a half-mile beyond the pickets.

The transport was still a nightmare. Despite the continuing rains, Chelmsford dispensed with all tentage and he was only carrying rations for ten days, plus a month's supply for the advanced base. Even the scant minimum of equipage, however, with the ammunition and rations needed 44 carts and almost a hundred wagons, with close to 3,000 oxen and another herd to bring out the Eshowe wagons. The convoy took up more than two and a half miles of track on the march, and while the coastal road promised smoother country than the inland track Pearson had taken, the drifts were just as numerous and even wider, and the column could not expect to better ten miles a day.

The relief finally marched at six in the morning on the twenty-ninth of March. By noon the head of the convoy was at the Inyoni River, nine miles away, but it was dusk before the tail of the wagon train was up, and the inexperienced conductors botched the laager, which would only hold a third of the cattle. The next morning was wet and so foggy that the oxen could not go out to graze until after five, and it was eight before the column started. By evening, however, the Advance Division was in an adequate laager on the southern bank of the Amatikulu, seven miles farther along. Barrow's scouts had been encountering Zulus during the day, and an impi seemed to be gathering off to the northwest. Chelmsford had reason to fear an attack while he was on the march, or even worse, in a laagered camp while the oxen were out grazing, and he could only hope that the attack would come in the evening or at dawn, with man and beast behind his shelter trench.

The Amatikulu was in full flood, forty yards across and four feet deep. Barrow's men and Dunn's scouts got across in the morning, after torrential rains had fallen in the night. The Advance Division crossed in two hours, the men wading in water up to their armpits, with their boots tied about their necks and their rifles and ammunition pouches held over their heads. They established a camp a mile and a half past the drift, in the shelter of a river bend, and sat down to await the transport. Every cart and wagon had to be double-yoked, and six hours passed before Pemberton's Rear Division could start the crossing. By dusk the whole column was in a laagered camp, soaked to the skin and less than two miles from their morning's camp, with eleven hours of hard work behind them.

Captain William C. F. Molyneaux, 22nd Regiment, was Chelmsford's A.D.C., and he was assigned as laager-master on the first of April. He had been through the Ninth Kaffir War with Chelmsford but had been invalided home and had only returned to Natal when the news of Isandhlwana reached England. He had reached Durban on the twenty-second of March, pausing only long enough to purchase two miserable nags which he named "Lampas" and "Poll Evil" after their most prominent ailments, and had gotten to Fort Pearson just as the column was about to start. He now rode out of camp on Lampas, accompanied by John Dunn, to pick a laager site on the Inyezane. The two men found one on a grassy rise a mile south of the river, hard by the burned military kraal of Gingindhlovu. Molyneaux marked out the corners and by the time the first wagons came up, he was ready to guide each one into place. By five in the evening the laager was formed, and the men cooked dinner before they started the shelter trench.

Barrow's scouts had reported the Zulus massing behind Umisi Hill to the west, and Dunn thought there might be more warriors farther up the Inyezane. He rode out of camp with Molyneaux to see later in the evening, and both men were thankful for a blinding rainstorm that hid them from enemy scouts. They found no Zulus along the southern bank, and Dunn then stripped and gave his horse and clothing to Molyneaux to hold while he worked his way across the river with the aid of a fallen tree, carrying only his rifle and a handful of cartridges. It was quite dark before he returned to a somewhat shaken Molyneaux, with news of an impi and bivouac fires beyond the river.

The night was quiet but far from comfortable. The shelter trench filled with water, and over 5,000 men and 3,000 animals had churned five acres of sodden soil into an evil-smelling compost. The wagons could not be moved until the ground dried, so Chelmsford decided to spend the following day in camp, sending the NNC out to provoke the expected attack.

The morning of the second of April broke in a white rainless mist that presaged a hot day. The camp rose at dawn to stand to arms, but before the Natal Kaffirs could leave the camp, the advanced pickets fell back with the news that the impi was coming. The bugles sounded the alarm, and the Imperial infantry and the Naval Brigade, two deep, manned the waist-high rampart behind the shelter trench, with the rockets, fieldpieces and Gatling guns posted in the corners. The mounted men and the NNC waited behind the infantry, and conductors, drivers and other noncombatants scrambled up on the wagons to watch. Chelmsford, still wearing a red woolen nightcap, paced up and down behind the infantry with his mounted staff behind.

The impi came into sight as the mist cleared. The horns had already raced far ahead and were almost separated from the loins. The left wing trotted along the northern bank of the Inyezane until it was abreast of the laager and then wheeled to splash across the stream in two columns, splitting again as it emerged from the water to plunge into the long grass, so that three separate regimental masses began the approach to the northern laager faces. The loins and the right wing dropped over Umisi Hill to the west and also split into three groups, so that no less than six Zulu regiments were deployed in simultaneous attacks against three of the laager faces. These were all regiments that had been at Isandhlwana or Rorke's Drift: the uVe, the inGobama-khosi, the umCijo with the incorporated drafts of the umHlanga, the uMbonambi and Dabulamanzi with his headringed uThulwana. An in-Duna named Somopo commanded, and he dropped 2,000 reserves a mile to the west before advancing with the remaining 10,000 warriors. The attack was ill conceived. Cetshwayo had ordered Somopo to prevent the column from linking with the garrison at Eshowe, and he had waited as long as he dared. He had failed to attack the column while it was crossing one of the drifts, and he was now attacking a strong laager before the draft oxen had been turned out to graze; if he had been able to drive them off, he might have immobilized the column.

A Gatling gun opened the fight with a sighting burst that ripped into a group of warriors as they disappeared into the tall grass a thousand yards away. They were only three and four hundred yards off when they emerged again, and the infantry companies opened with volley fire. The ordered crashes were ragged at first—the ranks were filled with young recruits who had hardly fired a rifle in practice before—but they stopped most of the charges where the grass ended a hundred yards away. The company officers took great pains with the firing, and one, Captain Charles Kennedy of the 99th, sprang clear over the shelter trench to make sure his men could see him.

The Zulu attack stalled, halting before the awesome but harmless rocket tubes, and Chelmsford ordered Barrow out to push the left horn back. The movement was premature; Zulus on either side pressed forward and threatened to cut off the mounted men, and Chelmsford sent Molyneaux out to call Barrow back. The men had to fight their way into the laager; Barrow and two others were wounded, and a Zulu put a bullet through Lampas just as Molyneaux put him at the shelter trench. The horse faltered and then somersaulted, pitching Molyneaux into the mud. He picked himself up, pistoled the horse and then cleared him of bridle and saddle, which he carried around the laager to his batman Noot, whom he ordered to saddle Poll Evil.

Noot was perched on a wagon, loading rifles for John Dunn, who was calmly picking off the Zulu inDunas he could recognize. An enormous Boer conductor was seated in a chair in the bed of a nearby wagon, alternating accurate shots with swigs from a gin bottle. Norris-Newman and Hamilton-Browne were firing from other wagons. The scourge of the 3d Regiment, NNC, had taken a few days' leave from his new unit to visit friends at Fort Pearson after the column left, and had prevailed on the officer commanding to let him take dispatches on to Chelmsford. As the Zulus began to break cover, Dunn noticed that the infantry companies still had their rear-sight leaves raised for long-range firing and the volleys were passing well over the heads of the attackers. He caught Chelmsford's attention to point this out, and the sights were promptly lowered.

The rushes pressed forward for twenty minutes or so, but there was little heart in them and hardly a Zulu reached to within twenty yards of the trench. The regiments had only reassembled a week or so ago, after resting from the Isandhlwana campaign; their ranks were thinned and the bitter knowledge of what the massed rifles leveled against them could do was heavy upon them. One knot of warriors attacking the northern face broke cover and charged, falling to a man before they reached the trench. Only an uDibi boy, a mat-carrier ten or twelve years old, raced through the fire and hurdled the trench to fall, confused and weaponless, against the outer face of the rampart. A brawny sailor from H.M.S. *Boadicea* leaned over to collar him and dragged him, kicking and squirming, into the laager. He was cuffed into submission and sat on by his captor until the engagement was over; he was then adopted by the crew as a mascot and eventually passed into the Royal Navy.

As the rushes died down, the warriors took shelter in the grass and behind clumps of bushes and opened a wild fire on the laager. A few shots struck home. A bullet grazed Crealock and another dropped Lieutenant Johnson of the 99th in front of his commanding officer. A slug struck Lieutenant Colonel Northey deep in the right shoulder. He fell and recovered himself. Turning the command over to a major, he walked around the laager to the medical wagon, where a naval surgeon extracted the bullet. Northey then returned to his battalion and resumed command. He started to cheer his men, shouting to be heard over the din. A sudden hemorrhage choked him off, and he collapsed in a spray of arterial blood. Four days later he was dead.

The Zulus were now wavering openly, so Chelmsford sent Barrow out again and ordered the NNC to follow him. The Zulus fired a few last shots and then turned to flee, casting aside their weapons to run the faster. The reserve joined the route, and by half past seven the last warrior had disappeared over the Inyezane or behind Umisi Hill. Chelmsford had issued cavalry sabers to the Mounted Infantry, but this was a weapon that took practice to use effectively. The Zulu shields easily turned the great slashing cuts that the men tried at first, and one man severed the ear of his own horse as he swung on a warrior. A few Zulus turned at bay with their assegais and were finally ridden down by men who had learned to use the point.

The Zulu losses had been heavy. Almost 700 bodies lay in the grass around the laager, Barrow's men and the suddenly enthusiastic Natal Kaffirs had accounted for several hundred more, and scores of dead warriors littered the track of the retreat. Over 400 guns were recovered, many of them dropped as the Zulus recrossed the Inyezane, and a number of Martini-Henrys bore the stamp of the 24th Regiment on the stock. A dead inDuna carried an English officer's sword; Crealock's clerk recognized it and returned it to Lieutenant Porteous's family.

Chelmsford had lost two officers and eleven men killed, and a further 48 had been wounded. Stray bullets had killed or wounded 34 oxen and a dozen horses, including Poll Evil. Most of the companies had only expended six or seven rounds of ammunition per man in the carefully controlled volleys, a bitter reminder of what might have been made of the opportunity at Isandhlwana had the troops been kept together. Chelmsford was more than satisfied; it was precisely the kind of battle he wanted and which he would continue to seek until the Zulu power was broken.

Eshowe was relieved the following day. Chelmsford decided to abandon the site, preferring an advanced base nearer the better coastal road. Before starting back, Chelmsford heard that Dabulamanzi had retired to his Esulwini kraal six miles to the north, and he took Barrow's men out in an effort to catch him. Dunn, still clinging to his unofficial status, ignored the general order and pouted until Chelmsford sent him a personal invitation. The Zulus were gone by the time they arrived, but Dunn spotted Dabulamanzi on a high cliff a half-mile away, and the two old friends traded fruitless shots at 1,200 yards. The troops fired the huts and retreated as cartridges hidden in the thatch began to explode.

Pearson had started south on the fourth, laagering a scant four miles away near the Inyezane. Chelmsford followed on the fifth, camping on his heels, but the track was so bad and the garrison's progress so slow that the General sent them on by the old track, while he swung wide to regain the coastal road. He laagered farther down the Inyezane on the sixth, and as the men turned in, they could see Eshowe, fired by the vengeful Zulus, in flames behind them.

Each regiment put pickets out 400 yards from the laager, and Dunn's scouts occupied the open fields beyond. The night was quiet and dark, but shortly before dawn a single distant shot sounded. A picket squad of the 3d/60th, clad in dark green, bolted for the laager, followed by Dunn's natives. The startled guard company along the shelter trench fixed bayonets and then fired at the silent men rushing out of the night, killing one man and wounding four others before they realized their mistake. The survivors of the picket tumbled into the laager, and when Dunn's scouts followed them, the flustered guard caught them on the bayonet. Dunn had taught them to answer "Friend!" on challenge, but their frantic cries of "Flend! Flend!" failed to halt the slaughter. Dunn rushed up from his wagon, crying, "My God! They're killing my people! Oh, my children!" He found three of his men dead and another eight wounded. Chelmsford convened a court-martial, which reduced the sergeant of the picket to the ranks and sentenced him to five years' penal servitude, but the proceedings were eventually quashed.

The column reached Gingindhlovu on April seventh, moving a mile and a half past the battlefield to avoid the stench, and laagering near the coastal road. Here the General left Pemberton to establish the new advanced base, to be called Fort Chelmsford, while he himself rode south with his staff to return to Fort Pearson. On the road they passed Dunn's main residence, which had been looted and burned. Dunn regarded the devastation stoically; the furniture—even his piano—could be replaced, but his journals could not. Writing came hard to him, and he valued the few records he had. Molyneaux heard him muttering as he poked at the wreckage, "I have not done with the Zulus yet."

By the twelfth of April all but Pemberton's force were back in Natal. There had been mixed news from Wood's area, but all the reinforcements had arrived and the aftermath of the first invasion had been dealt with. It was time to plan the second.

THE LEFT FLANK COLUMN

T HE DISASTER to the Central Column left the flanking columns deprived of any meaningful strategic role. Pearson was stranded high and dry at Eshowe, and while Evelyn Wood had extricated his 4th Column from Zululand, he had retreated to a defensive position at Kambula. Wood was now at liberty to occupy himself as he saw fit until the reinforcements arrived from England and Chelmsford was once again ready to move on Ulundi.

The area offered a number of interesting possibilities. It swarmed with semiautonomous chieftains who had not thrown in with Cetshwayo, and Wood was intrigued by the idea of defecting several of them to the British cause. The principal inDuna thereabouts was Uhamu, Cetshwayo's half brother, now forty-five years old and enormously fat, who had never been reconciled to his monarch's policies. Uhamu commanded some 6,000 adherents and had always been friendly to the English, and Wood entertained hopes of bringing him and his people into Natal. Uhamu, however, had left his kraal and was hiding far to the east near the Swazi border, waiting to see how the fighting went.

Two smaller clans demanded immediate attention. The Swazi freebooter Mbilini commanded a band of renegade Zulus who infested the Zungi Range to the east of Kambula and who were raiding to the northwest as far as Luneberg, 25 miles away. They had been joined by a petty Zulu chieftain named Manyanyoba, and the two marauders, beyond any control from Ulundi, were pillaging small kraals and isolated homesteads for miles about. The main road into the eastern Transvaal led up from Luneberg, crossed the Intombi River at Myer's Drift five miles past the tiny settlement, ran through Derby and finally reached Middleburg, 130 miles to the north, and Lydenburg in the heart of Sekukuni's country. Military supplies and produce moved back and forth between Natal and the Transvaal along this road, and its lower reaches passed through mountainous terrain and were under continual attack by the freebooters. Mbilini and Manyanyoba between them did not command sufficient weight to justify a concentration of troops, but they were strong enough to paralyze all traffic that tried to move without a strong escort.

Under the original invasion scheme, Colonel Rowland's 5th Column had been based at Luneberg, concerned not so much with Zululand as with the unsettled frontier of the eastern Transvaal and just such problems as these marauders in the disputed territories of northwest Zululand. Rowland began to lash out at these gadflies in February, and as soon as Wood was settled at Kambula, Buller took the Frontier Light Horse and the Boers under Piet Uys over to Luneberg to help. Rowland and Buller twice attacked the marauders at Eloya Mountain and in the caves where Manyanyoba was hiding; they killed forty Zulus and captured 200 head of cattle but failed to break either band. Late in February the Transvaal Boers began to congregate on the high veld, and Rowland started for Pretoria with his staff, turning the troops at Luneberg over to Wood's command.

There was work for Buller to the east of Kambula as well. The Frontier Light Horse had little rest, and young George Mossop, now known as "Chops," welcomed the days "A" Troop was left in camp to provide pickets. Between raids to the west, Buller led his men on long forays into the hills north of the Black Umfolozi. On the first of February he struck at the emaQulusini, and on the tenth, between his rides with Rowland, he harried the kraals at the foot of Hlobane Mountain and brought 500 head of cattle back to Kambula. Hlobane itself was much on his mind, ever since the day he stood atop Zunguin and watched 4,000 warriors drilling on the lower slopes of the grim table top. His men came under fire from the steep cliffs on every raid to the east, more and more cattle were being driven to the safety of the upper plateau and more and more Zulus were seeking shelter on the lower plateau.

If an occasional troop of the Frontier Light Horse was left in camp, Buller himself took no rest. He was in the saddle every day, riding forty and fifty miles, and no one ever saw him asleep, hardly ever saw him dismounted, so that the legend of his restless and inexhaustible strength grew apace. Wood drove himself as hard as Buller. Sleeping fully clothed for weeks on end, he had a fixed habit of rising twice nightly to visit all the outlying pickets on foot, returning soaked to the waist from the wet grass. He had forbidden his staff to accompany him, but he was growing deaf, and Captain the Honourable Ronald George Elidor Campbell, Coldstream Guards, the second son of the Earl of Cawdor, feared he might miss a challenge and be shot, and followed him silently on all his rounds. Wood's health was no better than it had ever been, and the lawn tennis, polo and tugs-of-war he insisted on organizing added to the strain of the incessant work in the wet camp. Fever prostrated him several times, and the devoted Campbell nursed him back to his feet.

His amiable correspondence with Chelmsford continued. Wood wrote long, chatty letters, commenting freely on the shortcomings of various officers in Natal and offering sage and sometimes patronizing advice on matters that were no concern of his. Chelmsford let all this pass, including repeated recommendations to start hiring additional transport for the coming campaign; the General already controlled every draft animal he could locate. Wood finally took matters into his own hands and sent officers to the Orange Free State with a cheque for £56,000 to hire mules. The War Office later complained that he should have drawn smaller cheques at intervals to save the interest; Wood retorted that the loss was more than covered by the salary of the paymaster he had saved.

Wood's original position proved unsatisfactory. He had 2,700 men jammed in his camp, fuel was scarce and the drainage poor. The Zungi Range was rich in coal, and parties went afield to pick at seams that broke the surface, but the nearest timber was ten miles away. Despite taut latrine discipline, the soggy campground was soon fouled. Manure from the horse lines was carted to a dump, and the European troops used trenches, but the hundreds of Natal Kaffirs of Wood's Irregulars defecated at will in camp and nothing could induce the Boers to use the assigned trenches. In the middle of February Wood gave up the struggle and moved two miles along the spur toward the timber on Ngaba ka Hawane, establishing a sprawling encampment atop a wide, uneven ridge. The 1st/13th and the 90th light Infantry settled into an irregular, hexagonal wagon laager, just to the west of a wagon kraal for the cattle perched on a terrace at the edge of the low cliff forming the southern face of the ridge. A long, narrow redoubt, large enough to shelter several companies of infantry, topped an eminence above the terrace. The disselboom of each wagon was run under the bed of the wagon next ahead, the wheels were chained together, and kraal and laager were surrounded by shallow trenches and earthen parapets. The approach between the redoubt and the kraal was blocked by a stout palisade of stakes, while four guns posted in the open commanded the slopes to the north. The Natal Kaffirs were banished to a huddle of grass huts to the east, and a fresh manure heap was started to the west. Within a fortnight the incessant rain had crowned it with a stand of grass four feet high.

Reinforcements continued to trickle in. Schermbrucker's Kaffrarian

Vanguard, transferred from Luneberg, followed Raaf's Transvaal Rangers, and Lieutenant Colonel John Cecil Russell rode in with the Mounted Infantry from Helpmakaar, accompanied by Captain Alan Gardner, who joined the Frontier Light Horse. Colonel Frederick Weatherley came in from the Transvaal with his two sons, fourteen and sixteen, and fifty lancers of the Border Horse. Wood, a stickler for correct social usage and a bit of a snob to boot, found Weatherley somewhat too flamboyant for his taste. He had served in the Austrian cavalry, he had been involved in a dubious messroom affair in India, and he was just fresh from a divorce court, in which he had been awarded the custody of his sons.

In mid-February two native messengers arrived from Uhamu, stating that he was anxious to surrender. He had visited Ulundi, and the mistrustful Cetshwayo had ordered him to stay there, but he had slipped away and was hiding to the north of the Black Umfolozi. Buller rode out past Hlobane to meet him, but Uhamu failed to keep the appointment. A few days later a European trader named Calverley rode into Kambula under a flag of truce. He was a friend of Uhamu's who had sought shelter in Swaziland when the war broke out and he had ridden alone across northern Zululand to report that Uhamu still wished to come in, but he was fearful of being caught and too fat to move fast. Calverley was a little uncertain of his own reception and anxious to make amends; there were persistent rumors that he had been at Isandhlwana with a party of Uhamu's retainers. Buller rode out again and again found no sign of the chieftain or his clan, and Wood then asked Captain Norman Macleod, the Political Agent in Swaziland, to help. On the second of March Macleod found Uhamu in a Swazi kraal and sent him on to Kambula via Derby and Luneberg with 700 of his followers. He could not ride and could barely walk, and Wood sent an escorted wagon to meet him at Myer's Drift on the Intombi River.

The party reached Kambula on the tenth of March. Wood promptly disarmed the warriors, finding three Martini-Henrys that had belonged to the 24th Regiment. He then questioned Uhamu himself, who announced that the bulk of his clan was still hiding in northern Zululand and wanted to come out; he was especially interested in his 300 wives, having brought only two with him. Wood was acutely aware of the effect the defection of Cetshwayo's half brother and his entire clan would have in Zululand, but the expedition to escort them out would be risky. They were holed up in caves in a mountainous region between the Black Umfolozi and the Mkusi Rivers, almost fifty miles to the east and less than forty miles from Ulundi itself. Uhamu was willing to lend 200 of his warriors to the enterprise, and Wood finally decided to chance it.

He started on the fourteenth of March, with 360 of Buller's men and Uhamu's retainers. It was long after dark before they reached the area Uhamu had described. The troopers bivouacked, while the warriors spread out to find their wives and children. Wood for once slept through the night—he had suffered a mild sunstroke during the day—but Buller never lay down. All through the night old men, women and children hurried to the bivouac, and at dawn the escort started back with 958 refugees. Loyal Zulus had speared a few last stragglers within sight of the camp, but Wood could wait no longer. He started to march at half past six, and fifteen hours later camped at the foot of Zunguin, still ten miles from Kambula. The following morning Russell, who had just reached Kambula, started out with the Mounted Infantry and all the mule transport to fetch the exhausted children. Scores of them, many less than five years old, had walked the entire way, and one woman had given birth beside the track but reached Kambula before the rear guard with her new infant on her hip. Buller, after an initial mutter about verminous brats, rode in at the end with six toddlers clinging to his back and his saddlebow.

A month and a half had passed since Isandhlwana, and England was growing impatient for good news. The defense of Rorke's Drift and Pearson's skirmish on the Inyezane had been heartening, but they could not wipe out the sting of a major defeat or the enforced subsequent inactivity. The night before he started after Uhamu's people, Wood heard that a fresh blow had fallen.

Brevet Major Charles Tucker commanded five companies of the 80th Regiment at Luneberg. Late in February a convoy of eighteen wagons laden with ammunition and provisions started from Lydenburg for Natal. On the first of March Tucker sent "D" Company to meet the convoy at Derby to escort it down the lower reaches of the road, and then, on the fifth, he decided he wanted "D" Company back and sent it orders to return. Two days later he dispatched Captain David Barry Moriarity with another company to bring the wagons in. Moriarity, a forty-two-year-old Irishman who had seen service in India and had spent five years on half pay, set out with two lieutenants, a civilian surgeon and 103 N.C.O.'s and enlisted men. He reached Myer's Drift on the Intombi in an hour or two, and found the river, fifty yards across, swollen by the recent rains. The drift lay in a large open area surrounded by high, broken ground. Seven of the convoy wagons had reached the far bank, but the drift was impassable, and Moriarity cast about for materials with which to construct a raft. By the next day he had ferried the bulk of his command across, leaving one of his lieutenants with two platoons to work on the approaches to the south bank, which were dissolving into mud.

Moriarity left a small detail on the north bank to pitch his tents, and marched on with the bulk of his company to find the missing wagons. He came up with them several miles to the north of the river, and the eleven civilian conductors were glad to see him. Suddenly abandoned by their escort on the most dangerous stretch of the road, they had laagered in the rain with about thirty native voorloopers to await rescue. Natives from a neighboring kraal had pilfered some of the wagons and run off 46 oxen, and they were now trying to move the wagons down to the drift a few at a time with the remaining teams. Moriarity got them all down to the river on the ninth, to find the torrent in spate with a seven-knot current and still rising.

The men he had left behind had gotten two of the first wagons across in a short lull, but there was nothing more to be done until the river fell. Moriarity had apparently learned nothing from recent events in Zululand. He formed the sixteen wagons into a large inverted V, with the apex on the road and the base legs twenty yards from the riverbank, leaving open gaps between the wagons. He pitched his own tent by the road outside the laager and put his three ammunition carts and the oxen inside the V. The 71 men with him on the north bank pitched four bell tents in a neat line between the last wagon in the upstream leg of the V and the riverbank; the 35 men on the south bank had already pitched three tents next to the two wagons that were already across. The European conductors slept in their own wagons on top of the stores, and the native voorloopers slept under the beds.

It finally stopped raining on the afternoon of the eleventh of March, and Major Tucker rode out from Luneberg to visit the camp, bringing Lieutenant Henry Hollingworth Harward, 80th Regiment, with him. Tucker criticized Moriarity's arrangements, pointing out that the wagons were too far apart and the legs of the V were too far from the riverbank, but Moriarity, who hoped to get the rest of the wagons across the next day, simply shrugged his shoulders. The river was falling by now, so Tucker rode back to Luneberg, taking with him the two lieutenants on the south bank and leaving Harward behind. Harward, a veteran of the Ashanti campaign, saw no reason to entrench two wagons virtually within sight of the troops at Luneberg. Moriarity was not expecting an attack and had put a single sentry on either side of the camp without bothering to post advanced pickets, so Harward did the same on the south bank and the men turned in for the night.

It began to rain after dark, and a thick fog set in during the course of the night. Shortly after four o'clock, while it was still pitch black, one of the sentries on the south bank heard a shot from the north bank. There was no further sound, but Harward had his men fall in and sent a messenger across to check with Moriarity. The messenger returned and stated that he had informed Moriarity of the shot, and that the captain had ordered his men to turn out. Moriarity, in fact, had gone back to sleep and the order never reached his troops.

Shortly after five o'clock the rain ceased and the mist began to lift, so that the men on the south bank were able to distinguish the wagon sails across the river. The silence was suddenly broken by a crashing volley a bare seventy yards from the upstream leg of the laager on the north bank, and the horrified men on the south bank, straining to see in the faint light, saw a mass of eight or nine hundred Zulus charging down on the wagons. Harward opened fire at once, disclosing his presence, and several hundred Zulus broke away from the charging impi and plunged into the river to cross to the south bank.

Josiah Sussens, one of the conductors on the north bank, had risen just before dawn to see if the drift was down. He had no sooner slipped out of his wagon than he heard the volley and discovered the charging impi. He ran back to his wagon to get his rifle and heard Moriarity, outside the laager, cry, "Guards out!" It was much too late. The men, still asleep in the bell tents, were butchered as they stumbled out, and hundreds of Zulus swarmed through the laager, hacking and stabbing at the conductors and voorloopers and at the few soldiers who had escaped from their tents. Moriarity was surrounded by a mob of warriors and put up a tremendous battle alone. He pistoled the first three Zulus to reach him—all, oddly enough, sons of Manyanyoba—and then grabbed an assegai and started to fight his way down the side of the laager. A spear thudded into him, but he continued to slash away until a rifle ball caught him in the chest. He cried out, "I'm done! Fire away, boys! Death or glory!" and fell as a second assegai finished him off.

Sussens reached his wagon, calling to his friend Whittington, but Whittington was speared as he emerged, and Sussens had to abandon his rifle. The interior of the laager was alive with Zulus, and he decided to dodge through the oxen to make for the river. Weaponless and clad only in a nightshirt, he reached the bank and dived in head-first as several assegais whizzed past him. He surfaced to find Zulus lining the bank and firing at every head that emerged, so he ducked under again, struggling to shed his shirt. Swimming under water most of the way, he emerged gasping and spluttering and stark naked on the south bank, to find himself in the midst of a battle worse than the one he had just escaped. Zulus dodging through the tents and wagons had smashed Harward's two platoons, and isolated knots of soldiers were trying to fight their way clear of the shambles. For an instant Sussens considered throwing himself back into the river, preferring drowning to the prospect of imminent disembowelment. He then decided to make a dash for Luneberg. Skirting the camp and keeping to the road, he trotted off to the south, scampering away whenever a Zulu approached him. Three soldiers he attempted to join were shot just as he reached them, and then he saw an organized party of infantry retreating down the road ahead of him. This was Colour Sergeant Anthony Booth, who with Lance Corporal Burgess and ten men had gotten clear of the camp and was falling back on a deserted farmstead two miles south of the river. The men were completely accoutered, with full pouches. Booth had them well in hand and was directing volleys at every group of Zulus that approached. Several other survivors had joined them, and Sussens finally caught his breath and then commandeered an overcoat from one of the voorloopers who had also escaped.

Lieutenant Harward had stayed with his men until his stand dissolved. Ordering Booth to try for the farm, he then caught and saddled his horse to gallop to Luneberg for help. He reached Fort Cleary before six, and Tucker mounted every man for whom he could find a horse and started for the river, followed by two of the three garrison companies. Booth had lost four men by the time the rescue reached him, and the impi, which Mbilini had led, melted into the hills as the riders approached. The troopers rode into the camp in shocked silence. The wagons had been looted and the stores destroyed; Captain Moriarity, Surgeon Cobbins, three European conductors and fifteen native voorloopers, and sixty N.C.O.'s and men were scattered amidst the wreckage. All had been slashed and hacked to ribbons.

Chelmsford was furious. The disaster had been caused by sheer negligence and had been marked by cowardly conduct to boot. Moriarity was dead, but Harward was tried by a general court martial which finally convened the following February. He was accused of abandoning his men while under attack and riding off at speed, and of having failed to take proper precautions for the safety of his camp as well. He put up a spirited defense. He had only joined the camp on the south bank the night before the attack, and he could hardly laager with two wagons. He had taken every precaution he could, and had certainly been better prepared for the attack than Moriarity had been. He had not ridden away until his command had disintegrated, and then only because help was urgently needed to ward off total destruction; he owned the only horse on the south bank and Booth—who had since received the Victoria Cross—had done everything he himself could have done. The court acquitted him on both counts and the proceedings eventually came before Sir Garnet Wolseley for review. Wolseley could not reverse the verdict, but he disapproved the findings and refused to confirm them.

Had I released this officer without making any remarks upon the verdict in question, it would have been a tacit acknowledgment that I concurred in what appears to me a monstrous theory, viz., that a regimental officer who is the only officer present with a party of soldiers actually and seriously engaged with the enemy, can, under any pretext whatever, be justified in deserting them, and by so doing, abandoning them to their fate. The more helpless a position in which an officer finds his men, the more it is his bounden duty to stay and share their fortune, whether for good or ill. It is because the British officer has always done so that he possesses the influence he does in the ranks of our army. The soldier has learned to feel, that come what may, he can in the direst moment of danger look with implicit faith to his officer, knowing that he will never desert him under any possible circumstances.

It is to this faith of the British soldier in his officers that we owe most of the gallant deeds recorded in our military annals; and it is because the verdict of this Court-Martial strikes at the root of this faith, that I feel it necessary to mark officially my emphatic dissent from the theory upon which the verdict has been founded.

Harward was released from arrest and restored to duty, but the Duke of Cambridge heartily approved Wolseley's remarks. He ordered the findings and the comment to be read at the head of every regiment in Her Majesty's service.

On the twentieth of March Chelmsford sent Wood a letter outlining his planned march to relieve Eshowe and asking the 4th Column to demonstrate to draw off some of the strength from the impi reportedly congregating to attack Chelmsford. Wood had firm reports of another impi planning to attack Kambula, but the request gave him an excuse to carry out a project that he and Buller had long considered.

The abaQulusi on Hlobane had been reinforced by a detachment of royal troops from Ulundi, and almost a thousand warriors were by now perched on the lower plateau. They had been a thorn in the flank of the 4th Column ever since Wood had arrived in the area, and while their weight was hardly sufficient to hamper his movements, both Mbilini and Manyanyoba drew strength from their defiance, and northwest Zululand would remain in turmoil as long as their bastion stood. Only the apparently unscalable cliffs had stopped Buller from launching an attack before, but on the fifteenth of March Wood had reconnoitered the approaches and he had marked two possible routes to the top. The western slope from Zunguin Nek to the lower plateau was too steep to ride up, but Wood thought a dismounted force might be able to lead its horses up, especially if it were unopposed. At the eastern end of the mountain Ityenka Nek gave onto a high, rocky terrace, and the cliffs above it were deeply notched and honeycombed with caves. A path

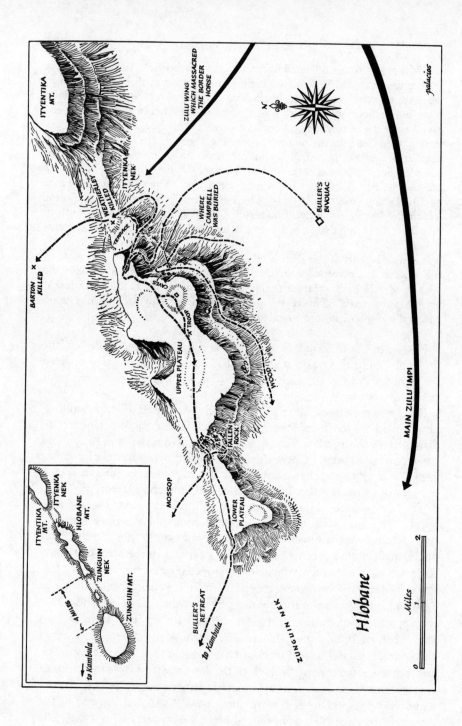

ITYENTIKA MT.

ZULU WING WHICH MASSACRED THE BORDER HORSE

ITYENTIKA NEK

WEATHERLEY KILLED

TERRACE

BARTON KILLED ×

WHERE CAMPBELL WAS BURIED

CAVES

BULLER'S BIVOUAC

N

'X' TROOP

UPPER PLATEAU

IGQOZA

MAIN ZULU IMPI

MOSSOP

FALLEN ROCK

LOWER PLATEAU

BULLER'S RETREAT

to Kambula

ZUNGUIN NEK

Hlobane

Miles

0   1   2

ITYENTIKA MT.

ITYENTIKA NEK

HLOBANE MT.

ZUNGUIN NEK

ZUNGUIN MT.

4 MILES

to Kambula

palacios

led across the face of the cliffs, twisting in and out of the notches and crossing a mountain stream that splashed across the jumbled rocks, but it promised passage of sorts.

The exact nature of the high razor-back ridge that connected the lower plateau to the upper one could not be seen from the plain below, so Wood decided to launch a pincer attack, with Buller taking a strong force up the eastern trail while Russell created a diversion at the western end. It was far from certain that either force could gain the summit even unopposed, and a handful of determined Zulus at either end could obviously stop any force of climbers. Since the main Zulu strength was on the lower plateau, Wood planned to throw the greater weight against the upper plateau, and he ordered Russell not to attack if he encountered serious opposition. The latest reports from Ulundi, moreover, indicated that a massive impi was about to leave to attack Kambula, and the road led directly along the southern flank of Hlobane. Wood frankly referred to his vague plan as a reconnaissance in force. It was risky in the extreme; he stood to gain little and he was overstepping by far the generous freedom of movement that Chelmsford had granted him.

Kambula was astir long before daylight on the twenty-seventh of March. The corporal of the guard passed through the Frontier Light Horse lines, awakening the men with a gentle kick on the foot, and as they stumbled out they were told that another patrol in force lay ahead. They were to pack three days' rations, and each man was issued four packets of ammunition—twice their usual allowance. Chops Mossop saddled his Basuto pony "Warrior," a sure-footed, well-trained bay he had brought from the Transvaal, and took his place in "A" Troop, serving as rear guard for the four troops that rode out in column of half-sections. Captain Gardner was second-in-command to Buller, and the two men mustered the units as they started the long ride ahead. Major Edmund Tremlett, R.A., took a single rocket tube with seven gunners, and Piet Uys with two of his sons and thirty Boers rode with the 156 men of the FLH, under Captain Robert Barton of the Coldstream Guards. Commandant Raaf led seventy Transvaal Rangers in a straggling mob, followed by the eighty Cape Colony volunteers of Baker's Horse. Weatherley was late in starting with his Border Horse, and rode out even after the 277 Natal Kaffirs of the 2nd Battalion of Wood's Irregulars, who were shepherded along on foot by Major William Knox Leet of the 1st/13th. There were, all told, 400 mounted men, and the column offsaddled for an hour's lunch early in the afternoon to the south of Zunguin. They were under way again by three, skirting the southern slopes of Hlobane; a few shots from an elephant gun plunged down from the lower plateau and the abaQulusi lit three large signal fires, but no enemy movement was visible. At six in the evening, as the sun was setting, the men bivouacked near a deserted kraal south of Ityenka Nek, five miles beyond the eastern extremity of Hlobane and almost thirty miles from Kambula.

The men built roaring fires from timber found in the kraal, boiled coffee and roasted green mealies. Buller never entrenched his bivouacs, but the sun never found him on the same ground he had been camping on when it set. The moon was down by eight, and Buller fed all the bivouac fires and then moved his column north to the foot of Ityenka Nek. By ten he was in place at the first slope, and his men caught what rest they could for the next five hours, huddled on the stony ground with the bridles of their saddled horses looped over their arms.

Long before four the column was moving again, riding up Ityenka Nek four abreast. A few stars were visible, but a cold wind from the north was piling thick clouds across the arch of the heavens. The stony ground rose steeply and it was no longer possible to ride. The men dismounted and led their horses forward; the footing grew worse, and the men began to slip and flounder, with their horses plunging and rearing behind them. The wind brought a rumble of distant thunder, and the loom of lightning flashes to the north silhouetted Hlobane. A sudden blast of icy wind struck the column, and a vivid flash of lightning with a terrific peal of thunder illuminated the column. Mossop caught a glimpse of a solid white wall of rain sweeping down the mountain, and an instant later the storm struck, drenching the men to the skin, while the incessant flashes blinded the men and frightened the horses.

The storm lasted for hours, while Buller urged and goaded his command along. The climb was an unending nightmare as the men fought their way onto Ityenka Nek, crossed the terrace, and edged forward along the travesty of a trail that skirted the cliff face. Water was streaming over the rocks, washing the footing out from under them, and several horses slipped off the trail to crash onto the rocks below. The head of the column was still a hundred yards below the summit when the storm finally subsided, but the stars were already paling as the clouds passed. As the light strengthened, a sporadic fire broke out from Zulus hidden in caves along the upper reaches of the trail and on the rim of the plateau, and the column surged forward to close with them, making for the close red flashes amidst the rocks. By the time it was light enough to see, the exhausted men had finally gathered on the upper plateau. Lieutenant von Stietencron, an Austrian baron serving with the FLH, lay dead on the rocks below, Lieutenant Williams was mortally wounded as he reached the plateau, two troopers had been killed as well, and the route below was marked by the carcasses of a dozen horses, shot or smashed to death on the rocks.

The men sorted themselves out, and Buller took stock. The upper plateau was a world apart; open pasturage and thick bushes studded gentle rises and shallow gullies that blocked a clear view of the distance, and a few yards from the edge of the cliffs all view of the plain below was lost. Buller led his men to a low ridge several hundred yards in from the edge of the eastern cliffs, and there he made an unsettling discovery. He found that the Zulus, supposedly camped on the lower plateau three miles to the west, were all on the upper plateau, and, moreover, they had already slipped in behind him and blocked his retreat. Alerted by his advance the preceding afternoon, they had seen the start of his ascent by the lightning flashes and had congregated in force on a long finger of the upper plateau that jutted out to the north of the notch from which the trail emerged. As soon as the end of the column moved inland, they had moved forward to block the trail, and if he wanted to retreat by the same route, he would have to fight. The Zulus were not in sufficient force to endanger the column as long as it kept its cohesion, but they were strong enough to attack small detachments, and he would have to keep his men in hand.

Buller dismounted "A" Troop and spread it out along the ridge, with its horseholders in the hollow behind. He then sent Wood's Irregulars to flush cattle out of the bush and drive them to the western end of the plateau. Leaving the rest of his force to drift westward behind the Irregulars, he himself rode on ahead with a few officers to out the pass to the lower plateau and to meet with Russell. As soon as the column had disappeared behind the next rise, several hundred Zulus closed with "A" Troop, which checked them with a sharp fire, but the bulk of the warriors poured westward after the retreating column to the north of the short line of dismounted men. "A" Troop continued to fire for a while, but the Zulus in front of them were persistent and worked their way forward through the thick bush. Presently the troopers grew aware of firing behind them, somewhere to the west, and still more Zulus appeared to the north, on their unprotected flank. They realized, rather suddenly, that they were isolated and almost surrounded and neither in a strength nor a position to make a stand. Suddenly they broke and ran for their horses, riding off in small groups in search of their parent unit. The Zulus they had been facing, and those that had guarded the head of the trail, began to move forward.

Lieutenant Colonel Russell, in the meantime, had ridden out of Kambula at noon on the preceding day, taking 640 men with hm. He had a rocket tube under Lieutenant Arthur John Bigge, R.A., eighty Mounted Infantry under Lieutenant Edward Stevenson Browne, 1st/

24th, Schermbrucker's forty Kaffrarian Vanguards, and seventy mounted natives from the Edendale Mission under Captain Cochrane, most of them survivors of Durnford's stand in the donga. Commandant Loraine White commanded the 240 Natal Kaffirs of the 1st Battalion of Wood's Irregulars, and 200 of Uhamu's warriors, distinctly less enthusiastic about attacking the abaQulusi than they had been on the rescue of their wives and children, streamed along under the general direction of Lieutenant Cecil Williams of the 58th Regiment. Buller had a twelve-mile start, and when he bivouacked five miles to the east of Hlobane in the evening, Russell was camping four miles to the west of the mountain, on the ground where Wood had bivouacked on the fifteenth.

Wood himself followed two hours after Russell, taking only his personal staff and an escort of eight mounted men from the 90th Regiment and seven mounted Zulus under Mtonga, Cetshwayo's half brother and the last of Mpande's brood with a valid, if long dormant, claim to the throne. Although he had lived two decades in Natal and the Transvaal, Mtonga spoke no English, and Llewellyn Lloyd, Wood's Political Agent, interpreted for him. Lieutenant Henry Lysons of the 90th rode with Captain Ronald Campbell; just twenty years old, he had only joined the regiment a few weeks before and was orderly officer for the day.

Wood joined Russell's bivouac at dark and spent the night there. As the storm began to die away before dawn, Russell led his column across Zunguin Nek and began to ascend the western slope of Hlobane. The climb was long and increasingly steep, but it was not impossible for dismounted men leading their horses, and by the break of day the column was assembled on the lower plateau. Russell sent Uhamu's men out to round up the cattle, and he then cantered ahead with a small party to reconnoiter the pass to the upper plateau, reaching the razorback ridge leading to it at about the time Buller had arrived at the far end of the upper plateau.

As Russell's column left its bivouac, Wood set out with his escort to ride the five miles along the southern foot of Hlobane to Ityenka Nek to follow Buller up to the summit. He was more than halfway, and the bulk of the mountain was just emerging from the gloom, when he encountered Weatherley and his Border Horse, riding aimlessly to the west. Weatherley should have been on the summit by then, and Wood asked him what he was doing. Weatherley replied that he had lost Buller in the storm and was looking for him. The tail of Buller's column was just visible high on the trail above the terrace, so Wood turned Weatherley sharply about and bade him ride for the sound of the firing that was even then breaking out at the head of the trail. The men of the Border Horse, for the most part English settlers from the

Transvaal, had not followed Weatherley for such risky business, and they showed a reluctance to move. Wood left them in disgust and rode on for Ityenka Nek, dismounting on the rocky terrace and veering toward the Zulus firing from the rim of the plateau and the caves ahead. He missed the easier gradient Buller had found in the dark, and eventually came to a stop a hundred yards from the summit, with snipers in the jumbled rocks ahead and the Border Horse finally coming up to the small stone kraal where he had left his horses and the mounted Zulus, 200 yards below.

The Border Horse now began to fire at the distant snipers, and Wood waited to see what effect the shots might have. A Zulu suddenly popped up from a rock a scant fifty yards away and fired. Wood noted that the shot seemed low, but Lloyd fell back, exclaiming, "I'm hit—badly! My back is broken!" Wood and Campbell caught him and carried him down to the stone kraal. Wood then started back up, leading his horse, but a shot struck it and killed it, and when he regained the kraal he found that Lloyd had died. Wood now ordered Weatherley to take the Border Horse up to clear the trail, but the men balked again. Campbell then picked up Lysons and four privates from Wood's escort and started up the trail in single file, making for a cave from which several Zulus were firing. The narrow passage was only two feet wide between towering rock walls, and as Campbell plunged into the mouth of the care, a Zulu fired a shot into his forehead, killing him instantly. Undaunted, Lysons and Private Edmund Fowler sprang over his body, driving the Zulus into the recesses of the mountain. Lysons then held the mouth of the cave while the others dragged Campbell's body back to the kraal.

Wood had been extremely close to Campbell, and his death stunned him. The false trail to the summit was still blocked by other snipers, and Wood temporarily lost all interest in the battle while he concentrated on giving his friend a proper burial. The fire from the rocks was striking home among the horses, and Wood decided to move the bodies back down to the terrace to dig a grave. Walkinshaw, his bugler, helped him to hoist the bodies onto a pony, and Wood then remembered his own horse, dead on the trail ahead. In the saddle wallet was a small prayer book belonging to Mrs. Campbell, which he had borrowed from the captain before leaving Kambula, his own prayer book being too large for the wallet. He sent Walkinshaw back to get it, telling him not to get shot for the sake of the saddle, but to take all risks to retrieve the prayer book. The bugler walked erect through a hail of fire to the dead horse, tugged the saddle out from under the carcass, and returned with it on his head. The party then moved 300 yards down the terrace to clear soil, and Wood set Mtonga's retainers to digging a grave with their assegais.

Some of Buller's men had returned to the edge of the plateau, and their fire soon stilled the snipers along the trail. Weatherley could now see the proper track to the summit, and with a curt farewell from Wood he took his men up to the plateau, arriving soon after "A" Troop had abandoned its ridge. The grave was barely finished when the small party on the terrace saw a group of 300 Zulus a half-mile to the east, coming toward them along the crest of Ityenka Nek. They opened a long-range fire, and Mtonga's men hastily tumbled the bodies into the grave, but Wood, judging the distance the attackers still had to come, made them lift them out and finish the digging. Only when he was certain that Lloyd and his friend could rest without their legs doubled up would he permit the bodies to be lowered and the grave to be closed. He then read an abridged burial service and ordered his escort to mount. Weatherley's men had all disappeared, and Wood decided to ride back to the western end of Hlobane to see how Russell was faring.

He dropped off Ityenka Nek and started back along the southern flank, taking with him a lancer of the Border Horse who had been shot in the thigh. Mtonga's Zulus had rounded up a small herd of goats and sheep on the terrace and were driving them along. With Lloyd gone, no one could speak to them and they were left to their own devices. The Zulus on Ityenka Nek broke off the pursuit and started to ascend the trail to the plateau, and Wood was soon well along the southern flank, with his view to the south across the plain blocked by a low ridge.

Mtonga was riding along the crest of the ridge, keeping the goats from straying, when he suddenly called out and beckoned for Wood to join him. Wood cantered up the rise, glanced over the plain to the south, and got the shock of his life. Less than three miles away, trotting straight as an arrow for Kambula, was a gigantic impi. Some 22,000 warriors were arrayed in five dense columns, glistening black masses speckled with bobbing white shields, with the sun sparkling on the assegais. All heads were turned to Hlobane, the body of the impi was already abreast of the mountain, with the flank columns advanced, and the right horn was breaking away and heading for the western end of the mountain. The eastern route was already blocked, and when the head of the impi reached the slope that Russell had ascended, whoever was still atop Hlobane would be trapped. The long lines extended far back to the east, and several regiments had already broken away from the rear and were headed for Ityenka Nek.

The situation had changed in a twinkling. All thought of attack was gone, and whatever was happening on the upper plateau would have to stop at once. Both Russell and Buller would have to be brought down, and the entire force would have to retire on Kambula before the impi reached it. Wood had impressed on both columns the necessity of keeping a sharp watch to the south, but there was no way of telling if either force had as yet seen the danger. He scribbled a note and ordered Lysons to take it to Russell:

> Below the Inhlobane. 10.30 A.M. 28/3/79
> There is a large army coming this way from the south. Get into position on Zunguin Nek. E. W.

Both Russell and Buller were aware of the impi's approach. Russell had left his men rounding up cattle and had gone forward to inspect the pass. He saw at once that it was impossible for mounted men and even impractical afoot. The lower plateau came to a salient point surrounded by virtually vertical slopes; and the razor-back ridge, a grassy fifteen yards across, ran forward to butt against the tip of the upper plateau, which came to a point to meet it. The end of the ridge terminated in an almost vertical slope of rocks and bare earth that rose 150 feet to the upper level, and the bare slope in the center was flanked by enormous masses of jumbled rock, as large as small houses, which had crumbled from the sheer escarpment of the upper plateau and extended far below the level of the razor-back ridge on either side. The fall concealed crevices into which a horse might fall from sight, and the hollows were choked with a thick tangle of shrubs and vines which would hamper rather than aid a climber. On either side of the lower plateau, of the ridge, of the rock falls and the upper plateau, the ground fell vertically for almost 500 feet before it met the steep but easier gradients of the lower slopes. All the cattle above had been taken up by the trail Buller had used, and to prevent animals from straying off the upper plateau to tumble down the central slope, the Zulus had erected a low stone wall across the top of the pass.

Russell sent Lieutenant Browne with twenty of his dismounted men up the pass to find Buller. Slipping and scrambling, with their carbines slung on their backs, they picked their way carefully up the slope and set out to find Buller. Browne first encountered Tremlett and Leet, who had ridden ahead of Buller to inspect the pass. Both men were aware of skirmishing behind them to the west, but all appeared to be quiet, so Browne slid back down the pass and reported to Russell, whose scouts, posted on the southern rim of the lower plateau, had just discovered the approaching impi.

It was obvious to Russell that he would not be able to get his force onto the upper plateau, so that there was nothing he could do to support Buller. He left a few men to guard the pass in the event Buller was forced to try it, gathered the rest of his men and descended to the plain by the same route he had used to reach it. Wood's Irregulars and Uhamu's people, engrossed with the captured cattle, lagged behind to round up strays and to work the herd down the steep slopes. Calverley, who had ridden out with Uhamu's warriors, remained behind at the pass. When Russell reached the western foot of Hlobane, he met Lysons with Wood's note ordering him to Zunguin Nek.

A nek, in Boer parlance, was a sloping saddle of ground between two rises. Zunguin Nek was actually the land between Hlobane and Zunguin Mountain, but the ground was several miles across and relatively level, and Russell, who had not been east of Zunguin before, was not sure what Wood meant. A much more clearly defined saddle connected Zunguin itself with the next hill to the west, and after conferring with his officers Russell decided that Wood wanted him there. He consequently set out with his 200 mounted men and rode six miles to the northwest, past Zunguin and out of sight of Hlobane, and sat down to await further orders.

Buller had also seen the impi. He had inspected the pass himself shortly after Browne left, realized its difficulties, but had nevertheless decided to send his Natal Kaffirs home by this route. Afoot and unencumbered, they could pick their way down, and in any event they were already at the western end of the upper plateau, and to send them back to descend by the eastern trail would add more than ten miles to the distance they would have to march to regain Kambula. Buller then started back to the east, sending Captain Robert Barton on ahead with thirty troopers of the Frontier Light Horse. Barton was instructed to descend to the terrace by the eastern trail, to find and bury Williams, Von Stietencron and the troopers who had been killed on the ascent, and then to find Weatherley and head the Border Horse off, since there no longer was any point in their climbing to the summit. Barton and Weatherley were then to make their way back to Kambula by the route of the preceding day's advance, along the southern flank of Hlobane. Barton, his face blackened from a carbine discharge, rode off with his troopers, taking with him Lieutenant Cecil Charles Williams and Calverley, who had left Uhamu's people and had managed to get his horse up the pass. On his way to the head of the eastern trail, Barton encountered the Border Horse, who had reached the top after all and were riding along the northern cliffs, trying to avoid the swarming Zulus and looking for a place to descend. Barton turned them around and took them with him down the eastern trail, picking up the bodies he was to bury on the way.

Barton had no sooner left than Buller himself saw the impi. He realized at once that retreat was imperative, and that he would have to leave by the pass or not at all. The impi was still five miles away, but by the time he collected his command and took it down the eastern trail it would be on him and pinch him against the mountain. Barton, moreover, with orders to retire along the southern flank, was in dire peril, and Buller sent two troopers pounding after him to change his retreat to the north of Ityenka Nek and along the northern side of Hlobane. He was, unfortunately, facing west when this thought struck him, and without thinking he ordered the troopers to tell Barton to retire "by the right of the mountain." Barton, busy with his burial detail on the terrace below, was equally unfortunately facing east when the messengers found him. He had not yet seen the impi, and he took the message for a confirmation of his original orders to retire by the south side of Hlobane. When he was finished, he dropped off Ityenka Nek and followed the same path that Wood and his escort had taken several hours earlier.

The various units on the upper plateau were now all drifting to the west, stopping occasionally to skirmish with groups of the ubiquitous Zulus, who, encouraged by the apparent retreat and then emboldened by the sight of the approaching impi, were beginning to harry the smaller units. Only solitary riders were in danger as yet, mostly the men from "A" Troop who had scattered in their retreat. Mossop had caught Warrior in the scurry to the horseholders, but the pony bolted and carried him off to the north and into a small knot of Zulus. Mossop shot one as he rode the man down, but not before the Zulu had slashed his arm open. Casting about for his unit, Mossop then fell in with the Border Horse on the northern precipice, but he left them as soon as he realized they were not closing with the Frontier Light Horse. Riding westward alone, Mossop soon overtook several hundred Zulus who were trailing the retreat of the other units. The Zulus had formed an extended line, so Chops dug his spurs into Warrior and gave the pony his head. When the Zulus bunched to stop the horse, Warrior swerved suddenly and bolted through the gap. Only Mossop's experience dodging ant-holes on the veld saved him from a fall, and he did not slacken his pace until he had finally reached the men converging on the head of the western pass.

The situation here had deteriorated completely. Buller had already started to put the Natal Kaffirs over the pass, and a disorganized mob of them was slipping down the slope, racing across the ridge below, and scattering to flee in all directions. Numbers of abaQulusi had emerged from various crevices after Russell had departed, and they were attacking both Uhamu's people and the fresh arrivals. Other abaQulusi had worked back along the ridge and clambered into the rock falls on either side of the pass to attack the men attempting to descend, and they were soon joined by numbers of Zulus from the upper plateau, who dropped down baboon trails behind the men trapped at the tip and worked their way forward to join the attack. Most of the Natal Kaffirs who finally reached the plain were trapped or run down by the impi below, over eighty of them were killed and few ever reached Kambula. The unit was never reconstituted, and in effect ceased to exist from the instant it dropped down the pass.

Buller's entire command was now jammed into the narrow salient at the end of the upper plateau; the units were totally disorganized and were intermingled with the bellowing herd of cattle that Wood's Irregulars had driven there and abandoned. The sides of the point fell in a sheer drop to the lower slopes, and the men at the head of the pass were first held back by the Natal Kaffirs crowded ahead of them and, when their own turn came, balked at committing themselves and their horses to the appalling slopes and were going over by twos and threes, slipping and rolling and under continual attacks from the Zulus in the rocks lining the sides. The overhanging jumble hid the attackers from the upper plateau, and Zulus darting forward speared and slashed at the slithering horses and men.

The Zulus on the upper plateau were pushing forward as well, firing into the thick of the press at the head of the pass and snatching at laggards. An organized rear guard might have held them off, but Buller and all his officers were putting men down the slope in the van, and no one behind turned to stand. A small party from "A" Troop, still some distance away, was trapped against the southern cliffs by a sudden rush of warriors who threw themselves on the horses and pushed them bodily into the void. Mossop dismounted and wormed his way forward to the head of the pass, which was strewn with struggling bodies. He nudged the man beside him, asking if he thought they could get down. "Not a hope!" the man replied, and to Mossop's horror put the muzzle of his carbine in his mouth and pulled the trigger. His brains spattered Chops, who dropped Warrior's bridle and jumped down the center of the pass. He landed on a dead horse, fell over the carcass, slid past a slain Zulu and scrambled down to the frantic jam of bodies on the ridge. As he rose to his feet, an iron hand gripped his shoulder and a tremendous clout landed on his ear. "Where's your horse?" someone yelled. He looked up into Buller's contorted face, and pointed back at the upper plateau. "Go back and get him," Buller shouted. "Don't leave him again." Mossop dutifully started back up, dodging the bodies that hurtled by and edging out into the rocks as he neared the top. As he crawled over the rim, he heard Warrior's whinny and grabbed the pony's bridle.

The bulk of the men were over by now, and the Zulus had pushed forward to the head of the pass, hacking and stabbing at abandoned horses and at men who still hesitated at the descent. They were fighting between Mossop and the pass itself, so he sprinted to the edge of the rock fall to the south and jumped down to a tremendous boulder, dragging Warrior with him. The horse lost its footing, knocking Mossop off the rock, and with a shower of sparks from its skidding shoes it slid off to the other side. Mossop clutched at the rough surface, banged his head on a jutting knob, and fell, completely dazed, into a narrow crevice. He was feebly trying to claw his way out when the carcass of a dead horse descended from above and jammed itself over his head. In total darkness and almost suffocated, he began to inch his way out from under. He finally got clear and rolled over the ledge to drop to the next rock, dropping from boulder to boulder until, battered and bruised, he fetched up on a steep rock ledge far below the level of the razor-back ridge. His arm and his head were bleeding and he had lost his hat and his carbine, but the overhang hid him from the upper plateau and for the moment he was safe. He sat up, and to his utter astonishment saw Warrior standing a short distance away, perched on a thin patch of soil among the rocks. The horse had survived two fearful drops without breaking a limb. He had a bad cut over one eye and blood was oozing over his hoofs, but he could still walk. Mossop caught his bridle and led him to a level space below the rocks and then inspected him carefully. His saddle was under his belly, the saddletree had broken into two jagged pieces of iron and one stirrup was gone. Mossop took the saddle off, folded his jacket to protect the withers from the broken iron, resaddled him and knotted the reins over his neck.

The impi below had by now swept past the upper plateau and it was no longer possible to descend to the south. Mossop's only hope was to climb back to the ridge, cross it, and descend to the north of the mountain. The side of the ridge below the rock fall was a steep grassy slope, and a switchback trail led up to the lower plateau. Mossop mounted, noting vaguely that Warrior's gait was peculiar, and he was just considering the easiest gradient when a mob of Zulus burst around the jutting rocks to the south and charged him. Their shields were up and their stabbing assegais held high, and Mossop dug his spurs into Warrior, who bounded sixty yards up the slope before he came to a sudden halt. The Zulus were climbing after them, so Mossop spurred him again and again until they had regained the ridge where it broadened to meet the lower plateau.

The upper plateau was clear, but fighting was still in progress among the rocks bordering the pass and along the ridge itself. Buller had stayed aloft until his men were fairly started, and had then descended himself, leading his great, bloodstained, cream-colored horse. Taking his stand on the ridge at the foot of the slope, he had controlled the rout as best as he could, sending men on to the lower plateau and down to the safety of the plain to the north. Isolated men were still picking their way down through the rocks, beset by Zulus, and Buller time and again went to their rescue, raging up the pass with pistol and saber.

The Boers had reached the pass hard on the heels of the Natal Kaffirs. Well-mounted and superior riders, they had all gotten clear before the jam started and rode on to Kambula without pause. Only Piet Uys and his sons stood by Buller, and Uys stayed with him on the ridge as well. They were well clear of the Zulus amongst the rocks, when Uys glanced back and saw his eldest son at the foot of the pass struggling with two led horses. He rode back to help him, and a Zulu sprang from the rocks and speared him in the back.

More horses than men had been killed, and no man could hope to reach Kambula afoot, or even to get clear of the ridge and the lower plateau. Survival depended on a mount, and it took raw courage to take an additional rider behind on an exhausted horse, infinitely more so to turn back to snatch a man afoot from closing Zulus or to turn a horse over to a wounded man. Lieutenant Cecil D'Arcy, FLH, started down the rock fall beside the pass, and a boulder dislodged somewhere above struck his horse and took its leg off. He pistoled it and started to take the saddle off, when the abaQulusi in the rocks started toward him. Wearing heavy boots and carrying his carbine, revolver, field glasses and seventy rounds of ammunition, he slithered over the rocks and ran for the foot of the pass, where a trooper named Francis caught a riderless horse and gave it to him. D'Arcy had no sooner mounted than he spotted a wounded trooper, and he promptly dismounted, put up the trooper and sent him to safety. He turned to face the Zulus, but just as they reached him he found Buller by his side, jumped up behind, and was taken to the safety of the lower plateau. He got off at once, as Buller turned to plunge back into the fight, and was then taken up behind by Lieutenant Alfred Blaine, FLH, whom Buller had previously rescued from the pass when he lost his horse. Blaine got D'Arcy down to the plain, and the thrice-rescued lieutenant finally reached Kambula riding behind Major Tremlett. Buller rode into the rocks twice again, once to pull out Lieutenant Everitt and then to rescue Trooper Rundell. Knox Leet charged to the rescue of Lieutenant Smith, FLH; and Lieutenant Browne, who had stayed behind when Russell rode off, rescued two troopers.

Buller finally noticed Mossop, and ordered him off the ridge to the north. Chops left as Leet and Buller were lifting a wounded man onto a horse, with D'Arcy urging them on. One or two men were still fighting groups of Zulus by the pass, and the Zulus on the upper plateau were pouring down. Warrior jolted down the steep slopes to the north, finally reaching the grassy slopes below and stopping by a trickle of muddy water. Groups of two and three horses, most of them with two riders up, were fleeing across the plain. The main impi was already rounding the western foot of Hlobane, and a solid mass of Zulus was streaming down from the lower plateau behind. Mossop was feeling faint, so he slid off his horse and plunged his face in the pool. The cold water revived him, but when he pulled Warrior's muzzle up, he found that his injuries and exertions had finally overtaken him. His legs would not support him, and try as he might, he could not mount. He tugged at the saddle and only succeeded in pulling it over. Spent, he lay there for the moment, and then the yells of "uSuthu!" from the approaching Zulus galvanized him. An instant later he was seated in the slipping saddle, fumbling with his single stirrup and urging his injured horse forward. His coat had fallen out and he was conscious of the broken saddletree digging into Warrior's withers, but there was neither time nor material to fashion a replacement. The horse was in obvious pain and jerked and stumbled, but he warmed to the work and settled into a jog that strengthened with every stride. Zigging and zagging to avoid the Zulus swarming over the plain, Mossop rode to the north of Zunguin and entered the hills beyond. He dared not halt for miles, and when he did, he clutched the saddle until he was sure his legs would bear his weight. The saddletree had dug a hole in the pony's withers, so he cut his shirt off, wet it and folded it and placed it over the laceration. Then, alternating short rides with shorter walks, he continued to Kambula, arriving late in the evening. He took Warrior to the horse lines and washed and fed and watered him. Then he stumbled to his own tent. Only one man, who had not gone out that day, was left; he bound up Mossop's arm and gave him some supper.

Barton, with "C" Troop of the Frontier Light Horse, and Weatherley with his Border Horse had barely descended from the terrace when they discovered the main impi a half-mile away. The van was far past them, pinching them against the mountain, and there was no escape to the south. They wheeled and rode back to cross Ityenka Nek, and found their way blocked by the flank column that had broken away from the body of the impi before. More Zulus were pouring down the trail, and with 83 men they could not hope to regain the summit. They dressed their lines and charged up the nek to cut their way out to the north, and the inGobamakhosi regiment stood up to the charge and stopped it in its tracks. The lines dissolved into a swirl of savage fights, and Zulus closed in from all sides and dragged the men down. Four troopers of the Frontier Light Horse and eight of the Border Horse broke out and escaped to the north, but 66 men died, including all the officers of the Border Horse. Calverley was killed, and so was Cecil Charles Williams. Weatherley won through, and then turned and rode back to find his fourteen-year-old son, taking with him a trooper on whose horse he ordered the boy to leave. The lad refused to leave his father, so Weatherley took him on his own crupper and put his arm around him, slashing with his saber at the encircling Zulus, and the two died together.

Barton was wounded and his horse was speared, but he cut his way out and descended to the northern plain. Then he stopped to take Lieutenant Poole up behind him and started out to the north. A Zulu named Tshitshili saw him go, called up several warriors, and trotted behind him for seven miles until the exhausted horse could struggle no farther. As the animal foundered, the men slipped off and separated; Tshitshili overtook Poole and shot him and then ran after Barton, who stopped and pulled out his revolver. It misfired three times, and Tshitshili, who had washed his spear several times that day, called on him to surrender. Barton, not understanding, lifted his hat and waited for death. A Zulu coming up fired at him and he fell, mortally wounded, so Tshitshili finished him with his assegai. The bodies lay there until May of 1880, when Wood visited the area again, and Tshitshili told him the tale and led him to the mummified corpses.

Wood, unable to find Russell's column on Zunguin Nek, scaled Zunguin to watch the retreat, remaining until dusk and riding into Kambula in the dark. The main impi had bivouacked on Zunguin Nek and it would obviously be coming on in the morning. It was raining heavily by nightfall, and the last of the survivors was stumbling in, when a late arrival reported that some survivors from Barton's force had been driven far to the north and were lost in the vicinity of Potter's Store. Buller had just reached camp. He had been riding forty miles and more every day for the last week, and he had not slept or even lain down for the last 42 hours, but he saddled up at once and rode out into the rain with led horses. He returned after midnight with seven men he had found wandering in the hills eight miles away.

Fifteen officers and seventy-nine men had been killed, one officer and seven men wounded. Scores of Natal Kaffirs had been killed, and Wood's Irregulars and Uhamu's people were gone. The Border Horse had been wiped off the rolls, and with 32 casualties and scores of horses killed or wounded, the Frontier Light Horse was temporarily crippled. Wood took full responsibility for the luckless foray, and in his report refused to mention that he had moved at Chelmsford's request—even if the General had not been informed of the objective. Chelmsford chided him gently, corrected the omission and added the responsibility to his own heavy load.

Wood recommended six men for the Victoria Cross: Lieutenant Lysons and Private Fowler for charging the cave where Campbell was killed, and Buller, Browne, Knox Leet and D'Arcy for their rescues at the pass. Knox Leet had wrenched his knee in one of Wood's tugs-of-war the week before the foray; he was barely able to hobble and had not dared to dismount during the fighting. He had been the only man in the column to ride up the eastern trail and then to descend the pass without getting off his horse, and at the foot of the pass he had taken Lieutenant Smith up behind and had then ridden down off the lower plateau and brought him into camp. All of the awards were approved except D'Arcy's; he was turned down on the grounds that he was a volunteer and not a member of the Imperial forces.

The night of the twenty-eighth was quiet and cold after the rain finally stopped, and a chill fog blanketed the hills. Wood, who calculated that he had ridden over ninety miles in the last two days, made his usual rounds of the outlying pickets, while Buller finally snatched a few hours of sleep. The mist still curled over the camp as the dawn broke, and the men stood to arms as usual. As the bugle sounded, 400 men crowded into the narrow redoubt twenty feet over the level of the ridge, a company of the 1st/13th shouldered its way through the 2,000 penned oxen to man the wagons of the cattle kraal, and the rest of the force took its assigned positions in the main laager. Lieutenant Frederick Nicholson, R.A., commanded the two guns in the redoubt, standing on the parapet to control them, and Lieutenants Arthur Bigge and Frederick Slade each commanded a section of two guns on the open slope between the redoubt and the laager. Wood snapped his watch shut with satisfaction; only seventy seconds had elapsed between the alarm and the final reports.

The mist began to clear, the light strengthened, and the men stood down. The night pickets came in, and the men gathered for breakfast. Mossop hurried down to the horse lines. He was bruised and aching, he had a black eye and a cut head and his wounded arm was stiff, but he passed fit for duty. He found Warrior lying down and obviously far gone. Chops knelt and took his head in his lap; the horse recognized him, whinnied once and died.

The day's work started. Commandant Raaf took a troop of Transvaal Rangers out to find the impi, and the cattle were driven out to graze. After a moment's reflection Wood ordered two companies of the 1st/13th to the slopes of Ngaba ka Hawane five miles to the west to cut timber. With luck, they would be back before the impi arrived, and the risk of their being caught in the open was balanced by the need for wood; if they missed a day's supply, the camp would be without fresh bread.

There were defections in the course of the morning. Uhamu's men dispersed, streaming off toward Utrecht to find their wives and children, and the rest of the Natal Kaffirs Knox Leet had trained as Wood's Irregulars dispersed as well, leaving less than fifty natives in camp, although the Edendale contingent stood fast. Piet Uys lay dead on Hlobane, and the forty Boers who had come with him had lost all desire to aid the British cause. They bid Wood adieu and rode away, leaving only the half-dozen wagon owners whose property was chained and lashed into the laager walls.

The men policed the camp while Wood occupied himself with his report of the preceding day's action and with letters to the families of the officers who had fallen. By eleven o'clock most of Raaf's men were back, bringing with them one of Uhamu's men, whom they had encountered near Zunguin Mountain. He had wandered away from the column attacking Hlobane and the preceding afternoon had fallen in with friends in the Zulu impi, who were unaware that he had joined the British. Learning that the impi hoped to attack Kambula about noon, he had drifted off to carry the news to Wood. Another scout, who had been waiting for Wood on his return to camp the preceding evening, had already brought a detailed account of the impi's composition. As at Isandhlwana, the fierce and aged Tshingwayo commanded, and Mnyamana, the premier inDuna, again marched with him. There were nine regiments, and except for the abaQulusi, who had joined at Hlobane, all had come from Ulundi.

The impi itself hove into sight shortly after eleven, still five miles away. The timber detail scurried in with its load and the cattle guards drove the main herds back to the kraal, abandoning 200 head that stampeded at the last minute. Wood, secure in the knowledge that the defenses could be manned at a moment's notice, insisted on dinner. The meal was over by noon, and the Zulus were drawing near. They were holding to the same five columns in which they had marched past Hlobane, moving west through the valley to the south of the ridge on which the camp stood. Wood opened boxes of reserve ammunition and placed them in the redoubt and along the laager walls and then, at the last instant, finally sounded the alarm. As the men fell in, the Zulu columns diverged; three continued west until they were directly south of the camp, while the two forming the right wing split away and moved to circle to the north of the camp.

The ridge sloped off gently to the north, and the Zulu right horn was in place on the next rise long before the center and the left horn had worked their way to the south of the camp. Wood, standing with his staff in the open below the redoubt by the palisade, had one bad moment. The inhabitants of Utrecht had besought him to abandon Kambula and to base his column on the settlement, but he had insisted he could protect the village as well from the camp. For a few minutes he feared that the impi would bypass him completely to fall on Utrecht, but the right wing halted and faced the camp, and he knew he had been right.

The left horn was still moving, and Buller, with all his mounted men standing to their horses in the center of the main laager, suggested that he induce an attack by the right wing before both wings could launch a simultaneous attack. Wood consented, a wagon gate was rolled aside, and at one thirty the mounted men sallied. Mossop had been given an old hat, a saddle and another carbine to replace his losses, and he had just been introduced to Warrior's replacement. His corporal had assigned him a huge, bony beast with a coffin head and a Roman nose, so high he could barely mount, and when he did get up, he could not reach the stirrups.

The Frontier Light Horse trotted down the slope to within a few hundred yards of the right wing, slid off their horses, and fired a single volley. The men then sprang into their saddles and fled for the laager, while by prearrangement every tent pole in the camp was jerked down. With a sudden roar, 11,000 warriors of the uNokenke, the uMbonambi, the umCijo and the umHlanga surged forward and started up the long northern slope of the ridge. Mossop's horse had wheeled at the volley, and only the boy's firm grip on the double bridle saved him; as it was, he could not mount and was simply dragged along in the retreat, dancing by his horse's head. They skirted a marshy area by a pool where the horses watered, and several troopers started to cross it. Their mounts bogged down, and Mossop saw the leading Zulus splash through the shallows to assegai steeds and riders. A long finger of Zulus had almost overtaken him when his captain, Oldham, saw his plight, wheeled, and raced back to his rescue. Oldham placed his mount squarely in front of Mossop's brute, who stopped prancing just long enough to allow the boy to vault into the saddle, and with stirrups flying he followed Oldham back to the laager. As they galloped for the gate, the four guns between the redoubt and the laager thundered out a salvo that passed right over their heads. The Edendale men retreated to the west, making an offing of several miles and staying outside the camp during the ensuing battle.

The men left their horses in the center of the laager and ran for their assigned section of the walls. Mossop clambered into a wagon bed—

Piet Uys's, he noted—and slit the sail with his knife. Thrusting his head out, he saw the Zulu van crash into the wagons to the north and then sweep around the corner to race along the western face. A sheet of flame and smoke rippled out of the wagons, dropping warrior after warrior and forcing the Zulus away from the wagons.

It was a windless day, and the laager was soon wreathed in a thick cloud of smoke that blotted out the attack. Mossop fired into the agitated swirls, and then felt his wagon rock as a press of Zulus smashed into one beyond him. He heard someone shout, "They're in!" and tumbled out of his wagon in time to see a company of the 1st/13th, brought up from the eastern face, thrust a few Zulus out with their bayonets.

Wood, on the rise behind the guns, had borrowed a carbine that threw high, but he was making good practice. He noted a handsome inDuna, wounded in the foot, assisted out of the attack by two comrades, and watched as all three fell. Finally the guns and the fire from the laager beat the Zulus back and the attack subsided. Wood ordered "Cease Fire."

The respite did not last long. The left horn and the center were in place by now, and shortly after two o'clock they attacked. As the fire started, the right horn came in again from the north, while the Undi corps, the inGobamakhosi and the abaQulusi poured across the valley to the south and began to mount the ridge. The main laager and the cattle kraal were perched on impassable rock faces, but a broad, steep slope led up between them. The ridge was steep, and the fire from the camp could not reach the dead ground in the ravine, and the Zulus scrambling up the slope were sheltered until they reached the crest. They breasted the lashing cross fire that hit them from the redoubt and the laager, forced their way into the cattle kraal, and fell on the company of the 1st/13th posted there. A vicious little fight developed amongst the maddened cattle crammed into the kraal, and then the infantry extricated itself and retreated along the palisade to the shelter of the redoubt. Wood stood in the path of the retreat and hurried the men streaming past him to safety. A private, late in leaving the kraal, was hit in the leg and fell, and Wood started down the slope to his aid. Captain Aubrey Maurice Maude, 1st/90th, restrained him. "Really, sir," he exclaimed, "it isn't your place to pick up single men." He went down himself with Lysons and Lieutenant Francis Smith, and the three officers brought the man in, although Smith took a bullet in the arm that invalided him out of the fight and all the way home to England.

Wood now sent Maude across the back of the guns to the laager, to ask Brevet Major Robert Henry Hackett to bring out two companies to sweep the Zulus to the south off the ridge and down the slope by the cattle kraal. Hackett was a bachelor with 23 years of service in the 90th Light Infantry; he lived only for his regiment and had once refused to take the newly instituted examinations for officers on the grounds that he was competent to perform all regimental duties and was totally uninterested in a staff appointment. He brought out his men at once, dressed his lines, fixed bayonets and charged for the lip of the slope. "G" Company was under Lieutenant Arthur Tyndall Bright, just twenty-one years old, who had inherited the command when Maude transferred to the staff to replace Campbell.

The advancing infantry swept the Zulus off the crest and down to a small terrace below the ridge, but then Hackett in his turn was forced to retreat. Masses of Zulus were pressing up out of the ravine onto the terrace, and the fire from the laager and the redoubt slackened as the infantry masked the head of the slope. Both ravine and terrace were in dead ground that the fire from the entrenchments could not reach, and the Zulus were sheltered while their numbers built up to charge again. Hackett started back in good order to the laager, which was only a few yards behind him, but a stinging rifle fire caught him in the flank. A party of Zulus had taken possession of the manure heap and burrowed into the grass that crowned it, and a small knoll hid them from the laager. Zulus with rifles were generally wildly inaccurate, but for once a few marksmen had been granted an opportunity to strike an effective blow. The two companies regained the laager with the Zulus from the terrace pressing hard on their heels, and the flanking fire struck a score of men as they were crossing the level. Colour Sergeant McAllen had been hit in the arm defending the laager against the first attack. He had his wound dressed and came out with Hackett, and a bullet from the manure pile killed him. A shot drilled through Arthur Bright's thigh, missing the bone but drenching him in blood, and he was dragged through the wagon gate by the men beside him. At the last moment Hackett himself was struck; a bullet passed through his head from temple to temple, starting his eyeballs out of their sockets and destroying his sight. Dazed and confused, he remained conscious and was led to the waiting surgeons.

The Zulus on both sides of the ridge had seen a sally retreat before their advance, and the illusion of imminent victory sustained their spirits. Time and again the warriors of the right horn regrouped and started for the northern face of the laager, and time and again the rifle fire and the four guns in the open beat them back. Time and again the center and the left horn massed in the sheltered valley and surged up the slope into the withering cross fire, and time and again the booming guns from the redoubt hammered them back to the ravine. The streaky smoke billowed about the laager and rose in a column from the redoubt, and the carnage continued for the space of three hours. Then the relentless tempo faltered and died, and Wood pulled two companies of the 1st/13th out of the laager to line the edge of the ridge, sweeping a few remaining Zulus out of the cattle kraal on the way. Their fire drove the Zulus off the terrace and the massed regiments in the ravine began to drift back to the east. The fire hurried them along, and Wood ordered Buller out to harry the retreat. The mounted men pursued the impi until dark, and the Frontier Light Horse followed the abaQulusi all the way to Hlobane before turning back. Mossop rode with the remnants of his troop, but he had collared a more suitable mount before he left the laager.

The battle had lasted a full four hours, and 29 men were dead or mortally wounded, and another 55 were wounded. Lieutenant Nicholson, struck down on the parapet of the redoubt, was dying, and so was Lieutenant Loraine White of the Transvaal Rangers, the son of a Waterloo veteran. The hospital tents, already crowded with the wounded from Hlobane and the camp's sick, were inundated, and the surgeons worked through the night. They dressed Arthur Bright's wound, but in the confusion did not notice that the bullet that had passed through his thigh had lodged in the other one, smashing the femur and severing an artery. He bled to death before morning. Hackett, unaware that he was blind, was complaining of the dark and begging for a candle, and it was more than a week later, in a hospital in Pietermaritzburg, before a doctor prevailed on a visiting lady to break the news to him.

It began to rain at dark, and the exhausted troops were turned out at three in the morning when a wounded Zulu fired at a sentry and the alarm was sounded. Wood sat out the incident in an ambulance until bullets began to snip through the sail, when he decided that he preferred getting wet to being shot by his own men.

Some 800 Zulus were piled around the ridge and hundreds more lay on the terrace, in the ravine and along the retreat; over 2,000 had died in all. Wounded prisoners told the impi's tale. The warriors had been faint with hunger when the attack started; they had marched without the uDibi boys and no Zulu had eaten a mouthful for the last three days. The dead in the cattle kraal were found with their mouths stuffed with the stiff porridge scraped from the voorlooper's cooking pots.

The Zulu army never took the field again after the march to Kambula. The warlike spirit of the nation had only existed in the thoughtless minds of thousands of ignorant young men who had never been blooded but who had all been raised on the legend of Shaka and the exploits of their fathers. Like youth the world over, they had a supreme confidence in their own strength and courage and their own abilities to best all trials, and there was none to tell them that they were ignorant and inexperienced and that war with the abeLungi was more than a sporting contest. Their truculent exuberance had carried their king into war, and they had brought their raw strength and high courage to Isandhlwana, to Rorke's Drift, to the Inyezane and to Gingindhlovu and to Kambula, and there they had learned that strength and courage meant nothing to massed breech-loading firearms. The regiments had all been blooded by now, and all the warriors had washed their spears. Between six and eight thousand of them lay dead on the bright green hills of Zululand, and a higher number had been wounded. Almost half the warriors who had assembled at Ulundi in January for the First Fruits ceremony had felt the touch of a bullet, the abeLungi were pouring into the country in greater numbers than ever before, and no Zulu impi could hope to stop them.

Cetshwayo had suspected it from the first, and now the entire nation knew the truth. The king knew nothing of strategy or of tactics or of the ways of European diplomacy, and he had given no direction to the war into which he had drifted. He had an army, and it had wanted to fight, and he had sent it to try conclusions with the invaders. It had failed, and he now waited for the inevitable end, temporizing in the fashion of his people by sending messengers to search for Chelmsford with pathetic offers of tempting bargains. It was far too late.

THE SECOND INVASION

W HEN Lord Chelmsford returned to Durban on the
ninth of April, he was at last ready to plan his sec-
ond invasion. The situation had altered radically since the dark days
after Isandhlwana. The flanking columns were safe, and the fear of a
Zulu invasion of Natal had receded. The Zulu army had been sorely
battered and was considerably less enthusiastic about fighting, although
it was still dangerous. The bulk of the reinforcements had landed; there
were fifteen Imperial infantry battalions to draw on as well as a naval
brigade and two regiments of English cavalry. There were hordes of
mounted volunteers, all manner of military oddments, swarms of unattached officers available for special services and four general officers.
Chelmsford commanded some 16,000 European troops, 7,000 armed
Natal Kaffirs and several thousand civilian transport conductors. Only
wagons and oxen were in short supply.

There was, in fact, a surfeit of strength, and the new operational
plan reflected it. Chelmsford's objective was still Ulundi; neither England nor the Zulu nation would be convinced the war was over until
the royal kraal had been burned and the king captured. Only one
column was really needed for this task; additional columns now added
little to the safety of Natal, and they were impossible to co-ordinate
and simply represented a drain on the available transport. Chelmsford,
moreover, naturally intended to command the force that reached
Ulundi and he could hardly afford another disaster brought on by an
unsupervised subordinate. Three or four Imperial battalions, fleshed
out with artillery and cavalry, would be ample for the main striking
force, which would in any event be limited to a crawl but could not be
expanded without multiplying the supply problems out of all proportion.

The main column could either strike east from upper Natal or north
from the Lower Drift of the Tugela. The distances to Ulundi were

about equal. Chelmsford chose upper Natal largely because he could move parallel to the main rivers, crossing only small headwaters instead of the lower reaches of a score of major streams. The upper country also held more firewood than the coastal region, but the decision meant that all supplies had to be moved several hundred extra miles from Durban before they could enter Zululand and in the event added six weeks to the campaign.

The plan left eleven or twelve surplus battalions for whom gainful employment had to be found—not to mention the four general officers. Chelmsford had asked for a single general officer to replace him should his own health break; he was now gaunt and tired but his health was splendid and although the numbers of troops in Natal appeared to justify the presence of five generals, the amount of work to be done did not. Chelmsford had not been consulted in the choice of the generals, and the Duke of Cambridge had sent him a mixed bag. The senior of the four new arrivals was Major General the Honourable Henry Hugh Clifford, V.C., C.B., and Chelmsford set about reducing his surplus by making Clifford Inspector General and placing him in command of the base and all the troops in Natal, as well as of all lines of communication in the colony up to the borders of Zululand, turning over to him for disposal the whole of the 2nd/24th, the 2nd/4th and the equivalent of another battalion in odd companies drawn from the other regiments as well as part of the Naval Brigade and the cavalry and two battalions of the Natal Native Contingent.

Clifford, fifty-two years old, had been in the Army since 1846. He had fought in the Kaffir Wars and had won a Victoria Cross in the Crimea, but continual staff assignments had removed him from the main stream of regimental life. He was highly intelligent and a gifted artist, but he was also brusque and tactless and tended to ignore channels. The Duke of Cambridge had specifically chosen him to ease Chelmsford's administrative burdens in Natal, where Strickland had been struggling to provide transport in the face of Bulwer's hostility and the incompetence of most of the junior officers assigned to him. Clifford, however, was aware that Chelmsford was living on borrowed time. He made a hard task no easier by the barrage of complaints, requests and gratuitous suggestions he leveled at Chelmsford and the other field commanders, and he fiercely resented the decision to chop his authority over the lines of communication at the borders of Zululand.

The best of the three remaining generals was Henry Hope Crealock, C.B., the elder brother of Chelmsford's military secretary. He had also fought in the Crimea, in the Sepoy Rebellion and in China, and he had been with Wolseley on the Red River expedition in Canada. He was also an artist, and for a spell had actually left the army in a futile effort to earn a living as a painter in Rome. Chelmsford now organized what he called the South African Field Force into two divisions and he turned command of the Ist Division over to Crealock, giving him the 2nd/3d, the 88th and the 99th Regiments for a 1st Brigade under Colonel Pearson, and the 57th, 3d/60th and 91st Regiments for a 2nd Brigade under Charles Mansfield Clarke, the colonel of the 57th. Headquarters for the Ist Division were at Fort Pearson on the Lower Drift of the Tugela, where Crealock would also find the bulk of the Naval Brigade, John Dunn's scouts, 564 mounted volunteers and fifteen fieldpieces.

The other two generals were Edward Newdigate, a likable if lackluster and somewhat indecisive man who had been in the Army 37 years—longer than Chelmsford himself—and Frederick Marshall, the most junior if not the youngest man on England's list of 249 Major Generals. Chelmsford's presence with the striking force would keep Newdigate in the shade, but he was given command of the IInd Division, with six companies of the 2nd/21st and six of the 58th in the 1st Brigade under Colonel Glyn and six companies of the 94th and seven of the 1st/24th in the 2nd Brigade under William Pole Collingwood, colonel of the 21st. Twelve fieldpieces, including Harness's reconstituted battery, a battalion of the NNC and 210 mounted volunteers were included as well. Marshall was given a Cavalry Brigade subordinated to the IInd Division and consisting of the 17th Lancers and the 1st (The King's) Dragoon Guards.

Evelyn Wood was far too valuable to be placed under Newdigate, and Chelmsford owed him a debt of gratitude going back to the Perie Bush, which London as yet had done nothing to acknowledge. Chelmsford gave him a local rank of Brigadier General, left his column intact and relabeled it the Flying Column. It was to move with the IInd Division, keeping a sufficient distance to maintain the fiction of a separate command but actually an integral part of the striking force. Wood took four companies of the 80th Regiment from Luneberg to add to the 1st/13th and the 90th, welcomed four Gatling guns to go with his four fieldpieces, and finished with 784 mounted men from various volunteer units. Despite past experiences, he also began to recruit again for Wood's Irregulars and he bade Buller relinquish command of his beloved Frontier Light Horse to Cecil D'Arcy to assume command of the collective mounted volunteers.

The proliferation of units in Natal was unwieldy, but the reorganization was sound and made effective use of what was available. The assignments had all been announced by the middle of April, but the troops were still scattered over the face of Natal and several weeks would elapse before the new echelons could take form. The English cavalry and the bulk of the artillery were still at Durban, Crealock's 1st Brigade was at Fort Pearson and his 2nd Brigade in the new camp at Gingindhlovu, the Flying Column was at Kambula, and the IInd Division was strung out along the back roads on the march to upper Natal.

Their progress was slow. Most of the battalions were fresh from England, weighted down with needless impedimenta and unused to field conditions. Almost 600 men had been recruited and scraped out of the depot battalions to reform the 1st/24th, for example; they were still soldiers in name only, and they were late in arriving to boot. Their transport, the *Clyde*, ran aground on a reef off Dyer's Island on the third of April, and although all hands were landed before the vessel sank, the battalion had to return to Capetown before proceeding to Natal. The men were eager to reach the front, but delays were endless. The battalions shook down at Durban, and officers limited to forty pounds packed in a valise regretfully abandoned hammocks, washstands and India-rubber mattresses with bellows to inflate them. Chelmsford had issued an edict against pipe clay, but even with spit and polish relaxed the men found the new life hard. They were taken to Pietermaritzburg by train and commenced the march upcountry through a colony that regarded them with indifference and offered few amenities. Feet soon hardened—the standard treatment for blisters was to draw a needle threaded with worsted through—but the routine was depressing. After a day of marching it took hours for unaccustomed troops to form a wagon laager and entrench it, there was a stand-to at dusk and another that started two hours before dawn, and what little sleep could be snatched on the bare ground was broken by frequent and unnecessary night alarms or by the eternal round of duty on the outlying pickets, where every passing shadow was magnified into an attacking impi. The officers messed by company groups of three and four, learning from experience to simmer chunks of stringy slaughter beeves and not to parboil them, and breakfasting off cold tea and the greasy remnants of their suppers. The men were forbidden hard liquor, and the officers guiltily broached a bottle or two in their tents, or paid a shilling a glass for "squareface" Hollands gin in the dreary public houses that studded the roads, tended by surly keepers, whose prices rose as the distance from Durban grew, and thronged by half-sodden loafers ready to exchange misinformation about the Zulus for a drink. Untended gear was "jumped" and disappeared at once; Natal Kaffirs ran off horses and transport oxen at night, and even Chelmsford's horse was stolen, to turn up several days later hidden near the camp of a mounted volunteer unit.

The Imperial cavalry made a poor initial showing. The regiments had brought out their own highly trained mounts, and the horses looked like tucked-up whippets when they landed after three weeks below decks in the transports. It took them several weeks to recover. Cavalry in England was fed on cut fodder, and the horses had never learned to support themselves by grazing. They would not touch the rank grass of Natal at first, and the pasturage around Durban was played out. The average trooper weighed 160 pounds and carried dress and accouterments weighing another forty; the saddlery and the equipment carried in the wallets added sixty pounds more. This gave each undernourished horse a load of more than 260 pounds, an amount that startled the colonists. When Marshall finally left Durban on the seventeenth of April, he found that his regiments could only cover ten miles a day and had to rest every third day. Detachments of the Army Service Corps accompanied the column to carry fodder for the mounts, and it was early May before he finally reached Dundee.

Chelmsford stopped in Pietermaritzburg on his way upcountry to make a final effort to secure martial law for Natal. His situation was critical. He had almost 25,000 men to feed and thousands of animals to care for; produce was scarce and prices were still rising. Scores of farmers had ridden off to the war, and there was no transport left to move what little produce there was into the towns. The roads were rutted and the drifts quagmires, and there was no more pasturage within easy reach of the tracks, cutting the time teams could spend inspanned to a few hours a day. Great numbers of native voorloopers had simply deserted, and few of those that remained would take their teams near the border of Zululand. Overworked oxen were dying in droves, each costing the Crown an indemnity of £20, and there were no replacements in sight. Bulwer remained obdurate, and would only back an appeal to colonists to sell transport to the forces, which netted Chelmsford 674 additional oxen at £15 a head.

General Crealock reached Fort Pearson and took command of the Ist Division on the eighteenth of April. His only orders from Chelmsford were to burn the military kraal at emaNgwene and the great kraal at Undi, some forty miles into Zululand, but before he could do so, he was to establish an advanced base with supplies for two months on the Inyezane and an intermediate post on the Amatikulu. He was eventually to move to the mission station of St. Paul, seven miles past Undi and still twenty-five miles from Ulundi, but the planning beyond this stage, which lay many weeks in the future, would depend on the progress the IInd Division had made in the meantime.

Crealock was a reasonably energetic man, but he was as careful as Chelmsford had been in the first phase, and he had more men and even less transport at his disposal. His 2nd Brigade was already on the Inye-zane, his 1st still at Fort Pearson. He had 250 wagons and 3,500 oxen, and there were approximately 1,200 wagonloads of supplies to be fer-ried across the Tugela and taken to the advanced depot. What fresh transport Chelmsford could squeeze out of Natal was going to the IInd Division, and the previous movements along the coastal route had ham-mered the tracks and the approaches to the drifts into muddy sinks. The grass was already gone, and long daily drives under heavy escort were needed to bring the oxen to their daily grazing. Crealock estab-lished his intermediate depot on the Amatikulu and named it for him-self; this was acceptable practice, although there was some muttering at the amount of personal baggage that he brought, scattered through 27 wagons. The main depot on the Inyezane was a knottier problem. The drainage along the banks of that stream was poor; the stench of rotting bodies at Gingindhlovu had driven the first force five miles downstream, and within a fortnight the ground there was foul as well. Crealock was casting about still farther downstream for a fresh site when Norris-Newman visited the tentless camp with a private request from Clifford in his pocket to report on conditions. The correspondent produced a long letter deploring all the arrangements, which Clifford forwarded to Crealock, asking to have the complaints attended to. Crealock, naturally furious, scribbled "Read and returned" on the back and sent it back to Clifford, but a month later the Inspector General was sending a party of inspectors to sniff into the work of Crealock's overburdened transport officers. The commander of the Ist Division, as he put it, "cut up rusty," and Clifford added another complaint to his growing collection.

The overworked punts at the Lower Drift were replaced by a pon-toon bridge in May and the greater part of the stream was bridged by a semipermanent trestle in June, by which time the telegraph from Dur-ban and Pietermaritzburg had been strung to the Inyezane. There was talk of establishing a base on the coast north of the advanced depot, which Crealock had tactfully named Fort Chelmsford, but the idea came to naught and Crealock placed no reliance on the hope of landing men and stores from the sea. Scouting naval vessels selected a sandy stretch of open beach south of Point Durnford, but the only advantage it offered was the absence of the usual rocks, and the slightest breeze turned the surf into an impassable barrier. H.M.S. *Tenedos* was se-verely damaged in an accidental grounding during the survey and retired to Capetown, calling in her sixty men from the Naval Brigade before she returned to England.

Crealock sent the first convoy of 110 wagons off to the Amatikulu on the twenty-first of April, but it was the seventeenth of June before the last of twelve such trains had been staged on to the Inyezane. By then his oxen were walking skeletons that needed doubled teams to draw lightened loads five miles a day. Even with the advanced depots provisioned, the 1st Brigade was still at the Lower Drift, and enteric fever had struck at Fort Crealock and Fort Chelmsford. Eighteen officers and 479 men were invalided back to Natal; three officers and 68 men died. In two months of hectic activity along the coastal road, not a single hostile Zulu had been seen.

The Flying Column had a few weeks of relative inactivity while the IInd Division took shape. On the fifth of April Captain John Prior of the 80th Regiment took a mounted patrol out of Luneberg. Natal Kaffirs near the Intombi informed him of a party of raiders sweeping horses and cattle out of a valley ahead, and Prior gave chase. The marauders released their loot and ran, and Prior rode after two of the refugees, bringing one down with a lucky shot. He turned out to be the celebrated Mbilini, mortally wounded.

On the sixteenth of April another patrol under Commandant Rudolph, sometime Landdrost of Utrecht, came across a near-naked European wandering half-crazed over the veld far to the east of Kambula. He was a Frenchman, and after he had been given a slug of brandy, his wits returned and he identified himself as Henri Grandier, a trooper of Weatherley's Border Horse. He had been caught in the trap on Ityenka Nek, and claimed that he had given his mount to a wounded comrade. All the men on the ridge were killed, but for some reason the Zulus spared him and toward evening he was taken to Mbilini's kraal on the terrace, near the spot where Lloyd and Campbell had just been buried. Mbilini attempted to question him, and the next morning sent him to Mnyamana, before the impi left the Hlobane bivouac. Mnyamana ordered him sent to Ulundi, and four men had escorted him there and taken him before Cetshwayo. The king wanted to know the name of the British commander, the reasons for the British invasion, and the whereabouts of the errant Uhamu. He had then been held under guard in a hut for upwards of a week. According to Grandier, he had been beaten almost continually and well-nigh starved, until Cetshwayo had heard of the death of Mbilini. The king then ordered him returned to Mbilini's kraal to be put to death. He started back under another escort of two warriors, and near Hlobane one of them wandered off in search of food. The other began to doze, and Grandier seized his chance. Grabbing an assegai, he pinned him to the ground and then chased the other Zulu away when he returned to the camp. He had then started for Kambula but had lost his way, and had been searching the hills for three days when Rudolph found him.

The English press made much of the sensational story, which stood for six months. Then Colenso began to collect an account of events at Ulundi during the war. He eventually heard from a native named Klaas, who had been one of Grandier's escort. The Frenchman had not been mistreated, and Cetshwayo had given him two horses and an oxen and ordered the escort to release him in the vicinity of Kambula. Hero or liar, Grandier was at any rate the only European prisoner of war taken by the Zulus during the campaign.

In the middle of April the task of policing the camp at Kambula reached a point of diminishing returns, and Wood again shifted a half a mile to the west. Buller was making long forays to the south, reconnoitering the tracks but encountering few Zulus, and Wood's major activity was gathering fuel. He had long since exhausted all timber in the vicinity, and he soon had two companies of infantry camped at the Doornberg thirty miles to the south hacking at the thorn thickets, which he denuded so thoroughly that the local Boer settlers eventually changed its name. Four other companies were scattered about picking at the surface coal seams. A pound of coal was worth three of wood, and the fueling parties were soon supplying the needs of the IInd Division as well as those of the Flying Column.

Chelmsford now wasted six weeks in posting the IInd Division in upper Natal. His line of advance lay by the old road to Ulundi, and although the laager had been struck by fever, his natural base should have been at Helpmakaar at the head of the road. He had been carrying a well-nigh intolerable load for over a year, pushing one antlike column after another against his elusive and exasperating foe, from the Perie Bush to Gingindhlovu, and while he had carried the burden well and alone, without flinching and without complaint, he could not bring himself to return to the field of Isandhlwana. He may be forgiven for shrinking from the prospect of marching a fresh column along the track where the bones of a first column still lay unburied, but the detour around the crossing at Rorke's Drift led him into protracted difficulties. The next crossing to the south lay at the Middle Drift of the Tugela, but a belt of impassable country beyond barred him from striking north to the Ulundi road. The only solution was to move upstream, crossing the headwaters of the Buffalo and then the Blood to work through the hills beyond before dropping down to the Ulundi road in the vicinity of Ibabanango. A possible track still farther north along the valley of the White Umfolozi was vetoed because it led under the shadow of Inhlazatye Mountain, an enormous table top that dwarfed Hlobane.

The want of information concerning the interior of Zululand led to a false start. The abandoned farms that comprised the settlement of Dundee lay twenty miles north of Helpmakaar on the Border Road, and from Dundee a good hunting road led east, crossing the Buffalo River at Landman's Drift and passing between the Doornberg and Koppie Allein before swinging north along the right bank of the Blood. Fifteen miles north of Koppie Allein the track crossed the Blood below Conference Hill, across the river from Bemba's Kop, leading from thence on to Kambula. Buller had found a track that led south from Kambula between Bemba's Kop and Munhla Hill, well to the east of the Blood, but there did not appear to be a road through the hills beyond the Blood at Koppie Allein, and it looked as if the IInd Division would have to move north to Conference Hill before crossing. Chelmsford consequently named Conference Hill the advanced depot for both the Flying Column and the IInd Division, and for the last half of April and for most of May scores of small convoys crawled laboriously along the rough tracks from Dundee to stock the base.

By mid-May the battalions of the IInd Division had reached upper Natal, and were camped at Dundee, at Landman's Drift and the Doornberg and at Conference Hill itself, waiting for the straining transport to build up the supply dump. On the sixteenth of May a squadron of the 17th Lancers left Dundee, crossed Landman's Drift and bivouacked at Vecht Kop, where Pretorius had smashed Dingane's impi forty years earlier. The next day they crossed the Blood below Koppie Allein and mounted the foothills that lined the left bank. By evening they had reached Itelezi Hill, a half-dozen miles into Zululand, and had rendezvoused with Bettington's Third Troop of the Natal Horse, which had ridden down the left bank from Conference Hill. The combined patrols scouted far past Itelezi before turning south to recross into Natal near the junction of the Blood and the Buffalo. They reported that a practical wagon route led across the Blood River at Koppie Allein past Itelezi Hill and from thence on toward Ibabanango, which meant that there was no need for the IInd Division to move fifteen miles north to Conference Hill before crossing the Blood. Chelmsford therefore canceled his plans to concentrate on Conference Hill and shifted his advanced base to Koppie Allein, and all the stores that had been dragged to the north were repacked and started back to the south.

All through May the IInd Division sat in its laagers at Landman's Drift, waiting for the stores to accumulate. Early in the month Chelmsford visited Wood at Kambula, and on the fifth the Flying Column finally abandoned the ridge on which it had been perched since the thirty-first of January and started south. By the twelfth it was at Wolf's Hill, where Wood entrenched a camp and brought supplies up from his own depot on Balte Spruit. Buller made two more scouts to the south, tracing out a practical route for the column to follow to the south. He reconnoitered the valleys of the Tombokala and the

Ityotyosi to the east of Itelezi Hill, crossed the Nondweni and penetrated to within six miles of Ibabanango. Here, on the nineteenth of
May, he dropped down on the traders' wagon track that was said to
lead to Ulundi, just past Isipezi Hill, which Chelmsford had been trying to reach when the impi attacked Isandhlwana.

The cavalry had finally reached upper Natal, and Marshall now used
it to carry out a long-overdue chore. All through the long months that
followed the massacre at Isandhlwana, the bodies of the slain had lain
where they had fallen. Wilsone Black had paid the field a hurried visit
on the fourteenth of March and he rode back again on the fifteenth of
May to find all as it had been before. His patrols were too small to
police the wrecked camp, and as the weeks passed, public pressure to
bury the dead mounted. Chelsmford was forced to ignore it; the job
would take several hundred men the better part of a day, and while a
mobile patrol of twenty or thirty men might ride in and out in safety,
thrusting a large force without transport ten miles into Zululand was a
risky proposition. In mid-April Colenso proposed to Bulwer that he go
to Isandhlwana in a private capacity with a party of civilians to dig the
graves. Bulwer received the offer politely but declined it on the score
of the Bishop's safety—an apprehension which John W. Natal scorned.
Only when the cavalry began to reach Dundee did Chelmsford feel
that the project was feasible.

On the twentieth of May Marshall took the 1st Dragoon Guards and
half the Lancers to Rorke's Drift, picking up two guns, five companies
of the 2nd/24th and a large force of mounted volunteers. At four in
the morning on the twenty-first Colonel Drury Lowe crossed the
Buffalo with half the cavalry, moved up the valley of the Bashee past
Sihayo's burned kraal and worked up to the Nqutu Plateau, descending
to Isandhlwana along the spur down which the attack had rolled. Marshall crossed an hour and a half later with the rest of the force, riding
to the camp along the track and leaving the infantry to guard the
heights to the east of the Bashee.

The two forces met in the wrecked camp at half past eight, found
the area deserted and posted vedettes before setting to work. The
spilled grain had sprouted, and oats and mealies grew thickly about the
vicinity of the wagon park, concealing the bodies of the men who had
died in the final stand. The fluttering pennons on the nine-foot bamboo
lances dipped and rose as the mounted men poked through the growth,
searching for corpses. Most of the bodies were little more than skeletons, but here and there the skin on a skull had mummified to preserve
recognizable features. The volunteer units were able to identify most
of their dead, but there was none to recognize the privates of the 24th
Regiment, because Colonel Glyn had begged Marshall not to touch

them on the grounds that the regiment wanted to bury its comrades in the presence of both battalions. The 2nd Warwickshire were left where they had fallen, and the rest of the dead were placed in shallow graves scraped in the rocky soil and marked with cairns. The entire force was back at Rorke's Drift by evening, bringing out forty of the abandoned wagons with led horses. It was late June before detachments of the 24th were able to march in from Rorke's Drift to finish the job.

As on previous visits, unoccupied men wandered through the camp, searching for personal belongings or for trinkets to send survivors. Norris-Newman found the remnants of his own tent, with the dried corpses of his Natal Kaffir servant and his spare horses beside it. Theophilus Shepstone, Jr., had ridden in with the Natal Carbineers to search for his brother George, and while removing the bodies of the men who had died in the last stand on the saddle, he recognized the corpse of Anthony Durnford. Before it was buried, he removed two rings and a pocket knife, and, knowing Durnford's relationship to the Colenso family, he sent them on to the Bishop. Seaward Longhurst, veterinary surgeon of the 1st Dragoon Guards, was watching him, and several months later he fell into the clutches of Frances Ellen Colenso, who was systematically interviewing every man she could find who had been at the camp. Under her questioning, Longhurst claimed to recall that Shepstone had also removed a packet of letters from the body, which, he judged from their contour, might have contained official papers. Frances seized on the point and jumped to the conclusion that the packet held the still-missing orders from Chelmsford to Durnford and, no doubt, the "proof" that Durnford had not been ordered to take command of the camp. In her inflamed imagination, Shepstone would naturally wish to conceal such evidence, which he had no doubt sent to Chelmsford. She prevailed upon Longhurst to describe the incident to Durnford's brother Edward, and it was 1882 before Shepstone heard of the story. He immediately denied it to the Colensos, to Longhurst and to Edward Durnford, pointing out that the body was coatless when he found it and producing affidavits from two of the men who had been with him. The missing order itself, although Shepstone did not know it at the time, had actually been found on the same day in Durnford's portmanteau in his wagon where the escort had abandoned it, and Edward Durnford by 1882 had also received Crealock's order book with the copy of the message. Edward Durnford and the Bishop at once accepted Shepstone's statement and apologized, but neither Frances Colenso nor Longhurst bothered to reply. Four years later, in 1886, the implacable Frances Colenso was still hard at work trying to clear Durnford's name. She had by now enlisted the aid of Lieutenant

Colonel Charles Luard, who held Durnford's old job of Colonial Engineer at Pietermaritzburg. Although Luard had not even been in Natal during the campaign, he began to malign Shepstone, and when the fresh slanders finally reached his ears the long-suffering Captain of Volunteers demanded an official court of inquiry. The story finally came out into the open, and, faced with a general court-martial, Longhurst and Luard hastily retracted.

By the end of May Chelmsford was finally poised to strike. Four infantry battalions, the 17th Lancers, a squadron of the 1st Dragoon Guards, twelve fieldpieces, Bengough's 2nd Battalion of the NNC, Bettington's troop of Natal Horse and the Edendale contingent, now under Offy Shepstone, were all congregated on the bank of the Blood River at Koppie Allein. Wood lay at Munhla Hill eighteen miles to the northeast across the river with three infantry battalions, four fieldpieces and four Gatlings, 485 Natal Kaffirs and 780 mounted volunteers. Newdigate had supplies for a month, and Wood for six weeks, and Chelmsford had struck his headquarters at Utrecht and moved on to join the IInd Division. The two forces would join near the junction of the Tombokala and the Ityotyosi, slanting from thence to the southeast to cross the Nondweni before picking up the Ulundi road south of Ibabanango.

Newdigate crossed the Blood River on the thirty-first of May with his 1st Brigade and Harness's battery, moving on the next day to camp at Itelezi Hill while the rest of his division crossed. The Flying Column marched down from Munhla Hill to camp a few miles from Newdigate on the Umvunyana River. The first of June was a Sunday, and the men were given a day of rest. Lieutenant Colonel Harrison, R.E., was Assistant Quartermaster General, and responsible for scouting the path of the morrow's march. Early in the morning he sent a small mounted patrol out past the site of the new camp at Itelezi Hill to reconnoiter the valley between the Ityotyosi and the Tombokala, where the IInd Division was to bivouac the following day.

Toward evening the IInd Division was camped at Itelezi Hill and the Flying Column just to the north at Incenci Hill. The water supply for the Flying Column was inadequate, and Wood and Buller rode out from their camp with a few mounted troopers to search for a pool or a rivulet to relieve the strain. A mile or so from the camp a distant rider caught their eye, and they reined in as the dancing dot resolved itself into an officer galloping up on a lathered horse. He had been in command of the morning's patrol, and an hour earlier he had been ambushed by a party of Zulus. His native guide and three of his seven men were missing. The four survivors were coming on behind him, and far beyond them a few Zulus could be seen leading several horses off into the late afternoon light. Buller spoke briefly with the officer, and then he and Wood turned white. Hardly waiting for the other survivors, they wheeled their horses and started back to the camp. A blow even heavier than the disaster at Isandhlwana had again descended on the British forces in Zululand.

Two of the missing men were from Bettington's troop of the Natal Horse. The third had been Napoleon Eugène Louis Jean Joseph, the son of Napoleon III and the Prince Imperial of France.

THE PRINCE IMPERIAL

SHORTLY AFTER three on the morning of March 16, 1856, the guns at the Invalides began to boom. The populace stirred uneasily in its sleep, but hardly any of the inhabitants of Paris bothered to count the full hundred and one shots. It was morning before they learned that the Empress Eugénie had been safely delivered of a son.

Napoleon III was beside himself with joy. He loved his wife dearly (although constancy was somewhat beyond his powers), and the labor had lasted a full 36 hours. The birth had been a semipublic affair with hordes of official witnesses, including the Emperor's cousin Prince Napoleon, known as "Plon-Plon," who had just been lowered to third place in the line of Imperial succession. Plon-Plon was so consumed with rage at the successful culmination of the birth that he broke the nib of the pen with which he signed the official witness book, leaving a large blot to posterity.

The father's joy went far beyond that of a simple paterfamilias. Continental royalty regarded him as little more than an upstart, and at home his throne still rested on the fickle foundation of public adulation. The nephew of the great Napoleon, he had lived in exile as a child, had returned to France to plot revolt, and had fled to America when discovered. He had returned, only to spend six years in prison following another conspiracy, and had finally escaped to England. In 1848, aged forty, he came back to Paris after the revolution and before the year was out had been elected President of the Republic. In 1852 he proclaimed himself Emperor. The following year he married Eugénie de Montijo, the daughter of a penniless Spanish hidalgo, and the Second Empire was fairly launched. The respective backgrounds of the Imperial couple, however, militated against their complete acceptance, and while the Queen of England found them personally charming, the Tsar of Russia pointedly omitted the usual *Mon Frère* from his correspondence. Their child, on the other hand, was born to the purple, and he would enjoy from birth the advantage of a legitimacy his father had never possessed.

The nation was not to forget for an instant that this was the Prince Imperial, the Child of France and the future sovereign. The Pope graciously consented to stand as godfather, and Napoleon announced that he in his turn would be godfather to all legitimate French children born that day. Before the hapless infant was six hours old, he had been exhibited to the diplomatic corps in the throne room, draped with the ribbon of the Legion of Honour and with a large crucifix resting on his umbilical knot. Count Otto von Bismarck, the second plenipotentiary for Prussia, found the ceremony vulgar.

The infant was known as "Lou-Lou," and he had an indulgent father and a rather unstable mother, who, if she was somewhat inept in dealing with small children, truly loved her only child and spared him most of the barbarities that Victoria and Albert inflicted on their royal brood. Lou-Lou had a devoted, affectionate tutor who made few scholastic demands on his charge, and the general course of his education was directed by a father who had only one thought in his mind.

The population of France would lose its heart to a soldier while it spurned a statesman, and a soldier Louis must be. He was enrolled as a Grenadier at birth and commissioned in the 1st Imperial Guard Regiment at nine months. He was introduced to horses before he was out of his cradle, and he attended his first military review, mounted, before he could walk. It was a strange childhood, and the boy grew up with an acute awareness of his position, but was somehow untrammeled by the weight of it. Frail and rather delicate, he was nevertheless an exuberant extrovert with a daring spirit and a generous, open nature. Although it blossomed late, he had a sure touch; hearing of a pensioned soldier who had lost his life savings, he made good the sum with a note reading, "From a Grenadier to a Voltigeur." Dignity was not his forte, nor was reserve, and he was in some danger of turning into a thoroughly spoiled royal brat. Only one threat would bring him to heel, but from infancy it sufficed: he must not "disgrace the uniform."

His character was cast by the time he was fourteen. His father's constant companion, he lived in a dream of future glory with the example of his illustrious great-uncle ever before him. He was a master of military trappings, surrounded by uniforms and flags and regiments. He reveled in drill, he was a superb horsemen and a master swordsman. Of strategy, of staff work, of the true wellsprings of military power, he knew nothing.

When the war with Prussia came, he rode off to the front with his father in a fever of excitement. Napoleon III was to take personal command of his armies; Eugénie was left behind in Paris as Regent.

Had the boy observed his father closely for even a moment, he might have been prepared for the shock of what was coming. The Emperor was not a good general, and a view of the stricken field at the bloody victory of Solferino had cured him of a romantic attitude toward war. The slaughter had horrified him, and he regarded the present conflict as a pure catastrophe. He also had an inkling of the monumental chaos that lay behind the façade of a few glittering regular regiments. He was in any event in no physical condition to lead an army; he suffered from hemorrhoids and a bladder stone and could not sit a horse nor even ride in a carriage over any but the smoothest roads. He endured continual agonies that sapped his strength, his will and almost his reason.

Louis rode through the fringes of a successful initial action at Saarbrücken, where 60,000 Frenchmen dislodged 1,000 Prussians from a town and then retired. The fourteen-year-old boy capered in the wake of the advance in an ecstasy of delight; he had seen shells explode and wounded men with bandaged heads and he had picked a spent bullet off the ground. The debacle began immediately afterward. The French had tried to mobilize almost a million men without the slightest trace of organization, and hordes of bewildered and ill-supplied conscripts suffered several shattering defeats. Eugénie issued a series of resolute but unrealistic edicts to which no one but her husband paid much attention. She abruptly disposed him from command, and then forbade him or her son to leave the front. For a few humiliating days the two rode back and forth, jostled by the debris of the disintegrating armies which mocked and jeered them in their confusion. Louis' world was breaking apart and he could not understand what was happening. His father finally sent him with a small escort to seek shelter near the Belgian border, and he clung to French soil for a while, moving from village to small village and risking capture by roving Prussian patrols. When the end was clear, the escort took him into Belgium, made for a channel port and sent him to England. His mother arrived a few days later. She had fled Paris disguised as a madwoman, and an Englishman brought her off in his yacht and carried her to Hastings in a raging storm. There was neither a military nor a political role to maintain any longer, and Napoleon III drifted into captivity. The Republicans continued to resist for a while, but the Second Empire had been swept away.

Eugénie rented Camden Place, a country estate at Chislehurst, and waited for her husband to join her. He was released soon enough, and the royal family settled down to await an opportunity to return to France, joined by a small clutch of retainers who nursed the mirage of a shadowy Imperial court. To their surprise, the English public received them with enthusiasm. The Prince of Wales set the fashion. Without consulting his mother, he visited Eugénie to welcome her to England. Victoria was furious. She was genuinely fond of the royal exiles, and she pitied their plight, but she was Queen of England and the refugees were an acute political embarrassment. Republican France was as touchy as Imperial France had been, and the slightest gesture of kindness to the Bonapartes was easily misinterpreted.

No such considerations bothered her people, who did not like Republicans but dearly loved royalty. Eugénie and Louis were accepted at once, and when Napoleon finally landed, expecting God knows what fresh humiliations, he was, to his astonishment, cheered to the echo. The Queen finally thawed, established cordial relations, and admitted the Bonapartes to the homely round of her extensive family ties.

The next three years were hard ones for Louis. He had neither a past to support him nor a future to give him hope. Filon, his tutor, could interest him in nothing, and his mind, sharp enough when he wanted to use it, drifted aimlessly. Only a visit to the Royal Military Academy at Woolwich, where the artillery and engineering officers were trained, fanned a momentary spark of interest. His boyhood was gone and his manhood had not yet arrived.

Napoleon insisted that something be done to educate his son, and for a term Filon took him to King's College, Strand. Louis was bored and hopelessly unprepared, and he had no desire to change. Then an English friend made a suggestion; why not send him to Woolwich? Louis perked up at once, and the Duke of Cambridge smoothed the way. Faced with entrance examinations, Louis turned to and bested them, giving a sudden glimpse of a hitherto unsuspected flair for mathematics.

There were 200 Gentlemen Cadets at the "Shop" in 1872, and Louis took his place among the "snookers" of the lowest class. Louis Conneau, his best friend and the son of a doctor who had followed Napoleon into exile, entered with him, and the two moved into a small house with Filon the tutor and Xaviar Uhlmann, an ex-dragoon who had been Louis' valet since his early childhood. He was not recognized at first, and he had the sense to realize that he would have to win the acceptance of his English schoolmates as a cadet and not as a French prince. He took his full share of the "roshing" to which all the snookers were subjected; early in the game a group of upperclassmen tossed him fully dressed into a cold bath for an infraction of class rules. Conneau, appalled by the affront to the Imperial dignity, at once jumped in beside him.

Despite his success at the entrance examination, Louis' feeble academic background was a tremendous handicap. When his troubled tutor went to the superintendent he was reassured; there had been precedents, and a prince need not fear rustication for academic failure. Louis would not have it that way, however, and to Filon's delight the drowsing intellect suddenly awoke. As his slippery grasp of English improved, Louis began to make progress.

His fellow cadets accepted him as an equal. He was un-English enough to enjoy showing off, but his riding and fencing were worth exhibiting, and he never swanked. Two of his pet expressions gained currency: "Is it an insult?" whenever he was chaffed, and "What the divel 'eapened?" at any unusual event. His only difficulties were in military history, where his violently partisan views on Waterloo conflicted with the English version and disrupted the class. The dispute did not interfere with his popularity, however, and he was even admitted to the highly unofficial Alpine Club, whose practice it was in midnight climbs to decorate the towers and spires of Woolwich with chamberpots on the eve of the annual inspection by the Duke of Cambridge.

His status changed appreciably during his sojourn at the Shop. During a lecture in 1873 an aide appeared at the classroom door to call him back to Camden Place, and when he arrived, he found his father dead after a long-delayed operation. Thousands of Frenchmen crossed the Channel for the funeral, and when Louis slipped quietly back to his classes, many of his countrymen regarded him as Napoleon IV. In 1874 he reached his majority with his eighteenth birthday, and Chislehurst was again thronged with visiting Frenchmen, to the great embarrassment of the English Cabinet. In a surprisingly mature and emotional speech, Louis took his place as the head of the Bonapartist party.

The changes did not affect his work. He continued to grind away, improving his standing every term, until Uhlmann worried about his health. His mother glowed with pride over his achievements, and the Empress became a familiar figure during her frequent visits to the Shop. Once she was almost brained by a stray cricket ball.

At graduation in 1875, Louis stood first in riding, first in fencing, and seventh in over-all merit in a class of 34 cadets. He had been a phenomenal success after all. He might have stood fourth had he sat officially for the examination in French, but he refused to take unfair advantage of his classmates. Then he sat unofficially, out of curiosity, and to everybody's amusement was beaten by an English cadet.

The ten ranking graduates were allowed to opt for the coveted commissions in the Royal Engineers, regarded as a much more preferable career than that in the Royal Artillery, to which the rest of the class was consigned. Louis was not to be commissioned, but he stood in the line of precedence. To everyone's surprise, and the incredulous delight of the eleventh member of the class, he spurned the "Sappers" and opted for the artillery. He was, he explained simply, only carrying on a tradition; he came from a family of gunners.

The years following his graduation were a letdown. He drew closer to his mother, never an easy woman to live with, and together they bided their time. France had achieved a measure of political stability, and the death of the Emperor had dashed the hopes of an immediate recall, although neither of them doubted for an instant the reality of an eventual return. In the meantime he could only wait, guiding the destiny of his small but fanatically loyal political party and suffering in silence the gibes of the French press, which called him "Napoleon III½" and the "Imperial Baby." He was never allowed to forget the spent bullet he had pocketed at Saarbrücken, and no one in France believed that his career at Woolwich had been anything but a farce. He was labeled the *fruit sec,* an idiot, and it was reported that his fellow cadets had shunned him. Even his own party was scandalized by his military career; it was bad enough that the Imperial sword should be placed at the disposal of the English crown, but what really galled was the idea of the French Prince Imperial placing himself on an equal footing with nameless English cadets. Louis ignored the furor, and when his age group was called for conscription—Frenchmen abroad who ignored the summons were outlawed—he quietly submitted his name. He was, needless to say, not called, but the gesture did not pass unnoticed.

He was immensely popular in England. He was a riotous guest at the endless weekend parties in the country houses, his name was linked romantically with Princess Beatrice, and as his manhood came he was drifting slowly into the empty existence of royalty in exile. He visited Italy and Scandinavia, shocking royal hosts with high jinks and practical jokes. He asked for and was granted permission to join a battery during annual maneuvers, and it was the Shop all over again. Foreign potentates were generally nuisances, but Louis' riding and his zest for drill won him a place in the mess and even surprised the rank and file. He made several close friends, including Arthur Bigge, his battery commander, and Frederick George Slade.

By the beginning of 1879 he was twenty-two years old. He was still bumptious and impulsive, but there were increasing flashes of a strange maturity. The tearing spirits could still be checked by the old call, and in his limited role as a political figure Louis appeared in a different light. He made a few speeches, writing and editing them himself, and to the uncritical adulation of the English populace he began to add the admiration of English men of affairs and even a grudging respect from the few Republicans who crossed his personal path. As the year started, he faced a future filled with no prospect more exciting than the possibility of a marriage to Beatrice.

Then came the news of Isandhlwana. The reinforcements were mustered and departed; Bigge and Slade called at Camden Place to say goodbye. Louis at once wrote the Duke of Cambridge and begged permission to go. He had valid public reasons; he wished to show his gratitude to the Queen, and to fight his first campaign for England. There were, of course, other reasons, private and urgent. A military record would back his claim to the throne of France as nothing else possibly could, but he might not fight indiscriminately for a foreign nation. If he joined England in a Continental or even an Indian war, the political repercussions would be tremendous. The Zulus were the perfect foe, however; no Frenchman could possibly take umbrage at his fighting a savage nation. Above all, he was a soldier, his friends were going to war, he was young and the smell of powder smoke was in his nostrils.

The Duke of Cambridge was willing enough, but Disraeli—on whom the brunt of the inevitable French reaction would fall—"had never heard of anything more injudicious." The project appeared to be stymied, until Eugénie entered the fray. Her motives were political, mixed with genuine dismay at her son's evident distress. It was inconceivable that Louis could come to any harm, and the experience would strengthen his hand enormously. She visited the Duke, she enlisted the aid of the Queen. Cambridge was struck by a sudden, happy thought. Louis might go out in a private capacity as a "spectator"; if he subsequently appeared in uniform, that was his business. Chelmsford could be asked to keep an eye on him, and all parties would presumably be satisfied. The Queen was delighted. It never crossed her mind that the slightest risk was involved—perhaps from the climate and the rough camp life, but certainly none from the Zulus. He was only to be a spectator, and the entire British Army was there to protect him. Disraeli capitulated before the onslaught of two obstinate women.

The Duke of Cambridge suffered a mild twinge of conscience at the additional burden he was tossing to Chelmsford. He made the position quite clear to the General.

February 25th/79

My dear Chelmsford

This letter will be forwarded to you by the Prince Imperial, who is going out on his own account to see as much as he can of the coming campaign in Zululand. He is extremely anxious to go out and wanted to be employed in our army, but the Government did not consider that this could be sanctioned, but have sanctioned me only to you and to Sir Bartle Frere to say that if you shew him kindness and tender him a position to see as much as he can with the columns in the Field I hope you will do so. He is a fine young fellow, full of spirit and pluck, having many old cadet friends in the Artillery, he will undoubtedly find no difficulty in getting on and if you can help him in any other way please do so. My only anxiety on his conduct would be, that he is too *plucky* and *go ahead*.

I remain, my dear Chelmsford,
Yours most sincerely,
George

The French exploded. They had always been of two minds about Louis. To his own party, of course, he was already Napoleon IV, and while the Republicans feared him as a political threat and ridiculed him as a person, they still took a proprietary interest in him and regarded him as a Frenchman of Frenchmen. Now, on two days' notice, he was deserting his party to risk his valuable neck for the hated English in a petty dispute with some obstreperous blacks at the ends of the earth. He, a Bonaparte, was to serve as a rankless member of a foreign battery, at the beck and call of every junior British officer. A host of rumors swept the country. He was being sent away to escape a love affair, as a landless exile he wanted to prove his right to the hand of Princess Beatrice, he simply wished to get away from Eugénie. Louis ignored the storm. His reasons, he told his party, were political; the Bonapartist hopes were centered in his person, and he wished to gain experience and improve his knowledge of military affairs.

In two days he was gone, sailing on the twenty-eighth of February on the *Danube* from Southampton with drafts for the 3d/60th Rifles. The night he left Camden Place he wrote his will, and in casting it he was able to see himself as already dead on the field of honour. All were to know that he died in the Roman Catholic and Apostolic faith in which he had been born, that he wished to be buried beside his father until such a time as their bodies could rest in French soil, that his last thought was of his mother and his country, and that he died filled with gratitude for his partisans and for the Queen of England, her family and her people. There were generous bequests to all his friends and retainers, and he left his weapons and uniforms to his closest comrades, "all but the last I shall have worn, which I bequeath to my Mother." Prince Napoleon had behaved abominably to Eugénie after the death of Napoleon III, and a codicil cut Plon-Plon out of the line of succession, passing the mantle to the elder of his two young sons. It was the first and last document Louis signed as "Napoleon."

A score of ardent young Frenchmen wished to accompany him, but he would not go *en Prince* and he took only the faithful Uhlmann.

Eugénie saw him off bravely enough, weeping intermittently and collapsing in a dead faint when the steamer was hull down on the horizon.

The *Danube* touched at Madeira but not at St. Helena—a bitter
disappointment—and Louis reached Table Bay on the twenty-sixth of
May. All of Capetown was in the streets for a glimpse of him, but he
remained quietly at Government House, dining with Lady Frere. The
ship left the next day and reached Durban on the evening of the thirty-
first.

Every ship in the anchorage was beflagged and most of civilian
Durban was down at the Point to greet him as he came ashore. He
stood the welcoming speeches and then moved in with English friends
to don the undress uniform of a British lieutenant, without any insignia
of rank. Lord Chelmsford was still north of the Tugela with the
Eshowe relief column, and no one else could give him a place. Major
Butler, the Assistant Adjutant-General, attached him to an artillery
battery to mess, and Louis impatiently waited for Chelmsford's return.

One of his horses had been killed in a landing accident, and the other
was taken ill. Visiting the lobby of the Royal Hotel, Louis happened to
glance out a window, and a civilian trotting by on a magnificent gray
caught his eye. The demands of the campaign had snapped up every
suitable horse in Natal, and broken-down crocks were going for fabulous prices. The gray looked like everything Louis' practiced eye
could ask for, and he sent Uhlmann out to buy the animal on the spot.
The rider turned out to be Meyrick Bennett, the managing director of
Randles, Brothers & Hudson, the horse was named "Percy," and Mr.
Bennett did not wish to sell. Uhlmann then identified his master and
appealed to the owner's feelings, and Mr. Bennett reluctantly let the
horse go. Percy, he added, was apt to be skittish.

Not even Uhlmann was to accompany Louis to the front, and he
acquired a soldier named Lomas to serve as a valet, a groom named
Browne, and when his second English horse died, another mount
which he named "Fate." He met a few classmates from the Shop, and
discovered that the ranks of the mounted irregulars, recruited from
transients all over southern Africa, were studded with Frenchmen who
had left their homeland after the collapse of the Second Empire. He
made friends with all he met, and he encountered a French journalist
for whose presence in Natal he was actually responsible.

Deléage was a nominal Republican who worked for *Figaro*. His
feelings toward Louis were even more ambivalent that those of the
majority of his countrymen; biased by the tone of the French press, he
feared to find a dull-witted, Anglicized pretender, and he cringed in an
agony of shame at the thought of the embarrassment such a Prince
Imperial might cause his country if he cut a ridiculous figure. He had

talked his newspaper into sending him all the way to Natal so that at least one pair of French eyes might report on Louis' conduct, but the instant they met, Deléage realized that his fears had been groundless. Louis might be a fifth wheel in an English battery, but he could appear in a different light to his rightful subjects. Deléage recognized him for a true prince, with the simplicity and charm of a distinguished, superior spirit. Eight years in England had not Anglicized him a whit, he spoke the Parisian argot, and Deléage correctly diagnosed the ardent nature which an acquired calm was just learning to control. He capitulated on the spot, and he was to view what he saw of the Zulu campaign through the strangest eyes in Natal; neither Zulus nor English nor the issues at stake had the slightest significance for him—the entire uproar was only a demented charade through which moved the Prince Imperial of France, whose true worth the callous British could not recognize. Louis for his part saw only a pleasant fellow countryman, who spoke little English and knew nothing of military matters or camp life. He resolved to keep a kindly eye on him, if possible.

Then he caught the prevalent fever and collapsed, and Uhlmann nursed him back to a shaky convalescence before Chelmsford arrived. Louis presented his letters, which the harassed General could hardly ignore. He was faced with the reorganization of his entire force and the job of mounting a second invasion of Zululand, and he had little time to spare for a feverishly enthusiastic young man fit only to serve as a subaltern of artillery, the one job he could not be offered. He wanted to be in the thick of the campaign, but his neck was too valuable to risk, and every letter he bore harped on his impulsive ways. Eugénie was set against the mounted volunteers, the best place to dump civilians. He could at least ride and he seemed intelligent, and according to the superintendent of the Shop he was a quick observer and could sketch ground tolerably well. Chelmsford asked him if he would care to serve on his personal staff as an extra A.D.C., and Louis accepted at once.

Chelmsford rode off to attend to more pressing matters, and Louis joined him in Pietermaritzburg. When the General continued upcountry, Louis was again left behind for three days. He had tried to ride a horse that had thrown Longcast, the interpreter, and was bucked onto a pile of stones for his pains, suffering a mild concussion. It was late April before Louis caught up with the General at Dundee.

On the second of May the General took his staff by way of Landman's Drift, Koppie Allein and Conference Hill to visit Evelyn Wood at Kambula. Here Louis met his friends Bigge and Slade, who had served their guns in the open during the attack on the camp. He was, in fact, meeting old friends and making new ones at every stop. It was impossible not to like him, his enthusiasm was so infectious. He gloried in roughing it, refusing what few amenities camp life offered, and he volunteered for everything. He continued to show off. He habitually vaulted into his saddle, and he was determined to master any horse that gave his rider trouble. He also sliced potatoes flung at him as he rode past, using the sword his great-uncle had carried at Austerlitz.

The Flying Column broke camp and moved south when Chelmsford rode back to Conference Hill on the fifth of May. On the eighth, at his new headquarters in Utrecht, Chelmsford appointed Colonel Richard Harrison, R.E., his new Acting Quartermaster-General, responsible for supplies and transport and for reconnoitering the track into Zululand for the IInd Division. Harrison was a stolid, experienced officer who had served in the Sepoy Rebellion and in China, and the appointment was aimed at Clifford, whose department would normally have carried out these functions if he had not been blocked at the borders of Zululand. Since the supplies and the transport were procured outside of Zululand, the bulk of Harrison's duties consisted of supervising the transport actually with the troops and of finding a suitable route for the IInd Division.

He had no staff at all except for a lance corporal named Martin, and Chelmsford gave him one of the 162 special service officers unattached to regiments who were available for odd jobs. The batch that came out in time for the first invasion were known as *aasvogels*, or vultures, because they had eaten up all the good assignments, and those that only arrived with the April reinforcements were known as *boomvogels*, because they were up a tree and were generally assigned to transport duties.

Lieutenant Jahleel Brenton Carey was a boomvogel, but he had been fourteen years in the Army and was well suited for staff duties. The son of a Devon vicar, he had been educated in France, had passed through Sandhurst, and had then received a free commission in the 3d West India Regiment, an Imperial unit although regarded as a social notch below the regular infantry of the line. He had accompanied an expedition to Honduras in 1867, and in 1870 went on half pay to serve with an English ambulance unit in France. Captured three times, he was invariably released when it was noted that he succored German wounded as rapidly as French. (The young Horatio Herbert Kitchener had also served with the Red Cross but, holding an active commission he had just received, had been severely rebuked by the Duke of Cambridge for risking a diplomatic incident.) Carey eventually transferred to the 98th Regiment, and then passed through the staff college before volunteering for the Zulu campaign. He was not disliked by his fellow officers, but they had already noted a peculiar tenderness in his character. He was ostentatiously pious and utterly devoted to his mother, his wife and his two young daughters. He carried their photographs on campaign, and even in an age when sentimentality flourished, his public adulation of his family caused comment. Even with Carey's assignment, Harrison's staff was weak, and Chelmsford suddenly realized he had found a suitable billet for the Prince Imperial. The employment would take him off Chelmsford's back and put him under supervision in a job that entailed a minimum of risk. Louis was delighted to get work into which he could sink his teeth, and Harrison put him to work at once.

Louis busied himself at Utrecht for a few days, trotting through the sprawling encampment and asking scores of questions, jotting the answers down in a memorandum book. Deléage appeared again, and Louis devoted a morning to showing him the laager of Boer refugees from the borderlands, the kraal where Uhamu was drinking himself into a daily stupor, and the hospital, where he chatted with all the sick Frenchmen. Then the correspondent left to visit Newcastle and Dundee, reassured that the English were concerned about Louis' safety after all. A week later, to his acute horror, Deléage heard that the Prince Imperial had ridden deep into Zululand on patrol.

It was true enough. Harrison's major concern was to find a way east into Zululand from Koppie Allein for the IInd Division, while Wood was using Buller to find a way south from Wolf's Hill for the Flying Column. Harrison decided to accompany Buller on the next foray, for which the Flying Column was to send 200 men of the Frontier Light Horse and the Edendale contingent to Conference Hill. Louis applied to Chelmsford, who decided there was little enough risk with an escort that strong, and on the thirteenth of May Harrison rode to Conference Hill with the Prince Imperial and William Drummond as staff interpreter. They spent the night at Conference Hill, where one of the entrenchments going up was named Fort Napoleon, and the following day the patrol set out, riding south to Koppie Allein and crossing the Blood River into Zululand on the sixteenth.

Louis was in a transport of delight. He was young, healthy, armed and well mounted, riding through the magnificent open hills under a wide blue sky, and the enemy he had come so far to meet might be encountered at any moment. All his immaturity came to the fore. He was thrilled when a few Zulu scouts were seen on a rise near Itelezi Hill, dejected when the pursuit was called off because the Zulus retired in a direction Buller did not wish to explore. Louis had charged far in advance of the Light Horse, searching for a straggler to engage, and before the troopers caught up with him he had taken off again in solitary chase of a lone Zulu he had spotted on a nearby knoll. Buller, who for all his bulldog impassiveness had a first-rate imagination, was disgusted with him. They were on a patrol, not a Zulu hunt, and if Louis got entangled he would draw the others in after him. Buller could control the men assigned to him—none better—but a Prince of France in a private capacity was something else again. The whole arrangement was fantastic, and he determined to get his charge off his hands as soon as possible. He led the way north until dark fell, bivouacking in a tight ring without fires. Louis, unaware of Buller's reaction, was too excited to sleep. The men had named the site of the morning's incident Napoleon Koppie, and the proud youth paced up and down through the cold night, warming himself with snatches of French martial airs, to the great annoyance of the others.

By the sixteenth they were back at Wolf's Hill camp. The scout had solved the problem of a track south for the Flying Column, but it had not helped Harrison, who still had to find a way east from Koppie Allein for the IInd Division. He decided to go out again, taking only six mounted volunteers and twenty men from the Edendale contingent. Buller had communicated his unease to Harrison, and was about to complain directly to Chelmsford—he categorically refused to assume responsibility for Louis again. Harrison consequently ordered Louis back to Conference Hill, but agreed to relent if Chelmsford gave permission. Louis set out for Utrecht at top speed, falling in with Wood on the way and inducing him to intercede with the General. When Harrison started from Wolf's Hill, Louis was with him again.

Although Harrison was the senior officer, he turned the practical control of the men over to Commandant Bettington, who led Troop 3 of the Natal Horse. Bettington had grown up in New Zealand, working as an ostler and keeping a livery stable before coming to Natal. A mature man of vast common sense, he made better use of mounted irregulars than many a leader with greater military experience, and he knew the country well. To Louis' astonishment, he disdained swords, claiming they got in the way on horseback, and he carried only a revolver and a riding crop. Like all irregulars, the troopers were lightly armed, each carrying only a Martini-Henry carbine and a hunting knife. They were capable of a hot fire afoot—although no one expected them to engage in a stiff fight unsupported—but their mounted firepower was drastically reduced. The Martini-Henry had no safety catch and was habitually carried empty, and in any kind of a fight it had to be loaded while managing a horse and was then fired with one hand, held like a heavy, awkward pistol. Accurate fire was of course impossible except at point-blank range, and the men depended on their mounts rather than their guns for security.

The patrol rode forty miles the first day, crossing at Koppie Allein again and riding south of Napoleon Koppie to within a mile or two of Sihayo's kraal on the upper Bashee. Buller was to meet them there with a larger force, and the two patrols were then to scout to the east, riding along the northern edge of the Nqutu Range to inspect the valley south of the Ityotyosi. Buller, however, failed to appear, and the party bedded down to spend a chill night in a donga. There was still no sign of Buller in the morning—he had turned east at Incenci Hill ten miles to the north to scout east between the Ityotyosi and the Tombokala—so Harrison decided to continue alone, moving east along the ridge and passing just north of the ravine in which the Zulu impi had hidden the day before Isandhlwana. Carey was along, and he and Louis stopped at intervals to make sketches of the ground spread below them to the north. As the patrol approached a small kraal perched on a rocky kop, a spatter of shots rattled off the surrounding boulders. Bettington judged the opposition to be only a handful of Zulus, and ordered the troopers forward. Louis, in great excitement, had dismounted and drawn his sword; he now sprang back on his horse and as the gaggle of charging horses funneled into single file on the narrow trail that led to the top, he found himself second in line. The Zulus scrambled off through the rocks, loosing a few more shots before running away. The patrol searched the huts before burning them, finding a few stores from Isandhlwana and Wilsone Black's saddle. Louis had now proved himself under fire and was exultant, although the longed-for chance to close with the enemy was still eluding him. Since there was already a Napoleon Koppie marked on the maps four miles to the north, the men named the rise Harrison Kop, throwing a sop to the Prince by calling the huts Napoleon Kraal. Louis was, in fact, collecting the lion's share of the honours; another entrenchment the Ist Division would erect on the Umlalazi would also be called Fort Napoleon.

The patrol continued to the east, penetrating to the headwaters of the Nondweni. The stream, which was also marked the Upoko on some maps and caused endless confusion, marked the end of Harrison's scout, and he turned back in the late afternoon. The men captured a few stray horses, and once Harrison rode forward to intercept three Zulus wearing red coats who were walking toward them. Bettington, marking them for hostile, overtook him, pistoled one and drove the others off.

The patrol stopped at sundown at a deserted kraal to cook a meal, leaving the fires lit and moving off as soon as it was dark. Small groups of Zulus were beginning to congregate in their wake, so they rode through the clear night, working north by stars and compass to cross the Blood and reach Conference Hill before dawn. They came up to the camp during the morning stand-to, listening to a distant officer shouting, "Now boys, be ready—when I give the word to fire, fire low—I see them coming—look out, boys—remember to fire low!" They showed themselves cautiously, making sure they had been identified, before riding in for breakfast.

Louis rode back to Utrecht with Harrison, turning out a long and careful report as soon as he arrived. The patrol had in fact found a practical route for the IInd Division as far as the Nondweni, but Buller had found another one ten miles to the north, and Chelmsford, better acquainted with Buller's abilities than with Harrison's, chose to move between the Ityotyosi and the Tombokala. Buller had also made his complaint about Louis, and Chelmsford issued orders in writing to Harrison to keep Louis in camp at all times unless he was accompanied by a strong escort. Harrison in turn passed the orders in writing to Louis.

Deléage had also had an adventure. He had set out alone from Conference Hill to ride to Wood's camp and had lost his way, wandering through the hills for a day and a night before finding his way back. Louis, on his way to Utrecht, stopped at his tent to scold him, frightening the journalist out of his wits by the story of his own patrol. After Louis had gone, Deléage passed the scolding on to the nearest English officers, berating them for their indifference to the value of a Prince Imperial. To his surprise, they all agreed with him vigorously, and one even came after him to discuss Louis in fluent French. This was Carey, and, discovering a receptive audience, he warmed to his task. He elaborated on the patrol, expanding on Louis' ardent spirits and the friendship that was developing between them, and glossing over the night in the donga, when a false alarm from Carey had needlessly interrupted everybody's sleep. Deléage was fascinated. He found Carey most un-English—a great compliment in his eyes.

On Sunday, the first of June, the advanced force of the IInd Division marched from the left bank of the Blood River to its new camp just to the north of Itelezi Hill, five miles away. On the same day Wood brought the Flying Column down from Munhla Hill to a camp south of Incenci Hill, just a mile or so away from the new camp of the IInd Division. The day's orders called for the cavalry to scout ten miles ahead of the new camp into the valley between the Ityotyosi and the Tombokala, to pick a campsite for the following day. Carey had scouted this very path on the twenty-ninth, riding out from Koppie Allein with an escort of eighty mounted men; he had seen no Zulus at all and on his return had been twitted unmercifully about the size of the escort he had requested.

As a result of Chelmsford's orders, Harrison had set Louis to sketching the ground that the column was traversing and occupying, and on the evening of the thirty-first Louis came to Harrison's tent and requested permission to extend his completed sketch the following day past the projected site of the new camp, to the area the column was to reach on the second of June. Harrison considered. The fresh ground Louis wanted to cover had just been pronounced free of Zulus, and the target area was less than ten miles ahead of the morrow's campsite and would be virtually in sight of the combined laagers of the IInd Division and the Flying Column. Various units of mounted men would be crisscrossing the ground between the Blood River and Itelezi Hill, guarding the marching column, and their scouting would naturally extend somewhat beyond the new campsite. Harrison finally decided that there would be no harm, providing Louis took a proper escort, and he specified at least six of Bettington's troopers and six men from the Edendale contingent, because the natives were notoriously quicker to spot movements in the landscape than the Europeans were. Since Louis was not an officer, he naturally could not command the patrol, but Harrison did not specify a particular officer, because he presumed that Bettington would be going himself. Louis departed to find the cavalry brigade major, who co-ordinated requests for mounted men.

Shortly thereafter Carey poked his head into Harrison's tent and asked for permission to accompany the Prince. Harrison was inclined to say no; he was badly overworked and would have his hands full the next day, but Carey wheedled, and Harrison finally gave in. Louis' topographical sketches left something to be desired, and Carey could supervise his work and look after him at the same time. Harrison said nothing about the command, because he was under the impression that Louis was already arranging for an escort with an officer, and Carey was simply to accompany the party.

By nine o'clock the next morning six of Bettington's troopers reported to the staff tent. Bettington had been under orders for another patrol, and while he had hand-picked the men, he had not assigned another officer. He had chosen Corporal Grubb, a veteran of sixteen years in the Royal Artillery and a decade's farming in Natal—he spoke fluent Zulu and had been on the Langalibalele expedition—Le Tocq, a French-speaking Channel Islander, and Troopers Abel, Rogers, Cochrane and Robert Willis. He had also sent along a friendly Zulu who knew the area to serve as a guide, and Louis, seeing that he had no horse, lent him Fate while he mounted Percy. There was no sign of the Edendale men. The camp was in a state of confusion, breaking up to start the move to Itelezi Hill, and they had reported to the wrong tent. The cavalry brigade major had taken no steps to provide another officer when he heard that Bettington could not come, but since Carey was now present there was no harm done. He told Carey that the bulk of the mounted natives were already patrolling the flanks of the day's march, and to commandeer six of them as he passed.

Louis and Carey started off with the seven men already in hand, with Louis' little terrier trotting behind Percy. Just ahead of the camp they came across Harrison and Major Francis Wallace Grenfell, 3d/60th Rifles, who was the staff officer for the day. The two were proceeding to the new campsite to search for a watering place for the column, and the patrol rode with them for an hour or so. Harrison noted Bettington's absence but did not comment on it, since Carey was obviously replacing him. He did ask where the Edendale men were, and Carey pointed to the mounted patrols several miles ahead, explaining that he would pick them up when they overtook them at the site of the new camp.

Louis rode far ahead while the others chatted. Carey started to call him back, but Harrison told him not to interfere and motioned him on. Carey and the troopers rode after Louis and the two groups parted. Grenfell shouted a farewell to the Prince. "Take care of yourself, and don't get shot!" Louis waved back. "Oh no," he called. "Carey will take very good care that nothing happens to me."

Harrison stopped at the new campsite, inspected the watering places, and busied himself for the rest of the day in guiding the arriving units to their assigned places and drafting orders for the morrow's march. Newdigate arrived later in the morning, and when Chelmsford came, Harrison showed him around the laager, not bothering to mention that Louis was out on patrol. Chelmsford was under the impression that he was busy elsewhere in the camp, as was Deléage when he came, and the General had no idea that Louis in effect had been entrusted with the task of choosing the exact site for the next day's camp. This was a job for an experienced staff officer who had to judge the drainage and the access to wood and water as well as general suitability for defense. Chelmsford, with the horror of Isandhlwana burned into his soul, would never have allowed his main column to march to a site selected by a young man whose military experience consisted of two years at the Shop.

Louis rode down the valley with Carey, climbing a gentle ridge as they neared the Ityotyosi. The mounted natives had moved away, and for a moment the two men considered chasing them to collect the rest of their escort. They decided against it; Louis felt the men in hand sufficed and Carey, still smarting from the jibes over the size of his last escort, acquiesced. The cavalry brigade major, moreover, had promised to send the original six men galloping after them as soon as he located them. He had in fact done so, but the men lost Louis' trail and proceeded no farther than the site of the new camp.

By noon the patrol had reached the end of the ridge, six or seven miles ahead of Itelezi Hill, and about twelve thirty they halted for a while. The new camp was out of sight behind them, and the landscape ahead was empty. Louis made a quick sketch, pointing with pride to Napoleon Koppie across the Ityotyosi to the southwest. Then he ordered the waiting troopers to offsaddle. As they dismounted, he changed his mind and ordered them only to loosen their girths. He had seen a deserted kraal a mile or two ahead, near the Ityotyosi, and he had decided to descend from the bare ridge to boil coffee with the fuel they would undoubtedly find in the huts. Carey demurred—the kraal stood near a deep donga that ran down to the Ityotyosi and it was surrounded on three sides by a tall stand of tambookie grass—but Louis overruled him. The men tightened their girths, mounted, and started down toward the kraal.

By three o'clock they had reached it. The cattle pen was a chest-high circular stone enclosure, 25 yards across, with five empty huts standing outside the pen. The grass on the east, south and west, six feet tall, grew up to the vicinity of the huts and cut off the view. The ground to the north was bare, and ran for 200 yards to the lip of an arm of a deep, seamed donga that in wet weather carried water to the Ityotyosi. The huts had been recently occupied; some dogs were skulking about, and there was a pile of freshly chewed sugar cane by the entrance to one of the huts. The men did not intend to stay long, and they had had the surrounding country in clear view during their descent from the ridge. They offsaddled and knee-haltered their horses, and Grubb and Le Tocq pulled thatch from one of the huts while the guide wandered down to the river to get water. Coffee was soon boiling and the men stretched at ease, drinking and smoking. Louis and Carey corrected their maps, and were soon engaged in an animated discussion of Napoleon Bonaparte's campaigns. Neither man had bothered to scout the vicinity of the kraal or to post a lookout, not even when the Zulu guide drew their attention to a pile of warm ashes in front of one of the huts.

At half past three Carey suggested that they resaddle. Louis saw no reason to hurry, and announced that they would take another ten minutes, but just then the guide, who had been poking around behind the huts, returned to report that he had seen a solitary Zulu moving over a nearby rise. Carey could not understand him and called Grubb over to interpret, and as soon as Louis heard the report, he ordered the men to collect their horses. They had scattered in grazing, and it was ten minutes or so before they were all together and saddled, with the men standing at their heads. Louis called out, "Prepare to mount!" and the men gathered the reins, grasped their saddles, and put their left feet in the stirrups.

Either Louis or Carey cried out, "Mount!" but the command was lost in the earsplitting crash of a volley that ripped out of the tambookie grass a few yards away, stampeding the horses and destroying in a split second the bonds of discipline that linked the men. Forty Zulus burst out of the edge of the grass, screaming "uSuthu!" and bounding after the frantic horses. Most of the men had reached the saddle, and their horses carried them off to the main donga. Rogers' horse had drifted farther than the others, and he was still adjusting his girth when the commands came. His horse bolted, and from the corner of his eye Grubb saw him dodging around one of the huts, his carbine leveled at a Zulu close upon him as he fumbled to load. Le Tocq was up, but he dropped his carbine as his horse shied. He slipped off to pick it up, got his left foot in the stirrup and threw himself across the saddle on his belly as his horse bounded away. Grubb was up, but not firm in his saddle, and just after his glimpse of Rogers he saw Carey put spurs to his horse. Then a bullet whistled past his ear and smacked into Abel's back below his bandoleer. Abel threw up his hands and slid back off his horse.

Louis could not mount. His foot was raised as the command was given, and the restive Percy shied violently and then dashed forward. Only Louis' grip on the holster saved him from a fall, and he could neither get his foot into the dancing stirrup nor slow the horse. For over a hundred yards he clung to the holster, gripping the stiff leather so hard that it collapsed. To a rider of his talents, the situation hardly qualified as an emergency; a firm grip on the pommel and a hard shove and he could easily vault into the saddle, but his grasp on the tapered leather was far from firm, he dared not shift his grip and he could not gain leverage for a thrust. Le Tocq thundered by, calling out, "*Dépêchez-vous, s'il vous plaît, Votre Altesse!*"—so that the last intelligible words he heard were in his native language—and then the strap holding the holster gave way, tearing almost across, and Louis slipped and fell under the horse. Grubb saw Percy trample on his right arm as he flashed by, and then they were all gone and Louis was alone.

He rose to his feet, groping for his great-uncle's sword. It was gone; it had slipped out of the scabbard as he tried to mount. He drew his revolver with his left hand and ran down the sloping bed of an arm of the donga. The Zulus, far fleeter, raced after him, and in a widening of the ravine, by a little mound, he turned at bay. Seven Zulus were coming up and a man in the lead named Langalabalele threw an assegai that caught Louis in the thigh. Louis pulled it out and rushed at him, but he turned and dodged behind a man named Zabanga, coming up behind him. Louis fired twice and missed, and Zabanga hurled his assegai and struck Louis deep in the left shoulder. For a moment he held them back, fighting desperately with the assegai and using his left arm to ward off blows, so that he was unable to fire again. More Zulus were dropping into the donga, and he finally sank to a sitting position, exhausted by loss of blood. There was a brief hacking flurry, and it was all over.

When the volley was fired, the stampeding horses had started a *sauve qui peut*. The panic lasted until the survivors had crossed the main donga, perhaps 200 yards away and hardly fifty yards from the branch where Louis was killed. During the flight no member of the patrol was in a position to make himself amenable to command, and while several troopers had snatched fleeting glimpses of the men who were down, Carey had no reason to believe that any member of his command was in sorer straits than he. Carey had not been entirely wrapped up in the matter of his own safety; as the horses bolted for the donga he had shouted "Bear to the left!" at the others and he reined in shortly after he had crossed the ravine. He had left the kraal with the bulk of his men and was no more guilty of abandoning them than the Prince himself, for Louis' running struggle with Percy and his flight afoot had taken him a full 200 yards from the kraal, and neither he nor Carey had stopped to help Rogers and Abel, if, indeed, they had seen them go down. The conduct of all of them, if unheroic, had been more or less unavoidable.

Grubb, Willis, Le Tocq and Cochrane all scrambled out of the far side of the donga at widely separated points, and they all gathered around Carey. Grubb had managed to unsling his carbine, but he had pitched onto his mount's neck as the horse plunged into the donga and he had dropped the gun in regaining his seat. The riderless Percy emerged from the donga near him, so Grubb caught him and shifted horses, leading his own. There was no sign of the Zulu guide.

Carey was now in a dilemma. The broken ground hid all sight of the four missing men and the three missing horses, but the arms of the donga were obviously alive with Zulus. Carey quickly learned that the three missing Europeans had last been seen dismounted; Abel was probably dead and Rogers almost certainly so. Except for Louis' two shots, not a single man had fired a gun, and no one seems to have heard Louis' shots. As the seconds passed and the Prince did not appear, Carey must have known with awful certainty that he was dead.

There were only five survivors. Carey carried a sword and a revolver, but the four troopers with him had only three carbines amongst them. A nimble man afoot with an assegai was almost an even match for a mounted man with a single-shot carbine, especially in broken ground, and Carey shrank from the idea of riding back across the donga to face an unknown number of Zulus while he searched the branches with only three carbines at his back. His situation would be even worse if he dismounted. He would have to leave an armed horse-holder with the six mounts and the unarmed Grubb as well, to go back with only two men. There was nothing at all to be gained by staying, and nothing to do but to ride back to the new camp at Itelezi Hill. The five men wheeled and rode north away from the donga, splashed through the shallow Tombokala and set out at a gallop for Itelezi, ten miles to the west.

Carey rode alone with his thoughts while the others lagged behind. He would be alone for the rest of his life—he would never get away from that kraal—and he must have realized it during the ride, for the grotesque injustice of what had happened colored his speech and action from that point on. The damage had been done long before the Zulus attacked; the inadequate size of the escort and the failure to scout the ground and to post a vedette had killed Louis as surely as the shoddy strap of the holster or the patrol's failure to go back in. Carey was certain in his own mind that no one could have altered the outcome after the attack, and his soul quailed at the thought of what he now had to face.

While still five miles from the camp, he saw a small mounted party to his right, and he swerved to close with them. Of all the men in Africa, he had the ill fortune to meet Evelyn Wood and Redvers Buller. Neither of them ever again referred to the exchanges of the next few moments, but the escort had ears, and the tale soon spread.

Buller saw him first and exclaimed, "Why, the man rides as if the Kaffirs were after him!" spurring forward even as Carey tried to wave him back.

"Whatever is the matter with you?"

"The Prince Imperial is killed!"

"Where's his body?" Carey pointed at the valley behind, and Buller, searching the ground with his glass, saw half a dozen Zulus leading three horses off some four miles away.

"Where are your men, sir?" he asked sharply. "How many did you lose?"

"They're behind me. I don't know."

"You ought to be shot, and I hope you will be. I could shoot you myself."

Buller was brave, almost to the point of madness, and he had shown time and again that he would stand in the face of all the impis of hell for the least of his troopers, but not even Buller saw any point in

returning to the fatal donga in the failing light. The party turned and
started for the camp at Itelezi.

Carey, by now sullen and surly, entered the staff tent just as dinner
was starting. Grenfell looked up and greeted him.

"Why, Carey, you're late for dinner. We thought you'd been shot!"

"I'm all right, but the Prince is killed." He left them struck dumb
and sought out Harrison, who was stunned. Harrison at once informed
Chelmsford, and asked for permission to go search for the body.
Chelmsford could scarcely credit the news and called for reports from
all the troopers. He turned down the idea of an immediate sally but
ordered a major force to search at daybreak, canceling the move to the
next camp. Harrison left him white and trembling, and Grenfell later
found him in an absolute misery of despair, slumped at his desk with
his head buried in his arms.

The news flashed though the camp, treated at first as a wild rumor.
Harrison thrust his head into one tent to announce it and someone
threw a crust of bread at him, all of them laughing until Archibald
Forbes caught sight of his face. Deléage, under the impression that
Louis had been in the new camp all along, heard it from a passing
artillery officer. He grabbed his arm and asked him to repeat it in
French, and then ran off to find Chelmsford, who could only confirm
it. Deléage then sought out Carey, who was eating his dinner and who
chose to treat him as an inquisitive reporter, having already beaten off
Forbes and several others. Deléage would have none of that, took his
stand as a fellow countryman of the Prince Imperial, and got the full
story out of him.

There was a brilliant moon, and Deléage was certain that the relief
would leave at once. It might still be possible to save Louis. The
English were never more alien to him than that night, and the best he
could do was to secure permission to leave with the column at five in
the morning.

Carey slept alone in his tent that night, if he slept at all. Long after
midnight, when the rest of the camp was finally bedded down, he
bared his miserable soul to his wife:

My Own One:
  You know the dreadful news, ere you receive this, by telegram.
  I am a ruined man, I fear, though from my letter which will be in the
papers you will see I could not do anything else.
  Still, the loss of the Prince is a fearful thing. To me, the whole thing
is a dream. It is but eight hours since it happened.
  Our camp was bad, but then, I have been so laughed at for taking a
squadron with me that I had grown reckless and would have gone with
two men.

To-morrow we go with the 17th Lancers to find his body. Poor fellow! But it might have been my fate. The bullets tore around us and with only my revolver what could I do?

The men all bolted and I now fear the Prince was shot on the spot as his saddle is torn as if he tried to get up. No doubt they will say I should have remained by him, but I had no idea he was wounded and thought he was after me. My horse was nearly done, but carried me beautifully.

My own darling, I prayed as I rode away that I should not be hit and my prayer was heard. Annie, what will you think of me! I was such a fool to stop in that camp; I feel it now, though at the time I did not see it.

As regards leaving the Prince, I am innocent, as I did not know he was wounded, and thought our best plan was to make an offing.

Everyone is very kind about it all here, but I feel a broken-down man. Never can I forget this night's adventure! My own, own sweet darling, my own little darling child, my own little Edie and Pelham! Mama darling, do write and cheer me up! What will the Empress say? Only a few minutes before our surprise he was discussing politics with me and the campaigns of 1800 and 1796, criticising Napoleon's strategy, and then he talked of republics and monarchies!

Poor boy! I liked him so very much. He was always so warm-hearted and good-natured. Still I have been surprised; but not that I am not careful, but only because they laughed at all my care and foresight.

I should have done very differently a week ago, but now have ceased to care.

Oh, Annie! How near I have been to death. I have looked it in the face, and have been spared!

I have been a very, very wicked man, and may God forgive me! I frequently have to go out without saying my prayers and have to be out on duty every Sunday.

Oh! for some Christian sympathy! I do feel so miserable and dejected! I know not what to do!

Of course, all sorts of yarns will get into the papers, and without hearing my tale, I shall be blamed, but honestly, between you and me, I can only be blamed for the camp. I tried to rally the men in the retreat and had no idea the poor Prince was behind. Even now I don't know it, but fear so from the evidence of the men. The fire on us was very hot, perfect volleys. I believe thirty men or more were on us. Both my poor despised horses have now been under fire. The one I rode today could scarcely carry me, but did very well coming back.

Oh! I do feel so ill and tired! I long for rest of any kind . . .

If the body is found at any distance from the kraal tomorrow, my statement will appear correct. If he is in the kraal, why then he must have been shot dead, as I heard no cry. *Enfin, nous verrons.* Time alone will solve the mystery.

Poor Lord Chelmsford is awfully cut up about it as he will be blamed for letting him go with so small an escort.

The *Times* and *Standard* correspondents have been at me for news, also the *Figaro* . . .

My own treasure, I cannot write more. Good night, my own one; I will try and let you know a few words tomorrow. I will now try to sleep, till reveille at 5 A.M.; and it is now nearly one and so very cold!

Deléage was at the General's tent at the appointed time, angered by the size of the escort that was assembling. Louis alive had ridden out with seven companions and a Zulu guide; over a thousand men were going to bring his body back. All the English cavalry and all the mounted volunteers, the NNC battalion and an ambulance unit—a force so large that the departure was postponed until nine o'clock. Deléage exploded and appealed to the English correspondents. They went to the General, and the force began to move at seven. Carey acted as guide and Molyneaux, Lomas and Dr. Scott, who had treated Louis in Durban, rode on ahead with a few troopers.

They fanned out to search as they neared the donga. Abels was lying a hundred yards from the kraal, horribly mangled and naked except for a flannel cloth wrapped around his butchered face. Rogers was propped against a bank near him, also naked with his belly ripped open. Then Captain Dundonald Cochrane of the Edendale contingent shouted, and they saw him remove his helmet. Louis had been found.

He lay stiff and cold on his back, naked except for a thin, golden chain with a medal of the Virgin and his great-uncle's seal twisted about his neck. There were no less than seventeen separate wounds in his thin body. At least two of them had obviously been mortal; the assegai thrust over his heart and one that had cut his brow and pierced his right eye to the brain. His left arm was battered and hacked, his right hand still clutched a fistful of Zulu hair. They had slashed at his belly but had barely grazed the skin. The ground was bloody and trampled for yards about, and a few yards away lay a bloodied light blue sock embroidered with an *N*. Beyond were his spurs, twisted out of shape. His terrier, also speared, was close by. The others came up silently. Deléage threw himself on the ground and wept.

Dr. Scott lifted him tenderly to inspect his back, since Carey thought he might have been shot as the rout started, but the only marks were from two of the thrusts that had pierced his sides. All the wounds were in front, and he had died facing his foes. They took off the golden chain, wrapped him in a cotton sheet, and carried him out of the donga to the waiting ambulance on a stretcher fashioned from a horse blanket and four lances. The ranking officers fell in behind the ambulance and the slow procession returned to the camp.

Chelmsford wrote at once to Frere:

The body has been recovered. . . . I shall bury it here with such military honours as are possible. I have always felt that it was somewhat unfair to saddle me with the responsibility which naturally would be attached to such a charge, but I had to accept it with all the rest.

It was the only complaint he made on the subject, but the troubles Louis had caused him were barely starting. When he gave the order for the funeral, his staff urgently talked him out of it, pointing out that the body would have to be sent to England. Deléage, to whom the debate was barely credible, began to breathe again.

There was a funeral service in the camp that afternoon, the first of a seemingly interminable series. Louis had been wrapped in a Union Jack and strapped to a gun barrel, and the entire force stood in formation while Father Bellard, the Catholic chaplain, read prayers for the dead. As chief mourner, Chelmsford stood behind the gun, grim and silent with red-rimmed eyes, leaning on a cane. The body went to Koppie Allein, and that night surgeons embalmed it as best they could, packing it in a rough deal casket with straw and sand to steady it. The next day it was placed in an ambulance and started back on the long road to Durban.

Natal lingered over every foot of its progress. When the coffin crossed Landman's Drift it came under Clifford's aegis, and the religion he shared with the Prince fitted him admirably for the task. There were imposing ceremonies in Pietermaritzburg—where Colenso, Macrorie and Green made a rare mutual appearance at a public ceremony—and in Durban, where the whole town turned out to do Louis honour. Uhlmann had collapsed on hearing the news and had then traveled to Pietermaritzburg to meet the body. His reason trembled at the thought of facing the Empress, his grief aroused universal pity and so prostrated him that he was unable to accompany the cortege to Durban. The body had been transferred to a zinc coffin in Pietermaritzburg, and on the eleventh of June the tug *Adonis* carried it across the bar to H.M.S. *Boadicea*, where the Commodore of the naval squadron had given up his cabin to serve as a *chapelle ardente*. Colonel Pemberton of the 3d/60th Rifles was to accompany the body, and Deléage and Uhlmann were allowed to travel on the warship, as was Lomas.

The coffin was transshipped to H.M.S. *Orontes* at Capetown, and there were further ceremonies, attended by all who could reach the ships. Deléage, for all his grief, must have had his fill of the "Dead March" from *Saul* by then, but the worst still lay ahead.

The news had reached England by telegraph on the nineteenth of June. It came to London first. The Duke of Cambridge had attended a dinner of the Scots Guards that evening, going on to join his eldest son, Princess Augusta and Lady Geraldine Somerset at the theater. He arrived in the middle of a complicated French play, and his party tried unsuccessfully to brief him on the plot during a short entr'acte. He had barely settled down for the fourth act when an aide entered the box to whisper to the Duke, who gave a tremendous start and hurried to the anteroom to read the telegrams that had been brought. He returned to the box only to pass the news and then left again to arrange how best to break the news to Eugénie.

Queen Victoria was at Balmoral and about to retire. At twenty minutes to eleven the Highland gilly John Brown knocked with the news. She could barely comprehend it, and it was Beatrice, as distraught as she, who got it across. The two women did not get to bed until dawn, and the Queen almost forgot that it was the forty-second anniversary of her accession.

Victoria's first thought was for Eugénie, and her brimming personal sympathy was heightened by a lively sense of the political ramifications for both of them. Eugénie was an emotional and dramatic Spanish woman, who had lost first her throne and then her husband and now not only her beloved only child but with him all hope of ever seeing the Napoleonic dynasty restored to the throne of France. The cause was dead. Louis had rightly held every hope of returning some day, but, as he himself had recognized, Plon-Plon was only a bad joke and his eldest child a totally unknown boy. To top it off, Eugénie and Louis had been guests of England, and the Queen herself had approved—nay, enabled—Louis to go to Natal. Now he had gotten himself killed, despite the presence of an entire British Army to protect him, and the only English officer who had been with him at the end had abandoned him and survived unscathed. Victoria made immediate plans to go to Chislehurst.

Camden Place was stricken to the core. Eugénie had taken the separation hard from the start, and she was actress enough to play her role to the hilt. There had been only two letters from Louis, filled with vitality; and the energies that had once directed an empire at war were now focused on a far narrower front. A relative who had failed to offer her timely consolation for her great sacrifice in letting Louis go was attacked furiously; an innocent request from her own mother for news drew an exasperated and detailed reply. Eugénie would transmit all news instantly; there was no need to ask for it. Now the role was to be in grim earnest.

Lord Sydney drew the painful task of informing Eugénie, and he traveled to Chislehurst at the crack of dawn to beat the morning newspapers. (The same thought had already occurred to an editor of the *Morning Post,* who arrived even earlier to intercept them.) In an extreme state of agitation, Sydney rang at Camden Place and was admitted by the elderly Duc de Bassano, who demanded his business. Sydney blurted it out; Bassano was staggered but agreed to inform the Empress.

She was still in her dressing gown when Bassano knocked and was admitted. One look at his face sufficed.

"Louis is ill?" she gasped.

Bassano only hung his head.

"He is wounded!"

Silence.

"I shall go out to Africa at once!"

Bassano broke down.

"*Hélas, Madame! C'est trop tard!*" He buried his face in his hands and sobbed convulsively. Eugénie stared at him. Then she uttered one terrible cry and sank to the floor. She was senseless for several hours, and was only semiconscious for the next two days, neither eating nor speaking.

The news horrified the population of England as Isandhlwana had never done. By press coverage alone, it ranked as the most stirring event of the year. (The second most important event was the marriage of the Duke of Connaught to Princess Louise of Prussia; Isandhlwana ran a very poor third.) It was in France, however, that the storm burst in all its fury. Alive, Louis had been a considerable threat to the stability of the Republican government and an object of derision to all but the Bonapartist press; dead, he was no threat at all but quite suddenly a tragic and romantic figure. He was once again the "Little Prince," the Child of France, and an Anglophobia that was never far from the surface burst forth in a frenzied rage. Traveling Englishmen scurried for the shelter of a channel port or the nearest hotel; English firms shuttered their windows. The wildest stories gained substance and were firmly believed. The death of the Prince Imperial could not have been accidental—it had been a deliberate plot arranged by someone: the French Cabinet, the English, the Freemasons. The last theory flourished for years and appeared in book form in 1891. Rostand, only eleven years old in 1879, eventually wrote a play entitled *Napoleon IV* to prove that Louis had been led into ambush with the connivance of Queen Victoria.

Filon the tutor lay ill and almost blind in his home in Paris. He heard newsboys shouting the death of a prince, leaped out of bed and sent the nurse for a paper. She managed to convince him he had heard wrong—it was the Prince of Orange and not the Prince Imperial. The neighbors abetted the deception for two months, stopping the newsboys at each end of the street. Then his sight returned and he saw his wife in black and knew.

The faithful rallied at Camden Place, but only a very few were received, and even these were not spoken to; Eugénie communicated by notes. A spasm in her throat prevented swallowing and she subsisted on liquids.

At the end of the second day the Empress attended a mass in Louis' room, and the next day Victoria arrived. The Queen did not stand on ceremony; she swept into the house and was admitted to the darkened boudoir at once. It is clear from her journal that she fully expected to be personally berated, and she was braced for any reproach. There was none. Eugénie only wanted assurance that Louis had not suffered. A fortnight before an enthusiastic visitor from Natal had shown her a sheaf of assegais and she had suddenly realized what Louis had been facing. His friend Conneau, however, had firmly stated that Louis would have been so excited in the heat of combat that he could not possibly have felt anything, and to this theory the Queen subscribed her opinion. The meeting was short but comforting; both women had suffered tragic losses, they understood each other, they were truly sisters at last. It was the Queen who induced Eugénie to take nourishment, and she sent her personal physician to treat her.

The ordeal had barely started. Letters from Louis arrived at intervals for weeks, full of his young enthusiasms and vibrant with life. Even the hasty note he had penciled with a saddle for a desk as he started on the last patrol arrived in due course. Party affairs demanded attention, and Plon-Plon caused endless trouble. Eugénie did not bother to reply to his letter of condolence.

Victoria wanted a state funeral and intended to lay the Order of the Bath on the casket herself. Her Cabinet was scandalized. She finally won the first point but lost the second, and when the Cabinet refused to attend, she flew into such a furious passion that in the end two ministers agreed to go.

H.M.S. *Orontes* reached England on the tenth of July, the coffin was transferred to the Admiralty yacht *Enchantress* and landed at Woolwich on the eleventh. It was taken to a mortuary chapel in the Arsenal and the Prince of Wales and the Dukes of Connaught, Edinburgh and Cambridge came to pay their respects. They all exhibited, the papers said, signs of profound emotion. Then the English departed and the French undertook a necessary legal ceremony—the formal identification of the remains.

The casket was pried open and the observers leaned forward. Uhlmann collapsed again in a dead faint and the others recoiled in horror. The embalming had failed, and the hideously ravaged face was unrecognizable. Grimly, the medical men completed the inspection. Dr. Conneau recognized the scar of a childhood abscess he had lanced on the hip, and Dr. Evans, an American dentist who had treated Louis, identified the teeth. The body was transferred to a magnificent casket, placed on a gun carriage and drawn to Chislehurst. It lay in state throughout the night, and Eugénie maintained a sleepless vigil beside it. She retired to her room at five in the morning and did not attend the funeral.

Forty thousand others did, coming from London to brave the rain and swamping the small village. Queen Victoria was there, with Beatrice beside her and four royal dukes as well. The entire diplomatic corps, with the exception of the French Ambassador, crowded in behind. Plon-Plon stood stolidly through the entire ceremony, refusing to identify himself by crossing or genuflecting with the mass celebrated by Cardinal Manning. Not so Beatrice, who was unfamiliar with the service and remained kneeling so long that a bishop finally sent an assistant to request her to rise. Before noon the booming minute guns and the volleys of musketry fired by Gentlemen Cadets from the Shop told Eugénie that her son had been laid to rest beside his father.

There was still more to be endured. Louis' effects had been sent home. The day after the funeral Eugénie entered his room and found the fatal saddle. She fainted at the sight of it. Then some officious idiot recalled the will. She opened a box that arrived and was greeted with the sight of the last uniform her son had worn, recovered in Zululand and slashed, bloodied and smeared with the mud of the donga.

Carey meanwhile was reaping the whirlwind that his moment of panic had sown. He continued his duties under Harrison for a week, but his situation was growing impossible. The entire corps of officers, furious at the stain on their collective honour, blamed him for what had occurred. There was only sympathy for Chelmsford—not even Deléage held him responsible—and there was an undercurrent of thought that Harrison might have taken a stricter view of the General's charge. Carey finally requested a court of inquiry, and on the eleventh of June he was suspended from duty and the court convened. It recommended a trial by general court-martial, which met the following day.

Carey's defense was a peculiar one. The letter he had written his wife, virtually *in res gestae*, shows clearly that he was lying, but it was a lie he was undoubtedly forced to maintain in order to be able to live with himself. Carey claimed that he had never been in command of the patrol; it had been led by the Prince, and he himself had only accompanied it because it presented an opportunity to correct his sketches. Louis had decided to go on without waiting for the rest of the escort,

Louis had chosen the resting place, Louis had failed to post a lookout. As for the panic, it had been common to all, including Louis; he, Carey, had attempted to guide the rout, and when he had finally discovered that the Prince was down, it had been impossible to go back to his aid. Aside from the plain fact that Carey had known perfectly well that he was in command, the argument was specious. Louis held neither rank nor position within the Army, while Carey was a commissioned officer with full authority over the mounted volunteers. The defense, however, put up a good case. Louis had habitually worn the uniform of an officer of the Royal Artillery and he had acted like and had been treated as an officer, which in the eyes of most of the force invested him with the status of an officer. Louis had never been a soldier, he had only been a boy playing at soldier, and because he was a prince and because it was impossible not to like him, they had let him play. He had not held official command of the patrol but he had held *de facto* command; he had given orders to the men which had been obeyed and Carey, his head turned by his blossoming friendship with a potential emperor, had acquiesced without a murmur. Harrison, furthermore, had not specifically charged Carey with the command; he had not learned that Carey was the only officer along until after the patrol had started, and then he had even mumbled something about not interfering with the Prince.

The court rejected the argument with a fury compounded by Carey's air of unconcern and his readiness to shift every iota of responsibility to Louis. He was found guilty of misbehavior in the face of the enemy and shipped home at once.

Chelmsford assigned the only sentence that would cleanse the escutcheon; Carey was to be cashiered. At the same time, the court unanimously recommended mercy, and even Chelmsford stretched a point by stating that Carey was not deficient in personal bravery but "might have lost his head in the crisis." The ambivalence was not caused by any consideration for Carey himself. His conduct had been despicable, but he was a victim of circumstance and immolating him would appear as if a junior officer were being made the scapegoat for a national catastrophe. It was a point the English press had already seized on, and when an account of the trial reached England, the newspapers sprang to Carey's defense. The blame must lie with Harrison, with Chelmsford, or with the Duke of Cambridge, who had let him go out in the first place.

The sentence had to be reviewed before it was published, and Carey arrived in Plymouth at the beginning of August, aware that he had been found guilty but with his fate still in doubt. He was a Devon man, and to his astonishment the ship was met by a brass band and a deputation with a public address. He was kept on the ship to avoid a scandal, but once ashore he could not be kept quiet. He already had sympathy, but the public support induced him to try for justification as well, and he made himself available to every sensation-seeking reporter. His numerous statements were contradictory and in extremely bad taste. Louis had been immature, he had presumed on his birth, he had been insubordinate. Carey had prayed for forgiveness and God had granted it.

He was a captain now—he had been gazetted on the sixth of June, before news of the tragedy reached England—and for a fortnight he played the ill-used hero. His career had in fact been saved, for whatever it was now worth, but it had not been the press that had saved him. It had been Eugénie.

She had gathered at once that Carey had abandoned her son, if he had not actually caused his death, but she spurned revenge and even in her grief, and long before Carey reached England, she appealed to Victoria. She wanted no recriminations; her sole consolation was the thought that her son had been found useful and competent by those who employed him, and that he had fallen as a soldier under orders and obeying commands. Nothing must be done to the man who happened to be with him at the time. Victoria hesitated, pointing out that the matter was not entirely in her hands—but of course it was. She wrote to the reviewing authorities.

Carey had still not reached England before Eugénie discovered that her generosity had been grossly misplaced. Shortly after the funeral she turned to a great pile of unopened correspondence, and as she opened the very first letter, an attendant saw her face whiten and her hands begin to tremble. A Miss Olivia Scotchburn of Dartmouth had once had some contact with Eugénie, and she had gratuitously undertaken to collect a few details of Louis' last days for her. She had applied to Mrs. Carey, who with no thought of what she was doing to her husband handed over the terrible letter he had written at Itelezi Hill. By his own pen he was a craven and a liar; Eugénie had in her hands a signed confession of his guilt. She could only interpret its arrival as a naked plea for mercy from Annie Carey.

As soon as he arrived in England, Carey had the impudence to write to Eugénie, offering his sympathy and suggesting that she receive him. He had as yet no idea that his letter to his wife was in her possession; he was unaware that she was filled with loathing and disgust. Bassano answered him frigidly, fending off the visit and informing him that Eugénie would be grateful if he would publicly disclaim some of the statements he had been making about Louis. Carey ignored the hint and continued to press his suit.

On the sixteenth of August the proceedings of the court were published. The Adjutant General announced that the charge had not been sustained by the evidence, Her Majesty had not confirmed the proceedings, and Carey was to be relieved of all consequences of the trial. He was released from a technical state of arrest and ordered to his regiment for duty. The announcement went on to state that Lord Chelmsford was completely exonerated, but that Harrison's orders had not been sufficiently explicit, and that Carey's mistaken notion of his position was largely due to the defective orders—although his professional knowledge should have sufficed to rectify the error.

It was a shade too hard on Harrison and much too easy on Carey. Under the circumstances, it had to be a compromise, and like all compromises, it satisfied no one—except, perhaps, Carey himself. The Army was disgusted; the theory that British officers might abandon their posts in moments of stress had received official sanction. Harrison, who was doing a very good job, did not learn of his reprimand for some time, and when he did, simply issued a forthright statement that cleared him as far as the War Office was concerned. He came out of the campaign a Companion of the Bath and eventually retired as a full general. The same forces that blamed Chelmsford for the disaster at Isandhlwana naturally added the death of the Prince Imperial to his slate, and the public, to the amazement of men returning from Zululand, continued to cheer the mention of Carey's name. The French were wrought up over a minor point—the command of the patrol. Louis' death had been caused by the choice of the halting place and the failure to post a lookout, and national honour insisted that these be English and not French decisions. Someone eventually produced a penciled note, allegedly found in the ticket pocket of Louis' light waterproof coat and sent home with the rest of his personal belongings. It read: "1:30 1st June—Started from Itelezi to find camping ground for the IInd Division; party under Captain Carey." It was the clincher, and even Wood was taken in by it and quoted it in his autobiography. It was, unfortunately, a forgery. The patrol had started from the old camp on the left bank of the Blood River and Louis had left his kit there, not at Itelezi. By one thirty the patrol had been halted for an hour on the ridge overlooking the kraal. Carey, furthermore, had not been a captain on the first of June, no one in Natal knew of the promotion until after he had been sent home, and no one in the field ever referred to him by that rank. England and France, however, knew him only as a captain, because the gazette had been out for a fortnight before he came to public attention.

There the matter might have rested, except for Carey himself. To impudence he now added arrogance, and he took the view that his character had been officially certified stainless. He continued to write to Camden Place, for only if the Empress received him would he feel vindicated in the eye of the public. Eugénie never answered him personally, and he finally received a chilling note from Camden Place: "*L'Impératrice juge inutile de poursuivre cette correspondance.*" Even that failed to stop him. He continued to post his unanswered letters, floundering deeper and deeper into a morass of contradictory hypocrisy. Then Eugénie released the letter he had written his wife.

He was finished. He rejoined his regiment, which did not want him, and he was put in Coventry for the rest of his life. Officers turned their backs on him when he approached; conversations he tried to join ceased. He had neither the sense nor the courage to resign, and six years later he died in Bombay.

Eugénie made a pilgrimage to Zululand in 1880. Evelyn Wood escorted her—he went on half pay to do it and was never paid for the six months the trip took. The party took a number of heavy stone monuments along. Wood took them all to Kambula, and they rode out to Hlobane, ascending the eastern end of the mountain, riding west along the top, and descending by the pass where Buller had retreated. They descended on foot, letting the horses pick their own way down, and of the fourteen the only one that did not fall was Wood's, and that because he led it and positioned its feet himself. They marked Campbell's grave, found Barton's body, and put up a monument over Piet Uys's grave on the razor-back ridge.

Then they traveled to the Ityotyosi and camped there, erecting an enormous stone cross from Queen Victoria. They sent packing an American woman correspondent, who had come a long way for her copy, and they found Sobuza, who owned the kraal, and purchased the site from him. Wood interviewed eighteen of the Zulus who had taken part in the attack, and Eugénie met Zabanga. Langalabalele had been killed in battle with the British. Zabanga said they would never have killed the white man, who fought like a lion, had they known who he was.

Bigge and Slade were in the party, as were Lady Wood and the Honourable Mrs. Campbell. Wood's bugler, Walkinshaw, was still with him, and he took advantage of the trip to fall in love with one of Eugénie's maids. Before they left, the Empress planted a willow and an ivy shoot in the donga. Wood was later invited to Balmoral to report on the trip, and was able to return £3,600 of the £5,000 Victoria had given him to cover all expenses. She also met Bigge, and was so impressed by his talents that she put him to work under Sir Henry Ponsonby as the Assistant Royal Secretary. He never returned to the Army.

There was a final flurry. A committee proposed a statue to Louis in Westminster Abbey. The project was well advanced before political opposition scotched it. It would be an affront to the honour of France; Louis, furthermore, had gone out to advance his own cause and not for the love of England. The dispute reached the floor of Parliament and the Abbey was voted down. Victoria at once announced that the monument would go in St. George's Chapel at Windsor. Eugénie could not endure the thought of further wrangling, or the idea that the Queen might be compromised by her own eternal kindnesses. She offered to leave English soil, but Victoria talked her out of the idea.

Eugénie gave up Camden Place and moved to Farnborough. She retired from public life, she traveled. She visited Egypt and Ceylon, timidly crossing France on the way. She was received kindly and quietly, and she returned often after that. In the end she was even reconciled with Plon-Plon. He had gotten himself arrested by demanding a plebiscite, and she crossed to France to intercede for him.

She aged gracefully. She bought a yacht and cruised the Mediterranean. She was one of the first to use a motor car, she was enthusiastic about airplanes. She finally died in 1920, aged ninety-four.

ULUNDI

O N JULY 8, 1878, the Duke of Richmond announced in the House of Lords that the Sultan of Turkey had consented to the British occupation and administration of the island of Cyprus. British government, the Duke added, would be inaugurated by Sir Garnet Wolseley.

The new administrator had been in England since his return from Natal in October of 1875. After a year as Inspector General of the Auxiliary Forces he had been appointed to the Council of India, where his views on the policy to be pursued in Afghanistan clashed with those of the Viceroy and his Quartermaster General. The new assignment was much more to his liking, since he foresaw a practically free rein and he would, furthermore, be directly under the Foreign Office and not under the irksome jurisdiction of the Duke of Cambridge.

The General Commander in Chief had been consulted neither in the matter of Wolseley's appointment nor in those of the officers to serve on his staff. The latter were all members of the Ashanti Ring and provided clear evidence that Sir Garnet had been negotiating out of channels again. The Duke's temper was not improved by the sobriquet that Wolseley had lately acquired in the press: "Our Only General." He was a superior commander, but he was far from the only competent general on the list, and the Duke, with more than 12,000 officers available for staff assignments, failed to see why the claims of the thirty or forty men whom Wolseley regarded as the only reliable men in the entire Army should always be pre-eminent.

Wolseley was a military genius, and his intellectual capacities far surpassed those of any other officer of his time, but he was a tragic figure. He was fiercely ambitious and drove himself at a furious pace, but it was his fate to be embedded in a system which never gave him the scope he needed, and he spun out his productive years in a period when no worthy antagonist appeared on the horizon. He had risen to general rank a full two decades earlier than the run of his colleagues, for all of whom he had a withering and injudiciously expressed contempt. He was convinced he could manage a battle, a war or a colony better than anyone else, and he sincerely believed it was in his country's best interests to give him command whenever danger threatened.

He had no hope of getting such postings from the Duke of Cambridge, and the Queen found him uncouth and disliked him intensely. His own worst enemy, he was a bombastic egoist, a snob and a parvenu. His incessant flattery of his social betters was crude and transparent. His one hope of preferment lay in the Cabinet, which could override the Duke's prerogative of making military assignments whenever the work at hand required a political role, and although Wolseley loathed politicians almost as much as journalists, he was able to make effective use of both. Civilians found his common-sense approach refreshing, and he had the smell of success. There were, however, dangers in depending on civil support, and while Wolseley was sage enough to avoid an open commitment to either party, his talents and jingoistic views were more congenial to the Liberals than to the Conservatives.

The Only General's enthusiasm for his new post evaporated as soon as he reached it. A third of the island's 180,000 inhabitants were Turks, under whose corrupt administration the bulk of the Greek Cypriots lived in utter stagnation. There were no public buildings fit to live in and no reliable Turks to eke out the small British staff. Within weeks Wolseley was bogged down in a bewildering succession of unappetizing problems which failed to succumb to his vaunted powers. He was inundated with questions of land reform, currency, crops, customs, judges, consuls, religious properties and public sanitation, and caught between the Foreign Office in London and the British Ambassador in Constantinople, where the Sultan could not resist interfering in his holdings. Within months Wolseley was angling for fresh employment. Distant rumblings in Afghanistan drew his attention to the Indian command; he begged both the Foreign Minister and the Duke of Cambridge not to let his present position block his consideration, and he let the Viceroy of India know he was ready to leave at a moment's notice. When he learned that trouble in Afghanistan would be handled by officers already in India, he was reduced to eying the situation in Natal. It began to look promising by January of 1879, and the news of Isandhlwana threw him into a fever of anticipation. Less than a week after his receipt of the news his impatience overcame him and he appealed to the Foreign Office: "Telegram just received says that a new commander is to be sent to the Cape of Good Hope. Will you send me?"

On the twenty-seventh of April Wolseley returned from a picnic to find a cipher telegram ordering him to return to London and to report to the War Office. The ostensible reason was to join a committee investigating the effect short service had had on the Army, but Wolseley nourished a hope that Cyprus would see him no more and he packed his trunks to be sent after him. It took a fortnight to break away, much of it devoted to an undignified squabble with the Royal Navy. The quickest way home was by ship to Marseilles and then by train to a channel port, and Wolseley hoped for the prestige of a warship to carry him to France. The Admiralty thought him somewhat junior for such an honour and offered passage only as far as Syracuse. Wolseley countered with Venice, and a compromise was finally reached with Brindisi. He spent two days in Paris, and finally reached London on the twenty-first of May.

The Duke of Cambridge greeted him with a gloating lecture on the evils of the short service system. Regarded by Wolseley as an absolute necessity if England was to have a reserve force, the system had caused havoc in the small volunteer army and the Duke viewed it as the principal cause of all the difficulties in Zululand. He obviously regarded Wolseley's recall from his post in Cyprus to investigate the matter fitting justice, but Wolseley paid little attention to his complaints. He had just learned from Lord Salisbury that the Cabinet had secretly decided to send him to Natal.

Although the campaign in Zululand occupied the center of the stage, it was far from the only problem besetting southern Africa. The inevitable cessation of hostilities would have to be followed by some sort of peace settlement, the Transvaal Boers were on the verge of revolt, both Sekukuni and the Basuto chieftain Morosi were in arms and there were minor disturbances in the Cape Colony as well. The command in southern Africa was divided amongst four men: Sir Bartle Frere as High Commissioner held the supreme civil power in both British and native territories, Sir Henry Bulwer was Lieutenant Governor in Natal, Colonel William Owen Lanyon had replaced Shepstone as Administrator of the Transvaal, and Lord Chelmsford, with a local rank of Lieutenant General, held the military command. Such a division in the face of crisis was bad enough, and in the eyes of the Cabinet all four men were handicapped as well. The Zulu campaign was not a popular cause in the months following Isandhlwana, and the public shared the Cabinet's feeling that Frere had rushed the country into an expensive, unnecessary and unjust war. Once under way, the war had to be prosecuted, and Bulwer's opposition to Frere and Chelmsford had not passed unnoticed. Owen Lanyon had opposed Evelyn Wood's efforts to supply his forces from the Transvaal, and he was only a substantive major in the 2nd West India Regiment and far too junior to administer a territory beset with a native war of its own and an erupting European population. Chelmsford was at best unlucky, and even if the Cabinet was not ready to charge him with incompetence, a number of newspapers had done so and he was losing a large measure of public confidence.

The Cabinet had already hedged. They might have used the opportunity of Isandhlwana to make a clean sweep, but they let the chance pass, largely because Disraeli stood firm in the face of political pressure. Chelmsford had been reinforced, and he still enjoyed the support of the Duke of Cambridge, who in turn held the Queen's ear. Frere had been severely rebuked, but he had not been recalled. By the twenty-seventh of April, when the Cabinet called Wolseley to London, they were only aware of the situation in Natal as it had been at the beginning of the month. Frere was off to the Transvaal, and Chelmsford had won the battle of Gingindhlovu and had extricated the column at Eshowe. The reinforcements had not yet arrived, and Chelmsford had as yet had no opportunity to use the second chance he had been given. Wolseley's recall, in other words, had been merely a precaution.

By the time Sir Garnet reached London, the news of Hlobane and Kambula was in hand and Chelmsford's plans were clear; but the process of mounting his second invasion was obviously going to be protracted, and his dispatches were filled with his difficulties with Bulwer. Finishing the campaign, imposing a peace settlement on Zululand, and dealing with Sekukuni and the incipient revolt in the Transvaal could best be accomplished by one man with the power to cope with all related problems, and Sir Garnet Wolseley was the obvious choice. His military record was outstanding, he had considerably more experience in civil administration than any other general, and he was already well acquainted with Natal. His choice, moreover, would be greeted with public enthusiasm and would help shore up a government under heavy Conservative attack.

That Sir Garnet should go to Natal was an easy decision to reach; on precisely what terms he should go and what should be done with the men he was to replace were considerably harder nuts to crack. Despite the reprimand, Sir Bartle Frere still technically enjoyed the confidence of the Cabinet, and he was a truly exalted personage with a brilliant record. Having balked at recalling him in February, the Cabinet could not in good conscience do so in May. Chelmsford also retained the ostensible support of the Cabinet, although Disraeli's opinion of his military capacity was sinking rapidly. Despite the tragedy of Isandhlwana and the dragging campaign, he had been performing creditably against all manner of obstacles and dreadful luck ever since his arrival in the Perie Bush. To recall him after the reinforcements had been consigned to his command and just when he was on the verge of bringing the campaign to a successful conclusion would have been grossly unfair and would have precipitated a crisis with the Duke of Cambridge and with the Queen herself.

The solution adopted was pusillanimous, and the manner of its announcement shameful. Frere, Chelmsford, Bulwer and Owen Lanyon were left with their ranks and titles intact. Wolseley was given the local rank of full General and commissioned both as Governor of Natal and of the Transvaal and as High Commissioner "for Native and foreign affairs to the Northward and Eastward of these Colonies" as well. This gave him plenary civil and military powers; as a full General he outranked Chelmsford and as Governor of Natal and of the Transvaal he outranked both Bulwer and Owen Lanyon. As High Commissioner he outranked Frere in Zululand and Sekukuni's territory, and only in the Cape Colony itself was he still outranked by Frere.

The announcement in England was withheld until the twenty-sixth of May, by which time Wolseley had picked the dozen officers who were to form his cortege. He was, of course, triumphant. England, in her hour of peril, had again sent for her Only General. The Duke of Cambridge was stunned, outraged far more by the shabby Cabinet maneuver and the list of Ashanti Ring staff officers than he was by the choice of Wolseley himself. The Queen made no secret of her dislike for Wolseley and pointed out to Disraeli that he was a braggart and an egoist. "So was Nelson, Ma'am," replied her Prime Minister.

The choice was greeted with approbation in the press, but the Government's transparent hypocrisy earned them little credit. "It is a fortunate circumstance that Sir G. Wolseley's presence at home had enabled the Government to avail themselves of his services," the Secretary of State for War announced blandly, and the press lost no time in pointing out that it would have been wiser to state frankly that the appointment was the result of deliberate intention and not merely a happy accident.

To the Secretaries of State for the Colonies and for War fell the task of breaking the news to Frere and to Chelmsford. Sir Michael Hicks Beach composed a lengthy telegram for Frere, full of labored explanations and tactful phrases which softened not a whit the effect of the blow. Colonel Stanley addressed Chelmsford in blunter terms: "The appointment of a senior officer is not intended as a censure on yourself, but you will, as in ordinary course of service, submit and subordinate your plans to his control." Wolseley sailed two days after the announcement was publicized and he reached Natal long before either message. The first news of his impending arrival came to Sir Bartle

Frere at Capetown on the sixteenth of June in a public Reuters news cable which he at once forwarded to Chelmsford.

Wolseley did not reach Capetown until the twenty-third of June. The heady effects of the last few days in London, of the crowds at Paddington Station and the throngs at every stop on the way to Dartmouth, had worn off, and it was coming home to him that if Chelmsford reached Ulundi before he arrived on the scene, he would cut a rather ridiculous figure, and his enemies would be greatly comforted. Even before the *Edinburgh Castle* docked, his staff had shouted to the pier "Is the war over?" and when he stepped ashore he knew of the Prince Imperial's death and that he still had a fair chance to reach the front in time.

He spent the night with Frere and sailed the following evening for Durban in the first available ship. The news from Natal had placed him in a quandary, and aside from sending Clifford a confidential telegram asking for information, he had been able to take no action in Capetown.

In both the Red River expedition and the Ashanti campaign Wolseley had been able to plan his movements down to the last detail far in advance, so that when the time for action came, he had been able to devote his energies to maintaining a schedule of his own devising. He was now to arrive on a scene where a major campaign, the concept of which he strongly objected to, was so far advanced that he could not cancel it to start afresh. Two strong columns, well supplied with rations and ammunition, were deep into Zululand, virtually out of touch with each other and attached by long lines of communications to a base in Natal commanded by a general who had no authority over the lines beyond the enemy's border. Chelmsford was with a column almost within sight of Ulundi, and the previous history of the campaign and Wolseley's personal opinion of Chelmsford's capabilities gave him no assurance that some fresh disaster might not yet strike either or both columns. "He is a gentleman and a very nice fellow," Wolseley observed, "but the Lord forbid that he should ever command troops in the field."

Frere judged Wolseley correctly in the hours they spent together. Sir Bartle was a remarkably perceptive man, and barring his obsession with the Zulu threat (which stemmed from his preoccupation with confederation), he was able to view men and events with a detachment few working statesmen of his generation could attain. He understood perfectly that power in Africa had to be concentrated in the hands of one man, and, ignoring the public mortification he himself had endured, he was even able to regret for Chelmsford's sake that the change had not been effected earlier. He had known Wolseley for years and had a high regard for his shrewdness and sensibility. He was filled with contempt for the Cabinet that had humiliated him, but none of his natural resentment was directed at Wolseley personally. He saw at once, however, that Sir Garnet lacked the requisite patience and experience to frame the future administrations needed in Zululand and the Transvaal, and he knew there were no competent advisers in Natal to whom he could or would turn. Wolseley had reached his present position in life by slicing Gordian knots; it was the only technique he had mastered, and he would continue to hack at them even when they could be easily untied.

Chelmsford had started his advance from Itelezi Hill the day after the Prince Imperial's body was sent back to Durban. The IInd Division moved on the third of June to the vicinity of the kraal where Louis had died, and the Flying Column crossed the Ityotyosi and camped half a mile ahead. The next day the Flying Column crossed to high ground beyond the Nondweni, and the IInd Division, slowed by a sandy drift, crossed the Ityotyosi and camped on the foul ground the Flying Column had just vacated. There were no reliable maps of the ground ahead, and no one knew whether the small stream beyond Wood's camp was the Upoko or the Tenemi, but scouts reported a large band of Zulus on the other side, and whatever it was called it would have to be reconnoitered.

Before dawn on the fifth of June General Marshall rode out of the IInd Division camp with a squadron each of the 17th Lancers and the King's Dragoon Guards. He moved past the Flying Column camp, from which Buller had already departed with the Frontier Light Horse, and when the sun was full face, he stood five miles away over a mimosa-studded slope seamed with stony ravines that dropped to a green valley through which the shallow river trickled, its surface a golden sheen in the morning light. Buller had already fired a few kraals in the valley, and he was eying a large force of Zulus who were moving down the slopes across the river. He finally took his men across the stream and dismounted his force.

Horseholders took the mounts to the bank while the men opened out and plunged into the tall dry grass beyond, opening a hot fire on the Zulus bunched at the foot of the slope. Buller perched on an antheap to watch, while the Zulus melted into the brush. They began to return the fire and their dark shapes were hard to tell from the aloes in the eddies of smoke. Then a flanking fire burst out of a mealie patch, and Buller ordered his men to fall back; dismounted fire-fights were not in their line, and there were several thousand Zulus swarming down the slopes and through the bush in the fields by the river.

General Marshall splashed across the stream as the volunteers retired.

It was bad country for cavalry, barring a few open patches near the banks, but having come this far from England, no cavalry regiment could resist a rare chance for action. The dragoons moved right and left along the bank to guard against flanking parties, and Colonel Drury Lowe trotted his squadron back and forth through the mealie patches, charging with leveled lances across the open stretches. He encountered no Zulus, since they had all taken to cover on the slopes, and they now began to fire at the dragoons. Drury Lowe dismounted a troop to return the fire, and the unnecessary skirmish cost him the life of a promising officer. His adjutant, Lieutenant Frederick John Cokayne Frith, suddenly threw up his arms and fell forward on his saddlebow. Drury Lowe spurred up to him, but he was already dead, shot through the heart by a Martini-Henry. Marshall finally extricated the cavalry and started back to camp, with a half a dozen men wounded and Frith's body flopping across the saddle of his led horse. The Zulus followed for miles, keeping to the ridges and firing down at the exasperated troops. It was late afternoon before they rejoined their columns, which during the day had advanced to the right bank of the Nondweni.

They buried Frith by the river that night, all of the officers turning out for the funeral, and shortly after dark the camp was plunged into one of the frequent alarms that continually plagued the bivouacs. An outlying native picket fired three shots at a shadow. This was the agreed alarm signal and the soldiers of the 58th Regiment ran in on their supports. The officer in charge fired two volleys and retired to an unfinished earthen fort, and the whole camp, now thoroughly aroused, pulled down tent poles and manned the wagon laager. Newdigate, fearing for the rest of his pickets, sounded "Close," but the battalion commanders suddenly started a volley fire and even the artillery loosed two rounds. Five men had been wounded before the uproar was stilled, and the earthen entrenchment was christened "Fort Funk." Patrols searched the surrounding hills in the bright moonlight, but there were no Zulus for miles about.

Chelmsford had brought the column 25 miles from the Blood River in less than a week, but his supply depots lay twelve miles behind the Blood, and he now had to establish the first of his intermediate depots and stock it with rations and ammunition before he could move on. He started a stout stone entrenchment named Fort Newdigate on the sixth of June and the next day moved the bulk of the IInd Division on to the valley where Frith had been killed, leaving two companies of the 2nd/ 21st and two Gatling guns to garrison the new post. At the same time he unloaded all his wagons and started them back to Koppie Allein, sending all of Wood's wagons back in the same convoy.

The move was a prime example of the difficulties he faced in operating in the trackless hills of Zululand. There were 660 wagons in the convoy, and it took the entire Flying Column to escort them: three Imperial battalions, four guns, 740 mounted volunteers and Bengough's battalion of the NNC—4,000 men in all. They reached Koppie Allein on the ninth, and Wood sent his wagons on to Conference Hill to replenish while those of the IInd Division went on to Landman's Drift. It was the twelfth before they were back at the Blood River and another five days before the laden wagons had been dragged through the crumbling drifts to Fort Newdigate. Chelmsford had been forced to wait for ten days, using the time to establish Fort Marshall nine miles to the south, at Isipezi Hill on the Ulundi track, where Russell's patrol had just missed the main impi as it slipped up to the Nqutu plateau. Before Wood was back, Chelmsford had gotten a long letter from Colonel Stanley hinting that he might be superseded, and a private telegram from his brother a few days later announced that Wolseley was on his way.

This was the crowning indignity. He had been struggling one way or another with the problem of Ulundi for the last ten months. He was now forty miles from his goal with 10,000 men, supplies for a month and sufficient transport, and the sole opportunity to retrieve his reputation was about to be snatched away. Chelmsford determined to make the most of whatever time was left. With close to 700 wagons and more than 12,000 lumbering oxen he could hardly sprint, but for the next ten days he pushed ahead with dogged determination, leapfrogging the IInd Division and the Flying Column along the meandering traders' trail to Ulundi. Four miles, three miles, a heart-lifting five miles and once a whole day crossing a silted drift that had to be firmed with bundles of grass thrown into the riverbed. By the twenty-eighth of June he was bivouacked on the heights of Mtonjaneni, with the Mahlabatini plain and Ulundi itself plainly visible sixteen miles ahead across the White Umfolozi, and the Indian Ocean glittering in the distance fifty miles to the east.

Crealock's Ist Division had made less progress. The fault was not entirely his, but he was no driver and his men were known as "Crealock's Crawlers." His transport problem was considerably worse than Chelmsford's; he had fewer oxen to begin with and they were in the last stages of exhaustion. What replacements Clifford could find were going to Chelmsford, and Crealock's convoys grew smaller and smaller and the distance they could move in a day shorter and shorter. The major drifts took a day to cross, and time and again he was stopped in his tracks and forced to wait until his dwindling, bony teams were fit to continue. It was the nineteenth of June before his entire division and the needed supplies were finally assembled at Fort Chelmsford on the Inyezane.

The next stream was the Umlalazi, six miles ahead. Crealock got his division across on the twenty-second, naming a rise on the right bank Napoleon Hill and the camp on the left bank Fort Napoleon. The next morning he set out to explore the beach in search of Port Durnford. The coast line of Zululand north of the Amatikulu was a long sandy beach, blocked off from inland by a low coastal ridge, on which the long rollers from the Indian Ocean crashed in a ceaseless thundering surf. Chelmsford had explored this coast the preceding August, hoping to find a place where an expedition might land. There was none; there was only an area where supplies might possibly be brought to shore to obviate the need of supplying a coastal column by ox wagons. Port Durnford was no port at all, but simply a stretch of beach along which some quirk of the bottom had lessened the violence of the surf. Its latitude was known, but there was no accurate map of Zululand, and Crealock was not certain where it lay. He had asked for a naval vessel to be there on the twenty-third of June, and assumed that the area was near the mouth of the Umlalazi.

It was not. The surf below Fort Napoleon was even worse than elsewhere, and Crealock set out to ride north along the low ridge. He found Port Durnford five miles to the north, backed by a narrow break in the ridge and surrounded by salt marshes. The surf was gentle and the naval vessel was riding to anchor 1,500 yards offshore. Crealock signaled the ship to return in a week with the loaded transports and then rode back to camp to start cutting a track through the marshes to the beach.

Fort Napoleon was finished on the twenty-sixth, and the following day Crealock spent over ten hours moving his column a scant three miles. By the twenty-ninth he was finally camped a mile from the beach, and the next day the warship was back with two transports and a tug with two decked-over surfboats. The Naval Brigade marched down to the beach, stacked arms, and set to work. By evening they had run two stout hawsers out 400 yards past the breakers and buoyed them, and the surfboats had warped in eighteen tons of supplies. The Ist Division was no longer dependent on oxen to bring up rations 25 miles from the Lower Drift of the Tugela.

The campaign had, in fact, reached a stage at which not even Sir Garnet Wolseley could readily impress his authority upon it. He was still at a loss during the run from Capetown to Durban. He considered for a space recalling both Chelmsford and Crealock, on the grounds that the separate columns constituted an invitation to disaster and that the winter grass was too dry to support the oxen; he could then mount a campaign of his own devising the following summer. The columns, however, were too far advanced to justify such an extravagant delay and, as he must have known, were actually in little danger. It would, he confided to his wife, be a fearful disappointment to the Cabinet if he did postpone the campaign, but they would have only themselves to blame for not having sent for him three months earlier.

By the time his ship touched at Port Elizabeth, he had decided on his course, and he fired off a series of telegrams to Chelmsford, Crealock and Clifford which were couched in terms of outrageous brusqueness. Neither his manners nor his motives were admirable. He clearly wished to give the authorities in England the impression that Chelmsford's campaign was teetering on the brink of disaster, and at the same time, without actually ordering him to do so, he hoped to intimidate Chelmsford into halting long enough to allow him to reach the front himself.

The telegram to Clifford demanded information and bade him remember that "all operations for peace are to be referred to me, as I have full powers to act without reference to England, and that [Chelmsford] is not to correspond either by telegraph or in writing with the authorities in England or the Cape except through me. This last applies to yourself also."

Clifford sniffed the prevailing wind early. Much of Chelmsford's dislike for the man stemmed from an incident that occurred shortly after Clifford's arrival in Natal in April. Chelmsford had sent a lengthy dispatch from Utrecht to the Secretary of State for War, requesting three additional battalions and explaining his need for them, which was based not on the situation in Zululand but on the future requirements in the Transvaal and elsewhere. The document passed through Clifford's hands in Pietermaritzburg, and he calmly cut the explanations out, inserted requests for various Army Service Corps units and supplies he wanted for Natal, and forwarded the whole in Chelmsford's name. The dispatch drew a stinging reply from Colonel Stanley which threatened to supersede Chelmsford unless he retracted the requests, and Wolseley was already on his way to Capetown before Chelmsford had the reply in hand and was able to send Stanley a correct copy of his original dispatch. Clifford now answered Wolseley's cable with a long, fawning reply which Sir Garnet got when he landed in Durban. It expressed relief at his arrival and sharply criticized all of Chelmsford's arrangements not only in Natal but in the field as well. Clifford was idiotic enough to send a copy to Chelmsford himself, but he suddenly realized what he had done and hastened to make amends in a private letter to Chelmsford protesting his loyalty and good faith. Chelmsford got the cable to Wolseley on the eve of his final advance, but he at once took time to pen a lengthy memorandum to Sir Garnet outlining Clifford's antics since his arrival. It was hardly necessary; Wolseley intended to replace Clifford with his own man, Colonel George Pomeroy-Colley, as soon as he arrived from India, but for the moment Clifford's views coincided with his own.

Wolseley's cable to Chelmsford asking him to report on his situation reached him at Mtonjaneni on the evening of the twenty-eighth of June. He was then almost a hundred miles from the terminus of the wire at Landman's Drift from whence cables had to be forwarded by special messenger. It came before he got the copy of Clifford's reply, and Chelmsford sent Sir Garnet a detailed account of his own position and what little he knew of Crealock's, pointing out that he was on the verge of attacking Ulundi. Despite Wolseley's peremptory tone, his reply was friendly and although he had still not received any official word from London concerning Wolseley's official position, he gave no hint of resentment or of a lack of willingness to subordinate himself to a superior officer on the scene. He admitted frankly that he was making no effort to control Crealock, with whom he was not in direct touch, and added that the commander of the Ist Division was at full liberty to direct the activities of the coastal column under the guidelines he had given him in April. The reply started back to Landman's Drift the following morning, but before Wolseley got it he fired off a second telegram:

Concentrate your force immediately and keep it concentrated. Undertake no serious operations with detached bodies of troops. Acknowledge receipt of this message at once and flash back your latest moves. I am astonished at not hearing from you.

The message reached Chelmsford on the evening of the second of July. He had already moved down off the heights of Mtonjaneni to a sandy, cactus-covered plain by the White Umfolozi, and he was only four miles from the royal kraal of Ulundi. His reply was noncommittal.

Wolseley landed at Durban on the twenty-eighth of June, barely paused to listen to an address of welcome from the Mayor and Corporation and caught a special train for Pietermaritzburg. He abandoned it short of the terminal and rode at top speed for Government House, arriving before the guard of honour could be mustered and while the flustered Bulwer was still buttoning himself into his uniform. At five that evening he was sworn in as Governor of Natal and took stock. The reports from Crealock and Clifford were in hand and they did nothing to ease his dilemma. For once in his decisive life Sir Garnet Wolseley was at a loss and did not know what to do next.

There was obviously going to be a Battle of Ulundi in the next few days, and the war was then going to be over. It would not be a particularly dangerous battle, because the Zulu enthusiasm for combat was played out and both British columns were large, experienced and alert. A statesman might have let the war come to its inevitable conclusion and then devoted himself to the problem of a peace settlement, but Wolseley was only a soldier. He had an expectant audience in England and he desperately wanted to be present in personal command when the troops reached Ulundi.

He spent the twenty-ninth at Pietermaritzburg, waiting impatiently for Chelmsford's answer to his telegram. No one was quite certain where the IInd Division actually was. Despite the string of garrisoned posts between Landman's Drift and the head of the column, there was no regular system of dispatch riders, and the last telegram from Chelmsford had placed the column at Fort Evelyn, thirty miles short of Ulundi, on the twenty-third. It was precisely this system that put Clifford's nose so far out of joint; Chelmsford had cut himself loose from his base with a self-sufficient force and made use of the outpost string to communicate with his base only when he needed additional supplies. Wolseley could either join Crealock's Ist Division or Chelmsford with the combined IInd Division and Flying Column, and he naturally wanted to join the column that would reach Ulundi first. He could not make a choice until he heard where the IInd Division was, and his mounting frustration spilled over into the telegram he sent Chelmsford on the morning of the thirtieth.

Wolseley held an inDaba on the afternoon of the twenty-ninth, calling in such Natal Kaffir chieftains as he could reach to tell them that he intended to end the war, that his enemy was Cetshwayo and not the Zulu people and that the Great White Queen would send one army after another until the impis submitted. The following morning he heard the news of the successful landing at Port Durnford. There was nothing to be gained by waiting at Pietermaritzburg, and Wolseley made up his mind. He would join Crealock.

He had little actual choice. To join Chelmsford he would have to ride a full 250 miles along the Estcourt road to Dundee, and thence by Landman's Drift and Koppie Allein over the Blood and on past Fort Newdigate and Fort Evelyn perhaps fifty additional miles to wherever the IInd Division was. It would take two full days of hard riding to reach Dundee alone, and after Landman's Drift he would be in enemy territory and could not move without a strong cavalry escort. He could hardly count on reaching Chelmsford in much less than five days, but he could be in Durban in two hours by special train and off Point Durnford six hours after he embarked. His presence would be considerably less embarrassing to Crealock than it would be to Chelmsford, and he had little doubt of his ability to take the Ist Division to Ulundi in short order, although the entire history of the campaign should have warned him that the task was much more difficult than he seemed to think.

He reached Durban on Tuesday, the first of July, and embarked in the evening in H.M.S. *Shah*. By dawn they were anchored off Port Durnford in the midst of a small cluster of transports and tugs which had landed sixty tons of supplies and thirty mules the previous day. The wind had freshened, however, and the surf on the beach was high. With some difficulty, Wolseley and his staff were transferred to one of the surfboats and battened down in the cramped, smelly interior. The crew struggled for two hours to catch one of the warp lines, while the horribly seasick General and his staff were pitched and tossed about. The Commodore finally refused to allow further attempts, and the surfboat returned to the *Shah*, where even more difficulty was encountered getting Wolseley and his shaken staff back aboard. The surf by now was tremendous, and so heavy a sea set in toward dark that the Commodore weighed anchor and stood out from the coast. The weather showed no sign of abating, and Wolseley finally demanded to be taken back to Durban. He landed on the third and on the morning of the fourth set out to ride the ninety miles to Port Durnford. He reached Fort Pearson on the fifth, but before he could cross the trestle bridge to continue on to Crealock, someone handed him a telegram Archibald Forbes had posted that morning at Landman's Drift. Lord Chelmsford had crossed the White Umfolozi the preceding day. He had smashed a large Zulu impi and burned the royal kraal. Wolseley had missed the Battle of Ulundi and the war was over.

Chelmsford had gotten his battle after all, but he had been forced to outwit not only Sir Garnet but also Cetshwayo himself to get it. The Zulu monarch had never had much stomach for the war, and there is evidence to show that he was genuinely bewildered by the precise nature of the issues at stake—a reaction that was shared by a growing number of Europeans. The terms of the ultimatum had been completely impossible, and he had been invaded before he had time to comply with even the conditions over which he did have a measure of control. He had no very firm command over the various factions in his domain and hardly any at all over the sequence of military events. He simply sent impis in the direction of the invading columns, and the results of the first victory at Isandhlwana appalled him. The Zulu losses had been tremendous, and what until then had been a dispute which he hoped temporization, concession or a display of force might still settle had been turned into a war of sheer extermination. The British burned every kraal they reached and ran off all the cattle. Cetshwayo could not have ordered the impis to cease resistance even if he had been so inclined; they would attack whenever they felt strong enough and an opportunity presented itself, and until the war spirit was utterly drained, they would continue to fight as long as there were British forces present in Zululand.

Since Cetshwayo could not quench the war spirit, he took the only course open to him to stop the fighting: he sent messengers to find a person in authority who could name the price for the withdrawal of the British forces. He started as early as March, but his imperfect grasp of the nature of the political structure arrayed against him insured his failure. Somtseu, who had always represented the Crown, was gone and Sobantu and Jantoni were unavailable for advice. Early messengers, trying to make their way to the conference site of the ultimatum, were turned back and advised to seek out Lord Chelmsford, of whom they had never heard. They returned to Ulundi. Messengers trying to reach Bishop Schreuder at Kranz Kop were first fired on because they did not display a white flag and then held for six weeks. A messenger sent to Pearson at Eshowe was locked up as a spy and taken back to the Lower Drift when the column was finally relieved. No one troubled to listen to any word that was sent, and all the messages were regarded as insincere tricks to halt the advance.

It was the end of May before Cetshwayo finally understood that only Lord Chelmsford had the power to halt the invasion and that he was with the column coming in from Koppie Allein. Even these basic facts were confused by Chelmsford's shift from the coastal column to the inland forces; there were several generals in the country, interpreters used euphemisms to describe them, and the envoys were not always certain that they were approaching the right man. On the fourth of June three envoys from Ulundi reached the Flying Column's camp on the Nondweni, and Chelmsford talked with them that evening. The message from Cetshwayo was not very clear. He simply wished to know why the war was being waged, and it was impossible to say if this was a genuine request for information or a rhetorical device based on the knowledge that the British could have no good answer. Chelmsford gathered, however, that Cetshwayo also wanted to know what he would have to do to stop the war, and he specified the terms on which he would cease hostilities pending a discussion of the final peace settlement. He wanted Cetshwayo to restore all the horses, oxen and arms captured since the war started, and several regiments, which Chelmsford would name, would have to surrender by approach-

ing within a thousand yards of his camp and laying down their weapons. The messengers protested—the captured material was scattered
through every kraal in Zululand and would take weeks to gather, and
no regiment would obey such an order from the king while hostile
forces were in the land. The discussions continued through the next
day and Chelmsford finally conceded; he would settle for the oxen
actually at Ulundi and the two guns captured at Isandhlwana, and only
one regiment need surrender. According to the envoys, there was a
Zulu-speaking European trader living in the vicinity of Ulundi, so
Colonel Crealock wrote out the terms and placed them in an envelope
addressed to "The White Trader Reported to be at Ulundi" and sent
the messengers back, telling them that Cetshwayo's reply should be
brought back by one of the inDunas who had been present at the
reading of the ultimatum.

There was indeed a European living in Zululand, but he was not at
Ulundi. Cornelius Vijn was a lame twenty-three-year-old Dutchman
who had come to Natal in 1875 and had spent most of his time trading
into Zululand. Paying little heed to rumors of war, he crossed the Tugela in November of 1878 with a wagon and six Natal Kaffir servants.
Trading cotton goods, beads and knives for cattle and hides, he worked
his way from kraal to kraal until the outbreak of the war found him far
north of the Black Umfolozi. Jeering Zulus stripped him of his wagon
and cattle and killed two of his servants, and he was in terror for his life
when Cetshwayo heard of his plight and ordered his goods restored.
He settled down to wait for the end of the fighting and he was keeping
a journal of sorts, although he had lost track of the exact date several
months before. Crealock's letter was delivered to him, and Cetshwayo
ordered him to report to Ulundi. He got there about the twelfth of
June.

The king dictated a rambling answer, but if he made any mention of
Chelmsford's terms, Vijn, whose English was fragmentary, failed to
record it. Cetshwayo complained that he could not negotiate while the
British forces were burning his kraals and raiding his cattle. He wanted
Chelmsford to withdraw, and then he wanted Somtseu, his brother
Misjan and Sir Henry Bulwer all to come to Ulundi to discuss the
situation. To this message Vijn added a note of his own: "His Wor-
ship—I'm short of paper, if you will send me some paper, ink, and pens,
I will write you state of the Zulus."

The envoys bearing this reply left Ulundi no later than the fourteenth of June, but it was the twenty-second before they reached a
British camp. Chelmsford by then had advanced to the Umhlatuzi,
more than twenty miles past the camp where the messengers had left
him on the sixth. They missed him and tried to approach Fort Mar-

shall, but Colonel Collingwood threatened to shoot them if they tried to come in. He directed them to Chelmsford's camp, but they were so frightened by their reception that they returned to Ulundi.

Cetshwayo at once dictated another letter and sent it to Chelmsford, who was by now at Mtonjaneni. He sent a hundred of the captured oxen and two enormous elephant tusks and stated that the two guns were on the way to Ulundi. Another tusk and more cattle had gone to Crealock; these were not gifts but earnest money to demonstrate good faith. Ignorant of Zulu custom, both generals misread the gesture. Chelmsford announced that he would continue to advance, since his conditions had not been met, and he returned the tusks. He sent word that he would not cross the White Umfolozi for another day, but that a Zulu regiment would have to surrender by the following evening.

Cetshwayo got this answer on the thirtieth of June and at once called for Vijn to dictate his reply. The IInd Division was actually in sight on the heights of Mtonjaneni and he was growing desperate. He could not order a regiment to surrender, but the two guns from Isandhlwana were coming in from an outlying kraal and would start for the British camp in the morning. He had also heard of the death of the Prince Imperial, whom he thought to be an English nobleman, and he returned Louis' sword. There were no more British oxen at Ulundi, but the next day he sent a hundred white oxen from the royal herds.

Vijn was also growing desperate and added a few notes of his own: "Sir—P.S.—if the English Army is in want for the country, please do me a favour to call for me by bearer, that I may get out of the country. I went into the country to buy cattle for blankets. And be your obedient servant—C.V." Another note did his royal protector a disservice: "P.S.—my really believing is, that the king wants to fight, but the princes or his brothers they want peace; also the people wants to fight." On the envelope he scribbled, "Be strong, if the King send in his army, they are about 20,000."

When the messengers with the royal cattle approached the White Umfolozi, the umCijo regiment was guarding the fords. They let the messengers through but they refused to allow the surrender of the royal cattle and drove them back to Ulundi. The king left Ulundi on the third of July, taking Vijn with him, and the Dutchman wrote another letter outlining the situation. He marked the envelope, "For my life keep this secret to natives," but he had no chance to deliver it.

Chelmsford would wait no longer. Before him lay Ulundi and some-where behind, straining every nerve to stop him, was the ominous figure of Sir Garnet Wolseley. On the twenty-ninth he formed a large wagon laager at Mtonjaneni and the following morning marched down into the valley of the White Umfolozi with the bulk of the IInd

Division and the Flying Column, carrying neither kits nor tents and with rations for only ten days. Left with the garrison were two companies of the 1st/24th, furious at the loss of their opportunity to take revenge for Isandhlwana. Between Mtonjaneni and the river lay a sandy, waterless plain covered with cactus and thorn, and the troops spent the night in a cold, comfortless bivouac. The march resumed the next morning, and toward noon the messengers with the Prince Imperial's sword reached Chelmsford. He sent them back with a written note offering to accept the surrender of a thousand Martini-Henrys from Isandhlwana in place of a Zulu regiment. He also added that he was advancing to the riverbank because of the scarcity of water, but he would not cross until noon on the third of July, to give Cetshwayo time to comply with the conditions. To show that partial compliance was not satisfactory, he tried to return the oxen the king had sent before, but the messengers would not accept custody of the herd, claiming it would only delay their return to the king. Before they reached Ulundi, an inDuna at an outlying kraal informed them, incorrectly, that the king had already left the Mahlabatini plain, taking Vijn with him. Since no one else at the royal kraal could read English, the messengers never delivered Chelmsford's letter.

The column slogged over the sand during the morning of the first of July, pushing its way through the thickets of thorn. Wood reached the riverbank about one thirty, to find a large Zulu impi approaching the opposite bank. The IInd Division was still a mile behind him, and it laagered on its leading wagons at once, while the Flying Column went into square by the river. The Zulus moved off toward evening, however, and the next morning Chelmsford brought the IInd Division up to the Flying Column and started work on a fortified position. The wagons were laagered and surrounded by a trench, and a small stone redoubt was built on a rise beside it. The brush was cleared away for several hundred yards around, and the position was ringed with distance markers.

There was a long low bluff covered with bush across the river from the camp, with a shallow drift at either end. Zulus armed with rifles had occupied the hill and maintained a desultory fire at the watering parties that came down from the camp, but return fire soon drove them away from the thirsty horses and cattle. One officer disregarded orders and indulged in a long-awaited bath. Picking what seemed to be a secluded stretch of the river, he stripped and entered the water, but he had no sooner submerged than bullets from the bluff began to kick up spouts around him. He emerged hastily and spent a moment trying to pull his trousers over his wet and sandy legs and then abandoned his dignity and ran for the camp clutching his clothing. During the day pickets at the upper drift saw a herd of white cattle approaching across the Mahlabatini plain, but an impi stopped them while they were still some distance away and turned them around. This was the umCijo regiment, barring the cattle Cetshwayo had sent.

Chelmsford put the finishing touches on his laager and redoubt on the morning of the third of July, and when no further word had been received from Cetshwayo by noon, assumed that his proposals had been rejected. To signify the end of the negotiations, he drove back across the river the cattle captured at Isandhlwana which Cetshwayo had already returned. Then, at one thirty, he ordered Buller to take the mounted volunteers across the river to reconnoiter the Mahlabatini plain. With him went Captain Lord William Leslie De la Poer Beresford, 9th (The Queen's Royal) Lancers, a noted sportsman who had taken leave from his job as A.D.C. to the Viceroy of India to fight in Zululand.

For the last time in the campaign the Frontier Light Horse rode out of camp to scout. They splashed through the knee-deep drift below the bluff that concealed the snipers, and as soon as they were over, Buller sent Baker's Horse off to the left behind the bluff. The Zulus had assumed they were only a watering party headed for the lower drift and had not seen them cross. They were still in their hiding places amongst the rocks along the riverbank when Baker's men suddenly appeared on the crest behind them, pinning them against the river. Thirty or forty Zulus burst out of their niches and scattered in terror, and the men dismounted and dropped them as they ran. Baker shot one, who tripped and fell headlong into a pool in the shallows, purpling the water as the splash subsided. Five Zulus rounded the upper end of the bluff and set out across the plain, but a knot of mounted men rode after them, killing four and capturing the fifth. They were leading him back with a riem around his neck, when one of the men saw him trying to ease a pistol out of his captor's saddle holster and shot him.

Buller himself led the Frontier Light Horse, the Transvaal Rangers, Whalley's Natal Light Horse and the Edendale contingent straight across the plain toward Ulundi. The Mahlabatini was a vast, gently rolling basin of sandy soil covered with patches of long grass, ringed with seven or eight gigantic kraals. The military kraal of Nodwengu stood on the slopes of a gentle rise to the right of the track, and ahead, three miles from the White Umfolozi and across a small stream, Ulundi itself lay on the slopes of the basin. The plain was alive with small parties of Zulus, but no major impi could be seen. Buller rode forward, driving small groups of Zulus off the track and searching for a strong position for the morrow's battle. The men left Nodwengu on their right and beyond it spotted a party of warriors driving a herd of goats toward a grassy hollow. Beresford spurred forward, overtaking a laggard Zulu, who turned and raised his shield over his head. It was a sign of surrender, but Beresford did not know this and spitted him with a tremendous downward thrust that pierced shield and body. He then dropped him deftly off the point and cantered back with the pig-sticking cry of "First spear!"

The men were spreading out to surround the goats, but Buller noticed that the herders were in no hurry to reach the hollow and seemed to be slowing. Suspecting a trap, he checked his force and had no sooner ordered his men to fire without dismounting than a crackling volley burst out of the grass 150 yards away and 3,000 concealed Zulus sprang to their feet and charged forward in a loose semicircle.

The fire was as usual high, but half a dozen horses were hit and as the mounted men turned to retreat, three troopers fell from their saddles in the path of the charging impi. Trooper Pearce was dead as he crashed to the ground, but Sergeant Fitzmaurice of the 24th, serving with the Mounted Infantry, was only wounded. His horse was hit as well, and he fell heavily as the animal dropped and then staggered to his feet stunned and dizzy with pain. Beresford saw him and wheeled to ride back, reaching him just as the leading Zulus arrived. Sergeant Edmund O'Toole of the Frontier Light Horse rode back as well, and with saber and carbine the two men beat the Zulus back. Beresford ordered Fitzmaurice up behind him, but the man was dazed and did not understand. Beresford finally slid off his horse and threatened to punch him if he did not obey, and he turned and began to fumble at the saddle. He was a huge man and Beresford could not hoist him, and O'Toole, who had been firing at the Zulus who reached them, finally dropped his carbine and dismounted as well. Between the two of them they got Fitzmaurice up and then remounted and rode off just as the main weight of the charge reached them. Fitzmaurice, a dead weight, slumped against Beresford and clutched his waist, and twice he fainted and pulled Beresford from the saddle. Keeping just ahead of the Zulus, all three men reached the river in safety.

Cecil D'Arcy saw Trooper Raubenheim fall from his horse and raced back alone to the rescue. Raubenheim could not stand, and D'Arcy dismounted to help him. He had no sooner hoisted him to the saddle and remounted himself, however, than his horse bucked them both off. The Zulus were only a few yards away, and D'Arcy's horse was in a frenzy. He nevertheless calmed the horse and then attempted to pick up Raubenheim again, but he strained his back so severely trying to hoist him to the saddle that he was forced to drop him. In agonizing pain, he was just able to hold off the leading Zulus long enough to regain his saddle. Barely able to ride, he fell back on the retiring force and left the still living Raubenheim to his fate.

The Zulus who had gotten away from the bluff had returned with several thousand reinforcements, and Baker was in position on the reverse slope near the lower drift, checking their advance with a heavy fire. Buller sent a messenger ahead, ordering him to hold the drift at all costs, and then brought his column past the end of the bluff and over the river, halting on the far bank to cover Baker's retreat. The Transvaal Rangers at the end of the column splashed over, and Baker's men abandoned the bluff to follow them. Both impis closed in behind, and for a few minutes the surface of the shallow river was whipped to a froth as Buller's men and the Zulus stood on the banks and fired across. Then Buller broke off to ride to the laager, and the last British shot killed a tall Zulu who had stepped down to the water's edge and stood alone in the open to fire at the retreating riders.

During the day a messenger had brought Chelmsford the telegram Wolseley had posted in Durban on the first. It ordered him to retire on the Ist Division if he were compelled to retreat and objected strongly to the two forces operating separately. Chelmsford replied with his plans for the morrow and promised to retire on Crealock if need be. It was clear by now that Wolseley would not reach the front in time, and his bombastic messages were greeted with hilarity by the staff. Especially amusing was Sir Garnet's imperious demand for the whereabouts of the Ist Division; Chelmsford had not heard from the Crawlers for several weeks and was himself unsuccessfully plying Clifford for information. Wolseley announced his intention of joining Crealock, and wanted Chelmsford to send him daily reports in cipher; if Chelmsford and Crealock did not hold a common cipher, he was to send his messages in French.

Chelmsford issued his orders that evening. The entire force would cross the river at daybreak to attack Ulundi. Colonel William Bellairs, unattached, would hold the laagers with the last five companies of the 1st/24th. The officers of the battalion were outraged, but the ranks were filled with untrained boys from the recent drafts, and Chelmsford did not wish to hazard the regiment again.

There was a full moon that night, but by the time it rose the men had bedded down in the open and soon thereafter a thick mist set in. The night was cold and what little rest the men got was broken by a continuous din from across the White Umfolozi. A new Zulu regiment had reached the Mahlabatini plain and was being doctored, and nearby kraals were mourning the day's dead. Listening Natal Kaffirs interpreted each fresh outburst. During the night they announced that

Raubenheim had been turned over to the women and was being tortured.

The noise did not subside until reveille, when the men rose and breakfasted in the dark. Offy Shepstone was awakened early. The men of the Edendale contingent, as was their invariable practice, had risen before the bugle and had gathered by the river for a prayer service. His grandfather had been a Wesleyan missionary—Somtseu became an Anglican only at his marriage—and the hymns brought back memories of his grandfather's mission. During breakfast Archibald Forbes wandered about offering £100 that there would be no battle that day. The money was covered at once. By first light the Frontier Light Horse had ridden through the drift without encountering any opposition and had fanned out to cover the column as it crossed. As soon as the units were clear of the bluff and on open ground, Chelmsford formed an enormous hollow square. Five companies of the 80th Regiment formed a line abreast four ranks deep with Owen's two Gatling guns in the center, eight companies of the 90th Light Infantry and four of the 94th formed a column of twos behind the left end of the 80th, and eight companies of the 1st/13th and four of the 58th formed behind the right. Two companies of the 94th and two of the 2nd/21st closed the rear. The lines were carefully dressed, and twelve fieldpieces under Harness, Tremlett and Major Le Grice studded the corners and sides. Chard with his company of Royal Engineers and Major Bengough's 2nd Battalion of the Natal Native Contingent marched in the center, surrounded by a tight square of fifty ox wagons and mule carts laden with engineers' tools, medical supplies and the regimental ammunition reserves with all the copper bands carefully loosened. Buller's mounted men, a squadron of the 17th Lancers and a troop of the 1st Dragoon Guards rode ahead and on the flanks, hunting through the long grass and firing the kraals as they passed them. There were, all told, 4,165 Europeans and 1,152 natives in the force, including 899 mounted men. Company officers maintained the dress and kept the lines closed up as the square moved forward, and Chelmsford needed only to halt and to face the sides out to be ready to fight.

The ponderous formation moved out slowly across the Mahlabatini plain along the well-worn foot track to Ulundi, marching toward the gentle rise beyond Nodwengu that Buller had found the preceding day. The bandsmen of the 1st/13th, who would serve as ammunition carriers and stretcher-bearers during action, were playing the regimental marches: "The British Grenadiers" for the 2nd/21st and "The Gathering of the Grahams" for the 90th. The 2nd/21st—the Royal Scots Fusiliers—had their Colours uncased, and only many years later would realize that they could claim the distinction of being the last regiment that ever carried Colours into action. The great plain and the enormous kraals seemed to be deserted, but groups of Zulus were massing on the heights in the distance, and as the black swarms grew, they moved down the slopes and disappeared in the low ground that rimmed the basin. The track was strewn with warriors killed on the preceding day, and the Frontier Light Horse, riding in the van, came across Pearce's body and then, near a small kraal, the mutilated remains of Raubenheim. He had been scalped, and his nose and right hand and his genitals had been hacked off before he, like Pearce, had been slit open.

The sun was well up by eight o'clock, and the Frontier Light Horse was a mile or so ahead. The Edendale men fired a large kraal as the formation lurched past, and the long column of smoke rolled out across the stony ground, shredding itself on the mimosa and the weird euphorbia trees. Beyond Nodwengu Chelmsford eased the formation to the right, and the square began to ascend the gentle knoll in the center of the plain. Buller's men were already crossing the Mbilane, the small stream that trickled across the plain below the royal kraal, and Ulundi lay just ahead beyond a thick belt of tall grass. As the mounted men scrambled out of the donga, the inGobamakhosi regiment silently rose from the midst of the grass and, as if on signal, other regiments appeared at wide intervals on either side. The silent black masses parted the waving grass, displayed their shields and began to move forward, joining the regiments coming down from the heights as they reached them, until the center of the basin was ringed with the dark groupings. There would be a battle after all, and Archibald Forbes had lost his bet.

Cornelius Vijn had made a good estimate; the Zulus were 20,000 strong. All that remained of the young manhood of the nation had gathered at Ulundi: the decimated units from Isandhlwana and Rorke's Drift, from Gingindhlovu and Kambula, and as yet unblooded youngsters who still hoped to wash their spears. The regiments were all there: the isaNgqu, the uThulwana and the rest of the Undi corps, the umXhapho, the uDloko and the amaKwenkwe from the Gqikazi kraal, the umCijo and the uDududu and the inTsukamngeni. They moved forward slowly, converging on the square patch of bright red that topped the green rise in the center of the ring. The irregular masses were marked by their distinctive shields—black, white, red, black on white, and red on white—and they finally merged to form a vast, sprawling semicircle that ran from the west through the north to the east, cutting off the track to the White Umfolozi and pressing the mounted men back toward the square. A great reserve of warriors moved behind the square to the burning kraal of Nodwengu, seated itself and waited to close the ring. The warriors began to move faster, and here and there a regiment began to trot until the movement became general. The silent men in the square could hear a distant hum that rose as the ring contracted: assegais rattling against the stiff cowhide shields, bodies streaming through the grass, and thousands upon thousands of feet stamping the ground. For the last time the warriors moved toward the massed and leveled rifles, for the last time in their brief history they charged to defend their kraals and cattle, king and country.

The mounted men fell back slowly at first, riding perilously close to the advancing Zulus to fire their carbines and then wheeling to reload. Buller sent Captain Parminter of the Frontier Light Horse with only twenty men squarely into the path of a lagging regiment to goad the warriors on. Rockets were already swishing out of the British square to burst near Ulundi, and as at Kambula, Buller was using his men to sting the impi wherever he could, trying to commit them to a charge that would carry them full into the fire that awaited them. One of Parminter's men dismounted to better his aim, and his horse, terrorized by the fire, swerved wildly and would not let him mount. The Zulus sensed his danger and surged forward with a yell, and Parminter spurred back to steady the horse until the man could mount. Then Buller gave the order to retire, and the men all wheeled and cantered for the square. The ground by the track was pitted with innumerable potholes, and the Zulus had covered them with sticks and grass. Here and there a horse stumbled, but George Mossop noticed that even the worst of the riders clung to their saddles and not a man fell.

The square had wheeled half to the right, halted, faced out, and closed its ranks tightly. The guns were unlimbered, and as the troopers rode up the knoll the red patch was suddenly ringed by a glittering band of steel as the men fixed bayonets. There was a moment's confusion as the horsemen approached; no unit would break ranks to let them in, but Chelmsford made an opening and the riders pressed in, bunching by the carts behind the lines and dismounting to stand by their horses' heads. Some of the men scooped cartridges out of the open boxes and passed them out to their comrades.

The Zulus came on slowly at first, and the British made their final arrangements. The rest of the boxes were opened wide, and the bandsmen piled packets of cartridges behind each company. The men opened their pouches, and their officers ordered them to fix bayonets and to load. The lines were all four-deep now, and the front two knelt while the crowded ranks edged back and forth, searching for a clear field of fire. Wood had suggested entrenching, but Chelmsford turned him down. "They'll only be satisfied if we beat them fairly in the open," he said. "We've been called ant-bears long enough." There was no need to specify who "they" were; not only the Zulus but all England had to be shown that the impis could be beaten without an entrenchment, that the disaster at Isandhlwana had stemmed from faulty troop dispositions and not from a failure to fight from a laager. Chelmsford also refused to dismount, so that Wood and Newdigate and the officers of all three staffs had no choice but to remain up as well. It gave them an uncommonly fine view of the battle.

Then, just before the first spatter of shots, a small gray duiker sprang from a clump of bushes and fled along the front of the square, followed by a ripple of shouts from the soldiers. It was a fleeting glimpse of the old African heritage; no other wild ungulate could have made its home and survived on the thickly settled Mahlabatini plain.

The British movements had trampled down the grass for a hundred yards about, but the oncoming warriors were half hidden in the growth beyond. The artillery opened fire, and the red-laced puffs of dirty white smoke began to explode in the black lines. There was a story current amongst the Zulus, few of whom had ever seen an artillery piece or understood the principle of shrapnel or shell, that the death dealt by a shell was caused by British soldiers who sprang from the burst, and warriors advancing through the mangled remains could be seen converging to jab and poke at the smoke. Then as the regiments began to charge, the battalions opened with rifle fire and the rattling bursts from the Gatling guns stitched the crashing volleys together.

Regiment after regiment surged forward, and the lines began to melt away in the hail of bullets scything the slopes. Succeeding waves charged over the contorted bodies that littered the grass, and the shining faces of the warriors, with gleaming eyes and set teeth, bobbed up and down over the rims of their shields. Raw courage had brought them that far, but bravery alone could not force a way through the crescendo of fire, and the warriors sank to their knees to crash full length in the dust or tumble head over heels in mid-stride. Not a Zulu reached to within thirty yards of the British lines.

The crowded interior of the square, wreathed in the greasy smoke and beset by an unceasing wave of sound, hummed with activity. The Natal Kaffirs huddled in terror at the very center, crouching under their raised shields while their officers jeered at them and kicked them back when they tried to crawl under the wagons. The Native Horse was yelling encouragement at the firing line, and many of the men were perched precariously atop their saddles to see better and to add their carbine fire to the battle. The regimental surgeons had established a dressing station and were already at work on the mounted men who had been hit during the retreat, but the Zulus had opened a wild, high fire from the grass and the bandsmen were soon bringing men from the lines to the station. Most of the Zulu fire passed overhead, endangering only the mounted men, but here and there a shot struck home and a man fell back out of the lines or a horse whinnied in pain and thrashed wildly about the square. The treatment for man and horse was the same: cold water on the bullet hole and a compress to stop the bleeding. Some were already dead when the stained litters reached the surgeons, and Mr. Coar, the chaplain, read burial services at the height of the battle over a large pit that had been dug as soon as the square had halted to receive Pearce and Raubenheim. Forbes, undismayed by his loss, moved back and forth with an open notebook jotting down impressions, and Melton Prior was furiously sketching the rough details from which he would work up a general view of the action as soon as it ended.

There was little for Chelmsford to do. He trotted around behind the lines, his staff at his heels, dodging the wounded and the bandsmen struggling up with the heavy ammunition boxes. Once or twice he ordered a company to fire faster, shouting to make himself heard above the din, and once he pulled a Gatling gun out of the line to send it to a hard-pressed corner. Morshead, one of the gunners, was hit in the thigh, pouring blood over the frame that held the chattering barrels. He waved the litter-bearers aside, and sank down behind his gun to help load the drums. Buller sat motionless on his horse, a cigarette in his mouth, watching the Zulu rushes through a small telescope and waiting for the next call for the mounted men.

The regiments in reserve by Nodwengu finally rose to their feet and, led by an inDuna on a white horse, formed a long curved line and charged for the right rear corner of the British square. The fire of a square was weakest at the corners, but there were two nine-pounders at this one and they blasted a wide gap in the center of the line, while eight infantry companies on the flanking sides poured an oblique fire into the charge. For a few moments the Zulu momentum sustained the charge, and then, in the very instant that a hand-to-hand melee, bayonet against assegai, seemed imminent, the fire shattered their order and hurled them back, and the debris of the reserve turned and fled.

The attack had lasted a scant half-hour, but the embattled square was ringed with the Zulu dead. Some of the wounded warriors were crawling back down the slopes, dragging themselves toward the grass; others were dodging and circling, shrieking defiance and searching for an opening in the deadly lines they faced. The charges had never developed the ferocity of the rushes at Rorke's Drift or Kambula—most of the Zulus here had known that their cause was hopeless from the start and no real hope of victory lay behind their courage—and Chelmsford soon sensed the change in the tempo of the attacks. He had misjudged it once, ordering the cavalry to mount just before the reserve charged and then hastily ordering them down again, but when the reserve fled, he waved his helmet at the commander of the 17th Lancers and cried, "Go at them, Lowe!"

The 94th and the 2nd/21st edged aside, and the blue-jacketed lancers with their brass-buttoned white plastrons moved out in column of fours, with the troop of dragoons and the mounted volunteers behind them. Drury Lowe took them around the square to the broad slope leading down to the donga. Addressing himself to his squadron, he ordered, "Form troops, form squadron—trot," and the sections shook out into line abreast, two deep, surmounted by the steel tips with the fluttering red and white pennons. Then, as the lines straightened, "Form line— Gallop— Cha-a-arge!"

A roaring cheer burst from the square as the lances lowered to the rest and the pennons streamed beside the horses' manes. Drury Lowe had no sooner given the order than a spent bullet fired by a distant Zulu struck him squarely in the back of the belt, and he slid from his horse, certain that his spine was broken. A cautious inspection showed him his tingling legs were uninjured, so he got to his feet, clambered back in the saddle, and followed the charge he hoped to lead. A bullet from the grass ahead struck Lieutenant Herbert Jenkins in the face, shattering his jaw. It might be years before he had another rare chance for action, and he had no intention of abandoning the charge. Veering aside to clear the pounding horses behind him, he paused long enough to bind his face together with his handkerchief and then spurred on after his men.

It was a riding-school exercise. Hardly breaking formation, the lancers rode down the slope through the retreating Zulus, picking their men from the ruck. The momentum of the horses spitted the warriors on the points, and as they passed, a strong outward flick of the wrist cleared the weapon, which swung back, up and forward again to point, with stained tip and dyed pennon, at the next victim. George Mossop, following in the wake of the charge, was fascinated by the movement, almost too fast for the eye to follow, as lance after lance flipped through its deadly arc. One or two of the lances fouled in a shield, which would not drop off, and the lancers slowed and tried to slough them off against their horses.

The charge stopped at the donga, and the Zulus scrambled across. Just beyond, some 500 warriors were still concealed in the grass and they rose and poured a volley into the lancers as they picked their way across the shallow ravine. Captain the Honourable Edmond Verney

Wyatt-Edgell fell from his horse, dead, and several of his men were wounded, but the lancers formed again and plunged into the grass after the Zulus. These warriors stood their ground, grabbing at the lances and stabbing at the bellies of the horses, and before the Zulus turned to run, the charge had disintegrated into a series of individual fights. Most of the men jammed the lance butts into the leather sockets on their right stirrups, thrust their arms past the elbow through the haft loops and drew their sabers to continue the slaughter, and the mounted volunteers overtook them and fanned out to fire at the refugees. The formal charge was over and the 17th Lancers, who had last fought in the Crimea, had justified their existence for another twenty years.

The pursuit continued to the heights, until the last knot of Zulus had been driven from the Mahlabatini plain. The artillery was leisurely shelling the hills as the Zulus poured over the passes, and the Natal Native Contingent, its courage restored, was hunting through the grass to dispatch the wounded and the hale Zulus feigning death in the hopes of a later escape.

Chelmsford finally ordered the guns to limber up, broke the square and marched the men to the banks of the Mbilane, where the force rested and dined on the contents of its haversacks. A surprising number of officers had packed a bottle or two of champagne into their kits for just this occasion, and they toasted the victory in the warm and gassy wine. A few working details were still busy on the knoll; the engineers were gathering equipment, and the dressing station was preparing the wounded for the trip back to the laager. The outline of the square was perfectly marked on the rise by the thick windrows of expended cartridges; the troops had fired over 35,000 rounds. The surgeons made their report. Wyatt-Edgell was dead and Lieutenant George Astell Pardoe of the 1st/13th had been shot through both thighs. Eighteen other officers had been wounded more or less seriously, including four of the mounted staff officers. Chelmsford's aide, the naval lieutenant Milne who had climbed a tree to observe the camp at Isandhlwana, had been grazed by a bullet. Ten men had been killed and 69 wounded. There was no accurate count of the Zulu dead, and not even an estimate of their wounded, but over a thousand bodies lay on the slopes and in the path of the mounted pursuit.

The column started back toward the White Umfolozi as soon as the men had eaten, its pace slowed by the long line of litters. The wounded faced a grim ordeal: more than a hundred miles of rough, trackless country lay ahead to be traversed in the springless, jolting ox wagons. Pardoe started to hemorrhage before he reached the laager. His left leg was amputated the following day, but he never rallied and he died ten days later.

The mounted men flushed a few last Zulus out of the grass. Five warriors were found submerged to their nostrils under an overhanging bank in the Mbilane; all were killed. Then the pursuers abandoned the search and began to converge on the kraal of Ulundi. Suddenly there was a race as Buller shouted, "Now then, who's to be first in Ulundi?" The men put spurs to their horses and galloped for the gate, but Beresford put his horse at the thorn barrier that surrounded the great kraal—it covered almost ninety acres—and sailed over to land amidst the huts. (He was known as "Ulundi" Beresford until the day he died.) Whilst Beresford was maneuvering his horse through the huts, others had ridden to the isiGodlo at the upper end of the kraal, and Captain Baker dismounted and dodged through the welter of fenced passageways to the rude single-story mud hut that had served Cetshwayo for a palace. A kick demolished the unpainted door and Baker burst in, with Beresford at his heels.

There had been vague tales of treasure at Ulundi, but the hut was filled with trash. Empty champagne and gin bottles littered the floor, but the orgy the looters surmised had taken place the night before the battle had never occurred; Cetshwayo drank very little and the bottles represented the collection of years. A locker in a corner was filled with old English and Dutch newspapers, and a photograph of the coronation ceremony in 1873 hung on the wall. A silver snuffbox lay under more rubbish, and here too was the tinsel crown that Shepstone had brought to Zululand. Adjutant Tomasson of the Frontier Light Horse picked up an assegai which he idly plunged into the polished dirt floor. It struck metal, and in great excitement he dug up a large iron box. It was filled with old boot-blacking brushes. Men were already firing huts around the perimeter, so Tomasson returned to his horse, pulled a bottle of champagne, which he had hoarded for more than four months, out of his saddlebag and drank a toast himself. Then he scribbled a few lines for the post he knew would leave the laager that night and rode out of the kraal.

There were still a few Zulus skulking amongst the 1,500 huts. Melton Prior, busily sketching, suddenly found himself alone and looked up to spy a warrior slipping toward him through the labyrinth of passageways. He left the kraal hastily. William Drummond, the staff interpreter, was riding Percy, which he had purchased after the Prince Imperial's funeral. He too jumped the thorn wall, but he lost his way in the huts. He was never seen alive again, and months later his charred corpse was found in the ashes of the kraal.

The mounted men started off after the retiring column, while a few men tarried to fire the other kraals. By midafternoon they were all ablaze, the entire British force was safely back across the White Um-

folozi, and the Mahlabatini plain was deserted except for the Zulu dead
and the fresh British graves.

Archibald Forbes left the camp soon after the troops were back at
the laager. He was laden with personal mail, and although Chelmsford
had not yet written his official report, he carried several messages from
his staff. The nearest telegraph terminus lay at Landman's Drift a
hundred miles away, but Forbes took only a lead horse and set out to
ride it alone. It was an act of considerable courage. Four days earlier an
overcast sky stopped the heliograph, and Chelmsford had sent his answer to Wolseley's telegram back from Mtonjaneni to Fort Evelyn
twenty miles behind by Lieutenant James Henry Scott-Douglas, 2nd/
21st, who rode back late in the afternoon with only Corporal Cotter of
the 17th Lancers for an escort. Scott-Douglas did not want to miss the
march to Ulundi, so as soon as the message was delivered, the two men
started back at dusk. They lost the path in the dark and at dawn found
themselves at kwaMagwaza fifteen miles from Mtonjaneni. A party of
500 Zulus on their way to Ulundi surprised them there and killed them
after a brief fight. Their bodies had not yet been found, but Forbes
took the same track, losing his way time and again in the patches of
intermittent fog in the hollows. The country was far from pacified and
still swarmed with small bands of Zulus who had naturally not heard
the news of Ulundi. Stopping only to change horses at Fort Evelyn
and Fort Newdigate, Forbes crossed the Blood River at sunrise and
before noon had filed his story at Landman's Drift. He then pushed on
to catch the mail and reached Pietermaritzburg, almost 300 miles from
the White Umfolozi, fifty hours after he started. His mud-plastered
clothing was in tatters from the thorn country, and the tale lost nothing in his telling of it. The account was heralded in the English press as
the "Ride of Death," and George Augustus Sala, with more admiration
for a colleague than knowledge of military protocol, suggested he be
awarded a Victoria Cross. When Forbes applied for the South African
campaign medal, however, on the grounds that Chelmsford had entrusted him with official dispatches, the General indignantly denied it,
and the War Office turned him down.

The camp on the White Umfolozi was quiet that night. The war was
over, and the battalions would soon be sailing for England. Chelmsford
slept the sleep of the just. He had successfully concluded two arduous
campaigns in a year and a half. Providence had been very good to him
and he could hold his head high in the future. Sir Garnet Wolseley was
welcome to whatever remained of the Zulu campaign.

The flames across the river died away, and the drifting black smoke
was hidden by the soft night. A few miles to the west of the sleeping
camp stood the kwaNabomba kraal, where Shaka had arrived 63 years

ago to claim his inheritance. He had found an apathetic clan no one had ever heard of, who numbered less than the Zulu dead that now lay unburied across the river, and out of them he had fashioned an army and on that army he had built an empire. The proud and fearless regiments had carried their assegais south to the Great Kei River, west to the high veld over the Drakensberg Range and north to Delagoa Bay. He had smashed more than a thousand clans and had driven them from their ancestral lands, and more than two million people had perished in the aftermath of the rise of his empire, which had survived him by a scant fifty years. The last independent king of the Zulus was now a homeless refugee without a throne, and his capital lay in ashes. His army had ceased to exist, and what remained of the regiments had silently dispersed to seek their home kraals. The House of Shaka had fallen, and the Zulu empire was no more.

THE CAPTAINS
AND THE KINGS DEPART

L ORD CHELMSFORD awoke on July 5, 1879, feeling like a man
       from whose shoulders a considerable burden had been
lifted. Twenty-four hours earlier his entire future had been hanging in
the balance, and if the Zulu impi had failed to attack him, or if Sir
Garnet Wolseley had sent him a peremptory telegram forbidding him
to fight, he would have had to return to England in disgrace. The victory of Ulundi, however, had given him the right to retire on his own
terms, and while his self-control was too great to permit a long-overdue
outburst of temper, there was no longer any need to act the role of
Wolseley's compliant subordinate.

Chelmsford spent the fifth of July in the laager beside the White
Umfolozi. The message from the Secretary of State for War announcing Wolseley's appointment finally reached him there, and he fired off
an immediate and acerbic answer. Colonel Stanley had blandly written
that the appointment of a senior officer was not intended as a censure.
Chelmsford replied:

> I regret that I cannot view the appointment in that light. Instead of being,
> as when appointed to this command, the General Officer Commanding the
> Forces in S. Africa, my command under the orders of Sir G. Wolseley is
> now reduced to the force with which I have been fortunate enough to
> defeat the whole of the Zulu army, but which as regards numbers can
> scarcely be regarded as a Lt-General's command.

He also requested permission to return to England with his personal
staff. It would, of course, be granted, and his one desire was to get
away from Sir Garnet and out of South Africa as soon as he possibly
could.

He set about making his last tactical arrangements. He could not
stay where he was. He had brought his force down from Mtonjaneni

576

without tents and with rations for only ten days, and half of these were now gone. It was customary to occupy a defeated enemy's capital, but there was no point in leaving a garrison at Ulundi. Too small a force would entail a risk and too large a force could not be supported, and Ulundi in any event no longer existed. The best information available indicated that Cetshwayo had left Ulundi about noon the day before the battle, taking Cornelius Vijn and a small party of retainers. He would have to be captured, but Chelmsford had neither the force, the rations nor the inclination to organize the search and to push small columns into the wild country north of the Mahlabatini plain. Wolseley was welcome to that job.

Wolseley, moreover, had publicly criticized him for operating with separate columns and had ordered him to join the Ist Division at once. Very well, he would leave the White Umfolozi and retire toward the coast by kwaMagwaza, St. Paul's mission station and the old Undi kraal. On the sixth of July he broke camp and moved back to Mtonjaneni, where the Flying Column bivouacked while the IInd Division ascended the heights to the fortified laager that guarded the stores. The next day Chelmsford started to dismantle the laager and issued orders for the IInd Division to accompany the wounded back to Fort Newdigate, while the Flying Column set out for kwaMagwaza. That night, however, a fierce storm of bitterly cold wind and driving rain broke, which rendered all movement impossible until the ninth. The storm finished the job overwork and poor feeding had started and scores of oxen and horses died.

Chelmsford telegraphed his resignation to Wolseley from Mtonjaneni. He opened the message with an opportunity Colonel Stanley had unwittingly provided him: "The inferior command accorded me in your General Order of 28 June does not agree with the position which the Sec. of State for War in his dispatch received last night states I was to occupy consequent upon your appointment." It was a telling point; the Cabinet had simply given Wolseley a superior rank and sent him out without defining his relationship to Chelmsford or changing Chelmsford's own status. Sir Garnet's commission, therefore, gave him the right to issue orders to Chelmsford but it did not, technically, give him the right to bypass Chelmsford and issue orders directly to the troops under Chelmsford's command. Wolseley had of course done precisely that and had in fact treated Chelmsford as simply a column commander. Colonel Crealock, Chelmsford's Military Secretary, prepared the communication and sent it off.

Wolseley's attitude toward Chelmsford had changed as soon as he heard the news of Ulundi. He sent an immediate, and for him a generous, telegram of congratulations, and he dropped the imperious, carping tone he had used until then. Chelmsford's resignation flicked him, however, and while he still struggled to maintain his generosity, he could not let it pass. He took instant umbrage at Colonel Crealock's use of the title "Military Secretary," since this was a staff billet reserved for the General Commanding and Wolseley of course had his own. He also pointed out something that Chelmsford had overlooked; his rank of Lieutenant General was a local one that held only while he was the General Commanding in southern Africa, and on Wolseley's arrival he had actually reverted to his old rank of Major General. Since Wolseley now had more Major Generals than he could really employ, Chelmsford was free to leave and Wolseley would accommodate him in any manner he wished.

Wolseley reached the Ist Division on the seventh of July, prepared to be thoroughly nasty. He greeted Crealock with the remark that the Ist Division might as well have been in England for all the good it had done during the campaign, a remark he had apparently been saving for the occasion, as he had already used it in a letter to his wife a week earlier. Crealock might well be uncomfortable. Wolseley was an unorthodox dresser who designed his own campaign uniforms, but he was a stickler for neatness, and Crealock had been affecting a sombrero with an artistic puggaree and a peacock feather. Wolseley, who wore only a mustache, also disliked beards and long hair, and officers who had not shaved in months hunted their razors out of their kits and honed them. Crealock, a finicky eater, had seen no reason to adjust his customary standards to the austerity of the field. Sir Garnet's staff found an ox wagon fitted as a mobile hen house, and among the files was a telegram from Major Butler in Natal, who had been striving to provide transport for the division, drawing the line at six milch cows.

Wolseley now experienced some of the transport difficulties that had plagued Chelmsford for a year and a half, and he tackled them in typical fashion. The transports from Durban were able to land 120 tons of supplies a day at Port Durnford, so Wolseley simply cut the Ist Division loose from the line of forts to the Lower Tugela—Pearson, Tenedos, Crealock, Chelmsford and Napoleon—and turned them all over with their garrison troops to Clifford. On the thirteenth, after a two-day delay by the surf, the transport *Natal* landed three of Wolseley's prime favorites from the Ashanti Ring: Captain Ederic Frederick, Lord Gifford, of the 57th; Lieutenant Colonel Baker Creed Russell, 13th Hussars, who was still only a substantive captain; and Colonel George Pomeroy-Colley, 2nd (The Queen's Royal) Regiment, who had gotten the summons in Afghanistan and left on three days' notice. They were no sooner ashore than Wolseley pushed on to St. Paul's with 1,600 troops.

Chelmsford met him there and on the sixteenth Sir Garnet inspected the Flying Column. There were a number of ceremonial parades. Chelmsford bade his troops farewell, and so did Wood and Buller, who were both going home on medical certificates. Wood had not had a full night's sleep in eight months and was on the verge of a breakdown, and Buller for weeks had been spending more time in the saddle than on his own two feet and his legs were covered with suppurating sores. He broke into tears as he left the Frontier Light Horse. Rarely had such unlikely material been welded into as effective a force, and every trooper knew it. Wolseley distributed several decorations awarded for the early part of the campaign.

Chelmsford and his staff rode to Durban via the Lower Drift of the Tugela. On the twenty-first he reached Pietermaritzburg, where the colonists met his carriage outside town and drew it in. He was received with enthusiasm. He had been the outstanding figure in the colony for close to a year, he had made few enemies outside of Bulwer, and he was closely identified with Sir Bartle Frere, whose policies had been popular. With few exceptions, the colonists were willing to attribute Isandhlwana to ill luck rather than to incompetence, and Natal as a whole wished Chelmsford well. By the twenty-seventh of July he had sailed from Durban, free at last of his burdens and ready to meet whatever awaited him at home.

Chelmsford had taken the Flying Column clear across central Zululand, fighting the battle of Ulundi on the way and leaving a chain of fortified outposts at intervals of twenty miles. The southern half of the country was pacified, and not a hostile Zulu had been seen in the coastal area since the battle of Gingindhlovu in early April. There had been no word from the chieftains north of Ulundi, however, and while Cetshwayo was at large, Wolseley could not regard the campaign as over. By the eighteenth of July he had decided on a course of action. He would reoccupy Ulundi, abandon the last of Chelmsford's organization, and push two small columns into central Zululand from which strong patrols could search for the king. Lieutenant Colonel Clarke of the 57th would command one column, and Baker Russell would take over a new Flying Column to be formed at Fort Newdigate. By the twenty-third of the month the Ist Division had ceased to exist, and the IInd Division and the original Flying Column were gone by the end of the month as well.

The exodus of the surplus troops started. Eleven hundred men of the Royal Marine Light Infantry, sent in answer to an earlier request of Chelmsford's, were still embarked at Capetown. Wolseley sent them back to England and he also let the last of the Naval Brigade rejoin its ships. Detachments of troops were marching all over Natal and lower

Zululand to join the new columns or to start the long voyage back to England.

Wolseley had also disclosed the outlines of his peace settlement, which fulfilled all of Sir Bartle Frere's forebodings. Wolseley had brought no clear instructions with him, and he seems to have had a free hand. Hicks Beach was adamant on one point: Zululand was not to be annexed to the Crown, for the days of the Disraeli administration were numbered, and the Cabinet was once again disassociating itself from fresh territorial commitments in Africa. On the eighteenth of July Wolseley called an inDaba at his camp on the Umhlatuzi—only a handful of compliant coastal chieftains appeared—and called for the surrender of all arms and all cattle belonging to the king. He then announced that Cetshwayo would never rule over the nation again, that the Zulu army was to be abolished, and that the country would be partitioned. His objective was obviously the destruction of the House of Shaka, and a balkanization of the country that would prevent its ever again becoming a threat to its neighbors. He had not yet announced the details of his plan, and in working them out he took counsel with no one in authority, consulting neither with John Shepstone, the Acting Secretary for Native Affairs, nor Theophilus Shepstone, still technically Secretary although now largely inactive. Bulwer's advice was not sought and Colenso, naturally, was ignored. When Frere finally asked for information, Wolseley's reply was patronizing and barely civil. What advice Wolseley did seek, on the basis of which he intended dictating a peace settlement which would affect the future of several British colonies and territories and the kingdom of Zululand, came, of all people, from John Dunn.

Throughout July Baker Russell and Clarke struggled to move their columns across central Zululand. The transport difficulties continued. The IInd Division had to rest for a full week on its way back to Landman's Drift before the oxen and the English cavalry horses were fit to continue, and on the eighth of August a terrific storm broke over Mtonjaneni again, where 3,000 draft animals had been collected. More than 450 oxen died in the next three days, and an additional 200 were incapable of any further work. Since Natal could provide no further animals, even under the martial law that had finally been instituted, Wolseley commandeered 2,000 Natal Kaffirs and organized a chain of carriers between Port Durnford and St. Paul's. The system had served him well in the Ashanti jungles, but in Zululand it proved even less satisfactory than the inefficient ox teams, each man's head pack being limited to 56 pounds.

By early August the troops were in garrison in a new series of fortified posts. Fort Victoria was constructed at Mtonjaneni and Fort

Robertson at kwaMagwaza. Wolseley, who was on a visit to Pieter-maritzburg late in July, had ruffled feathers in London to smooth, and he hastily ordered the depot at kwaMagwaza renamed Fort Albert, while the next two forts, over the White Umfolozi, were named George and Cambridge. Organized resistance was clearly at an end, but few chieftains were coming in to surrender, neither arms nor royal cattle had been given up, and the king's whereabouts were still un-known. Wolseley, loudly and most unfairly blaming the delay on Chelmsford's retirement from Ulundi, reached the Mahlabatini plain himself on the tenth of August, determined to direct operations in person until Cetshwayo was captured.

Clad in tatters, Cornelius Vijn walked into Ulundi the same day with the first positive news. The king was north of the Black Umfolozi; he had stayed first with his chief inDuna Mnyamana and for the last fortnight with his half brother Ziwedu. He had heard he was to sur-render in person but was afraid to come in, and he sent word by Vijn that he no longer had an army and was engaged in collecting the royal cattle to hand them over.

Patrols were already searching for the king. Baker Russell had pushed into northern Zululand with 340 mounted men on the strength of a rumor, but he carried no feed for his horses and soon had to retire. Wolseley now took Vijn aside and secretly offered him £200 if he would return to Cetshwayo and induce him to surrender. He promised not to come after him for three days, and Vijn, nothing loath, started before dawn on the eleventh. That morning, in a small kraal just north of Ulundi, a mounted patrol finally found the two guns captured at Isandhlwana. The Zulus had never fired them. Not understanding the lock mechanism, they had tried to screw musket nipples into the vents.

Vijn reached Ziwedu's kraal after dark, but the king had already moved on. Ziwedu provided guides in the morning, and by noon Vijn found his quarry in a small kraal ten miles farther along. Cetshwayo, already aware that he had lost his throne, refused to surrender. A deposed chieftain in Bantu society was automatically killed, and Cetsh-wayo could conceive of no other reason for wanting his person. Vijn was also unable to clarify his confusion over the new "Great Chief-tain." Cetshwayo knew neither Chelmsford nor Wolseley, whom he now confused with Crealock. He had originally assumed that the Great Chieftain was with the column to which John Dunn was at-tached and had sent his messengers to the Ist Division. Chelmsford had left by then, and it took Cetshwayo several months to grasp that he was the general with the IInd Division column. Since Dunn was now with the general who had sent Vijn, the king could not see how that general could be the Great Chieftain. Vijn, unable to follow his reasoning, left him to tell Wolseley that the king would not surrender but that Ziwedu and two other half brothers would come in as soon as they had informed Cetshwayo they were doing so.

Wolseley at once sent out Major Percy Barrow with a squadron of the 1st Dragoon Guards, sixty Mounted Infantry and enough natives to make up a force of 300 men. They left Ulundi on the afternoon of the thirteenth of July with Vijn to guide them, and they were across the Black Umfolozi by midnight. Barrow was in a fever of impatience but made slow progress. The men continually blundered off the trail in the dense brush of the broken hills and Vijn, who had only traveled the track once in the opposite direction, was vague about distances and landmarks. The district was alive with game which made mysterious noises in the night—John Dunn had specifically warned Barrow to beware of lions—and by sunrise the force was in a foul temper, and the scarlet jackets of the dragoons were in shreds. The column had floundered along for less than three miles since midnight, trying to light its way with rush torches, and at dawn Vijn was not certain of their exact location. Barrow wrangled with him about directions and distances—the Boer "mile" was worth four English ones—and it was noon before Vijn led the sullen men up to the kraal where he had left Cetshwayo two days before. It was empty, but three Zulus in the vicinity admitted that the king had departed only the afternoon before. There were more kraals across the shallow Mona river, which wandered through a deep gorge hereabouts, and Barrow pushed on at once with the mounted infantry and the natives. The dragoons and their English horses were played out and stayed behind.

The first kraal they reached was also deserted, but an ox had been slaughtered there that morning. It was late afternoon, but Barrow followed the spoor off through the hills and at dusk came up to the kraal of a Zulu named Mbopa. As he approached, he saw the distant flash and puff of white smoke as someone fired a gun to warn of his coming. Barrow was making an interesting discovery. Aside from Theophilus Shepstone, John Dunn and Bishop Colenso, few Europeans had a first-hand knowledge of the king's character, and Natal had largely accepted the distorted account peddled by most of the missionaries and Sir Bartle Frere that Cetshwayo was a hated tyrant who ruled by terror. The inhabitants of these kraals knew that the king's power was gone and he was a refugee amongst them, but they were fanatically loyal and would give Barrow no concrete news.

The following morning Barrow made Mbopa guide the force to the kraal of his son Nkabanina, five miles away. Ederic Frederick, Lord Gifford, rode ahead with a small patrol to beat through the bush, and during the course of the morning, while Barrow was questioning the

Zulus at Nkabanina's kraal, he sent in forty prisoners. A small boy had inadvertently disclosed that beer and food were going to the king, but Barrow, who had plundered the huts and was browbeating the inhabitants, could discover nothing. Then Vijn recognized an old man whom Gifford had sent in as one of the servants who had been with Cetshwayo when he left him on the twelfth, and Barrow concentrated his efforts on him. It was long after dark before the servant, who was severely handled, agreed to guide them farther.

They set out at dawn, Barrow and Gifford following two different trails until the sun was well up. While Barrow was transiting a thick patch of bush, the guide escaped. They were on the spoor of a small party by then and they followed it for a while, finding a broken beer pot, but they lost all trace of the refugees as they approached the left bank of the Black Umfolozi. There was quicksand at the drift, and the men had to rest their horses before they could cross. Gifford took twenty men and rode on ahead to investigate still another kraal. At sunset he sent two messengers back; he had hard information and wanted Barrow to join him.

Barrow started out to find him but lost the trail in the dark. He spent the night in an open bivouac and in the morning he started back. His rations were exhausted and he could go no farther. Vijn, his mind on the reward, wanted to ride after Gifford, but he was mounted on Barrow's spare horse and Barrow would not let him go. By the eighteenth they were back at Ulundi.

Gifford had captured five men and brought them back to their kraal to question them. He flogged two, who then escaped, leaving three brothers in his hands. They refused to talk, even when Gifford threatened to shoot them, so he finally blindfolded all three, led one off into the bush and then fired a rifle in the air. Returning to the kraal, he threatened to shoot one of the others and the man agreed to lead them to the kraal where the king had been that morning, fifteen miles away. It was almost midnight, but Gifford ordered his men to saddle up and started off, leaving the one brother behind to maintain the deception.

During the day Gifford recrossed the White Umfolozi below its juncture with the Black, and near the river he captured a Zulu carrying a long canvas case. It contained a mirror, a few cartridges and an expensive rifle, which Gifford was convinced belonged to the king. He pushed on with his recalcitrant guides, but his quarry had given him the slip again. Cetshwayo had doubled back on his tracks, and from a hiding place in the bush had actually watched Gifford crossing the river that morning.

Gifford had no intention of abandoning the chase. He had earned a Victoria Cross on the Gold Coast by organizing Wolseley's native scouts and ranging far into the jungle with them for days at a stretch, the only European for scores of miles about. He was living off the country by now, plundering supplies from the kraals he passed and crisscrossing the hills in pursuit of every chance rumor. Wolseley, still camped at Ulundi, sent out patrol after patrol and stationed guards at all the drifts, but Cetshwayo had seemingly vanished. "If I could only capture him I should be happy," he wrote his wife, "or if some kind friend would run an assegai through him."

On the twentieth Gifford met one of the patrols from Ulundi on the Black Umfolozi, drew provisions, and plunged back into the bush. His clothing was in rags and his horses and men were exhausted, but his tenacity was undaunted. Three days later another rumor reached Ulundi, and Wolseley sent out Colonel Clarke with the 3d/60th Rifles and two companies of Natal Kaffirs under Captain Barton. On the twenty-sixth Clarke got wind of a story that Cetshwayo was in a remote district of the Ngome forest, and Wolseley at once sent out Captain John Frederick Maurice, R.A., the son of Colenso's sometime friend, and the following morning Major Richard James Combe Marter followed with a squadron of his 1st Dragoon Guards, a company of the Natal Native Contingent, ten Mounted Infantry and Lonsdale's Mounted Rifles. With him, as an interpreter, rode Martin Oftebro, the son of the missionary who had been Cetshwayo's friend since before 'Ndondakusuka.

Marter crossed the Black Umfolozi and began to ascend the valley of the Ivuna, and that evening he bivouacked near a small kraal on Ngenge Hill. During the night lions killed three of his horses, and he moved on in the morning, halting during the forenoon at a small stream. While the horses were watering, a Zulu appeared, and Oftebro engaged him in a friendly conversation. He finally asked him casually if he knew where Cetshwayo was, and the Zulu considered for a while. He then pointed and replied, "I have heard that the wind blows from this side today, but you should take that path until you come to Nisaka's kraal." Marter started out at once, and on the trail he encountered a native runner bearing a letter in a cleft stick. It was from Gifford, who was only a few miles away, and it was addressed to Maurice. It gave neither Gifford's location nor that of the king, but indicated that Gifford knew the hiding place and was closing in. Marter released the messenger to deliver the note to Maurice and pushed on himself.

Gifford, who had now been scouring the bush for a fortnight, had finally run the king to earth. The day before he had found Cetshwayo's sleeping mat at another kraal and then captured two young boys loitering near the huts. Using the same ruse that had succeeded before, he broke down one of the boys, who agreed to lead him to the kraal where the king was. The party moved on until dusk, the men bivouacked and Gifford went on alone with the boy. At dawn they reached the edge of a steep cliff and far below lay the small kraal of kwaDwasa. People were moving about, slaughtering an ox, and Gifford recognized the portly figure of the man for whom he had been searching so long. There was no practical path down the cliff for mounted men, and Gifford decided to return to his camp, waiting for late evening so that he could descend and surround the kraal after dark.

Marter in the meantime had reached Nisaka's kraal about noon, and found two Zulus, who, although they would not disclose the king's hiding place, led the party to the kraal of Nisaka's brother, on the ridge overlooking kwaDwasa. Oftebro began a casual conversation and in a few moments had again accomplished what Gifford had failed to do in a fortnight. Two of the men beckoned Marter and Oftebro to follow them and led the way to the edge of the ridge, dropping to their hands and knees and crawling to the lip on their bellies. Almost 2,000 feet below they saw a small kraal of about twenty huts standing in a small rocky glade. Dense bush surrounded three sides and the guards posted about were not watching the steep slopes behind them.

Marter returned to his command and gave his orders. The men dropped their kits by the kraal and took off all accouterments that might make a noise. The Natal Kaffirs started down by a roundabout trail, with orders to hide in the bush and guard the head of the glade until the cavalry closed in. Then the dragoons, carrying unscabbarded sabers, started down the precipice past a bend that hid kwaDwasa. Two of the horses slipped and crashed to their deaths below, and it was three o'clock before the men had slashed their way down through the creepers that girdled the rocks.

Still hidden from the kraal, the dragoons remounted and then charged forward, bracketing the huts as the Natal Kaffirs ran forward to close the trap. The Zulus were taken by surprise and not a shot was fired. Oftebro shouted that the kraal would be burned and the inhabitants shot down at the slightest sign of resistance. He then dismounted and followed Marter into the kraal. Umkozana, an aging inDuna who had followed his king throughout the flight, was waiting inside. Oftebro asked him to take them to Cetshwayo, and he pointed to a hut at the upper end of the enclosure. The men hurried forward and Oftebro called out, demanding the king's surrender. A voice from the hut asked for the rank of the officer who made this demand. Oftebro described him as best he could, and Cestshwayo, gathering only that this was a subordinate and not a general, bade them enter and kill him. Oftebro assured him that he was in no danger and would be well treated, and the two men stooped and crawled into the dark interior.

The last king of Zululand was seated on the far side. Even in the gloom he recognized the interpreter and he asked bitterly, "Was your father a friend of mine for so long that you should do this to me?" Oftebro started to explain that he was only doing his duty, but Marter broke in and ordered the king out of the hut. He emerged into the daylight and his captors examined him. He had lost weight, he was drawn and tired, and the insides of his thighs were chafed raw from his travels. Marter gave orders to move on at once, and when someone pointed out that Cetshwayo could hardly walk, he had a horse saddled and brought forward. The king would not trust himself to this mode of travel, and the column set out with its pace tied to Cetshwayo's painful hobble. Marter brought along the nine men, five women and two young children he had found at the kraal.

Long after dark they bivouacked at a small kraal and in the morning they continued the march. Gifford, cheated of his prey, had heard the news the previous evening. He overtook them and rode on at once to Ulundi to report to Wolseley and to send back a mule cart from Clarke's force. Just before Marter reached the kraal where he intended to bivouac for the night, three of the men and one of the women bolted for the bush. The escort, alert alike for rescue and escape, fired at once and cut down two of the men. The following afternoon they reached the Black Umfolozi and joined Clarke, and they reached Ulundi the next morning with the king riding in a mule-drawn ambulance.

Cetshwayo dismounted stiffly, and Marter led him to Wolseley's tent through a corridor of troops paraded with fixed bayonets. Officers with drawn swords preceded them, and a company of dragoons closed the passage behind. Sir Garnet officially informed Cetshwayo that he was deposed for breaking the pledges he had made at his coronation. His kingdom was to be divided, and he himself would be held a prisoner to await the pleasure of the Queen. Within four hours he was on his way again, riding with his four women and a young girl in a grass-strewn cart drawn by ten mules and escorted by two infantry companies and two troops of volunteer horse.

The route led to kwaMagwaza and from there by St. Paul's to the sea, and as the party neared Port Durnford and cut across the trails leading south, Cetshwayo realized that his captivity was not to be spent in neighboring Natal, but in exile across the seas. They reached the coast on the fourth of September and the transport *Natal* was waiting offshore. The king paused in alarm. He had never seen a ship before. A surfboat waited by the buoyed hawser, with a stout plank resting on a rock at the water's edge. Cetshwayo, clad in an umuTsha and a damask tablecloth that served him as a cloak, paused for a moment on the plank and leaned on his stout staff. His eyes lingered on the bare expanse of beach and stared at the low ridge that blocked his view of the rolling hills beyond. The escorting infantry was drawn up in formation, the officers stood by the gangplank. The king's bearing was regal and his conduct dignified, as it had been since his capture. He bade the officers farewell and stepped down into the surfboat. He was violently seasick long before the *Natal* was under way.

He recovered during the voyage to Capetown. A photographer asked him to pose on a bench on deck, which he did with great good humor. The photographer took several pictures and then asked for another pose. Cetshwayo shook his head. "I have played the fool enough for one day," he said.

He landed at Capetown clad in an ill-fitting suit of European clothes and wearing a tall black hat. A carriage bore him through the streets to the old Castle, where Colonel Fairfax Hassard, R. E., took formal custody of the king and his three attendants and four wives. Throngs had gathered to watch him pass, and he was first startled and then touched and pleased when they cheered him.

At the entrance to his quarters he paused to gaze down at the first modern town he had ever seen, and to inspect the shipping that crowded the bay. "I am a very old man," he whispered softly. He was fifty-two years old.

His kingdom had already disappeared. On the first of September Sir Garnet Wolseley held an inDaba at Ulundi, where more than 200 chieftains had congregated. After a long harangue which John Shepstone translated, Sir Garnet announced that Zululand was now split into thirteen separate kingdoms, over each of which he had appointed a chieftain. The appointed men might rule in native fashion and they could commence their reigns as soon as they had subscribed to the conditions he now set forth. Each was to observe his appointed boundaries, and none was to permit the existence of a military system. All men were to be free to marry when they chose, and to come and go freely to Natal or to the Transvaal to hire themselves out for labor. No arms or ammunition might be imported. No life could be taken without fair trial and sentence passed by a council of inDunas, and smelling-out was to cease. Those wanted by British justice were to be sought out and surrendered, and no British subject was to be tried by a native court. No part of the land might be sold or in any way alienated. A British Resident was to be appointed who would hold authority over all thirteen kingdoms, and none might make war nor succeed to a chieftainship without his sanction. The thirteen chosen chieftains signed or made their marks, and the war was over.

The cost had been high. The House of Shaka had been overthrown and the Zulu kingdom fragmented. Some 8,000 Zulu warriors had died and more than twice that number had been wounded, to perish or recover without medical attention. Thousands of Zulu cattle had been run off into Natal or slaughtered to feed the invaders, scores of kraals had been burned and the fields had gone untended.

Over 32,400 men had taken the field in the Zulu campaign. The official British returns listed 76 officers and 1,007 men killed in action and 37 officers and 206 men wounded. Close to a thousand Natal Kaffirs had been killed; the returns were never completed. An additional seventeen officers and 330 men had died of disease, and 99 officers and 1,286 men had been invalided home. In all, 1,430 Europeans had died. The war cost the Crown £5,230,323 beyond the normal expense of the military establishment; the naval transport alone had cost £700,000. A tremendous sum had gone for the land transport, which had employed over 4,000 European and native drivers and leaders, more than 2,500 carts and wagons, and had seen as many as 32,000 draft animals on the establishment at one time. No one ever counted the tens of thousands of oxen that had died.

The world took little note of the war. The Zulu power was gone, and the colonists of Natal and the Transvaal Boers were free of the pressure on their flanks. The roads of Natal lay in ruin and transport was at a standstill, but these were transient problems, and the Crown had spent freely in the colony. There was little effect beyond the seas. The warriors at Isandhlwana had dealt Disraeli's administration a mortal blow, and no man can say what unwritten chapters of European history died with Louis Napoleon.

By the end of September the last detachment of British troops was out of Zululand, and by Christmas only the garrison regiments were left in Natal. The volunteer units disbanded. The Natal Native Contingent returned to its kraals. Commandant Montgomery was bitten by a black mamba and died at Fort Pearson. The Frontier Light Horse rode to Landman's Drift, where its horses were taken away, and it then marched to Pietermaritzburg to be disbanded. George Mossop was discharged on the Blood River and was given something less than £80 for his services. He promptly bought a horse for £7 that the seller had just stolen from a cavalry unit. Mossop had been forced to turn in all his equipment except the ragged corduroys on his back, and when he reached Utrecht, the keeper of the miserable hotel informed him that he did not cater to his class and refused to sell him even a bundle of forage for his horse. He spent his first night as a civilian stamping up and down the frosty street and the next day he started back to the Transvaal and his old life as a hunter.

There were honours and awards for many. Private Samuel Wassall received the Victoria Cross for his rescue of Westwood at Fugitive's Drift. Redvers Buller, Major Leet, Lieutenants Lysons and Browne and Private Fowler were awarded the Cross for their work at Hlobane, and Cecil D'Arcy, whose V.C. for Hlobane had been disapproved, was given one for his unsuccessful attempt to rescue Trooper Raubenheim at Ulundi. Lord Beresford was awarded a V.C. for rescuing Sergeant Fitzmaurice, but when he was commanded to Windsor he informed Queen Victoria that he could not accept the decoration unless the man who had shared the danger could share the award. The next Gazette announced Sergeant Edmund O'Toole's V.C. as well.

No less than eleven Victoria Crosses were given to the defenders of Rorke's Drift, far and away a record for a single action. Wolseley brought the medals with him; Chard and Bromhead topped the list, with Privates John Williams, Henry Hook, William and Robert Jones, William Allan and Frederick Hitch behind. Hook was still stationed at Rorke's Drift, and Wolseley pinned the medal on his tunic at the scene of the fight. There were Crosses for Surgeon Reynolds, James Dalton and Corporal Schiess of the NNC. Chaplain George Smith was not decorated, but he was offered and accepted an appointment as a regular Army chaplain.

Both Chard and Bromhead were promoted to brevet major. Since Bromhead was the senior surviving lieutenant of the 2nd Battalion of the 24th Regiment, he had actually succeeded to the command of "G" Company when Charlie Pope died at Isandhlwana before the fight started at Rorke's Drift, so his promotion was technically not a double jump. Chard, however, was still a lieutenant and could only be promoted to captain. It was the Duke of Cambridge who authorized promotion to the next rank, and Chard became the first Royal Engineer to skip the rank of captain.

Both men were invited to Balmoral together on their return to England. Chard attended and was given a gold signet ring by Queen Victoria. Bromhead had gone on a fishing trip to Ireland and did not receive his invitation until the date had passed. He tendered his apologies at once, but he was not invited again.

There were, in 1879, no provisions for the posthumous award of the Victoria Cross, nor any benefits for survivors. There were not even provisions to insure that the dependents of enlisted men killed on active service received what back pay might be owing. A listing of such names appeared from time to time in the London Gazette, a publication hardly likely to come to the attention of the families concerned, and public-spirited gentlemen would insure that these lists were carried in the popular press. The best that could be done for Nevill Coghill and Teignmouth Melvill, therefore, was an announcement in the *Gazette* that both men "would have been recommended to Her Majesty for the Victoria Cross had they survived." Melvill left a widow with two young sons, and the Queen placed her on the Civil List with a pension of £100. Coghill had been Sir Bartle Frere's aide, and although he was a poor man, Frere erected a large stone cross and a tablet on the rock beneath which the two had died. Only during the reign of Edward VII were the regulations finally changed, and in 1907 the first two posthumous Crosses ever awarded were sent to the families of these two officers.

The war had raised a few men from obscurity into the limelight, and many of them quickly sank back again. Frederick Hitch, his shoulder shattered, was discharged from the Army and finished his days as a London cabman. Henry Hook became a guard at the British Museum, and Corporal Schiess, an itinerant worker in Natal, was destitute and ill by 1884. He was offered passage to England on a troopship and the cost of his rations was raised by public subscription, but he did not survive the voyage and was buried at sea.

Chard subsequently served in Cyprus, India and at Singapore, but he was only promoted once again. He developed cancer of the tongue and retired from the service in August of 1897. Three months later, aged fifty, he died near Taunton, Somerset. Gonville Bromhead's fame overcame his handicap, and he was allowed to soldier on despite his deafness. He was never promoted again, however, and still a major, he died in Allahabad on February 9, 1891, aged forty-six.

Others fared better. William Knox Leet and Edward Browne both became generals. So did Horace Smith-Dorrien, and in August of 1914 he was commanding the IInd Corps of the B.E.F. during the retreat from Mons. Cut off from flanking corps by a headquarters error, he disobeyed staff orders and turned to fight. His courageous action allowed the B.E.F. to extricate itself intact, but it came at a moment when the erratic Sir John French was in a frenzy of despair, and he never forgave his subordinate for his level-headed action. He drove him out of France the following year and hounded him further in his memoirs. Smith-Dorrien saw no further active service and died in 1930, aged seventy-two.

Evelyn Wood was in the field during the First Boer War in 1881 and again in Egypt in 1882, but he never again commanded troops in battle. He spun out the tail of his useful career in a series of important administrative posts, working to better the lot of the enlisted man. He rose to Field Marshal and died in 1919, aged eighty-one.

Redvers Buller left his honeymoon in 1882 to join Wolseley in Egypt, and two years later was again in action at Suakin. At a battle in which *two* brigades were in hollow squares, a volley from one struck the other, and Buller distinguished himself by rallying the men as the flank began to cave in. Wolseley sent for him again during the Gordon Relief expedition, but a character quirk which his personal courage had always masked before now became apparent for the first time. Buller was a resourceful subordinate and a lion in battle, but he had never held a major independent command and he did not trust himself enough to make important decisions. He was aware of the difficulty himself, but no one else in England was. In 1899 he was given command of the British troops in southern Africa, and he arrived at Capetown to find Boer commandos exploding out of the Transvaal in all directions and even threatening Natal. The advance was contained—barely—and Buller then abandoned his over-all control and moved to Natal to take personal command on that front. His advance met with disastrous checks, and part of his force was bottled up in Ladysmith. The decisions that had to be made were pressing, but Buller would not or could not make them. He did nothing and in due course he was relieved by Lord Roberts. He was not in disgrace, but he had failed by far to measure up to the grossly inflated image of himself that the public and officialdom alike held. He died in 1908, aged sixty-nine.

Wolseley's fate was the most tragic of all. England again sent for her Only General in 1882, and he won an easy victory at Tel el-Kebir. In 1884 he was sent to relieve Gordon and failed, because the government had delayed outrageously in its decision to mount the expedition. In 1895 the Duke of Cambridge was finally maneuvered out of office after 39 years as General Commanding in Chief, and the prize for which Wolseley had thirsted for so many years was finally in reach. There were a number of candidates for the post; the Queen favored her son Arthur, Duke of Connaught, and Lord Roberts had recently returned to England after 41 years of service in India. Wolseley, who loathed Roberts, was in an agony of apprehension and intrigued shamelessly—he came within an ace of eliminating himself from consideration. He need hardly have worried. The post of Commander in Chief was his, but even as he entered it, the Cabinet stripped it of much of the power the Duke of Cambridge had wielded. In the years that were left to Wolseley he was unable to institute the sweeping reforms on which his heart had always been set. Then the brilliant intellect which had always been his pride and which had made him so contemptuous of all opinion save his own began to fail him. His memory started to go, at first in little lapses that his frantic aides tried to conceal and then in a fashion that could no longer be hidden. He failed to recognize officers who had served him for years and denied he had ever met them. What influence he had began to fade. He had chosen Buller for the command at the Cape, and when Buller failed, the government did not consult Wolseley on the choice of his replacement, which went to his great rival Roberts. He retired in 1900 and died in 1913, aged eighty. His potential had been enormous, but he was born scant years too late, forever out of phase with the events that might have led him to the heights, and he spent his life trying to close the gap.

Gladstone came into office in 1880 after a campaign during which he had bitterly attacked Sir Bartle Frere. Hoping he would resign, he did not recall him. There was growing pressure to do so, however, and in June the government tried to nudge him by cutting his salary, on the grounds that Wolseley's appointment had diminished his duties. Frere had no private means and had already anticipated his pay in the interests of his post, but he refused to resign under circumstances that would make him look like a man held to his job by the salary alone. The government finally recalled him in August, and his 45 years of devoted service came to an end. He was in debt and his policies were discredited. The complexities that had led him into the Zulu war, that had broken his integrity and made a mockery of his objectivity, were too great to explain to a public that no longer cared to listen. What Sir Bartle Frere had done could only be justified if Cetshwayo had in fact been a bloodthirsty tyrant who oppressed his people and menaced his neighbors, and against all reason and beyond all comprehension Cetshwayo had suddenly turned into a noble and popular figure who had been cruelly wronged. Frere died in 1884, aged sixty-nine.

Sir Theophilus Shepstone's day was over. He lived in retirement until his death at seventy-six in 1893. His monument was the native reserve system of Natal, which alone had permitted the colony to survive its infancy. He was a man of greater sagacity than Wolseley and he had a bar better control of his own personality, but his flaws were even more glaring. More than any single individual he had been in a position to win the allegiance of the Transvaal, which might have averted the Boer Rebellion of 1881 and in turn the Boer War itself, and he had failed utterly. He must also bear a share of the responsibility for the Zulu war, for even from Pretoria his influence would have been sufficient to deflect Frere, but far from stopping him he pushed him forward.

Colenso's day was done as well. He was aging and tired, and the number of fronts on which he heard the call to battle had multiplied beyond any hope of response. Every newspaper and every speech and every private letter put something before him that demanded an answer, and a single pen that wrote more and more slowly could not cope with the flood. The climate for once was sympathetic; Frere's policies had probably been wrong, Chelmsford must obviously bear some of the responsibility for Isandhlwana, Wolseley's peace settlement was patently disastrous and Cetshwayo was not the cruel savage he had been painted. For the sake of whatever future the Zulu people faced, the record had to be correct. Colenso and his family did what they could. The Bishop took down Vijn's story and published it with detailed annotations. With Edward Durnford's help, his daughter Frances published a history of the war, with the first accurate accounts of the Langalibalele Rebellion of 1873, Wolseley's mission of 1875, the Matyana inquiry, the annexation of the Transvaal and the history of the disputed territories, and a patient answer to the immediate charges on which Frere had based his ultimatum. The British were hardly out of Zululand before the inevitable consequences of Wolseley's folly began: the thirteen kingdoms he had established were at one another's throats like so many Kilkenny cats. No one seemed to care, a quarter of a million people were sliding toward anarchy, and a Crown which had wantonly destroyed their society and their political institutions would not permit them to seek stability. Colenso was powerless to save them, but he could at least preserve their story. A stream of forgotten pamphlets began to flow from the press at Bishopstowe, recording and commenting on every turn of events, and analyzing the statements of English and colonial officials and of the scores of Zulus Colenso had interviewed.

It was his last service, and he died in 1883, aged sixty-nine. He was buried below the altar of his Cathedral in Pietermaritzburg under a slab that bears the single word "Sobantu." All his life he had regarded the power of the Crown in Natal as a sacred trust to be discharged for the benefit of European and native alike, and as a churchman he had striven to ensure that the Crown fulfilled its obligations impartially.

Frances Sarah Colenso and her three daughters stayed at Bishopstowe until a fire destroyed the home a year later. She could not bear to leave and moved to a neighboring farm where she died in 1893, aged seventy-seven, just after her return from a final visit to England. Frances Ellen Colenso had seized the pen her father dropped, and if her passion for a cause exceeded the Bishop's, she failed to reach even his occasionally dubious level of objectivity. Under the pseudonym Atherton Wylde she published a eulogy of Anthony Durnford, and in 1884 she continued her history of the Zulu war with two volumes covering the story of the nation after 1879. In 1886 she moved to England to supervise the preparation of her father's biography, but she died of tuberculosis the following year before it was completed.

Agnes and Harriet Colenso continued to champion the Zulu cause. They managed to secure the election of a second Bishop of Natal—Colenso's biographer, in fact—but the Archbishop of Canterbury declined to consecrate him and the vacancy was never filled. Macrorie resigned in 1891, and he was followed by a man chosen to be acceptable to both parties. The move was only partially successful and the problem of two separate churches in South Africa was never fully resolved.

The two sisters lost their homesite at Bishopstowe in the Church Properties Act of 1910 and moved into Pietermaritzburg. They continued their activities, and every fresh crisis in Zululand found Harriet ready with counsel and support. She and Agnes, the eldest and the youngest and the last of the five children of John William Colenso, died within a few weeks of each other in 1932.

Lord Chelmsford's later years were quiet. He never quite escaped from the field of Isandhlwana, but his own clear conscience and the battle of Ulundi were sufficient protection. He defended his course in the House of Lords, and when Archibald Forbes attacked him in a vitriolic and grossly distorted article in the *Nineteenth Century Magazine*, Arthur Harness made effective reply in *Fraser's*.

Chelmsford enjoyed the warm support of Queen Victoria. He was made a Knight, Grand Cross, of the Order of the Bath, and he was, of course, invited to Balmoral on his return to England. (The Queen asked him to bring a photograph of John Dunn along.) When Victoria asked Disraeli to invite Chelmsford to Hughenden, however, her Prime Minister refused point-blank and could not be budged. He would grant an official interview at Downing Street, but he would not open his private home to one of the authors of his current political troubles. (When Buller learned of Disraeli's stand, he returned his own invitation to Hughenden.)

There was no question of further active service, however, and although Chelmsford was promoted to Lieutenant General in 1882, he remained on half pay until 1884. Then, with compulsory retirement staring him in the face, the Queen appointed him Lieutenant of the Tower of London. Victoria had at her disposal, in fact, an almost bottomless bag of honorary comfits, and Chelmsford continued to enjoy them. In 1884 his son was appointed a Page of Honour, and in 1888 he himself was promoted to full General. The following year he generously relinquished the Tower appointment to make way for a needy successor, but he had already started to collect a fair share of honorary colonelcies: in 1887 of the 4th Middlesex (West London) Rifle Corps and then in 1893 of the Bedfordshire Regiment, in 1898 of the Sherwood Foresters (the Derbyshire Regiment), and in 1900, a great plum, of the 2nd Life Guards. Edward VII continued to support him; he retained the appointment as Gold Stick he had received from Queen Victoria, and in 1902 he was gazetted a Knight, Grand Cross, of the Victorian Order. In 1905, at a ripe seventy-eight, he died suddenly in the middle of a billiards match at the United Service Club.

EPILOGUE:
THE RUIN OF ZULULAND

CETSHWAYO was still on his way to the coast when Sir Garnet Wolseley called the inDaba at Ulundi on September 1, 1879, to announce the terms of his settlement. The nation had lost its army and its king; it had no voice, nor even a will of its own for the moment, and it was prepared to submit to the authority of the Crown. It was still territorially intact and it thought of itself as a nation, and while it knew that the king had been deposed and the country was to be divided, the details of the terms came as a shock.

As Frances Colenso aptly expressed it, the settlement was made with Wolseley's "habitual promptitude and entire indifference to the results of his actions beyond the immediate present." Sir Garnet had a single objective in mind: to reduce Zululand to a condition from which it could not possibly unify itself and thus ever again pose a threat to its neighbors. To this end he created an excessive number of petty kingdoms, placed them under chieftains who owed their position to the Crown and not one of whom had a claim to the loyalty of the entirety of even his own subjects, and he took care to settle the leading survivors of the House of Shaka, who might claim such loyalty, under men who had good reason to oppose the uSuthu faction. No other factor received the slightest consideration, and Wolseley utterly destroyed a viable nation and forced it down a road that led to thirty years of anguish for the Zulu people.

He showed an appalling lack of foresight in his arrangements. He had, to begin with, completely disregarded the agreement reached by the Boundary Commission in 1878. Even Sir Bartle Frere had accepted the territorial decisions, albeit with bad grace, but Wolseley ran his kingdoms up to the Buffalo and the Blood Rivers only, and in effect made a present of all the disputed land to the west to the Transvaal. It seemed at the moment a neat way to add to Crown lands, but the Boers were about to rise and within two years would be independent. The choice of the kinglets was also unfortunate. Wolseley deliberately chose them for their subservient attitudes or demonstrated hostility to the uSuthu faction, or simply to pay off debts acquired in the course of the war. Some were outright aliens and hardly one enjoyed the confidence of even the district over which he had been set to rule. Worst of all, the British Resident who was to serve as a channel for all communications with Natal and the Crown and who was to act as a final court of appeal did not have his functions defined and had not a shred of power to enforce his decisions.

The largest of the thirteen kingdoms was simply a buffer state between Zululand and Natal. It comprised a broad belt of land south of the Umhlatuzi running inland from the sea well to the west of the confluence of the Buffalo and the Tugela. Wolseley gave it to the one chieftain he had reason to trust fully: John Dunn. For the first time in his life, Jantoni's position was now recognized by the Crown; he ruled over more than double the land he had held from Cetshwayo and his title ran from the Queen of England. He was at last and officially the White Chief of Zululand, and the British Resident established his office in his territory at Eshowe.

His position was nevertheless peculiar. He had tried to live in two worlds and neither would accept him. He was not welcome in Natal, and although the Zulus in the kraals he had built up accepted his authority, he was still an *umLungu*—a European—and because Chelmsford had forced him to sacrifice his neutrality he was regarded as a traitor by the rest of the Zulu nation. He accepted his appointment only after extracting from Wolseley a personal guarantee that Cetshwayo would never be permitted to return, and Sir Garnet, who had no authority to make such a promise, gave it because his entire settlement was predicated on the permanent exile of the king. Despite its inevitability, the appointment touched off a storm of protest. A letter to a Capetown paper expressed sentiments held by men as disparate as Shepstone and Colenso, who had seen eye to eye on little else for years: "A white man who for twenty years or more has lived the Zulu life, wedded Zulu wives and chosen their society in preference to that of such women as a white man should love and honour, is not a man to represent the Queen of England in a nation of savages."

Other appointments were equally unpopular with the Zulus, who had no choice but acquiescence. Natal owed the Basuto chieftain Hlubi a debt of gratitude that went back twenty years and more. His men had cleared the last of the Bushmen out of the Drakensberg and had served Durnford staunchly at Bushman's River Pass and at Isandhlwana. He could not be given land from the native reserves in the colony, but Wolseley carved out a small kingdom for him to the northwest of

Dunn's, along the Buffalo and the Blood Rivers. It covered the important crossing at Rorke's Drift and included the territories of Sihayo and Matyana and the site of Isandhlwana. Although they spoke no Zulu, Hlubi brought his people with him, and their advent was naturally resented by the original inhabitants.

Uhamu, regarded by the majority of the Zulu people as a deserter and a traitor, was restored to his border district in the north. Mnyamana, the former prime minister, was also offered a kingdom, but he refused out of loyalty to his king. Under the impression that Uhamu was to replace Cetshwayo, he expressed a willingness to submit to him and both his own people and the abaQulusi, fervently loyal to the former monarch, were placed under Uhamu.

Two other kinglets reflected Wolseley's desire to destroy the House of Shaka. The Zulu nation had been hammered together from hundreds of former clans, and while they had long since lost all political independence, several still existed in shadowy form and their kraals were ruled by hereditary chieftains. Mlandela was the paramount chieftain of the Mtetwa people, whose chieftain Dingiswayo had given Shaka his start, and to the north of his kraals Somkele ruled the Mpukonyoni. Wolseley had hoped to revive the pre-Shakan clans by restoring these two, but the attempt was doomed to failure, since, while the people were still aware of their ethnic origins, they had long since grown accustomed to thinking of themselves as Zulus.

The rest of the chieftains were nonentities, except for Usibebu, now thirty-five years old and in his prime. He had quarreled violently with his cousin Cetshwayo before the war, and he was noted for the civility with which he treated Europeans. He had, nevertheless, stayed loyal to his king during the war and had been wounded commanding the u-Dloko at Isandhlwana. He had recovered shortly before Ulundi, had guarded the river crossings (it was he who had turned back the royal cattle), and had been one of the commanders in the final battle. By firing across the river just before Buller's last patrol, he had technically violated Chelmsford's truce, but Dunn spoke highly of his character and Wolseley gave him a mountainous kingdom east of Uhamu and north of the Black Umfolozi.

Aside from Uhamu, the major representatives of the House of Shaka were Cetshwayo's eldest son Dinuzulu, a boy of eleven, the king's full brother Ndabuko and his half brother Ziwedu. Wolseley ignored their hereditary status and placed them under Usibebu and, since all the royal cattle were forfeit, he stripped them of their means of sustenance as well. Dabulamanzi, who had also supported the king, found his territories in John Dunn's kingdom.

The first British Resident was a man named Wheelwright, but as soon as he had time to take the temper of the country, and realized that his own position, undefined and powerless, was little more than a sham, he resigned. He was replaced in March of 1880 by Melmoth Osborn, a competent official who had been on Shepstone's staff in the Transvaal. Osborn filled a difficult post as best he could, and by September of 1880 had at least secured jurisdiction over the actions of the various Europeans who were beginning to attach themselves to the kinglets as advisers and traders. It was a full three years, however, before he was able to establish the *Nongqai*, an armed native police force.

Had the Crown annexed Zululand outright, the people might have accepted the kinglets as British inDunas set to rule over them. It was at once clear, however, that the kingdoms were on their own and that there was no interest in regulating their internal affairs. The new kinglets, in other words, were not Crown officials but were apparently intended as replacements for the hereditary chieftains, and few Zulus would accept them on these terms. The people still looked to the old order, and only the kraals still under their hereditary chieftains were content.

It took almost two years for the extent of the discontent to manifest itself fully, and the process was hampered on every hand by the natural desire of the colonial officials to abide by the terms of Wolseley's settlement. The first overt moves were instigated by Mnyamana and Ndabuko, whom Usibebu had set to menial labor. In February of 1880 four Zulu envoys arrived at Bishopstowe to see Colenso. They spoke for three of the kinglets and represented four of Cetshwayo's brothers and half brothers. They carried "Cetshwayo's Book," an elaborately bound presentation copy of the speeches Shepstone had made at the coronation, and they wanted to have pointed out what pledges the king had allegedly violated. The book had been dropped during the king's flight from Ulundi, and Mnyamana had sent a large party of men to scour the Mahlabatini plain to find it. Cetshwayo had sent a similar mission to Natal during the war, but Bishop Schreuder had turned it back at the border.

Colenso sent the deputation to Pietermaritzburg to see John Shepstone, who was naturally evasive and announced that all complaints must be submitted to Osborn. Before the envoys left, Colenso carefully explained the charges that had been leveled in the ultimatum, and for the first time Zulus were able to put a vehement, detailed denial into sympathetic hands. The deputation then returned to Osborn, who refused to listen to complaints about Usibebu's ill treatment of Ndabuko and Dinuzulu, claiming he was only competent to deal with the provisions of the settlement. He did, however, give the envoys permission to return to Natal, but on their arrival John Shepstone sent them back to Eshowe, stating Osborn would be instructed to deal with them in the future. The emissaries had by now covered more than 500 miles afoot to no avail, but it was clear to them that the war had been caused by serious misunderstandings, that European council was divided and that the case for the king's return was fairly strong.

Cetshwayo and his attendants were confined to a dingy suite in the Castle, where General Clifford, now his jailer, treated him kindly. For the first few months of the king's captivity Frere had granted access to a stream of visitors out to satisfy their curiosity. Many of the officers homeward bound from the war had stopped to see him, but Frere had denied Frances Colenso and the Bishop's two sons permission to visit him.

Cetshwayo had adopted an artless pose and played his role well. "I am only a child," he declared, "and the British government is my father." He could scarcely have chosen a better attitude for the British public, which had digested the nine days' horror of Isandhlwana and was beginning to suffer twinges over the justice of the war. Thousands of citizens were now ready to look on the king as a noble savage who had been cruelly used, and reports from the early visitors abetted the process. The turn infuriated Frere and colonial officials, who for years had faced his truculence and the threat of his impis. The ogre they had vainly warned against, when not one Englishman in ten thousand could have identified his name, the barbarian whose power had annihilated a modern military expedition, was suddenly a gentle, childlike creature.

Colenso finally secured permission from London to pay Cetshwayo a visit, and arrived with his daughter Frances in November of 1880. He brought the king up to date on recent events in Zululand and collected a further rebuttal of Frere's charges. Cetshwayo had not even been informed of the birth of his eighth child, a daughter born several months earlier, nor was he aware of John Dunn's enmity. There was also discussion of an idea that had already taken seed; Cetshwayo might be able to visit England to make his peace with the Queen and beg the return of his throne.

The effects of Wolseley's settlement began to be felt in 1881. The status of what royal cattle still remained in northern Zululand was still in doubt, although it was clear that Uhamu was holding at least 2,000 that rightly belonged to Ndabuko. A Natal Kaffir named Sitimela appeared in Mlandela's kingdom. He claimed to be Dingiswayo's grandson, and appropriated the family herds. He used them to purchase adherents and drove Mlandela out to seek refuge with John Dunn. Mnyamana and Ndabuko were still trying to get Osborn to let them take their case to Pietermaritzburg, and they could now speak for eight of the thirteen kinglets, all of whom wanted Cetshwayo returned. Hlubi was governing his district wisely and stayed neutral, and only John Dunn, Uhamu and Usibebu were opposed to the king's return, joined by a kinglet named Fanawendhlela, whose kingdom included the Ulundi site. Osborn had no power to alter arrangements and no force to maintain order, and he could only refuse to see visitors, deny passes to visit Natal and tell plaintiffs to settle their problems themselves. Even Zulu custom added to the growing tensions; the king was "dead" as long as he was in exile and his subjects could not mention him by name. They could only petition for the return of his "bones," a turn of speech which several officials deliberately misunderstood.

In August of 1881 a Zulu deputation visited Bishopstowe without Osborn's permission. Their timing was unfortunate. Before Wolseley had left the scene, he had managed to provoke the Transvaal Boers, who took advantage of a Cape Colony–Basuto war to rise themselves. They cut several British columns to pieces with long-range rifle fire, killing Pomeroy-Colley at Majuba Hill, and the Crown was even then working out a face-saving formula to give the Transvaal control over its internal affairs. Bulwer left Natal in April of 1880 and before he returned in March of 1882, no less than seven generals had served as Officers Administrating or Governors of Natal, including Clifford, Pomeroy-Colley, Evelyn Wood and Redvers Buller. Just as the Zulu deputation reached Colenso, Evelyn Wood announced an inDaba in Zululand to hear complaints, and Colenso packed the deputies off to present their petitions to him. Delayed by bad weather, they reached the inDaba a day too late, and Wood dealt with them brusquely.

For once he did more harm than good. He first explained that the Transvaal was again enjoying a measure of independence, and the Crown was therefore no longer responsible for the territories the Boundary Commission had awarded the Zulus in 1878. Swaziland was also independent—to block the Boers from the sea—and the Zulus would have to respect the new boundary north of the Pongola. Wood then dealt with the internal disputes, holding rigidly to Wolseley's formula. He ordered Usibebu to return a third of the cattle he had seized from Ndabuko and Ziwedu, providing those two men moved to John Dunn's kingdom and took Dinuzulu with them. Uhamu was to return something less than half the cattle he had taken from Mnyamana and was not to treat him so harshly in the future. The verdicts were interpreted as carte blanche to harry Cetshwayo's adherents. Usibebu hurried home to seize the rest of the uSuthu cattle before they were taken to Dunn's district, but a neighboring chieftain rescued them and drove Usibebu away. Dunn then plundered Ndabuko and Ziwedu still further when they arrived in his territory. The abaQulusi had been supporting Mnyamana, and Uhamu fell on them, burned their kraals and drove them out of his kingdom. With Osborn's approval, Dunn then attacked Sitimela, slaughtered his followers, and restored Mlandela to his district. By the end of the year the country was in an uproar, and several of the petty thrones were on the verge of collapse.

There was a ray of light on the horizon for Cetshwayo. Sir Hercules Robinson came to Capetown as High Commissioner in January of 1881 and moved the king from close confinement to Oude Moulen, a run-down farm in the suburbs. The life here was easier; the king could meet friends and roam the countryside on long walks. Langalibalele lived nearby, still hoping after eight years for permission to return to his amaHlubi, and the two exiles hunted together, coursing a deer hound at rabbits and jackals and throwing sticks Zulu-fashion at birds. The official custodian rarely visited the farm, and the wardens were surly ex-enlisted men, but when Cetshwayo finally refused to walk abroad guarded by common policemen, his new interpreter secured permission to take him out alone. Robert Charles Samuelson was the son of a Norwegian missionary who had known Cetshwayo since his early manhood, and his company was congenial. He was expected to remain with the king day in and day out, and he would soon have quit had not Cetshwayo begged him to stay. The visitors continued to come; once it was Prince Albert and Prince George, the future George V, on a world tour as midshipmen in H.M.S. *Bacchante,* and again Lady Florence Dixie, a scatterbrained enthusiast who adopted the cause of the exiled king.

Cetshwayo now pinned his hopes on the Queen, and Samuelson spent ten days taking down his defense from beginning to end. Robinson brought good news in September: the king was to go to England the following May and in the meantime was free to come and go as he liked. Samuelson took the announcement to mean he no longer need submit the king's correspondence to Robinson for censorship, and within months he was in trouble. The king had dictated a letter to Lady Florence, which she gave to a newspaper after inserting slurring remarks about Henrique Shepstone. When Cetshwayo denied them, Samuelson took her to task, but while she admitted adding the phrases she claimed she had taken them from an earlier letter, which she blandly stated must have been a forgery. Samuelson lost his job.

Cetshwayo and three of his inDunas, with two attendants, his new interpreter and Henrique Shepstone, arrived in England on July 12, 1882, and moved into a rented house in Kensington. He was immensely popular, attracting great crowds outside his house who hoped for a glimpse of him and stopping all traffic when he was taken shopping. He had learned to wear European clothing well, and his bearing was regal. He was taken to Osborne for a hugely successful luncheon with Queen Victoria and on the seventh of August finally met with Lord Kimberley at the Colonial Office.

The wind was blowing his way, and he made the most of it. Wolseley's settlement was a patent failure, and the Crown obviously wanted to restore him to a unified Zululand. The terms would be roughly similar to those the thirteen kinglets had signed, and Kimberley wanted a portion of the country set aside for any of his people who did not wish to come under his rule. Cetshwayo assented at once, but pointed out that a large portion of his land had already been lost when Wolseley gave the disputed areas to the Transvaal. Kimberley was evasive; that land was no longer under British control and it was obvious that Uhamu, Fanawendhlela, Usibebu and above all John Dunn could not be turned over to the mercy of the uSuthu. Cetshwayo departed before the details were settled, trusting Kimberley to work out the size of the sanctuary district, and by the twenty-fourth of September was back at Oude Moulen eagerly awaiting the call to return to his kingdom.

It was four weary months before the call finally came. The delay had been caused by Sir Henry Bulwer, again Governor of Natal and Special Commissioner for Zululand, whose task it was to accommodate the desires of Downing Street to the realities of the local scene. Bulwer was by no means opposed to the return of Cetshwayo, but his desire to see justice done was as strong as ever, and there were a very large number of conflicting factions. Bulwer took immense pains to inform himself, but his sources were not always reliable and his knowledge of the complex situation in Zululand suffered in consequence.

There were a number of compelling reasons to modify the vague, generous terms Kimberley had offered. To begin with, Zululand obviously could not be restored to the conditions of 1878. Chastened or not, it would in time pose exactly the same threat to Natal as before, the more so because the Crown still refused to hear any talk of annexation. Then, no matter how Cetshwayo's return was structured, provision would have to be made for the chieftains who had accepted their appointments only on Wolseley's guarantee that the king would never return. Even within the districts whose kinglets had petitioned for his return there were large elements of the population who clearly did not wish to see him back, and here Bulwer's sources failed him, so that he greatly overestimated the size of the opposition to the restoration.

Even with the bulk of the country in favor of the return, there were still several thousands of Zulus who would need protection from the uSuthu faction. Bulwer provided them with a sanctuary in the form of a vast Native Reserve that took in the kingdoms of John Dunn and Hlubi. Both men might remain where they were, but Dunn in effect was stripped of his expanded territories and cut back to the corner in the southeast from which he had started. Usibebu could not possibly be returned to Cetshwayo's control, nor did Bulwer feel that he could be dispossessed. The most Bulwer would do was to adjust his district, restoring Ndabuko and Ziwedu to their kraals and adding this territory to Cetshwayo's domain. To compensate Usibebu for this loss, he gave him a territory to the north which Wolseley had orginally assigned to a chieftain named Mgojana, who had never occupied it. Bulwer attributed this to a lack of interest, and missed the fact that the land in question was inhabited by a group of ultra-uSuthu clans who had been in the forefront of the agitation for the king's return.

Uhamu's territory was restored to Cetshwayo, and his position was most unpleasant. Even if Cetshwayo could be persuaded to leave him in peace, Mnyamana would return to power, and the abaQulusi would not be slow to seek revenge.

When Sir Hercules Robinson finally announced the results of the settlement to Cetshwayo, the king was appalled. Bulwer's solution bore little relation to the liberal terms Kimberley had spoken of in London. Cetshwayo was not only to lose half his kingdom—including the best of the cattle country and the heartland of the uSuthu faction—but his truncated domain was to be bracketed north and south by large enclaves sheltering his most bitter enemies. With Usibebu and John Dunn removed from the country he had no doubts of his ability to impose order on all of it, but the present proposal was unworkable and would lead to immediate disorders he could not control. There was no help for it, however, and Robinson gave him his choice: sign or chance permanent exile. Under strong protest, hoping to regain what he had been promised in London and anxious in any event to return to his country, the king signed.

On January 10, 1883, H.M.S. *Briton* dropped anchor off Port Durnford and Cetshwayo landed through the surf. The return was far from triumphal. Hardly a Zulu was to be seen, for Sir Theophilus Shepstone, who was waiting on the beach with an escort from the 6th Dragoon Guards, had kept the time and the place of the landing secret until the last moment. It took the party a week to reach Mtonjaneni, where the ceremony was to be held, and another week before the aged Mnyamana arrived.

During the fortnight, Cetshwayo saw how seriously his power had been impaired. Few chieftains in distant parts cared to commit themselves openly to him for the moment, and it was clear from the attitude of the inDunas who did come that the respect he had once enjoyed was gone. Usibebu rode in with a party of unlawfully armed men, paid his respects to Somtseu and rode away before the ceremony. Uhamu refused to come at all. Only Dabulamanzi voiced wholehearted support. The restoration took place on the twenty-ninth of January, and Cetshwayo was not allowed to voice a protest at the terms, although Dabulamanzi railed at Shepstone until the king stopped him. Usibebu's borders had still not been defined, and the power of the throne was weakened still further. Much of the uSuthu strength was drawn from the new Reserve area south of the Umhlatuzi, and Shepstone now announced that this area would come under Natal law and its inhabitants would need a pass from Osborn to cross into the king's territory. The British Resident at Ulundi was to be Henry Francis Fynn II, and Osborn was finally given permission to recruit an armed native police force, the Nongqai, to guard the border. Shepstone then retired and left Cetshwayo to make his way as best he could.

Trouble broke out almost at once. Cetshwayo built a new kraal on the Ulundi site, but his control hardly extended beyond the Mahlabatini plain. His support stemmed entirely from chieftains who hoped for a redress of grievances; he dared not provoke them and he could not stop them from attacking their oppressors. The abaQulusi turned on Uhamu's people, and the uSuthu clans placed in Usibebu's district began to attack his kraals. For a few weeks Usibebu contented himself with reporting the raids to Pietermaritzburg, and then he assembled a large force of his Mandhlakazi faction and demanded the submission of the worst of the gadflies. The effect was electrical. The uSuthu clans, the emGazini and Mnyamana's Butelezi suddenly rose and moved on Usibebu's chief kraal, outnumbering the Mandhlakazi three to one. Cetshwayo could not control the uSuthu and could only appeal to Fynn. Usibebu abandoned his kraal and retreated to the Umsebe valley, luring the triumphant uSuthu forces after him. Then, on the thirtieth of March, he turned and fell on his pursuers. There was no cover in the valley, where a series of dongas separated by low ridges limited visibility, and the beaten uSuthu van spread panic through the rest of the force. Before the sun had set, more than 4,000 uSuthu supporters had been slain during their retreat across the open plain below the valley, to a Mandhlakazi loss of less than a dozen men. In no other fight did so many Zulu warriors perish, not at 'Ndondakusuka nor in any of the battles with the British.

Cetshwayo suffered both the calamity and the blame. Bulwer naturally accused him of aggression, and Usibebu was absolved. The situation continued critical and was beyond the king's control. Mnyamana had attacked Uhamu, who drew support from the Mandhlakazi and could not be beaten. Cetshwayo needed the support of the uSuthu clans in the Reserve, but he was forced to hold their chieftains at Ulundi and dared not let them go. The Colonial office had repudiated Shepstone's claim that the Reserve was Natal territory, but if the chieftains were allowed to return, some might defect with their clans and even the loyal ones could cause him further trouble by attacking John Dunn or Hlubi. Osborn, trying to maintain order in the Reserve, issued repeated demands for the chieftains to return to their home kraals, and Cetshwayo was forced to ignore them.

The tension rose steadily until July, and then the crisis came. An uSuthu clan struck at one of Usibebu's outlying kraals, and the Mandhlakazi crossed the Black Umfolozi and marched twenty miles to Ulundi in the course of a single night. At dawn on the twenty-first Usibebu was less than five miles from Ulundi and he was not discovered until he was in sight of the kraal. Cetshwayo had not dared to revive the latent regimental system, and his retainers were little more than a loose mob disheartened by the defeat at the Umsebe valley. They scattered at once and Usibebu swept into the kraal and burned it. Cetshwayo mounted a sorry nag to ride to safety, but he fell off and sought shelter in a clump of trees. A Mandhlakazi warrior named Ralijana found him there and, under the impression that he was Ziwedu, cast an assegai which pierced his thigh. He was stabbed in the leg again before he could identify himself, and Ralijana then let him go. There was no mercy for the inDunas found at the kraal. Most of them were old and fat, and fifty of the nation's leading inDunas perished. Tshingwayo, one of Wolseley's kinglets and the man who had commanded at Isandhlwana, died in his hut, and Seketwayo, another kinglet, was also killed. Sihayo died and so did the aged Mbopa, who had killed Shaka 55 years before.

There was no sign of Cetshwayo for a fortnight, while Osborn searched for him high and low. Then word reached Eshowe; the king was convalescing in the remote kraal of a chieftain named Sigananda Cube in the Nkandhla forest. The news that the king was hiding in the Reserve south of the Umhlatuzi made Osborn uneasy. If Cetshwayo had fled to seek asylum in the Reserve the Zulu throne was vacant; if he had gone to Sigananda simply because he was an uSuthu, he was ignoring the purpose of the Reserve. Neither the uSuthu nor the Mandhlakazi were amenable to British control; Usibebu was clearing out pockets of uSuthu supporters north of the Black Umfolozi and Cetshwayo time and again refused to emerge from the forest to report to Eshowe. Osborn went to get him in person but the king evaded him, and while the British Resident had sent for troops, he hesitated to attack. Loyal uSuthu from all over the Reserve were congregating in the forest, and Osborn could not afford to lose even a skirmish. Then

Fynn volunteered to enter the Nkandhla and on the fifteenth of October he emerged with Cetshwayo in tow.

The king had now lost even the little authority to which he had been restored. He moved into a hut at the Gqikazi kraal near Eshowe while Bulwer and the Colonial Office sought some solution to the problem. There was none. It would take British troops to put Cetshwayo back on his throne, and by his attitude since his flight he had forfeited all claim to such support. Usibebu was walking rampant through the king's territories, but he could not be proclaimed king of all Zululand without grave injustice to the scores of clans who would not accept him as a paramount chieftain. The Reserve territory could not be extended to the whole of Zululand—tantamount to the annexation which the Colonial Office still refused to consider—unless Cetshwayo were sent into permanent exile, and this would touch off an open revolt of the uSuthu clans. The only course that commended itself to the Colonial Office was to give Usibebu the whole of the country north of the Black Umfolozi and to proclaim the fifteen-year-old Dinuzulu king in place of his father under a regency of inDunas. Bulwer soon discovered that even this solution was unworkable; Uhamu would no more live under Usibebu than he would under Cetshwayo, and a score of major uSuthu chieftains and their clans, from Mnyamana down, would have to be moved off hereditary lands north of the Black Umfolozi.

Then, late in the afternoon of February 8, 1884, a messenger summoned Osborn to the Gqikazi kraal. He arrived with his medical officer to find Cetshwayo stretched on his back in his hut. The body was cold and he had been dead for some hours. When the medical officer prepared to perform an autopsy the king's horrified attendants stopped him. Under the circumstances he attributed death to "fatty disease of the heart," but privately he thought Cetshwayo had been poisoned. He may well have been.

The last hope of independence for the Zulu people died with Cetshwayo. The country was in a turmoil and even the line of succession was confused. Dinuzulu was almost sixteen and Cetshwayo's only surviving son, but his mother, Msweli, had been a commoner, and the king had later married a Great Wife who was pregnant when he died. Her child, born several months later, was a son named Manzolwandhle, whose claim to the throne was considerably better than that of his elder half brother. Many Zulus refused to recognize Dinuzulu's claim, and the Crown never recognized him as king of the Zulus. Mnyamana and Ndabuko, however, were acting as regents and they knew the uSuthu cause would never survive without a leader until Manzolwandhle came of age. They simply disregarded the infant, and the tattered mantle of sovereignty descended to Dinuzulu. Manzolwandhle eventually moved to Natal and played no further role in the history of his people.

Bulwer's hope of extending the Reserve to the Black Umfolozi was scotched by the Colonial Office, which refused to condone any extension of British territory beyond the Tugela. No one in Natal or in London could see a solution. John Dunn made an offer to serve as Chief of all the Zulus, but it was firmly rejected. Then the Transvaal Boers broke the impasse. Two of them sought out Dinuzulu and offered Boer assistance to drive out Usibebu. The offer was foolishly accepted. Hundreds of Boers poured into northwest Zululand and on May 21, 1884, Dinuzulu knelt in a wagon while four men placed their hands on his head, pronounced him king and swore to protect him from his enemies. On the fifth of June the heartened uSuthu, supported by about a hundred mounted Boers, attacked Usibebu at Etshaneni in the Lebombo Mountains. A few volleys at long range finished the Mandhlakazi cause and Usibebu and his surviving supporters sought refuge in the Reserve.

Then the bill was presented. Some 800 men demanded farms—George Mossop arrived just in time to add his name to the list—and almost 3,000,000 acres disappeared into a New Republic which laid out a capital at Vryheid near Kambula and proceeded to survey claims clear across Zululand to the sea. Dinuzulu was left with little more than Usibebu's original district.

Settlers flooded into the north and the west, and clans emplaced on hereditary lands were treated as so many squatters and began to drift into the forced labor and semislavery of the Boer domains. Then a German trading firm bought St. Lucia Bay and the adjoining 100,000 acres and announced that they had annexed the land to Germany. The British awoke with a start, a gunboat arrived to haul up the Union Jack, and a flurry of agitated notes passed between London and Berlin.

By January of 1886 the Zulus were growing desperate and they petitioned the British for help. They made a second appeal in April, and the Crown invited a delegation of New Republic officials to Durban. The Boers refused to discuss either their boundaries or their relations with the Zulus, and the talks broke off. Dinuzulu complained again in May. The Boers had even settled in the traditional "cradle" of Zululand, where they had desecrated the graves of the early kings and driven the traditional guardian clans away. Dabulamanzi tried to protest in October. A field-cornet arrested him and shot him when he tried to escape.

Later that month the British met with a second delegation of Boers. In return for recognition, the New Republic abandoned its claims of sovereignty over the Zulus and agreed to a new boundary. St. Lucia returned to British control and the Boers were again blocked from the sea. The Zulus had not been consulted and Dinuzulu complained bitterly. Such uSuthu clans as the abaQulusi, the eGazini and the Butelezi were still on New Republic lands and the sacred cradle had been given to the Boers as well. Osborn finally met with Dinuzulu's representatives, but he could hardly satisfy the complaints. The Imperial government was by now ready to annex the country—seven years too late to do any good—but no Zulu would give a firm reply. The envoys stated they had been "children of the Crown" since the day Shaka sent Sotobe to meet King George, but none was willing to assent to an outright transfer of what remained of the nation to British control. Dinuzulu at least did not voice opposition, so Osborn and Theophilus Shepstone finally decided that tacit approval had been implied. In February of 1887 the Zulus were informed that their country was a British Protectorate and on the ninth of May Dinuzulu's land and the Reserve finally became a British possession.

The Native Law of Natal was extended to the whole of Zululand and Ndabuko and Mnyamana were present when the law was promulgated at Eshowe. Dinuzulu did not enter the negotiations himself and it is clear that he regarded his status as unchanged. He ignored the newly appointed magistrates and continued to administer the affairs of his nation as if his authority were still supreme.

In August he sentenced a man to death for witchcraft, killed his wife and seized his cattle. Osborn summoned him to appear in person and, when he failed to come, fined him thirty head of cattle and sent the Nongqai to collect them. Dinuzulu let them go and then appealed to the Boers for help, later spreading a rumor through the kraals that a commando was coming to help him against the British. Now thoroughly annoyed, Osborn summoned him to Eshowe again and this time he came. The Resident read him a stern lecture and fined him fifty head of cattle. He also informed him that he was sending Usibebu and the survivors of the Mandhlakazi back to their former territories.

This was a mistake. When Usibebu and 700 followers arrived, they found their old kraals occupied by the uSuthu. The crops had not been harvested and the usurpers refused to move. The local magistrate, working with inadequate numbers of the Nongqai, managed to evict enough uSuthu to make room for the newcomers, but both factions began to build up strength and prepared for a clash. In March of 1888 an uSuthu chieftain refused to vacate a kraal, and when a European subinspector appeared with eight Nongqai troopers, he found over a thousand armed Zulus waiting for him. He prudently withdrew, and Osborn issued warrants for the arrest of Dinuzulu and Ndabuko.

The Resident attempted to serve the warrants on the first of June. A strong column set out from Eshowe with 64 of the Nongqai reinforced by 140 British soldiers from the Natal garrison and 400 Zulus provided by Mnyamana. The force met an impi of 1,800 uSuthu and, because it was not prepared for a pitched battle, was forced to retire after a sharp skirmish in which two soldiers were killed. The country promptly exploded. The uSuthu murdered two traders, father and son, who had guided the British column, and then fell on the returning Mandhlakazi. An impi threatened the small Nongqai garrison at Nongoma, and when Usibebu marched to the rescue, the uSuthu drove him off in a battle at Ndunu Hill in which he lost a quarter of his followers. Osborn pulled all his forces out, and the country rose behind him, killing traders and burning the rude magistracies.

By July Osborn was back with 2,200 men and on the second he defeated the uSuthu under Dinuzulu's uncle Tshingana in a hot little fight that cost him two Europeans and more than sixty native levies. Dinuzulu, Ndabuko and Tshingana escaped to Vryheid and tried to surrender to the Boers, and when they were not accepted, they boarded a train and sheepishly rode to Pietermaritzburg. Dinuzulu went straight to Bishopstowe, and Harriet Colenso brought him in to the police in the morning. A long and complicated trial started in October before a specially constituted court at Eshowe, and because it appeared that they were fully aware of the law and had deliberately contravened it, they were convicted of treason and public violence. Dinuzulu was sentenced to ten years' imprisonment, Ndabuko to fifteen, and Tshingana to twelve, and early in 1889 they were deported to St. Helena.

The next decade saw several changes in Zululand. A commission finally delimited the border between the uSuthu faction and the Mandhlakazi, and a long-overdue peace settled over northern Zululand. A few rough roads were pushed into the country, and some settlers secured land grants and followed the traders who had already established permanent stores near the new magistracies and the major kraals. Theophilus Shepstone died on June 23, 1893. His son Henrique had replaced his brother John as Acting Secretary for Native Affairs in 1884, and despite his semiretirement the office of Secretary was left vacant until his death. John Dunn died on August 5, 1895, at the age of sixty-one. He left 49 recorded wives and 117 children (unofficial counts ran as high as 65 and 131), and the area north of the Lower Drift of the Tugela was populated by thousands of Zulus who owed him allegiance. Several of his daughters had married Europeans, who settled in their father-in-law's domains. Not one of his own sons was strong enough to replace him, and for a time his Zulu inDunas continued to control the area, but in the year following his death the rinderpest struck down the herds that held his survivors together. His descendants and his followers scattered, and only a few returned to settle on the Dunn Reserve a later land commission established. The next generations were driven still further apart by the law; some of Dunn's descendants had reverted to Native status, many were Coloured and a few, descended from his children by Catherine Pierce, were Europeans.

By 1897 Britain was ready to shed control of Zululand. In November Tongaland was annexed to Zululand and on the thirtieth of December the combined territories were presented to Natal. On the same day Dinuzulu and his two uncles landed at Durban, free to return to their homeland. Usibebu had been living near Eshowe during Dinuzulu's exile, and he was also permitted to return to his hereditary lands in the north. The ablest Zulu general since Shaka, he died in 1905.

Despite the heavy fighting in Natal, Zululand was virtually unscathed by the Boer War. Both sides generally refrained from using combatant native levies, although the Natal Native Horse came out 350 strong, and Robert Samuelson proudly led the Dreifontein Scouts, recruited from the Edendale men, on patrols through the Drakensberg. An occasional commando raided into Zululand to seize supplies from the kraals, and in 1902 the Zulus retaliated, attacking a commando that had bivouacked in a cattle pen and killing 56 of the 59 Boers, while losing 200 warriors themselves.

In 1902 Natal opened Zululand to European settlement, after a land commission had set aside reserves for the clans. Settlers poured in, and a coastal railroad sent a daily train to Somkele's district, where coal had been found. The line was a dead loss and Natal took it over, and in 1905, overextended financially, the colony passed a Poll Tax Bill to collect £1 from all unmarried male natives.

The bill cost Zululand dearly. The country had been peaceful since 1888, but locusts, rinderpest, erosion, shrinking land and a growing population had reduced many of the clans to the verge of destitution, and the tax was the last straw. Sundry clans refused to pay and unrest spread through the reserves of both Natal and Zululand. Dinuzulu was in a difficult position. Natal recognized him only as a district chieftain, but most of the clan heads regarded him as their king and sent to him for advice. He could give none, and he made his own kraals pay the tax. Then a petty Natal Kaffir chieftain named Bambatha, who lived near Greytown, refused to pay. Several other Natal Kaffir chieftains had refused as well, and two members of the Natal Mounted Police had already been killed by an excited mob when they tried to arrest a man near his kraal at dark. Bambatha had a record of cattle theft and faction fighting, and when the police came to arrest him, he slipped into Zululand with his wife and three small children and sought out Dinuzulu. What followed is not quite clear. As a salaried district chieftain, Dinuzulu should have arrested the man, but Bambatha returned to Natal with two of Dinuzulu's henchmen, while his family stayed behind in the uSuthu kraal. Bambatha was now ready to foment rebellion in Natal, and on the night of April 4, 1906, he ambushed a police patrol 172 strong with a party of 150 followers, killing four Europeans and driving the rest into flight. He then recrossed the Tugela and made for Sigananda Cube's kraal in the Nkandhla forest.

Sigananda Cube was ninety-six years old, and he had fought with Shaka's impis as an uDibi boy. He asked Dinuzulu for advice, and when Dinuzulu refused to counsel him, he decided to cast his lot with Bambatha. Several Europeans, including a magistrate, were murdered in sporadic violence, but by the second of May one hundred troops from Natal were in Zululand. There were several sharp fights before Bambatha's force was trapped in the Mhome gorge on the tenth of June and virtually wiped out. Bambatha was killed, as was Mehlokazulu, the son of Sihayo, and Sigananda Cube was captured.

It was the last Zulu rising, and the first campaign a British colony had ever conducted without calling for Imperial help. Twenty-three European volunteers and six Natal Kaffirs had died, and over 2,300 Zulus had been killed.

Sigananda Cube died in jail, but almost 5,000 Zulus were brought to trial. Dinuzulu had taken no active part in the rebellion, but most of the Zulus were convinced that the outbreak had his blessing, and the prisoners implicated him time and again. Then Bambatha's wife surrendered and reported that she had heard her husband plotting with Dinuzulu before the rebellion. Natal had not known that Bambatha's family had been staying at his kraal, and Dinuzulu was arrested and brought to trial at Pietermaritzburg. Despite a spirited defense waged by a committee that included Robert Samuelson and Harriet Colenso, he was again found guilty of treason, on the grounds of sheltering Bambatha and failing to report the presence of his family, and sentenced to four years' imprisonment. He was first incarcerated at Newcastle, and in 1910 was moved to the Transvaal and allowed to live freely on £500 a year. He died in 1913, aged forty-five, without ever returning to Zululand.

Dinuzulu's son Maphumuzana, better known as Solomon, was proclaimed principal heir and in 1916 was permitted to return to Zululand as paramount chieftain of the uSuthu. Since Union, Zululand had become little more than a series of native reserves akin to those of Natal, under Native Law administered by European magistrates, and while the chieftains still exercised authority in the domestic affairs of the kraals, the office of paramount chieftain was without political significance and hardly more than honorary. Solomon's function was largely ceremonial, he caused no troubles and was even permitted nominally to form two Zulu regiments to maintain the old traditions. He built a corrugated-iron house near Nongoma, married 65 wives (one of whom was a Christian who demanded and obtained a divorce), developed an interest in sports cars, and died in 1933.

Solomon left a minor son, Cyprian Bhekezulu, who served under a regent until he became paramount chieftain in 1945. He still holds the office today.

The hills of Zululand have changed little since Shaka's day. A railroad skirts the coast, unpaved roads crisscross the land, and small settlements have sprung up to serve the magistracies and the Europeans who farm there. Eshowe, Nongoma, Babanango, Mtubatuba and Nqutu all look like sleepy villages in the American South: small clusters of stores and a single hotel, with the main street running out into the ancient land beyond. The kraals still dot the slopes, and if most of the huts have cylindrical mud walls with conical thatched roofs, here and there in the remote districts the beehive huts can still be seen.

Civilization has barely touched the landscape, and 85 years have not yet eradicated the traces of the fighting in 1879. There are neat little cemeteries by the battlefields and whitewashed stone cairns to mark the mass graves at Isandhlwana, but the rains still wash up bullets and badges, buttons and bones, and the British bivouacs are still marked by shards of dark-green glass from the ration beer bottles. Coal mines have burrowed into the flanks of Hlobane, and Piet Uys's grave on the razorback ridge has been desecrated, but the windy heights on the plateau above look just as they did when Buller led his men down the pass.

There is a large mission cathedral on the slopes of the Oskarberg, and below it a stone dwelling, curiously like Jim Rorke's, stands on the exact site of the hospital that burned down during the fight. The storehouse and the cattle kraal are long gone, but a local resident has traced their outlines and marked them with bricks, and the lines of the front wall and the final mealie-bag redoubt can still be seen in the tall grass.

There is an ugly stone archway to mark the site of Chelmsford's square at Ulundi, where Zulu children offer the chance passerby the expended Boxer cartridge cases they can still kick up on the Mahlaba-tini plain. In one wall of the structure is set a small plaque that reads:

IN MEMORY OF THE BRAVE WARRIORS WHO FELL HERE IN 1879
IN DEFENCE OF THE OLD ZULU ORDER

It is the only memorial that has ever been erected to honour the Zulu nation.

NOTES ON
ZULU ORTHOGRAPHY

SOURCES

BIBLIOGRAPHY

INDEX

NOTES ON ZULU
ORTHOGRAPHY

The transliteration of Zulu is studded with phonetic and grammatical pitfalls. The major difficulties stem from certain sounds not used in English—chiefly three tongue clicks, an imploded *b* and a voiceless fricative represented by *hl*.

The dental click (represented by the letter *c* and formed with the tip of the tongue and the upper front teeth) is equivalent to the sound usually rendered in English by "tut-tut" or "tsk-tsk." The lateral click (represented by *x* and formed with the side of the tongue and the upper side teeth) is akin to the "cluck-cluck" sound used to "giddiyap" a horse. The palatoalveolar click (represented by *q* and formed by withdrawing the tongue from the back of the hard palate) was used by children in simpler times to represent a gun shot; it has also been compared to the noise a cork makes coming out of a bottle. All three clicks can be unvoiced, voiced (indicated by a preceding *g*), nasalized (indicated by a preceding *n*) or aspirated (indicated by a following *h*). Since *c*, *x* and *q* can all be rendered by other letters in English, these conventions cause no difficulties except with the diphthong *ch*, which in Zulu represents an aspirated dental click. "Church" must therefore be spelled "Tshurtsh."

The imploded *b* is usually represented by a plain *b*, the English exploded *b* by *bh*. Official Zulu orthography uses a *ɓ* for the imploded *b*, which I have disregarded.

The voiceless fricative *hl* is similar to the Welsh *ll*. It resembles an English *sh-l*, with the tongue held somewhat back so that the air leaks to the sides.

The grammatical difficulties arise from the Zulu system of prefixial concords; those associated with the nouns are inflected to indicate class, number and case. Neither prefix nor the inflexible root can stand alone, and the prefix also serves as an article. The use of an English article is therefore redundant, but since its elimination is impossibly awkward I have decided to chance the tautology. Thus "the emaLangeni clan" in preference to "the Langeni clan," and "emaLangeni" rather than "Emalangeni." I have, however, omitted the slight prefatory hum that precedes most personal names;

thus "Shaka" rather than "uShaka" and the common spelling "Mpande" rather than the more correct "umPande."

I have not, however, been entirely consistent with this usage. Many proper nouns are so well known even to non-Bantu linguists that an attempt to align them with the official orthography would appear to be an affectation. Hence "Zulus" rather than "amaZulu," "Umfolozi" rather than "um-Folozi" and "Basuto" rather than "baSuto" or the older "baSotho." (We are here, in fact, dealing with another language in which an individual is properly "moSuto," people collectively "baSuto" and the language itself "seSuto.")

The use of *h* to represent aspiration must also be noted. Unaspirated *t* sounds like *d*, and unaspirated *k* like hard *g*; *th* and *kh* must be used to get the English sounds *t* and *k*. "Tugela" is thus an accurate rendition of the officially spelled "Thukela."

Stress is almost invariably on the penultimate syllable, but in syllabification *n* usually goes with the following consonant rather than the preceding vowel; it simply indicates nasalization.

The following breakdown may be helpful:

Cetshwayo	Tsk-tsh-*why*-o
Dingane	Di-*nga*-nyeh
Dingiswayo	Di-ngis-*why*-o
Isandhlwana	Ee-sahn-djil-*wha*-na
Mpande	Mm-*pahn*-de
Shaka	Oo-*sha*-ge
Hlobane	Shlo-*bah*-nyeh
Uhamu	Oo-*hahm*-oo

The spellings employed are personal choices, and I cheerfully accept responsibility for their selection. The interests of clarity for the general reader have been regarded throughout as more important than the sensibilities of the specialists. Before the lynx-eyed reader pounces, however, I would warn him that several apparent errors are deliberate; "eGazini" and "emGazini" are two different clans, for example, and "Langal*i*balele" ("the sun, it *is* glaring") and "Langal*a*balele" ("the sun, it *was* glaring") are two different names.

SOURCES

After considerable deliberation I have decided to dispense with detailed text notes, primarily because I do not wish to claim for this work an academic status to which it is not entitled. All sources used are listed in the bibliography, the sources for quoted material in the text are self-evident, and speculative passages are clearly labeled. For the general background material, especially that concerning the shaping of British colonial policy toward southern Africa, I have relied more on competent secondary sources by trained historians than on any attempt of my own to reinterpret the primary sources. Both primary and secondary sources for much of the ground covered present more than the usual number of pitfalls. There are no written native annals, early European observers were usually untrained and rarely motivated by a passion for accuracy, and a depressing percentage lacked objectivity when dealing with European-native, Boer-Briton or High Church–Low Church materials or with the controversies of the Zulu Campaign of 1879. The history of southern Africa, moreover, has not been noted for the care it devoted to its archives.

Of the general histories of southern Africa, Eric Walker's is the most complete in one volume, although it is so packed with detail as to present heavy going to the casual reader. Arthur Keppel-Jones' is among the best of a number of more compact surveys. The multivolume giants of Theal and Cory that long dominated the field predate modern historiography and are little read today.

Very few authors—and no professional historians—have attempted a general history of the Zulu nation. Gibson's *Story of the Zulus* was first published more than sixty years ago and is little more than an uncritical narration for popular consumption. T. V. Bulpin's *Shaka's Country*, with its companion, *To the Shores of Natal*, is also for popular consumption, but presents an eminently readable account on a regional basis.

Among the anthropological studies Eileen Krige's *Social System of the Zulus* is a superbly written account of the daily life of the people—among the very best surveys of a particular native civilization by a trained anthropologist. A. T. Bryant's *The Zulu People* is even more detailed, but it is marred by the author's frequent excursions into speculative waters in which he was far beyond his depth. A missionary with a thirst for accurate detail and enormous sympathy for the people amongst whom he lived, he lacked formal training, and his attempts to relate Nguni Bantu civilization to classic cultures must be disregarded.

The pre-Shakan history of the Zulus rests largely on what the early observers were able to glean from the Zulus themselves. Nathaniel Isaacs, an utterly untrained observer, published within eight years of Shaka's death. Henry Francis Fynn, a more reliable recorder, lost his journals and was forced to reconstitute them in later life from rough notes. They were first published in 1950, after D. McK. Malcolm finished the editing James Stuart had started. Bryant's massive *Olden Times in Zululand and Natal* utilizes both sources, but depends primarily on tribal lore garnered during four decades of exhaustive interviews with native elders, starting in 1883 when the Shakan era was still within living memory. Bryant traced out the origins of hundreds of eastern Nguni clans, and since the source has now vanished, it is safe to say his work will never be exceeded. Almost everything published on the subject since depends on him, but his rambling work, cut by more than a third to permit publication, suffers from his quaint style and chaotic organization. His material is badly in need of modern editing.

Stow's *Native Races of South Africa* does for the Bushmen and the Suthu clans of the high veld something of what Bryant did for the eastern Nguni, but it depends on fragmentary European references rather than the direct debriefing of natives and it was written almost a generation before publication in 1905. Read with Msebenzi's *History of Matiwane* (a direct native account) and Tylden's *Rise of the Basuto* (an excellent secondary source that brings the Basuto to 1946), however, it gives a fairly complete picture of the early inland plateau.

Bird's *Annals of Natal* is a compendium of primary sources dealing with that colony through 1845. Boxer's *Tragic History of the Seas* covers the material of the shipwrecked Portuguese mariners. Gardiner's *Journey to the Zoolu Country* deals with early Port Natal and Dingane, as does Owen's journal, which contains an eyewitness account of the massacre of Retief's party. Mackeurtan's *Cradle Days of Natal* is far and away the best secondary source for the colony through 1845, while Eric Walker's *The Great Trek* is the best account of that event by a professional historian and also covers in detail the short-lived Boer Republic of Natal.

The history of Natal after 1845 is stony ground for the general reader. Most modern historians were drawn to other areas of southern Africa and few bothered to untangle the story of Natal from the complexities of the broader scene. De Kiewiet's *Imperial Factor in South Africa* concentrates on the fluctuations in British colonial policy and gives by far the clearest picture of the forces that shaped Natal's history. I have relied on it heavily.

There is an astonishing lack of good biographical works for the major figures of Zulu history, although no lack of primary sources squirreled away in nooks and crannies. Both Shaka and Cetshwayo have been the subjects of recent uncritical popular biographies. Ritter's *Shaka Zulu* is marred by the insertion of Zulu personages of dubious historical authenticity. Elizabeth Watt's *Febana* is a virtually fictionalized account of Francis Farewell drawn largely from Isaacs. Oliver Walker's two popular books on John Dunn are usually classed as novels.

A ponderous "Life" or "Life and Letters" was almost a standard concomitance of Victorian obsequies, but most of these were written at the instigation of the bereaved family and they will not serve as definitive biographies. Cox's *Life of John William Colenso* was written with Frances Colenso at his elbow and is a forbidding theological jumble, chiefly valuable for its extensive quotations. A magnificent trove of Colenso materials is housed in the Campbell Library, but to date no use has been made of it except for Wyn Rees's *Letters from Natal*—the correspondence of Mrs. Colenso edited with excellent annotations and commentary.

There is no biography of Theophilus Shepstone—a glaring omission. Uys planned one, but he was only able to publish a single volume of the three he planned. Several of Shepstone's early journals had previously been entrusted to a visiting American professor and mysteriously disappeared from his custody; Uys delayed further work in the hope that they would reappear. *In the Era of Shepstone* is a detailed study of several aspects of his work at mid-career—especially confederation and the annexation of the Transvaal—but it of necessity skimps his work in Natal itself. It is carefully documented and objective—something of a rarity in this field—and it is a pity the author was unable to continue.

Martineau's *Life of Sir Bartle Frere* is valuable for its extensive quotations but violently partisan and unreliable. The same is true of Wirgman's *Life of James Green* and the life of Bishop Gray by his son. Lady Hicks Beach's life of her husband is somewhat more reliable and allows the correspondence to carry his colonial work.

The literature of the Zulu campaign of 1879 is in sorry condition. Except for John William Colenso and his daughter Frances, no one has concerned himself much with an examination of its origins, and although the Colensos were voluminous, they—and especially Frances—were so concerned with defending Cetshwayo and Durnford and refuting Frere, Shepstone, Chelmsford or Wolseley that they must be read with enormous caution. (Frere's own papers on this subject are simply a continual polemic.) Allowing, however, for an industrious belaboring of dead horses, the Bishop's *Langalibalele and the amaHlubi Tribe* and *Cetshwayo's Dutchman*, the Frances Colenso—Edward Durnford *History of the Zulu War*, and Edward Durnford's *A Soldier's Life and Work in South Africa* among them contain detailed accounts of the Langalibalele operations, the course of the boundary dispute, and the various incidents which led to the ultimatum of 1878.

Most military accounts of the campaign rest squarely on the official *Narrative of Field Operations*. A reasonably objective summary, it skirts controversial material but is neither complete nor free from error. Norris-Newman's *In Zululand with the British* by a working journalist is brisk and accurate for what the author actually observed but fills in gaps with hearsay. A freshet of popular accounts appeared in the 1880's, none of any particular merit, and then there was a long lull broken only by an occasional biographical work. MacKinnon's and Shadbolt's *South African Campaign* devotes only a few pages to the operations; the bulk of the book consists of a cabinet photograph and biographical sketch of every Imperial officer who died as a result of active service and a valuable list of all special service officers who participated in the campaign, with a summary of their activities. It also has an excellent map, unfortunately not to scale.

In 1936 Clements, a retired journalist, published *The Glamour and Tragedy of the Zulu War*, a sloppy account of almost libelous irresponsibility. It rehashed irrelevant arguments condemning Lord Chelmsford, which the author neither understood nor bothered to explore, and its only value lay in anecdotal material identifying colonial volunteers whom English writers had tended to ignore. This gratuitous attack led to the publication in 1939 of the Honourable Gerald French's *Lord Chelmsford and the Zulu War*, which for the first time made extensive use of the general's military correspondence for 1879. (The papers, however, had been edited and annotated many years after the campaign by Major Gosset—a far-from-disinterested party in the controversy.) This work teetered as far to one side as Clements had to the other; it is basically the *Narrative of Field Operations* all over again, eked out by extensive quotations from Lord Chelmsford's correspondence to answer the specific charges Clements had bandied about, and the continual air of righteous indignation and triumphant vindication mars what might have been a better book. Clements had best been ignored; a battleship had been used to sink a rowboat.

In 1948 the Zulu campaign finally attracted the attention of the only professional historian to write on the subject; Sir Reginald Coupland published *Zulu Battle Piece*, with a brief genesis of the war and a detailed, objective account of Isandhlwana. He dealt with the major charges leveled against Chelmsford but limited himself to putting the controversy into perspective, without digging very deeply. His account of Rorke's Drift is a short recapitulation of the official report, and he repeats the popular belief that Chard and Bromhead were young and inexperienced—going out of his way to label them "barely out of their teens."

Rupert Furneaux's *The Zulu War: Isandhlwana and Rorke's Drift*, published in 1963, is a sketchy, anecdotal throwback to Clements, inaccurate in detail and dismissing Chelmsford as a "delightful donkey."

Of the men who survived the massacre in the camp at Isandhlwana, published accounts were left by Smith-Dorrien (in his autobiography and in the form of a slightly more detailed letter to his father which Coupland quotes) and by Wallie Erskine (whose testimony at the enquiry is quoted in Moodie's *Battles in South Africa*). Unpublished accounts held by the 24th Regiment Museum at Brecon include those by Privates J. Williams, J. Bickley and E. Wilson and by Glyn's interpreter, Brickhill. Of the men out with Chelmsford who returned to the camp after the massacre and who reached

Rorke's Drift just after the fight, published accounts were left by Norris-Newman, Henry Hallam Parr and Hamilton-Browne, whose *A Lost Legionary in South Africa* is valuable through no fault of the author's. He was writing more than thirty years after the event, with ingrained prejudices and a memory refreshed at dubious sources. He performed creditably on the twenty-second of January, however, and was the only man to witness the attack on the camp from the plain. Henry Francis Fynn (the son of the early settler) also published an account in the Natal *Witness* on January 22, 1913. Unpublished accounts in the Campbell Library include those by Henry Harford, W. J. Clarke, J. P. Symons, and a detailed account by a mounted volunteer signed only with the initials "J. M." Penn Symond's account is at Brecon, and the letters of Arthur Harness are also relevant.

There are five detailed accounts by men who fought at Rorke's Drift. The best known is Chard's official report written three days after the fight. It is a small masterpiece of detail and organization, but Chard could not keep 140 men under his own eyes during the long hours of battle, and his version is both incomplete and in several details understandably in error. (For reasons I suspect but do not care to speculate on here, he maintained silence afterward and never amended or expanded the original report.) Surgeon Reynolds and Chaplain Smith left accounts which add nothing substantive to Chard. Private Hook published an account in *The Royal Magazine* in 1905 which goes into considerably more detail about individual activities than the others did; he was the only eyewitness of the grim fight within the hospital to leave a record. Harry Lugg left two detailed letters which the Bristol *Observer* published a few weeks after the fight. My suspicion that Adendorff did not stay to aid the defense is based on an analysis of all the sources listed for both battles. Space precludes a review of the evidence, which I hope to publish separately.

George Mossop's *Running the Gauntlet* is the only autobiography by an enlisted man; it has a good account of Kambula and the only account by a man who came down the pass at Hlobane with Buller.

Sir Garnet Wolseley published a distressingly incomplete autobiography which stops in 1873—just before he entered controversial waters. His biography by Maurice and Arthur, published in 1924, is outrageously partisan and hopelessly inadequate. His letters to his wife, edited by Arthur, add little to the life and leave the unfortunate impression of an egotistical, name-dropping snob. The picture may be valid but it is incomplete; he deserves better. (A fresh biography which I have not seen is being published as this goes to press.)

Evelyn Wood left a brisk, candid autobiography, but he displayed little interest in the causes of the events in which he participated.

Katherine John and E. P. Tisdall have written popular biographies of the Prince Imperial. The information about the horse "Percy" stems from Dr. George Campbell of Durban. Testimony of the survivors at Carey's court-martial is quoted by both Moodie and Norris-Newman. Far and away the best analysis of the circumstances of the Prince's death appears in Whitton's *Service Trials and Tragedies*.

Several general reference works were invaluable. Tylden's *Armed Forces of South Africa* traces out the proliferation of volunteer units in a country addicted to the commando system—he identifies 628 of them. The names, ranks, units and service dates of the Imperial officers are taken from Harte's 1878 Army List. The *Natal Almanac* for 1879 is a fertile source of information about that colony's institutions and people. D. C. F. Moodie's three volumes are a curious hodgepodge; the author collected every newspaper clipping and private letter he could find describing military actions, and the details of long-forgotten skirmishes are mixed with more important battles. The last volume chronologically was actually published a decade before the two-volume set describing actions up to 1878, and it contains letters to newspapers by participants in virtually every action of the Zulu campaign—eyewitness material mixed in with much hearsay rubbish. The two-volume set contains (as "John Dunn's Notes") the material that was later published separately as *John Dunn and the Three Generals*—all of an autobiography that gentleman left.

The postwar trials of the Zulu nation can be found in Frances Colenso's *Ruin of Zululand* (to be treated with the same caveats that must accompany all her work), in Samuelson's autobiography, and in Gibson's *Story of the Zulus*. James Stuart's *History of the Zulu Rebellion* is the standard work on the rising of 1906. Bulpin's books bring the story up to recent times.

BIBLIOGRAPHY

(A) *UNPUBLISHED SOURCES AND PRIVATE INFORMATION*

ANONYMOUS. Manuscript account by unidentified officer of Vause's Troop, Natal Native Horse. (Campbell Library.)

BICKLEY, J., Bandsman, 1st/24th. Manuscript account. (24th Museum, Brecon.)

BRACKENBURY, HENRY. Letter to Arthur Harness. (Margaret Stewart Roberts, great-niece of Arthur Harness.)

BRICKHILL, JAMES. Manuscript account. (24th Museum, Brecon.)

BROMHEAD, GONVILLE. Letter to family, private information. (Lt. Col. Sir Benjamin Bromhead, great-nephew of Gonville Bromhead.)

BULWER, HENRY. Assorted dispatches. (Public Records Office.)

CAMBRIDGE, H. R. H. Duke of. Letters to Lord Chelmsford. (Chelmsford Papers.)

CHELMSFORD, GENERAL LORD. Assorted letters and papers, private information. (Chelmsford Papers and family members.)

CLARKE, W. J., Natal Mounted Police. Manuscript autobiography. (Campbell Library.)

COLENSO, JOHN WILLIAM. Colenso Papers. (Campbell Library.)

CREALOCK, JOHN NORTH. Letters to Arthur Harness. (Margaret Stewart Roberts.)

DURNFORD, ANTHONY WILLIAM. Private information. (Muriel Durnford, great-niece of Anthony Durnford.)

DURNFORD, EDWARD C. L. Letters to John William Colenso. (Colenso Papers.)

FIELDING, JOHN W. (true name of John Williams). Documents and private information. (Denis J. Pratley, grandson of John Fielding.)

FRERE, BARTLE. Assorted dispatches. (Public Records Office.)

HARFORD, HENRY C. Journal. (Campbell Library.)

HARNESS, ARTHUR. Collected letters, 1878–79. (Margaret Stewart Roberts.)

HEAD, R. (true name of private at Rorke's Drift, enlistment name unknown). Letter from Rorke's Drift. (24th Museum, Brecon.)

HICKS, WILLIAM (mounted volunteer, unit unknown). Letter. (Campbell Library.)

HITCH, FREDERICK. Private information. (Mrs. W. Oxford, daughter of Frederick Hitch.)

"J.M." (unidentified mounted volunteer, unit unknown). Manuscript account. (Campbell Library.)

LUGG, HARRY. Letters and family information. (H. C. Lugg, son of Harry Lugg.)

NAPOLEON, LOUIS, Prince Imperial. Private information. (Dr. George Campbell.)

PARSONS, CHARLES S. B. Letter to Arthur Harness. (Margaret Stewart Roberts.)

SCHEVEGMAN, W. R., Natal Hussars. Manuscript account. (Campbell Library.)

STUART, JAMES. Assorted items from the Stuart Papers. (Campbell Library.)

SYMONDS, WILLIAM PENN, 1st/24th. Manuscript account. (24th Museum, Brecon.)

SYMONS, J. P., Natal Carbineers. Manuscript account. (Campbell Library.)

WEATHERLY, LOUISE. Manuscript account, letter to Charles W. Thesiger. (Mr. Justice Gerald Thesiger.)

WERNER, A. Manuscript memorial of Harriette Colenso. (Campbell Library.)

WILLIAMS, J., Private #139, 1st/24th. Manuscript account. (24th Museum, Brecon.)

WILSON, E., Bandsman, 1st/24th. Manuscript account. (24th Museum, Brecon.)

WYNNE, WARREN R. C. Journal and private information. (Charles M. Wynne, son.)

(B) NEWSPAPERS AND PERIODICALS

(i) Natal

The Natal Witness (founded 1845 by D. D. Buchanan).
The Times of Natal (originally *The Courier,* edited by R. Ridley).
The Natal Mercury (founded 1852, by John Robinson and R. Vause).

(ii) United Kingdom

The Daily Telegraph.
The Evening Standard.
The Graphic.
The Guardian.
The Illustrated London News.
The London Gazette.
The London Times.

(iii) Specific Articles

BOND, BRIAN. "The Effect of the Cardwell Reforms on Army Organization, 1874–1904," *Royal United Service Institute Journal*, November, 1960.

FORBES, ARCHIBALD. "The Conduct of the Zulu War," *Nineteenth Century Magazine*, February, 1880.

FRIPP, C. E. "Reminiscences of the Zulu War," *Pall Mall Magazine*, 1884.

FYNN, HENRY FRANCIS. "My Recollections of a Famous Campaign," *The Natal Witness*, January 22, 1913.

HARNESS, ARTHUR. "The Zulu Campaign," *Fraser's Magazine*, March, 1880.

HOOK, HENRY. "How They Held Rorke's Drift," *The Royal Magazine*, February, 1905.

REYNOLDS, JAMES HENRY. "The Defence of Rorke's Drift," reprinted 1928 in the *Royal Army Medical Corps Journal*.

SOUTHEY, R. J. "The Battle of Isandhlwana," *The Springbok*, 1949.

WHITTON, F. E. "Rorke's Drift," *Blackwood's Magazine*, February, 1934.

(C) PUBLISHED SOURCES

AGAR-HAMILTON, J. A. I. *The Native Policy of the Voortrekkers*. Cape Town, 1928.

ARTHUR, GEORGE (ed.). *The Letters of Lord and Lady Wolseley, 1870–1911*. London, 1922.

ASHE, MAJOR, and WYATT-EDGELL, E. V. *The Story of the Zulu Campaign*. London, 1880.

ATKINSON, C. T. *The South Wales Borderers, 24th Foot, 1689–1937*. Cambridge, 1937.

AXELSON, ERIC. *Portuguese in South-East Africa 1600–1700*. Johannesburg, 1960.

AYLIFF, JOHN, and WHITESIDE, JOSEPH. *History of the Abambo Generally Known as Fingoes*. Fingoland, 1912.

BARNES, R. MONEY. *A History of the Regiments and Uniforms of the British Army*. London, 1950.

————. *Military Uniforms of Britain and the Empire*. London, 1960.

———— and KENNEDY ALLEN, C. *The Uniforms and History of the Scottish Regiments*. London, 1956(?).

"A PLAIN WOMAN" (CHARLOTTE BARTER). *Alone Among the Zulus*. London, 1866.

BECKER, PETER. *Path of Blood—The Rise and Conquests of Mzilikazi*. London, 1962.

BELLAIRS, WILLIAM. *The Military Career*. London, 1889.

BINNS, C. T. *The Last Zulu King—The Life and Death of Cetshwayo*. London, 1963.

BIRD, JOHN. *The Annals of Natal, 1495 to 1845*. Pietermaritzburg, 1888.

BLACKMORE, HOWARD L. *British Military Firearms 1650–1850*. London, 1961.

BLOOD, BINDON. *Four Score Years and Ten.* London, 1933.

BOND, JOHN. *They Were South Africans.* London, 1956.

BOXER, C. R. *The Tragic History of the Seas, 1589–1622.* Cambridge, 1959.

BRAATVEDT, H. P. *Roaming Zululand with a Native Commissioner.* Pietermaritzburg, 1949.

BROOKES, EDGAR. *The History of Native Policy in South Africa from 1830 to the Present Day.* Cape Town, 1924.

BROOKS, HENRY (edited by R. J. Mann). *Natal: A History and Description of the Colony.* London, 1876.

BRYANT, A. T. *A History of the Zulu and Neighboring Tribes.* Cape Town, 1964.

————. *Olden Times in Zululand and Natal.* London, 1929.

————. *The Zulu People.* Pietermaritzburg, 1949.

BUCHANAN, BARBARA I. *Pioneer Days in Natal.* Pietermaritzburg, 1934.

BULPIN, T. V. *Shaka's Country.* Cape Town, 1952.

————. *To the Shores of Natal.* Cape Town, n.d.

BURROWS, H. R., and others. *The Dunn Reserve, Zululand.* Pietermaritzburg, 1953.

BUTLER, LEWIS. *Redvers Buller.* London, 1909.

BUTLER, WILLIAM F. *The Life of Sir George Pomeroy-Colley.* London, 1899.

CLEMENTS, W. H. *The Glamour and Tragedy of the Zulu War.* London, 1936.

COLENSO, FRANCES ELLEN. *The Ruin of Zululand.* London, 1884.

COLENSO, FRANCES ELLEN, and DURNFORD, EDWARD C. L. *History of the Zulu War and Its Origin.* London, 1880.

COLENSO, JOHN WILLIAM. *Digest on Zulu Affairs 1878–1883.* Bishopstowe, 1883.

————. *Langalibalele and the amaHlubi Tribe.* London, 1874.

————. *Natal Sermons.* London, 1866.

————. *Ten Weeks in Natal.* Cambridge, 1855.

————. *Three Native Accounts of the Visit of the Bishop of Natal in September and October, 1859, to Umpande, King of the Zulus.* Pietermaritzburg and Durban, 1901.

CORY, GEORGE E. (ed.). *The Diary of the Rev. Francis Owen, M.A.* Cape Town, 1926.

COUPLAND, REGINALD. *Zulu Battle Piece—Isandhlwana.* London, 1948.

COX, GEORGE W. *The Life of John William Colenso, D.D., Bishop of Natal.* London, 1888.

CUNYNGHAME, ARTHUR. *My Command in South Africa 1874–1878.* London, 1880.

DEKIEWIET, C. W. *The Imperial Factor in South Africa.* Cambridge, 1937.

DEVITT, NAPIER. *Galloping Jack, Being the Reminiscences of Brigadier-General John Robinson Royston.* London, 1937.

DE WATTEVILLE, H. *The British Soldier.* New York, 1952(?).

Dictionary of National Biography. London, 1953.

DOKE, CLEMENT M. *Text-Book of Zulu Grammar.* Johannesburg, 1950.

————, MALCOLM, D. McK., and SIKAKANA, J. M. A. *English and Zulu Dictionary.* Johannesburg, 1958.

DURNFORD, EDWARD. *A Soldier's Life and Work in South Africa 1872 to 1879, A Memoir of the Late Colonel A. W. Durnford, Royal Engineers.* London, 1882.

ELLIOT, W. J. *The Victoria Cross in Zululand and South Africa and How it Was Won.* London, 1882.

FAYE, CARL. *Zulu References.* Pietermaritzburg, 1923.

FITZHERBERT, CUTHBERT (ed.): *Henry Clifford. His Letters and Sketches from the Crimea.* New York, 1956.

FITZPATRICK, J. P. *The Transvaal From Within.* London, 1899.

FORBES, ARCHIBALD. *Barracks, Bivouacs and Battles.* London, 1892.

————. *Memories and Studies of War and Peace.* London, 1895.

FORTESCUE, J. W. *A History of the 17th Lancers.* London, 1895.

FRENCH, GERALD. *Lord Chelmsford and the Zulu War.* London, 1939.

FULLER, CLAUDE, and FOUCHE, LEO. *Louis Trigardt's Trek Across the Drakensberg, 1837–1838.* Cape Town, 1932.

FURNEAUX, RUPERT. *The Zulu War: Isandhlwana and Rorke's Drift.* 1963.

————. *The Siege of Plevna.* London, 1958.

FYNN, HENRY FRANCIS (edited by James Stuart and D. McK. Malcolm). *The Diary of Henry Francis Fynn.* Pietermaritzburg, 1950.

FYNNEY, F. B. *The Zulu Army.* Pietermaritzburg, 1878.

GARDINER, ALLEN. *Narrative of a Journey to the Zoolu Country in South Africa Undertaken in 1835.* London, 1836.

GIBSON, J. Y. *The Story of the Zulus.* London, 1911.

GILLMORE, PARKER. *On Duty, A Ride Through Hostile Africa.* London, 1880.

GODLONTON, R., and IRVING, EDWARD. *A Narrative of the Kaffir War of 1850–51.* London, 1851.

GRANT, JAMES. *British Battles on Land and Sea.* London, n.d., 1886(?).

"Ex C. M. R." A. K. GRANVILLE. *With the Cape Mounted Rifles.* London, 1881.

GRAY, CHARLES. *Life of Robert Gray, Bishop of Cape Town and Metropolitan of Africa.* London, 1876.

HAGGARD, H. RIDER. *A History of the Transvaal.* New York, 1899.

————. *Cetywayo and His White Neighbors.* London, 1882.

HALFORD, SAMUEL JAMES. *The Griquas of Griqualand.* Cape Town and Johannesburg, n.d., 1950(?).

HAMILTON-BROWNE, G. *A Lost Legionary in South Africa.* London, 1912(?).

HARRISON, RICHARD. *Recollections of a Life in the British Army During the Latter Half of the 19th Century.* London, 1908.

HART, H. G. *The New Annual Army List, Militia List and Indian Civil Service List, for 1878.* London, 1878.

HATTERSLEY, ALAN F. *Carbineer, the History of the Royal Natal Carbineers.* Aldershot, 1950.

HERRMAN, LOUIS (ed.). *Travels and Adventures in Eastern Africa by Nathaniel Isaacs.* Cape Town, 1936.

HICKS BEACH, VICTORIA. *The Life of Sir Michael Hicks Beach.* London, 1932.

HOLDEN, W. CLIFFORD. *British Rule in South Africa.* London, 1879.

————. *History of the Colony of Natal, South Africa.* London, 1860.

————. *The Past and Future of the Kaffir Races.* London, 1866.

HOLT, H. P. *The Mounted Police of Natal.* London, 1913.

HURST, GODFREY T. *Short History of the Volunteer Regiments of Natal and East Griqualand.* Durban, 1945.

JOHN, KATHERINE. *The Prince Imperial.* London, 1939.

KEPPEL-JONES. ARTHUR. *South Africa, A Short History.* London, 1949.

KIDD, DUDLEY. *The Essential Kaffir.* London, 1925.

KIRBY, PERCIVAL (ed.). *Andrew Smith and Natal.* Cape Town, 1955.

————. *The True Story of the Grosvenor.* Cape Town, 1960.

KOTZE, D. J. *Letters of the American Missionaries 1835–1838.* Cape Town, 1950.

KRIGE, EILEEN JENSEN. *The Social System of the Zulus.* Pietermaritzburg, 1957.

LAGDEN, GODFREY. *The Basutos.* New York, 1910.

LEYDS, W. J. *The First Annexation of the Transvaal.* London, 1906.

LISTER, MARGARET (ed.). *Journals of Andrew Geddes Bain.* Cape Town, 1949.

LUCAS, THOMAS J. *Camp Life and Sport in South Africa.* London, 1878.

————. *The Zulus and the British Frontiers.* London, 1879.

LUDLOW, W. R. *Zululand and Cetewayo.* London, 1882.

LUGG, H. C. *Historic Natal and Zululand.* Pietermaritzburg, 1949.

MACKEURTAN, GRAHAM. *The Cradle Days of Natal (1497–1845).* Pietermaritzburg, 1948.

MACKINNON, J. P., and SHADBOLT, SYDNEY. *The South African Campaign, 1879.* London, 1880.

MACMILLAN, WILLIAM MILLER. *Bantu, Boer and Briton.* London, 1929.

MACQUARRIE, J. W. (ed.). *The Reminiscences of Sir Walter Standford, 1850–1885.* Cape Town, 1958.

MARTINEAU, JOHN. *The Life and Correspondence of Sir Bartle Frere.* London, 1895.

MAURICE, F., and ARTHUR, GEORGE. *The Life of Lord Wolseley.* London, 1924.

MAURICE, FREDERICK. *The Life of Frederick Denison Maurice.* New York, 1884.

Minutes of Proceedings of the Court of Enquiry into Certain Charges Preferred Against Langalibalele. Pietermaritzburg, 1874.

MITFORD, BERTRAM. *Through the Zulu Country.* London, 1883.

MOFFAT, ROBERT. *Missionary Labours and Scenes in Southern Africa.* New York, 1843.

MOLOJA (dictated to J. M. Orpen). *The Story of the "Fetcani Horde."* (n.d., n.p.).

MOLTENO, P. A. *The Life and Times of Sir John Charles Molteno.* London, 1900.

MOLYNEAUX, W. C. F. *Campaigning in South Africa and Egypt.* London, 1896.

MONTAGUE, W. E. *Campaigning in South Africa.* London, 1880.

MOODIE, DUNCAN CAMPBELL FRANCIS. *The History of the Battles and Adventures of the British, the Boers, and the Zulus, etc., in Southern Africa from the Time of the Pharaoh Necho, to 1880.* Cape Town, 1888.

————. *Battles in South Africa Including the Zulu War.* Adelaide, 1879.

MOSSOP, GEORGE. *Running the Gauntlet.* London, 1937.

MSEBENZI (told to Albert Hlongwane, edited by N. J. Warmelo). *History of Matiwane and the Amangwane Tribe.* Pretoria, 1938.

The Natal Almanac, Directory and Yearly Register, 1879. Pietermaritzburg, 1878.

NEILL, STEPHEN. *Anglicanism.* London, 1958.

NORBURY, HENRY F. *The Naval Brigade in South Africa during the Years 1877–78–79.* London, 1880.

NORRIS-NEWMAN, CHARLES L. *In Zululand with the British Throughout the War of 1879.* London, 1880.

PAGE, JESSE. *Captain Allen Gardiner—Sailor and Saint.* London, 1883(?).

PARR, HENRY HALLAM. *A Sketch of the Kafir and Zulu Wars.* London, 1880.

PEARSON, HESKETH. *Dizzy, The Life and Nature of Benjamin Disraeli.* London, 1951.

REES, WYN (ed.). *Colenso Letters from Natal.* Pietermaritzburg, 1958.

REYHER, REBECCA HOURWICH. *Zulu Woman.* New York, 1948.

RITTER, E. A. *Shaka Zulu, The Rise of the Zulu Empire.* London, 1957.

RIVETT-CARNAC, DOROTHY E. *Thus Came the English in 1820.* Cape Town, 1961.

ROGERS, H. C. B. *The Mounted Troops of the British Army 1066–1945.* London, 1959.

————. *Weapons of the British Soldier.* London, 1960.

ROTHWELL, JOHN SUTTON (compiler). *Narrative of Field Operations Connected with the Zulu War of 1879.* HMSO, London, 1881.

ST. AUBYN, GILES. *The Royal George 1819–1904, The Life of H.R.H. Prince George Duke of Cambridge,* London, 1963.

SAMUELSON, R. C. A. *Long, Long Ago.* Durban, 1929.

SCHAPERA, I. (ed.). *The Bantu-Speaking Tribes of South Africa.* London, 1937.

SCHAPERA, I. *The Khoisan Peoples of South Africa.* London, 1930.

SHUTTER, C. F. *Englishman's Inn.* Cape Town, 1963.

SMITH, EDWIN W. *The Life and Times of Daniel Lindley (1801–80).* London, 1949.

————. *The Mabilles of Basutoland.* London, 1939.

SMITH, WALTER H. B. *The NRA Book of Small Arms.* Harrisburg, 1948.

SMITH-DORRIEN, HORACE. *Memories of Forty-Eight Years' Service.* London, 1925.

STANLEY, HENRY M. *Coomassie and Magdala.* London, 1874.

STOW, GEORGE W. *The Native Races of South Africa*. London, 1905.

STREATFEILD, FRANK N. *Kafirland: A Ten Months' Campaign*. London, 1879.

STUART, J. *A History of the Zulu Rebellion 1906*. London, 1913.

SYMONS, JULIAN. *Buller's Campaign*. London, 1963.

TABLER, EDWARD C. *The Far Interior*. Cape Town/Amsterdam, 1955.

TALBOT-BOOTH, E. C. *The British Army*. London, 1937.

THEAL, GEORGE McCALL. *The Republic of Natal*. Cape Town, 1886.

————. *The Yellow and Dark-skinned People of Africa South of the Zambesi*. London, 1910.

TISDALL, E. E. P. *The Prince Imperial*. London, 1959.

TOMASSON, W. H. *With the Irregulars in the Transvaal and Zululand*. London, 1881.

Trial of the Bishop of Natal for Erroneous Teaching. Cape Town, 1863.

TYLDEN, G. *The Armed Forces of South Africa*. Johannesburg, 1954.

————. *The Rise of the Basuto*. Cape Town and Johannesburg, 1950.

TYLER, JOSIAH. *Forty Years Among the Zulus*. Boston, 1891.

TURNER, E. S. *Gallant Gentlemen—A Portrait of the British Officer 1600–1956*. London, 1956.

UYS, C. J. *In the Era of Shepstone*. Lovedale, 1933.

VIJN, CORNELIUS (translated and edited with notes by J. W. Colenso, Bishop of Natal). *Cetshwayo's Dutchman*. London, 1880.

WALKER, ERIC ANDERSON. *The Great Trek*. London, 1948.

————. *A History of Southern Africa*. London, 1959.

WALKER, OLIVER. *Proud Zulu*. London, 1949.

————. *Zulu Royal Feather*. London, 1961.

WATT, ELIZABETH PARIS. *Febana*. London, 1962.

WEBBER, C. E. *The Lines of Communication of an Army in the Field and Their Working*. London, 1882.

WHITTON, F. E. *Service Trials and Tragedies*. London, 1930.

WILKINS, PHILIP A. *The History of the Victoria Cross*. London, 1904.

WILKINSON, T. E. *A Lady's Life and Travels in Zululand and the Transvaal during Cetewayo's Reign*. London, 1882.

WILLIAMS, CHARLES. *The Life of Lieutenant-General Sir Henry Evelyn Wood, V.C., G.C.B., G.C.M.G.* London, 1892.

WILMOT, A. *History of the Zulu War*. London, 1880.

WIRGMAN, A. THEODORE. *Life of James Green*. London, 1909.

WOLSELEY, GARNET J. *The Soldier's Pocket-Book for Field Service*, 3d edition. London, 1874.

————. *The Story of a Soldier's Life*. London, 1903.

WOOD, EVELYN. *From Midshipman to Field Marshal*. London, 1906.

————. *Winnowed Memories*. London, 1918.

WORSFOLD, BASIL. *Sir Bartle Frere*. London, 1923.

"WYLDE, ATHERTON" (pseudonym of FRANCES ELLEN COLENSO). *My Chief and I*. London, 1880.

WYNDHAM, HORACE. *The Queen's Service*. Boston, 1899.

YOUNG, P. J. *Boot and Saddle*. Cape Town, 1955.

INDEX

ABOUT THE AUTHOR

DONALD R. MORRIS was born in 1924 and raised in New York City. He enlisted in the Navy in 1942, entered the U.S. Naval Academy at Annapolis in 1944, and graduated in 1948 with a B.S. in Electrical Engineering. (Of 410 men in his class, he stood first in Naval History, second in English and 409th in Electrical Engineering.)

Mr. Morris served on several destroyers, then went on to Naval Intelligence School and Russian language training and was detailed to the CIA in 1956. He remained with the CIA and continued in the Naval Reserve until 1972, when he retired as a Lieutenant Commander with eighteen years active and twelve years Reserve service. He earned two battle stars in Korea and holds the Navy Commendation medal. His seventeen years with the CIA were spent almost entirely in Soviet counterespionage operations. He was stationed for lengthy periods in Berlin, Paris, Kinshasa (Zaire), and Vietnam.

Mr. Morris is the author of two novels: *China Station* (1951) and *Warm Bodies* (1957), which was a *Reader's Digest* Book Club selection and was made into a motion picture called *All Hands on Deck*. *The Washing of the Spears* (1965) was a History Book Club and a Military Book Club selection. Mr. Morris has also written for the *Victory at Sea* television series, *Encyclopaedia Britannica*, *The Atlantic*, *Argosy*, *True*, *Verbatim*, and a number of aviation and computer periodicals. He is a member of Mensa. He holds a Commercial Pilot's License and is a Certified Flight Instructor.

A news analyst for *The Houston Post* since 1972, Mr. Morris writes an op-ed column four times weekly on national and foreign events. He has taught writing and African history at the University of Houston, and lectures frequently on foreign affairs.